COLUMBIA PROJECT ON

ASIA

IN THE   CORE CURRICULUM

MASTERWORKS
OF ASIAN LITERATURE
IN COMPARATIVE
PERSPECTIVE

The 1980s witnessed the introduction of Asia into the core curriculum at undergraduate institutions throughout the United States, and Asian materials are now at the threshold of general knowledge in literature, history, and the social sciences. THE COLUMBIA PROJECT ON ASIA IN THE CORE CURRICULUM was inaugurated in 1984 under the sponsorship of Columbia University to support this integration of Asian materials into the general education curriculum. The project, chaired by Wm. Theodore de Bary, Ainslie T. Embree, and Carol Gluck, has received ongoing support from the National Endowment for the Humanities, the Henry Luce Foundation, the Panasonic Foundation, and the U.S. Department of Education.

The three Guides that we are pleased to announce here are designed for faculty members who are integrating Asian material into general education courses primarily focused on the Western tradition or canon. Each Guide contains approximately forty essays, written by leading specialists, and each essay conforms to a common format that makes the Guides useful to those who are integrating these materials into introductory courses in the various academic disciplines. The Guides will be an invaluable resource for course preparation. And each will be an indispensable reference for faculty and students alike.

Columbia Project on Asia in the Core Curriculum

ASIA: CASE STUDIES IN THE SOCIAL SCIENCES
A GUIDE FOR TEACHING
Myron L. Cohen, editor

MASTERWORKS OF ASIAN LITERATURE IN COMPARATIVE PERSPECTIVE
A GUIDE FOR TEACHING
Barbara Stoler Miller, editor

ASIA IN WESTERN AND WORLD HISTORY
A GUIDE FOR TEACHING
Ainslie T. Embree and Carol Gluck, editors

Roberta Martin
Project Director

Wm. Theodore de Bary, Ainslie T. Embree, Carol Gluck
Project Chairmen

COLUMBIA PROJECT ON

ASIA

IN THE CORE CURRICULUM

MASTERWORKS
OF ASIAN LITERATURE
IN COMPARATIVE
PERSPECTIVE

A Guide for Teaching

Edited by
Barbara Stoler Miller

An East Gate Book

M.E. Sharpe
Armonk, New York
London, England

An East Gate Book

Copyright © 1994 by Trustees of Columbia University in the City of New York

*Grateful acknowledgment is made to the following for permission to reprint
previously published material, which has been adapted for the present volume:*

Columbia University Press for "An Account of My Hut" by Paul Anderer,
"Kālidāsa's *Sakuntalā*" and *"The Mahābhārata"* by Barbara Stoler Miller, and
"The Poetry of Matsuo Bashō" and *"The Tale of Genji"* by Haruo Shirane, from
Approaches to the Asian Classics, Wm. Theodore de Bary, ed., copyright © 1987
by Columbia University Press.

Encyclopaedia Britannica, Inc., for *"The Tale of Genji"* by Edward Seidensticker,
and "Tang Poetry" by Burton Watson from *The Great Ideas Today*,
copyright © 1987 by Encyclopaedia Britannica, Inc.

Permission for reprinting the translations of the waka
by Ono no Komachi has been granted by:

Grove/Atlantic Monthly Press, *Anthology of Japanese Literature*,
edited by Donald Keene, copyright © 1955 by Grove Press.

Stanford University Press, *Japanese Court Poetry*, by Robert Brower
and Earl Miner, copyright © 1961 by the
Board of Trustees of the Leland Stanford Junior University.

Stanford University Press, *Kokin Waka Shū: The First Imperial Anthology
of Japanese Poetry*, translated by Helen Craig McCullough, copyright © 1985
by the Board of Trustees of the Leland Stanford Junior University.

Library of Congress Cataloging-in-Publication Data

Masterworks of Asian literature in comparative perspective :
A guide for teaching / edited by Barbara Stoler Miller.
p.   cm. — (Columbia project on Asia in the core curriculum)
Includes index.
"An East Gate book."
ISBN 1-56324-257-5 (C).—ISBN 1-56324-258-3 (P)
1. Oriental literature—Translations into English. 2. Literature, Comparative.
3. Chinese literature—History and criticism.
4. Japanese literature—History and criticism.
5. Indic literature–History and criticism. 6. Asia in literature.
I. Miller, Barbara Stoler. II. Series
PJ409.M38   1993
809'.8895—dc20
93-24473
CIP

BM (c)   10   9   8   7   6   5   4   3   2   1

BM (p)   10   9   8   7   6   5   4   3   2   1

This volume is dedicated to the memory of its editor
Barbara Stoler Miller
1940–1993
whose lifelong commitment was to make
the literature of Asia accessible to all.

Contents by Country

IV. Japanese Texts

Lyric

Narrative

Drama

Postscript

Contents by Genre

China

Japan

DRAMA

India

China

Japan

Preface

The Project on Asia in the Core Curriculum began in 1984 to support the introduction of material on Asia into the core curricula of undergraduate institutions throughout the country. Three "Guides for Teaching" are the result of dialogue between Asian specialists and colleagues specializing in the Western tradition who most often teach the introductory, general education courses in the various academic disciplines. There was no attempt to stress Asia at the expense of the West. The purpose was to identify texts, themes, and comparative concepts that would provide avenues of entry for Asian material into core courses in literature, history, and the social sciences.

The guides are entitled: *Masterworks of Asian Literature in Comparative Perspective, Asia in Western and World History,* and *Asia: Case Studies in the Social Sciences*. Each volume contains approximately forty essays by leading specialists that suggest a range of possibilities for introducing material on Asia. The essays are arranged to provide the widest choice of approaches to meet the reader's pedagogical needs. While the guides are discrete publications, they form a series that facilitates interdisciplinary teaching: An instructor who chooses, for example, to draw upon Rajagopal Parthasaraty's essay on "*Samskara*: The Passing of the Brahman Tradition," in this volume on literary masterworks, will also find much of interest in Ainslie Embree's review of South Asian history (in *Asia in Western and World History*), in Lawrence Babb's overview of religion in India and in Owen Lynch's discussion of the caste system (both of which are in *Asia: Case Studies in the Social Sciences*).

The Project on Asia in the Core Curriculum has involved over one hundred scholars from seventy-five public and private undergraduate institutions throughout the United States. It has been chaired at Columbia University by a panel composed of Wm. Theodore de Bary, Ainslie T. Embree, and Carol Gluck.

The National Endowment for the Humanities, the Henry Luce

Foundation, the Panasonic Foundation, and the U.S. Department of Education have sponsored the project. We are deeply indebted to these sponsors for their continuing support.

We welcome any and all contributions to this ongoing curricular dialogue.

Roberta Martin
Project Director

Guide to the Reader

Masterworks of Asian Literature in Comparative Perspective
includes two tables of contents, one which groups the texts by
country and a second which groups them by genre. The "Summaries of the Masterworks," found at the end of the volume, provide
brief background on each of the texts discussed for the instructor
seeking the appropriate text(s) for a specific course. The reader is
also referred to the first section of the volume, "The Worlds of
Asian Literature," where introductory essays on the imaginative
universe of each of the three literary traditions can be found.
These essays provide both context for reading the individual texts
and points for comparison among the three traditions.

Topics for discussion follow each essay. A list of references,
containing recommended translations and other background
works, concludes each entry. The list of references is designed to
facilitate the compilation of a syllabus, whether the work is being
chosen for a core reading in a literature course or a supplemen-
tary reading in a history course.

To illustrate the complex issues involved in translation of lyric
texts, transliterated poems are translated and explicated in the
essays on lyric. In addition, specifically for classroom use, there
are four examples of poems in Hindi, Urdu, Chinese, and Japanese,
giving the original language, the transliterated version, a word-for-
word translation, and one or more poetic renditions in English.
These can be found on pages 93, 104, 244, and 376.

Timelines of Indian, Chinese, and Japanese history are included at the end of the volume for reference.

Principles of Transliteration and Pronunciation Guide

TRANSLITERATION

Because the English renderings of Chinese, Indian (Sanskrit, Bengali, Hindi, Tamil, Urdu), and Japanese words are not always consistent, certain spelling variations require explanation.

In this volume, non-English words which appear in *Webster's 3rd International Dictionary, Unabridged* are written with Webster's spelling. Non-English words not included in this dictionary are written in italics with diacriticals where appropriate, proper names excepted.

Spelling variations occur particularly in the transliteration of Chinese words because there are two systems of transliteration still in use for Chinese words. The older is called Wade-Giles after its two originators and the more recent, developed in the mid-twentieth century by the People's Republic of China for international use, is called *pinyin*. In this volume, the pinyin system of transliteration is used to render Chinese terms. In some essays, however, when the primary references listed at the conclusion of the essay employ the Wade-Giles system of transliteration, then in the essay the pinyin is followed by the Wade-Giles rendering given in the brackets: for example, *Shi jing* [*Shih ching*]. The exception to this format is the essay "Chuang Tzu" by Shuen-fu Lin. Professor Lin requested that the primary transliteration of certain names and titles be given in Wade-Giles. In these cases, the *pinyin* follows in parentheses: for example, *Chuang Tzu* (*Zhuang zi*). (This procedure has also been noted at the end of the chapter.)

Further spelling differences occur in Chinese, Japanese, Sanskrit and other Indic language words that appear in titles of works under "References" or within quoted sections of works under discussion. These spelling differences reflect inconsistencies in translations in either romanization or diacritical usage.

PRONUNCIATION

CHINESE

Contributed by David D. W. Wang

Vowels in Chinese are mostly like continental Spanish-German vowels with exceptions (as shown) occuring especially near final *n* or *ng*. (Note: In spoken Chinese, vowels are given one of four tonal inflections. Since such linguistic expertise is beyond the scope of this guide, information on the tonal system is not included here.)

a	as *a* in father	thus *ai* as *eye* in *eye*
		ao as *ow* in how
		an, *ang* as *a* in father plus *n*, *ng*
	exceptions:	*ian*, *yan* as *yen* in *yen*
e	as *u* in *up*	thus *en*, *eng* as *u* in *up* plus *n*, *ng*
	exceptions:	*ie*, *y* as *ye* in *yes*
		ei as *ei* in *eight*
i	as *ee* in beet	thus *in*, *ing* as *ee* in bee plus *n*, *ng*
		ui as *ui* in French "*oui*"
	exceptions:	*i* as *i* in fir in *shi*, *chi*, *zhi*, *ci*, *si*, *zi*
o	as *o* in dog	thus *uo* as *wa* in *wall*
	exceptions:	*ou* as *o* in code
		ong as *o* in code plus *ng*
u	as *oo* in book	thus *you*, *iu* as *yeo* in *yeoman*
	exceptions:	*un*, *ung* as *oo* in boot plus *n*, *ng*
ü	as German *u* in *über* or French *u* in *une*	

Note: a *u* in *ju*, *qu*, *xu*, *yu* is always pronounced as *ü* and never *u* thus it is not necessary to spell these words with an umlaut.

Consonants are mostly as in English, except that some letters are put to separate use, because there are two kinds of *ch* (*q*, *ch*), two kinds of *sh* (*x*, *sh*), and two kinds of *j* (*j*, *zh*), and a single letter to represent *dz* (*z*) and *ts* (*c*).

b	as *b* in bottle
c	as *ts* in cats
d	as *d* in dot
f	as *f* in food
g	as *g* in gun

h	as *h* in *h*and
j	as *j* in *j*eep
k	as *k* in *k*id
l	as *l* in *l*aw
m	as *m* in *m*oon
n	as *n* in *n*ine
p	as *p* in *p*en
q	as *ch* in *ch*urch
r	as *r* in *r*unner
s	as *s* in *s*ong
t	as *t* in *t*op
w	as *w* in *w*ay
x	as *sh* in *sh*eet
y	as *y* in *y*ellow
z	as *dz* in a*dz*e
ch	as *tch* in ca*tch*ing
sh	as *sh* in *sh*oe
zh	as *j* in *j*oke
ng	as *ng* in lo*ng*

SANSKRIT AND HINDI

Contributed by Barbara Stoler Miller

Words in Sanskrit (a classical language) and Hindi (a modern language) are rendered in Roman script, using international conventions for transliteration. In the pronunciation of Sanskrit and Hindi words, the accent is usually on a syllable when this is heavy. A syllable is heavy if it contains a long simple vowel (*ā, ī, ū, ṛ*), a diphthong (*e, o, ai, au*), or a short vowel followed by more than one consonant. It should be noted that the aspirated consonants *kh, gh, ch, jh, ṭh, ḍh, th, dh, ph,* and *bh,* are considered single consonants in the Sanskrit/Indic phonetic system.

Vowels, except *a,* are given their full value as in Italian or German:

a	as *u* in c*u*t
ā	as *a* in f*a*ther
i	as *i* in p*i*t
ī	as *i* in mach*i*ne
ṛ	a short vowel; as *ri* in *ri*ch, but often rendered *ri* in Anglicized words
e	as *ay* in s*ay*

ai	as *ai* in *ai*sle
o	as *o* in *go*
au	as *ow* in c*ow*
ṁ	nasalizes the preceding vowel and makes the syllable heavy
ḥ	a rough breathing vowel, replacing an original *s* or *r*; *occurs only at the end of a syllable or word and makes the syllable heavy*

Most consonants are analogous to the English, if the distinction between aspirated and nonaspirated consonants is observed; for example, the aspirated consonants *th* and *ph* must never be pronounced as in English *th*in and *ph*ial, but as in ho*th*ouse and she*ph*erd (similarly, *kh, gh, ch, jg, dh, bh*). The differences between the Indic "cerebral" *ṭ, ṭh, ḍ, ḍh, ṇ, ṣ* and "dental" *t, th, d, dh, n, s* are another distinctive feature of the language. The dentals are formed with the tongue against the teeth, the cerebrals with the tongue flexed back along the palate. Note also:

g	as *g* in *g*oat
ṅ	as *n* in i*n*k, or si*ng*
c	as *ch* in *ch*urch
ñ	as *ñ* in Spanish se*ñ*or
ś	as *s* in *s*ugar

Aside from the above, special conditions in some of the Indic languages require further detailed explanation.

In the case of Hindi, spoken in Northern India and relevant to the chapter "Devotional Poetry of Medieval North India" by John Stratton Hawley, the following pertains: The standard system for transliterating Indic words into the Roman alphabet was devised for Sanskrit, and certain modifications are required for Hindi. Two innovations are especially prominent. First, in spoken Hindi the neutral vowel "a" is usually inaudible, and is therefore not indicated in transliteration. Therefore one sees, for example, *rām* rather than *rāma* to indicate the name of the god of that name (cf. also *sāvak* and, from a derivation outside of Sanskrit, *harām*). There are, however, instances when the final "a" is sometimes audible, as when preceded by the semivowel "y," and in that case the final "a" appears in transliteration (e.g., *vinaya*). I also retain the final "a" in the words *saguṇa* and *nirguṇa*, because it has become customary to use them in their Sanskrit form. Finally, one often meets an audible final "a" in Hindi poetry. In the sample chosen for analysis here, however, Tulsidas apparently intends to keep close to the rhythms of speech. I have therefore transliterated as if it were spoken prose, omitting the final "a."

The second innovation involves nasalization. Whereas Sanskrit indicates nasalization in a variety of ways, depending on the value of the succeeding consonant, Hindi simplifies. That simplification is registered in transliteration through the uniform use of a tilde (˜). If a vowel is both long and nasal, both the macron and the tilde appear (˜). If a diphthong is nasalised, the tilde appears over the first letter of the transliteration (ãi).

Other variations from standard Sanskrit usage occur in a variety of ways, sometimes in response to metrical needs (e.g., *ātmārāma* > *ātamarãm*), but there issues of transliteration as such need not be involved.

In the case of Urdu words, relevant to the chapter "Lyric Poetry in Urdu: the Ghazal" by Shamsur Rahman Faruqi and Frances W. Pritchett, the following should be noted: The Urdu sound system basically corresponds to that of Hindi. Special non-Indic diacritics used in this chapter include *kh*, a voiceless fricative (the sound of "ch" in Loch when said by a Scotsman, or the sound made when clearing one's throat); *gh*, the voiced counterpart of *kh*; ᶜ, an Arabic letter, romanized as *ain* or *ayn*, and pronounced in Urdu as one of a number of vowel sounds; and ᵓ, a sign called a hamzah indicating a glide between two vowels. The Urdu *ṛ* indicates a modern retroflex liquid, a sound made by flipping the tongue forward against the roof of the mouth and is not to be confused with the Sanskrit semivowel *ṛ*.

For information on Tamil, see the beginning of "Classical Tamil Poetry and Tamil Poetics" by Rajagopal Parthasarathy.

JAPANESE

Adapted from H. Paul Varley, A Syllabus of Japanese Civilization, *New York: Columbia University Press, 1972*

Japanese words and names have been transcribed according to the Hepburn system of romanization.

Vowels in Japanese are similar to those in Italian:

a	as *a* in *a*rm
i	as the first *e* in *e*ve
u	as *u* in r*u*de
e	as *a* in ch*a*otic
o	as *o* in *o*ld

Long marks or macrons over the vowels *u* and *o* (*ū, ō*) require that the sound be held for twice its normal duration. Since there are no true diphthongs in Japanese, each vowel must be pronounced separately. For example, the word *kai* is pronounced *ka-i.*

Consonants are pronounced as in English (*g* is always hard) with the exception of *r*, which is rendered like the unrolled *r* of Spanish. Double consonants should be sustained in the same fashion as the lengthened vowels mentioned above.

Introduction

Masterworks of Asian Literature in Comparative Perspective

Barbara Stoler Miller

"The very thought of a superior European culture is a blatant insult to the majesty of Nature," wrote the eighteenth century German philosopher Johann Gottfried von Herder in his *Ideas on the Philosophy of the History of Mankind*. Herder's study questioned the assumption of most historians of his time that "civilization" was a unilinear process, leading to the high point of eighteenth century European culture. The critique seems relevant two centuries later, in view of the debates going on in American educational circles between academics who interpret multicultural curricular changes in the humanities as a lapse into cultural relativism, and opponents who contend that the cultural imperialism that still dominates Western attitudes towards Asian, African, and Latin American cultures is at best anachronistic.

The issues are complex, but radical changes in American society over the past half century, wrought by factors of war, migration, and global communication, have altered what we call "Western culture," the range of beliefs and values that anthropologists refer to as patterns of and for behavior. New research in archaeology, geography, and literature suggests that the cultures of Asia and the West have historically been less indifferent to one another than is generally supposed. It has become increasingly clear that in order to understand what Western culture is, we need some understanding of non-Western cultures. Most of us live in multi-cultural environments in which we are constantly faced with ideas and practices that challenge our personal values. To be truly educated in the modern world demands the ability to make translations from one time frame to another, from one language to another, from one code of communication to another. Human communication in its highest forms involves the translation of ideas, emotions, forms across barriers of time, place, and language.

The tendency to overgeneralize conclusions and judgments about a foreign culture can be countered by careful study of concrete examples of that culture, such as works of imaginative literature. When confronting literatures as vast and complex as those of Asia, it is impossible to limit the unit of understanding. One must pay attention to words, figures of speech, verses, episodes, epics, and whole imaginative universes. To some extent every reader of literature is a literary translator. In order to capture the meaning of a single image or concept the translator must draw in the entire culture and find ways to connect aspects of that culture with appropriate aspects of his or her own culture. This creates a dialogue between the original and the translated version, so that every modification of the translation takes its own context and the context of the original into fresh account. Like the translator, the reader is of necessity a comparatist, shuttling back and forth between ways of seeing the world, struggling to transcend the constraints of his or her own experience of time and place.

The essays in this teaching guide were written as part of a project on Asia in the Core Curriculum, based at Columbia University since 1984, but involving faculty from various colleges and universities throughout the country. The project included components on literature, history, and the social sciences. These essays reflect the collaboration of scholars of Asian literature with literary scholars of English and European literature. We examined Asian texts in translation as potential works for inclusion in courses surveying world literature. The essayists are translators and critics of Chinese, Japanese, and Indian literatures who have taught in undergraduate comparative literature programs.

Throughout our discussions, we confronted the conceptual challenges of comparison and cultural imperialism. The social critics of our time have made us acutely aware that cross-cultural understanding is ultimately grounded in one's experience and ideology. Hermeneutical sophistication and sympathetic imagination certainly enhance the possibilities of cross-cultural understanding, but the obstacles are significant. We recognized that the non-specialist is particularly handicapped by a lack of knowledge of the original texts and contexts. There is a difference between

Asian texts as artifacts of a specific culture and as works in the context of world literature. To address these issues, specific "masterworks" are recommended in the teaching guide on the basis of their literary value within their own cultural contexts, their literary value as expressions of the human condition, and the quality of available translations. We also include introductory essays on the "imaginative universe" of each of the three major literary traditions represented in the guide.

David Damrosch of Columbia's Department of English and Comparative Literature set the tone of our discussions by raising the general question of how students and teachers come to terms with material from foreign cultures, when a detailed knowledge of the cultural context cannot be assumed. Damrosch observed that the issues raised by the inclusion of Asian works in surveys of literature are also present in any course which attempts to discuss works from a variety of periods and countries. He identified the double problem of dealing with perceptions of difference and sameness in a comparative approach. Readers may fail to appreciate the foreign literary values, modes of representation, or they may too readily appreciate similarities, assimilating the foreign material to familiar terms without perceiving its particularities. He advocated what he called "a dynamic reading, one which can see points of similarity and dissimilarity not statically but as moments on a larger trajectory."

Damrosch used the epic genre as an example of the challenges posed by difference and similarity. He pointed to the degree of continuity within the Western epic tradition, grounding direct comparison of works like the *Aeneid* and the *Divine Comedy* in a substantial core of similarities. By contrast, the Indian epics, the *Mahābhārata* and the *Rāmāyaṇa*, are only loosely related to the wider Indo-European epic tradition and work so differently that any broader definition of epic must be modified to accommodate their elements of structure, action and character. On the other hand, the absence of anything that can be called epic in Chinese literature raises issues about genre as the basic category of comparison.

In view of such questions, our purpose in the guide is to suggest alternatives for different types of literature courses and provide a basis for selecting works. Each of the Asian works presented is meant to stand on its own or combine with others to suit the needs of a particular course. We offer different strategies for reading these Asian works and for integrating them into general education curricula. The approach is meant to enable readers to gain access to some of the major concepts of Asian civilizations by studying examples of lyric, dramatic, and narrative works from classical and modern Asian traditions. The pedagogical intent of the guide made the choice of works highly selective in another way. The longevity and influence of the literary traditions of China, Japan, and India identify them as the dominant literatures of Asia. Each tradition has its own mechanisms for establishing and transmitting cultural values by selection and exclusion. These processes determined what it meant to be a "classic" in various parts of Asia at different times. Out of the bewildering array of extant literary works, we have selected those works from the past that have endured as "classics" in each civilization, as well as works of modern literature widely regarded for their literary merit. Despite our reservations about genre classification across cultures, the classical Asian works do fall within the broad categories of lyric, drama, and narrative. In the modern period, attention is focused on narrative works, which have been the main medium of literary innovation and experimentation.

All participants in the project, both essayists and discussants, contributed to these essays through their critical questions and ideas.

The success of the project at every level owes a great deal to Roberta Martin. I know that readers of this volume will join us in thanking her for bringing this material to a wider audience. Madge Huntington admirably managed every stage of the production process with the able assistance of Lynette Peck. Lori Stevens thoughtfully edited the essays and Barbara Gombach provided guidance in bringing consistency to diacritical usage in Indic terms. Nadine Berardi prepared the background notes on the literary works discussed in the essays. The project has been generously supported by grants from the National Endowment for the Humanities, the Henry Luce Foundation, the Panasonic Foundation, and the U.S. Department of Education.

ESSAYISTS AND DISCUSSANTS

Joseph Roe Allen III
Washington University

Paul Anderer
Columbia University

Gene A. Barnett
Fairleigh Dickinson University

Paula S. Berggren
Baruch College, City
University of New York

Michael C. Brownstein
Notre Dame University

David Damrosch
Columbia University

George Doskow
St. John's College

Shamsur Rahman Faruqi
University of Pennsylvania

Robert P. Goldman
University of California,
Berkeley

Thomas Blenman Hare
Stanford University

John Stratton Hawley
Barnard College, Columbia
University

C. T. Hsia
Columbia University

C. Harold Hurley
Roberts Wesleyan College

Theodore Huters
University of California, Irvine

Wilt Idema
University of Leiden, The
Netherlands

Ken K. Ito
University of Michigan

Barry Douglas Jacobs
Montclair State College

Richard A. Johnson
Mount Holyoke College

Donald Keene
Columbia University

Robin Jared Lewis
Columbia University

Michael Liberman
East Stroudsburg University

Shuen-fu Lin
University of Michigan

Lucien Miller
University of Massachusetts

Steven J. Mocko
Mohawk Valley Community
College

Donald Morton
Syracuse University

Bharati Mukherjee
University of California,
Berkeley

Rajagopal Parthasarathy
Skidmore College

Thomas A. Pendleton
Iona College

Andrew H. Plaks
Princeton University

Judith Abrams Plotz
George Washington University

Frances W. Pritchett
Columbia University

William Radice
University of London

David Rubin
Columbia University

Barbara Ruch
Columbia University

Margery Sabin
Wellesley College

George L. Scheper
Essex Community College

George Sebouhian
New York State University
College, Fredonia

Edward G. Seidensticker
Columbia University

Carole M. Shaffer-Koros
Kean College of New Jersey

Haruo Shirane
Columbia University

James Shokoff
New York State University,
Fredonia

Marilyn Sides
Wellesley College

Richard Torrance
Ohio State University

John Whittier Treat
University of Washington

Robert L. Vales
Gannon University

Judith Vassallo
Moore College of Art

David Der-wei Wang
Columbia University

John W. Ward
West Chester University

Burton Watson
Columbia University

Stephen H. West
University of California,
Berkeley

Bruce M. Wilson
St. Mary's College of Maryland

Anthony C. Yu
The University of Chicago

Pauline Yu
University of California, Irvine

I

The Worlds of Asian Literature

THE IMAGINATIVE UNIVERSE OF INDIAN LITERATURE

Barbara Stoler Miller

INTRODUCTION

Westerners have been "discovering" India since antiquity, when members of Alexander the Great's expedition to India in the fourth century B.C.E. recorded their responses to the exotic fabulousness of the subcontinent. This was amplified through the centuries in the writings of Arab historians and Portuguese missionaries. In the thirteenth century, the Venetian traveler Marco Polo visited India on his way to China; the account of his journey, as related to Rusticello, draws on a tradition of myths and fables that combined some fact with much fiction. The reports of Marco and others who followed him aroused some European interest in the institutions and customs of the distant peoples of Asia, but there were no serious Western attempts to study Indian literature until the last half of the eighteenth century. Sir William Jones (1746–94), a judge of the British high court in Calcutta and a superb linguist, recognized the relationship of European languages to Persian and Sanskrit, rejecting the orthodox eighteenth-century view that all these tongues were derived from Hebrew, which had been garbled in the Tower of Babel. With Charles Wilkins, Jones produced the first direct translations of Sanskrit works into English: the *Bhagavad Gītā*, the *Hitopadeśa*, the *Śakuntalā*, the *Gītagovinda*, and the *Laws of Manu*. These formed the basis of early Western conceptions of ancient Indian culture and, through Schlegel and Goethe, were influential in the development of German Romanticism. The same early translations and studies that circulated in Europe were read by Emerson and Thoreau in America. Yet, despite growing sympathy for Indian literature in certain quarters, European response was generally more ethnocentric.

Even after centuries of "rediscovery" and scholarship on India, what seems to linger in the Western imagination are images of romantic exoticism or extreme social chaos. Contemporary responses to Indian literature and art often echo the views of Englishmen like Thomas Babington Macaulay (1800–59), whose desire to "improve" India colored his judgments, as in these remarks from a speech made in the House of Commons in 1843:

> The great majority of the population of India consists of idolators, blindly attached to doctrines and rites which are in the highest degree pernicious. The Brahmanical religion is so absurd that it necessarily debases every mind which receives it as truth; and with this absurd mythology is bound up an absurd system of physics, an absurd geography, an absurd astronomy. Nor is this form of Paganism more favourable to art than to science. Through the whole Hindu Pantheon you will look in vain for anything resembling those beautiful and majestic forms which stood in the shrines of Ancient Greece. All is hideous, and grotesque and ignoble. As this superstition is of all superstitions the most irrational and of all superstitions the most inelegant, so it is of all superstitions the most immoral.[1]

The powerful and often paradoxical religious imagery that one finds in much of Indian literature encourages the formation of such stereotypes among uninitiated Western readers. Even scholars who are usually more judicious can distort Indian literature when they ignore indigenous categories of culture and representation in favor of prevalent Western interpretive ideas. Yet, when they are exercised with appropriate caution, well-honed critical tools can provide a framework of questions that make the reader self-conscious about the biases she or he brings to any reading. Contemporary Western critical attitudes that insistently focus on linguistic dimensions of the human condition dovetail in some basic ways with ancient Indian ideas about the origins and experience of literature.

It is difficult to deny that the cultural and literary history of India, with its predominant pattern of cultural and linguistic pluralism, is bewildering at many levels. During the past four thousand years, India has produced a vast body of oral and written literature in more than twenty languages and innumerable local dialects. The complexity of the linguistic situation alone makes any attempt to provide a brief overview of Indian literature impossible. However, amidst the linguistic, historical, and geographic diversity of Indian literature, there are enduring characteristics, many of which have their origin in the ancient traditions of Sanskrit and Tamil poetry. Sanskrit belongs to the eastern, or so-called Indo-Aryan, branch of the Indo-European family of languages, which was spoken by tribes who seem to have migrated into the regions of Iran and India toward the end of the second millennium B.C.E. The earliest preserved evidence of Sanskrit literature is the body of ritual hymns collectively known as the *Ŗg Veda*, which were guarded and orally transmitted by a priestly class known as brahmans, who remained the main repository of Sanskrit traditions through the centuries. Tamil, whose earliest preserved literature dates to the second century B.C.E., belongs to a wholly distinct family of languages, known as Dravidian. Among the four Dravidian languages, which are geographically located in the southern part of the Indian subcontinent, only Tamil has a literary tradition to rival that of Sanskrit.

From the time of the earliest attempts to collect and codify the hymns of the *Ŗg Veda*, Indian literature is characterized by a preoccupation with the nature of language. In order to assure the precise pronunciation, transmission, and preservation of the hymns, the brahman scholars carefully analyzed the language of oral poetry in these sacred texts and began to speculate on the structure and function of speech. Linguistic science developed in India in the middle of the first millennium B.C.E. and achieved its first major expression in the work of Pāṇini, a grammarian of the fifth century B.C.E. By basing his analyses not only on the sacred language of the *Ŗg Veda*, but on the spoken language of his time and region, Pāṇini was able to liberate the older linguistic techniques from their narrow purpose and to apply them to a codification of the language of his day. The language he codified is called Sanskrit, which means "put together, codified, classified." It is the classical language of India, and this language itself became the standard medium of what is classical in Hindu culture. Sanskrit broadly refers to the language and the cultural values associated with it. But Sanskrit never really supplanted other languages. Various other Vedic dialects continued to develop independent of Sanskrit; the grammarians referred to them by the collective term Prakrit, which means "original" or "natural." Among them is Pali, the language of early Buddhist texts. These Prakrits form the basis of the modern languages of North India, among which the literatures in Hindi and Bengali are the richest.

In modern times, the basic dichotomy between Indo-Aryan and

Dravidian languages and literatures has been complicated by the introduction into India of two major languages of conquest. Persian gained widespread use from the thirteenth to the nineteenth century and left its mark in the development of the Urdu literary culture of Islamic India. English, the language of the British Raj from the late eighteenth to the twentieth century, like Persian, has greatly complicated issues of linguistic and cultural identity that are reflected in contemporary literature.

In an attempt to introduce Indian cultures through literature, difficult choices have to be made among works from different languages and periods. One of the most glaring omissions is the absence of any work from the Indian Buddhist and Jain traditions. Though Buddhism and Jainism have left indelible marks on every aspect of Indian thought, Buddhist and Jain texts are characteristically more didactic than literary. The preponderance of works of Sanskrit epic, lyric, and dramatic literature is based on the widespread cultivation of Sanskrit throughout the subcontinent for several millennia (from about 1000 B.C.E. to 1800 C.E.), during which time it enjoyed high status and served as the vehicle for continuous exchanges among various literary cultures. Sanskrit was not only the hieratic language of the brahman priests from ancient times, but, under various rulers, it was also the status language of royal administration and poetry. Even those who never mastered the intricacies of Sanskrit knew its poetry through vernacular translations and oral performances.

AUTHORSHIP AND POETICS

In India few records exist that document the historical reality of ancient authors, but rich legendary traditions surround the names to which poems in various genres are attributed. The legends reflect a fundamental Indian preoccupation with the origin of things, often involving vast expanses of mythic time and space in contrast to the concrete nature of historical time and place. Whereas historical narrative is characteristic of Chinese literature, mythic narrative dominates in India. Concerns about the origin and traditions of literature are expressed through the legends of authorship, which often point to aspects of the texts that might otherwise be ignored. The process by which these texts "create" their authors highlights the theoretical sophistication found in the poems themselves, where careful reading consistently reveals embedded theories of aesthetic experience.

Early Indian literature employs two variant ways of representing authorship. An author may literally exist as a character within the text attributed to him (making explicit the author implied by the work), as is the case in the Sanskrit epics and in the *Gītagovinda*. Otherwise the author may be the hero of a legend that is attached to the text, as is the case with Bhartṛhari and Kālidāsa. Sometimes the legends surrounding the verses are mythical contexts for the poetry. A literary legend dramatizes the poetic personality in the text. It may also point to the work's dominant poetic structures, in much the same way that the prologue of a Sanskrit drama announces its dramatic structures. Legends explain the poetry by means that are different from academic analyses of Sanskrit poetics, which characteristically focus on formal elements of individual stanzas. The mythic structure of the legends sometimes complements the content and language of the poetry so well that it is possible to imagine that the legends were self-consciously elaborated by the poets themselves, though textual evidence is uniformly against this. In any case the accounts are informed by the same attitudes toward language and literature that govern the texts themselves.

Legends of authorship often involve transformations in which authoritative knowledge and poetic inspiration are acquired through divine intervention. In the *Ṛg Veda*, poetry is a means of establishing relations between the world of humans and the world of the gods. In the Vedic hymns, which were composed as invocations to accompany offerings poured on the sacrificial fire, speech is personified as a goddess who gives inspired priests the power to communicate with the world of the gods. The Vedic poets stress that their language does not serve the function of separating elements of the cosmos. Instead it is a unifying force, and speech is a manifestation of the poets' own power to communicate with the divine, to unify humans with nature and the cosmos. By gaining insight into hidden correspondences between the human and divine realms, the seer-poet (*kavi*) attained the special power to give his visions concrete expression in poetry (*kavya*). Fascination with expressing hidden correspondences between experience and imagination lies at the base of the metaphorical language that is exploited throughout the history of Indian literature. Although kavya narrowly refers to "poetry," in its broadest sense it signifies imaginative literature, works in verse or prose that exploit metaphorical language and show self-conscious ideas of art.

Throughout Indian literature the power of speech is deemed crucial to the production of aesthetic experience or *rasa*, a concept that is central to Indian theories of literature and art. Though usually translated as "sentiment" or "mood," rasa more literally means the "flavor" or "taste" of something. Rasa is essentially the flavor that the poet distills from a given emotional situation in order to present it for aesthetic appreciation. Human emotion, the basic material of rasa, is divided by early theorists into eight categories, each of which has its corresponding rasa. The eight are the romantic, the heroic, the comic, the pathetic, the furious, the horrible, the marvelous, and the disgusting. Every poem or drama has a dominant rasa; of these the romantic and the heroic are of central importance throughout Sanskrit literature, beginning with the two great Sanskrit epics, the *Mahābhārata* and the *Rāmāyaṇa*.

CATEGORIES AND CONTROLLING METAPHORS

In addition to its concern for linguistic and aesthetic subtleties, Indian culture has systematically developed various categories that attempt to order and reconcile conflicting aspects of society, life, and art. Sets of four elements are particularly common. Early Indian thinkers speak of the four cyclic ages of the cosmos (*kṛta* or *satya, tretā, dvāpara, kali,* named for dice-rolls in gaming), the four ranks of society (brahman priest, warrior, community member, menial laborer), and the four stages of life (celibate student, householder, forest dweller, wandering ascetic). One of the most enduring of these sets is that which enumerates the four spheres of human life (*puruṣārtha*). These are an idealized tetrad of culturally acceptable pursuits that inform much of Indian civilization and specifically circumscribe the life of a Hindu: (1) *dharma,* the sphere of duty, virtue, law, social responsibility, and order—individual, social, and cosmic; (2) *artha,* the sphere of worldly profit, wealth, and political power; (3) *kama,* the sphere of pleasure, sensuous love, and art; (4) *moksha,* the sphere in which one seeks liberation from the constraints imposed by the three worldly pursuits. The significance of these categories is expressed not only by their durability, but also by the profusion of theoretical and imaginative literature that has clustered around them. They inform many of the major texts of Indian literature, whose controlling metaphors developed with reference to them.

Associated with each of the four spheres is a textual tradition of learned theories. In the sphere of dharma, there are the brahmanical law books (*dharmaśāstra*) that codify Hindu religious activity. In the sphere of kama, various theoretical texts and manuals elaborate highly developed theories of literature. These include texts on the science of love (*kāma-śāstra,* the most famous of which is the *Kāma-sūtra* of Vatsyāyana), as well as on the sciences of poetics (*alaṃkāra-śāstra*) and dramaturgy (*nāṭya-śāstra*). In the sphere of moksha are the texts of speculative philosophy and logic. These texts were composed in very technical Sanskrit and have been the property of a small class of Hindu academicians throughout their history. They remain inaccessible to the majority of educated Hindus as well as to Western readers. Although the theoretical texts are inaccessible, the imaginative works in which these spheres of life are explored provide contexts replete with concrete examples.

Because it is so central to Indian civilization, the concept of dharma has attracted various and complex interpretations throughout history. Derived from a Sanskrit form meaning "that which sustains," dharma generally refers to the law that sustains the cosmos, human society, and the individual. On the human scale, it is religiously ordained duty, that is, the code of conduct appropriate to each group in the hierarchically ordered Hindu society. In theory, right and wrong are not absolute; in practice, right and wrong are decided according to kinship, social rank, stage of life, and occasion. There is the general notion that if each unit or group performs its functions correctly, the whole universe will function harmoniously. This relativity of values and obligations is perhaps the most difficult aspect of Hinduism for modern Westerners who are raised on ideals of universality and egalitarianism. Yet if no attempt is made to understand it—which does not mean to approve it—much of Indian culture remains opaque.

Just as Greek culture has drawn on the Homeric epics to confirm its values, so Indian culture has drawn upon the *Mahābhārata* and the *Rāmāyaṇa* to confirm its own. Within these two epics, dharma is represented through the characters' actions and their consequences, that is, their karma, another fundamental concept of Indian thought. Appropriate to the authority of their social position as warrior-kings, the epic heroes embody order and sacred duty (dharma), while their foes, whether human or demonic, embody chaos (adharma). The ritualization of warrior life and the demands of sacred duty define the religious and moral meaning of heroism throughout the *Mahābhārata* and the *Rāmāyaṇa*. Acts of heroism are characterized less by physical prowess than by dharma, often involving extraordinary forms of sacrifice, penance, devotion to a divine authority, and spiritual victory over evil.

Although the religion of the epics had not yet assumed many of the features that are today recognized as "Hinduism," it is convenient to look at the epics as the repositories of many features that India's dominant Hindu culture emphasized and developed. It is well to remember that Hinduism was not founded by any historical personage, such as the Buddha, Christ, or Muhammad. It evolved from a variety of cults and beliefs, of which some have their foundations in Vedic religion, and others are based on local cults. Hinduism is fundamentally a complex of attitudes and rituals integral to the routines of daily existence. In Indian languages, the religious life and its demands are referred to as "the eternal dharma" (sanātana-dharma), the way that keeps order in the universe.

Despite the overwhelming evidence of a preoccupation with sacred duty and order in what was felt to be a dark age of the cosmos, the practicalities of worldly life have been given ample attention in Indian literature from ancient times. Techniques for gaining wealth and power are presented in various collections of fables, stories, and romances. The most famous of these is the Pañcatantra, which is essentially a didactic book, meant as a delightful manual for young rulers. Each of the five chapters stresses a different aspect of human conduct, such as "The Loss of Friends," and "The Winning of Friends." The characters are both humans and animals whose actions demonstrate the value of a constant cagey presence of mind and preparedness for any eventuality. Accompanying the prose narratives are moral maxims in verse, meant to be memorized; many of these have found their way into collections, such as the poems attributed to Bhartṛhari, of which this verse is characteristic:

> A piercing hiss augurs swift end
> of a drop of water touching molten iron,
> but a drop resting on a lotus-leaf
> assumes a mellow pearl-like hue.
> And if in light of some auspicious star
> it falls into an oyster shell, it turns into a pearl.
> A man attains to vile or mean
> or lofty ways through the company he keeps.

The attitudes expressed in the fables and romances of ancient India are characteristic of many modern Indian writers, but nowhere are they more graphically expressed than in the satirical novels and stories of R.K. Narayan. One of Narayan's most engaging characters is the "financial mystic" Margayya, the hero of The Financial Expert, a comic novel of life in a small Indian town, in which the hero suffers characteristic Indian conflicts over the demands of wealth, love, and religious duty. Margayya articulates his own obsession: "It's money which gives people all this (authority, dress, looks). Money alone is important in this world. Everything else will come to us naturally if we have money in our purse."

Margayya begins his adventure as a financial adviser to peasants who come to borrow money from the Malgudi Central Cooperative Land Mortgage Bank; his office is an old tin trunk placed under a banyan tree in front of the bank. He meets a devilish character named Dr. Pal who magically appears in answer to his prayers and helps him on the way to prosperity by publishing a book on sex. His shady business activities propel him to wealth, but the fragile magic finally fails, and he returns to his place under the banyan tree, ready to start again.

In ancient literature emotional feeling (kama) is recognized as the source of all action. The Buddha and some Hindu religious thinkers considered it the source of attachment to the world and an impediment to freedom. For the classical Indian poets, emotional feeling was at the center of human existence and its highest manifestation was through aesthetic experience.

In Indian literature emotion is not an isolated human phenomenon. The natural world of birds, flowers, and forests in their seasonal transformations expresses human emotions. The role that nature plays in Indian poetry is closely associated with the Indian attitude toward erotic love. Erotic emotion is in the cycles of the seasons as well as in the lover's eyes. If Kāma, the god of love, can use lovers as his weapons, he has a powerful ally in nature.

This power of Kāma and the relationship between erotic and ascetic aspects of life are explored by Kālidāsa in his lyric narrative poem *Kumārasaṃbhava, The Birth of Śiva's Son.* It is a celebration of the creative love of Śiva for the goddess Pārvati, the daughter of the Himalayas. Kālidāsa sets the scene by evoking the potent, sensuous divinity of the mountains:

> Far in the north divinity animates
> the majestic mountain range called Himalaya,
> a place of perpetual snow
> that sinks deep into the seas
> on its eastern and western wings,
> a towering barrier standing over earth.

> Himalayan herbs shine at night
> deep inside cave shelters
> where wild forest men
> lie with their rustic women—
> herbs like lamps burning without oil
> to excite sensual love.

The mythic theme of the long narrative lyric poem is the threat posed to the gods by the demon Tāraka, who is practically invulnerable since he can be overcome only by a son born to Śiva and Pārvatī. When the god of love, Kāma, accompanies Pārvatī to Śiva's Himalayan retreat in springtime to seduce him, Kālidāsa describes Śiva as Kāma sees him in the trance of yoga. Śiva's yogic power is expressed in poetic imagery suggestive of an impending dance of creation or a destructive burning of the universe. Śiva wakes from his "volcanic stillness" to take part in the world of creation. Paradoxically, he burns the god of love with his fiery third eye, but in so doing catches a glimpse of Pārvatī's beauty and only waits for her trial by religious austerity to strengthen and purify her for the sacred marriage and extravagant erotic rite of creation that follows. In every section of the poem the sacred landscape of India is intertwined with the power and beauty of Śiva and Pārvatī enacting sacred rites of love.

The underlying idea here is that the passions of nature can be transmuted in art to energize the world and reestablish harmonies of feeling and form. This is an Indian classical ideal, but not every poet subscribed to it. The poet Bhartrihari was renowned in his own time as a philosopher who continually vacillated between the secluded life of a monk and the world of courtly pleasure, delighting in his own contradictory position. Bhartrihari, in his characteristic irony, worshipped an idealized female who was simultaneously poison and ambrosia; he loved her lustily, only to find himself deceived by life's transience and woman's trickery.

Although theoretically each sphere of life could be enjoyed by man in his time, skeptics like Bhartrihari raised doubts about the reality of the model. His sense that none of life's possibilities are what they seem to be gives pattern to his irreconcilable attractions. In his poems he expresses dreams of finding salvation as a hermit meditating on the god Śiva in a mountain cave on a cliff whose stones are washed by sprays of the sacred river Ganges, or lying as a hermit embraced by Nature. Yet despite moments of calm, the sensuality of Nature continues to disturb him. Bhartṛhari remained obsessed with the fact of life's transience and felt that choice among the spheres of activity was imperative. Any possibility of a harmonious balance of dharma, *artha*, and kama in an ordered life leading to concentration on moksha in old age seemed absurd to him.

Recognition of the ephemeral nature of worldly laws, wealth, and pleasure underlies much of the Indian preoccupation with liberation from mundane existence (moksha, "release"; or nirvana, "extinction" in Buddhist terms). This preoccupation is compounded by the Indian belief in rebirth and transmigration, which serves to exaggerate the pain of a single mortal life. Elaborate philosophies and practices have been devised throughout Indian history to present ways of achieving liberation. Extremely different ways are found in the renunciatory traditions of Buddhism and Hinduism, preserved in the stories and sermons of the Buddha and the Hindu sages, in contrast with the erotic mystical poetry of medieval devotional cults, addressed to Krishna, Śiva, or the goddess Devi. The lyric poems of medieval devotional literature, which exist in every Indian language, give expression to a religion that is predominantly emotional. For example, the Bengali devotional cults center chiefly on episodes in the early romantic life of Krishna as they are described, not in the *Mahābhārata*, but in medieval sectarian epics known as puranas. These are a favored subject in Indian miniature painting as well as in popular art forms. By admitting into the sphere of religious salvation intense human emotions, such as had usually been associated only with passionate human love, the devotional traditions allowed for the harmony of religious duty (dharma), liberation (moksha), and love (kama). The tension Bhartrihari suffered between the life of passion and the life of religious devotion is here resolved in passionate devotion to Krishna, Śiva, or Devi. Centuries earlier the *Bhagavad Gītā* had advanced a compromise between worldly action and renunciation, but in the *Gītā* self-surrender to Krishna comes from a mystical friendship, through which Arjuna learns the martial qualities of disciplined self-control over desire.

In the later devotional poetry addressed to Krishna, the emphasis is on complete surrender to the love of Krishna, accompanied by all the emotions of attachment. What makes Indian devotional poetry unique is the notion that the god may be enticed by the love of the devotee and reciprocate in passionate ways. The notion of incarnation makes it possible to think of the god in human ways and in human relationships, upon which Krishna depends.

Although the promise of Krishna's embrace exists, what inspires the poets is not the satisfaction of love, but the passionate yearning of a lover separated from his beloved—a suffering of such intensity that it liberates the devotee from worldly concerns. Jayadeva's Sanskrit poem *Gitagovinda* and the devotional lyrics of bhakti poetry in every Indian language suggest how completely religious, erotic, and aesthetic meanings are integrated in this popular tradition.

Exploration of the tensions and relations among dharma, *artha,* kama, and moksha dovetail with discussion of the themes and motifs that are recurrent through various levels of ancient and modern Indian literature. Notable among these are themes of cultural polarities whose dynamic relations to each other provide the ground for many myths and ideas. These include ideas of order and chaos, often described in naturalistic terms, or in terms of heroes and demons; ideas of nature and culture, city and forest, secular life and religious pursuit; concepts of action (karma) and fate (daiva), involving curses, boons, penances, death, rebirth, and sacrifice; concepts of time and immortality, focusing on the paradox of man's bondage in the phenomenal world (samsara) and his infinite potential for freedom (moksha, nirvana); notions of male and female creativity and destructiveness, related to fertility, family, power, and love. All of these inform the work of Indian authors—the bards of the *Mahābhārata* and the *Rāmāyaṇa*, the ancient Tamil poets, Kālidāsa, Bhartrihari, Jayadeva, the devotional poets of medieval India, even Urdu poets of the Indo-Islamic tradition and modern writers in various languages, such as Tagore, Premchand, R. K. Narayan, Anita Desai, U. R. Anantha Murthy, and Salman Rushdie.

NOTE

1. Quoted by E.M. Forster in a review of Benjamin Rowland's *Art and Architecture of India* in *The Listener*, September 10, 1953, p. 419.

REFERENCES

Chatterji, S. K. *Languages and Literatures of Modern India.* Calcutta: Prakash Bhavan, 1963.
de Bary, Wm. Theodore, et al. *A Guide to the Oriental Classics.* 3d ed. Section 2, "Classics of the Indian Tradition." New York: Columbia University Press, 1989. Contains bibliography and topics for discussion.
Dharwarkar, Vinay, et al. "Indian Poetry." In *The Princeton Encyclopedia of Poetry and Poetics.* 2d ed. Princeton: Princeton University Press, 1990.
Dimock, Edward C., et al. *The Literatures of India: An Introduction.* Chicago: University of Chicago Press, 1974.
Embree, Ainslie, ed. *Sources of Indian Tradition.* Vol. 1, *From the Beginning to 1800.* 2d ed. New York: Columbia University Press, 1988.
Hay, Stephen, ed. *Sources of Indian Tradition.* Vol. 2, *Modern India and Pakistan.* 2d ed. New York: Columbia University Press, 1988.
Warder, A. K. *Indian Kāvya Literature.* 4 vols. Delhi: Motilal Banarsidass, 1972–83.

A NOTE ON MODERN INDIAN LITERATURE

David Rubin

The literatures of India in the twentieth century, and particularly since independence in 1947, have flourished both in English and in the many Indian regional languages. Fiction and poetry are probably the most widely cultivated genres, though drama and criticism are gaining in both frequency and maturity. Only a small amount of this writing has been translated into English. Therefore, ironically, it is mainly works written originally in English, called Indo-Anglian, that have become well known in the West.

Both the abundance and the variety of twentieth-century Indian literature make a brief survey of it next to impossible. Getting an accurate overall picture of writing in the entire Subcontinent is rendered still more complicated by the fact that few critics command more than two or three of the many regional languages in which worthwhile literature is being produced. (This explains why most of the references in this essay will be to works written in Hindi, Urdu, and Bengali, in addition to English.) The following remarks are meant to serve as a very general guide for the interested Western reader.

In the five decades preceding Indian independence, fiction in both English and regional languages tended to focus on the discussion of social and political questions—rising nationalism, religious reform, caste, the status of women, the struggle against traditional restraints—and often took a didactic and doctrinaire approach, as in the novels of Mulk Raj Anand. Among notable exceptions are (in Bengali) Tagore's fiction and B. Bandopadhyay's *Pather Panchali* (1929) and *Aparajito* (1931), which were to become known worldwide through Satyajit Ray's film trilogy; in them one finds an emphasis on the personal and psychological rather than the ideological. This development is more radical than it might at first appear to a Western reader, for it marks a heretofore unfamiliar growing sense of selfhood among Indian writers. The psychological and social emergence of the individual, as distinct from group or caste, becomes a worthwhile subject for literary treatment in its own right. In Hindi, Premchand's later work is less reformist, reflecting greater objectivity and universal concerns, as well as pessimism about humanity in general and India in particular. His darkened outlook anticipates that of many Indian writers after the first euphoria of independence in 1947 had given way before the harsh realities besetting the country.

In the first half of the century, popular British, and particularly Victorian, literature had established the superficial forms for the development of Indian fiction (as well as Indian poetry written in English). After independence, younger Indian writers were increasingly influenced by such Continental figures as Baudelaire, Camus, Sartre and Kafka. In both Indo-Anglian and Indian-language novels the city tends to replace the village as the favored setting. Though social and political themes persist, more often than not the approach is subjective (frequently autobiographical), the mood one of existential despair or baffling absurdity. Unfortunately, some of the best Indian fiction either remains untranslated (e.g., Shrilal Shukla's *Rāg Darbāri* in Hindi) or is found in inadequate and clumsy English versions. Among the best literary translations to date are Gordon Roadarmel's *The Gift of a Cow* (Premchand) and A. K. Ramanujan's *Samskara* (Anantha Murthy). (Incidentally, these two works provide an interesting contrast: the former representing the culmination of the naturalistic regional novel before World War II, and the latter, more recent fiction in an allegorical and existentialist mode.) There are good translations of Mohan Rakesh[1]—one of the finest short story writers in Hindi in the postindependence movement known as *nai kahāni*, or "new story"—and of Saadat Hasan Manto's imaginative and iconoclastic Urdu stories.

Before World War I, poetry in the regional languages most typically reproduced the time-honored patterns of Indian narrative verse (often with subjects drawn from mythology) and devotional songs. The experience of the war, which afforded many new and unexpected contacts with the West, along with the growing nationalist movement, accounts in part for the radicalism in both form and subject matter of Indian poetry in various languages. Contemporary political and social problems, along with autobiographical topics, were now grist for every poet's mill. Free verse, as well as a great variety of styles and forms that defy the usual typologies, was soon cultivated in Hindi and Bengali. The revolutionary new Hindi poetry known as Chayavad, for example, has elements which might be classified as romantic, realistic, symbolic, and metaphysical. The influence of the past is not lacking in Prasad and Nirala, to cite two of the leading Chayavad poets, as well as in Tagore (where Upanishadic concepts and allusions to the epics and myths are frequent), but the treatment by all three poets is highly personal and the ideas sometimes revolutionary. For example, *Sacrifice* (1917), one of Tagore's most famous plays, reinterprets Hindu concepts of worship and condemns the practice of animal sacrifice to Kali.

The poets of succeeding generations (e.g., Muktibodh in Hindi, Jibanananda Das in Bengali) have a more tenuous connection with the Indian past; in translation their poetry will often be difficult to identify as specifically Indian, but for passing references to a tropical tree or bird. Though many Urdu poets have maintained a somewhat closer tie with their literary tradition, they may sometimes put the structure and conventions of *ghazal* to unexpected uses.

The question will arise as to whether Indian literature written in English can be considered authentically "Indian." For general readers the question may well be irrelevant, as their main concern will probably be simply how good, in absolute terms, each novel or poem is in its own right. But anyone particularly interested in India may quite naturally wonder for whom Indian writers, working in the medium of a non-Indian language, can speak. It can be said, all too glibly, that English is not a foreign language in India—it is, for example, the original language of the Indian constitution, the legal language of administration at the federal level, and the medium of much of the most respected press. But it cannot be denied that English remains the language of an elite class that constitutes a small percentage of the total population of the country. Many of the Indo-Anglian writers (B. Rajan, Raja Rao, and Santha Rama Rau, for example) have been longtime émigrés, living the greater part of their adult lives abroad. They are understandably concerned with problems of identity ("Indianness") and the confrontations and misunderstandings that beset them in their relations with non-Indians—all in all, paralleling the concerns of Anglo-Indian novelists from Kipling and Forster to Paul Scott and Ruth Jhabvala. Their fiction often seems to be an exercise for solving private crises, with India serving as a distant background against which Indians and Europeans are drawn as predictable stereotypes. The international theme remains subjective and personal rather than being used as an objective (and unpolemicized) basis for an examination of manners and morality (such as one finds in Henry James, for instance). Though the international theme is treated also by Indo-Anglian novelists like Mulk Raj Anand and Manohar Malgonkar who have resided mostly in India, in their novels it is subordinate, while in fiction written in Indian languages it is virtually nonexistent.[2]

The best of the Indo-Anglian novelists either ignore the international theme or raise it above the limitations of highly personal musings to a level of universal significance. In the first instance, R. K. Narayan's work is concerned at the immediate level with his own Mysorean world, viewed in an apparently (and deceptively) comic mode familiar in English fiction. The West is remembered only as, for example, a statue of an Englishman that survives the Raj ("Lawley Road") or has become a subject of purely vocational interest (*The English Teacher*, first published in America as *Grateful to Life and Death*), but his fictional Malgudi, corresponding to Mysore (where he has lived much of his life) is profoundly rooted in the traditions of Indian culture and society, from which all its values (and the author's as well) are derived. Similarly, while Ahmed Ali's fine novel *Twilight in Delhi* (1940), set in the early days of this century, notes the presence of the British as an important historical phenomenon and some of the characters are affected by the gathering momentum of the independence movement, the main burden of the book is the elegiac description of the intimate lives of old Muslim families in Delhi, who live out the last days of a society and culture in decay.

In the second instance, Kamala Markandaya, whose numerous novels are divided almost equally between works dealing entirely with India and others on the international theme, treats the latter as a dramatic device for the development of complex individual characters; Anita Desai, who usually deals with a mainly Indian milieu, takes as her subject a European refugee living in straitened circumstances in India (in *Baumgartner's Bombay*). These two novelists elevate the Indo-Anglian novel of East-West problems from the limited sphere of introspection and private failure, with its dependable cast of racial and national stereotypes, to a high level of serious and original moral fable.

As more and better translations become available (along with the few noted here) writers of fiction in the regional languages should eventually command greater interest for the Western reader. This is not only because their understanding of India and specifically Indian problems is apt to be deeper and more sympathetically felt than that of the émigré novelist or the writer whose orientation has been largely toward the West, but also because in purely literary terms Indians writing in an Indian language usually possess a fresher and surer instinct for the linguistic medium they have chosen.[3] The same may be said for those Indian poets who write in their mother tongues, though here too there are exceptions, most notably A. K. Ramanujan's own poetry and brilliant recreations of classical Tamil and Kannada verse.

It should be noted finally that many Indo-Anglian novels, even when of limited literary value, can serve as a source of vividly and dramatically presented information for students of modern Indian history and social developments; see, for example, the catastrophe of the Partition as described in Khushwant Singh's *Train to Pakistan* or Chaman Lal Nahal's *Azadi* ("Freedom"—an Indo-Anglian novel despite its Urdu title). In a few novels the powerful recreation of historical events is happily matched by literary excellence. *Kanthapura*, Raja Rao's evocation of the effect of the Gandhian independence movement on a village in Southwest India, is such a work.

Throughout the twentieth century, the main direction in the development of the various Indian literatures has been toward the abandonment or modification of traditional forms in favor of Western genres and techniques. The romance and *dāstān* have been replaced by the realistic novel and short story, the *ghazal* and devotional poem by highly personal unified lyrics. Though its future developments cannot be predicted, it is fairly certain that Indian literature will continue to reflect (perhaps more accurately than any sociological research) the upheavals and major changes in Indian society and thought.

NOTES

1. See particularly the two Mohan Rakesh issues of the *Journal of South Asian Literature* (v. 10, nos. 2 & 3, Fall/Winter 1973, and v. 14, nos. 3 & 4, Summer/Fall 1979).

2. For example, in Nirmal Verma's *Ve Din* (*Days of Longing*) there is no element of racial or cultural malaise, and scarcely even any mutual curiosity, in the relationship of the Indian narrator and his Austrian lover.

3. Readers interested in comparing Indian-language and Indo-Anglian writing may like to consider the treatments of similar subjects in each medium: for instance, T. Sivasankara Pillai's *Scavenger's Son* and Anand's *Untouchable*.

REFERENCES

This brief list of modern Indian literature available in translation is meant to supplement the References accompanying the other essays on Indian literature.

Ali, Ahmed. *Twilight in Delhi.* Bombay: Oxford University Press, 1966.

Anand, Mulk Raj. *Untouchable.* New Delhi: Orient Paperbacks, 1970.

Bandopadhyay, Bibhutibhusan. *The Song of the Road (Pather Panchali).* Translated by T. W. Clark and Tarapada Mukherjee. London: Allen & Unwin, 1968.

Bhandari, Mannu. *The Great Feast.* Translated by Richard Alan Williams. New Delhi: Radha Krishna Prakashan, 1981

Journal of South Asian Literature 9, no. 2/3 (Fall/Winter 1973); 14, no. 3/4 (Summer/Fall 1979). Special issues devoted to Mohan Rakesh.

Manto, Saadat Hasan. *Kingdom's End and Other Stories.* Translated by Khalid Hasan. New Delhi: Penguin, 1987.

Markandaya, Kamala. *The Golden Honeycomb.* New York: Thomas Y. Crowell, 1977.

Nahal, Chaman Lal. *Azadi.* Boston: Houghton Mifflin, 1975.

Narayanan, Gomathi. *The Sahibs and the Natives: A Study of Guilt and Pride in Anglo-Indian and Indo-Anglian Novels.* Delhi: Chanakya Publications, 1986.

Nirala, Suryakant Tripathi. *A Season on the Earth: Selected Poems of Nirala.* Translated by David Rubin. New York: Columbia University Press, 1977.

Pillai, T. Sivasankara. *Scavenger's Son.* Translated by R. E. Asher. New Delhi: Orient Paperbacks, no date.

Rao, Raja. *Kanthapura.* New York: New Directions, 1963.

Renu, Phanishwar Nath. *The Third Vow and Other Stories.* Translated by Kathryn Hansen. New Delhi: Chanakya Publications, 1986.

Roadarmel, Gordon, ed. and trans. *A Death in Delhi: Modern Hindi Short Stories.* New Delhi: Penguin Books, 1987.

Sahni, Bhisham. *Tamas.* Translated by Jai Ratan. New Delhi: Penguin Books, 1988.

Singh, Khushwant. *Train to Pakistan.* New York: Grove Press, 1961.

Vaid, Krishna Baldev. *Steps in Darkness.* Translated by the author. New York: Orion Press, 1962 (reprinted New Delhi: Orient Paperbacks, 1968).

Verma, Nirmal. *Days of Longing.* Translated by Krishna Baldev Vaid. New Delhi: Orient Paperbacks, 1972.

THE IMAGINATIVE UNIVERSE OF CHINESE LITERATURE

Pauline Yu and Theodore Huters

Any understanding of the fundamental principles and assumptions underlying the writing and reading of Chinese literature should begin with a consideration of the larger cultural context in which those conceptions were embedded and which they to a large extent articulate. Indeed, it is no mere coincidence that the very word for writing in classical Chinese, *wen,* embraces a multitude of meanings beyond that of literature alone—among them culture, civilization, learning, pattern, refinement, and embellishment. The notion of literature as the primarily aesthetic phenomenon of belles lettres arose only very late in China—as indeed was the case in the West as well—and never took deep or exclusive root in the tradition. Much more compelling were the presumptions that literature was an integral element of the cosmos and of the sociopolitical world, and that in writing of the self one spoke ineluctably to and of society as well: the forms and patterns of one's writing corresponded naturally with those of the universe itself.

Needless to say, the tradition was not a monolithic one: significant voices were heard over time to question some of these presuppositions, and it could also be argued that the very need to reiterate them constantly suggests some fundamental uncertainty as to their validity. Moreover, these presumptions became increasingly tenuous and problematic over time. But it is undeniable that they represent the vision that the dominant literati culture continued to perpetrate of itself.

By examining what was at one time considered to be an important creation myth of the culture we may find an example of the worldview that is implicit in notions of the nature and function of literature in China. According to this legend, the universe was once an enormous egg that one day split open, with its upper half becoming the heavens, its lower half the earth, and the first human, Pangu, emerging from within it. Each day the heavens grew ten feet higher, the earth ten feet thicker, and Pangu ten feet taller until, after eighteen thousand years, he died. His head then opened up to form the sun and the moon, his blood filled the rivers and seas, his hair became the fields and forests, his breath the wind, his perspiration the rain, his voice the thunder, and his fleas became our ancestors.

Even the most cursory reading of this myth allows us to infer certain basic presumptions about the world that produced or received it. We might conclude, for example, that the universe is an uncreated one, generating itself spontaneously from a cosmic egg whose own origins are unspecified; that the elements of the universe are, from their very beginnings, organically and inextricably linked with one another; and that within those relationships the human being does not occupy a particularly glorified position. These conclusions are further confirmed by evidence that the myth is not indigenous to China at all, since it appears so late in the tradition and has so many well-known parallels in Indo-European cultures. The Chinese evidently were not concerned earlier in their history with questions of creation at all, or at least not creation by the hand of some divinity or force outside the cosmos itself—the ultimate sanctions for human activity could therefore be sought solely within the mundane realms of nature, human society, and human history. To be sure, recent archaeological discoveries have suggested that creation myths of other sorts did arise and circulate, but they never occupied the prominent place within the culture that, for example, the Book of Genesis held in the West, which indicates a relative lack of interest in the question itself.

Although the Pangu legend has been shown to possess roots in foreign soil, its implications are nonetheless borne out by other evidence of more assuredly Chinese origin. These implications of the legend can be suggestively extended to the realm of literature, where they yield a number of immediately apparent observations. In what follows the foreign myth simply serves as a useful focus for the isolation of what were pre-existing and prevailing ideas within the Chinese tradition—this may also, of course, explain why it eventually appealed to Chinese sensibilities.

A first observation might be that the tradition lacks the figure of some anthropomorphic deity whose creative actions and products serve as the model for human literary activity, as in this well-known formulation from Sir Philip Sidney's *Apology for Poetry*:

> Only the poet, . . . lifted up with the vigour of his own invention, doth grow in effect another nature, in making things either better than Nature bringeth forth, or, quite anew, forms such as never were in Nature. . . . Neither let it be deemed too saucy a comparison to balance the highest point of man's wit with the efficacy of Nature; but rather give right honour to the heavenly Maker of that maker, who, having made man to His own likeness, set him beyond and over all the works of that second nature: which in nothing he showeth so much as in Poetry, when with the force of divine breath he bringeth things forth far surpassing her doings . . . [1]

In contrast to the modern Western tradition, Chinese theories of the arts did not emphasize the notion of creation ex nihilo—Sidney's "invention," and its attendant values of originality and uniqueness—choosing instead to stress the importance of continuity and convention. It is important to keep in mind that these were emphases rather than exclusions: the culture was by no means a static or unimaginative one, but the privileging of tradition and pattern shaped critical discourse in powerful ways.

Second, the Chinese evidently did not view the work of art itself as the image or mirror of some suprasensory reality, whether successful, as in Rom. 1.20 ("For the invisible things of Him from the creation of the world are clearly seen, being understood by the things that are made, even His eternal Power and Godhead"), or inevitably incomplete or flawed, as in the Platonic theory of mimesis. Literature did not claim to represent a realm of being fundamentally other from that of concrete phenomena; it embodied principles transcendent to any one individual object in the sensory world (dao [tao]), but the very essence of those principles lay in the fact that they were at the same time immanent in and inseparable from those objects, rather than residing on some altogether different level of being. In contrast to the dualistic view of the universe that lies at the basis of Western notions of poiesis, mimesis, and fictionality, there was in early Chinese literary theory no true dichotomy between the real and the ideal. Rather, literature spoke of the things of this world—and it was but a short step to the assumption that it spoke of the actual personal, social, and political circumstances of the historical author. From this arises the persistent impulse to contextualize the elements of a literary work—to assume that they referred directly, even if veiled, to the author's empirical world, rather than representing the products of a fictive imagination. Thus a poetic oeuvre could serve to construct a biography, and known biographical facts, conversely, could explicate the poetry; extended works of fictional narrative would similarly be construed as chronicles—no matter how disguised—of the author and his or her personal circumstances.

Another way of understanding this attitude, or a third implication of the Pangu myth, is to see it as a manifestation of the holistic, unitary notion of the universe, within which all things are organically connected. Just as our human ancestors are only one small yet integral element of a larger whole, so the writer in traditional Chinese formulations exists in a network of relations with the worlds of nature and society that provide the impetus, forms, and subject of his or her works. We can see this totalizing view clearly in the following passage from the "Great Preface" to the sixth-century B.C.E. canonical anthology of poetry, the *Book of Songs*:

> Poetry is where the intent of the heart goes. What in the heart is intent is poetry when issued forth in words. An emotion moves within and takes form in words. If words do not suffice, then one sighs; if sighing does not suffice, then one prolongs it [the emotion] in song; if prolonging through song does not suffice, then one unconsciously dances it with hands and feet.
>
> Emotions issue forth in sounds, and when sounds form a pattern, they are called tones. The tones of a well-governed world are peaceful and lead to joy, its government harmonious; the tones of a chaotic world are resentful and arouse anger, its government perverse; the tones of a defeated state are mournful to induce longing, its people in difficulty. Thus in regulating success and failure, moving heaven and earth, and causing spirits and gods to respond, nothing comes closer than poetry.[2]

This is a classical statement of the expressive-affective conception of poetry that the Chinese tradition shares with other Asian literatures as well. Certain basic ideas resemble those in the West—the importance in poetry of song, emotion, and patterning—but others seem quite distinctive. Later texts would make explicit the tacit assumption here that the "intent" or emotion that moves within represents a natural response to the stimulus of the external world, be it that of nature or the body politic. Certainly the "Preface" emphasizes the latter and thus takes for granted that what is internal (emotion) will naturally find some externally correlative form or action, and that song can spontaneously reflect, affect, and effect political and cosmic order. We should not underestimate the pervasive power of this assumption throughout much of the tradition—that a seamless connection between the individual and the world somehow enables the poem simultaneously to reveal feelings, provide an index of governmental stability, and serve as a didactic tool. Whether or not these could be demonstrated to everyone's agreement, the literary work certainly was never regarded as a heterocosm—an autonomous being that could serve as an end in itself and be read independently of its context and tradition. The very notion of "literature" itself embraced pragmatic forms such as epitaphs, mnemonics, dispatches, and memorials to the throne that the West generally does not include. And the act of writing even such a "high" form as poetry was an eminently social and political, as well as personal and interpersonal, form of communication. It was a skill any educated person was presumed to possess and be able to use on a regular basis—at social gatherings large or small, court festivities (and there often on command), leave-takings and reunions, births and deaths, and at any of the countless events that merited commemoration. The earliest historical works also recount incidents when allusions to poems provided a means of conveying information and opinions obliquely in delicate diplomatic situations. For several hundred years, furthermore, the ability to write poetry to set topics was tested on the civil service examinations that represented the officially sanctioned route to government office—the only acceptable career for the well-born and educated individual. This emphasis on the didactic function of all writing and the obsession with the political dimension of expression distinguishes the Chinese tradition notably from that of Japan, with which it otherwise shares several basic ideas.

A fourth possible set of implications for literature centers on the attitudes to history that the Pangu myth reveals, both overtly and implicitly. Even the myth itself demonstrates the typically felt need to place its account within some precise if meager temporal framework—note the specific mention of the "eighteen thousand years" that elapsed until Pangu's death. More important is the tacit assumption that the passage of time inevitably involves a movement from fullness to diminution, here literally from the wholeness of the original egg to its fragmentation into the elements of the cosmos. At the same time, however, no element of causality or true linear sequencing enters into the account; the egg simply opens up, and the myth focuses on what comes into existence through natural transformation rather than exploring or exploiting the possibilities of a more "vertical" set of relationships. This leads to the fifth implication: the absence of some divinity or demiurge who, like the God of the Judeo-Christian tradition, not only brings the world into being but also provides it with its laws. The lack of such a god places the burden for providing those norms and values on history itself.

These notions are related to each other and were enormously influential and persistent within the culture as a whole. The belief that history is the story of decline from some earlier golden age is basic to Confucianism. This tradition locates the perfection of sages in some dim era of mythical culture heroes, and more recently in the founding years of the Zhou dynasty, whose ideals Confucius (six hundred years later) claims merely to "transmit." This belief is shared as well by early Daoist texts like the *Dao de jing* (*The Classic of the Way and Its Power*), which advocates a return to values and modes of behavior that were possible—unself-consciously, at least—only at some prior stage of civilization. These attitudes are certainly not unfamiliar to Western culture, which locates itself somewhere and sometime after the Fall. However, the Chinese—and more particularly the Confucian—responses to this given differed significantly. Perfection did lie in the past, and earlier works were generally by definition superior to those that followed. The impulses in favor of archaism and imitation were powerful ones; innovations were therefore often best disguised as "returns" to some prior mode. At the same time, however, as the notion of "return" suggests, perfection was recuperable to the extent that one was able truly to study and emulate the past, because the exemplars were not only human—of the same order of being and therefore in theory totally imitable—but also carefully demonstrated to be genealogically related to the founders of the political order. History thus served much the same function that revelation did in the West, providing didactic models and principles to be studied and, perhaps even more importantly, embodying those ideals in concrete human figures to whom one could trace one's lineage directly and thereby be assured of the possibility of return. In literary terms these attitudes are particularly evident in the fondness for allusions to and reiterations of past texts and in the obsession with tracing the progenitors of one's own works; the descent lines are rarely fleshed out in any coherent chronological fashion, but the sources are identified. And finally, this lack of interest in a fully developed logical or temporal sequencing is significant especially for later narrative, as discussed below.

Despite this concern with history and historicity, that is, the impulse to place literature both within its own tradition and within a larger cultural context, we should note that linearity—at least in the Aristotelian sense of a shaped movement from beginning to middle to end—is conspicuously absent as a structuring principle in traditional Chinese literature, historical or otherwise. The reasons for this are extremely complex, and one can only speculate at best. It may have something to do with the primary place of the short lyric, with its values of brevity, immediacy, and momentariness, as the first and foremost paradigm for written expression (as opposed, say, to longer narrative forms like epic or drama), although here one runs into classic chicken-and-egg type questions. It may have something to do with the Chinese view of history itself. Although history suggests a linear mentality in positing a diminishment of the perfection of some distant past, it does not in Chinese formulations possess a determinate point of origin or a clear line of devolution, and does not move teleologically toward some future apocalypse or redemption. This lack of linearity certainly also has something to do with the absence mentioned earlier of a distinct creator figure who might suggest that literature itself, analogously, creates an autotelic world as well. Rather than representing a metaphoric substitution for some realm of an ontologically different order, the work—and its author as well—are construed as being metonymically related to the only world there is. Indeed, the characteristic mode of reading a poem in traditional China consisted of a synecdochic filling-in of what had only been suggested.

Most of these notions are associated most directly with the Confucian tradition in China, although many are also shared with Daoism and, later, Buddhism as well. Daoism certainly takes for granted the integral relationship of all beings in the universe while denigrating, of course, the primary position Confucianism assigns to the human. And while the other-worldly orientation of Indian Buddhism is undeniable, the uniquely Chinese development thereof that proved to be the most enduring, Chan (better known by its Japanese pronunciation, Zen) shared with the indigenous systems of belief the notion that insight into true, transcendental reality was best gained by an appreciation of the concrete things of daily life.

While the actual extent of the impact of these philosophical and religious traditions cannot be measured here (they have been and are still being examined in a number of scholarly works), a few general points can be made, with particular reference to poetry. The interest in Daoist texts as a mystical, intuitive apprehension of reality proved attractive to early literary theorists, who then wrote of a transcendence of sensory perception and spatiotemporal limits that precedes the act of composition. Discussion of the ineffability of writing itself, its curious blend of conscious craft and spontaneous outpouring, found prototypes in anecdotes centering on the marvelous accomplishments of various artisans in texts like the *Zhuang Zi* [*Chuang Tzu*]. Classical Chinese poetry was an extremely demanding and highly crafted form, but the ultimate goal came to consist in producing a poem that, exquisite, left no visible traces of the artistry that had labored to produce it.

Daoism and Buddhism also shared a distrust in the power of language to express meaning with any degree of adequacy, an issue that obsessed poetic theorists as well. The preference for short lyric forms throughout the tradition may reflect not only certain conditions imposed by the language itself—its heavily monosyllabic character, the proliferation of homophones, and the resulting limited number of rhymes—but also an acknowledgment of the incommensurability of words and meaning and a consequent preference for the evocative and unstated, for suggesting a "meaning beyond words." A slightly different version of this ideal was embraced by Confucius himself as well, who expressed an impatience with students for whom everything had to be spelled out in its entirety. Indeed, the overlaps among systems of thought that to Western eyes might appear to be mutually exclusive and antagonistic are numerous. Perhaps the most important point to be made in connection with the relationship of these systems to the culture and literature of China is that they are best viewed as mutually necessary complements. There is a strong disinclination historically to extremism and an equally strong preference for harmony, evident on as minute a level as the love for balanced pairs and parallelism in both poetic and narrative forms. Thematically, especially in poetry, the most persistent issue focuses on the obligation of the scholar-bureaucrat to serve the state versus the powerful attraction of life in retreat. Confucianism dictated the former, except in extraordinary circumstances; Daoism and Buddhism sang the lure of the latter. In some instances the two possibilities were able to coexist: the integration of public and private was presented as the image of culture from its very origins. Yet in other cases, the contradictions between the public and the private, the needs of society and those of self, began to call into question this integration of the two.

Indeed, such questions were posed from the inception of the written tradition, in poems like "Encountering Sorrow" (fourth to third centuries B.C.E.), whose author, Qu Yuan, was forced to confront an inexplicable unwillingness of those around him to recognize the true nature of his self and to trust the motives behind his public actions. He was left with no recourse but escape, whether into death or shamanism, depending on what tradition of reading one follows. The poem expresses the disjunction between the individual and the body politic; later commentary tried to put them back together. Similar questions are suggested in the first comprehensive work of history, the *Records of the Historian* of Sima Qian (145–90? B.C.E.). Like Qu Yuan, Sima Qian had been unjustly accused of disloyalty to the state and suffered the severe penalty of castration in order to be able to continue pursuing his craft. Understandably, his work often focuses on the nature of justice in the world, or—more to the point—on why there seems, on the whole, to be so little of it. He delves into this issue by repeatedly asking why, if people behave honorably, they are not thereby guaranteed at least recognition of their virtue, if not conspicuous success in life. Sima Qian allows himself to ponder this matter at some length in his biography of Bo Yi and Shu Qi, two earlier and paradigmatic victims of this noncoincidence of virtue and happiness (loyal to the Shang dynasty ruling house, they refused on principle to eat the grain of the usurping Zhou rulers, retired to "eat ferns" on Mt. Shouyang, and died there of starvation). Toward the end of the essay he quotes Confucius and comes to the sensible conclusion that since the rewards of riches and glory appear to be in no way correlated to virtue, one might as well choose the path of virtue: one prefers it, after all, and it will as likely lead to worldly success as any other approach. He seems at this point to be heading toward the larger conclusion—one very comfortable for the contemporary Western reader—that living out his own shame for the sake of his writing and pleasing himself by doing good is thus a good in and of itself. Sima Qian sums up this attitude by saying that "When the whole world is in foul and muddy confusion, then is the man of true purity seen. Then must one judge what he will consider important and unimportant."

The biography does not end there, however; instead it goes on immediately to lament that "the superior man hates the thought of his name not being mentioned after his death," and that merely doing good is a waste if others do not learn of it. The ultimate value of virtue is measured in a public sphere—the only place where it really gains any meaning. In considering the question of why anyone does anything—and this must be seen, finally, as a meditation on the nature of his literary art—Sima Qian ultimately concludes that public recognition is prerequisite to any real private value. Sima Qian and his attitude here, already adumbrated in the situation of Qu Yuan, loom large in the Chinese literary history and thought of later centuries. This is so owing both to his position as one of the first writers in China to manifest self-consciousness concerning one's very creative motivation and to his paradigmatic role as someone concerned in equal measure with his own integrity and with the political health of the realm.

The historian's ultimate valorization of a public life has an important theoretical dimension behind its practical side. In granting precedence to the context in which one lives rather than to any individual existence that can subsist outside that context, Sima Qian points to the pervasive feature of Chinese literature mentioned above: the sense that the individual exists more as part of a network of other beings than as an entity unto himself. This overwhelming sense of context also helps explain why Chinese narratives are characterized more by metonymic progression from a given point to a closely related point within an extremely broad range than by stories that develop a limited number of elements to reach a definitive climax and denouement.

The very form of Chinese history writing best illustrates this point. Chronological sequences centered around a story with a beginning and an end are rare; more common instead are collections of a large series of individual essays and biographies. These are accompanied perhaps by a bare listing of significant dates and events, all of which taken together provide a picture of a period as a whole. Later, when novels developed, they tended to take the same shape; often they did not focus on a single set of characters for more than a few chapters before introducing a completely new group. And even when the same protagonists are retained throughout (as in The Story of the Stone/Dream of the Red Chamber), whole sequences of events and characters that bear very little apparent causal relationship to or acknowledgment of the needs of straightforward plot development occupy large portions of the narrative. This is also the case with Journey to the West, where the series of episodes in which the book's heroes are tested continue with little regard for how the events in each episode move the plot toward its conclusion. As with history, the metonymic universe of narrative discourse encompasses the whole sweep of earthly existence and is thus theoretically infinite; narrative closure becomes an arbitrary and almost insignificant act. That many novels also present themselves as either real or imagined elucidations of historical writings illustrates, in turn, how the whole genre of *xiaoshuo*—in fictional narrative—in itself exists in a contiguous relationship with other forms of narrative. Rather than being a distinct and clear-cut entity circumscribed with definite and definitive conventions, fiction shades imperceptibly into the more "factual" genre that it so much resembles. It is perhaps needless to say that the converse holds for early history writing in China as well.

With history at the forefront of narrative concern, and with the persistent assumption that interests of the individual inevitably implicate a larger context, it is perhaps only natural that politics often comes to dominate novelistic discourse. One reason for this, of course, is the position of Confucianism within Chinese thought, already adumbrated above. As an ideology concerned above all else with the happy survival of the state, Confucianism inevitably placed concerns of state in the foreground within all varieties of written expression, while subordinating all other discourses. Given the extremely broad definition of concerns of state, however, the politics of the novel are at once broader and more subtle than we are accustomed to thinking of them. Since everything has a political dimension, for an author to introduce political concerns into his work does not require the overt signification that political literature has taken in the West; on the other hand, everything, whatever else it has, has a political reading as well. The point at which these horizons merge, however, was concern for maintenance of the overall context that guaranteed meaning to each fragment of life that was represented.

Since Confucianism harbored at its core the faith that state and society could perfectly mirror one another, depiction of any sort of discord, no matter how personal it might seem to us, automatically had profound social overtones. The relations of contiguity implicit within the structure of Chinese thought wrought its effect on the arrangement of values within the system. While the paramount values were assuredly positioned within a decidedly hierarchical order, they existed at the top of this order side by side in such a way that it was almost impossible to adjudicate among them. For instance, loyalty to family and loyalty to state were seen as complementary, but certainly of a higher order than loyalty to self. If, however, family and state loyalties happened in practice to come into conflict, choosing between them was an almost impossible task—particularly in light of the virtually universal narrative awareness that the major Confucian values were usually debased in their actual historical existence. The necessity of choosing between two imperfect values provides the major source of tension in traditional Chinese narrative, in both its ironic and pathetic modes. Chinese irony and Chinese pathos both force people to make untenable choices between ideals that have become seriously flawed somewhere in the course of their implementation, but irony makes light of the result while pathos stresses how unfortunate the consequences can be.

This type of structure is in a sense writ small within *Journey to the West*, in which each major character represents a particular concatenation of imperfect values that clashes with that of each other character. The final submergence of these differences through realization of the transcendent doctrines of Buddhism finally confirms the comic nature of the earlier episodes, but only perfunctorily resolves the problems raised by the juxtaposition of the differing virtues. What renders *The Story of the Stone* so painful is the degree to which the faulty implementation of the dominant values of Confucian society destroys any possible honorable accommodation to them. In Cao Xueqin's novel, the belief that society and its ideology faithfully represent one another has turned into a disabling fear of the consequences that would ensue if the claim were true. The characters' corrosive inability to find alternative means to lodge their subjective impulses accompanies this disillusion with the prevailing order. This inability is a powerful foreshadowing of the crisis of modern literature, in which the fabric of traditional values has become so tattered that there can be no meaningful response to the situation.

CHINESE LITERATURE IN THE TWENTIETH CENTURY

With the widespread realization among the educated that traditional culture was increasingly unable to meet the political challenge presented by the coming of Western power, a sense of cultural crisis marked intellectual discourse in China after 1895. For a variety of reasons, but perhaps primarily because it was the only field of endeavor regarded as having the broad scope required, literature became a focal point of efforts to meet the new demands made upon the Chinese conceptual order. The years after 1895 witnessed the publication of a spate of novels that wove their net of social relations with an irony calculated to demonstrate the bankruptcy of the network as a whole. This gloomy picture of the whole is punctuated by tentative efforts to establish the possibility of individual perception independent of what was seen as the tyranny of a received wisdom that insisted upon a uniform view of social events. More often, however, the cause of individual perception is mocked by a relentless epistemology that puts true understanding of events at a level of complexity far beyond the capacity of the individual knowing mind.

In this sense, the wide metonymic scope of the traditional conceptual order presents a devastating paradox at its moment of crisis: the very comprehensiveness that had at one time insured a place for everything now defeated any attempts to separate out discrete perceptions that would shape events into some new order. If the old order could continue to move along on its own terms by not changing its conception of the relationship of parts to whole, the new context represented by the wider world had rendered the old context radically contingent and finite by making Chinese civilization merely one narrative among others. It was at the point where the relentless exploration implicit within the old system suddenly discovered its new boundaries that the ultimate cultural crisis exploded in modern China.

Of the writers of the iconoclastic period that began around 1917, Lu Xun comes closest to the crux of the problem in his brief accounts of individual failures to communicate at any level with the rest of society. His characters are continually obsessed with their inability to transmit their own notions about a society that is constitutionally unable to live up to its own promises to itself. This in turn casts a negative light upon the tradition of a literature that had always vowed to itself that depicting a representative sample of experience would satisfactorily encompass the whole—and it is decidedly negation that Lu Xun seeks. For if to be understood one must become part of an extended network of meaning, Lu Xun and his various personae would emphatically reject the invitation. Thus another paradox of literature in modern China centers on the desire of authors to escape being integrated within the framework of traditional understanding by destroying the relationships of meaning they find around them. But the destruction of these networks in an important sense also destroys the possibility of representing any entity beyond the writer's own tormented self-consciousness. In response to the pervasive objectivity of events that no longer seem to add up to anything, writers retreat into denial and intransitive subjectivity. This inability to move the focus beyond themselves painfully blocked out any possibility of fulfilling the desire to express the full dimensions of the cultural crisis that had caused them to turn to literature in the first place.

The extraordinary frustration implicit in this reduced posture perhaps best explains why Chinese writers were so drawn to Marxism. As an ideology that offered powers of rational explanation of the same order as Confucianism, while at the same time—at least initially—utterly rejecting the particulars that the tradition had based itself upon, Marxism offered a restoration of context that took into account the extraordinary changes that had so disordered the Confucian worldview in its final years as the orthodoxy. Marxism also had the considerable virtue of building a context that included the whole world and all its history. With the metaphoric sweep of its dynamic view of historical change, Marxism turned Confucianism on its head even as it maintained the contextual range of old patterns of thought. That the ideology of revolution had a ready explanation as to why intellectuals were restricted to wallowing in their subjectivity only made it that much more appealing. The literature that Mao called for in his famous utterances of 1942 (*Talks at the Yan'an Forum on Literature and Art*) specifically denied the legitimacy of any further explorations of the personal worlds of the authors; the remarkable acquiescence this prohibition encountered testifies as powerfully to the desperate situation writers had worked themselves into as it does to the brute power of state enforcement.

With literature now enlisted in the campaign to create a new context for China, it was at the same time reinvested with tremendous powers of signification. It was the job of literature to demonstrate the existence of the new order, and writers, well aware of the alternative, threw themselves into the task. But as the new context either failed to materialize or, far worse, began to manifest alarming similarities with the tradition, writers were also assigned the duty to find out why—with the important caveat that the Communist Party could never be at fault. Ruling out the Party and its class allies left writers with a set of familiar targets: the bourgeoisie, the intellectuals, and, above all, themselves—or perhaps more accurately, other writers. The sad reality left to literature by the time of the Cultural Revolution combined the worst features of the traditional and the modern: a vulgar and utterly mechanical didacticism combined with the renewal of doubt about the legitimacy of the authorial voice. It is no wonder that literature after 1979 began with a veritable orgy of subjectivity: denied both subjectivity and objectivity for so long, writers quite naturally began the painful task of reconstruction by attempting to gain a new sense of themselves. This new subjectivity, however, had it remained fixated upon itself, threatened to take Chinese literature back to the indulgences of the May Fourth period.

In the past several years a number of new voices have come on the scene, working out new techniques to explore a broader horizon. Perhaps the happiest result of this reaching outward is represented by the work recently translated as *Chinese Lives*.[3] Superficially a collection of reportage, this work, in presenting the profound differences among a variety of people, perhaps marks the beginnings of the sense of a new context that modern Chinese literature has promised itself for so long.

NOTES

1. Walter Jackson Bate, ed., *Criticism: The Major Texts*. New York: Harcourt Brace Jovanovich, 1970, pp. 85, 86.
2. Author's translation.
3. Zhang Xinxin and Sang Ye, *Chinese Lives*, ed. W.J.F. Jenner and Delia Davin. New York: Pantheon Books, 1987.

REFERENCES

Anderson, Marston. *The Limits of Realism: Chinese Fiction in the Revolutionary Period*. Berkeley: University of California Press, 1990.

Birch, Cyril, ed. *Studies in Chinese Literary Genres*. Berkeley: University of California Press, 1974.

Chan, Wing-tsit. *A Source Book in Chinese Philosophy*. Princeton: Princeton University Press, 1963.

Chen, Kenneth. *Buddhism in China*. Princeton: Princeton University Press, 1965.

Chen, Kenneth. *The Chinese Transformation of Buddhism*. Princeton: Princeton University Press, 1972.

Chow, Tse-ts'ung, ed. *Wen-lin: Studies in Chinese Humanities*. Madison: University of Wisconsin Press, 1968.

Dawson, Raymond, ed. *The Legacy of China*. London: Oxford University Press, 1964.

de Bary, Wm. Theodore, ed. *Sources of Chinese Tradition*. 2 vols. New York: Columbia University Press, 1960.

Frankel, Hans. *The Flowering Plum and the Palace Lady: Interpretations of Chinese Poetry*. New Haven: Yale University Press, 1976.

Fung, Yu-lan. *A History of Chinese Philosophy*. 2 vols. Princeton: Princeton University Press, 1953.

Graham, A. C. *Disputers of the Tao: Philosophical Argument in Ancient China*. Lasalle, IL: Open Court, 1989.

Hsia, C. T. *The Classic Chinese Novel*. New York: Columbia University Press, 1968.

Hsia, C. T. *A History of Modern Chinese Fiction*. New Haven: Yale University Press, 1971.

Lin, Shuen-fu, and Owen Stephen, eds. *The Vitality of the Lyric Voice: Shih Poetry from the Late Han to the T'ang.* Princeton: Princeton University Press, 1986.

Liu, James J.Y. *The Art of Chinese Poetry.* Chicago: University of Chicago Press, 1962.

Liu, James J. Y. *Chinese Theories of Literature.* Chicago: University of Chicago Press, 1975.

Liu, Wu-chi. *An Introduction to Chinese Literature.* Bloomington: Indiana University Press, 1966.

Mote, Frederick. *Intellectual Foundations of China.* New York: Alfred A. Knopf, 1972.

Nienhauser, William H., ed. *The Indiana Companion to Traditional Chinese Literature.* Bloomington: Indiana University Press, 1986.

Owen, Stephen. *The Great Age of Chinese Poetry: The High T'ang.* New Haven: Yale University Press, 1981.

Owen, Stephen. *Traditional Chinese Poetry and Poetics: Omen of the World.* Madison: University of Wisconsin Press, 1985.

Plaks, Andrew, ed. *Chinese Narrative: Critical and Theoretical Essays.* Princeton: Princeton University Press, 1977.

Plaks, Andrew. *The Four Masterworks of the Ming Novel.* Princeton: Princeton University Press, 1987.

Rickett, Adele, ed. *Chinese Approaches to Literature from Confucius to Liang Ch'i-ch'ao.* Princeton: Princeton University Press, 1978.

Rolston, David, ed. *How To Read the Chinese Novel.* Princeton: Princeton University Press, 1990.

Ropp, Paul, ed. *Heritage of China: Contemporary Perspectives on Chinese Civilization.* Berkeley: University of California Press, 1990.

Schwartz, Benjamin. *The World of Thought in Ancient China.* Cambridge: Harvard University Press, 1985.

Waley, Arthur. *Three Ways of Thought in Ancient China.* Reprint. New York: Doubleday Anchor, 1956.

Watson, Burton. *Chinese Lyricism: Shih Poetry from the Second to the Twelfth Century.* New York: Columbia University Press, 1971.

Watson, Burton. *Early Chinese Literature.* New York: Columbia University Press, 1962.

Yu, Pauline. *The Reading of Imagery in the Chinese Poetic Tradition.* Princeton: Princeton University Press, 1987.

THE IMAGINATIVE UNIVERSE OF JAPANESE LITERATURE

Haruo Shirane

Japanese literature can be traced back to the seventh and eighth centuries, when the Japanese first began employing the Chinese graph system to write. In this early period, when China represented the model for almost all aspects of civilization, the most esteemed literary genres were, as in China, histories, religious and philosophical writings, and poetry, all of which were written in Chinese, the official language of government and religion. Of these genres, only poetry developed a significant native counterpart. The first major works are the *Kojiki* (*Record of Ancient Matters*, 712), a historical narrative that records many of the early Japanese myths, and the *Man'yōshū* (*Collection of Ten Thousand Leaves*, 745–759), a vast compendium of over four thousand Japanese poems. Like almost all other early Japanese prose works, the *Kojiki* is written almost entirely in Chinese, while the *Man'yōshū* primarily employs Chinese graphs phonetically, to record poetry in Japanese. It is not until the development of a Japanese syllabary, or kana, in the late ninth and early tenth centuries, that the Japanese begin writing "Japanese" prose literature, that is to say, vernacular prose written in the native syllabary. This development, which was pioneered by aristocratic women who were largely excluded from the world of Chinese writing, led to the great flowering of Japanese prose literature in the late tenth and early eleventh centuries, to Murasaki Shikibu's *Tale of Genji* (*Genji monogatari*), Sei Shonagon's *Pillowbook* (*Makura no sōshi*), and to such literary diaries as the *Gossamer Years* (*Kagerō nikki*), by the Mother of Michitsuna, and the *Sarashina Diary* (*Sarashina nikki*), by the daughter of Takasue.

Though the Chinese literary tradition continued to have a profound impact on Japanese views of literature and though prose and poetry written in Chinese (by Japanese) remained an integral part of the Japanese literary tradition until the modern period, from the tenth and eleventh centuries the Japanese wrote primarily in their own language and developed a wide variety of native genres—poetry, essays, literary diaries, prose fiction, historical narratives, folk narratives (*setsuwa*).

One of the salient characteristics of Heian kana literature, particularly that written by aristocrats, was the close relationship between the writer and the audience. The kana preface to the *Kokinshū* (*Collection of Old and New Poems*, early 10th c.), generally considered the first defense of Japanese poetry, reminds its readers that giving voice to one's emotions and thoughts through poetry is a universal and inevitable response to nature and life. Japanese poetry in the ancient period, the age of the *Man'yōshū*, had a public, political role in the ritual affirmation of those in power (especially the emperor), as well as a private role as a form of intimate dialogue. In Heian aristocratic society it was impossible to function, either in public or in private, without the ability to write a thirty-one-syllable *waka* (sometimes referred to as a *tanka*). Indeed, no serious courtship or intercourse between the sexes could take place without an exchange of poetry, which became an epistolary medium. A number of the literary diaries in the classical period—for example, *The Gossamer Years* (*Kagerō nikki*, 10th c.)—grew out of private records of poems that had been exchanged between the author and his or her acquaintances. Even the seventeen-syllable hokku (later called *haiku*), which became popular in the early Edo period (17th-19th c.), often functioned as a personal address, usually as a gesture of appreciation and acknowledgment to the poet's host. Even in the modern period, in which waka and haiku remain immensely popular, it is often said that more people write poetry than read it.

Japanese linked verse (*renga*)—the dominant poetic form in the Muromachi period and popular throughout the Edo period in the form of comic linked verse (haikai)—encapsulates the notion of audience as author. A linked verse sequence as a rule required two or more participants. The sequence opened with a seventeen syllable (5/7/5) verse (the ancestor of the modern haiku), to which another poet adds a fourteen-syllable (7/7) verse. The second verse was in turn capped by a seventeen-syllable (5/7/5) verse, and so forth, until a sequence of thirty-six, fifty, or one hundred links was completed. Here the poet and the reader play both roles, exchanging places on a regular and formal basis. Reception becomes a form of creation, and creation a form of reception.

Even in classical prose fiction, where it was not possible for every reader to be a writer, an intimate relationship existed between the author and the audience. The author often wrote for a specific individual, such as a princess or empress, whose response was critical to the future development of the narrative. The early eleventh-century prose masterpiece, *The Tale of Genji*, was written by Murasaki Shikibu for the empress and her ladies-in-waiting. Encouraged and aided by her readers, who copied, bound, and distributed each new chapter, Murasaki Shikibu wrote one sequel after another. The literary diaries that flourished in the Heian period, beginning with *The Gossamer Years* by the Mother of Michitsuna, resembled open letters to friends or relatives. Only a reader intimately acquainted with the author's private circumstances would have been able to follow the original text, since proper names and events are implied but not stated. As we shall see, there existed another narrative tradition, in which Buddhist priests and minstrels narrated or chanted to a largely uneducated, popular audience. Yet in the literary mainstream derived from the Heian classics, the ties between the audience and the author remained extremely close. Even as late as the modern period, when the novel came under the heavy influence of Western fiction, one of the most dominant prose forms has been the "I-novel" (*watakushi-shōsetsu*). In the I-novel, the author, who appears thinly disguised as the protagonist, assumes that the reader is already familiar with his or her private circumstances. From the earliest times, Japanese readers (or listeners) have closely identified with the life of the author, who frequently engaged them in an extended and intimate dialogue through a variety of literary forms.

Many Japanese literary and aesthetic forms, particularly those that stress brevity, condensation, and overtones, assume an intimate audience. The paring down of form and expression occurs in a wide variety of traditional (particularly late medieval) aesthetic forms: Noh drama, poetry, landscape gardening, bonsai, tea ceremony, and ink painting, to mention only the most obvious. Historically, Japanese poetry evolved from the *chōka* (literally "long poem"—the dominant form of the ancient period) to the thirty-one-syllable *waka*, the central form of the Heian or classical period; to linked verse in the medieval period; and finally in the Edo period, to the seventeen-syllable *hokku*, the shortest poetic form in world literature. A similar phenomenon occurs in the tea ceremony. Originally held in a large hall, it evolved into a highly refined, spare ritual in a small two-and-a-half-mat (10′ × 10′) room designed by Sen no Rikyū, the great tea master. A similar condensation of form can be found in Noh drama. Medieval drama as it evolved under Zeami, the greatest Noh playwright, was a drama of elegance, restraint, and suggestion. Human actions were reduced to the bare essentials, to highly symbolic actions such as tilting the mask to express joy, or sweeping the hand to represent weeping. In one essay (Kakyō), Zeami writes that "if what [the actor] feels in the heart is ten, what appears in movement should be seven." Zeami stresses that the point at which physical movement becomes minute and then finally stops is the point of greatest intensity. The physical and visual restrictions—the fixed mask, the slow body movement, the almost complete absence of props or scenery—create a drama that must occur as much in the mind of the audience as on the stage. On the role of the audience, Zeami notes: "Among those who witness Noh plays, the true connoisseurs see with their minds while the untutored see with their eyes."

In each instance, the artistic or literary form evolved toward extreme abbreviation or an "open" text that invited, if not demanded, the active participation of the audience. The "open" space in Japanese poetry is apparent in the "cutting word" (kireji), a formal requirement of the seventeen-syllable hokku. The cutting word severs the semantic, grammatical, and rhythmic flow of the poem, creating a "gap" that the reader must bridge. Like the cadenza in pre-Romantic music, a blank section of the musical notation which allows the performer to add to the composer's work, the cutting word entrusts a significant part of the meaning to the reader. Matsuo Bashō, the great master of the seventeen-syllable hokku, illustrates this: "The hokku that reveals seventy to eighty percent of the subject is good. Those that reveal fifty to sixty percent, we never tire of." The blank canvas in the sparsely painted medieval ink-brush paintings and the expanses of white sand in the "dry river and mountain" (karesanzui) gardens serve similar functions. A profound awareness that the meaning of a literary text is indeterminate and changeable, dependent on the particular reader and circumstance, is perhaps most conspicuous in the genre of linked verse (renga): Each new verse, or link, deliberately alters the meaning and context of the previous verse, usually in an unexpected and surprising manner. The editors of such poetic anthologies as the Kokinshū were also highly conscious that the meaning of *waka* could be altered when they were taken out of their original contexts and juxtaposed, as they often were, with other poems on similar topics.

In *Essays in Idleness* (*Tsurezuregusa*, 17th c.), often considered the ultimate compendium of classical aesthetics, Yoshida Kenkō argues that what is not stated, cannot be seen by the eyes, and is incomplete in expression is more moving, alluring, and memorable than what is directly presented. "Are you only to look at flowers in full bloom, at the moon when it is clear?" "No, to look out on the rain and long for the moon, to draw the blinds and not see the passing of spring—these arouse even deeper feelings." Visually, Kenko's aesthetics stress shadows—for example, dusk and early dawn, the favorite temporal settings of Heian court literature—which have more depth than noon or darkness. Musically, attention is drawn to silence and echoes, the space (*ma*) between notes. From ancient times, the Japanese have prized the social capacity for indirection and suggestion, meaning without saying. Poetry was recognized for overtones, connotations, and subtle allegory, rather than for what was stated (as subjects were restricted to little more than love and the four seasons). This particular literary and social mode depends, in large part, on a close bond between the artist and the audience. They have the capacity to communicate on a profound, subtle, and extralinguistic level, a form of communication perhaps possible only in the kind of hermetic, homogeneous society found in Japan.

This kind of suggestiveness depends on a commonly shared, highly encoded literary tradition. *The Tale of Genji* unfolds over three generations and four imperial reigns, yet it gravitates toward intensely emotional and meditative scenes in which language, rhetoric, and themes of poetry are foregrounded. The primary reference is to other literary and poetic texts rather than to an external world. From the middle of the Heian period, poetry was primarily restricted to certain topics—such as the unhappiness of love, the cry of the cuckoo, the coming of spring—with fixed aesthetic associations. Without intimate knowledge of the many poems in the canon, it was impossible to appreciate the subtle variations that such poetry depended on. What distinguished a poem on the scattering of cherry blossoms from the thousands that preceded it? In the poems of the great *waka* anthology of the Kamakura period, *Shinkokinshū* (early 13th c.), the primary technique is allusive variations (*honkadori*) on earlier classical poems (particularly those found in the first imperial *waka* anthology, *Kokinshū* [early 10th c.]). Likewise, Zeami's best Noh plays derive much of their depth and elegance from the elaborate interweaving of themes and phrases from earlier classics. On the surface, even medieval and Edo travel literature, the greatest of which is Matsuo Bashō's *Narrow Road to the Deep North* (late 17th c.), appears to be personal accounts of journeys around Japan, but in fact is elaborate meditations on *utamakura*: poetic places and their literary associations. This kind of literature assumes that the author shares with the reader a common body of literary knowledge and associations, which can be communicated with the slightest hint. Without a deep awareness of literary conventions, rules, and models—often only accessible to practitioners—it becomes difficult, if not impossible, to judge the quality of the work. Indeed, it is the intertextual space, the play between a literary text and prior texts, or between a stage movement and its *kata* (fixed pattern), that frequently becomes the aesthetic focal point.

In linked verse each new verse completes or complements the previous verse. However, the third verse must break away from the world of the first verse, moving the sequence in a new and often surprising direction. It is also critical to alternate between striking and less conspicuous verses. This musical movement of association and disassociation, surprise and juxtaposition, intensification and relaxation, is characteristic of a broad range of prose literature. The pensée (*zuihitsu*—of which the two most famous examples are Sei Shonagon's *The Pillow Book* (*Makura no sōshi*, early 11th c.) and Yoshida Kenkō's *Essays in Idleness*—is a collection of quasi-independent passages of varying length that are related by the kind of metonymic association found in linked verse rather than by a unifying theme or perspective. An even closer structural resemblance to linked verse can be found in Matsuo Bashō's *Narrow Road to the Deep North* and in the prose fiction of Ihara Saikaku, one of the great linked-verse poets of the Edo period. Even in the modern period we find writers such as Kawabata Yasunari, the Nobel Prize winner, juxtaposing images and passages in linked-verse fashion.

Traditional Japanese architecture, in contrast to Western architecture (which generally starts with a fixed space and divides it), is like the Japanese narrative: It tends to begin with a single element to which more parts are added until a larger whole is arrived at. Works such as *Tales of Ise* or the monolithic *Tale of Genji* began as a sequence or collection of short stories that were augmented until they grew into longer narratives. Like the verses in linked verse, or the poems in carefully ordered imperial anthologies, each of the narrative parts can be appreciated both in isolation and as an integral part of a larger narrative. The famous garden at Versailles is designed so that the entire vista is visible from a single, unitary perspective. In contrast, Japanese medieval gardens, like Japanese traditional narratives, are constructed in such a way that the setting and perspective change as one moves through it, leaving no center or dominant point of view.

Many of the characteristics of Japanese literature described so far are directly related to its strong poetic roots. In the ancient period, the Japanese intelligentsia, closely following the Chinese model, considered poetry, history, and philosophy to be the classical literary genres. But at least initially, literary masterpieces failed to materialize from either history or philosophy, both of which had to be written in Chinese, the official language of religion and government. Of the three ideological centers—Buddhism, Confucianism, and Shinto—two (Buddhism and Confucianism) were borrowed from the continent. Shinto, the indigenous religion, while containing a body of intriguing myths, did not develop a self-conscious textual tradition. The Japanese priesthood and intelligentsia considered the central texts of Buddhism and Confucianism to be literary classics, but these currents of thought did not directly generate great literature, at least not in the beginning. Nor do we find epic or drama, the literary genres associated with the wellspring of the Western literary tradition. Instead, there is poetry, and in particular the thirty-one-syllable lyric, which tended to be personal in focus. The emergence in the Heian period of a large and influential body of women's literature that centered on poetry and focused on private affairs (particularly male-female relations) further deepened the lyrical and private orientation of Japanese traditional literature. It is significant that the poetic diary, an autobiographical form based on the verse exchanged between the author and his or her acquaintances, became the mainstay of the women's prose tradition.

The lyrical orientation of Japanese literature should not obscure the fact that Japanese prose fiction also was rooted in an oral tradition. This tradition included a wide assortment of myths, legends, anecdotes, and folk tales often of strange, supernatural, or divine events (lumped together by Japanese scholars under the term *setsuwa*). Japan's first vernacular tale, *Tale of the Bamboo Cutter* (late 10th c.), is about a shining princess who descends from the moon to become the daughter of a poor bamboo cutter, and consists largely of oral material woven together by a writer at court. The role of the oral tradition became particularly prominent in the medieval period, when Buddhist priests gathered and used popular stories for didactic purposes, to preach to a largely illiterate audience. *The Tale of Heike*, a medieval epic chanted to the accompaniment of the *biwa* (lute) by minstrel/priests, draws heavily on the oral tradition. The largest and probably the best collection of oral literature, *Tales of Times Past* (early 12th c.), is divided into secular and religious tales: both types depict a popular, rough-and-tumble society far removed from the courtly world of *The Tale of Genji* and *The Pillow Book*.

One of the recurring plot paradigms derived from the oral tradition is the "exile of the young noble." A young god or aristocrat, having committed a transgression or sin, undergoes a severe trial in a distant and hostile land. In the process the young man proves his mettle, meets a woman, and acquires the power necessary to become a leader and hero. The myth of "The Luck of the Sea and the Luck of the Mountain," one of the key stories in the eighth-century *Kojiki* and *Nihonshoki*, is one example. Fire-fade (Luck of the Mountain) is forced to look for his brother's fishhook that he has lost. His search takes him to the bottom of the sea, where he meets and lives with the daughter of the God of the Sea, who gives him jewels that later enable him to defeat his brother and control the land. In *The Tale of Genji*, the hero likewise commits a sin (having a secret son by Fujitsubo, the consort of his father, the emperor). He is exiled to Suma, where he meets a woman (the Akashi lady) who eventually bears his only daughter, a key to his subsequent political success and triumph. As in other narratives, the exile functions as a means of atonement, a ritualistic coming of age, and a means of discovering a woman who can provide a channel to power.

The cluster of ancient, native beliefs commonly referred to as Shinto underlies the traditional Japanese literary hero known as the man of *irogonomi*, an emotionally and aesthetically sensitive but socially and politically vulnerable, if not weak, paramour. He emerges in the early Japanese myths, comes to the fore in the Heian classics, and reemerges in the "floating world" of Edo literature, particularly in Jōruri and Kabuki drama. One famous example is Ariwara no Narihira, protagonist of *Tales of Ise*, who like the shining Genji, discovers love where it is most unexpected and difficult, if not impossible, to be fulfilled. The *irogonomi* hero lends himself to a picaresque narrative, but Narihira, like the shining Genji, is not a lustful or crafty paramour. Rather, he is an overly delicate and refined individual who expresses his often unhappy and frustrated state in moving verse.

Much of Japanese literature from the classical period through the medieval period stands in a larger Buddhist context that regards excessive attachments—especially the deep emotions of love—as a serious deterrent to individual salvation, particularly in a world in which all things are viewed as impermanent. The universe, as portrayed in medieval literature, contains Six Realms (*Rokudō*)—gods, humans, warriors, animals, hungry ghosts, and creatures of hell—a cosmological hierarchy that pushes creatures up and down according to a principle of karmic reward and retribution. Each individual is bound to a cycle of life and death in the Six Realms, to a world of suffering and illusory attachment, until he or she achieves salvation. In the Heian and medieval periods, the Japanese believed strong attachments, particularly at the point of death, would impede the progress of the soul to the next stage, which, hopefully, would be the Pure Land, or Western Paradise. In a typical Noh play by Zeami, for example, the protagonist is caught in one of the lower realms—often as a wandering ghost or as a person suffering in hell—as the result of some deep attachment or resentment. For the warrior, the attachment is often the bitterness or ignominy of defeat; for women, jealousy or the failure of love; and for old men, the impotence of age. In *Tadanori*, one of Zeami's finest warrior plays, the cause of Tadanori's suffering is dissatisfaction with a politically influenced decision to omit his name from a famous poetic anthology (one of his poems was included, but anonymously). In the manner of Zeami's "dream" plays, in the second half of the play the protagonist reenacts or recounts the source of his attachment to the visiting priest, who offers prayers for his salvation and spiritual release.

Except for purely didactic literature composed by Buddhist priests, traditional Japanese literature usually takes a highly ambivalent view of Buddhist ideals—focusing on the beauty of passion, especially single-minded devotion, as well as on the dangers of excessive attachment. Indeed, at the heart of Japanese classical literature, particularly from the mid-Heian period onward, lies the conflict between Buddhistic aspirations of selflessness and self-denial (which eventually merged with samurai ideals), and the sensual, aesthetic, and emotional orientation of early native beliefs. For example, the first vernacular fiction, *Tale of the Bamboo Cutter* (late 10th c.), establishes a dichotomy between the world of the moon, devoid of attachments or suffering, and the secular world of impermanence and illusory attachments. The princess finally returns to the moon, but only after a painful parting that brings out an emotional tenderness that, as a creature of the moon, she had hitherto lacked. In *A Ten-Foot Square Hut* ("An Account of My

Hut," early 13th c.) the poet Kamo no Chōmei, confronted with a world of suffering and impermanence—natural disasters, famine, destruction of the capital—retreats to a small hut outside the capital. In the process of preparing for the next world, however, he becomes attached to the tranquillity and pleasures of his rustic retreat: he then fears his attachment to the beauty of nature and to writing poetry will hinder his salvation.

Conflict tends to be internalized when it occurs in Japanese literature, often creating a highly psychological work. In Zeami's lyrical Noh drama, for example, there is usually no substantial conflict between characters. In a typical Zeami Noh play, the climax occurs when the protagonist is freed of his or her attachment or reconciled to himself or herself, not when the opposition, if there is any, is vanquished. When the influence of Buddhism abated in the Edo period, more secular plot paradigms came to the fore, such as the conflict between human desire or love (ninjō) and social duty or obligation (giri). Even so, the ultimate focus of literature and drama was on the intense emotions (ninjō), generated by or in conflict with the irreconcilable pressures of society and giri. This does not mean that Japanese drama is lacking in dramatic conflict. (One has only to think of Chūshingura, the great revenge drama.) Dramatic conflict exists, but the primary objective of drama is not the pursuit and development of dramatic conflict to its logical consequences (as it usually is in Western drama), nor is it the raison d'être of prose fiction. Japanese drama and prose fiction, while sometimes possessing extended plot structures, are like the lyric, which is concerned with the elaboration of a particular mood or emotion rather than narrative development. In vernacular fiction, the poetic diary, and drama (Kabuki, Jōruri, and Noh) it is no accident that one of the most popular scenes is the parting: a poetic topos that can be traced back to the ancient poetry of the Man'yōshū. The Tale of Genji is highlighted by a series of partings, which culminate in the climactic parting—the death of the heroine. The same can be said of The Tale of Heike, a complex and detailed military epic that repeatedly focuses on the terrible partings that war forces on human beings. The closeness of traditional Japanese social ties—between parent and child, lord and retainer, husband and wife, individual and group—make the parting an emotionally explosive situation, but it is the lyrical presentation of the parting that is most noteworthy.

The lyricism of classical Japanese literature derives, in significant part, from a fusion of genres and media that in Western literature are generally thought of as being intrinsically separate.

First of all, prose fiction is extensively interwoven with poetry and poetic diction, both in the dialogue and in the descriptive prose. In fact, one cannot find a single work of premodern Japanese prose literature that does not include poetry. A more obvious fusion of media occurs in Japanese drama. Since the Renaissance, Western theater has been split into three basic forms— drama, opera, and ballet—whereas traditional Japanese theater has combined these elements (acting, music, and dance) in each of the major dramatic forms: medieval Noh drama, Kyōgen (Noh's comic counterpart), Jōruri (puppet theater), and Kabuki. Of these, only Kyōgen does not depend on music, but even this dramatic form includes song and dance. One of the central principles of Noh and Jōruri, *jo/ha/kyū* (introduction, development, and finale), refers to the rhythm and tempo of the play, particularly in relation to dance and song (as opposed to Aristotle's beginning, middle, and end, which in Greek drama refers to the three stages in the action's development). This synthetic quality often makes the literature or drama more performative than mimetic: instead of emphasizing a represented, "recreated" world, the work calls attention to itself as a performative or dramatic medium.

Japanese prose fiction tends to have a strong narrational voice: a narrator (or narrators) describes and comments on the action from a subjective point of view. The conventions of the oral storytelling tradition are evident in almost all prose fiction (*monogatari*), including such highly sophisticated, stream-of-consciousness narratives as *The Tale of Genji*. Even *The Great Mirror* (11th c.), a vernacular history of the Heian period, is presented as a story heard and told by elderly raconteurs. In Japanese traditional drama, this type of narrational voice flows over the action, dialogue, and scenery. In the Noh, for example, the dialogue alternates with descriptive passages narrated by both the chorus and the protagonist. The position of the narrator is most prominent in Jōruri, where the chanter (*gidaiyū*), on a dais separate from the puppet stage, performs both the puppet dialogue and the narrative description.

This double structure—action enveloped in descriptive narration—lends itself to extremely powerful lyric tragedy, in which the tone is elegant, poetic, and uplifting even as the subject matter or situation is unpleasant and sorrowful. The love suicide (*shinjū*) plays by Chikamatsu Mon'zaemon, the greatest Jōruri playwright, are one example. The climactic travel scene (*michiyuki*)—a subcategory of the parting topos—is one of tragedy and pathos: the lovers, who are traveling to the place of their death, have resolved to be united in death rather than live under their present circumstances. The overriding narration is chanted to music and interwoven with references to *utamakura* (poetic places) and allusions to classical poetry. The narration consequently elevates the hero—who is usually a weak *irogonomi* figure—even as he dies on the stage. The same can be said of the climactic scenes in *The Tale of Genji*, when the heroine dies, and in the final chapter of *The Tale of Heike*, when Kenreimon'in reflects on the destruction of her clan. In most of these scenes the exquisite and poetic descriptions of nature and the seasons, so central to Japanese lyricism, suggest that death is not an end but a return to nature.

Like the structure of its prose narratives, the history of Japanese literature tends to be accretionary. Every major historical era gave birth to new literary and artistic genres, but usually without destroying or abandoning the earlier forms. The thirty-one-syllable *waka* emerged in the classical period, linked verse appeared in the medieval period, the seventeen-syllable hokku came to the fore in the Edo period, and free verse was created in the modern period (under the influence of Western poetry). With the exception of linked verse (the rules of which are difficult to follow), all of these poetic forms continue to flourish today in Japan, with hundreds of thousands of serious practitioners. The same is true of Japanese drama. Noh drama and its comic counterpart, Kyōgen, emerged at the end of the medieval period; Jōruri (puppet theatre) and Kabuki, which were rival forms, became dominant in the Edo period; and modern theater (Shingeki) came to the fore in the twentieth century. Instead of each new form displacing or absorbing the previous one, these dramatic forms have continued to coexist even today.

Much of this remarkable continuity, not only in literature but in the other arts (tea ceremony, flower arrangement, archery, etc.), can be attributed to the establishment of schools with close master-disciple relationships—a phenomenon with such deep roots that it continues today. Even highly independent modern writers such as Yukio Mishima claim to have a "teacher" (*sensei*)—in Mishima's case Kawabata Yasunari, who acted, if only nominally, as a patron. The disciple system was influenced by Buddhist practice and directly reflects the primogenitary "house" (*ie*) system found in premodern Japanese society at large. It enabled the performing arts, which included poetry, to be transmitted almost unchanged over long stretches of time. It is thus possible for anyone in modern Japan to see drama that has remained essentially unchanged for over five centuries.

As in China, writers have always shown a great reverence for tradition and precedent, change often occurring in the name of the past, as "restoration." The ideal of continuity that we find in other areas of Japanese culture—for example, the political myth of unbroken imperial succession going back to the Sun Goddess—applies equally to Japanese literature, which continually refers to the past for both inspiration and authority. The process of learning is critical to the notion of audience as author. Learning begins with imitation and reproduction of the classics, and mastery of the forms (*kata*) and movements established by the great masters. The object of traditional art and literature is not (as so often in the West) the representation of nature, society, or some other ideal world, but rather the "re-presenting" of the classics.

Such a system makes it difficult for innovation to occur rapidly and for originality to be identified. If the literary child, whether poet or performer, is attempting to possess the same heart as the parent (the opposite of Harold Bloom's artistic Oedipal struggle and the "anxiety of influence"), what is to distinguish between the two? The line between imitation and originality, craft and art, school and individual, master and disciple, becomes quickly blurred. Such literature and art would seem to be hopelessly beyond the comprehension of a Japanese general public, not to mention those attempting to read and understand Japanese literature in translation. However, the result of this system is often a work that is greater than that of any single individual, a culmination of generations of talent that has a universal appeal. This process led to the creation of such enduring classics as *Tales of Ise* and *The Tale of Heike*, which were not written by a single author but instead are the products of generations of writers and listeners, and ultimately of a particular society. It has also led to a "living tradition" of Japanese arts and literature.

REFERENCES

de Bary, Wm. Theodore, et al. *A Guide to Oriental Classics*. 3d Sect. IV. New York: Columbia University Press, 1989. Contains bibliographies and topics for discussion.

Keene, Donald. *Dawn to the West: Japanese Literature in the Modern Era*. 2 vols. New York: Holt, Rinehart and Winston, 1984. An extensive study of modern literary movements and writers, in fiction, drama, poetry, and criticism.

Keene, Donald. *The Pleasures of Japanese Literature*. New York: Columbia University Press, 1988. A brief introduction to the major genres.

Keene, Donald. *Seeds in the Heart: Japanese Literature from Earliest Times to the Late Sixteenth Century*. New York: Henry Holt and Company, 1993.

Keene, Donald. *World Within Walls*. New York: Holt, Rhinehart and Winston, 1976. A broad survey of all genres from 1600–1867, with bibliographies.

McCullough, Helen, ed. *Classical Japanese Prose: An Anthology*. Stanford: Stanford University Press, 1990. Anthology of prose genres with introductions.

Rimer, J. Thomas. *A Reader's Guide to Japanese Literature*. New York: Kodansha International, 1988. A brief guide, with translated modern and classical texts, plot summaries, and bibliography.

Tsunoda Ryusaku, Wm. Theodore de Bary, and Donald Keene, eds. *Sources of Japanese Tradition*. 2 vols. New York: Columbia University Press, 1958. A source book of key excerpts from major texts in Japanese religion, thought, and aesthetics from the earliest times to the present, with extensive historical introductions.

A NOTE ON MODERN JAPANESE LITERATURE

Paul Anderer

For our purposes (and following period distinctions observed widely by scholars both here and in Japan), "modern literature" refers to writing produced after the Meiji Restoration of 1868. It is literature of an enormous range and output. Donald Keene has observed that "the Japanese literature written in the century or so since 1868 exceeds in volume all the Japanese literature that survives from the preceding millennium" (the introduction to his history of modern Japanese literature, *Dawn to the West*, provides other useful background detail). There is a substantial number of literary works available, even in English translation, and the lists grow at a steady rate.

The following six examples by no means exhaust even that smaller selection of writings that are regularly cited as being great or representative or seminal. At the least, these examples have been chosen to convey a sense of how many fine, distinctive, and frequently challenging voices have emerged on the literary scene in modern Japan. Arguably, the finest contemporary writers have committed themselves to fiction, which has become the preeminent genre of the post-Restoration era. Yet even in fiction whose "theme" is of the loss of tradition or the oppressiveness of the past, the legacy of the classical, lyrical mode remains a strongly felt presence controlling both imagery and plot.

Presumably, readers of this guide will not be able to use more than one or two of the works discussed in any given course. With this in mind, the basic themes or issues of each work are noted:

Sōseki. *Kokoro.* A tale of coming of age as a modern intellectual in a world where traditions are disappearing, and people are free to express their innermost thoughts, even as they deceive and betray each other. The moral tone in its disposition to explore the dark places of the modern heart is reminiscent of Conrad.

Tanizaki. *Seven Japanese Tales.* Tanizaki is so unconcerned with judging the often strange, indeed perverse, behavior of his characters that he is nearly an antimoralist. If Sōseki is groping toward a dark truth, Tanizaki relishes the possibility fiction offers to tell pleasurable, beautiful lies—to disguise the banalities of contemporary life or retreat imaginatively into various idealized pasts.

Kawabata. *Snow Country.* A haunting poem in prose about love and manipulation in a world removed from the ordinary. The language is as beautiful as the details of the love affair are sordid. Acknowledged as a traditionalist, Kawabata's effects are analogous to those achieved by literary "modernism" in the West.

Enchi. *The Waiting Years; Masks.* Enchi is one of a number of powerful women writers who emerge in the modern era; her novels make extensive use of the forms and structures of traditional writing, but their themes take revenge on an oppressive, stifling past.

Abe. *Woman in the Dunes.* Abe is the quintessential postwar writer, allegorizing ruins and stretches of barren emptiness, and confronting his solitary characters with choices rightly called existential. His writing invites comparison to Kafka and Beckett.

Mishima. *The Sailor Who Fell from Grace with the Sea.* In the West, Mishima is well known, as much for his suicide, his nationalism, and his sexual politics, as for his writing. He was haunted first by postwar emptiness, then by the economic recovery: both threatened a certain spiritual essence that Mishima sought, often melodramatically and luridly, to recapture.

II
Indian Texts

CLASSICAL SANSKRIT LYRIC: POETRY OF LOVE AND LOSS

Barbara Stoler Miller

The courts of ancient and medieval India delighted in eloquent speech. Words of counsel, as well as erotic and philosophical musings, were recited before the king in witty and elegant language. Among the languages of ancient India, Sanskrit and Tamil had the most highly developed linguistic structures and literary means. Within the cultures of both languages, the systems of grammar and poetics were the foundation for poetic activity. Lyric was especially prized among the forms of poetry. Lyric poetry in Sanskrit is defined as a form—kavya, "imaginative literature." A great deal of Sanskrit literature is written in verse, but would not qualify as kavya. In contrast with epic poetry, which is characterized by redundancy of words and formulas and a pace carefully measured to the listening audience, kavya poetry is marked by a brilliant condensation of independent stanzas, metrical complexity, compound words, and intricate figures of speech.

Sanskrit lyric poetry is expressed through three codified genres: fragmentary lyric (khaṇḍa-kāvya), narrative lyric (mahā-kāvya), and dramatic lyric (dṛśya-kāvya). The latter is represented by Kālidāsa's drama, the Śakuntalā. The three genres are not always totally distinct and are blurred in Jayadeva's Gītagovinda.

Much Sanskrit poetry has come down to us in anthologies of fragmentary lyrics compiled in medieval India from varied, and now largely untraceable sources—the fragmentary stanzas were drawn from earlier collections, from longer narratives, and from dramas. These verses are short and aesthetically complete—ideally an isolated verse should be appreciated on its own, without any larger context. Most commonly the verses are quatrains in which the lines are structured into uniform, quantitative metrical patterns, based on ancient Vedic and epic meters. As in Indian

55

miniature painting, brevity is not poverty: abundant detail and complexity of thought can be compressed into a simple metrical pattern. Larger contexts are created within these miniature molds by varied devices, such as densely compounded words, complex grammar, and rhetorical ornamentation. Metaphor, simile, allegory, synecdoche, antithesis, hyperbole, and punning abound. Poets deliberately exploit the suggestive overtones of words and images, so that they resonate in the mind of the audience like the tone after a bell has been struck, what critics call *dhvani*, or overtone. Repetitions of sounds are also used to increase the metrical sonority of a verse.

A simple verse from the erotic section of Bhartrihari's collected poems will suggest structure of the Sanskrit stanza. The metrical pattern here follows the most common pattern of a fixed sequence of long and short syllables repeated in each quarter of the verse. As in Latin and Greek prosody, rhythm depends on the amount of time required to pronounce a syllable, not on stress. The basic unit is a line of eleven syllables in the pattern known as Indravajrā:

> - - u | - - u | u - u | - -
> *viśramya viśramya vanadrumāṇām*
> wandering wandering of trees
> *chāyāsu tanvī vicacāra kācit*
> in shadows slender woman roamed one
> *stanottarīyeṇa karoddhṛtena*
> with a breast-cloth held in hand
> *nivārayantī śaśino mayūkhān*
> warding off moon's rays
>
> A certain slender woman was wandering,
> seeking solace in shadows of forest trees,
> warding off the moon's scorching rays,
> with the silken shawl held by her hand. [B 121][1]

The poets convey emotion through the sensuous nuances of the changing natural world, and they luxuriate in the rich colors, scents, and sounds that nature provides. The classical poetic ideal is to compress the profusion of nature's qualities into a palpable, thick, emotion-laden atmosphere, so highly controlled that the audience participates in the aesthetic experience.

> Lovers scented with sandalwood,
> flashing antelope eyes,
> arbors of fountains, flowers,
> and moonlight,
> a terrace swept with breezes

of flowering jasmine—
in summertime they fan the flames
of passion and arouse the god of love. [B 98]

The role that nature plays in Indian poetry is closely associated with the Indian attitude toward erotic love. Each season has its special eroticism, but the lush sensuality of the rainy season is particularly stimulating. The season of the rains is most poignant for parted lovers:

Clouds shade the sky,
plantain lilies mask the earth,
winds bear lingering scents
of fresh verbena and kadamba,
forest retreats rejoice
with cries of peacock flocks,
and love's yearning overpowers us—
with happiness or sorrow. [B 140]

The luxuriant dreamworld of erotic romance first comes to mind when we think of Indian love poetry. However, this is but one aspect of the complex universe of love represented in the vast body of poetry that exists in various Indian languages, such as Sanskrit, Prakrit, Tamil, Hindi, and Bengali.

In India, poetry in the classical genre of the fragmentary lyric has usually been preserved anonymously. Despite this, several collections of miniature poems are attributed to known authors by rich legendary traditions surrounding their names. Bhartrihari is prominent in Indian literature for the quality of his verses and the power of his legend. He was a philosopher of the fifth century C.E. and the legendary author of the Śatakatraya, a three-part collection of Sanskrit poems about political wisdom, erotic passion, and renunciation. Bhartrihari was renowned in classical India as a philosopher who continually vacillated between the secluded life of an ascetic and the world of courtly pleasure. The poetry attributed to him shows love's darker side. With characteristic irony, he worshipped an idealized female who was simultaneously poison and ambrosia; he loved her lustily, only to find himself deceived by life's transience and love's trickery. He says:

I prefer being bitten by a terrible serpent,
long, wanton, tortuous, gleaming like a black lotus,
to being smitten by her eye—
healers are everywhere to cure one of a serpent bite,
but there is no spell or remedy for me;
I was struck by the glance of a beautiful woman! [B 129]

Woman is love's victorious seal,
imprinting his triumph on all things—
deluded men who forsake her
are fools pursuing illusory fruits,
fools condemned without pity by the god of love
to become naked mendicants, wearing shorn
or tufted or shaggy hair
and bearing begging bowls of skull bone. [B 113]

In his poetry Bhartrihari does not simply vacillate between worldly indulgence and asceticism; he concurrently experiences delight in the fullness of the world, anxiety over its cruel transience, and the feeling that this tension defies resolution. When he dreams of tranquility in the forest, it is not as a romantic setting for love, but as a refuge from the pain of its delusion—and yet, the calm of lying in Nature's embrace is like the weariness of a lover in the arms of his mistress after love making:

Earth his soft couch,
arms of creepers his pillow,
the sky his canopy,
tender winds his fan,
the moon his brilliant lamp,
indifference his mistress,
detachment his joy—
tranquil, the ash-smeared hermit
sleeps in pleasure like a prince. [B 190]

Throughout Indian poetry, the beloved, whether female or male, is lyrically composed of the elements of nature, whose creative energies he or she personifies for the lover. Parts of the female body are conventionally equated with natural objects. The prevalent poetic view is subjected to Bhartrihari's cynical analysis:

Her breasts, those fleshy protuberances,
are compared to golden bowls;
her face, a vile receptacle of phlegm,
is likened to the moon;
her thighs, dank with urine,
are said to rival the elephant's trunk—
this despicable form is made venerable
by the ornaments of poets. [B 159]

The acknowledged master poet of Sanskrit is Kālidāsa, about whom we lack clear historical evidence. However, throughout the centuries the quality of Kālidāsa's poetry attracted many legends to his name. These are known from sources in Sanskrit and other languages. The legend is a tale of Kālidāsa's transformation from fool to poet through a series of events that bring him under the grace of the goddess Kālī. It is a parable of magic, paradox, transformation, and allusions to the power of speech.

Though details vary from version to version, the basic story is recognizable throughout. It begins with the King of Banaras offering his daughter in marriage to a certain Brahman pandit. She refuses on the grounds that she is a greater scholar than the pandit and therefore cannot serve him. Determined to trick her, the pandit finds a handsome cowherd whom he has dressed in the garb of a pandit and makes him memorize a Sanskrit greeting. Though he tries to carry out these instructions, the cowherd only utters nonsense syllables, but the pandit cleverly construes a benedictory verse to Śiva out of them and the princess is tricked. When she discovers that he is a fool, she angrily assigns him to gather flowers for her. Each day he stops before an image of the goddess Kālī and offers a few flowers to her with reverence. One of the palace maids, in order to tease him, conceals herself behind the image, chewing a ball of betel nut. When the cowherd finishes his usual prayers, the maid puts the remnants of her chewing into his hand. He thinks the goddess herself has presented it to him, so he swallows it. Instantly, unlimited knowledge of logic and grammar dawns in him, and he becomes a great poet, endowed with the power of speech. From his great reverence for the goddess Kālī, he came to be known as Kālidāsa, the servant of Kālī.

Among the six surviving works that are generally attributed to Kālidāsa by Indian critics and commentators is the lyric monologue *Meghadūta* (*The Cloud Messenger*). In the one-hundred-eleven stanza poem, a passing cloud arouses the memory of love in a demigod of nature, a yakṣa, who is exiled from his beloved. He begs the cloud to carry a message to her in their distant Himalayan home.

> A demigod who was heedless in his office
> had lost his honored rank—
> his master cursed him to endure
> a year in exile from his love.
> He lived on Mt. Rāma
> in the hermit groves
> whose waters were pure from Sītā's ablutions. [1][2]

From this opening, an immediate correspondence is made between the demigod's separation from his beloved and the epic hero Rāma's separation from Sītā, a story well known to Kālidāsa's audience from the *Rāmāyaṇa*. As in his *Kumārasambhava,* Kālidāsa set the subtle movements of erotic emotion in a timeless sacred landscape, full of ancient mythological reverberations and natural beauty. In the first half of the poem, the demigod recalls in sensuous imagery the landscape that the cloud will traverse on its northward course. He gives striking, erotically charged descriptions of the cities and countryside. Kālidāsa's profound intimacy with nature allows his imagination to interpenetrate with the landscape; his vision is expressed in both simple and complex metaphors that relate the natural world in its seasonal transformation to the pain and joy of love. Nature is heightened by its association with the mood of an estranged, nostalgic lover. The desire of parted love is constantly straining for fulfillment in descriptions of the cloud's sensuous contact with creatures of the forest.

> Spying the first weak shoots of golden green valley flowers
> and plantains' tender buds along the riverbanks,
> scenting the rich fragrance of forest earth,
> mating deer will trace the path of raindrops that you lose. [21]

In the second part, the lover's sorrowing heart is framed in nature's beauty. The demigod evokes his own divine city on Mount Kailāsa and the charms of his sorrowing beloved—he remembers her in love and imagines her now tossing on her couch, sleepless and wan through the watches of the night.

> Demigods in the company of beautiful nymphs
> ascend to their palace balconies,
> crystal-paved and studded
> with reflections of flowerlike stars—
> they ascend to enjoy aphrodisiac wine
> pressed from a wish-granting creeper
> while drums gently beat with the deep sounds
> of muffled thunder. [66]

The culminating possibility of resolution is expressed in the message verse that concretely equates the demigod's beloved with aspects of nature, but reminds her of her unique place in his heart.

> In twining creepers I see your body,
> in eyes of frightened does your glance,
> in the moon, the glow and shadow of your cheek,
> in the peacock's crested plume your hair,
> in the flowing waters' quick ripples
> the sportive frown on your brow—
> but never in a single place
> can I find an image of your likeness. [101]

Indian poets realized the unique power and aesthetic potential of the emotions of passionate sexual love. The erotic mood that emerges from such love was expressed in the antithetical modes of "separation" and "consummation." To experience this mood in the interplay of its two modes was considered the height of aesthetic joy. In Indian poetry, an act of remembering is the focal technique for relating the antithetical modes of love-in-separation and love-in-consummation. This tone of love is dominant throughout the tradition. One finds it in stray verses scattered through the anthologies, as well as in longer poems and dramas.

The emotions of erotic love are close to the intensity of religious devotion. The poets Kālidāsa and Bhartrihari address their poems to the god Śiva, the erotically potent divine ascetic. Erotic poems thus become religiously powerful. Divinity is present in all Indian art—poetry, drama, and sculpture. In the earliest preserved literature of India, the *Rig Veda,* poetry is a means of establishing relations between the world of humans and the world of the gods.

The dramatic lyrical poem *Gitagovinda,* which I have translated as *Love Song of the Dark Lord,* is a unique work in Indian literature and a source of religious devotion in both medieval and modern Hinduism. Its author, Jayadeva, who composed it in eastern India in the twelfth century, makes explicit the relation between religious and erotic experience. The poem is dedicated in devotion to the god Krishna. It concentrates on Krishna's love with the cowherdess Rādhā in a rite of spring. Intense earthly passion is the example Jayadeva uses to express the complexities of divine and human love. For centuries since its composition, audiences in India have continued to appreciate the emotional lyricism of the poem in its variations on the theme of separated lovers' passion.

> Jayadeva, wandering king of bards
> who sing at Padmavati's lotus feet,
> was obsessed in his heart
> by rhythms of the goddess of speech;
> he made this lyrical poem from tales of the passionate play
> when Krishna loved Śri. [1.2]

However figuratively the *Gitagovinda* may be interpreted, erotic emotion is central to its religious aesthetic. By admitting into the sphere of religion intense erotic emotion, such as is ordinarily associated only with passionate human love, the poem allows for congruity of desire and religious experience. In the tradition to which the *Gitagovinda* belongs, devotion is not disciplined self-sacrifice, but rather complete surrender to the love of Krishna, accompanied by all the emotions of attachment. It expresses itself most characteristically in songs of devotional poetry and dancing, done in hope that Krishna will answer the devotee's plea for an embrace. A highly intensified sensuous delight is the source of the spiritual intoxication that raises the devotee above the world of everyday reason into the protection and embrace of the divine lover, who has been seduced by the love of the devotee.

It is the theory of incarnation (avatara) that basically makes it possible to think of god in human ways—but if we take the Gitagovinda as an example, we can see how the poet's mystical vision of incarnation involved a shifting duality between worshipper and god, making devotional love, like human love, a circular dance in which both parties participate in diverse relationships, a dance in which the line between human and divine are blurred in fundamental ways. In the Gitagovinda, Krishna, the embodiment of love, himself suffers from love's separation and so shares his consort's pain. Krishna's suffering softens Rādhā's angry pride and overcomes her psychic inhibition to expressing her sexual power over him.

Rādhā, Krishna's partner in the rite of spring, is neither a wife nor a worshipping rustic playmate. She is an intense, solitary, proud female who complements and reflects the mood of Krishna's passion. She is Krishna's partner in a secret and exclusive love. After their lovemaking, he stays with Rādhā to admire and ornament her, to play her humble servant in a reversal of the normal human-divine relationship.

> Then, as he idled after passionate love,
> Rādhā, wanting him to ornament her,
> freely told her love,
> secure in her power over him. [12.11]

The lyrical techniques of Jayadeva's songs combine with the conventional language of Sanskrit erotic poetry to express the intimate power of divine love. One of the opening verses of the Gitagovinda expresses the poet's conviction that aesthetic experience is the means by which his audience can experience the divine love of Rādhā and Krishna.

> If remembering Hari enriches your heart,
> if his arts of seduction arouse you,
> listen to Jayadeva's speech
> in these sweet soft lyrical songs. [1.4]

Jayadeva's conception is revealed by following the way he presents his characters through the movement of the poem's twelve parts. The *Gitagovinda* begins with a miniature play-within-a-play whose meaning is enigmatic. This opening continually flashes on the mind of the audience to remind them of the unique relationship between Rādhā and Krishna. The scene is set by an alliterative description of the clouds that veil the sky.

"Clouds thicken the sky,
Tamāla trees darken the forest.
The night frightens him.
Rādhā, you take him home."
They leave at Nanda's order,
passing trees in thickets on the way,
until secret passions of Rādhā and Madhava
triumph on the Jumna riverbank.

The darkness of the night in the forest is described in voluptuous sounds and imagery that echo through the entire poem. It is in this secret, sexually stimulating environment that Krishna and Rādhā enact the primordial triumph of their divine love and then suffer the long night of separation that ends in their reunion. They follow the path through the forest as a pair, which Jayadeva expresses in the dual compound Rādhā-Madhava. The triumph of their passions occurs in this dual state, which is the defining form of their relationship in the *Gitagovinda*. The "home" to which Rādhā brings Krishna is a forest thicket, the secret place of their divine love, in which they meet again at the end of the journey.

After evoking Rādhā and Krishna in their secret erotic relationship and stating his own aim, Jayadeva invokes the ten cosmic incarnations of Krishna. He proceeds to present increasingly intimate aspects of Krishna's relation to existence, focusing on the suffering he shares with Rādhā in the frustration of their love. Krishna's ecstatic reunion with Rādhā within the forest thicket in springtime allows the poet's audience to witness the center of existence—a vision of the soul of his erotic mood reflected in her.

Intense memory of Krishna's incarnate presence is the purpose of singing the *Gitagovinda*. Memory functions within the lyric drama itself as the creative means by which the poet, the audience, Rādhā, and Krishna recreate the original secret encounter—dramatically encouraged by a third character, Rādhā's friend, who acts as a go-between for the parted lovers and describes the condition of each to the other, thus enabling the audience to share the shifting perspectives of secretly participating in the play of divine love. The setting in which this remembering occurs is springtime, when Krishna ignores Rādhā in his lust for all the beautiful women of the forest. Rādhā vividly remembers minute details of how Krishna looked as he danced in the circle dance with the other cowherdesses, playing seductively to mock her. It is the power of Rādhā's memory of Krishna that triumphs over the capricious adolescent god and makes him reciprocate her love.

Rādhā's response to Krishna's love is the subject of medieval Indian devotional poetry in various languages. These poems express a religion, not of ascetic withdrawal, but of joy. Centuries later the Bengali poet Rabindranath Tagore speaks of this joy in his *Gitañjali* [73]:

"Deliverance is not for me in renunciation.

I feel the embrace of freedom in a thousand bonds of delight." [73][3]

TOPICS FOR DISCUSSION

1. Classical Indian lyric poetry may be approached in its own terms, focusing on the controlling metaphors, images, figures of speech, and structures of individual verses and longer forms.

2. Compare Indian lyric poetry with Western, Chinese, or Japanese lyric traditions, particularly in terms of the attitudes towards nature expressed in selected poems. What is the relation between nature and love in Indian poetry and what comparable role does nature play in other lyric traditions?

3. The qualities of love expressed in the poetry can also be explored. Why do the Indian poets concentrate their poetic energy on love-in-separation? Compare this with the same theme in medieval troubadour poetry of the West. What is the relation between love and religious experience? In this context compare the *Gitagovinda* with the "Songs of Songs" or the poems of St. John of the Cross.

NOTES

1. The notations in brackets refer to poem or verse numbers. Those beginning with B, as in [B 121], refer to "Bhartṛhari's Poems" in *Bhartṛhari and Bilhana: The Hermit and the Love Thief* (New York: Penguin, 1990).

A notation such as [1.2] indicates part one, verse two of the given text. The translations in many cases have been revised for this essay by Barbara Stoler Miller.

2. Opening verse of *The Cloud Messenger*, translation by Barbara Stoler Miller. For a complete translation, see L. Nathan, cited below under References.

3. *A Tagore Reader*, ed. Amiya Chakravarty (Boston: Beacon Press, 1966), p. 305.

REFERENCES

Ingalls, Daniel H. H., trans. *An Anthology of Sanskrit Court Poetry: Vidyakara's "Subhasitaratnakosa."* Cambridge: Harvard University Press, 1965.

Miller, Barbara Stoler, trans. *Love Song of the Dark Lord: Jayadeva's Gitagovinda.* New York: Columbia University Press, 1977.

Miller, Barbara Stoler, trans. *The Hermit and the Love-Thief: Sanskrit Poems of Bhartrihari and Bilhana.* New York: Columbia University Press, 1978; Delhi: Oxford University Press, 1990.

Nathan, Leonard, trans. *The Transport of Love: The Meghaduta of Kalidasa.* Berkeley: University of California Press, 1976. [This may be compared with Kalidasa's *maha-kavya*, the *Kumarasambhava*, translated by Hank Heifetz as *The Origin of the Young God* (Berkeley: University of California Press, 1985).]

CLASSICAL TAMIL POETRY AND TAMIL POETICS

Rajagopal Parthasarathy

THE TAMIL LANGUAGE

Tamil is the oldest of the four major Dravidian languages, and is spoken mainly in Tamil Nadu in southeastern India. The language was regularized around 250 B.C.E., and it is this standard language, *centamil*, that is described in the *Tolkāppiyam* (5th c. C.E.; The Old Composition), the earliest work on Tamil grammar and poetics. However, the earliest Tamil poetry goes back to a period between 100 B.C.E. and 250 C.E., and is found in numerous anthologies that were later gathered together in two great collections: the *Ettutokai* (The Eight Anthologies) and the *Pattuppāṭṭu* (The Ten Long Poems).

Throughout its history, Tamil Nadu was relatively isolated and free from the invasions that swamped the rest of the country, except for a brief Muslim interlude (1324–70 C.E.) in Madurai. Though the Aryanization of South India had been going on since the first millenium B.C.E., Tamil Nadu (and Kerala) were not united with the rest of India till the British period. Again, Tamil, among all the Indian languages, has resisted Sanskritization by preserving archaic features of phonology and morphology. As a result, the spoken and written forms are different from each other. Also, unlike other Dravidian scripts, Tamil orthography has resisted the inclusion of special characters for writing down Sanskrit sounds.

Tamil is an agglutinative language. Suffixes, themselves meaningful elements, are added to a noun or verb to inflect its meaning. For example, the word *paṭittatilēyiruntu*, "from what was read," comprises the following elements:

paṭi   *-tt*   *-at*
to read (past tense) (3rd per. sing. neuter)
-il -   *ē*   *-y*   *-iru*
(locative case) (emphatic) (phonetic insertion) to be
-ntu
(past tense)

Words are thus built up by piling one suffix on top of another.

Classical Tamil has eighteen phonemic consonants as opposed to twenty-four in Modern English. However, the dental stop /t/ (as in *tāmarai*, "lotus"), the retroflex stop /ṭ/ (as in *kaṭai*, "shop"), the retroflex lateral /ḷ/ (as in *kaḷvan*, "thief"), the retroflex palatal lateral /ḻ/ (as in *paḻam*, "fruit"), and the alveolar trill ṟ/ (as in *aṟivu*, "knowledge") are not found in English, as also the dental nasal /ṉ/ (as in *cantu*, "lane"), the retroflex nasal /ṇ/ (as in *kaṇ*, "eye"), and the palatal nasal /ñ/ (as in *pañcu*, "cotton"). Double consonants are frequent in Tamil (as in *kappal*, "ship"; *vaṭṭam*, "circle"). In English they are enunciated only between words (as in fast train, gold digger). Initial and final consonant clusters (as in splendid, tribe, hatch, plump), typical of English, are unknown in Tamil. On the other hand, Tamil has only two diphthongs (/ai/, /au/), whereas English revels in them. Again, Tamil has long and short vowels; English has stress which tends to forward whenever it can. Stress being phonemic, it determines, for example, noun and verb functions of the same homographs: PERmit (n.); perMIT (v.).

Turning to syntax, we find that the normal order of words in an English sentence is SVO (subject + verb + object). In Tamil and other Dravidian languages, the word order is SOV (subject + object + verb): *nāṉ puttakam paṭittēṉ* ("I a book read" instead of "I read a book"). Of course, such a construction is not unusual in English; it occurs in poetry as an inversion: ". . . thy sweet love rememb'red such wealth brings" (Shakespeare, "Sonnet 29").

The inversion of the normal order of words (anastrophe) is a rhetorical device used for dramatic effect. It takes many forms: (1) subject after verb ("Unkempt about those hedges blows / An English unofficial rose"—Rupert Brooke, "The Old Vicarage, Grantchester"); (2) object before subject ("Nature I loved, and, next to Nature, Art"—Walter Savage Landor, "Dying Speech of an Old Philosopher"); (3) verb after adverbial clause ("When lilacs last in the dooryard bloom'd"—Walt Whitman); (4) preposition after noun ("It was young David, lord of sheep and cattle / Pursued his fate, the April fields among"—Stella Benson, "Five Smooth Stones").

The verb, in Tamil, is usually in the final position. The inverted word order has to be normalized in English. Take, for example, the following lines from the poem "Tamil" by Cuppiramaṇiya Pārati (1882–1921):

yāmaṟinta moḷikaḷilē tamiḷmoḷipōl
initāvatu eṅkum kāṇōm.[1]

I-know [the]-tongues-[of-men]-among Tamil-language-as
sweet-as anywhere is-known-not.

Among the tongues of men I know,
There is none so sweet as Tamil.

THE MAKING OF A TAMIL POEM

Except for the thief, there was no one.
And if he lies, what shall I do?
A heron too was there,
its thin legs yellow as millet stalks,
looking out for sand eels in the running water
the day he took me.[2]

Kapilar, *Kuṟuntokai* 25

A woman confides to her friend, and we overhear their conversation. The memory of past intimacies overwhelms the present, now threatened by the fear of betrayal. Of all the elements that compose this scene, it is the heron with its rapacious appetite that stands out in her mind. The heron is oblivious of the world around it in its pursuit of food. The woman's lover is the heron, and she the helpless eel in its beak.

The heron is the only witness to their lovemaking—an indifferent witness at that. Likewise, the world too is indifferent to the private woes of individuals. The heron presides over her life as a bird of ill omen foreboding a lonely future for her, though it does not utter a sound. The stillness of the heron is in contrast to the flowing water. This contributes to its ominousness. The heron is totally absorbed in itself. So is her lover. Hence the danger and threat. The epithet "thief," referring to her lover, further reinforces the idea: he stole her innocence, and what is worse, from her point of view, he may even deny the whole thing, and then abandon her. And if he does so, she will not be able to call him to account. She is obviously in desperate straits.

The woman does not, however, openly accuse her lover of possible betrayal. To do so would be discourteous and in bad taste. She only hints at the possibility, obliquely, through her references to the heron and the thief. They are both predatory by nature. We are offered evidence of this in the heron's behavior towards its prey. A thief too, it is implied, behaves likewise. He takes what belongs to another, without right. Also implied is the notion of acting secretly or unseen. The figure of the heron, "looking out for sand eels in the running water," dominates the scene. The figure is not simply decorative; it is functional. It discreetly alludes to her lover's behavior and its implication for the future of their relationship. The *Tolkāppiyam* (*Pruḷatikāram* 48), the earliest work on Tamil grammar and poetics, refers to this device as *uḷḷurai uvamam*[3] (indirect suggestion). Only the object of comparison (the heron) is explicitly described. The reader is offered the barest of hints to establish relationships (the heron and her lover), and discover the subject (the fear of her lover's betrayal). A love poem such as this, which explores the inner world, is classified as *akam* (the inner), one of the two great categories of Tamil discourse. The other category is *puram* (the outer). In the *akam* poems the burden of the discourse is borne by the figure. Its resonances are knit into a mosaic, and inlaid into the poem. *Uḷḷurai uvamam* is thus a mode of understanding through indirect suggestion.

It is this unobtrusive drama in miniature, at once contemporary and perennial, that Kapilar (2nd c. C.E.) invites the reader to witness in turn. The reader can be expected to be more sympathetic than the heron. Though Kapilar works by the ground rules of convention, he is able to rise above them and, in the process, shape a poem that continues to resonate in the mind long after one has heard it. The entire poem of five lines is compressed into one sentence of twenty-five words. This is a common syntactic feature of the *akam* poems. The opening lines construct the frame in which the drama is enacted. The punch line (*maṇanta ñāṉṟē*, "the day he took me") appears at the end of the poem, and completes the sentence. Here and elsewhere, when a poet wishes to depict one of the phases of love, all he does is to conjure with a few deft strokes the appropriate landscape, including the several elements integral to it. Eventually, the poem that emerges is at once concrete and universal; all traces of personal accents have been refined away to a vanishing point.

A famous verse in the Song of Songs (4.16) offers a parallel:

> Awake, O north wind; and come, thou south;
> Blow upon my garden, that the spices thereof may flow out.
> Let my beloved come into his garden,
> And eat his precious fruits.[4]

She invokes the wind to arouse her physically to enable her lover to smell her out, and possess her completely. Social conventions inhibit her from being more explicit. So she withdraws behind the veil of language, and cries her heart out in metaphors. The garden is herself, its spices and fruits are her physical charms which are her lover's alone.

Literary traditions often overlap, and in the Song of Songs we have evidence of a remarkable cross-fertilization of two traditions—the Hebrew and the Tamil. 1 Kings 10:22 mentions imports of apes, peacocks, and ivory in Solomon's time, the trip taking three years. The Hebrew word for peacock, *tukki*, is borrowed from the Tamil word for peacock, *tōkai*. Further evidence of contact with Tamils early in the first millenium B.C.E. is found in the names of Indian products in Hebrew, like *ahalot*, for the spice-wood aloes, from the Tamil *akil*.

Both the Tamil and Hebrew poems share a common theme of women in love expressing their thoughts not explicitly—for that would violate social norms; women were expected to be chaste and not display their emotions—but implicitly through a set of poetical conventions. Both poems illustrate the paradox of the silent language in which women for centuries were conditioned by society to express themselves. Chaim Rabin, to whose scholarship I owe this insight, goes so far as to suggest that the genre of the Song of Songs may owe something to the Tamil love poems that probably made their way to Tharshish along with the apes, peacocks, and ivory.[5]

A *puram* poem, on the other hand, explores the outer world. It is firmly tethered to a specific place and time.

> "On the weak, shriveled arms of the old woman
> the veins stand out. Her stomach is flat
> as a blade of lotus. Unnerved by the fighting,
> her son had turned his back on it." So folks talked.
> "If he had fled in the heat of battle,"
> she thundered in a rage, "these breasts that nursed him
> I'll tear to pieces." Sword in hand, she groped
> in the bloodstained field, turning over
> one lifeless body after another. When

she saw her son lying prostrate, hacked to bits,
she rejoiced more than on the day he was born.[6]

Kākkaipāṭiniyār Naccellaiyār, *Puranāṉūru* 278

A woman, incensed by the rumor that her son had lost heart in
battle and fled, rejoices on discovering that he has died heroically
on the battlefield, his body hacked to bits. It is dishonorable to
perish with wounds in one's back. In *Puṟ.* 65, we learn of King
Cēramāṉ Peruñcēralātaṉ facing north and ritually starving himself to death to atone for the spear-wounds in his back.

The battlefield, soaked in blood and burdened with the dead, is
the object of the poet's praise. It is contrasted with the shriveled
old woman whose breasts and womb can no longer support life. She
vows to renounce that emblem of femininity, her breasts, should her
son prove to be a coward. If he had fallen, wounded in the back, she
would have cut up his body and dispatched him to heaven.

The poem oscillates between the *akam* and *puṟam* worlds, between a mother's love for her son and his heroic death on the
battlefield. In case of a conflict between the two, as is evident
here, *puṟam* takes precedence over *akam*, war over love, death on
the battlefield over death at home. The poem represents, in microcosm, the values of a heroic age when the sword was mightier
than the plow, and a good name was cherished above life itself.

A DISTINCT POETICS

Classical Tamil poetics are original, and not indebted to Sanskrit. It
comes as an exciting revelation to those who stumble across it. The
most comprehensive statement of Tamil poetics is the third book of
the *Tolkāppiyam*. It is basically a handbook for the making of
poems. Poetry is classified into *akam* and *puṟam*, categories which,
however, extend beyond poetry to permeate a whole way of life.

The *akam* poems have as their focus the individual within the
matrix of familial relationships, foremost among them being love
between man and woman, which is explored vertically, that is,
archetypically. The bias is impersonal: the experience itself is
rarefied and frozen in the shape of a poem.

The *puṟam* poems, on the other hand, are centered outside the
matrix of familial relationships, and are occasional in character.
They explore the relationship between man and the world around
him horizontally, that is, historically, with reference to a specific
place and time.

Women preside over the *akam* poems, which are redolent of their ambiance and sacred power (*aṇaṅku*). Premarital love (*kaḷavu*), marital and extramarital love (*kaṟpu*), and extramarital love in all their phases are the subject of *akam* proper, which includes the whole gamut of the experience: meeting, waiting, sulking, lamenting, and parting.

The characters of the *akam* poems include the heroine, her friend, mother and foster mother, the hero, his friend or bard, the concubine, her friend, and passersby. A typical situation would include the heroine speaking to herself or to her friend, as in *Kur.* 25 discussed above. The audience overhears what is said. The utterance is in the form of a monologue, the genre preferred by the poet who never directly addresses his audience. In fact, the poet himself is nowhere in the picture, a feature quite uncommon in much romantic verse. The monologue emphasizes the primacy of speech, the relation of poetry to the spoken voice.

Men preside over the *puṟam* poems, which reverberate with the exploits and prowess in battle of heroes. The two genres are not exclusive; they often overlap.

Three distinct elements blend together to shape a poem. They provide the specific context for its realization.

> When we study the contents of a poem
> only these three things excel in the act of composition:
> the first elements, native elements, and human elements.
>
> (*Tol. Poruḷ.* 3)[7]

The first elements (*mutal*) are place and time. Place refers to the five *tiṇais* into which the world of *akam* is divided, the *tiṇai* being a complex of "landscape, class and behavior pattern."[8] The *tiṇais* are named after their characteristic flowers or trees, and are presided over by deities. They are *kuṟiñci* (hills/conehead), *mullai* (forest/jasmine), *marutam* (farmland/arjuna tree), *neytal* (seashore/dark lily), and *pālai* (wasteland/ivory-wood tree). Time includes both the seasons of the year and the hours of the day and night. The seasons are the rains (August-September), the cold season (October-November), the season of early dew (December-January), the season of late dew (February-March), early summer (April-May), and late summer (June-July). A day has six parts: dawn, morning, midday, evening, early night, and the dead of night.

The native elements (*karu*) comprise an entire taxonomy of interrelationships between humanity and nature. They include human beings, their occupations and pastimes, musical instruments, ragas, animals, birds, trees, and flowers. One or more of these elements usually occurs in a poem as a concrete symbol of one of the phases of love.

The human elements (uri) are the phases of love (meeting, waiting, sulking, lamenting, and parting), which correspond to the five tiṇais. In practice, the elements of one tiṇai often blend harmoniously with those of another in a "fusion of tiṇais" (tiṇaimayakkam) to deepen the poem's resonance. Kur. 25, discussed above, is a poem that hovers between kuriñci and marutam, refusing to be tethered to the one or the other tiṇai. The elements that compose the text are drawn from both kuriñci (lovers' meeting, millet stalks) and marutam (fear of betrayal, heron, sand eels, running water). This indeterminacy of genres is characteristic of akam poems.

Two phases of love the Tolkāppiyam (Poruḷ. 1)[9] considers not suitable for love poetry are unrequited love (kaikkiḷai) and mismatched love (peruntiṇai). Their corresponding tiṇais, with identical names, are not included in the study of the five akam tiṇais.

In the poetics of akam, kuriñci for example stands for lovers' meeting in the hills, because of the secrecy they afford; the time frame is the cold season, the season of early dew, and the dead of night. "Millet stalks," in our example (Kur. 25), are one of the elements of the kuriñci landscape where millet is raised as a staple food. The phrase evokes at the same time the theme of lovers meeting.

The world of puram also comprises seven tiṇais. They correspond to those of akam. Six of them are named after flowers or trees. Flowers, appropriate to each phase of combat, are worn as garlands by warriors. They are veṭci (scarlet ixora), for cattle raiding; vañci (Indian willow), for invasion; uḷiñai (balloon vine), for siege; tumpai (white dead nettle), for pitched battle; and vākai (sirissa tree), for victory. Kāñci (portia tree), for the impermanence of life, and pāṭān, for the praise of kings, were not considered suitable for poetry. (For a chart showing the correspondences between akam and puram, see Ramanujan 1985.[10])

The akam and puram genres are not exclusive. They complement each other. Often, they overlap, even fuse together to speak passionately and with sophistication of an ancient way of life.

Elaborate as this "grammar of poetry" is, it is not mechanistic. It is a part of the received tradition of poets who put it to effective use in making poems, and in achieving their poetic effects. A knowledge of this grammar is, therefore, essential for understanding Classical Tamil poetry.

TOPICS FOR DISCUSSION

1. Read the poem, "When We Two Parted," by Byro (1788–1824).

When we two parted
    In silence and tears,
Half broken-hearted
    To sever for years,
Pale grew thy cheek and cold,
    Colder thy kiss;
Truly that hour foretold
    Sorrow to this.

The dew of the morning
    Sunk chill on my brow—
It felt like the warning
    Of what I feel now.
Thy vows are all broken,
    And light is thy fame:
I hear thy name spoken,
    And share in its shame
They name thee before me,
    A knell to mine ear;
A shudder comes o'er me—
    Why wert thou so dear?
They know not I knew thee,
    Who knew thee too well:—
Long, long shall I rue thee,
    Too deeply to tell.

In secret we met—
    In silence I grieve,
That thy heart could forget,
    Thy spirit deceive.
If I should meet thee
    After long years,
How should I greet thee?—
    With silence and tears.

Compare this love poem with Kapilar's "Except for the Thief." Their tone and attitude to love differ. One is romantic; the other, classical. Examine the ways in which the two poems differ from one another. What is distinctive about each poem?

2. Consider the view that *uḷḷurai uwamum* is a refinement of the metaphor. It also occurs in Chinese poetry, as in Ezra Pound's "The Jewel Stairs' Grievance." Pound's note on the poem makes explicit the use of this figure in Chinese.

The jewelled steps are already quite white
    with dew,
It is so late that the dew soaks my gauze
    stockings,
And I let down the crystal curtain
And watch the moon through the clear autumn.

Note: Jewel stairs, therefore a palace. Grievance, therefore there
is something to complain of. Gauze stockings, therefore a court
lady, not a servant who complains. Clear autumn, therefore he
has no excuse on account of weather. Also she has come early,
for the dew has not merely whitened the stairs, but has soaked
her stockings. The poem is especially prized because she utters
no direct reproach.

James J. Y. Liu refers to such a figure as a compound image (*The
Art of Chinese Poetry*, 1962: 106–11).

3. Choose one example from Ramanujan's *Poems of Love and
War* (pp. 5–10) of each of the five genres of *akam* poems: *kuṟiñci,
mullai, marutam, neytal,* and *pālai*. Show how each poem
illustrates the specific characteristics of its respective genre.

4. In "On the Weak, Shriveled Arms," Kākkaipāṭiṇiyār
Naccellaiyār sings of "arms and the man." So does the English
poet Keith Douglas (1920–44) in "Vergissmeinnicht." Douglas was
killed during the Allied invasion of Normandy on June 9, 1944.

Three weeks gone and the combatants gone
returning over the nightmare ground
we found the place again, and found
the soldier sprawling in the sun.

The frowning barrel of his gun
overshadowing. As we came on
that day, he hit my tank with one
like the entry of a demon.

Look. Here in the gunpit spoil
the dishonoured picture of his girl
who has put: *Steffi. Vergissmeinnicht*
in a copybook gothic script.

We see him almost with content,
abased, and seeming to have paid
and mocked at by his own equipment
that's hard and good when he's decayed.

But she would weep to see today
how on his skin the swart flies move;

the dust upon the paper eye
and the burst stomach like a cave.

For here the lover and killer are mingled
who had one body and one heart.
And death who had the soldier singled
has done the lover mortal hurt.

Tunisia, May–June 1943

The two poems differ radically in their tone and attitude to war. The reader is more likely to find himself drawn to the English rather than the Tamil poem, since Douglas speaks out against the inhumanity of war. Should the reader allow his own ideas about war to interfere with his appreciation of poetry? How detached from such concerns is it possible for a reader to be to have a fair understanding of Asian literature? Two well-known Chinese poems may also be compared with the Tamil poem: "Fighting South of the Ramparts" by Li Po (701–62), and "Song of the War-Chariots" by Tu Fu (712–70).

NOTES

1. Cuppiramaṇiya Pārati, "Tamil," in *Makākavi Pāratiyār kavitaikaḷ* [The Poems of Makakavi Bharati] (Madurai: Aruna patippakam, 1958), p. 50.
2. *Kuṟuntokai*, edited, with a commentary, by U. Vē. Cāminātaiyar, 4th printing (Madras: Śrī Tiyākarāca vilācam, 1962).
3. *Tolkāppiyam: Poruḷatikāram.* Old commentary by Pērāciriyar (Tirunelveli: Kaḷakam, 1961).
4. "The Song of Songs," in Ernest Sutherland Bates, ed., *The Bible Designed to Be Read as Literature* (New York: Simon & Schuster, 1936), p. 778.
5. Chaim Rabin, "The Song of Songs and Tamil Poetry," *Studies in Religion/Sciences religieuses* 3 (1973): 205–19. David Shulman brought this article to my attention.
6. *Puṟanāṉuṟu*, edited, with an old commentary, by U. Vē. Cāminātaiyar, 6th printing (Madras: Śrī Tiyākarāca vilācam, 1963).
7. *Tol.: Poruḷ.*
8. Maṇṭalapurutaṉ, *Cūṭamaṇinikantu* [The Crest-Jeweled Glossary], in Kamil Veith Zvelebil, *Tamil Literature*, vol. 10, fasc. 1, p. 37 of *A History of Indian Literature*, 10 vols., ed. Jan Gonda (Weisbaden: Harrassowitz, 1974).
9. *Tol.: Poruḷ.*
10. A. K. Ramanujan, trans., *Poems of Love and War from the Eight Anthologies and the Ten Long Poems of Classical Tamil* (New York: Columbia University Press/UNESCO (Translations from the Oriental Classics), 1985), p. 252.

REFERENCES

Hart, George L., III, trans. *Poets of the Tamil Anthologies: Ancient Poems of Love and War*. Princeton: Princeton University Press (Princeton Library of Asian Translations), 1979.

Hart, George L., III. *The Poems of Ancient Tamil: Their Milieu and Their Sanskrit Counterparts*. Berkeley: University of California Press, 1975.

Kailasapathy, K. *Tamil Heroic Poetry*. Oxford: Clarendon Press, 1968.

Liu, James J. Y. *The Art of Chinese Poetry*. Chicago: University of Chicago Press, 1962.

Marr, John Ralston. *The Eight Anthologies: A Study in Early Tamil Literature*. Madras: Institute of Asian Studies, 1985.

Parthasarathy, Rajagopal, trans. *Cilappatikarâm of Ilankō Atikaḷ*. New York: Columbia University Press (Translations from the Asian Classics), 1993.

Ramanujan, A. K., trans. *Poems of Love and War from the Eight Anthologies and the Ten Long Poems of Classical Tamil*. New York: Columbia University Press/UNESCO (Translations from the Oriental Classics), 1985.

Ramanujan, A. K. "Form in Classical Tamil Poetry." In *Symposium on Dravidian Civilization*, edited by Andre F. Sjoberg, 73–104. Austin, TX: Pemberton Press, 1971.

Ramanujan, A. K., trans. *The Interior Landscape: Love Poems from a Classical Tamil Anthology*. Bloomington: Indiana University Press, 1967.

Zvelebil, Kamil Veith. *Tamil Literature*. Band 2, Abschnitt 1 of Jan Gonda, ed. *Handbuch der Orientalistik*, Zweite Abteilung, *Indien*. Leiden/Cologne: E. J. Brill, 1975.

Zvelebil, Kamil Veith. *Tamil Literature*. Vol. 10, fasc. 1 of Jan Gonda, ed. *A History of Indian Literature*. 10 vols. Wiesbaden: Otto Harrassowitz, 1974.

Zvelebil, Kamil Veith. *The Smile of Murugan: On Tamil Literature of South India*. Leiden: E. J. Brill, 1973.

DEVOTIONAL POETRY OF MEDIEVAL NORTH INDIA

John Stratton Hawley

The language family that we today call Hindi is familiar to more people in India than any other. Upwards of 150 million inhabitants of North India speak it as a mother tongue, and at least that many more know it as a second language; as such it has been calculated to be the world's sixth most widely spoken language.

A language does not, however, make a literature. Just as English was not regarded as a subject fit for study in British and American schools until the nineteenth century (that honor was reserved for "the classics" in Greek and Latin) so Hindi was until quite recently overshadowed by its elder cousin, Sanskrit, at least in the context of formal education. Yet just as English had its Chaucers and Shakespeares long before its admission to the curriculum, so Hindi had a thriving literary tradition as early as the fifteenth to seventeenth centuries, when the religious poems that count as its major classics were composed.

The lyrics and epigrams that emerged in this period are conventionally called bhakti poetry, in that they have to do with bhakti, love or devotion in one's relation to God. Bhakti poetry did not originate then, however. A well-known passage, personifying bhakti as a woman, says that she was born long before in South India: the reference is not to any Sanskrit source—that would be too rarefied, too far from anyone's mother tongue—but to the intense devotional poetry that was produced in Tamil from about 600 to 900 C.E. The passage goes on to say that Bhakti matured as she wandered northward through the western provinces of India, ultimately shrivelling to an aged crone, but she experienced a sudden rejuvenation when she arrived in the Hindi-speaking regions.

The period when Bhakti regained her supple youth is the one that concerns us here, the time when compositions bearing (usually oral) signatures of poets such as Kabir, Ravidas, Nanak, Mirabai, Surdas, and Tulsidas appeared across North India. These poets are regarded as the great founding voices of the Hindi language, and their words are familiar throughout North India today, far more so than anything composed in Sanskrit. They are learned in schools, sung in homes and temples, and enacted in religious dramas. Depending on the poet and the mood, they are apt to be recited by anyone from a Brahman pundit to an illiterate, low-caste village woman.

The Sanskrit root *bhaj*, from which the word bhakti is formed, means broadly "to share, to possess," and the engagement described by bhakti, in which human beings share in the Divine, is an intense one. Often that intensity is expressed in personal terms: the Divine is thought of as disclosing itself in relationships that are built when human beings conceive of the Ultimate in sensory form, especially through the strongest sense, sight. Poets of this period most frequently saw God as Ram or Krishna, two anthropomorphic divinities that are understood to be related to each other as expressions of the more distant Vishnu. These poets' worship—and therefore their poetry—is said to be *saguṇa* ("with attributes"), because it cultivates a sense of the visible presence of the Lord. It is strongly associated with particular images, stories, and sacred places.

A second type of bhakti poetry has just the opposite impetus. Poetry of this sort is said to be *nirguṇa* ("without qualities") because it precisely questions the propriety of approaching God through icon, legend, and ritual. Such poems are often outspokenly critical of the superficiality and hypocrisy that seem so easily to infest the more routinized expressions of "with-attributes" religion. In India the guardians of public religion come in for especially harsh criticism, because they are often the same people who give definition to the caste system, with its gradations of personal and ritual purity (or impurity). In Hindu society these guardians of formal religion are mainly Brahmans, but the poets of *nirguṇa* bhakti were equally harsh in their attitude toward the hollow pretensions of Muslim religious authorities, the *qāzis* and mullahs so visible in North India at the time.

It is important to remember that tradition holds these *saguṇa* and *nirguṇa* poets together as members of a single family, united in the pursuit of immediate, interior religion. This is done in part with hagiography, for all the great bhakti poets are regarded not just as literary figures but as saints whose life stories are worthy of recall. These remembered lives intersect more frequently within the *saguṇa* or the *nirguṇa* clan than they do between the two groups, but there are some vignettes that break down this barrier. This is true in the poetry, too. All the poet-saints we have mentioned expressed themselves in a petitionary genre called *vinaya* ("humble submission"), and this served as a basis for the creation of anthologies that drew *saguṇa* and *nirguṇa* poets together in unified collections. Differences remain: the *saguṇa* poets Mirabai and Surdas frequently sing from a standpoint that suggests their being one of the milkmaid girls (*gopīs*) who surround Krishna with their love, while *nirguṇa* poets such as Kabir and Ravidas speak more out of their own experience. Yet the conceit by which a male poet assumes a female persona is to be seen on both sides of the *saguṇa/nirguṇa* divide, for the feminine sex was thought, at least by men, to be more naturally inclined toward devotional feeling than the masculine. Hence these medieval bhakti poets really do belong together as a single group, no matter how, divergent their individual emphases.

They are not, however, equally easy of access, especially outside their own cultural context. Often it is easier for outsiders to identify with the sorts of feelings that caused the *nirguṇa* poet Kabir to debunk the pretensions of Brahmans, *qāzīs*, or yogis than to imagine their way into the well-loved stories and ritual conventions that animate religious poetry of the *saguṇa* type. Consider, for example, this poem reliably attributed to Kabir:[1]

> Go naked if you want,
> Put on animal skins.
>   What does it matter till you see the inward Ram?
>
> If the union yogīs seek
> Came from roaming about in the buff,
>   every deer in the forest would be saved.
>
> If shaving your head
> Spelled spiritual success,
>   heaven would be filled with sheep.
>
> And brother, if holding back your seed
> Earned you a place in paradise,
>   eunuchs would be the first to arrive.
>
> Kabir says: Listen brother,
> Without the name of Ram
> who has ever won the spirit's prize?
>
>   (Hawley and Juergensmeyer, 50)[2]

Kabir's "rough rhetoric"[3]—confrontational, assaultive, abruptly familiar—is very much in evidence here, and it suits his purpose to be as direct as possible. Hence both mood and message come across quite clearly in translation. About all the Western reader needs to know is that for Kabir, like many *nirguṇa* poets, the word Ram refers not primarily to the heroic, righteous avatar of Vishnu (its original meaning), but to the Almighty in a much more general sense. In fact, Kabir himself fends off any such confusion by referring to "the inward Ram" (*ātamarām*, i.e., *ātmārām*) in the very first verse. Even if one knows little about Hindu culture, it is not difficult to piece together the rest: that yogis habitually wear animal skins or simply go naked; that the pious sometimes undergo tonsure as a sign of their devotion; and that celibacy is widely assumed—certainly among yogis—to be a precondition for spiritual purity. Outsiders may not know that in the original language of the final verse "name" rhymes with "Ram" (*rām nām*)—a fact that probably contributed to broadening the meaning of "Ram" in the first place—but they can scarcely miss Kabir's desire to reduce religion to its bare essential, the repeating of God's name, rather than letting it get lost in a labyrinth of pointless conventions. And the poet's arresting comparisons make it obvious why the poem became memorable to speakers of Hindi. Here ideas matter more that poetic artifice, and superciliousness and self-deception are sufficiently universal phenomena that Kabir's humor translates well from one century and one culture to another.

Unfortunately, humor is not always so easy to translate, as one can see by considering a poem that is in many ways similar to Kabir's, but was composed by a much more "refined" poet, Tulsidas. Like Kabir, Tulsidas (or Tulsi, for short) lived in the religiously complex city of Benares, but a century or so later, he apparently died in 1623. Kabir belonged to the *julāhā* caste, a low-ranked group of weavers, many of whom rejected their Hindu identity by embracing Islam; Tulsidas was almost certainly a Brahman. Hindi speakers would recognize this in his oral "signature" in the middle of the following poem, because it reveals Tulsi's reaction to someone from a much humbler station in Indian society than his own. The suspicion that Tulsi is looking down his nose is ultimately false, but it serves the poet well to have his audience think that at first. After all, if one is to learn that God cares more about love than about sect or status, a finicky Brahman makes a good teacher:[4]

A blind, mean-minded,
    dull-witted, withered-up
Old Muslim on the road
Got knocked down
    by a son of a pig.

As he fell, fear filled his heart.
"Oh God! Oh God! Unclean, unclean!
An unclean thing has killed me," he moaned
    and groaned as he fell
into the jaws of death.

Tulsi says, his sorrows vanished
And he went straightaway
To the land of the lord of all worlds.
As everyone knows, it is because
    of the power of the name.

That very name of God
Is what people say with love.
So how can they say its grandeur place it
    where it's impossible to go?

                      (Hawley and Juergensmeyer, 164–5)

A hallmark of Tulsidas's style, consistent with his Brahman learning, is its intricate use of language, even in a humorous poem like this. As such, its appeal is quite different from the rhetoric of Kabir. In the first two verses of the original, which look like stanzas when presented in translation, Tulsidas takes his love of alliteration to such extremes that the Hindi-speaking listener is bound to be amused. As Tulsi presents us with the picture of a pious old Muslim getting tripped up in an encounter with a pig, he spins a web of alliteration so dense that the audience too has trouble keeping its balance:

1   *ãdharõ adham jaḍ jājaro jarā javan*
      sūkar ke sāvak ḍhakā ḍhakelyo mag māi
2   *giro hiye hahari harām ho harām hanyo*
      hāy hāy karat parigo kāl phāg māi.

It would strain the limits of credibility in modern English verse to give a fully alliterative translation of the original, but Mark Juergensmeyer, my co-translator, and I hope some of the flavor comes across in the long string of hyphenated words that introduces the first verse, and in the repetitions, assonances, and alliterations of the second.

Embedded in the whirlwind of the first verse is the pivotal phrase *sūkar ke sāvak*, which we rendered "by a son of a pig." The translation is overly literal, but we hoped that echoes from the parallel English expression having to do with dogs would come in and supply the air of profanity that surrounds *sūkar ke sāvak*. In any case, it would have been awkward to use the English idiom—a figurative translation—because the rest of the poem depends on this unfortunate animal's being a little pig, not a son of a bitch.

The second verse presents a similar problem in the word *harām*, which is rendered as "unclean" or "an unclean thing." *Harām* does mean "unclean," but because it does, it can also actually mean "pig," and the original gains force from this. Juergensmeyer and I saw no way to reproduce the double meaning, and felt we had to choose one and not the other to carry the meaning. In doing so, however, we gave up some of the density of the original.

There was yet another problem. What was to be done with the fact that the old man's exclamation—*harām! harām!*, especially as amplified by *hāy hāy*—is a call of despair, a curse? Furthermore, how could we convey the idea that this Muslim curse contains a Hindu name for God (*rām*)? That, after all, is the whole point of the poem.

An earlier translator simply gave up at this juncture. F. R. Allchin, who translated this poem in 1964, himself cried *harām* and took recourse to a footnote, which begins, "This verse depends upon an untranslatable play on words . . . "[5] We made a try, for better or worse, by settling on the expression "Oh God! Oh God! Unclean, unclean!" Obviously this is not an altogether literal translation, but we hoped that by restructuring the puzzle somewhat, we could put hearers in a position where they could put the pieces back together themselves.

As for the word *rām*, there seemed good reason to render it "God," both in the expletive context of verse two, where *rām* is concealed in the word *harām*, and in the phrase *rām nām*, which comes at the beginning of verse four. When Kabir says "Ram," as we have seen, he does mean something quite close to "God," but when Tulsi says it there is not just God to factor in, but Ramacandra too, that is, Ram the hero and avatar. That element is lost in our translation, and it does figure in Tulsi's sense of the miracles Ram can bring about (v. 3). Yet by not trying to carry

Ram directly into English we hope to preserve the general meaning of a phrase like *rām nām* and in the same moment to make the poem as immediately intelligible as possible.

Our translation has other costs, too. I fear we have not given enough emphasis to the fact that this is Hindu salvation being foisted on a Muslim. How could we have made it clear that *harām*—the despairing curse—is the only Urdu word in the poem, while grace is mediated in Hindi? Suppose we had rendered *jan* (in the final verse) not in a broad way, as "people," but had instead highlighted its communal or sectarian sense—*jan* as devotees of Ram? Perhaps it would have been better. Yet Tulsi's point is that this Hindu god is kind not only to his own sect but to all people—*jan* in the wider sense, including even the pitiful Muslim outsider described in this poem. This point is made time and again in bhakti poetry by recalling the fate of Ajamil, the dissolute, womanizing Brahman who met death by calling desperately for his son Narayan and was answered instead by God, one of whose names, as it happened, was also Narayan. Here one has the same motif, but it is given an even more extreme expression. It is not just a fallen Brahman who is rescued, but a Muslim!

One final problem in rendering this poem relates to its last word, the clincher: *agamāi.* Tulsidas sets this word up for some considerable attention by breaking a convention he had established in the first three stanzas, where he distributes the final rhyme between two words: *mag māi, phāg māi, jag māi.* At the end, by contrast, rhyme and sense converge in a single word, *agamāi.*[6] Why is this word so critical? It frequently means "not to be gone beyond," hence "unsurpassable," but it can also mean "not to be gone to," hence a place "to where it is impossible to go," as in the current translation. That is the point here, that God's grace crosses all boundaries, especially the one that separates the all-knowing sheep (here, the Hindus) from the cursing goats.

The experienced listener would know a raft of other poems in which *agamāi* means "transcendent" and is surrounded by language that aspires to a similar loftiness. Here, by contrast, the poet is making the point that God cannot be God of the Universe without being God of the Gutter. We would have had to stretch the original even further to make this novel perspective explicit within the confines of the poem, and in the end it probably would not have worked: only a substantial reading of other bhakti poetry can truly give the reader a sense of why this poem and this ending stand out. No wonder a newcomer is apt to find more to appreciate in a "street" poet like Kabir than in a "literary" poet like

Tulsidas, who plays in delicate ways with an established genre.

In considering an "easier" and a "harder" *nirguṇa* poem, we have strayed some distance toward the *saguṇa* domain, for Tulsidas is normally understood as a distinctly *saguṇa* poet. In the poem just discussed, Tulsi speaks in a *nirguṇa* vein, drawing attention to the way in which God transcends the boundaries humans take for granted, but in his epic work, the *Rāmcaritmānas* ("Holy Lake of the Acts of Ram"), and in many of his short lyrics he shows himself to be a great devotee of Ram— not just Ram in the all-comprehending, formless sense but Ram as the storied hero who fights with demons. And there is a spectrum of "easier" and "harder" poems among *saguṇa* poets, too. As in the *nirguṇa* case, let us briefly consider an example of each, one by Mirabai, the other by Surdas.

Mirabai often presents a Western reader with verse that is more accessible than that of her *saguṇa* peers Surdas and Tulsidas. The reason is twofold. First, the manuscript corpus associated with her poetry is far more recent than what one finds with Tulsi or Sur. Only one of her poems appears in an anthology that can be reliably dated to any time near the sixteenth century, when she is said to have lived. A consequence of this is that the language of poems attributed to her tends to be much less dense than that of other bhakti poets. We often have reason to suspect that we are actually hearing not the voice of a famed poet, but rather the voice of the tradition that revered her. Apparently it was not so much a corpus of poetry that stimulated this veneration as a heroic life: Mira is said to have suffered great costs for the sake of her devotion to Krishna.

A second reason why Mira's poetry tends to be easier than that of the other great *saguṇa* poets is that tradition projects her as a woman, while the others are men. This means that she may speak simply and directly when she addresses Krishna, since she speaks for herself. A poet such as Surdas must project himself imaginatively into Krishna's world by taking on the role of one of Krishna's *gopī* milkmaids. One must know a fair amount about Krishna's world to appreciate the lyrics of Surdas, therefore, but one can sometimes hear Mira's voice as the voice of a woman— any woman—longing for her love. As if to account for this, the earliest hagiography of Mira already casts her in the role of a "latter-day *gopī* ";[7] she need feign no identity other than her own.

Both of these factors are in evidence in the following poem, in which Mira expresses the power of her separation from Krishna, her "dark Lord," even as she hears the sounds of his flute Murali beckoning from the banks of the Jumna River, where he loves to repair. In the body of the poem, Mira muses to herself about her lostness; then in the final line, here translated as a couplet, she summons her thoughts to address Krishna (however absent) directly. In doing so, she uses her favorite designation for him, "Mountain Lifter," referring to the moment when Krishna lifted Mount Govardhan to protect his people and cattle from the angry ravages of the rain-god Indra. Mira requests a similar presence and protection:[8]

> Murali sounds on the banks of the Jumna,
> Murali snatches away my mind;
> My senses cut loose from their moorings—
> Dark waters, dark garments, dark Lord.
> I listen close to the sounds of Murali
> And my body withers away—
> Lost thoughts, lost even the power to think.
> > Mira's Lord, clever Mountain Lifter,
> > Come quick, and snatch away my pain.
> > > (Hawley and Juergensmeyer, 136)

To contrast this poem with a *saguṇa* poem that is more difficult but belongs, nonetheless, to the same broad genre, one might quote a composition of the sixteenth-century poet Surdas that also concerns the River Jumna. This too is a poem of separation and longing (*viraha*). To understand Surdas's relation to the language of the poem, one must remember that he speaks through the persona of one of Krishna's *gopis*. Furthermore, he ("she") addresses another figure inside Krishna's dramatic world, the "wayfarer" Uddho (Skt. Uddhara), whom Krishna (here called Hari) has sent as a messenger to the *gopis*. By the time this poem is uttered, Krishna has departed for urban Mathura to fight the battles of righteousness that make for adulthood; in so doing he has left behind the forests and glades where he grew up with the *gopis*, who learned to love him so deeply. Through Uddho, he tries to urge them to become accustomed to his absence by focusing on his disembodied, spiritual presence, but the *gopis* are not persuaded that such an approach has any value. They respond in words that are intended to play on Uddho's (and Krishna's) sympathies, to bring back Krishna in the flesh:

1   Wayfarer, see how the dark Jumna's blackened.
2   Carry to that Hari of yours the word
        that she's scorched in a fever of longing.

3   From her couch she seems to have fainted to the earth,
        writhing with waves, her weight too great to lift.
4   The poultice of sand that stands on her banks
        has turned her torrent into rivulets of sweat.
5   Her hair: tangled grass and reeds rotting in the mire
        of her lotus-patterned sari blackened with mascara.
6   She flails about like aimless, restless bees,
        turning side to side, horrid and forlorn,
7   Babbling like a sheldrake night and day,
        subsisting on a diet of foam.
8   Surdas says, Lord, the sad state of the Jumna
        is not hers alone: it's also our own.[9]

This poem gains much of its strength from a specific canon of visual imagery. To appreciate the simile of a river that is like a suffering woman, a knowledgeable Indian audience can picture any of the thin, anguished women who drape themselves sleeplessly across divans in innumerable Mughal and Rajput miniature paintings. They are also shown—now as *gopis* specifically—in the *rās līlā* dramas of the Krishna tradition itself. Western readers must stretch further to understand this vision, familiar in one guise or another to almost every Hindi speaker, and to accept the notion that rivers are women—important women, indeed, goddesses. Certainly the Jumna is regarded in that way.

In the original, the poem draws upon and sharpens many of these features. First, the name of the river is feminine. Second, there is more than one name. In the refrain or title line of the original, the river is called Kalindi, a patronymic the Jumna earns by virtue of being descended from a Himalayan peak called Kalind. The poet brings that genealogy into play in the third verse when he depicts the river as having "fainted to the earth" from her (mountain) couch. In the first line he uses the name Kalindi in another way, saying that Kalindi looks *kārī* ("black"). Since the letters "l" and "r" are often interchangeable in Hindi, the words (though unrelated etymologically) themselves suggest this observation.

Unable to convey this web of connections, I simply avoided the name Kalindi in favor of Jumna, hoping at least to simulate a clear echo between the first and last lines: only at those points is the river actually named, and thus regarded as a river per se, not a woman suffering for her lover. As for the delicate interplay between convention and invention that the poet creates as he works out his comparison between river and woman, I fear this can only be approximated by first presenting English readers with many other *viraha* poems before they come to this more complex one, a proviso that was necessary also in regard to the *nirguṇa* poetry of Tulsidas.

Other aspects of the poem, fortunately, are not so recondite. Anyone who has known the taste of unrequited love or been parted from the person who, for him or her, makes the world cohere, knows *viraha* as a desiccating fever, a river run dry. Anyone can understand how the *gopis*, afflicted in this way, would want to enlist Uddho's (and, through him, Krishna's) sympathy for an archetypal other, the Jumna, before turning that sympathy to their own advantage in the typically redirective final verse. Finally, it takes no special expertise to see that when the poet brings his own name into the poem in the final verse, he is confessing that he, like any sensitive human being, often longs for God across a chasm like the one that separates the *gopis* from seemingly unreachable Mathura. This implicit comparison between the poet himself and his literary persona demonstrates the potential force of "with-attributes" religious verse.

For all their interconnectedness, then, the devotional poems of medieval North India are not equally easy for an outsider to appreciate. On the whole, the *nirguṇa* poems are more accessible than the *saguṇa* ones—more universal in their subject, less dependent upon a particular narrative world. And on both sides of the *nirguṇa*/*saguṇa* line there are also differences between "street" poets and their "literary" counterparts that make the former tend to speak more loudly through translation than the latter. Thus one has a grid in which the *nirguṇa* "street" poet is usually easiest to approach from the outside, and the *saguṇa* "literary" poet the hardest. Yet even at the most difficult corner of the grid, windows do open to the outsider, and the view one sees—sometimes of familiar, generically human terrain—often comes into especially sharp focus precisely because it is framed by an edifice that seems so new and strange.

	"street" poet	"literary" poet
nirguṇa	easiest access e.g., Kabir, "Go naked"	middle difficulty e.g., Tulsidas, "Blind, mean-minded"
saguṇa	middle difficulty e.g., Mirabai, "Murali sounds"	hardest access e.g., Surdas, "Wayfarer"

ISSUES FOR DISCUSSION

1. Since the religious dimension in medieval Hindi poetry is so prominent, a Western student may find it helpful to compare it with some of the poetry that appears in the Bible. Conveniently, the Bible contains poetry in both *nirguṇa* and *saguṇa* modes. For the former, one might turn to passages from such prophets as Isaiah or Jeremiah; for the latter, certain of the Psalms suggest themselves, especially those that address the theme of separation from God. Yet the biblical book that is most closely in tune with Hindi *saguṇa* poetry is undoubtedly the Song of Songs, with its oscillation between longing and celebration, and its unabashed romantic idiom. Western readers who have difficulty accepting the basic presupposition of *saguṇa* poetry—that the experience of love, especially erotic love, is a version of the experience of God—may be intrigued to see that the Song of Songs, a love poem, has been included in the Jewish and Christian canons, and may be interested to know that its history of interpretation within both religious traditions is among the most extensive accorded to any biblical book. One recent scholar, in fact, has given serious attention to the idea that a historical connection exists between the Song of Songs and earlier Indic poetry dedicated to Krishna.[10]

2. A difficulty in comparing Hindi religious lyrics with passages from the Hebrew Bible is that the periods of time being set alongside one another are so far removed. This difficulty is overcome if one turns to metaphysical poetry of the Protestant Reformation instead. To illustrate comparatively the complexities of poets such as Surdas and Tulsidas, one might want to quote from the sonnets of John Donne, as Kenneth Bryant has on occasion done.[11]

3. A comparison with Protestant hymns is especially appropriate, since bhakti poetry, especially the *saguṇa* type, is almost always sung (this is easy to forget when reading translations). Unfortunately, the quality of the poetry that is set to music in most Protestant hymns does not rival the best bhakti verse, and the musical treatment is often much more formulaic. One can, however, suggest the musical heights to which bhakti verse can rise by referring, for example, to some of the chorales and arias in the Passions and cantatas of Johann Sebastian Bach. One can even find in these places examples of a distinctively "Hindu" genre, the poem of darshan, in which a version of the beloved Lord is assembled in words. For Bach, of course, the awful yet beautiful Lord is Jesus in the last moments of his life, but the mode of meditation is comparable to what one finds in the poem-

songs of Krishna. As in Hindu bhakti, Bach's musical poems work out new and personal variations on an iconographic tradition established centuries before, and often the explicit purpose of the variation is to bring the tradition alive in the present. If one wanted to carry such a musical comparison further, one might recall that over the course of both Jewish and Christian history, the biblical texts most frequently set to music were precisely the texts savoring most strongly of bhakti: the Song of Songs and the Psalms. One might consider the sometimes mystical dimensions of so much of the romantic poetry that was set to music in German *Lieder*, where, as in bhakti poetry, the theme of *viraha* is often overwhelmingly prominent.

4. From a critical, Western point of view, serious textual problems attend the study of devotional poetry in medieval North India. A Western reader expects "authenticity": works attributed to an author should actually have been spoken by the person in question. As we have seen in the case of Mīrābāī, this condition cannot always be satisfied in regard to bhakti poetry. Rather, one finds a range of authenticities. Mira's case is the weakest, since we have for her but a single poem that can be reliably dated to the end of "her" century,[12] the sixteenth, while Surdas, for example, presents a considerably stronger case. Although Sur, like Mira, serves as the fountainhead for a tradition that evolved over centuries, more than two hundred poems bearing his name were in existence in a manuscript that dates to the sixteenth century, and others can by text-critical means be inferred to have existed at the same time.[13] With Nanak and Tulsidas, it seems we can come at least equally close to the "authentic" poets in question.

It is well for a Western reader to be aware of this text-critical dimension in the study of bhakti poets, since Indians have, on the whole, given it a low priority. Indian scholars have done excellent textual work, but have tended to focus on works written in Sanskrit rather than in vernacular languages. Readers interested in authenticity, rather than in the tradition of Mira or Sur as popularly received, will therefore want to be careful to determine the textual status of the verse used as the basis for any translations of these poets.[14] Vulgate editions tend to reveal far more about how a poet was perceived in the nineteenth or twentieth century than in the sixteenth or seventeenth, and typically they include many more poems than exist in early collections. In a tradition that has a strong oral component and involves large numbers of independent poems, and in which poets often "sign" their poems with the name of a poet to whom they feel indebted, fluidity over time is the norm rather than the exception.

On the other hand, if one's primary concern is with the perception of these poets in recent times, then the "vulgate" is exactly what one wants to consult. And if one cares about how traditions of poetry develop, both in composition and in performance, one will try to understand the full spectrum—from the earliest poems attributed to these poets, to the most recent. Unfortunately, the resources for doing this with full confidence are not yet available, even in Hindi itself. Many hands are now at work on sophisticated textual criticism of major works of Indian devotional literature, but it will take some time before the results are published.

NOTES

For further information on transliteration and pronunciation of the Hindi language discussed in this chapter, please refer to the guide at the front of this book.

1. Pārasnāth Tivāri, *Kabīr Granthāvalī* (Allahabad: Hindi Department of Allahabad University, 1961), *pad* 174.

2. All quotes with page numbers from Hawley and Juergensmeyer as cited in Selected Readings.

3. Linda Hess, *The Bijak of Kabir* (San Francisco: North Point Press, 1983), pp. 7–24.

4. Tulsidās, *Kavitāvalī* 7.76, as given in *Tulsī Granthāvalī*, vol. 2 (Varanasi: Nāgaripracāriṇī Sabhā, 1974), p. 181.

5. Allchin, *Tulsī Dās: Kavitāvali* (London: George Allen & Unwin, 1964), p. 160n.

6. Kenneth Bryant has analyzed a poem of Surdas in which the same technique is used, in *Poems to the Child-God* (Berkeley: University of California Press, 1978), p. 49.

7. Nābhādās, *Bhaktamāl* (Lucknow: Tejkumār Press, 1969), p. 712. The date of the text is about 1600, and the entire passage is translated in John Stratton Hawley and Mark Juergensmeyer, *Songs of the Saints of India* (New York: Oxford University Press, 1988), p. 123.

8. Paraśurām Caturvedī, ed., *Mīrābāī kī Padāvalī* (Allahabad: Hindi Sāhitya Sammelan, 1973), *pad* 166.

9. The poem, edited by Kenneth Bryant, corresponds to number 3809 in the standard *Sūrsāgar* of the *Kāśī Nāgaripracāriṇī Sabhā*, vol. 2 (Varanasi: Nāgaripracāriṇī Sabhā, 1976).

10. Chaim Rabin, "The Song of Songs and Tamil Poetry," *Studies in Religion / Sciences religieuses* 3:3 (1973), pp. 205–219.

11. Bryant, *Poems to the Child-God*, pp. 57–60.

12. The poem is *Manu hamāro bādhiu māi kaval nain āpne gun*, found in the Sikh *Ādi Granth*, which was compiled in 1604.

13. The manuscript, dated to the equivalent of 1582, is printed in a facsimile edition. See G. N. Bahura and K. E. Bryant, eds., *Pad Sūrdāsjī kā / The Padas of Surdas* (Jaipur, 1982).

14. Short statements about the textual status of poetry attributed to each of the poets mentioned in this essay can be found in the notes to J. S. Hawley and M. Juergensmeyer, *Songs of the Saints of India*, chapter by chapter.

REFERENCES

At the present time, only a few translations can be recommended as possessing both literary merit and an accurate assessment of problems involved in ferreting out "authentic" texts. For Kabir, readers of English will be delighted with Linda Hess's *The Bijak of Kabir*, translated with the help of Shukdev Singh and available in paperback (San Francisco: North Point Press, 1983). In her illuminating introductory essay and notes, Hess explains why she preferred to translate from a single collection of poetry attributed to Kabir (the *Bijak*, as edited by Shukdev Singh) rather than attempt a critical edition on the basis of a comparison of several traditions of transmission. A fine selection of poems translated from the "vulgate" Surdas is to be found as part two of Kenneth Bryant's *Poems to the Child-God* (Berkeley: University of California Press, 1978). The first part of the book is an analysis of major features that characterize some of the best poetry of the Sur tradition, without attempting to discriminate between poems that came into the tradition early and more recent arrivals.

Charlotte Vaudeville's translations of Kabir (*Kabir* [Oxford: Clarendon, 1974]) do not approach Linda Hess's in their literary quality as English verse, but they do render into English the edition that many scholars regard as currently the most reliable, Parasnath Tivari's *Kabir-Granthāvalī* (Allahabad: Hindi Department of Allahabad University, 1961). A more recent effort in the same direction, but for a less-well-known *nirguṇa* poet, is the edition and translation of Namdev presented by W. M. Callewaert and Mukund Lath in *The Hindi Songs of Nāmdev* (Leuven: Departement Oriëntalistiek, 1989). An English version of the poetry of Nanak is hard to recommend, though several exist and the poetry presents text-critical problems of a lower order than most other bhakti poets. Poetic translations of Nanak tend to carry a weight of verbiage that far exceeds the original, and the literal ones found in the works of W. H. McLeod (e.g., *Textual Sources for the Study of Sikhism* [Chicago: University of Chicago Press, 1990, paperback]) are, by McLeod's own admission, intended to present the sense, not the sound, of the original.

I know of only one anthology of bhakti poems from medieval North India, and that is *Songs of the Saints of India* (New York: Oxford University Press, 1988), by John Stratton Hawley and Mark Juergensmeyer. It is available in paper, contains introductory material for each poet presented, and attempts to be based on the best current scholarship, though it is not a work of textual or literary criticism as such.

Lyric Text: Hindi

Sample Text

Tulsidas, *Kavitāvalī* 7.76

1   *ãdharo*   *adham*   *jad*   *jājaro*   *jarā*   *javan*
   blind   dull-witted   old
     mean-minded   withered-up   Muslim

  sūkar   *ke*   *sāvak*   *dhakā*   *dhakelyo*   *mag*   *mãi*
   pig   son   road
     of   got knocked   down   on

2   *giro*   *hiye*   *hahari*   *harām*   *ho*   *harām*   *hanyo*
   (he)   worried   hey!   has killed (me)
   fell   in his heart   unclean   unclean
                   (thing)

  hāy   *hāy*   *karat*   *parigo*   *kāl*   *phãg*   *mãi*
   alas!   making   death   into
   [Oh God!]   alas!   [saying]   (he) went   trap
       [Oh God!]   [jaws]

3   *tulasi*   *bisok*   *hvai*   *trilokapati*   *lok*   *gayo*
   Tulsi   become   world
     sorrowless   three-world-lord   [land]   went

  nām   *ke*   *pratāp*   *bāt*   *bidit*   *hai*   *jag*   *mãi*
   name   power   known   world
     of   the matter   is   in

4   *soī*   *rām*   *nām*   *jo*   *saneh*   *sõ*   *japat*   *jan*
   that   name   love   repeat
    Ram   which,   that   [say]   people,
    [God]   if   devotees

  tāki   *mahimā*   *kyõ*   *kahi hai jāti*   *agamãi*
   its   why   unreachable
    grandeur   is said

A literary translation in English appears on page 82.

LYRIC POETRY IN URDU: THE GHAZAL

Shamsur Rahman Faruqi and Frances W. Pritchett

People are always tempted to compare the ghazal to the sonnet. Poems in the two genres are usually about the same length, and they share a basically romantic and introspective sensibility. A Western scholar, Paul Oppenheimer, has recently called the sonnet "the oldest poetic form still in wide popular use," and has proudly traced it back through a number of European languages to its origins in Italy in the early thirteenth century. He has failed to do his cross-cultural homework, however, for the ghazal antedates the sonnet by about six hundred years: it traces its origins back to seventh-century Arabic poetry. From Arabic it spread into a number of languages, most notably Persian, Turkish, and then Urdu—where it is thriving today not only as a sophisticated genre of modern poetry, but also in the popular media: "filmi" ghazals and "filmi" versions of classical ghazals have made themselves at home in the movie industry, and on radio, television, and cassette.

Throughout the ghazal's reign, which has extended over thirteen centuries of time and immense amounts of space, ghazal poets have cherished their genre and consciously maintained its coherence. Learning their art from a master poet (*ustād*) and passing it on in their turn to students (*shāgird*), ghazal poets have been proud to refer to and build on the work of their predecessors. Within the ghazal, the poet almost always adopts the stance of a romantic hero of one kind or another: a desperate lover intoxicated with passion, a rapt visionary absorbed in mystic illumination, an iconoclastic drunkard celebrating the omnipotence of wine. He presents himself as a solitary sufferer, sustained by brief flashes of ecstasy and defined by his desperate longing for some transcendent object of desire. This object of desire may be human (female or male), divine, abstract, or ambiguous; its crucial trait is its inaccessibility.

But if the worldview of the ghazal is romantic, its structure is classically precise. The following ghazal has been translated in a technically careful way, retaining as many formal features of the Urdu as possible. All translations here presented are our own.

> To hell with all hindering walls and doors!
> Love's eye sees as feather and wing, walls and doors.
>
> My flooded eyes blur the house
> Doors and walls becoming walls and doors.
>
> There is no shelter: my love is on her way,
> They've gone ahead in greeting, walls and doors.
>
> The wine of your splendor floods
> Your street, intoxicating walls and doors.
>
> If you're mad for waiting, come to me,
> My house is a store of gazing, walls and doors.
>
> I never called down a flood of tears
> For fear of my falling, pleading walls and doors.
>
> She came to live next door,
> Doors and walls adoring walls and doors.
>
> A lively house stings my eyes
> To tears, without you, seeing walls and doors.
>
> They greet the flood with rapture
> From end to end all dancing, walls and doors.
>
> Don't tell love-secrets, Ghālib
> Except to those worthy of hearing: walls and doors.

As can readily be seen, each of the ten two-line *shi͗rs*, or verses, ends in "walls and doors." This repeated end-refrain is called the *radīf*, and is present in most ghazals, though it is not compulsory. And in each verse the word before the *radīf* ends in "-ing"; the rhyme here is called the *qāfiyah* and is compulsory. The first verse, to set the pattern in a genre designed to be heard rather than read, repeats the rhyming elements at the end of each line, so that the hearer can at once tell how much is *radīf* and how much is *qāfiyah*. A verse of this special introductory form is called a *matla͗*, and most ghazals have one (though some may have more than one, and some may not have any). The last verse incorporates, by way of signature, the poet's pen name or *takhallus* (which in this case is Ghālib), and thus earns the special name of *maqtaᶜ*. The *maqtaᶜ* is optional: it is usually present in classical ghazals, but is no longer so popular today. What we could not show in English is the meter: every line of the ghazal is in the same rigorously defined Perso-Arabic quantitative meter.

The ghazal presents a blend of unity and autonomy that often seems paradoxical to Westerners. Formally speaking, the ghazal can be said to be unified: since its verses share meter, rhyme, and usually end-refrain as well, it has a powerful symmetry and cohesion. In terms of content, however, each two-line verse is an independent, free-standing poem, making its own effect with its own internal resources. Except for rare and special cases, there is no narrative or logical "flow" from one verse to the next; if the verses were rearranged, or one or two removed, usually this action would not even be detectable. While such treatment would fatally damage a sonnet, it would have little or no effect on most ghazals. Even today, lovers of Urdu poetry know hundreds and hundreds of two-line verses by heart, and can (and do) recite them for many conversational purposes; but no one can (or does) recite whole ghazals with all their verses in correct order. Plainly the pleasure of the ghazal dwells in each verse itself, and taking one verse "out of context" raises none of the problems that would be raised by so treating a verse from a sonnet. The ghazal acts largely as a kind of frame and showcase for its individual verses.

Yet the small two-line verse is not left entirely to its own devices, for it inhabits the long-established, well-developed ghazal universe. The ghazal universe is founded on the figure of the passionate lover, and faithfully mirrors his consciousness. The lover, while longing for his inaccessible (human) beloved or (divine) Beloved, reflects on the world as it appears to him in his altered emotional state. To him its highs are infinite heavens, its lows abysmal depths, its every scene and every moment charged with intense and complex meanings—meanings to which non-lovers, the ordinary "people of the world," are appallingly blind. The human inhabitants of the ghazal universe are stylized, and exist only to fulfill certain necessary functions: they include the lover's friends, his confidant, his rivals, his messenger, the beloved's cruel doorkeeper, the Shaikh full of reproachful and ostentatious piety, the Advisor with his unheeded words of caution, etc. This whole universe exists in the consciousness of the ghazal audience, who construct it by knowing verses and constantly refine it by hearing or reading, accepting or rejecting, yet more verses. The ghazal universe is thus filled with beings and objects so "pre-poet-icized" that they bear only the most incidental relationship to their natural counterparts.

The geography of the ghazal universe includes settings for the lover's every mood: the garden for dialogue between nature and human beings, the social gathering for human relationships, the wine house for intoxication and mystic revelation, the mosque for ostentatious impiety, the desert for solitary wandering, the mad-house or prison cell for intransigence and frenzy, the grave and its aftermath for ultimate triumph or defeat. Of all these scenes, the ghazal's single greatest source of imagery has long been the gar-den, with its inherent contradictions: nature cherished and na-ture subjugated, nature as both responsive and alien to human emotion, nature as flourishing and then decaying, nature as mir-roring both love and the failure of love. The flower of the garden, in every sense, is the rose. Here once again is the great poet Ghālib (1797–1869), on the rose:

> How murderous is the false faith of the rose!
> The nightingale's doings amuse the rose.
>
> Celebrate the breeze's freedom: everywhere lie broken
> The meshes of the desire-net of the rose.
>
> Deceived, everyone fell for its wave of color.
> Oh, the lament of the bloody-voiced lip of the rose!
>
> How happy is that drunken one who, like the rose's shadow
> Rests his head on the foot of the rose.
>
> They make me ashamed before the spring breeze—
> My cup without wine, my heart without desire for the rose.
>
> Your jealous beauty appears in such supreme glory—
> Mere blood in my eyes is the charming color of the rose.
>
> Even now, deceived, thinking it to be you
> The rose runs recklessly after the rose.
>
> Ghālib, I long to embrace her
> The thought of whom is the rose on the dress of the rose.

In each separate two-line verse, *Ghalib* shows us the rose in a fresh light: mocking her lover, the nightingale; losing her petals,

and with them, her hold on the breeze's affections; lamenting the
folly of those who mistake her inner grief for a mere show of color;
receiving a lover's submission; pleasing a human beloved; incar-
nating all beauty; suffering by comparison to a human beloved;
resembling a human beloved, and thus enchanting other roses;
and finally, offering such an ultimate symbol of loveliness that the
human beloved can be called the rose of the rose.

A second important source of ghazal imagery is the festive gathering, with its wine, poetry, romance, and conviviality. What the
rose is to the garden, the candle is to the gathering. And the
candle has at least as many dimensions as the rose.

> The beloved's face calls forth the deathless flame of the candle,
> The rose's fire is water of life to the candle.
>
> In the tongue of the knowers of tongues, death is silence.
> This shone forth in the gathering through the tongue
>   of the candle.
>
> The story was made explicit by the flame's suggestion alone:
> In the style of those who have died to the world, is the
>   story telling of the candle.
>
> Oh flame, it grieves over the moth's vain longing:
> Your trembling reveals the frailty of the candle.
>
> At the thought of you my spirit sways, I swear
> By the splendor-scattering of the wine, by the wing-fluttering
>   of the candle.
>
> Oh, the joyous bloom of the scar of love's grief!
> Flowering is in love with the autumn rose of the candle.
>
> Seeing me at the beloved's pillow, it burns—
> Why shouldn't my heart be scarred by the jealousy of the candle?

Here Ghālib has shown us the candle as a reflection of the power
of beauty; as a source of mystical illumination; as a revelation of
the nature of life and death; as a beloved moved by the passion of
its lover, the moth; as an image of the human lover's desire; as a
symbol of the irresistible beauty of the heart scarred with love; as
a rival of the human lover's.

While romantic and mystical themes may predominate in the
ghazal, it is important to note that they do not confine it. Since
each two-line verse (shiⁱr) is semantically independent, most gha-

zals contain verses in various moods and on various topics. Different individual verses of a single ghazal may contain abstract reflection, social commentary, pious exhortation, elegy, the poet's self-praise or self-deprecation, humor or satire, as well as punning and other, more complex forms of wordplay. While simplicity and melancholy have been very popular, metaphoric subtlety and verbal intricacy have also been cultivated. In theory, ghazal poets can say anything—and in practice, at one time or another, they have.

The Urdu ghazal is only technically an Iranian, and thus "foreign," genre. Its development reflects more than four hundred years of highly skilled practice by accomplished poets with an Indian sensibility—poets who imbibed Indian modes of thought, feeling, and expression through direct and indirect contact with Indian poetics and poetry. Such a history has fashioned the Urdu ghazal into a unique synthesis: its outer form is Iranian, but its mood and atmosphere are Indian. To be sure, Urdu ghazal continued to use most of the imagery and the topoi that it inherited from the Iranian ghazal. But it not only added new themes and new modes of thought, it also reimagined in many subtle ways the themes and metaphors and images that it had inherited. This transformation was achieved without any conscious effort at "rebellion." In fact, for a very long time, for reasons of strategy and respectability, Urdu poets continued to declare their allegiance to the "Iranian masters." This allegiance was, however, more de jure than de facto, for no distinction was made between early Iranian poets, medieval Iranian poets, and the "Indian style" (sabk-e hindī) Iranian poets who were Iranian-born but worked in India, and whose manner was more Indian than Iranian.

The cultural forces that shaped the Indian identity of the Urdu ghazal included the recitation gathering (mushācirah), the master-student (ustād-shāgird) relationship, and a remarkably interactive literary scene: almost every poet was bilingual, and many were proficient in three or four languages. Up to the middle of the eighteenth century, almost every Urdu poet was fluent both in Urdu and a local language, and/or Persian; many knew a fair amount of Arabic. This has given their work a richness of texture, a variety of imagery, and a wealth of intertextual connection not easily found elsewhere. As for the mushācirah and the ustād-shāgird relationship, they are forces of such importance that it will be worthwhile to take a brief look at them.

A mushācirah is an assembly of poets, generally quite formal in character, and with a small or large public audience. Mushācirahs existed in Iran, as occasions where participants, who were not necessarily poets, recited and capped verses. In late-medieval India, the *mushā^c̄irah* became an agonistic occasion, with poets reciting competitively, vying for the approval of an audience of connoisseurs. The agonistic element was reinforced in Urdu: a "model line" (*misrā^c-e tarah*) was specified beforehand, and ghazals were composed in strict conformity to its meter and rhyme. The themes, the mode of verbal presentation, the rhythmic effects of the poem, in fact the whole act of literary creation, became an affair of orality. Reputations could be made or marred faster, for instant interaction with, and response from, the audience was available. Poets could be—and were—criticized or ridiculed for bad verses or for errors; good ghazals, or good verses in a given ghazal, won instant praise and fame. The ghazals of the great eighteenth-century poet Muhammad Taqī Mīr (1722–1810) are full of references to his poems being sung or recited even in distant places.

A poet who was successful in *mushā^c̄irahs* also attracted another kind of attention—that of prospective patrons and students. Often the patrons were also students. A large number of patrons and students ensured at least three things: a fairly sustained means of income, a large reputation, and most importantly, the creation of an ongoing "writers' workshop" in which junior poets submitted their work to the master for advice and correction. The master not only suggested changes and improvements in the poems submitted to him; he also taught, by precept or example, the rules of the game.

Since the rules had evolved for the most part from the practice of major poets, or of individual masters, they were almost entirely oral, and were learned by direct instruction and rigorous practice. Lip service was of course paid to the Iranian masters, but in point of fact, the poetics was almost entirely Indian. The verses of the classical Urdu poets, especially those who wrote between about 1680 and 1850, are full of statements about the nature of poetry and what makes a good poem. These poets were conscious, on some level, of participating in the creation of a new poetics. The student imbibed the rules both from his own master and from the work of previous masters. For one of the necessary qualifications for a good poet was to know at least ten thousand verses of the classical master poets intimately. The good *ustād* held formal sessions with his students (*shāgirds*), and acted as arbiter, teacher, and guide.

Muhammad Husain Āzād gives, in his great literary history

Āb-e Hayāt (1880), the following account of how Shaikh Imām Bakhsh Nāsikh (1776–1838), a major poet of the early nineteenth century, presided over training sessions with his students.

> [Shaikh Nāsikh] was very scrupulous about the proper conduct of his sessions. He used to recline against a bolster. His *shāgirds* (many of whom were from rich and noble families) sat respectfully around the edges of the floor-covering. They didn't even dare to breathe. The Shaikh Sāhib would think for a while, then write something down. When he put down a paper he would say "Hmmm!" Someone would begin to recite a ghazal. When a word in a verse needed to be changed, or if it was possible after some thought to improve it, he would correct it. If not, he announced, "This is worthless, strike it out," or "Its first (or second) line is not good; change it," or "This rhyme is good but you haven't developed its full potential; cudgel your brain a bit more over the verse." When that person was through reading, another would read. No one else was allowed to speak.[1]

The training was so careful and technical that the atmosphere, as in this case, could be almost that of the schoolroom.

Changes enhanced the tightness, flow, and compressed meaning of the verse, integrating it into the traditional ghazal universe. In another of Āzād's examples, this process of correction is shown in more detail—in the context of a quarrel between the great Urdu poet Saudā (1713–1780) and the not-so-great Indo-Persian poet Makīn. Makīn had written the following Persian verse: "In this company my heart was constricted like a wineglass / The bloom on the wine's face made me blossom out." When Makīn heard that Saudā objected to this verse, he sent one of his senior *shāgirds*, Baqā, to defend his reputation.

> Mirzā [Saudā]'s objection was that it was inappropriate to speak of a wine-glass as having a constricted heart. Master poets had always used for the wine-glass the simile of a blooming flower, or that of laughter, because a wine-glass must necessarily be open. Baqā, in response, dripped with the "sweat of *shāgirdī.*" And at length he brought in a [Persian] verse of Bāzil's as a warrant (sanad):
> What pleasure would wine give to me, desolate without you?
> Because the wine-glass is like a constricted heart without you.
> When Mirzā Rafīᶜ [Saudā] heard this, he laughed heartily and said, "Tell your *ustād* that if he's going to keep examining the verses of *ustāds*, he should also try to understand them. For this verse supports my objection: although the wine-glass is

> proverbial for laughter and bloomingness, and the wine-glass is part of the equipment of pleasure, even it itself has the attributes of a sad heart."[2]

Saudā's objection is based on traditionally accepted patterns of imagery: the wineglass may be compared, by virtue of its wide, rounded shape, to a blooming flower or to an open, laughing mouth. In the ghazal world, it is sad hearts that become constricted, not happy hearts or wineglasses. Baqā tries to reply with a "warrant" (sanad), an authoritative precedent from the work of an accepted *ustād.* But Saudā points out that Bāzil's verse is deliberately taking advantage of the normal patterns of imagery for poetic emphasis: I am so desolate without you that even the wineglass itself—which is (by definition) always open and happy—seems to me to be constricted and sad. Makīn's verse, by contrast, violates the tradition while failing to create any special effect.

The theoretical approach of the classical Urdu ghazal was two-fold: it consisted of the pursuit of *"mazmūn"* and *"maᶜnī."* The former can roughly be translated as "theme." "Theme" is what one gets in answer to the question, 'What's the poem about?' *"Maᶜnī"* can be translated as "meaning." Meaning is what one gets in answer to the question, 'What does the poem say?' The poet's effort was to introduce new slants on old themes—and, if possible, even to invent new themes. His second goal was to pack as much *"maᶜnī"* into the poem as possible. All the resources of the language were his territory: the great poets never hesitated to use them. All kinds of wordplay, allusion, effects of assonance, devices suited to oral delivery, complexity of metaphor, simple, everyday speech rhythms—nothing was barred. The poem was seen more as a verbal artifact than a spontaneous, Wordsworthian "overflow of the powerful feelings of the heart." Poems were not treated as autobiography. Autobiography wasn't forbidden; it would, however, be frowned upon unless mediated to the audience through poetic devices.

Given the fact that the ghazal is basically a love poem, and its main theme is unrequited love, the poet has full liberty to deal with matters relating to love in the widest possible context. And since the ghazal is at its best when it implies or conveys more than it apparently says, any utterance in a ghazal can theoretically be interpreted in more ways than one, or on more levels than one. As Mīr says, "A single utterance has any number of aspects, Mīr / What a variety of things I constantly say with the tongue of the pen!" He finds another image as well: "Every verse is curled and twisted like a lock of hair / Mīr's speech is of an extraordinary kind."

Love consumes like fire—this is a fundamental, often-used theme for the ghazal. How this familiarity is made new, how it is turned into richness and variety, may be seen in the verses of the great masters. Of them all, Mīr was perhaps the greatest. Here are some of his *shi⁶rs*, drawn from a number of different ghazals, on the subject of burning and flame:

> The fire of love burnt Rāvan to death,
> Although that demon had his home in Lanka,
>   surrounded by water.

> Mīr, the sadness of a burnt-out heart never goes away,
> Faced with her beautiful face, the candle flame dies.

> The rose has taken on her color
> just as one candle is lighted from another.

> Fire eats away all that it encounters, wet or dry,
> But I, like the candle's flame, only consumed myself.

> Mīr, do not shed tears when the heart is on fire—
> It's no use sprinkling water on a conflagration!

> Bones shiver and burn away—
> What a fire has love lighted here!

> A splinter of lightning must still be lurking
> somewhere in my house.

> Today Mīr's house was an ash heap; he had been
>   smouldering for years,
> Perhaps last night he burnt himself away.

> Mīr, the scar of my ravaged heart is bright in the night—
> Love has lit a lamp even in such a wilderness.

With the advent of western ideas and education, the poetics of the classical ghazal lost its prestige, and fell into what Ghālib would call the "niche of forgetfulness." Yet the conceptual underpinnings of the ghazal remain unchanged. It is still basically a poem of unhappy love, or at least of unhappiness, and of dissatisfaction with life. Many of the more sophisticated traditional images are now used only by a few. Yet the ghazal still has a polyvalence that makes it piquant and effective. And, as Valī Dakanī says, "The road to fresh *mazmūns* is never closed / Till Doomsday the gate of poetry stands open."

Lyric Text: Urdu

YIH NAH THĪ HAMĀRĪ QISMAT
by Mirzā Asadullāh Khān GHĀLIB (1797-1869)

Meter: - - = - / = - = = / - - = - / = - = =

1.

It was not my fortune to attain union with the beloved

this	*was not*	*my*	*fortune*	*that*	*[union -with*	*beloved]*	*had been*
yih	nah thī	hamārī	qismet	kih	visāl-e	yār	hotā

If I had kept on living longer, it would have been this same waiting

if	*longer*	*(I) had gone on living,*	*this very*	*wait*	*had been*
agar aur		jīte rahte	yahī	intizār	hotā

2.

If I lived on your promise—well, know this: I knew it to be false

[if]	*[your*	*promise-on]*	*I lived,*	*then this*	*know:*	*false*	*(I) knew (it)*
	tire	vaᶜde par	jiye ham	to yih	jān	jhūṭ	jānā

For wouldn't I have died of happiness, if I had trusted it?

for	*[joy -from]*	*wouldn't (I) have died,*	*if*	*trust*	*had been*
kih	khushī se	mar nah jāte	agar	iᶜtbār	hotā

3.

From your delicacy I knew that your promise was loosely bound

[your	*delicacy -from]*	*(I) knew*	*that*	*was tied*	*promise*	*loosely*
tirī	nāzukī se	jānā	kih	bāndhā thā	ᶜahd	bodā

You never could have broken it, if it had been firm

you never	*could have broken (it),*	*if*	*firm*	*had been*
kabhī tū nah	toṛ saktā	agar	ustvār	hotā

4.

It's my heart that should be asked about your half-drawn arrow

someone	*[my*	*heart-from]*	*might ask*	*[your*	*arrow*	*-half-drawn*	*-about]*
koᵒī	mere	dil se	puchhe	tire	tīr-e	nīm-kash	ko

How could this pricking have existed, if the arrow had gone on through the liver?

this	*pricking*	*[where -from]*	*had been,*	*if*	*[liver*	*-beyond]*	*had been*
yih	khalish	kahāñ se	hotī	jo	jigar	ke pār	hotā

5.

What kind of friendship is this, that my /friend/Advisor/has become my Advisor/friend/?

this	*[what kind of]*	*friendship*	*is,*	*that*	*has become*	*friend,*	*Advisor*
yih	kahāñ kī	dostī	hai	kih	bane haiñ	dost	nāsih

If only there had been a helper for me, if only there had been a sympathizer!

[if]	*some*	*help -giver*	*had been,*	*some*	*sympathizer*	*had been*
	koᵒī	chārah sāz	hotā	koᵒī	gham gusār	hotā

6.

From the rock's vein would have dripped blood which would never have stopped
[vein- of rock -from] would have dripped that blood which then would not have stopped
rag-e   sang se   ṭapaktā   vuh lahū kih phir nah thamtā

> If the spark were what you are calling "grief"
> *[about which] "grief" (you) are assuming,   this if   spark   had been*
> jise   gham samajh rahe ho   yih agar sharār hotā

7.

Although grief is deadly to life, how can we escape, since we have a heart
grief although life -tearing is,   but (we) might escape how,   since   heart   is
gham agarchih jāñ gusil   hai pah bacheñ   kahāñ kih   dil   hai

> If there were not the grief of love, there'd be the grief of everyday life
> *[grief -of   love)   if   had not been,   [grief -of everyday life]   had been*
> gham-e ᶜishq   agar nah hotā   gham-e rozgār   hotā

8.

Whom can I tell what it is; the night of grief is a great disaster
might say (to whom] I,   that what (it) is;   [night of grief] bad disaster is
kahūñ   kis se   maiñ kih kyā   hai   shab-e gham burī balā   hai

> I wouldn't at all have minded dying, if it had taken place once!
> *[to me]   what harm was   to die,   if   one time had been*
> mujhe   kyā   burā thā   marnā agar ek bār hotā

9.

Since I became notorious after my death, why didn't I drown in the river!
became having died I   since   notorious, became why   not [drowned -in river]
huᵒe   mar ke   ham jo   rusvā   huᵒe kyūñ nah gharq-e   daryā

> There would never have been a funeral procession, nor a tomb anywhere
> *not   ever   funeral had occurred, nor anywhere tomb   had been*
> nah kabhī janāzah uṭhtā   nah kahīñ   mazār hotā

10.

Who could have seen him, for that One is unique
him who   could have seen, for   unique is that   one
use kaun   dekh saktā   kih yagānah hai vuh   yaktā

> If He had even a trace of twoness, then somewhere we would have encountered Him
> *if [twoness -of] whiff even had been, then somewhere "two-four" had been*
> jo dūᵒī kī   bu bhī hotī   to kahīñ   do chār hotā

11.

These subtleties of mysticism, this style of yours, Ghālib!
these [subtleties -of   mysticism],   this your speech, Ghālib
yih   masāᵒil-e   tasavvuf   yih tirā bayān   Ghālib

> We would have thought you a saint—if you weren't a wine-drinker!
> *you we saint would have thought, if not wine -drinker had been*
> tujhe ham valī samajhte   jo nah bādah khvār hotā

NOTES ON SELECTED VERSES

4. The beloved has given the lover a sidelong glance, eyes half-closed—she has shot an arrow from a bow not fully drawn back. Thus the prey has been merely wounded and left to suffer, rather than being put out of his misery at once. But the lover is defending her: she has given him a unique *frisson*, one obtainable in no other way.

5. There are two possible interpretations of the first line. First: the lover's friend, who formerly sympathized with him in his passion, has now become alarmed and taken on the role of concerned, reproachful Advisor, and is trying to persuade the self-destructive lover to behave more sensibly. Second: the Advisor, a stock figure in the ghazal who specializes in sensible worldly counsel and "I told you so" admonitions, has taken the lover in hand and is trying to befriend him and rescue him from his folly. In either case, the lover rejects such well-intentioned "friendship"; he does not want to be rescued from his passion, but to be supported in it, so that he can pursue it to the death.

6. Rocks have "veins" in Urdu just as they do in English. When you strike a person, blood appears from his veins; when you strike a rock, a spark appears—by analogy, from its veins. Thus fire lives in the heart of a rock, as blood in the heart of a person. The lover claims, "My grief is so far beyond normal grief that if my grief were inside a rock, the rock—which is strong enough to contain fire—could not endure it, but would melt down and drip an endless stream of blood."

8. The second line has two interpretations. I wouldn't at all have minded dying, if: (1) death had taken place only once—whereas in fact I find myself dying over and over again endlessly; (2) death had taken place even once—whereas in fact it never does, so that I long in vain for release from endless torment.

9. In Muslim culture, a proper tomb is of great importance. But the lover wants just the kind of oblivion that everyone else dreads. He wishes he had simply drowned, and the water had carried his body away. (To imagine oneself dead is an extension of the theme of passion as leading to death.)

10. The radical Oneness of God is the single most basic article of Muslim faith. The verse plays both on the number one, and on the expression "*do chār honā*," which literally means "to be two-four" and actually means "to encounter." Thus the second line has two piquant interpretations. If God had even a trace of twoness, then: (1) we would have encountered Him somewhere; or (2) there would have been two or four or more of Him.

11. The poet imagines other people addressing him, praising his lofty mystical themes (such as that in verse 10) and sophisticated style. They then, however, patronizingly reproach him for wine drinking—which itself, in mystical terms, can represent intoxication with the direct presence of God.

TOPICS FOR DISCUSSION

1. The ghazal can well be compared with a variety of romantic and lyric genres from other cultures. The autonomy and formal

rigor of the individual shi°r invite comparison with the Japanese haiku. In addition, the Urdu ghazal can also be compared with ghazals in other languages. Many well-translated examples of the Turkish ghazal, for example, are available in *The Penguin Book of Turkish Verse*, edited by N. Menemencioglu (1978), and lovely short Arabic lyrics in *Birds Through a Ceiling of Alabaster*, translated by G. B. H. Wightman and A. Y. al-Udhari (Penguin, 1975). Poems called "ghazals" have been written in Western languages as well, especially German; Garcia Lorca has written some in Spanish.

2. In recent years, some of the poets involved in the production of the Aijaz Ahmad volume (see Selected Readings below) have gone on to write English ghazals of their own. And earlier in the English poetic tradition, the Metaphysical poets, and especially John Donne, prided themselves on deliberately dense and complex imagery that invites comparison with the multivalent verses of Ghālib.

3. For English-speakers, the inescapable comparison, full of suggestive resemblances and striking contrasts, is with the sonnet. English sonnets of course present no translation problems—a good anthology like *The Sonnet*, edited by R. M. Bender and C. L. Squier (New York: Washington Square Press, 1967) provides ample material. For European sonnets, there is Paul Oppenheimer's recent *The Birth of the Modern Mind: Self, Consciousness, and the Invention of the Sonnet* (New York: Oxford University Press, 1989). Oppenheimer provides a provocative (and, in our view, overstated) thesis about the nature of the sonnet, followed by many Italian, German, French, and Spanish sonnets, with facing texts and good verse translations.

NOTES

For further information on transliteration and pronunciation of the Urdu language discussed in this chapter, please refer to the guide at the front of this book.

1. Muhammad Husain Āzād, *Āb-e Hayāt* (Lucknow: U. P. Urdu Academy, 1982), pp. 336–7.

2. Ibid., pp. 157–8.

REFERENCES

Ahmad, Aijaz, ed. *Ghazals of Ghalib*. New York: Columbia University Press, 1971. Contains Urdu texts, notes, literal translations, and fine English "transcreations" of a number of Ghālib's ghazals by Adrienne Rich, W. S. Merwin, and other modern poets.

Lazard, Naomi, trans. *The True Subject*. Princeton: Princeton University

Press, 1989. The work of the modern Pakistani poet Faiz Ahmad Faiz (1911–1984), elegantly translated by an American poet, with facing text in Urdu; this book won Princeton's worldwide translation competition. It contains both ghazals and structurally looser modern poems called *nazms*.

Russell, Ralph, and Khurshidul Islam, eds. and trans. *Ghalib, Life and Letters*. London: Allen & Unwin, 1969. A narrative of the great poet G̲h̲ālib's life—made up largely of excerpts from his irresistibly lively letters, with his views on poetry well represented, and excellent interpretive commentary.

Russell, Ralph, and Khurshidul Islam. *Three Mughal Poets: Mir, Sauda, Mir Hasan*. Cambridge: Harvard University Press, 1968. Although the poets are not "Mughal" but eighteenth-century, this book provides a good introductory look at the ghazal in the context of other Urdu genres.

THE POEMS AND STORIES OF RABINDRANATH TAGORE

William Radice

Rabindranath Tagore (1861–1941) was a poet on a huge scale. The sheer size of his collected works places him among the most prolific writers in the world; but more importantly the all-inclusiveness of his achievement is a reminder—in an age when Western poets have often set quite narrow limits to their work—that a creative artist can emulate the prodigality of Nature herself. He was, however, an epic writer who never produced an epic: there is no one work that one can point to as the summa of his art. This, and the fact that he wrote in Bengali (a language which very few foreigners learn), makes the task of projecting his genius outside his native Bengal formidably difficult. The English translations that he himself made—in particular his collection of devotional lyrics *Gitanjali* for which he was awarded the Nobel Prize in 1913—are now perceived to be inadequate both in quality and range. Other Bengali-speaking translators, for all that English is spoken fluently by many Bengalis, have generally been hampered by being too close to Tagore. Translation, like landscape painting, is an art that needs to be done at a distance.

Many have questioned whether Tagore can be translated at all. This is because his art had a deeply musical dimension. In addition to all his poetry and prose, he composed over two thousand songs, regarding them as his most natural and spontaneous form of creative expression; but his writing in prose and poetry is always musical in its verbal sound and rhythm, and how can one translate music? At the same time language was never for him an end in itself: in everything he wrote he had a clear idea or story or feeling that he wished to express. Despite his romanticism, there is a lucid rationality, directness, and honesty about his work that give confidence to the translator. Tagore is often complex, but he is never obscure; and sometimes he is breathtakingly simple. If the translator can rise to the challenge of understanding clearly what Tagore was saying, then the right words will come, and the right selection—from a mass of material which certainly varies in quality—will present itself too. If he then adds the introduction, notes, and appendices that the foreign reader requires to place Tagore in context, then, in time, a true portrait will probably emerge, as it has for, say, Tolstoy, another writer who combined sweep and abundance with lucidity. Of course every great writer will "lose" in translation; but if he is a great writer then more than enough will be left. What might, to those who know the original language, be a loss, is the world's gain. One thinks of the world-wide success of Shakespeare, in translations which presumably dilute his rich and musical Elizabethan English.

Where did Tagore's art come from? In essence this is, of course, an unanswerable (or theological) question. Tagore himself never doubted that his creative impetus came from a mysterious source outside himself. What Western writers have called "inspiration" or "the Muses," he described as his "life-god" (*jiban-debatā*). This force directed and harmonized all his work, not only his poetry, prose, drama, songs, and painting, but also his practical work: his experimental school and university at Santiniketan in West Bengal, his center for rural renewal at neighboring Sriniketan, his exhausting world tours to raise funds for these projects and promote his ideals. He never lost faith in his *jiban-debatā*; but it often bewildered and pained him. In poems and paintings he often imagined it as a woman luring him on but turning her face away, or gazing at him with an expression not unlike Keats's vision of Moneta in *The Fall of Hyperion*:

> Then saw I a wan face,
> Not pin'd by human sorrows, but bright-blanch'd
> By an immortal sickness which kills not;
> It works a constant change, which happy death
> Can put no end to; deathwards progressing
> To no death was that visage; it had past
> The lily and the snow; and beyond these
> I must not think now, though I saw that face—
> But for her eyes I should have fled away.
> They held me back, with a benignant light,
> Soft mitigated by divinest lids
> Half-closed, and visionless entire they seem'd
> Of all external things;—they saw me not,

But in blank splendour, beam'd like the mild moon,
Who comforts those she sees not, who knows not
What eyes are upward cast . . . .

Tagore has often been defined as a man of faith whose art was
dominated by mystical self-realization or spiritual joy, and his
dark, tormented paintings have seemed bafflingly at odds with
this. But when one studies him deeply one finds that his writings,
too, are full of "strangeness."

It is not, however, necessary to wrestle with unanswerable
questions in order to investigate the sources of Tagore's art. The
Ganges may, in Indian tradition, come down from Heaven; but in
practical, historicogeographical terms we can look at the mountains and tributaries that contribute to her flow. Among the most
important for Tagore were: (1) Sanskrit court poetry, especially
Kālidāsa; (2) the spiritual philosophy of the Upanishads; (3) medieval Bengali Vaishnava piety, i.e., the bhakti (devotional) movement that swept through Hinduism in the sixteenth and
seventeenth centuries and that in Bengal produced innumerable
songs (padas) celebrating the love of Rādhā and Krishna; (4) nineteenth-century religious rationalism, especially that of the
Brahmo Samaj, a reformed Hindu sect founded by Rammohan
Roy (1772–1833), which sought a Hinduism purged of superstition and idolatory; (5) evolutionism, owing something to Darwin
but finding in Nature's unfolding a benign and spiritual purpose;
(6) English Romantic poetry, though its influence has probably
been overemphasized by Bengali critics trained in English literature. A brief essay like the present cannot illustrate all these
strands, and one needs to go beyond Tagore's poems and stories
to perceive them all fully. The third, for example, is dominant in
his songs; the second and fourth in his essays and sermons. But
two famous poems, "The Wakening of Śiva" (tapobhaṅga) and
"Earth" (pṛthibī), will go some way towards showing how Tagore
blended his personal perceptions with his literary heritage.

"The Wakening of Śiva" could only have been written by Tagore,
but it could not have been written without Kālidāsa before him.
The mythology on which it is based found its locus classicus in
Kālidāsa's poem Kumāra-sambhava. The gods are in terror of the
demon Tāraka, and are told by Brahma that the demon can only
be destroyed by the son of Śiva begotten on Pārvatī, daughter of
the mountain-god Himālaya, also known as Umā. Śiva is at the
time engaged in ascetic penance (tapas), so Indra, king of the
gods, sends Kāma, the god of love, to "break his tapas"

(*tapobhaṅga*, the title of Tagore's poem) by smiting him with love for Pārvatī. The first attempt fails, and Śiva burns Kāma to ashes with a blast of flame from his third eye. Later he relents, restores Kāma, makes love to Pārvatī, and the war-god Kártikeya (also known as Kumāra) is born (*Kumāra-sambhava* is usually known as "The Birth of the War-God").

In Tagore's poem, the emphasis is on Kāma breaking Śiva out of his trance. The inertia of Śiva's ascetic penance is associated with a suspension of creativity; the erotic power that awakes in him is the creative power of Nature and of the poet himself. Nowhere else in his poetry did Tagore write of his own poetic purpose—and its origins in Nature—with such rapturous confidence:

> For I am Indra's messenger: I come to break your penance,
> O Śiva, fearsome ascetic; I am heaven's conspiracy against you.
>   Age after age I come,
> A poet, to your hermitage. I fill my basket with garlands
>   of victory;
> Irrepressible conquest shouts through the plangent
>   rhythms of my verse.
> By the force that drives my feelings, roses open;
> By the impulse of ecstatic discovery that opens new leaves,
>   I hurl forth my songs.
>
> O bark-clad anchorite, I know all your deceptions.
> Your bark is illusory armour: you joyfully anticipate defeat
>   At the hands of beauty.
> You may burn up Kāma again and again with your fire,
> But you always restore him to doubly blazing life;
> And because I fill and refill his quiver
> With passion, I am come with my snares of music, a poet,
>   Into the lap of earth.
>
> I know, I know, though you seem aloof, in reality you long
> For the agonized insistent pleas of your beloved
>   to wake you suddenly
>   Into new ardour.
> You hold yourself apart, sunk in seemingly impenetrable trance
> Because you want her to weep the fiery tears of separation.
> But the wonderful images of your union with Umā
>   on breaking your trance—
> I see them through all ages, play them on my vīṇā
>   in your consort's rāga,
>   For I am a poet.

The next stanza is a reminder that Tagore, partly because of his privileged and aristocratic background, had to struggle for recognition, and inspired enmity and jealousy:

> Your attendants, life-hating lovers of burning-grounds,
>   do not know me:
> They cackle with the devilish rancour of the mean in spirit
>   When they see what I am.
> But in the months of spring, when the time is auspicious
>   for your nuptials
> And sweet-smiling modesty blooms in Umā's cheeks,
> Then call your poet to the route of your wedding-procession,
> Let him join the seven sages who accompany you with trays
>   Of festive garlands . . . .

His battles with "the mean in spirit" had, however, largely been won by 1925, the publication date of "The Wakening of Śiva." Tagore had reached the height of his national and international prestige, and the energy of the poem reflects this. It is an energy controlled by Sanskrit learning and by long experience in handling words and rhythms. The language of the poem, rich in complex verbal compounds, can be described as Sanskritic, but there is nothing archaic or academic about it; Sanskrit words and Bengali syntax are combined with the muscular vigour with which Milton welded Latin to English: from two parents—classical and modern—comes a poetic offspring as vital and dynamic as the war-god Kārtikeya himself. One of the excitements of reading Tagore and other great modern Bengali writers is that we find in them language "being born," as in English writers of the sixteenth and seventeenth centuries—but less than a hundred years ago! The fluid vitality of literary language in the making has become unfamiliar to the contemporary English-speaking world, despite the efforts of Joyce and others to revive this quality.

"Earth" is written in a freer verse form than "The Wakening of Śiva." Tagore steadily worked towards greater freedom of form throughout his long creative life, culminating in the free verse of his final years. Yet, as Eliot put it, "No verse is free for the man who wants to do a good job," and the discipline and rocklike strength of Tagore's rhythm and diction in "Earth" matches his subject matter. In this poem, Hindu cosmology, vast in its imaginative reach, combines with Western evolutionism and historicism. One can even find in its harsh objectivity a kind of dialectical materialism, unsettling to those who think of Tagore as a gentle lyricist who, in Yeats's words, "like the Indian civilization itself, has been content to discover the soul and surrender himself to its spontaneity."

> At your footstool mounted on evil as well as good,
>   To your vast and terrifying beauty,
> I offer today my scarred life's homage.
> I touch your huge buried store of life and death,
>   Feel it throughout my body and mind.
> The corpses of numberless generations of men lie heaped
>   in your dust:
> I too shall add a few fistfuls, the final measure of my joys
>   and pains;
>   Add them to that name-absorbing, shape-absorbing,
>   fame-absorbing
>   Silent pile of dust.
>
> Earth, clamped into rock or flitting into the clouds;
>   Rapt in meditation in the silence of a ring of mountains
> Or noisy with the roar of sleepless sea-waves;
>   You are beauty and abundance, terror and famine.
>   On the one hand, acres of crops,
>   bent with ripeness,
> Brushed free of dew each morning by delicate sunbeams—
>   With sunset, too, sending through their rippling
>   greenness
>   Joy, joy;
>   On the other, in your dry, barren, sickly deserts
>   The dance of ghosts amid strewn animal-bones . . . .

Both "The Wakening of Śiva" and "Earth" are driven by what the Indians have traditionally called *shakti*, the creative energy identified with Śiva's consort and worshipped in Bengal as the mother-goddess Durgā or Kālī. There was lyricism and beauty in *Gitanjali*, Tagore's Nobel Prize-winning book, but very little wild energy; and the image of him as a woolly-minded dreamer has survived to this day. There is, of course, a quieter, dreamier, more meditative and introspective side of his poetry; he is the poet of peace (*śānti*) as well as energy; but at his best these two poles are balanced. In his poem "In Praise of Trees" (1931) he addresses the peace and shade of trees like this:

>   O profound,
> Silent tree, by restraining valour
> With patience, you revealed creative
> Power in its peaceful form. Thus we come
> To your shade to learn the art of peace,
> To hear the word of silence; weighed down
> With anxiety, we come to rest
> In your tranquil blue-green shade, to take
> Into our souls life rich, life ever

Juvenescent, life true to earth, life
Omni-victorious. I am certain
My thoughts have borne me to your essence—
Where the same fire as the sun's ritual
Fire of creation quietly assumes
In you cool green form . . . .

Among Tagore's most famous poems, "Shah-Jahan" (1916), addressed to the seventeenth-century Mughal emperor, is perhaps the finest example of how Tagore at his most spiritual is also Tagore at his most structured and tensile. Its sonorous, measured lines gradually take us closer and closer to the transcendent spirit that art as supreme as Shah-Jahan's Taj Mahal seems to evoke but can never quite capture, and we arrive at that perfect blend of feeling and form, movement and stillness, in which (as in Keats's "Ode on a Grecian Urn") Classic and Romantic become one:

Thus, Emperor, you wished,
    Fearing your own heart's forgetfulness,
To conquer time's heart
        Through beauty.
How wonderful the deathless clothing
        With which you invested
Formless death—how it was garlanded!
        You could not maintain
            Your grief forever, and so you enmeshed
            Your restless weeping
            In bonds of silent perpetuity.
            The names you softly
            Whispered to your love
On moonlit nights in secret chambers live on
            Here
    As whispers in the ear of eternity
        The poignant gentleness of love
Flowered into the beauty of serene stone . . . .

In countless poems and songs Tagore expresses himself directly: "I" is a frequent pronoun. Some have tried to dismiss him as a romantic egoist and his institution at Santiniketan as a projection if his own ego. He no doubt fervently believed, in line with Indian tradition, that the main purpose of his spiritual *sādhanā* (endeavor) was to control or shed the ego; but maybe as a man he never achieved this, remaining intensely self-absorbed till his very last hours. Given this self-absorption, it is all the more striking that he managed to control and subsume his ego in works of drama and fiction. He first broke through to the art of fiction in the 1890s. The Tagore family owned estates in East Bengal, and in 1889 Rabindranath's father Debendranath sent him to manage them. It was a crucial decade in his development. It brought him, for the first time, into contact with the landscape and people of rural Bengal. It acutely refined his sensitivity to natural beauty, to agriculture and crafts, and to different types of people. From this experience stemmed much of the practical work in later life, at Santiniketan and Sriniketan. He was also at the time closely involved in the expanding world of the Bengali literary magazine, and his writings for various journals included fifty-nine stories and twenty-seven narrative poems. Brilliant narrative poems like "Snatched by the Gods" were another aspect of his art that foreign readers in his lifetime never knew. Although many stories did appear in English (usually in versions by friends of Tagore "with the author's help"), the translations were insipid and truncated. Volumes such as *The Hungry Stones and Other Stories* (like the *Collected Poems and Plays*) also suffered from a complete absence of introduction and annotation.

Tagore's prose presents a challenge to the translator just as great as the poems. He did not himself create Bengali fictional prose. Bankimchandra Chatterjee (1838–94) had achieved eminence as a writer of highly original historical novels (Bankim was also the first Bengali writer to acknowledge Tagore's genius). But Tagore was the first Bengali to write realistically about Bengali life, and in order to convey all the shades of feeling, personality, and landscape that he observed in both rural and urban Bengal (Calcutta) he needed a richer and more flexible instrument than Bankim's elegant, clipped prose. When critics attacked his stories, comparing them adversely with European masters such as Maupassant or Chekhov, and dismissing them as idealized and overpoetic, he was always passionately defensive. He knew that his stories were based on a far closer observation of life than his critics were capable of, and he knew from experience the difficulty of creating a prose medium to match what he saw. Tagore's stories of the 1890s do indeed deserve to take their place among the classic short stories of the world. One can point to narrative flaws, to touches of sentimentality, but few writers have managed to create such memorable stories, so movingly alert to human hopes, sufferings, aspirations, and sensitivities, and also so observant of human shallowness, insensitivity, and cruelty. The complexity and musicality of his descriptive prose are sometimes the despair of the translator, but the essential directness of his narrative technique emerges effectively from accurate, careful translation. The most that the translator will need to do by way of departure from the original is sometimes to tighten sentences that are sonorously rhythmical in Bengali but can seem verbose in English. In "Resistance Broken," a literal translation of the description of Giribala would read like this:

> She found the wine of her overflowing beauty quite intoxicating. She would often be seen pacing restlessly and aimlessly on her roof, draped in a soft, brightly colored robe, as if she wanted to dance with every limb to the rhythms of some inaudible, unexpressed music in her mind. She seemed to possess a kind of joy, that drove and pressed and hurled her own body into all kinds of movement; she seemed to feel a strange, delightful pulsation in various facets of her beauty and in the various currents of her throbbing bloodstream. She would suddenly tear a leaf off a plant, and raising her right hand towards the sky release it on to the breeze—and at the same time her bangles would jingle, the end of her sari would fall off her shoulder, the graceful curve of her arm would soar towards the clouds like an unseen bird released from a cage into the boundless sky. . . .

Tightening it in English creates a momentum that comes closer to the effect of the Bengali:

> She was drunk with the wine of her beauty. She was often seen restlessly pacing on her roof, draped in brightly-coloured clothes: as if she wished to dance with every limb to an unexpressed tune in her mind. She had a kind of joy, driving and hurling her body into movement; she seemed to receive from the various facets of her beauty a strange pulsation, a throbbing in her blood. She would tear a leaf off a plant, raise it high and release it on the breeze: the graceful curve of her arm soared towards the clouds like an unseen bird released from a cage, while her bangles tinkled and her sari slipped from her shoulder. . . .

In *The Religion of Man*, the lectures he gave at Oxford in 1930, Tagore defined art as "the response of man's creative soul to the call of the Real." It is tempting to take "the Real" here in a theological sense: the "real" world of the Spirit that lies behind "apparent" reality (maya, "illusion" in Indian tradition). But this would be to distort the comprehensiveness of Tagore's vision. He was just as much concerned with material, prosaic reality as with ideal spiritual reality. Above all he was concerned with the meeting of the two. Again in *The Religion of Man*, he spoke of "the subject on which all my writings have dwelt—the joy of attaining the Infinite within the finite." Many of his stories are tragic: joy (*ānanda*) is overwhelmed by the sorrow (*duḥkha*) of mortal existence. But the possibility and reality of that joy is never entirely absent, even if it is lost or trampled on. Goodness suffers, but it definitely exists. Very often it is associated with vulnerable characters, such as Ratan in "The Postmaster," whose capacity for love and devotion is so tragically wasted by the Postmaster's obtuseness. In most of the stories we find a clash between the sensitive and the insensitive. The story "Ṭhākurdā" is an especially poignant and subtle example of this. One might say that it is not so much the protagonist Ṭhākurdā' himself who suffers as a result of the narrator's arrogant frivolity, protected as he is by innocent self-deception, but his granddaughter, whose feelings are so much deeper and finer than the young men who cruelly trick the old man:

> Finally, unable to bear any more, I ran into a room a bit further away: but no sooner had I collapsed into laughter when I saw a girl slumped on a low bed, sobbing. She stood up at once when she saw me. Choking with tears, darting fiery glances from her large, black eyes, she snapped, "What has my grandfather done to you? Why have you come to trick him? Why have you come?" Then, unable to manage anymore, she buried her face in her sari and burst into tears again.
>
> So much for my fit of laughter! All this time it had not entered my head that there was anything other than humour in what I had done. Now I saw I had hit a very tender spot; the revolting cruelty of my action was glaringly exposed; and I slunk out of the room, ashamed and embarrassed, like a kicked dog. What harm had the old man done me? His innocent conceit had never harmed anyone! Why had my own conceit been so malicious?

But at the very end, Ṭhākurdā's self-deception cracks, suggesting depths of suffering hidden by pride. The "tender, maternal deception" his granddaughter shows in humouring his delusions arises from her sensitivity to that pride. The narrator is humbled by them both:

> I didn't sleep at all that night. The next morning I crept like a thief to Ṭhākurdā's house, carrying all the valuable things we had taken from the old man; I intended to hand them back to the servant without saying anything.
>
> Flummoxed at not finding him, I heard the old man and his granddaughter talking somewhere inside the house. The girl was asking, with sweet affection, "Grandfather, what did the Lieutenant-Governor say to you yesterday?" Ṭhākurdā cheerfully spun a long panegyric to the ancient house of Nayanjor, supposedly

delivered by the Lieutenant-Governor. The girl received it eagerly.

My eyes filled with tears at the tender, maternal deception played by this young girl on her aged guardian. I sat silently for a long time; when at last Ṭhākurdā had come to the end of his story, I went up to his granddaughter with the things I had deceitfully stolen and placed them before her without a word. I had previously followed the modern custom of not specifically greeting the old man when I saw him; but today I did *praṇām* to him. He presumably thought this sudden show of respect was prompted by the Lieutenant-Governor's visit. He excitedly described it to me, and I happily fell in with his account. Others who were there listening knew that it was all made up, but merrily accepted it.

When everyone had gone I nervously and humbly made a proposal. I said that although my own lineage was in no way comparable to the Babus of Nayanjor, yet . . .

When I had finished, the old man clasped me to his breast and said joyfully, "I am poor—I never imagined I would have good fortune like this, my friend—my Kushum must have won great merit in heaven for you to take her like this." He wept as he spoke. This was the first time that Kailas Babu forgot his duty to his noble ancestors and admitted he was poor, admitted it would not do damage to the house of Nayanjor to accept me. I had plotted to humiliate the old man, but he now welcomed me with open arms as a worthy groom for his granddaughter, wishing me nothing but good.

Such writing can only come from a writer profoundly skilled in seeing through façades to essential human feelings. Human nature is laid bare in Tagore's short stories.

The effect of stories like "The Postmaster" and "Ṭhākurdā" is to persuade us that the highest truth we can perceive is contained in goodness, sensitivity, and love; but in responding "to the call of the Real," Tagore never blinded himself to life's tragic and evil aspects—and sometimes they seem victorious. In "Little Master's Return," we find very little to console us for the tragic series of events it describes, as Raicharan's devotion to Phelna is based on delusion, is rejected by Phelna himself and brings him no thanks from Anukul and his wife. In "Fool's Gold," success and respect elude Baidyanath to the bitter end, and the rattle of an empty treasure-jar in a cellar in Benares can be taken as a symbol of the hollowness, nihilism, and agnosticism that often seem to trail Tagore's faith and hope like a shadow. This is the "strange" side of the *jiban-debatā*. It is expressed above all in Tagore's paintings, which portray, as it were, the shadowy world which Yajnanath inhabits at the end of "Wealth Surrendered." His reaction, on learning from his son Brindaban that the boy he has entombed as a guardian spirit (yaksa) for his horde of treasure is actually his long-lost grandson, takes us close to the "Heart of Darkness":

> "Yes," said Brindaban, "Gokul. Now his name is Nitai Pal and my name is Damodar. You have a bad name with everyone round about, so we changed our names—otherwise no one would have talked to us."
> The old man clawed at the sky with all his fingers, as if struggling to clasp the air; then fell to the ground, fainting. When he came round again, he hurried Brindaban to the temple. "Can you hear the crying?" he asked.
> "No," said Brindaban.
> "If you strain your ears, can't you hear someone crying 'Father'?"
> "No," said Brindaban.
> The old man seemed relieved at this. From then on he would go round asking everyone, "Can you hear the crying?"—and they all laughed at his madman's words.
> About four years later, Yajnanath was on his deathbed. When the world's light grew dim in his eyes and breath began to fail, he suddenly sat up in delirium; groping with both hands, he murmured, "Nitai—someone has taken my ladder away." When he found no ladder out of the vast, lightless, airless cellar he was in, he slumped back against the pillows. Then he vanished, to the place which no one playing hide-and-seek on earth can discover.

Despite a series of personal bereavements which would have broken a lesser man, Tagore never succumbed totally to despair, and even in his last pronouncements from his deathbed on a world collapsing into war, he retained his hope for the future:

> As I look around I see the crumbling ruins of a proud civilization strewn like a vast heap of futility. And yet I shall not commit the grievous sin of losing faith in Man. I would rather look forward to the opening of a new chapter in his history after the cataclysm is over and the atmosphere rendered clean with the spirit of service and sacrifice. Perhaps the dawn will come from this horizon, from the East where the sun rises. A day will come when unvanquished Man will retrace his path of conquest, despite all barriers, to win back his lost human heritage . . . .
> (*Crisis in Civilization*, 1941)

It was, though, a measure of his range and seriousness as a writer that he could see life in the depths as well as the heights. Against the buoyancy, the energy, the joy of "The Wakening of Śiva" or

"Grandfather's Holiday" or "New Rain," we have dark poems such as "Africa" and "Question." Against the possibility of goodness and love represented by Ratan, Ṭhākurdā's granddaughter in "The Postmaster," Nilkanta in "Danger," Shashikala in "Elder Sister," and many more, we have the cry of the mad Meher Ali in "The Hungry Stones": "Keep away! All is false!" To read Tagore is not to encounter the "message" sought by those who seek a guru, but something much more real, human, and ambiguous. There is vulnerable uncertainty, as well as life-affirming creativity, in his tireless self-dedication to a life-god that never, finally, revealed its secrets:

> Is the path by which you come today
>> The same as I knew before?
>>> I see
>> Sometimes its faint outline;
> Sometimes not the slightest glimmer can be seen.
> You have brought in your basket flowers recalled or forgotten,
>> But others I have never hitherto known;
>> And in your fragrance you carry
>>> The message of a season new to me.
>>> A deathly dark suffusion
>> Obscures its coming revelation.
>>> O honour me
> With its garland, place it around my neck in this dimly
>> Starlit palace of silence. Let this our last
>>>> Tryst
>>> Carry me into the infinite night
>>> Beyond all earthly limit;
>>>> Let it make me one
>>>>> With the not known.

> ("Last Tryst," 1940)

TOPICS FOR DISCUSSION

1. "By the force that drives my feelings, roses open . . . " Have you felt, in translation, something of the extraordinary creative energy that readers of Bengali can experience in Tagore's writing? If so, in which poems or stories especially? What qualities of language, verse, and feeling convey this energy?

2. Compare Tagore's own translations—in the *Collected Poems and Plays* (especially *Gitanjali*) and in *The Hungry Stones and Other Stories*—with William Radice's two Penguin books. What differences do you find? What qualities do you find in the older versions that differ from Radice's versions?

3. Examine Tagore's ability to convey character by his use of dramatic monologue in poems such as "A Half-Acre of Land" and "Bride," or in stories such as "Ṭhākurdā" or "Kabuliwallah," which are told by a fictional narrator.

4. Examine Tagore's ability to build up suspense and horror in stories such as "The Living and the Dead," "Wealth Surrendered," or "The Hungry Stones," or in poems such as "On the Edge of the Sea" or "Snatched by the Gods." Compare Tagore's "ghost stories" with those of Western writers such as Edgar Allen Poe or M. R. James. Are you inclined to agree with those Bengali critics who have suggested that Tagore was influenced by Poe? Compare in particular Poe's story "Leigia" with "In the Middle of the Night."

5. Compare Tagore's poem "Deception" with any story by him where deception or self-deception are leading themes; or compare his treatment of human suffering in "Broken Song" with "The Postmaster" or any other of the stories.

6. Tagore is not generally perceived as a humorous writer, but in fact he was capable of great wit and irony. Find and analyze three stories where you feel these qualities are particularly strong. To what purposes does he use humor and irony?

7. Tagore is sometimes described as "a sort of Indian Tolstoy." Why? Do you think this is a useful label? Others have likened him to Goethe, Wordsworth, Shelley, or Whitman, and he is often contrasted with Gandhi [see Sibnarayan Ray, "Tagore-Gandhi Controversy" in *Gandhi, India and the World: A Symposium*, edited by Sibnarayan Ray (Philadelphia, 1970)]. Investigate the differences and similarities between Tagore and other Indian or Western figures you find comparable.

REFERENCES

The poems and stories by Tagore referred to in this essay are all in *Selected Poems* (Penguin, 1985, rev. 1987) and *Selected Short Stories* (Penguin, 1990), both translated, with introduction, notes, and appendices by William Radice.

Tagore, Rabindranath. *My Reminiscences.* New York: Macmillan, 1917.
Lago, Mary M., ed. *Imperfect Encounter: Letters of William Rothenstein and Rabindranath Tagore, 1911–1941.* Cambridge: Harvard University Press, 1972.
O'Connell, Joseph T., et al., eds. *Presenting Tagore's Heritage in Canada.* Toronto: Tagore Lectureship Foundation, 1989.

THE *MAHĀBHĀRATA,* INCLUDING THE *BHAGAVAD GĪTĀ:* INDIA'S GREAT EPIC

Barbara Stoler Miller

The two great Sanskrit epics of India, the *Mahābhārata* and the *Rāmāyaṇa,* have enchanted and instructed the people of India for thousands of years, deeply influencing the religious and cultural life of India and the rest of South Asia. Both epics were transmitted orally for centuries before being written down. They have their roots in events that took place in the period following the entry of the Indo-Aryan speaking nomadic tribes into northwestern India around 1200 B.C.E. The composition of the epics began as these tribes settled in the river valleys of the Indus and the Ganges during the first millenium B.C.E., when their nomadic sacrificial cults began to develop into the religious traditions known as Hinduism.

Most scholars would agree that the *Mahābhārata* was composed over the centuries between 400 B.C.E. and 400 C.E. The work has stylistic and mythological roots in the ancient ritual hymns of the *Rig Veda* and narrative sources in oral tales of a tribal war fought in the Punjab early in the first millenium B.C.E. As the tradition was taken over by professional storytellers and intellectuals, many sorts of legend, myth, and speculative thought were absorbed, including the *Bhagavad Gītā,* which belongs to the layer of the epic that took form around the first century C.E. In its present form the *Mahābhārata* consists of over one hundred thousand verses divided into eighteen books. The martial saga has been expanded into an encyclopedic repository of ancient Indian myths, ideals, and concepts. Indians say of it: "What is not here is not found anywhere else."

The *Mahābhārata* begins with a prologue on the creation of the epic itself. The main character is Vyāsa, the author to whom the epic is traditionally attributed. The story is narrated by the priest Vaisampāyana, a disciple of Vyāsa, at an assembly of warriors gathered for the snake sacrifice being held by Janamejaya, a descendent of the Pāṇḍavas. The birth of Vyāsa is narrated in response to Janamejaya's request to hear the whole epic text. Vyāsa's role penetrates deep into the epic; he is coexistent with it and intimately involved with the actors. He is both the epic's author and the sage grandfather of the epic heroes. He is a figure whose presence defines and animates the saga he inhabits. The story of Vyāsa's ancestry allows the reader to enter the imaginative universe of the *Mahābhārata* from its origin.

The narrator begins by telling of King Vasu, through whose city a river flowed. A mountain fell in love with the river, waylaid her, and begot twins on her. The king freed her by kicking the mountain with his foot. In gratitude, when her children were born she gave them to the king. He made the boy chief of his army and married the girl, whose beauty was so great that thought of her made him spill his seed, which eventually fell into the river Yamunā, where it impregnated a nymph who had been cursed by Brahma to become a fish. When she was in her tenth month she was caught by fishermen who pulled human twins from her belly and presented the marvelous pair to their king. He raised the boy as his son, but the girl, who smelled like a fish, he gave to a fisherman.

She plied a ferry on the river Yamunā, and so Parāśara caught sight of her when he was traveling on a pilgrimage. The "bull among hermits" was instantly smitten by her beauty and began making love to her. She protested that there were holy men standing on both sides of the river watching. Then he created a fog that "seemed to cover the entire region in darkness." Again she protested, pleading her virginity and filial piety. The great sage was pleased by her virtue and promised that his love would not ruin her virginity; then he granted her a boon. She chose as her boon that her body would always smell delicious. On the same day that she lay with Parāśara, she gave birth to Vyāsa on an island in the river Yamunā. He stood before his mother and set his mind on asceticism, telling her, "When you think of me, I shall appear to you if any task needs to be done."

The mating of the hermit with the fish-girl and the birth of Vyāsa is an epic play-within-a-play that echoes the obscure origins and kinship relations governing the entire *Mahābhārata*. The epic poet's birth and descent, like the birth and history of the epic heroes, is a story of seduction, restored virginity, and substitute fathers (human and divine). Vyāsa, like Karṇa, the first-born son of Kuntī and so the elder brother of the Pāṇḍavas, is born outside and before his mother's marriage. Just as Karṇa's mother, Kuntī, is the hub of a multivalent set of relations that constitute the epic story, so Vyāsa's mother, Satyavatī, is the hub of a set of relations that consitute the formal prologue of the poem. Later, when the continuity of the Bharata lineage is threatened, Satyavatī calls on Vyāsa to sire sons. Not only does he carry on the Bharata line, but he teaches the *Mahābhārata* to the bards so that the story will be passed down through the ages.

The story of Vyāsa's birth is not an isolated epic event. The births of the epic's main characters occur in equally dramatic episodes in which powerful desire initiates action. King Śantanu's passion for an irresistable woman, who is in reality the river goddess Gaṅgā, results in the birth of Bhiṣma, who later renounces his claim to the throne and takes a terrible vow of celibacy to allow Śantanu to marry Satyavatī, so sweet-smelling now that she seduces the king with her fragrance. These episodes, like the scenes of the births of Pāṇḍu and Dhṛtarāṣṭra and their sons (the Pāṇḍavas and the Kauravas), achieve their aesthetic and moral impact through the perennial human conflict between sacred duty (dharma) and desire (kama).

Vyāsa's eldest son Dhṛtarāṣṭra is heir to the Bharata throne, but he is born blind and so disqualified. His younger brother Pāṇḍu becomes king, but Pāṇḍu is also flawed as a king, since he has been cursed to die the day he makes love to a woman—once carried away by the bloodlust of hunting, Pāṇḍu killed a pair of mating deer and the buck hurled the curse in the throes of death. Again the Bharata lineage is threatened, because Pāṇḍu is barred from begetting sons. He renounces the kingdom, appoints his blind brother regent, and retires to the forest with his two wives. One of his wives is Kuntī, a princess whose intelligence and virtue endow her with a magic power—the power to call down a god at will and to have a child by him. The power terrifies her, but in a desperate attempt to save Pāṇḍu's life, she reveals it to him and invokes three gods to father her sons. She then lends her power to her cowife Mādrī and so the five Pāṇḍavas, the so-called sons of Pāṇḍu, are born. Each is endowed with an aspect of the god Kuntī invoked: Yudhiṣṭhira, the eldest, son of Dharma, the god of justice and order, embodies moral perfection; Bhīma, son of Vāyu, the god of wind, embodies the raw force of nature; Arjuna, son of

Indra, the chief of the gods, is the conquering warrior; the twins, Nakula and Sahadeva, sons of celestial twins, are as inseparable as patience and wisdom.

The Pāṇḍnavas' rivals, their cousins, the Kauravas, are also the sons of a weak man and a powerful woman. Gandharī, their mother, is tricked into marrying the blind king Dhṛtarāṣṭra. When she learns that her husband is blind, she ties a band on her eyes and vows to share his darkness forever—but her deep woman's rage is manifest in the ball of hard flesh, like a dense ball of clotted blood, which she aborts from her womb after a two-year long pregnancy. In her revulsion, she rejects it, but Vyāsa appears before her and instructs her to douse it with water and it falls into a hundred pieces, which are placed in a hundred pots, from which one hundred sons are born. Their births are accompanied by terrible portents. The first-born, Duryodhana, emerges howling like a wild jackal that feeds on carrion, foretelling his own lust for destruction.

The third extraordinary woman in the *Mahābhārata* is its heroine, Draupadī, a princess born out of a sacrificial fire. Dark and fiery by nature, she becomes the single wife of the five Pāṇḍavas and is the force that binds them to their heroic purpose.

Youthful rivalry between the Pāṇḍavas and their cousins, the Kauravas, explodes into adult rivalry for control of the kingdom. Though the cousins should be united by common blood and ambitions, instead they are deadly enemies. The blind Dhṛtarāṣṭra is legally regent for his brother and later, after Pāṇḍu's death, he becomes regent for his nephew Yudhiṣṭhira. But Dhṛtarāṣṭra is too weak to resist his own sons' treacherous desire for the throne. A plot is hatched to kill the Pāṇḍavas and their mother in a fire—they narrowly escape and live disguised as poor scholar-priests. It is their daily habit to beg for food and alms. While begging they hear about the upcoming wedding ceremony of Draupadī. Intrigued, they travel to the capital and establish themselves in the hut of a potter. On the day of the ceremony Arjuna, the gifted archer, wins her by performing a trial of marksmanship. The bride, not alms, is brought that day to Kuntī, who without looking up, tells them as usual to share whatever they have. When she realizes that it is a woman, Kuntī cannot retract her words, feeling that destiny made her speak. So the Pāṇḍavas take Draupadī as their common wife.

Attempts to rationalize the polyandry of Draupadī in terms of ancient social customs fail. In terms of the epic drama, it makes more sense to read the marriage of Draupadī as part of a vast cosmic drama. In the ancient Indian epic world, the king is the husband of the earth, related to the female power of fortune that is essential for sovereignty. In the *Mahābhārata*, Draupadī embodies Lakṣmī, the goddess of beauty and fortune. Her sexual power invites violence and her beauty threatens to produce chaos. But ultimately Draupadī, through her varied relationships with her five husbands, integrates conflicting aspects of their composite character and helps them restore order in the age of cosmic destruction.

Unbridled greed causes the Kauravas to frustrate their cousins' rights and eventually usurp their patrimony. Base desires motivate the Kauravas to engage Yudhiṣthira in a crooked dice game that he plays with ritual obsessiveness, losing everything, including his brothers and himself; finally in despair he wagers their wife Draupadī. Although the participants in the dice game are often warned about the danger of their course, once they begin the end is inevitable. Noble heroes become trapped in a degenerating world over which they have no control.

Draupadī is dragged into the dicing hall, stained with her own menstrual blood, to be the slave of her husbands' cousins. Before the entire court she questions Yudhiṣthira's right to pledge her since he did so after he had lost himself and so dissolved their relationship. But the court, including Gandharī, judges against her, refusing her claim of independence from her defeated husband. Her husband Bhima, seething with rage, vows to kill the man who disgraced her and to drink his blood. She for her part vows to leave her hair unbound until his death and to wash her hair in his blood. Her anger provides the energy that goads her husbands to the war that reestablishes order, symbolized by her act of binding her hair, soaked in the dead warrior's blood.

In its own terms, the purpose of the *Mahābhārata* is to teach the victory of dharma in an age of cosmic destruction, an inevitable era, beyond the ability of people to change it. The period lasts several thousand years—in the Indian view, it started with the *Mahābhārata* war and we are enmeshed in it today. Though we cannot change this cycle of destruction and decadence, even within it we can save something. In terms of the *Mahābhārata*, the chaos of destruction can be alleviated through the exercise of dharma. Dharma is the balance in the universe that often eludes commonsense understanding—we see gods, like Krishna, behaving in ways that shock us. The main role of Krishna in the epic is to save dharma, though every code of worldly conduct is violated in the process. But in the epic drama, dharma cannot escape the demands of the age, and it falls victim to the age of destruction. The scions of Vyāsa become engaged in a mutually destructive war, whose drama their ancestor himself is directing.

The Pāṇḍavas and Draupadī embody order and sacred duty (dharma), while their foes, the Kauravas, embody chaos (adharma). Acts of heroism are characterized less by physical prowess than by dharma, often involving extraordinary forms of sacrifice, penance, devotion to a divine authority, and spiritual victory over chaos.

For the epic warriors and the audience of the *Mahābhārata*, Krishna is a perplexing figure. He is a companion and teacher, as well as a potent god who commands devotion. He is a trickster whose seemingly capricious actions work to overturn all preconceptions about truth and falsehood, good and evil.

Krishna's mythology suggests that he was originally a tribal hero who was transformed into a cult divinity. The interweaving of his human and divine aspects reveals basic paradoxes inherent in the epic universe—in taking on the characteristics of a human being, Krishna becomes mortal and fallible. In the *Mahābhārata*, Krishna functions, not as an omnipotent god, but as an ambiguous, mediating figure whose power is dependent on the actions of his warrior companion Arjuna and his devotee Draupadī. The epic view of Krishna is all the more striking when we consider the violent reactions aroused by depictions of the human nature and fallibility of Jesus Christ in Martin Scorsese's film "The Last Temptation of Christ" and of Mohammed in Salman Rushdie's *The Satanic Verses*.

As for Krishna in the *Mahābhārata*—despite his human limitations—he acts with the authority of omniscience in the terrible spectacle of destruction. Peter Brook draws an interesting analogy between Krishna's role and that of an actor in the theater: "Krishna plays the part of a human being, which is not exactly the same as becoming one. An actor knows what is going to happen in the following scene, and yet knowingly plays to the best of his abilities a person who doesn't know."[1] Likewise, Krishna plays his part to stop a war he knows is inevitable, even when his words and actions seem contrary to dharma.

Despite the ultimate value of dharma in the Indian epic world, it cannot exist without its opposite, adharma. In the view of the ancient Indian poets, good and bad are always coeval and inextricably mixed, the universe has an ultimate order, but phenomenal existence appears turbulent. This notion of the world's complexity resonates with what modern mathematicians call "chaos," unpredictable behavior that defies our conventional linear notions of order. They say that nature is in a state of flux and any change in even the smallest component of the system changes the dynamics of the whole system, like the beat of a butterfly's wings that days later can result in a tornado. In a parallel way, we might see the world of the *Mahābhārata* as one of ordered randomness—truth and illusion turning into one another, twisting into intricate patterns that unpredictably emanate from apparently inscrutable origins.

The *Mahābhārata* war, which ends with the destruction of both armies, is represented in epicycles of dramatic confrontation and moral crisis. Exemplary among these is the *Bhagavad Gītā*. Before the war begins, the two opposing warriors Duryodhana and Arjuna approach Krishna to seek his alliance—he refuses to take arms, but allows them to choose between himself and his troops. Arjuna chooses Krishna as his charioteer, and Duryodhana is delighted to add Krishna's troops to the Kaurava army. In the face of doing battle against his relations, Arjuna's nerve fails.

Krishna's arguments on why Arjuna must overcome his uncertainty and fear of the battle contain ideas that resonate throughout the entire epic. We can understand the paralyzing conflict Arjuna suffers knowing that his own kinsmen and teachers are the enemies it is his warrior duty to destroy. We can sympathize with the warrior's impulse to shrink from the violence of the human condition and can also learn from what Krishna teaches him about his own and others' mortality. Krishna's exposition of the relationship between death, sacrifice, and devotion explores the idea that one must heroically confront death in order to transcend the limits of ordinary existence.

By purging his mind of attachments, Arjuna can continue to act in a world of pain without suffering despair. The core of Krishna's teaching is discipline (yoga), which enables the warrior to control his passions. Once Arjuna has been initiated into death's profound mysteries, Krishna gives him a divine eye with which to see the majesty of his cosmic form. The aspect of himself that Krishna reveals to Arjuna on the battlefield embodies time's deadly destructiveness: a fearsome explosion of countless eyes, bellies, mouths, ornaments, and weapons—gleaming like the fiery sun that illuminates the world.

It has been reported that the physicist J. Robert Oppenheimer was a serious student of Sanskrit and that he drew on the imagery of the *Bhagavad Gītā* to express his awe and fear at experiencing the explosion of the first atomic device at Alamogordo in New Mexico on July 16, 1945.

When he saw its dazzling white reflection in the sky and on the hills, he is said to have uttered, in Sanskrit:

divi sūryasahasrasya / bhavet yugapadutthitā |

yadi bhāḥ sadṛśi sā syād / bhāsas tasya mahātmanaḥ || 11.12

If the light of a thousand suns
were to shine in the sky at once,
it would be like the light
of that great spirit.

And, when the sinister and gigantic mushroom cloud rose up in the far distance over Point Zero, he quoted Krishna saying of himself:

kālosmi lokakṣayakṛtpravṛddho

lokān samāhartum iha pravṛtaḥ | 11.32a-b[2]

I am time grown old,
creating world destruction,
set in motion
to annihilate the worlds . . .

Imagery like this does more than put us in touch with something ancient and fundamentally Indian—it is the voice of our own moral crisis.

TOPICS FOR DISCUSSION

1. The Indian epics can be fruitfully considered in the context of Western epic literature, especially the *Iliad* and the *Odyssey*, with which they have much in common. General discussion can begin with the nature of epic, as distinct from lyric and drama. Exploration of the basic differences between epics of war, like the *Mahābhārata* and the *Iliad*, in contrast to epic romances, like the *Rāmāyaṇa* and the *Odyssey*, enhances students' perspective. In the latter case, it is illuminating to analyze the titles of the works in terms of the meaning of the names of the heroes—Odysseus means "one who suffers or causes pain," whereas Rāma means "one who causes delight."

2. One might discuss in the case of the *Rāmāyaṇa* and the *Odyssey* what characterizes the hero, what the relation of the hero is to his skills and his actions, what relation exists between

kingship and the social order, what kind of actions are repeated and "ritualized," what constitutes purity and pollution.

3. In the *Rāmāyaṇa* and the *Odyssey*, a comparison of the patterns in the travels of the heroes is significant. What kinds of places do they visit, whom do they encounter? How is time ordered in the epic?

4. How does the heroism of Odysseus and Rama differ from that of their counterparts in the *Mahābhārata* and the *Iliad*? In each case what is the relation of the hero to his wife and to other female characters? What is the nature of the reunion of the hero and heroine?

5. What part do the gods play in the course of events? What is the role of fate or destiny in contrast to personal responsibility for action (curses, boons, penances, death, and sacrifice are all motifs related to this issue)?

6. Certain recurrent themes provide bases for further analysis—order and chaos, culture and nature, the city and the wilderness, society and seclusion, time and immortality, power and impotence, legitimate rights of succession and the desire for offspring to carry on the lineages.

7. The *Bhagavad Gītā* can be approached in the context of the *Mahābhārata* or as a self-contained text, both of which are justified within Indian tradition. The dramatic moral crisis that is central to the *Bhagavad Gītā* has inspired centuries of Indian philosophers and practical men of wisdom, as well as Western thinkers like Thoreau, Emerson, and Eliot. Interpretations of the *Gītā*, as it is commonly referred to in India, are as varied as the figures who have commented on it. From Śankara, the classical Vedanta philosopher of the eighth century, to Mahatma Gandhi, the leader of India's independence struggle in the twentieth century, each thinker has emphasized the path to liberation suited to his own view of reality. These interpretations reflect the intentionally multifaceted message of Krishna's teaching.

8. The comparative possibilities for studying the *Gītā* are also varied. Following the suggestions provided by the afterword to my translation, entitled "Why Did Henry David Thoreau Take the *Bhagavad Gītā* to Walden Pond?" one could read the text with Thoreau's *Walden* or selected essays of Emerson. It could also be read with biblical works, such as *Job* or the Sermon on the Mount in *Matthew*.

9. One might consider Krishna and Arjuna as a pair of emblematic figures in Indian culture and compare them with such figures as Achilles, in the *Iliad*, or Socrates, as portrayed in the

early Platonic dialogues set at the trial and death of Socrates. Arjuna's questions involve the social results of personal actions as a reflection of more basic human problems of individual duty (dharma), personal desire (kama), and action (karma). Krishna's answers relate action to the real self (atman) underlying apparent contradictions of existence to the possibility of liberation from the constraints of mundane existence through various forms of discipline (yoga), including devotion (bhakti) to him, the incarnation of cosmic totality.

NOTES

1. *The Drama Review*, no. 109 (Spring, 1986): 61.
2. A single vertical line indicates the end of a half verse; two vertical lines indicate the end of a full verse; numbers separated by a period indicate chapter and verse; letters refer to verse segments. Thus, I 11.32a-b means the end of a half verse, chapter eleven, verse thirty-two, the first two segments of a four segment verse.

REFERENCES

Hiltebeitel, Alf. *The Ritual of Battle: Krishna in the Mahābhārata.* Ithaca: Cornell University Press, 1976.
Miller, Barbara Stoler, trans. *The Bhagavad Gītā.* New York: Bantam Books/Columbia University Press, 1986.
Narasimhan, C. V., trans. *The Mahābhārata.* New York: Columbia University Press, 1964.
Sharma, Arvind, ed. *Essays on the Mahābhārata.* Leiden: E. J. Brill, 1990.
van Buitenen, J.A.B., trans. *The Mahābhārata.* Books 1–5. Chicago: University of Chicago Press, 1973–78.
Zaehner, R. C. *The Bhagavad-Gītā,* with commentary based on original sources. London: Oxford University Press, 1969.

Indian Texts: Narrative

THE *RĀMĀYAṆA* OF VĀLMĪKI

Robert P. Goldman

> The story of the *Rāmāyaṇa* shall remain current among the people for as long as the mountains and rivers shall endure upon the earth.
>
> *Vālmīki Rāmāyaṇa*, 1.2.35[1]

THE SIGNIFICANCE OF THE RĀMA STORY FOR THE CULTURES AND SOCIETIES OF SOUTH AND SOUTHEAST ASIA

Although it is little known in the West, the ancient Indian epic poem the *Rāmāyaṇa*, attributed to the legendary poet-sage Vālmīki, is unquestionably to be included among the most popular, most imitated, and most influential works of literature ever produced. This monumental Sanskrit rendering of the moving and exemplary tale of Prince Rāma and the long suffering Princess Sītā—together with the innumerable later versions it has inspired in the folk, dramatic, and poetic literatures of virtually every significant language and nation of South and Southeast Asia—clearly places the tale of Rāma among the oldest, most widely known, and most deeply beloved stories of all time. As this statement may seem somewhat hyperbolic to those trained in the still powerfully Eurocentric academic culture of Europe and the United States, it will be appropriate here to dwell for a moment on the place and significance of this text in the intellectual, aesthetic, literary, religious, social, and general cultural history of the Indian subcontinent and the regions and peoples that surround it.

In the nearly three thousand years since its composition, the poem has undergone an extraordinary number of reworkings at the hands of authors and bards using every major language and belonging to every significant indigenous religious tradition of the diverse cultural domains of South and Southeast Asia. In one form or another, the text has been widely available and continually in use by hundreds of millions of people for as long as, or longer than, virtually any non-Indian text still known and read by other than a scholarly audience.

The staggering profusion of *Rāmāyaṇa* versions in the literary, folk, and, more recently, popular genres of the region is, first and foremost, a consequence of the importance the traditional cultures of South and Southeast Asia have placed upon the story and its central characters. The multiplication of these versions in Sanskrit, Prakrit, and the regional languages at every stage in their development, as well as the appropriation of the epic, its characters and central themes, by virtually every religious, philosophical, and sectarian tradition in the long history of Indian culture, is proof that the text was seen as seminally important to the culture, so much so that regional and sectarian audiences needed to have readily understandable versions that adapted the epic story to the changing needs of all segments of society.

From as far back as the tools of textual criticism can take us, the monumental Sanskrit poem had already been differentiated into a number of regional recensions and sub-recensions written down in virtually every area and script of India. In addition, the epic story was reworked many times for inclusion in other works such as the *Mahābhārata*, the other great epic of ancient India, and various puranic texts. Versions of this sort are the *Rāmopākhyāna* of the *Mahābhārata*, the *Ānanda-Rāmāyaṇa*, and the *Adhyātma-Rāmāyaṇa*. The Rāma story, moreover, became a favorite theme of the literary poets and playwrights of classical Sanskrit. Numerous Sanskrit literary works explore particular aspects of the complex *Rāmāyaṇa* story, and although some of these are now lost, or known only from fragments, such poetic masterpieces such as the *Raghuvaṃśa* of Kālidāsa, the *Bhaṭṭikāvya*, the *Rāmāyaṇacampū*, and important Sanskrit dramas such as the *Pratimānāṭaka* of Bhāsa and the *Mahāvīracarita* and *Uttararāmacarita* of Bhavabhūti, to name but a few, are still read and deeply enjoyed by those conversant in Sanskrit.

Nor are the versions of the *Rāmāyaṇa* restricted to the cultural universe of Hindu India. Despite, or perhaps because of, the fact that the epic's hero Rāma was worshipped as one of the principal avataras or earthly manifestations of the great Hindu divinity Vishnu (a central figure of devotional Hinduism), his story was of such importance and popularity that even non-Hindu and anti-Hindu groups, such as the Buddhists and the Jains, soon discovered the value of adapting the *Rāmāyaṇa* to serve the propagation of their own religious systems. Thus the Pali Jataka tales of early Buddhism contain several adaptations of portions of the *Rāmāyaṇa*, as can easily be seen in such texts as the *Dasaratha* and *Vessantara Jātakas*, while a more literary Buddhist work such as the *Buddhacarita* of Aśvaghoṣa clearly shows its author's knowledge of the Rāma story and his literary debt to Vālmīki. Jain authors are fond of using the epic, and a considerable number of Jain versions of the poem, such works as the *Paumacariya* and the *Triṣaṣṭiśalākapuruṣacarita*, have survived in Sanskrit and Prakrit.

In the regional languages of India, the influence of the *Rāmāyaṇa* has been even more profound. In virtually all of the major literary languages of early modern and modern India, there exists a significant and immensely popular version of the epic often regarded as marking the very beginning or pinnacle of that language's literary tradition. Such, for example, is the popularity and prestige of poems such as Kṛttibās' Bengali *Rāmāyaṇa*, Kamban's *Irāmāyaṇam* in Tamil, and the massively popular devotional rendering of the epic in the Old Avadhī dialect of Hindi, the *Rāmacaritamānasa* of Tulsī Dās known and loved by most of the three hundred million inhabitants of the "Hindi Belt" of North India.

Even these important regional versions of the poem do not exhaust the diversity of the poem. Each region has, in addition to this kind of major literary *nachdichtung*, many other versions— performative and literary, oral and written, folk and popular. In this category may be noted the various *Rāmlīlās* of North India, the *Jātra* plays of Bengal, and the many folk versions of the *Rāmāyaṇa* story current in all parts of India. One recent author, William Smith, has noted and described some fifty different literary *Rāmāyaṇas* from the eastern states of Bengal, Assam, and Orissa alone, each with a different religious, aesthetic, or ethical thrust.

A text of such wide diffusion—permeating the "high" and folk traditions of textual composition, as well as the visual arts of both pan-Indian and regional cultures, for nearly three millennia—can hardly have failed to make a profound impression on the popular culture of modern cosmopolitan India. The nature of this impression can be judged from an examination of the media of popular culture in both their elite forms and those that are consumed by a mass audience. A survey of modern Indian drama and fiction from the time of Michael Madhusudana Dutt down to Salman Rushdie reveals that the themes and characters of the *Rāmāyaṇa* story appear continually to haunt the Indian writer in the colonial and postcolonial period. A survey of Indian cinema yields similar results. Not only has the *Rāmāyaṇa* been exploited by the producers of popular Hindi musicals; it has also formed a rich source for the makers of the popular "mythologicals" such as Homi Wadia's *Hanuman Chalisa*, the Telugu *Sampoorna Ramayana*, and many more, including the art films of such *auteurs* as Aravindan in his *Kancana Sita* and the avant-garde Akshara Theater's production of *Ramayana.*

Nowhere, perhaps, has the immense popularity of the *Rāmāyaṇa* been demonstrated more dramatically than in the extraordinary success of the lengthy serialization of the epic created for Doordarshan (the Indian government television network) by the filmmaker Ramanand Sagar and broadcast throughout India and neighboring countries in weekly half-hour episodes over the past two years. The series has been widely marketed in Asia and throughout the world in the form of video cassettes. Newspapers and eyewitness accounts have been filled with descriptions of the way in which the showings would empty the bustling streets and bazaars of the country to the point of desolation, as people, often having bathed and dressed for worship, would gather in front of television screens to watch with rapt attention the slow unfolding of the ancient and well-loved tale. The political and cultural implications of this success have already been the subject of a considerable body of journalistic and scholarly analysis.

The influence of the *Rāmāyaṇa* has not been restricted even to so vast and populous an area as South Asia, but has extended widely into Southeast and even East Asia. In the former region it has provided the theme for much of the traditional poetry and puppet theater of Laos, Cambodia, Thailand, and the Malay-Indonesian world. Even in East Asia its influence, if more attenuated, is to be observed in a variety of forms ranging from the Chinese novel to the Japanese Noh drama.

Thus, although it is little known in the West outside a few areas of academic specialization, a number of Hindu-oriented religious groups, and the growing and influential community of South Asian origin now resident in Europe and North America, the *Rāmāyaṇa* of Vālmīki, the ultimate source of all known versions of the story, must be considered one of the most influential works ever composed. It has informed the literary imagination, defined the social consciousness, and focused the religious fervor of literally billions of people in dozens of cultures for perhaps three thousand years. In its longevity, diffusion, influence, and historical significance, it is perhaps comparable only to the Bible and the Qur'an. Given the extraordinary history and influence of the Rāmāyaṇa, some effort must be made to explain the reasons and significance of its remarkable and continuing success.

The influence of a text of the size and complexity of the Rāmāyaṇa, a work that has had so long and rich a history of intertextuality and multiple contextualization, cannot be accounted for in any simple fashion. Nonetheless, it is useful to isolate three domains in which the text has been and continues to be particularly influential both in and of itself and through its numerous descendants. These domains are the poetic, the social, and the religious.

The Rāmāyaṇa of Vālmīki holds a unique place in the literary and aesthetic history of India quite apart from its content or its antiquity. The particular literary piece, the poem ascribed to the sage, is widely regarded as constituting the origin of literature as an aesthetic category. For Vālmīki's fame is said not to derive from his invention of story or characters—the Rāmāyaṇa story being all but universally regarded as an account of historical, if not chronologically remote, events—but from the fact of his having, through divine inspiration, transformed a received narrative into true poetry, a genre that had not until then existed. The story of Vālmīki and the origin of poetry, and of how poetry came to be disseminated through bardic performance, is told at length in the poem itself and indeed constitutes a frame within which the epic narrative is contained. It is a popular story and is repeated or alluded to by many subsequent poets, playwrights, and literary theoreticians (writers of the stature of Kālidāsa, Bhavabhūti, Ānandavardhana, and Abhinavagupta), and a good deal of the prestige of the work is involved with its being regarded as the Ādikāvya (First Poem) and its author as the Ādikavi (First Poet). Its preamble, or upodghāta, in which the story of the work's origin is related, also puts forward in powerful form a central Indian notion of the nature of and connection between aesthetic and affectual experience. Its articulation of this seminal set of concepts, the theory of rasa (first fully elaborated in the Nāṭyaśāstra of Bharatamuni) is among the earliest recorded.

In the social realm, the influence of the work can hardly be exaggerated. A central and repeated thrust of the poem's narrative and characterizations is the creation of a set of normative exemplars for the principal roles in Indian familial, social, and political life. Thus its hero, prince Rāma, in all his sufferings and tri umphs, is made to represent the perfect ideal of the son, husband, brother, warrior, and king as these have been constructed in the traditional Hindu view of society. Indeed his heroism for the tradition is not so much tied up with his valor and martial skills, exhibited in the killing of *Rāvaṇa*, as in his stoicism and unwavering dedication to his father's promise despite its devastating effect upon him. In similar ways his wife, Sītā, his brothers Lakṣmaṇa and Bharata, and his servants, such as Hanūmān and Vibhīṣaṇa, have also come to be represented as models of their respective roles, while his arch enemy, the rapacious rakshasa lord Rāvaṇa, has become the very personification of a lack of sensual and social restraint and so of absolute evil. The presence of this powerfully acculturative instrument and its use for so many millennia cannot be underestimated as both a source of transregional unity in South Asia and as a device for reinforcing the hierarchical and authoritarian structures of the family, the society, and the state in traditional and even modern India. The *Rāmāyaṇa* is regarded as the "family epic" par excellence in the culture, and its characters and situations constantly inform the rhetoric of indigenous discourse from the nursery tale to the political speech. Moreover, its themes recur endlessly in hymns, sermons, popular theater, novels, films, and comic books. In this it has differed significantly from the other great Sanskrit epic of the ancient period, the *Mahābhārata,* which, with its themes of family discord and the subversion of normal patterns of deference, has traditionally been regarded as unsuitable for family use, a work seen as more appropriate to the "outside," i.e., larger political sphere only.

Finally, and perhaps most powerfully, the *Rāmāyaṇa* occupies an enormous role in the religious domain. Its hero Rāma is not merely a literary protagonist, a legendary warrior king, and an exemplar for a variety of normative roles, he is universally viewed by Hindus as God. Along with Krishna, a figure connected with the *Mahābhārata* cycle of stories, Rāma is considered one of the two most significant of the avataras ("descents") or incarnations of the great divinity Vishnu. Thus the poem, aside from being read or heard on the aesthetic and sociological levels, has a direct and powerful eschatological application. To recite or hear the work, or to witness a performance, is both to witness and to participate in the drama of God's salvific sojourn on earth, and the text is thus a focus for the exercise of the consuming devotion (bhakti) that is generally taught as the chief path to salvation in the dark and degenerate Kālī Age in which (Hindus believe) we now live. In this domain Rāma and Sītā, as well as their perfect devotee and messenger, the monkey Hanūmān, are major cultic figures of Hinduism, and their lives and deeds as recounted in the *Rāmāyana* are considered real by hundreds of millions of devotees for whom the worship of Lord Rāma or the repetition of His name (Rāmanāma) are seen as the sure path to salvation. The power of this vision of the *Rāmāyana* story as true and utterly relevant for the current age can be seen in such phenomena as Gandhi's appeal for the re-establishment of the *Ramrājya,* the kingdom of Rāma as a perfect norm for Indian society, and in the revival of Hindu fundamentalism in North India with its powerful and sometimes violent focus on the attempt to build a temple at the *Rāmajanmabhūmi,* the legendary birthplace of Rāma in Ayodhyā, a site currently occupied by a mosque.

THE EPIC STORY

Like the *Mahābhārata* and many other works of Indian literature, the *Rāmāyana* story is set in a narrative frame which, in this case, serves both to fix the composition of the poem in a historical context relative to the events it describes and to describe the events surrounding the work's creation and earliest performances.

The poem, as it has come down to us, begins in the midst of a conversation between the seer Vālmīki and the divine sage Nārada, a frequent traveler between the heavenly and earthly realms, who is visiting the ashram of the former. Vālmīki asks the sage if there is any truly virtuous and exemplary man in the world, and Nārada replies that such a person is King Rāma who was then reigning in Ayodhyā, capital city of the kingdom of Kosala. He then proceeds, in about seventy-five dense and often very elliptical verses, to describe Rāma's virtues and to provide an outline of his career from the time of his abortive consecration as king and ensuing exile to his ultimate recovery of his ancestral throne and perfect discharge of the duties of a Hindu monarch. This summary is sometimes referred to as the *samkṣipta* or abridged *Rāmāyana.*

Immediately following this conversation and Nārada's departure, Vālmīki sets out with his disciple to take his ritual bath at the riverbank. On the way he is enchanted with the beauties of the woodlands and is especially moved by the sight of a pair of cranes engaged in their mating ritual. As he watches, a tribal hunter, taking advantage of the birds' obliviousness to their surroundings, shoots and kills the male. Hearing the piteous cries of the female, the seer is overcome with both compassion and anger, and spontaneously pronounces a curse upon the hunter: "Since, hunter, you killed one of this pair of cranes, distracted at the height of their passion, you yourself shall not live for very long" (Rām. 1.2.14). The seer is puzzled to discover that this curse, uttered under the sway of his emotions, has spontaneously taken a form that is "fixed in metrical quarters, each with the same number of syllables, and fit for the accompaniment of stringed and percussion instruments." He discovers that somehow the grief (śoka) he has experienced for the sorrowing bird has been articulated as poetry to which he gives the term sloka, or verse. Pondering this strange event, the seer returns to his ashram, where he is visited by the great god Brahma who reveals to him that it was through his, the god's, power that he was inspired to create poetry and commissions him to render the exemplary tale of Rāma, which he had heard from Nārada, into well wrought verse. Gifted now with divine insight the sage "composed a poem that added to the glory of glorious Rāma with hundreds of slokas equal in syllables, their words noble in sound and meaning, delighting the heart" (Rām. 1.2.41). This, for the Indian tradition, is the creation not merely of a great poem but of poetry itself. And thus Vālmīki is immortalized as the ādikāvi, the first poet whose great work, the Rāmāyaṇa, as the ādikāvya, is literally the archetype of the genre.

Vālmīki teaches the poem to his disciples, the most outstanding of whom is a pair of twins, his foster sons who are in reality the sons of Rāma and Sītā, born to the latter in her last exile and raised secretly by the seer. The twins, Lava and Kuśa, become the first public singers of the epic tale and perform it throughout the country until, their fame having reached the court, they are invited to present the work before the king. As they do so, Rāma, the poem's hero and audience as well as the father of the bards, becomes enthralled by the poem and the performance and falls under the spell of their profound emotional appeal. It is at this point that the framing story (upodghāta) ends and the epic story proper begins.

The monumental poem of Vālmīki as it has been handed down contains approximately twenty-five thousand verses of two lines each. The great majority are in the typical, expository thirty-two-syllable sloka meter although, in the manner of long Sanskrit narrative poems, chapters (sargas) frequently close with one or more verses in longer meters, and occasionally, entire chapters or substantial portions of them, when highly figured, may be composed in the longer meters. The poem is also divided into seven books (*kāṇḍas*), each of which deals with a particular phase in Rāma's career or in the unfolding of the story.

Although it is difficult to convey the gravity and emotional tone of the work without providing some passages as examples, the basic narrative is not hard to summarize.

The epic story proper, as distinguished from the frame story, begins with the fifth *sarga* of the first book, the *Bālakāṇḍa*, which treats the hero's career from his birth to his marriage. Here we learn of the fair and prosperous realm of Kosala and its wise and powerful monarch, King Daśaratha, whose lineage derives from the Sun, and who rules from the splendid walled city of Ayodhyā. The king has attained every felicity a man could wish except the birth of a son and heir. On the advice of his ministers and with the assistance of the legendary unicorn sage Ṛśyaśṛṅga, he performs a great Horse Sacrifice as a consequence of which four splendid sons are born to him by his three principal wives, Kausalyā, Kaikeyī, and Sumitrā. As the gods assemble for the sacrifice we learn that they have been dispossessed from heaven and reduced to servitude by the dreadful and all-powerful lord of the rakshasa demons, the ten-headed Rāvaṇa. They beseech the great god Vishnu Nārāyaṇa to come to their aid, and he promises to take birth as a human so as to be able to circumvent the terms of a boon the demon king had secured that made him invulnerable to all but mortals. He urges the gods to incarnate themselves as great hosts of monkeys to assist him in his mission.

The king's sons Rāma, Bharata, and the twins Lakṣmaṇa and Śatrughna, are each imbued with a certain portion of the great god's essence and so represent partial avataras (incarnations). Rāma is the eldest and most fully endowed of the four. Lakṣmaṇa becomes his attendant and inseparable companion.

The princes are raised and educated uneventfully until, shortly before their sixteenth birthday, the great sage Viśvāmitra appears without warning at the palace and asks the king to lend him his favorite son Rāma, to guard a sacrifice the sage is performing from the depredations of a pair of fierce rakshasas who have been plaguing him. With great reluctance, and only through fear of the sage's curse, Daśaratha permits Rāma to accompany Viśvāmitra. The three, Rāma, Lakṣmaṇa, and Viśvāmitra, set out at once for the sage's forest ashram. On their journey, Rāma receives instruction in certain magical spells and, in response to his boyish questions, is told a series of mythological tales associated with the various spots through which they pass. At one point, following the sage's orders, Rāma slays a monstrous demoness who, having devastated a once prosperous region, now preys upon travelers. As a reward, Viśvāmitra confers upon the prince a set of supernatural missiles and the secret spells to control them. At length the three arrive at the sage's ashram where, in the course of his vigil, Rāma employs his newly acquired weapons to put an end to the rakshasas' harassment of the peaceful sages of the hermitage. One of the two demons is slain on the spot while the other, Mārica, is merely stunned. He will resurface in a critical role later in the epic.

Having accomplished his immediate goal, Viśvāmitra instructs the princes to accompany him to the city of Mithilā where, he tells them, King Janaka is in possession of a massive and powerful bow. No earthly prince has been able to wield the weapon, a feat of strength that the king has specified as the only acceptable bride-price for his beautiful foster-daughter, the earth-born Sītā.

The three proceed to Mithilā where Rāma easily bends the bow—in reality the great god Śiva's—and breaks it, thus winning the hand of the princess. A group marriage is arranged for all four of Daśaratha's sons and the two daughters and two nieces of Janaka. After the festive event, the wedding party returns to Ayodhyā. On their way they are accosted by the dreaded Brahmin-warrior Rāma Jāmadagnya, legendary nemesis of the warrior class, who has been enraged by the breaking of Śiva's bow. He challenges the upstart Rāma to wield the still more powerful bow of Vishnu. The king and his escort are numbed with fear; but Rāma faces the intruder down and, as an avatara of Vishnu, easily masters the second bow. The party proceeds to Ayodhyā, where the princes live in peace and contentment with their brides. Rāma and Sītā, in particular, are deeply absorbed in their mutual love. Thus the adventures of Rāma as a boy (bāla) come to a close, and with them the Bālakāṇḍa.

The second book, as its name (Ayodhyākāṇḍa) indicates, is set mainly in the city of Ayodhyā, and concerns itself with the political intrigues of the royal court and their tragic consequences. As the book opens we find that Daśaratha, feeling his age grow upon him, has decided, in the temporary absence of Prince Bharata, to retire from the throne and consecrate Rāma as heir-apparent. The announcement is greeted with general rejoicing and preparations for the ceremony are begun throughout the city. On the eve of the consecration, however, Kaikeyī, a beautiful junior wife with whom the aged king is deeply infatuated, allows herself to be worked into a jealous rage by her scheming maidservant Mantharā, and uses two previously unclaimed boons to extort the consecration of her own son Bharata in Rāma's place and the banishment of Rāma to the wilderness for fourteen years. The king tries pathetically to make Kaikeyī relent, but she is adamant. Daśaratha, compelled to honor his word, is forced to comply.

Informed of the sudden reversal in his fortune, Rāma betrays no distress but, arguing that his highest duty is deference to his father's promise, dons the garb of a forest ascetic, divests himself of all his wealth, and prepares to depart. Lakṣmaṇa is of course to accompany him, but when Sītā declares her intention to do so as well, Rāma forbids it. In a series of moving speeches, Sītā argues for the cultural norm of a wife's devoted accompaniment of her husband in joy and adversity, and in the end persuades Rāma. The three take leave of the heartbroken king and populace, and enter the wilderness.

Grieving for his beloved son, Daśaratha dies. Bharata is recalled from his prolonged visit to another country to be installed as his successor. But when the prince learns of the tragedy at Ayodhyā and of the machinations of his mother, he indignantly refuses the throne and instead leads his army into the woods to bring back his exiled brother to be king. The brothers meet, but Rāma, insistent upon obeying to the letter his dead father's word, refuses to return. Bharata, too, refuses the throne and the impasse is broken only when he agrees to serve as regent in Rāma's name for the period of exile. Rāma, Sītā, and Lakṣmaṇa then abandon their pleasant but overly accessible hilltop retreat and move on into the wild and demon-haunted forests of the South.

The third book of the epic, the *Araṇyakāṇḍa*, takes its name from the wilderness (*araṇya*) that is its setting. Here are recounted the dramatic events that occur during the period of Rāma's exile. In the forest, Rāma is approached by pious ascetics who appeal to him for protection against the savage man-eating rakshasas who have been attacking them. Soon Sītā is briefly carried off by a fearsome demon named Virādha, but the brothers manage to rescue her.

While they are living peacefully in the woodlands of Pañcavaṭī they are visited by a rakshasa woman, Śūrpaṇakhā, a sister of Rāvaṇa who attempts to seduce first Rāma and then Lakṣmaṇa. Rejected, she attempts to kill Sītā, whom she has been made to think of as the obstacle to the fulfillment of her passion for Rāma. At Rāma's behest, Lakṣmaṇa mutilates the demoness who flees to her brother Khara, the leader of the rakshasas of the region. Khara first sends and then leads punitive expeditions against the brothers, but Rāma exterminates the demons by the thousand.

News of these events reach the ears of Rāvaṇa, and, infatuated by the description of Sītā, he resolves to destroy Rāma by abducting her and keeping her as his concubine. He compels, on pain of death, the demon Mārīca, survivor of the fight at Viśvāmitra's ashram, to assist him in his plan. The latter, assuming the appearance of a wonderful deer, captivates Sītā's fancy and leads Rāma far off into the woods. When Rāma finally manages to shoot Mārīca, the demon mimics Rāma's voice to call desperately to Lakṣmaṇa for help. Sītā forces the skeptical Lakṣmaṇa to go after his brother, and soon after his departure, Rāvaṇa appears. After gaining Sītā's confidence by assuming the guise of a holy man, the demon-lord forcibly abducts her. A great vulture, Jaṭāyus, a friend of Daśaratha, accosts the fleeing demon, and a battle ensues during which the bird falls mortally wounded, surviving, however, long enough to tell Rāma and Lakṣmaṇa what has happened. Rāma succumbs to wild grief and searches the woodlands like a man bereft of his senses. At length he is directed to the monkey Sugrīva who, he is told, will be able to assist him in his quest for Sītā.

The fourth book of the poem, the *Kiṣkindhākāṇḍa*, takes its name from Kiṣkindhā, the cave-citadel of the monkeys which is its main setting. Wandering in the forest, Rāma and Lakṣmaṇa are accosted by Hanūmān, a great monkey hero and retainer of Sugrīva, the ruler of Kiṣkindhā who has been banished from the city as a usurper by his elder brother the monkey-king Vālin. Sugrīva tells Rāma a highly colored tale of his conflict with Vālin, and the two conclude a pact whereby Rāma agrees to aid the former in disposing of his rival in exchange for the monkeys' assistance in the search for Sītā.

The monkey brothers engage in hand-to-hand combat during which Rāma shoots and kills Vālin from ambush. Then, after much procrastination, Sugrīva, now reinstalled on the throne, dispatches search parties in all directions. The narrative then follows the strange adventures of the Southern party commanded by Vālin's son Aṅgada and Hanūmān. After spending some time in an enchanted underground realm, the monkeys, ashamed at the failure of their mission and in dread of the wrath of their king, resolve to fast themselves to death. They are spared at the last minute by the appearance of the vulture Sampāti, elder brother of Jaṭāyus, who reveals to them the fact that Sītā is being held captive on Rāvaṇa's island-fortress of Laṅkā. The monkeys take counsel as to which of them is powerful enough to leap the strait between it and the mainland. In the end it is clear that only

Hanūmān can undertake such a feat. He prepares for his great leap.

The fifth book of the poem is called the *Sundarakāṇḍa* for reasons that have not yet been adequately explained by scholars. The book is largely given over to a detailed, vivid, and often amusing account of Hanūmān's leap and his adventures in Laṅkā. Searching the city and the palace grounds, the monkey at length comes upon the despondent princess who has been alternately cajoled and menaced by Rāvaṇa and his rakshasa women. He gives Sītā Rāma's signet ring as a token, and she rejoices knowing that reunion with her beloved is at hand. The monkey offers to carry her back to Rāma, but she declines the offer, reluctant to allow herself to be willingly touched by a male other than her husband and arguing that it is only fitting that Rāma come himself to avenge her abduction.

Hanūmān then wreaks havoc in Laṅkā, shattering trees and buildings, and slaughtering servants and soldiers of the king. At length he allows himself to be captured and brought before Rāvaṇa. He is condemned, and his tail is set ablaze; but he escapes his bonds and, leaping from roof to roof, sets fire to the city with his tail. He then leaps back to the mainland and rejoins his search party. The monkeys return to Kiṣkindhā destroying, on their way, a grove belonging to Sugrīva. Hanūmān reports his adventures to Rāma.

The sixth book of the epic, the *Yuddhakāṇḍa*, as its name suggests, is chiefly concerned with the great battle (*yuddha*) before the gates of Laṅkā between Rāma and Rāvaṇa and their respective armies. Armed with Hanūmān's intelligence on the military disposition of Laṅkā, Rāma and Lakṣmaṇa proceed to the seashore accompanied by the monkey hosts of Sugrīva. There they are joined by Rāvaṇa's renegade brother Vibhīṣaṇa who has defected in his disgust with the former's immorality. The monkeys construct a causeway over the ocean, and the army crosses. A protracted and bloody battle ensues, with the advantage shifting back and forth until, in the end, Rāma slays Rāvaṇa in single combat. Installing Vibhīṣaṇa on the throne of Laṅkā, Rāma sends for Sītā but refuses to accept her now that she has lived in the house of another man. The princess is, however, shown to be faithful through a fire ordeal and so is taken back. Rāma, Lakṣmaṇa, and Sītā return to Ayodhyā in Rāvaṇa's flying palace. Having fulfilled the fourteen years of exile, Rāma is at last consecrated as king of Kosala.

The seventh and final book of the great epic is called simply the

"Last Book" (*Uttarakāṇḍa*), and it is somewhat heterogeneous in its contents. In general it functions as an extended epilogue to the epic tale proper. It provides narrative material on the prior history of significant characters other than the central figures in the story. Thus the first third of the book is devoted to accounts of the early careers of Rāvaṇa and, to a lesser extent, Hanūmān. In this section many of the critical events of the epic story are shown to have had their roots in relationships and curses from the past. Other passages relate legendary and mythological material of a general nature or involving ancestors of Rāma.

The remainder of the book tells of the last years of Rāma, his wife, and his brothers. After the struggles and sorrows of their years of exile, Rāma and Sītā find that their peace is to be once more shattered. It comes to Rāma's attention that, despite her ordeal by fire, Sītā has become the target of ugly gossip in the city concerning her alleged sexual infidelity with Rāvaṇa. In conformity with his duty of pleasing and serving as an exemplar for his subjects, Rāma has her banished to the forest despite the fact that she is pregnant and that he himself knows her to be innocent.

After some time Rāma performs a great Horse Sacrifice during which the two handsome and accomplished young bards appear at court to sing the *Rāmāyaṇa*. The bards are, of course, none other than Lava and Kuśa, the twin sons of Rāma and Sītā who have been fostered and trained by the poet-seer Vālmīki. Rāma now sends for Sītā, but rather than returning she calls upon her mother, the Earth, to receive her and as the ground opens, she vanishes forever. After a period of time, overwhelmed with grief, Rāma divides the kingdom between his long lost sons and then, followed by the citizens of Ayodhyā, enters the Sarayū river and returns at last to heaven as the Lord Vishnu.

TOPICS FOR DISCUSSION

1. How do the framing of the epic narrative and the text's treatment of the question of authorship compare with the way in which these matters are treated in other epic poetry with which you are familiar? What are some of the consequences of prefacing the poem with a straightforward synopsis of the plot? What does the frame story tell us about the understanding of the nature of literature in classical India, with specific reference to emotion and to performance?

2. How does the poem characterize the ideals for social behav-

ior? What does it teach us about the traditional relationships between generations? What is the relevance of the *Rāmāyaṇa* for our understanding of the characterization and role of women in traditional India? What characteristics distinguish Rāma as the ideal man from Rāvaṇa as the antithesis of this ideal? Discuss examples of such popular socially prescriptive literary works from other cultures.

3. How would you compare the characterizations of Rāma and Bharata with those of the heroes of the *Mahābhārata* such as Krishna, Arjuna, Bhīma, and Karṇa? How do they compare with the heroes of the Greek epics such as Achilles, Agamemnon, and Odysseus, and with the heroes of other Western literary works? What is the significance of the difference between, say, Rāma and Achilles for our understanding of literary and cultural differences between India and Europe?

4. Why is it that the *Rāmāyaṇa* is often regarded and treated as India's "family" epic in contrast with the much revered but less frequently read "outside" epic the *Mahābhārata?*

5. To what extent would you say that the poem's claim that its story would always be told on earth has proven true? How would you contrast the fate of the story with that of the Greek epics? What accounts for the difference? Why and by what means has the Rāma story survived in India and Southeast Asia?

6. Other than its aesthetic appeal and social message, what factor would you say most explains the survival and continuing massive popularity of the *Rāmāyaṇa* nearly three thousand years after the composition of Vālmīki's poem? Where would you look for parallels in Western literature?

NOTE

1. The three numbers, in this and later in-text citations, beginning from the left, refer to *kaṇḍa, sarga* and sloka. *Kaṇḍa* may be translated as "book," *sarga* as "section" or "chapter," and sloka as "verse." *Kaṇḍa,* literally "joint," is a broad division in the narrative the unifying feature of which may be the locus of action or a prominent character. *Sargas* contain episodes and are composed of individual slokas or verses.

REFERENCES

The *Vālmīki Rāmāyaṇa,* in its various recensions, has been translated— in whole or in part—many times since it first came to the attention of European scholars at the very beginning of the nineteenth century. Most of the English translations are difficult to find and still more difficult to read.

For the first three books of the poem, see Volumes 1–3 of the ongoing translation of the critical edition of the poem, published as *The Rāmāyaṇa of Vālmīki: An Epic of Ancient India*, edited by R.P. Goldman (Princeton: Princeton University Press, 1985; paperback, 1990).

Readable and accessible translations of books 4–7 are not available, although a variety of condensations and "retellings" of various *Rāmāyaṇas* can be had. Perhaps the most usable translation of the complete epic would be Hari Prasad Shastri's 1953 version published by Shanti Sadan, London (revised 1962).

Two useful overviews of the history of the Rāma story in India and in Southeast Asia are: Raghavan, V., *The Greater Rāmāyaṇa* (Varanasi: All India Kashiraj Trust, 1973), and Raghavan, V., *The Rāmāyaṇa in Greater India* (Surat: South Gujerat University, 1975).

ANITA DESAI: *FIRE ON THE MOUNTAIN* AND *GAMES AT TWILIGHT*

Robin Jared Lewis

Very few modern Indian writers have received as much international attention and acclaim as Anita Desai. Her eight novels and various short stories have expanded the dimensions of the Indian literary scene by giving voice to a range of characters previously relegated to the margins of Indian fiction: women, children, adolescents, and the elderly. Except perhaps for the Hindi writer Premchand, whose work emerged from the turmoil of the nationalist movement, and the energy created by the ideas of Mahatma Gandhi in the 1920s and 1930s, most modern Indian fiction has been dominated by writers who usually emphasize the dilemmas of adult males that mirror those of emergent India. This is true of major figures writing in English—Mulk Raj Anand, R.K. Narayan, and Salman Rushdie, to name a few—and also of many authors writing in the vernaculars.

Desai not only brought new characters to the forefront, but she also fixed her penetrating eye on the inner lives of the expanding urban middle class, delving deeply into the realms of imagination and fantasy through a variety of techniques relatively new to Indian writing. Her work has proved to be an inspiration to a new generation of women writers in the 1960s and 1970s, and there have been few serious critical accounts of modern Indian fiction in which she does not figure centrally.

That Desai comes from a highly cosmopolitan background is readily apparent in her work, which is infused with elements from Western, as well as Indian and other Asian, literary traditions. Born in 1937 to a Bengali father and a German mother, she was raised in Delhi in an atmosphere where reading and learning were highly valued, and she began writing around the age of seven. She has lived her adult life in India's three great cities—Calcutta, Bombay, and Delhi—and has received widespread recognition for her writing, beginning with the Royal Society of Literature's Winifred Holtby Memorial Prize in 1978, awarded for her novel *Fire on the Mountain*. Her works have twice been nominated for the Booker Prize, and she has also won the coveted Sahitya Akademi Award, given by India's national academy of letters.

All of Desai's works focus on characters who are at odds with society and the roles it imposes on them. This is certainly true of her early novels, two of which, *Cry, the Peacock* (1963) and *Where Shall We Go This Summer?* (1975), depict a sensitive woman trapped in an unhappy marriage with a callous husband. Two other early works, *Voices in the City* (1965) and *Bye-Bye, Blackbird* (1971), deal with educated Indians attempting to come to terms with the challenges presented by a difficult and at times hostile urban environment. The former is set amidst the disorder and dislocation of contemporary Calcutta, and the latter focuses on the cultural disconnection and racial animosity confronting Indian émigrés in London.

Desai's three most recent novels—*Clear Light of Day* (1980), *In Custody* (1984), and *Baumgartner's Bombay* (1989)—explore some of the same ideas, but they surpass the earlier works in complexity of both theme and structure. *Clear Light of Day* moves back and forth almost seamlessly between pre- and post-independence Delhi, chronicling the history of an extended family buffeted by the impersonal forces of history and diminished (but not defeated) by personal tragedy. *In Custody* represents a new direction for Desai, exploring the tragicomic efforts of an obscure university lecturer—and would-be poet—to interview an illustrious Urdu poet whose reputation for artistic achievement is equalled only by his public displays of dissolution and drunkenness. *Baumgartner's Bombay* tells the story of a German-Jewish refugee from the Holocaust and his melancholy exile in Bombay. It is Desai's boldest novel to date, a brilliant exploration of loneliness and aging set amidst the tragic dislocations of the postwar world.

The superb novel *Fire on the Mountain* (1977) and the contemporaneous collection of short stories entitled *Games at Twilight* (1978) lie at the heart of Desai's canon. Both works center on the notion of escape, of achieving a kind of radical singleness by fleeing from the social identities imposed by the traditions of India's upper classes. In sharp contrast to many modern Western works in which the protagonist struggles to escape from existential solitude into a new sense of community in Desai's work, the central characters seek to escape the powerful complex of social, religious, and familial obligations that hinders their search for individuality.

The best example of this is the principal figure in *Fire on the Mountain*: Nanda Kaul, the aging widow of a university president, has retreated to a house in the foothills of the Himalayas in search of a "pared, reduced, and radiantly single life." The setting is the town of Kasauli, a hill station built by the British as a refuge from the heat of the Indian plains, and Nanda's villa is named Carignano, evoking the more genteel holiday retreats of the Mediterranean. For Nanda, Carignano represents a sanctuary from the overwhelming responsibilities of her former identities as wife and mother. Her flight into the mountains is a defiantly feminist gesture that parodies the spiritual retreat into the Himalayas from worldly obligations that an aging male householder undertakes in accordance with the traditional Hindu life cycle. Desai's heroine is sharply etched, and her fierce determination to be free of the "relational" identity (which the Indian psychoanalyst Sudhir Kakar has delineated in *The Inner World*) drives the novel relentlessly to its climax.

Nanda Kaul's triumphant solitude is intruded upon by the arrival of the postman, who brings a letter announcing the imminent arrival of her great-granddaughter Raka. Raka, a tortured and unhappy child, has been packed off to Kasauli to remove her from the painful scenes engendered by the violent break-up of her parents' marriage. At the outset Nanda sees Raka as a burden, another wearisome reminder of her past. However, soon after the girl's arrival, Nanda realizes that her great-granddaughter represents the perfection of solitude to which Nanda can only aspire in vain: Raka has truly isolated herself from others as she wanders the mountainside, singing exultantly to herself, "I'm shipwrecked and alone . . . alone in my boat on the sea."

Against her will, Nanda soon finds herself inexorably drawn into a close relationship with Raka, whose wildness and independence arouse the nurturing instinct Nanda had renounced so emphatically. In order to bring the girl closer to her, Nanda creates a vivid fantasy of her own past that features thrilling journeys over remote mountain passes into Tibet, summers in verdant Kashmir, and most improbably, a happily romantic bond with her husband—who in reality had been unfaithful to her for the entire duration of their marriage. Although Raka soon becomes bored with her great-grandmother's elaborate tales, it is too late for

Nanda, who finds, to her disgust, that she is once again enmeshed in a web of relationship and need.

Just as the postman breaks into Nanda's treasured isolation to bring word of Raka's arrival in the book's opening scene, the final section begins with the "scream" of the telephone that announces the advent of Ila Das, an eccentric spinster whom Nanda has known since childhood. Ila, whose visit is a trial for Nanda, comes from humble origins, and in her old age she ekes out a living as a social welfare officer among the impoverished villagers of the hills. She is the target of cruel mockery and pranks by the local children, and she stands in the novel as an emblem of tangible failure in the social realm, an outcast with a sad and painful past—and an even more terrible end. Ila's shrill, grating voice is a symbol of her aloneness in a society that has no room for single women who do not follow the path of convention: her rape and murder (by a villager enraged at her attempts to prevent him from marrying his young daughter to a rich, elderly landowner) bring home to Nanda the utter futility of her own attempts to insulate herself from the pain and need that inevitably accompany human relationships. As Nanda sits stunned by the news of Ila's death, she is overwhelmed by shame at the lies she has told to Raka. But Ila's death liberates Nanda from *maya* (illusion in Hindu metaphysics), and she achieves a kind of metaphoric liberation at the end—as does Raka, who appears to proclaim that she has set the forest ablaze, providing a final, purificatory funeral pyre for Nanda's illusory solitude.

One of the most striking features of *Fire on the Mountain* is Desai's use of landscape. She derives this technique from a range of Asian imagistic genres in which the physical and the emotional landscapes are one. These include Tamil and Sanskrit poetry, and the vernacular feminine tradition of Heian Japan, exemplified by the terse miniatures in *The Pillow Book of Sei Shōnagon*, to which Nanda turns for inspiration. Desai's Kasauli is a terrain of stark desolation, of abrupt blooming and withering, that powerfully appeals to Nanda Kaul in her fierce desire for a simple style of living:

> Getting up at last, she went slowly round to the back of the house and leant on the wooden railing on which the yellow rose creeper had blossomed so youthfully last month but was now reduced to an exhausted mass of grey creaks and groans again. She gazed down the gorge with its gashes of red earth, its rocks and gullies and sharply spiked agaves, to the Punjab plains—a silver haze in the summer heat—stretching out to a dim yellow horizon, and said Is it wrong? Have I not done enough and had enough? I want no

more. I want nothing. Can I not be left with nothing? But there was no answer and of course she expected none.

The sere terrain also appeals to Raka, who shuns the neat paths carefully laid out by the British in the last century and instead plunges abruptly down the hillsides, secretively making her way through a succession of solitary adventures.

Perhaps the most notable aspect of Desai's novel is its quiet insistence on stripping away the veneer of sentimentality that often colors fictional depictions of the role of women in Indian society. Desai vividly evokes the crushing burden of responsibility frequently borne by Indian women in the joint family in her brilliant description of Nanda Kaul's ritual afternoon naps—her emblematic moments of solitude during her married life:

> . . . she had tried to shut out sound by shutting out light . . . she had spent the sleepless hour making out the direction from which a shout came, or a burst of giggles, an ominous growling from the dogs, the spray of gravel under the bicycle wheels on the drive, a contest of squirrels over the guavas in the orchard, the dry rattle of eucalyptus leaves in the sun, a drop, then spray and rush of water from a tap. All was subdued, but nothing was ever still.
>
> From all sides these sounds invaded her room, which was in the centre, and neither the wire gauze screens at the windows nor the striped Orissa cotton curtains at the doors kept them out. Everyone in the house knew it was her hour of rest, that she was not to be disturbed. She could hear a half-asleep ayah hiss at the babies "Quiet, go to sleep, you'll wake your mother." She could hear her husband tell someone in a carefully lowered voice "Later, I'll have to consult my wife about it. I'll let you know later." She could hear her sons tiptoe past in their great, creaking boots, then fling their satchels down with a crash.
>
> This would go on for an hour and she would keep her eyes tightly clenched, her hands folded on her chest—under a quilt in winter, or uncovered to the sullen breeze of the fan in summer—determinedly not responding. The effort not to respond would grow longer by the minute, heavier, more unendurable, till at last it was sitting on her chest, grasping her by the neck. At four o'clock she would break out from under it with a gasp. All right, she would say, sitting up on the edge of her bed and letting down her feet to search for her slippers, then straightening her hair—all right, she'd sigh, come, come all of you, get me, I'm yours, yours again.

Lying on her marriage bed at the very center of the house, Nanda is both mother goddess and sacrificial victim of her large family's insistent and unceasing needs.

In the awful moment after receiving news of Ila Das's murder, the harshest revelation Nanda must face is that her quest for solitude, an act of seeming willfulness, is not in the final analysis an act of will at all: "She did not live here alone by choice—she lived here alone because that was what she was forced to do, reduced to doing." Nanda sees that as an Indian widow she has no place in the world of active relationships; she can only be a passive onlooker, viewing the world coldly from her mountaintop retreat. Nanda is resigned to the fact of her own death ("Old, old—I am old"). On the other hand, Raka's final action is, in a curious way, an act of affirmation: the fire she sets is a womanly act of simultaneous destruction and creation. Raka brings down fire on the mountain in order to prevent herself from becoming another Ila Das, and from sharing Ila's dismal fate.

Desai's fine collection of short stories, *Games at Twilight*, offers a series of variations on the theme of escape. Her protagonists are women, children, widows, retirees, poets, artists, and dreamers: all figures who stand apart from the loud, onrushing urban society that surrounds them. Most of them seek to free themselves from the suffocating intimacy of the Indian family—like the children in the title story, who plead with their mother to let them play outside despite the staggering afternoon heat:

> . . . the children strained to get out. Their faces were red and bloated with the effort, but their mother would not open the door, everything was still curtained and shuttered in a way that stifled the children, made them feel that their lungs were stuffed with cotton wool and their noses with dust and if they didn't burst out into the light and see the sun and feel the air, they would choke.

Released into the yard, the children "burst out like seeds from a crackling, over-ripe pod." Their game of hide-and-seek, in which the older, stronger boys mercilessly hunt the weaker ones, becomes a metaphor for the social interactions of the joint family, where simply to be left alone is a kind of triumph:

> Ravi sat back on the harsh edge of the tub, deciding to hold out a bit longer. What fun if they were all found and caught—he alone left unconquered! He had never known that sensation. . . . To defeat Raghu—that hirsute, hoarse-voiced football champion—and to be the winner in a circle of older, bigger, luckier children—that would be thrilling beyond imagination. He hugged his knees together and smiled to himself almost shyly at the thought of so much victory, such laurels.

"Pineapple Cake" is another story in which a confined, protected child longs to escape into singularity. This terse vignette is set amidst the lace-curtain gentility of Bombay's Goan Catholic community. The ironically named Victor longs to flee from the clutches of his tyrannical mother, who has stuffed him into his best clothes and dragged him off to the wedding of two people he does not know. Upon leaving the church and heading for the reception, "Victor stupidly began a fantasy of slipping out of her hold and breaking into a toy shop for skates and speeding ahead of the whole caravan on a magic pair . . . losing his mother on the way." Victor's daydream is stupid because it is utterly futile, and he instead finds himself crammed into a taxi with three large, looming adults:

> The four of them sat squeezed together and the women made little remarks about how beautiful Carmen Maria had looked and how the de Mellos couldn't be badly off, tea at Green's, after all. "Green's," the woman in the purple net frock yelled into the taxi driver's ear and gave her bottom an important shake that knocked Victor against the door. This must have made him look peaked, for his mother squeezed his hand and whispered, "You've been a good boy—pineapple cake for you." Victor sat still, not breathing.

Desai has a remarkable talent for depicting children's fears and fantasies, and her sensitivity to the oppressive burden of expectation that a middle-class child faces in any society lends these stories their special power. The protagonist of "Studies in the Park" is a fugitive from the smothering attentions of both his mother, with her seemingly endless nurturing—" 'Suno, drink your milk. Good for you, Suno. You need it. Now, before the exams. Must have it, Suno. Drink.' "—and his omnipresent father, an Indian version of Gregor Samsa's imposing parent in Kafka's *The Metamorphosis*: ". . . my father appeared, bathed and shaven, stuffed and set up with the news of the world in six different languages—his white *dhoti* blazing, his white shirt crackling, his patent leather pumps glistening." Suno, whose name is the imperative form of the verb "listen," retreats to a nearby park. Here he discovers an entire subculture of adolescent fugitives who have fled their homes to seek a quiet place to study for their exams.

Desai's vision of urban India reflects a culture in which intimacy has become a form of suffocation; the quest for individual identity—separate from the socially determined roles to which her characters are often the unwilling heirs—is stifled. With consummate stylistic grace and innovation, Desai raises troubling questions about the adaptability of traditional Indian family structures to contemporary social pressures. Her writing has served as an inspiration to a new generation of Indian authors: its luminous clarity and subtle social insights have freed them from the deadening legacy of an essentially imitative fictional tradition. Desai's work has given new scope to the ongoing search for self-realization in modern Indian literature.

TOPICS FOR DISCUSSION

1. In what ways does Desai's work illuminate the question of identity, of the conflict between the desires of the individual and of society, in contemporary urban India?

2. What picture emerges from Desai's writing of the role of women in India today? How does this compare to the role of women depicted in contemporary Western fiction? In other Asian fiction?

3. How does Desai's style reflect the influence of other writers, and of other literary traditions? Do you see any resemblances to specific Western writers? To other Asian writers you have read?

4. Discuss Desai's use of natural imagery to express human emotion.

5. Looking at Desai's portraits of children and adolescents in contemporary Indian society, how do their dilemmas compare to those of youth in Western societies?

REFERENCES

Acharya, Shanta. "Problems of the Self in the Novels of Anita Desai." In *Explorations in Modern Indo-English Fiction*, edited by R. K. Dhawan. New Delhi: Bahri, 1982.

Belliappa, Meena. *Anita Desai: A Study of Her Fiction*. Calcutta: Writers Workshop, 1971.

Bliss, Corinne Demas. "Against the Current: A Conversation with Anita Desai." *Massachusetts Review* 29, no. 3 (Autumn 1988): 521–37.

Desai, Anita. *Fire on the Mountain*. Bombay and Calcutta: Allied Publishers Private Limited, 1977.

Desai, Anita. *Games at Twilight*. New York: Penguin Books, 1982.

Jain, Jasbir. *Stairs to the Attic: The Novels of Anita Desai*. Jaipur: Printwell, 1987.

Kakar, Sudhir. *The Inner World: A Psychoanalytic Study of Childhood and Society in India*. Delhi: Oxford University Press, 1978.

Krishna, Francine. "Anita Desai: *Fire on the Mountain*." *Indian Literature* 25, no. 5 (September-October 1982): 158–69.

Srivastava, Ramesh, ed. *Perspectives on Anita Desai*. Ghaziabad: Vimal Prakashan, 1985.

Indian Texts: Narrative

R. K. NARAYAN'S
THE FINANCIAL EXPERT

Bharati Mukherjee

In the main, R. K. Narayan is regarded lightly by Indian literary intellectuals—a frustration for those of us, Indian-born but not India-fixated, who find much to admire in his work. At the same time, he is often praised for the wrong reasons in the West.

To read Narayan is not to visit India or to understand Indians, although he is frequently cited by well-meaning foreigners (Graham Greene for example) as a trustworthy, even genial, guide. There is, finally, nothing gentle in Narayan's vision. I remember an impassioned West Indian critic once charging a number of Western (white) scholars at a Commonwealth Literature convention with "not having visited the West Indies, only having visited (V. S.) Naipaul," and I think the same holds for Western readings of Narayan. Before looking at *The Financial Expert* in depth, I would like to address "The Narayan Problem," at least as I perceive it.

The difficulty can partly be ascribed to an Indian prejudice against all English-language fiction written by Indians. The use of the colonial tongue is associated with a presumed pro-British, upper-class bias, and leads to a blanket condemnation of such writing as inauthentic in its very conception, cut off from the readership and imaginative resources of its homeland. From this assumption other judgments follow: the choice of English is a commercial search after a "world market" and foreign approval, and is thus a corrupt financial motivation; or else it is an open admission that the author is less adept at his or her mother tongue than the learned vernacular of the erstwhile ruler, which is a confession of inauthenticity. The true, mythic and tribal imagination cannot be evoked in a foreign tongue; characters cannot be conceived in foreign dress; customs cannot be fully appreciated when translated. All of these charges may hold some truth, though not to the pious extent they are often argued. Certainly they are not true in the case of Narayan.

Deep down, and less acknowledged, is the ancient fear of racial pollution: the use of English connotes impurity, even in outwardly "pure-culture" Indian authors. English imparts irony and duality; the artist's "sincerity," a touchstone of Indian criticism, is thus suspect. The choice of English, then, conjures up images of wealth, self-contempt, alienation, and secularism. It seems to imply a scorn for the native culture, which in turn responds defensively. "Indo-Anglian," the word used to describe native Indians like Narayan who write in English, is very close in the popular mind to "Anglo-Indian," the word used to describe the mixed-race (and English-speaking) genetic remnants of British colonialism.

It must be admitted that there is some justification in the charge. India's best-known writers in English—Kamala Markandaya, Arun Joshi, Anita Desai, Nayantara Sahgel, and the Polish-born longtime resident of India, Ruth Prawer Jhabvala (a dozen others of lesser talent could easily be included)—are natural mediators between East and West, and their characters do seem to occupy uneasy pinnacles of alien privilege and sophistication. One can imagine their characters, unlike Narayan's, speaking English at home, and their concerns being far removed from the cares of everyday Indians.

At best, such authors are seen as popular entertainers, light-weights. In keeping with that judgment, India's critics have far too often viewed Narayan's style as "journalistic" and pedestrian, his characters as clownish, his Malgudi a prettied-up tourist attraction; they do not realize that his style is a remarkable achievement, one of the wonders of the Anglographic world. He is not part of the same writing world as the authors mentioned above, who are really stylistic and thematic descendants of Forster, clones and competitors of British counterparts.

Only in one sense is Narayan a typical "Indo-Anglian." He is a natural translator of his experience, but not between his native Tamil and his fluent, flexible English. Narayan's imagination occupies two separate creations, two separate time schemes: the fabulous world of nearly pure essences—a timeless, godly realm—and a familiar (if idealized) South-Indian town called Malgudi, as it might have appeared a few decades ago.

This double vision requires a special language. English alienates the material, helps control it. Narayan's use of English is rather like Beckett's use of French; it imposes a rigid focus—dryness and distance—on an unruly imagination. It is a remarkably supple English: declarative, omniscient, comic, native, and distant, often sharing in the character's innocence and bluster. In *The Financial Expert* we read (in a sentence chosen at random), "He seemed to swell with his goodness, nobility, and importance, and the clean plans he was able to make for his son" (118).[1] ("Clean plans" reads to me as an importation.) Narayan's "reality," or what passes for it in the West, is the village grid of Malgudi with its recurrent landmarks and familiar shopkeepers (which lead to forced and misleading comparisons with Faulkner's Yoknapatawpha legend). This, along with his English prose style, is really his greatest invention. His further plot complications, such as the visiting movie companies (*The Guide* and *Mr. Sampath*), the man-eater (*The Man Eater of Malgudi*), the creative writing machine (*The Vendor of Sweets*), or Margayya's pyramid banking scheme in *The Financial Expert* really are distractions from each novel's major conflict, which is always and ever, human beings toying with divine perspective, their daring to demand more of the gods than they are prepared to give, their misinterpreting of God's bounty, and their pathetic attachment to maya (illusion).

These complex issues are present at every moment in the best of his work, often condensed into single sentences or paragraphs. In *The Financial Expert*, Margayya is borne along by bullock cart to get a lotus needed in a ceremony:

> The wheels crunched, roared, and bumped along. Margayya wondered if he was expected to reach his lotus by walking and not by riding in a cart. Would that in any way affect the issues and would it violate the injunction laid by the priest? "I don't think there is anything wrong in it. He'd have mentioned it. Anyway, better not raise the question. Perhaps this cart was sent here by God." (61)

It is not Faulkner who influenced Narayan; if one were to see a Western author with the same sense of tragic play, equally aware of the porous boundary between the human and the eternal, one might have to go all the way back to Ovid.

His world is populated by ghosts and demons, gods and their agents. As Margayya prepares to pluck a lotus from a fetid, overgrown pond green with scum (part of an elaborate and comic ritual for propitiating Lakshmi, the goddess of wealth), he is suddenly accosted:

> Far in a corner of the little *mantap* on the other bank, he saw someone stirring. He felt a slight shiver of fear passing through him as he peered closer. "Is it a ghost or a maniac?" He withdrew a couple of steps, and shouted: "Hey, who are you?" vaguely remembering that if it were a ghost it would run away on hearing such a challenge. But the answer came back. "I'm Dr. Pal, journalist, correspondent and author." Margayya espied a row of white teeth bared in a grin. (63)

("Dr." Pal's self-description earned an appreciative rephrasing by David McCutchion, in his *Indian Writing in English*, as: "trickster, pornographist and card-sharper.")

I know of no contemporary author, Indian or otherwise, who articulates so clearly the essence of his vision, and who adumbrates the vision with such charm and variety. He is simultaneously less familiarly Indian than the West may think, and more profoundly Indian than his native critics take him for.

The Financial Expert, published in 1952 but set ten years earlier in still-British India, is not an accurate portrait of Indian reality (the war time was tumultuous in India, with mass starvation in Bengal, open disputes over loyalty to the British war effort or to Independence, etc.), but it is, I submit, a moving and comic dramatization of the allowances built into the Hindu imagination to accommodate the roles of myth, mysticism, illusion, play, ignorance, and sheer human folly. In other words, Margayya is a fully human character (the only one in the book, with the possible exception of Balu), but he possesses the capacity, and dedication, for entering that timeless realm. The novel details the trial Margayya undergoes for that ambition.

Nearly all of Narayan's novels employ the same basic conflict: a weak (meaning limited, confined by maya) human figure, apparently trapped in an endless cycle of poverty, oppression, or frustration, is temporarily lifted into the world of his deepest desires. The agency for uplift is often the arrival, from outside Malgudi, of a new economic force. It promises liberation (financial or sexual), but it is, of course, yet another form of bondage. By luck, design, or cunning (or in the case of Margayya, prayer), the simple hero joins forces with the outsider, and is borne far above the world he has known, only to come crashing down, and back to the original point of departure.

At this stage, that of simple plot outline, it is easy to sympathize with Narayan's harshest critics: fatalism is too manifest, fate overpowers plot and character. Change is always illusory—why struggle? If we are attracted to novels for their rendering of character, and for the pleasures we take in their growth and change, for the rewards of following a complicated plot, then we are likely to feel shortchanged by Narayan's predeterminism. Indians, at least those critics to whom I have referred, feel embarrassed by Narayan's underlying Hindu chauvinism, and by his other-worldly inattention to India's persistent social and political squalor.

These points are well taken. I do not intend to argue them. The misery and injustice of Indian life is of as little consequence in Narayan's fiction as similar conditions are, say, in Jane Austen's. (In Indo-Anglian fiction they are the property of Narayan's contemporary, Mulk Raj Anand, in many ways his opposite number.) I intend only to demonstrate how he works to minimize their absence.

The central point that should not be missed by any critic or reader is that Narayan, in conventional novelistic terms, is a careful, skilled craftsman. Consider Part One of *The Financial Expert*, from its opening omniscience to its emergence of the transformed Margayya, the new devotee of Lakshmi (1–71). We learn from the beginning that Margayya ("one who showed the way") has lost his own "way," in having lost his original name of Krishna. (Krishna, incidentally, is the eighth incarnation of Vishnu; Vishnu's wife is Lakshmi.) The novel is about his rediscovery of his true nature. In setting scenes, introducing characters, and foreshadowing motivation, Narayan is impeccable.

At the novel's opening, Margayya is surviving under his banyan tree as a small-time money lender. He advances small sums to credulous villagers so that they might deposit them in the Co-Operative Bank and withdraw yet greater sums. He keeps all his records in his sacred little ledger. He secures his profit at both ends of the transaction. (The nameless narrator notes: "If the purpose of the co-operative movement was the promotion of thrift and the elimination of middlemen, those two were just the objects that were defeated here under the banyan tree.") His manner with the rustics is gruff and lordly. With the lowly Christian peon of the bank he is cruel and mocking; with the Co-Operative Bank Secretary, he is predictably servile.

When he is humiliated by the secretary, his life begins to fall apart. He is oppressed by signs of other people's wealth. In a long walk from the banyan tree to his house, he passes scavengers, corpse bearers, toddy tappers, and finally pauses to watch cars turning onto Lawley Extension. By then, he has convinced himself that money is the equal of air or food; without money, men are beasts. He thinks then of giving a car and education to his son, giving everything to his boy, and his mood brightens. By now, he has fantasized Balu through the local colleges and on to America for advanced degrees. "He would buy another bungalow in Lawley Road for his son, and then his vision went on to the next generation of aristocrats" (29).

And then, of course, the priest appears, "a cadaverous man, burnt by the sun, wrapped in a long piece of white cloth." He delays going home and "spoiling his son" in order to follow the priest on his round of duties. It is not in Margayya's nature to do so—he is ignorant of ritual, a thoroughly secular figure—but he is about to be transformed. The priest is one of Narayan's perfectly realized figures of human indifference, rather like Forster's Dr. Godbole ("We are so late!" "Late for what?"). He introduces Margayya to the goddess Lakshmi, in her form as a glass of milk. So the seed is planted. Lakshmi demands total devotion.

His son, a convincing portrait of the willful Indian boy-child, throws the ledger book down into the sewer. Without the sacred book, trusted by the villagers, Margayya is cheated by his clients. He cannot back up his bluster; he is forced to reassess his life. He returns to the temple, this time with the intention of propitiating Lakshmi. He can even take snuff in the temple; this shows that he is becoming a new man, for devotees of Lakshmi can do as they please, once she has bestowed her glance on them. When he returns for the third visit with his horoscope, the priest begins laying out the various rites he must perform. The priest seems to change personality: formerly mild and saintly, he grows increasingly mocking and irritable.

Honey, antelope skins, red lotus petals burnt with ghee from a smoke-colored cow—these strange protocols lead immediately to the meeting with Dr. Pal and the presentation of Pal's pornographic "sociology" that will launch him as a "publisher" and man of wealth. Everything is carefully prepared for; all scenes unroll with realistic credibility—yet everything is happening, simultaneously, in two worlds.

Narayan's heroes, like his style and dramaturgy, are far more complex than they first appear. Admittedly, they are not psychologically complex, nor are they provided with a compelling personal history. Of Margayya we know only his ancestors had been corpse bearers who ascended the ladder of caste (but fear detection), and that he despises his brother (whose property he shares) with the same irrational compulsion that he brings to loving his son, Balu. A line such as "He felt a desire to go home and spoil his son" in all its simplicity goes a long way to redeeming Margayya's character, at least for the Western reader. As we shall see, Margayya's stifling devotion to Balu is yet another form of maya, a veil of attachment and illusion that must be shed. By tracking Margayya's paternal love, from blind devotion to final indifference, Narayan is able to plot Margayya's spiritual growth away from maya towards enlightenment.

Margayya is memorable. He is a cheat and a fraud. He gained vision from the optician, then bullied him when the bill was presented. He is overbearing, tyrannical, and servile: in short, a comic creation, combining the earnestness, bluster, and clumsiness of a great comic straight man (like an Oliver Hardy) with a clownish tragedy akin to that of Gogol, Kafka, or Beckett. Very few authors could get away with as many damning observations about a hero—irritable, inconsistent, deceiving—yet still retain the reader's sympathy.

Above it all, Narayan communicates an essential truth about Margayya: gods are struggling for his soul. He is a foolish mortal who has prayed for wealth, and (alas!) his prayers have been answered. Goddess Lakshmi has granted him the vision of wealth:

> There was probably no other person in the whole country who had meditated so much on the question of interest. Margayya's mind was full of it. . . . It combined in it the mystery of birth and multiplication. . . . It was something like the ripening of corn. Every rupee, Margayya felt, contained in it the seed of another rupee and that seed in it another seed and so on to infinity. It was something like the firmament, endless stars and within each star an endless firmament and within each one further endless. . . . It bordered on mystic perception. It gave him the feeling of being part of an infinite existence. (116–17)

His body and soul have been taken over. Even as he journeys to Madras to pick up the body (as he understands it) of his son, he is calculating profit and loss. Agents of other gods are trying to reach him—Guru Raj, the unseen blanket salesman behind his pile of goods; Murti, the old tutor who teaches Balu the difference between Lakshmi and Saraswati; Madan Lal, the honest printer; his wife; the police inspector; the "madman" who sends postcards to Churchill, Roosevelt, Stalin, and even Margayya of Malgudi— but he is not yet ready to hear them.

He is in the grip of Lakshmi and she will not let go. We are told by the temple priest early in the novel that two goddesses are fighting over Margayya: Lakshmi and Saraswati (the goddess of enlightenment). No other gods will disturb the devotee of Saraswati (knowledge and enlightenment, in other words, are self-sufficient); Lakshmi is always on tiptoe, ready to flee. But after his arduous devotions, Margayya has banished Saraswati from his house. In his love of money he has gained the material world, the fortune he once dreamed of, but he has lost his son and wife, and his immortal soul. He has prayed for wealth and attained it; he has bent his son's horoscope, he has bribed his son's teachers, and his son has become a classroom donkey.

The loss of Balu to mindless, unredeemed pleasure and materialism (the legacy of Dr. Pal) is the true marker of Margayya's fall. Margayya's very late recognition of this fact, during his long-delayed duty-visit to Balu's wife, listening to her tears and confessions, leads to the eruption of his dormant humanity. He attacks the source of his, and Balu's, damnation: Dr. Pal. This attack leads to his financial ruin as his pyramid scheme collapses in the wake of Dr. Pal's malicious gossip.

The source of wealth is the source of misery; the deepest alienation is at the moment of greatest wealth; the hint of enlightenment is at the moment of prostrating grief and impoverishment. In the end, he once again is speaking to a recognizable human being—his son, Balu—no longer trying to bribe his love or shape his future. The only vision he can offer his son is a return to the banyan tree with a ledger and box. "I am showing you a way. Will you follow it?" When Balu shows his reluctance ("What will people say?") Margayya—or perhaps we should now say Krishna—asserts that he will go back to the banyan tree. Then he calls for Balu's baby ("I will play with him"), an echo of Krishna's own playfulness as a god. Margayya has been seduced and abandoned by the goddess Lakshmi (wealth), after an ardent courtship, only to be returned to the pinched, impoverished embrace of Saraswati (enlightenment).

Time, like plot, for Narayan is cyclical. Change is illusion. People cannot change their fate. They can, at best, deflect the gaze of the gods for a brief moment (years are but seconds in the eye of Brahma) before the inevitable reversal. Most of Narayan's characters accept their loss and have gained enlightenment.

The endings are, admittedly, moralistic, but they teach a moral that is very easy to misinterpret in the West. For all his celebrated geniality, Narayan is not Frank Capra. Balu's return from the dead, when he is "restored" from his putative death in Madras, leads only to his accelerated degeneration. Margayya's return to his senses at the close of the book is not an occasion for elation; it is sobering and detached. He will protect his house, but over the rest he has no control. Margayya's final offer to Balu is everything he has—the original pen and bottle of ink. It is a heartfelt gesture, but offered disinterestedly: take it or leave it. It is all he has.

He has finally achieved a god's perspective, that of detachment. He has overcome the maya of attachment, even to his son. He will no longer seek to save Balu from his destiny, nor to shape the world to accommodate his weaknesses. The propitiated gods— even Saraswati—demand total devotion. It will be recalled how even their agents, such as Dr. Pal, demand everything in Margayya's purse, in the selling of the pornographic manuscript, even rice and milk money. One rupee, if it is everything, is worth more than a share of several millions, as even Balu must learn in the end.

Readers might have the feeling, possibly intended by the author, that life beyond the banyan tree is itself an illusion. In other words, the contrast between meticulous realism in Part One and increasing trancelike fantasy (up to the final scenes of money sacks and the hordes of creditors descending on the house) never truly occurred. It is as though Margayya had been given a privileged glimpse—a divine perspective. Should he choose the tempting path of Lakshmi, only to see the rupture with his beloved son, the ruin of his name, and the inevitable return to the banyan tree and his scuffed little box of accounts?

Materially, his life has not changed. He has lost nothing, only the maya of great wealth. He ends with precisely the same possessions as he had when he began. But his tone, his love, and his acceptance are different. The transformation, true to the Hindu vision, is one of perspective; he has briefly shared a divine vision and the trace of this remains with him.

TOPICS FOR DISCUSSION

1. What is the relationship of the human and the divine realms in Narayan's work and how is this duality reflected in the structure of the novel? Does an apparently fatalistic vision impede his novelistic options with regard to plot and characterization?

2. Narayan portrays Malgudi as a sleepy middle class South Indian town without pressing social problems. Would it be fruitful to compare Narayan to recent writers of other cultures or is his idiom too peculiarly Indian and too idiosyncratic? How successfully does he convey the Indian experience for Western readers?

3. Does the novel have a mythic quality in spite of the low-key

depiction of everyday events? Do you see resemblances to specific Hindu myths or to classical Western mythology?

4. How pervasive is Narayan's humor and how is it realized in *The Financial Expert*? How well is it served by his dry, distant style?

NOTE

1. Page numbers refer to the University of Chicago Press, 1981 edition of *The Financial Expert.*

REFERENCES

Gerow, Edwin. "The Quintessential Narayan." *Literature East and West,* vol. 10, no. 1–2 (1966): 1–18.

Mehta, Ved. "Profiles [R.K. Narayan]: The Train Had Just Arrived at Malgudi Station." *The New Yorker,* 15 September 1962: 51–90.

Walsh, William. *R.K. Narayan: A Critical Appreciation.* London: Heinemann, 1982.

THE SHORT STORIES OF PREMCHAND

David Rubin

> I want the plots for my stories to be taken from life and to solve life's problems.

This statement of Premchand, from a letter written in 1930, expresses his fundamental conception of the short story: it should be both realistic and a medium for education and social reform. It is difficult to gauge how radical this conception was in Hindi literature when Premchand began writing fiction at the turn of the twentieth century. One should also note at the outset that at his best Premchand often happily transcends this formulation of the short story.

Some of the earliest (and best) storytelling known to the world had its origin in India. For hundreds of years before the common era, it flourished in the form of immense epics (which encapsulated countless digressive tales), and later in extensive anthologies, religious and secular fables, elaborate romances, and, from medieval times on, the *dāstān* or *qissā*—long, elaborate folk romances dealing with enchantments and adventure. Nevertheless, fiction as we understand it in the West is a fairly recent genre in India. From the middle of the nineteenth century, novels imitating English models began to appear in various Indian regional languages. These works are characterized by didacticism and moralizing, and are generally only of historical interest today. Realistic elements are not lacking in some of this fiction, especially in novels written in Bengali and Urdu, but it is Premchand who firmly establishes realism not only in Hindi but in modern Indian literature in general. In India, Premchand can be said to have created the genre of the short story (as distinguished from the tale), shaping it into a vehicle for the realistic portrayal of contemporary life and the exploration of its pyschological and social problems.

This vital new literature emerged along with what was basically a new literary language. Until the second half of the nineteenth century, serious literature in Hindi had been written mostly in Braj, a phase of the language substantially different from what we call Hindi today. Braj, still spoken in the districts around Mathura and Agra, had a long history as a highly developed literary medium. It is famed for the devotional songs of the bhakti poets, particularly Sur Das in the sixteenth century, and the secular poetry of Bihari Lal in the seventeenth. By the mid-nineteenth century, Braj literature was played out and writers began to experiment with *khaṛi boli* Hindi, the standard Hindi spoken around Delhi and Meerut. Though held by conservatives of the old school to be crude and incapable of refined literary expression, *khaṛi boli* Hindi soon attracted the best new writing talents, and by the second decade of the twentieth century the new Hindi literature was in full flower. The romantic-symbolist poetry of Prasad, Nirala, and Pant, and Premchand's realistic fiction were the first great creations of the new movement, and were quite unlike anything known before in Hindi of any type. The simultaneity of the literary and linguistic revolutions no doubt facilitated the adoption of new forms based on imported models, particularly the short independent lyric and the short story.

Dhanpat Rai, known after 1920 by his pen name Premchand, was born in 1880 in a small village near Banaras in the United Provinces (today Uttar Pradesh). Except for a few months in Bombay in 1933 to write scenarios for a film company and brief visits to other cities for literary conferences, he spent his entire life in eastern Uttar Pradesh, mostly in Banaras, Lucknow, and Allahabad. He belonged to a community, the Kayasths, known for its writers, lawyers, and teachers, and though his family was poor he had a good education in Persian and Urdu. By the time he began his career as a teacher in 1905 he had already had a novel serialized in a Banaras journal from 1903 to 1905. (Dating Premchand's early work is difficult, particularly as the author himself made conflicting statements about his earliest publications.)

Patriotism and romantic love dominate Premchand's first short story collection, published in 1908. Britain is not specifically mentioned in the patriotic tales because of the increasingly strict government censorship. Instead, Premchand chose subjects from medieval times or foreign history (one of the stories is about Mazzini), in which his opposition to British rule could be disguised by attacking past oppressors or glorifying other independence movements. This strategy did not forestall the banning of his collection in 1909 and the burning of all unsold copies. Soon after this, while continuing to write, he accepted a government post as Sub-Deputy Inspector of Schools. In 1921, partly as a result of Gandhi's call for noncooperation with the government, he resigned this position. From that time on, Premchand had to contend with severe financial difficulties (despite a steadily growing reputation) and chronic ill health that continued until his death in 1936. During his lifetime he published fourteen novels (preparing both Hindi and Urdu versions of most of them), short stories, plays, screenplays, translations, and criticism, and in addition worked virtually full-time as an editor, journalist, and press manager.

Early on, Premchand was influenced by Tolstoy and Chekhov, later by Gorki, and very likely by some of the other English and European writers he translated, including George Eliot, Galsworthy, and Anatole France. As early as 1910, Premchand began to write realistic fiction, although some romantic elements persist in his work for another decade or more. Social questions command his interest from this time on, and in both novels and short stories he deals with such subjects as poverty, prostitution, bribery, and corruption. Since his life span coincided with the most significant phase of India's independence struggle and the career of Mahatma Gandhi, his near contemporary, it is not surprising to find the impact of the noncooperation movement and Indian disillusionment with Western civilization (particularly after the outbreak of the European war in 1914) apparent in his writing. His patriotic impulse in the twenties took the form of satire of those Indians who, for material gain, cooperated with the British, as in "A Little Trick" and "A Moral Victory." His novels, like Dickens', often take a particular institution or social problem as the central theme—zamindari exploitation in *Premāshram* (*The Sanctuary of Love*), 1922; industrialization in *Rangabhūmi* (*The Arena*, 1924); the dowry system in *Nirmalā* (1926); educational reform and political oppression in *Karmabhūmi* (*The Field of Action*, 1931). But as Premchand matured as a writer, his attention was increasingly directed toward village life, not simply as a social problem but particularly as a stage for complex psychological drama of universal significance. This maturity is best revealed in his two finest achievements, *Godān* (*The Gift of a Cow*, 1936), his last completed novel, and *Kafan* (*The Shroud*), a collection of late stories (published posthumously in 1937).

Premchand's approximately three hundred short stories, some of which are still appearing for the first time in book form, have tremendous range. Leaving aside the very early romantic tales of India's past, the stories for purposes of discussion can be classified roughly as follows: the anecdotal or joke story ("A Lesson in the Holy Life" or, on a patriotic theme, "A Moral Victory"); the patriotic fable ("A Little Trick"); scenes or genre paintings of village life ("The Road to Salvation," "A Catastrophe"); the purely psychological story of human character (Chekhovian in "A Coward," Gandhian in "Penalty"); and the account of tragic human delusion and failure ("The Chess Players" and "Deliverance").

Premchand's stories bear a strong resemblance to Western models, but there are certain essential differences that stem from their cultural framework and historical circumstances. The basis for traditional Indian society, particularly in the village, is (at least theoretically) religious rather than economic. Westerners tend to think of "caste" as a social distinction, like "class," but in fact it is one of the basic modes of expressing the religious principles by which the Hindu world functions. The circumstances of one's birth in a particular community are immutably determined, and there is no question of mobility from one caste group to another, as there can be in even the most rigid Western social classes. The fulfillment of one's social obligations, or dharma, is therefore not a question of propriety, as it would be in the West, but—at least for the religious Hindu—a sacred imperative. (This explains in part the tremendous importance Premchand's village characters accord to "losing face," for to be disgraced is not merely a matter of social stigma but of sin.) Universal human nature being what it is, this extraordinarily codified, rigid social order does not prevent the emergence of individuals who turn out to be opportunistic, greedy, cruelly indifferent to the suffering of others, and so on. These individuals operate with mechanical efficiency within the religiously ordained patterns of society while they exploit it cynically, often without any apparent awareness of the monstrous contradictions their actions embody.

Premchand's rationalistic outlook viewed religious values as dehumanized, consisting of mere technical observances, a kind of dangerous insanity rife with destructive delusions. These values allowed the powerful and hypocritical to exploit the weak, and drove the decent man to destroy himself. The exploration of such confusions between real and illusory provides the basic material for his most successful stories.

In Western literature the conflicts of illusion and reality form the basis of both comedy and tragedy. The tragic hero learns the truth—discovers, for example, the nature of his hubris or the identity of those who actually love or hate him—at the expense of his life (or his capacity to fulfill his life); Lear and Oedipus are typical. In comedy the hero learns and survives. His basic search for reality leads him through a maze of deception, disguise, mistakes (about motives, identity, and even sex), culminating with his enlightenment. The forest of Arden, to cite an obvious example, is not Eden; and Rosalind and Orlando, with new knowledge of themselves and each other, return to the "real world" to try to create a more genuine pastoral dream in their hearts.

The confusion of illusion and reality in Premchand's stories is of a different order. The protagonists, tragic or tragicomic, rarely succeed in dispelling their illusions or attaining any kind of philosophical insight that would allow them to transcend, at least spiritually, the cruel limitations of their lives. Although Premchand set great store by the psychological development of his characters, he rarely allows them to achieve a breakthrough of understanding or a reversal of their circumstances. Only in the more decidedly comic stories are disillusionment and new insight possible. In "Intoxication," a young man is made to learn the absurdity of his snobbish pretensions, while in "My Big Brother" a boy comes to understand the love and devotion of his apparently tyrannical older brother. The protagonist of "The Writer," after a brief unhappy encounter with wealthy society, is content to return to his obscure and humble sphere. In "Ramlila," a child is disenchanted on discovering that his father, a police official, is corrupt. Small rewards are the most Premchand's characters can hope for. In the darker stories, which make up a proportionately larger number of Premchand's later fiction, the protagonist is often overwhelmed by adverse circumstances without understanding them.

"The Chess Players" (1924), one of Premchand's most famous stories, is an example of the author treating illusion in a somewhat allegorical way. It is also one of the few stories from his later period which harks back to an earlier historical era. The action is of the briefest: while Lucknow, capital of the kingdom of Avadh (Oudh), remains stupefied in irresponsible luxury and aestheticism, the kingdom becomes more and more chaotic, offering the British the opportunity to take over in a bloodless coup and send the king into exile. Rather abstract descriptions of Lucknow's decadence and the disorder in the countryside alternate with the specific fable of two nobles of the court, Mir and Mirza, whose obsession is chess. Ironically, their passion has made them as disciplined and austere as ascetics: they are capable of profound concentration and have become indifferent to food and the comforts of home, in contrast to the extreme sensual self-indulgence that typifies the city. Impatient with her husband's chess playing, which upsets the household routine, Mirza's wife puts an end to the games, whereupon the two continue for a while in Mir's house. But Mir's wife finds this inconvenient because she is engaged in a love affair with a cavalry officer. The lover contrives to drive the chess players away by making them think that they have been summoned to the king for conscription into the army. To avoid this the chess players leave their homes early every morning and hold their games in a desolate ruined mosque outside of town, an action that caricatures the holy man's genuine renunciation of worldly pleasures. As they play one day they observe the British army marching on Lucknow, but this only diverts the player who is losing. Later in the afternoon they see the army marching back, carrying the king off to exile. A dispute about chess moves leads them to exchange violent insults until they draw their swords—for although sensualists, as Premchand says, they are not cowards—and both die in the ensuing combat. The two kings on the chessboard survey the fallen heroes amidst the brooding ruins as darkness falls on the scene. The game, obviously, should be a part of life, but instead the players make life a part of the game. Their confusion of reality and illusion goes so far that while they remain indifferent to the fate of their king—except when one of the players becomes elegiac on the subject as a device to disrupt his opponent's game—they will die to defend their chess kings. The story might be seen as allegorizing the tragic situation of pre-independence India divided against itself and abandoned by an irresponsible upper class, but it is likely that Premchand intended merely to tell a story of destructive obsession. The (probably later) Urdu version even adds a line to the story's conclusion about the transience of human life.

In his best stories, Premchand most often deals with humbler people in less melodramatic circumstances. Consider "A Feast for the Holy Man" (ca. 1932) as a small example in the tragicomic vein. In this brief story (two pages in the Hindi), a "holy man" appears at the door of a virtually destitute farmer and bestows his blessing. Although they have almost nothing to eat themselves, the farmer and his wife put together a scanty meal for him. The sadhu asks for more, and finally for ghee. Losing patience, the farmer complains to his wife about this "beggar's" demands. But she replies, "After everything else, why make him angry with us just for this?" and he goes out to borrow the ghee. The sadhu has a fine repast, and while he sleeps the farmer scours his plate, pot, and ladle. That night, when he goes to bed hungry, the farmer reflects, "Well, he's a better man than I am!"

The conclusion remains ambiguous: is the farmer being ironic when he calls the sadhu the "better man"? He has shown some anger at the fellow's demands but accepts his wife's caution: "Why make him angry with us?" If the sadhu is angry he will not bestow his blessing, and may even curse them. The tradition of the angry sage (Durvasas in the *Shakuntala* and countless legends) is still strong, it seems, and since it is the religious obligation of everyone to support holy men, no matter how preposterous the circumstances, the sadhu must be fed. He is indeed the "better man" when it comes to survival. For Premchand the religious devotion that supports such sadhus defies common sense: illusion triumphs over reality, and Premchand's realistic art over the moralizing tendency that sometimes mars his work.

In "The Thakur's Well," (1932) Gangi, a low-caste woman, desperately looks for water for her sick husband because the water from the low castes' well is polluted and undrinkable. She attempts to "steal" water from the well used by the high-caste Thakurs but is frightened away. "You'll come back with your arms and legs broken," her husband has told her, "you'd better just sit down and keep quiet." She returns home to find her husband drinking the foul water from their own well. The story is replete with ironies: "Thakur" means "lord," and like the English word may refer either to a nobleman or to the supreme deity, while "Gangi" evokes the Ganges, the holy river. Like "A Feast for the Holy Man" the story is told without editorializing, but here the protagonist herself has a voice: Gangi has no illusions about the higher-caste people of the village. She knows that the priest, the landlord, and the shopkeeper—a symbolic triad of the three "twice-born" castes (Brahmin, Kshatriya, and Vaishya)—are all cheats, thieves, and debauchees who lust for her; they are cruel as well and, as she learns from an overheard conversation, treat their womenfolk like slaves. The "religious" structure of Hindu society is revealed as a fraud, in which the professed ideal serves to mask the most vicious egotism and provides a license for the rapacious exploitation of the poor. But even when, as here, the protagonist is free of the illusion, the general acceptance of that illusion by the rest of society makes it impossible to behave sanely.

Unlike the farmer in "A Feast for the Holy Man," Dukhi, the protagonist of "Deliverance," has no doubts about the superiority of the Brahmins and accepts without reservation their absolute claim on his devoted service. In this story, which is Premchand's most extreme treatment of caste-sanctioned inhumanity, Dukhi, a tanner (and hence untouchable), requires the Brahmin, Pandit Ghasiram, to fix an auspicious date for his daughter's betrothal. The action begins with what promises to be a comedy of the absurd: where will Ghasiram sit when he comes to Dukhi's hut? No Brahmin, Dukhi and his wife conclude, would consider sitting on anything so unclean as a tanner's cot; finally they decide that since Brahmins eat off plates made of leaves from the mohwa tree, a mat made of such leaves ought to be pure enough for him to sit on. For the Brahmin's food they will have to borrow flour, rice, gram, ghee, and spices, and of course be certain not to touch it when they offer it on leaf plates. Ghasiram agrees to come after Dukhi has done a variety of chores for him—sweeping, plastering, and chopping wood—while he himself goes in to have lunch and rest. But Dukhi meets his match in one particular block of wood that cannot be split. Exhausted, he decides to take a little rest and smoke. When he asks Ghasiram's wife for a light for his pipe, she is furious because he has stepped on her veranda. She brings him a burning coal in a pair of tongs and flings it at him, burning his head. His reaction: "This is what comes of dirtying a Brahmin's house. How quickly God pays you back for it!" Feeling a little remorse, Ghasiram's wife considers giving him something to eat, but she dismisses the idea when the Pandit reminds her that a couple of pieces of bread won't do for a tanner, and he will want at least two pounds. He suggests she make some pancakes, but she says, "Let's forget the whole thing. I'm not going to kill myself cooking in weather like this."

Dukhi in the meantime resumes his attempt to split the wood. His friend the Gond (a man of another low caste) tells him the Brahmin is a fraud who exploits the poor, a critical view which shocks Dukhi. Ghasiram comes out and encourages him to try a little harder with the wood. When Dukhi finally splits it he collapses. The Pandit exhorts him to split it into smaller pieces and leaves; when he comes back he realizes that Dukhi is dead. The problem now is how to dispose of the corpse, which he cannot touch. The Gond goes to the tanners' village and advises them not to go for the body if they want to avoid trouble with the police. The other Brahmins of the settlement are angry with Ghasiram because the corpse blocks access to their well. By the next day the stench is unbearable; the Pandit finally disposes of Dukhi's corpse by throwing a noose around the dead man's feet and hauling it out of the village, where the jackals and crows will take care of it.

The whole story is told with suppressed irony. Premchand writes: "When he saw the Pandit's glorious figure [Dukhi's] heart was filled with reverence. How godly a sight!—a rather short, roly-poly fellow with a bald, shiny skull, chubby cheeks, and eyes aglow with brahminical energy." Here the author faithfully reproduces Dukhi's naive reaction, generating irony in our response without imposing his own view. His only intrusion into the narrative is at the very end when he writes, "This was the reward of a whole life of devotion, service, and faith." This rather obvious moralizing is a flaw in an otherwise superb story, a kind of black comedy in which illusion triumphs over common sense. The Pandit and his wife are totally blind to the absurdity of their position, which Dukhi, equally blind because of his faith in their supposed godly superiority, perpetuates. Lives are destroyed by the illusion of "touch" as constituting contamination according to preconceived rules rather than actual cleanliness; on a grander scale, Hindu dharma itself has come to function in a way that can only be described as unholy. Premchand renders this shocking story bearable by wisely giving voice to our indignation through Dukhi's Gond friend, who expresses a normal, rational human reaction.

The name Dukhi means "sorrowful," a name bestowed sometimes by village people to ward off the envy of the gods; in "Deliverance" the irony is obvious enough as we see Dukhi earn his name all too literally. The protagonist of "The Price of Milk" (1934) is named, with equal irony, Mangal, "auspicious." With its theme of oppression on the basis of caste, this story offers a parallel to "Deliverance," but the mode is different. Mangal is an untouchable orphan whose mother, Bhungi, has acted as wet nurse for a high-caste landowner's son. While she is nursing, Bhungi is treated like the mistress of the house. After her death Mangal is allowed to live nearby under a tree and is fed with the leavings from the family table. The climactic action of the story comes when the upper-caste children, playing a game of horse-and-rider, refuse to give Mangal his turn as rider; Mangal rebels and throws Suresh, the landowner's son, off his back. Suresh complains to his mother that Mangal has touched him. She reprimands Mangal harshly and would like to beat him, but of course she cannot touch him without being contaminated. Mangal decides to run away, but after a day without eating he creeps back to the house to get his share of the leftovers from the servant. Unlike Dukhi, instead of a human friend he has only a stray dog for confidant. At the story's end he tells the dog how his own mother nursed Suresh—and this is the return he's getting for it.

Instead of black comedy here we have a naturalistic tragicomedy about the illusions spawned by caste. The landowner's family are not monstrous like Pandit Ghasiram, but ordinary people, normally decent, even affectionate and grateful toward Mangal's mother. Their mindless adherence to caste restrictions, at least in this particular instance, is not exploited for profit but is rather a kind of strict social etiquette. Given their mild nature, their concept of dharma (righteousness), which will condemn Mangal to lifelong serfdom, is even more astounding. When a Brahmin objects to an untouchable woman nursing Suresh beyond the prescribed time, the landowner teases him: "Until yesterday the child was nourished by the blood of this same untouchable, so he must already be contaminated. My my, that's a great religion you've got!" and even chides him for the way caste rules are broken to accommodate emergencies: "So . . . morality changes, sometimes one thing, sometimes another?" Yet in the long run he and his family accept the caste taboos, contradictions notwithstanding, as the way things must be. Premchand himself never intrudes in the story, although perhaps he intends to suggest a glimmer of hope in Mangal's rebelliousness and awareness of the inequality and injustice in the social order.

Despite the profound changes in Indian urban society (which constitutes the majority of the reading public), as well as in general literary taste, enthusiasm for Premchand continues to be strong in his homeland. Although contemporary writers focus on the urban scene and psychological problems (existentialist angst, for example), Premchand's panoramic portrait of Indian society in his stories and novels remains the outstanding accomplishment in fiction of the renaissance of Hindi literature.

TOPICS FOR DISCUSSION

1. How do Premchand's themes and attitudes relate to those of other works in the Indian tradition?

2. Is there evidence of the influence of Western ideas in his work?

3. How do Gandhian or Tolstoyan ideas and themes emerge in Premchand's work?

4. Examine the role of women in the stories, and the way it

compares with the role of women in other works of Asian literature.

5. Some Indians claim that Premchand is essentially Marxist in his outlook. Do you see any evidence of this?

6. Discuss Premchand's attitude toward religion.

7. Discuss Premchand's conflicting attitudes of idealism and realistic observation.

8. Premchand is often compared to Chekhov. In the short fiction of Chekhov (and many other twentieth-century short story writers, such as Mansfield, Joyce, and Hemingway), among the characteristics most often cited are: (1) unity of action; (2) psychological realism; (3) understatement; and (4) dispensing with conventional plot structure leading to a climax. Can any of these be applied to Premchand?

9. Premchand is acknowledged as a master in the portrayal of rural life. In this respect is he comparable to Western writers who deal with this subject—Hardy, for example, or Faulkner?

REFERENCES

Several collections of Premchand's short fiction have been published in India in paperback; the longest (thirty stories) and most readily available is *Deliverance and Other Stories*, translated, with introduction and notes, by David Rubin (New Delhi: Penguin Books India, 1988). A few other titles that may be of help in getting a wider sense of Premchand's achievement are:

Clark, T. W., ed. *The Novel in India*. London: Allen & Unwin, 1970.
Gupta, Prakash Chandra. *Premchand*. New Delhi: Sahitya Akademi, 1968.
Mukherjee, Meenakshi. *Realism and Reality: The Novel and Society in India*. Delhi: Oxford University Press, 1985.
Premchand. *The Gift of a Cow*. Translated by Gordon Roadarmel. Bloomington: Indiana University Press, 1968.
Premchand. *Nirmala*. Translated, with introduction, by David Rubin. New Delhi: Orient Paperbacks, 1987.

Filmography

Satyajit Ray, India's best-known film director, has made films in Hindi of two of Premchand's stories, "Śatrañj ke Khilāṛī" (*The Chess Players*) in 1977; and "Sadgati" (*Deliverance*) in 1981.

Indian Texts: Narrative

SALMAN RUSHDIE: *MIDNIGHT'S CHILDREN*

Robin Jared Lewis

In 1980, a new novel by an unknown Indian writer living in London burst upon the literary scene. It was received with enormous enthusiasm by critics both in India and abroad, and some went so far as to suggest that here at last was a viable candidate for the Great Indian Novel—if such a thing indeed existed. The novel was Salman Rushdie's *Midnight's Children*, and with its publication "the literary map of India," as Clark Blaise put it, was irrevocably redrawn.

Since that time, Rushdie has been violently thrust into the international limelight by the intense controversy surrounding his latest novel, *The Satanic Verses* (1989). Rushdie has always been a literary incendiary and his densely detailed and fantastically allegorical work has aroused the ire of orthodox Muslims in many countries. Both *The Satanic Verses* and effigies of its author were burned in several cities, numerous governments (including those of India and Pakistan) barred its importation, and Iran's late spiritual leader Ayatollah Khomeini issued a call for Rushdie's death, prompting the embattled author's disappearance into hiding somewhere in England.

It would be unfortunate, however, if the controversy over *The Satanic Verses* distracted readers and scholars from what is surely Rushdie's principal achievement: in a remarkably short period of time, he has altered our vision of the Indian subcontinent, both in *Midnight's Children* (1980) and in *Shame* (1984), his story of a country that is "not Pakistan, or not quite." All of the earlier portrayals—both Western, such as Kipling's *Kim* and *Gunga Din*, or the echo of the Marabar Caves in Forster's *A Passage to India*, and Indian, like Raja Rao's Gandhian myths, R.

K. Narayan's gently eccentric South Indian villagers, or Ahmed Ali's decaying, melancholy Old Delhi—have been simultaneously subsumed into, and surpassed by, Rushdie's passionate evocations of the recent history of India and Pakistan. Rushdie's vision of India is breathtaking in its sweep, encompassing far more historical and fictional territory than any of his predecessors, and it attempts to weave together the diverse strands of the Subcontinent's cultural and linguistic identity into one enormous tapestry of unparalleled richness and vitality.

Rushdie also deserves credit for laying to rest—for good, one hopes—the endless and elephantine post-1947 debate as to whether the English language can play a viable role in expressing Indian realities. *Midnight's Children* is a glorious jumble of linguistic energy and suppleness, and it settles the question rather decisively: the language of the novel mirrors its various subjects with uncanny precision. The ramblings of Rushdie's narrator Saleem Sinai recall those of Shakespeare's word-eaters in *Love's Labour's Lost*, of whom it is said, "They have been at a great feast of languages, and stolen the scraps." Rushdie's acknowledged inspiration in his use of English is G. V. Desani, whose remarkable novel *All About H. Hatterr* (1948) was written in what Anthony Burgess called "Whole Language, in which philosophical terms, the colloquialisms of Calcutta and London, Shakespearean archaisms, bazaar whinings, quack spiels, references to the Hindu pantheon, the jargon of Indian litigation, and shrill babu irritability seethe together."[1] But Rushdie surpasses Desani by making his language the touchstone of identity in the novel, and there can be little doubt that this linguistic exuberance has provided a model for future writers who seek to recast the English language in Indian terms.

Midnight's Children chronicles the family history of the narrator, one Saleem Sinai, beginning in 1915 with his grandfather and ending in 1978, when Indira Gandhi's Emergency ended with her defeat at the polls. Saleem's life story is meant to illuminate the central Indian question of identity, of the relationship between the individual and the larger whole, be it the family, the faith, or the nation. "To understand just one life, you have to swallow the world" is Saleem's credo, echoing the myth of the young god Krishna, in whose mouth his mother, looking for some purloined butter, found the whole world represented. Rushdie's novel moves seamlessly from the historical to the personal and back again through the device of Saleem's narration. It is a tribute to the novel's extraordinary structure that Saleem manages to turn up at nearly every major event in recent Indian history, without the merest hint of contrivance.

Saleem's enormous monologue, at times rambling and circuitous, at other moments terse and abrupt, takes us through a series of magico-realistic events that have led critics to compare Rushdie's work with Gunter Grass's *The Tin Drum* and Gabriel Garcia Marquez's *One Hundred Years of Solitude*. Indeed, magic lies at the heart of the book, for the "midnight's children" of the title, born all over India in the first hour of the country's independence on August 15, 1947, possess magical powers that represent both the awesome potential and the terrible fragility of the new nation:

> Midnight's children! . . . From Kerala, a boy who had the ability of stepping into mirrors and re-emerging through any reflective surface in the land—through lakes and (with greater difficulty) the polished metal bodies of automobiles . . . and a Goanese girl with the gift of multiplying fish . . . and children with powers of transformation: a werewolf from the Nilgiri Hills, and from the great watershed of the Vindhyas, a boy who could increase or reduce his size at will, and had already (mischievously) been the cause of wild panic and rumours of the return of Giants . . .

Two of these children are born at the stroke of midnight in the same Bombay nursing home, but a nursemaid shuffles the babies, producing two hopelessly confused identities: the narrator Saleem, of mixed Indo-British parentage but with a Muslim name and a Hindu homeland, and his nemesis Shiva, born a Muslim but saddled with a Hindu name and a Muslim nation. These two represent Rushdie's notion of the essential duality of the modern Indian reality—Saleem, whose distinguishing characteristic is his enormous nose, is gentle and sensitive, while Shiva ("for whom the world was things, for whom history could only be explained as the continuing struggle of oneself-against-the-crowd"), symbolized by his powerful knees, is, like his mythical namesake, a destroyer; he becomes a much-feared military hero in Pakistan.

Other modern Indian novelists have written of the dilemmas of new nationhood, but only Rushdie acknowledges the fragility of India as an idea, describing it as

> . . . a mythical land, a country which would never exist except by the efforts of a phenomenal collective will—except in a dream we all agreed to dream; it was a mass fantasy shared in varying degrees by Bengali and Punjabi, Madrasi and Jat, and would

periodically need the sanctification and renewal which can only be provided by rituals of blood.[2]

The notion of "unity in diversity," that metaphysical and political mystery which is today an unofficial motto of the Indian state, lies at the heart of Rushdie's troubled vision of his homeland. Just as Saleem's narrative struggles to fashion a coherent whole out of the shards of his personal history, Rushdie tries to make sense out of the seemingly senseless juggernaut of India's recent history, thereby expressing what he calls "the national longing for form." The creative tension in the novel—and in modern Indian society, for that matter—is between the forces of fragmentation, represented by Shiva's solipsistic individualism, and the powerful desire for oneness, which Saleem characterizes as "the Indian disease, this urge to encapsulate the whole of reality." Herein lies the great power of *Midnight's Children*, a novel that transforms the age-old Indian obsession with paradox—with the riddle of singularity and multiplicity, of one-into-many—into a dynamic metaphor for the continuing hope and pain that are the legacy of a people who are, in Rushdie's words, "handcuffed to history."

* * *

The chronology given below is an attempt to illustrate the extraordinarily detailed structure of *Midnight's Children* and its juxtaposition of the fate of Saleem Sinai with that of modern India. Historical events are in CAPITAL LETTERS, while fictional ones are in lower case; the locations indicate where the action in the novel takes place, but do not necessarily signify the same for the historical moments given. All quotations are from the text of the novel.

1915   Kashmir: Aadam Aziz and the story of the Perforated Sheet, whereby Saleem's grandfather meets his future wife ("a partitioned woman") during a medical examination conducted through a bedsheet in accordance with Islamic propriety.

1919   Amritsar: AMRITSAR MASSACRE. At the precise moment when General Dyer's troops open fire, Aadam sneezes and falls to the ground, saving his life.

1942	Agra (site of the Taj Mahal, "that mausoleum which has been immortalized on postcards and chocolate boxes and whose outdoor corridors stink of urine and whose walls are covered in grafitti and whose echoes are tested for visitors by guides, although there are signs in three languages pleading for silence"): Mumtaz and Nadir Khan are married and live underground in their own Taj Mahal.
August, 1945	Agra: ATOM BOMB DROPPED ON HIROSHIMA. Nadir Khan drops a bombshell by fleeing the conjugal nest, divorcing his wife ("Talaaq! Talaaq! Talaaq!") en route.
June, 1946	Agra: Mumtaz is remarried to Ahmed Sinai and changes her name to Amina.
January, 1947	Delhi: THE CRIPPS MISSION. Amina's pregnancy and Ramram Seth's deadly accurate prophecy of Saleem's birth (". . . there will be knees and a nose, a nose and knees . . . Newspaper praises him, two mothers raise him! Sisters will weep; cobra will creep! . . . Washing will hide him—voices will guide him! Friends mutilate him—blood will betray him! . . . Spittoons will brain him—doctors will drain him—jungle will claim him—wizards reclaim him! Soldiers will try him—tyrants will fry him. . . . He will have sons without having sons! He will be old before he is old! And he will die . . . before he is dead"); Ahmed Sinai's godown is torched.
June 4, 1947	Delhi-Bombay: MOUNTBATTEN ANNOUNCES THE PARTITION OF INDIA. Saleem's family moves to Bombay.
June 19, 1947	Bombay: THE INDO-BRITISH HERITAGE NEARS ITS END. William Methwold signs over his property to Indians (" 'Bad business, Mr. Sinai. . . . Never seen the like. Hundreds of years of decent government, then suddenly, up and off. You'll admit we weren't all bad: built your roads.

Schools, railway trains, parliamentary system, all worthwhile things. Taj Mahal was falling down until an Englishman bothered to see to it. And now, suddenly, independence. Seventy days to get out. I'm dead against it myself, but what's to be done?' ").

August 15, 1947 Bombay: INDIA BECOMES INDEPENDENT AT THE STROKE OF MIDNIGHT. Saleem and Shiva are born at the same moment, but the babies are switched; Prime Minister Nehru sends his congratulations (" 'You are the newest bearer of that ancient face of India which is also eternally young. We shall be watching over your life with the closest attention; it will be, in a sense, the mirror of our own.' ").

January, 1948 Bombay: GANDHI'S ASSASSINATION. The premiere of Uncle Hanif's film (starring Saleem's Aunt Pia).

1956 Bombay: SUEZ CRISIS. The Brass Monkey (Saleem's sister, later to become Jamila Singer) incinerates footwear, while Saleem's adventure in the washing chest leads to the formation of the M.C.C. (Midnight's Children's Conference) through the medium of Saleem's nose ("All-India Radio").

December, 1956 Bombay: INDIA'S FIRST FIVE-YEAR PLAN. India begins to turn white ("All over India, I stumbled across good Indian businessmen, their fortunes thriving thanks to the first Five-Year Plan, which had concentrated on building up commerce . . . businessmen who had become or were becoming very, very pale indeed! It seems that the gargantuan [even heroic] efforts involved in taking over from the British and becoming masters of their own destinies had drained the colour from their cheeks. . . . The businessmen of India were turning white."); Dr. Narlikar's tetrapods and his subsequent death.

January, 1957   Bombay: INDIA IS BESET BY REGIONALISM—
MARATHI VS. GUJARATI IN BOMBAY, THE
RISE OF A NEW REGIONAL PARTY IN TAMIL
NADU, THE ELECTION CAMPAIGN BEGINS IN
KERALA. Evie Burns arrives and the "cracks" in
Saleem begin to show.

February, 1957   Bombay: BOMBAY STATE IS PARTITIONED
INTO TWO LINGUISTIC STATES, MAHA-
RASHTRA AND GUJARAT. Saleem, showing off
on his bicycle for Evie Burns, careens into a procession of language marchers and sets off a riot
("In this way I became directly responsible for trig-
gering off violence which ended with the partition
of the state of Bombay, as a result of which the
city became the capital of Maharashtra—so at
least I was on the winning side.").

August, 1957   Bombay: COMMUNIST GOVERNMENT ELECTED
IN KERALA. Saleem's (AND INDIA'S) tenth birthday; Saleem discovers his mother's secret meetings at the Pioneer Cafe with Nadir Khan (now
Qasim the Red).

1958   Bombay: GOAN LIBERATION COMMITTEE
LAUNCHES   SATYAGRAHA   CAMPAIGN/
SPEAKER OF E. PAK. ASSEMBLY DECLARED
MANIAC/NEHRU CONSIDERS RESIGNATION AT
CONGRESS ASSEMBLY/RIOTS, MASS AR-
RESTS IN RED-RUN KERALA: SABOTEURS RUN
AMOK etc. The episode of Commander Sabarmati's Baton, wherein Saleem composes an
anonymous letter ("Commander Sabarmati, Why
does your wife go to Colaba Causeway on Sun-
day morning?") out of fragments of newspaper
headlines; Uncle Hanif's suicide; Mary Pereira's
revelation that it was she who switched the
babies.

September, 1958 Pakistan ("The Land of the Pure"): Saleem and
his family go into "exile" in Karachi.

October, 1958   Pakistan: GENERAL AYUB KHAN'S COUP. Zafar

Zulfikar wets his pants, but Saleem rises to the occasion by moving the tableware around to illustrate the logistics of the coup. He later accompanies Major Zulfikar on the midnight raid in which the President of Pakistan is routed naked from his bed.

1958–1962	Pakistan: U.S. ARMS TO PAKISTAN, SINO-IN-DIAN BORDER SKIRMISHES, CONGRESS PARTY WINS 1962 ELECTIONS. Saleem remains in exile.
1962	Back-to-Bombay: SINO-INDIAN BORDER WAR. Saleem returns to India; the Midnight's Children's Conference breaks into pieces; Saleem's "First Drainage" (his nose) takes place.
February, 1963	Pakistan: Saleem returns to Pakistan.
December 27, 1963	Kashmir: THE HAIR OF THE PROPHET MUHAMMAD IS STOLEN FROM THE HAZRATBAL MOSQUE IN SRINAGAR. Aadam Aziz returns home to die.
January 1, 1964	Kashmir: PRIME MINISTER NEHRU FALLS ILL (AND DIES IN MAY). Aadam Aziz dies.
April, 1965	Pakistan: FIRST INDO-PAKISTANI WAR BREAKS OUT OVER KASHMIR AND THE RANN OF KUTCH. Zafar Zulfikar kills his father.
September, 1965	Pakistan: INDIAN AIR FORCE BOMBS PAKISTANI CITIES. Saleem's family is killed in the bombings, while Saleem himself is brained by the family spittoon and forgets who he is.
1965–1971	Pakistan: THE FALL OF AYUB KHAN, THE SPLIT BETWEEN EAST AND WEST PAKISTAN INTENSIFIES. ("While Padma, to calm herself, holds her breath, I permit myself to insert a Bombay-talkie-style close-up—a calendar ruffled by a breeze, its pages flying off in rapid succession to denote the passing of the years . . . ").

1971   Pakistan to Bangladesh: THE BANGLADESH
                    WAR, THE CAPTURE (TEMPORARY) OF SHEIKH
                    MUJIB, THE MASSACRE OF CIVILIANS BY THE
                    PAKISTANI ARMY. Saleem is drafted into the Pa-
                    kistani Army's "Canine Unit for Tracking and In-
                    telligence Activities" (CUTIA, which means
                    "bitch" in Urdu); his unit becomes lost in the
                    depths of the Sunderban jungles, finally emerg-
                    ing just in time to witness the Indian Army's
                    triumphal entry into Dacca.

1972   Bangladesh to India: Saleem is made invisible by
                    Parvati-the-Witch and is transported to New
                    Delhi, where he is "reborn" as an Indian who
                    wants to save his country.

May, 1974   New Delhi: INDIA'S FIRST NUCLEAR EXPLO-
                    SION (AND FOUR MONTHS LATER, RAILWAY
                    MINISTER L.N. MISHRA EXPLODES WHEN A
                    BOMB IS PLACED IN HIS PRIVATE RAILWAY
                    CAR). Shiva appears and carries off Parvati; from
                    their "cosmic embrace" a baby is conceived.

February, 1975   New Delhi: Saleem marries Parvati.

June 12, 1975   New Delhi: PRIME MINISTER INDIRA GANDHI IS
                    FOUND GUILTY BY THE ALLAHABAD HIGH
                    COURT OF 1971 ELECTION MALPRACTICE.
                    Parvati goes into labor, which lasts thirteen days.

June 25, 1975   New Delhi: PRIME MINISTER DECLARES EMER-
                    GENCY. At the stroke of midnight, Saleem's
                    "son" Aadam Sinai emerges.

March, 1976   New Delhi: SANJAY GANDHI AND HIS "YOUTH
                    CONGRESS" SUPERVISE THE DESTRUCTION
                    OF SLUMS IN THE TURKOMAN GATE AREA
                    AND THE RELOCATION OF THE INHABITANTS.
                    Saleem and Shiva meet face-to-face for the first
                    time ("Shiva and Saleem, victor and victim; un-
                    derstand our rivalry, and you will gain an under-
                    standing of the age in which you live."); Parvati
                    is killed by the bulldozers.

April, 1976   Benares: Saleem, along with the other remaining Midnight's Children, is imprisoned in "the Widows' Hostel" by "the Widow" (Prime Minister Gandhi).

January 1, 1977 Benares: UNDER THE AEGIS OF SANJAY GANDHI, THOUSANDS OF FORCIBLE VASECTOMIES ARE PERFORMED. Saleem's "Second Drainage" (his penis), his vasectomy-"sperectomy" (draining-out of hope).

March, 1977   Benares-New Delhi-Bombay: MRS. GANDHI IS DEFEATED IN GENERAL ELECTION AND THE EMERGENCY ENDS. Saleem is released from the Widows' Hostel and returns to New Delhi and then Back-to-Bombay with Picture Singh ("the Most Charming Man in the World") and his son Aadam.

August 15, 1978 Bombay: Saleem's narrative ends in the Braganza Pickle Factory on the eve of his (AND INDIA'S) thirty-first birthday, on which he is to marry Padma—". . . it is the privilege and the curse of midnight's children to be both masters and victims of their times, to forsake privacy and be sucked into the annihilating whirlpool of the multitudes, and to be unable to live or die in peace."

TOPICS FOR DISCUSSION

1. How does *Midnight's Children* explore the relationship between history and the individual in the modern world? What does Rushdie mean when he describes Saleem Sinai as being "handcuffed to history"?

2. How does Rushdie attempt to blur the lines between fact and fantasy? Explain how the structure of *Midnight's Children* addresses this question.

3. What can Rushdie's novel tell us about modern nationalism, its pain and its triumphs? About the nationalist movements that created India and Pakistan?

4. How does Rushdie's use of the English language attempt to mirror the diversity of modern Indian society?

5. In what ways can Rushdie's style be said to reflect the influence of certain Western writers? Of specific Indian authors?

NOTES

1. G. V. Desani, *All About H. Hatterr* (1948; reprint, New York: Farrar Straus Giroux, 1970), p. 10.
2. Salman Rushdie, *Midnight's Children* (New York: Alfred A. Knopf, 1980), p. 111.

REFERENCES

Ali, Tariq. "*Midnight's Children*." *New Left Review* 136 (November/December 1982): 87–95.

Brennan, Timothy. *Salman Rushdie and the Third World: Myths of the Nation.* New York: St. Martin's Press, 1989.

Dissanayake, Wimal. "Towards a Decolonized English: South Asian Creativity in Fiction." *World Englishes* 4, no. 2 (1985): 233–42.

Nazareth, Peter. "Salman Rushdie's *Midnight's Children*." *World Literatures Written in English* 21, no. 1 (Spring 1982): 169–71.

Parameswaran, Uma. "Handcuffed to History: Salman Rushdie's Art." *Ariel* 14, no. 4 (October 1983): 34–45.

Reimenschneider, Dieter. "History and the Individual in Anita Desai's *Clear Light of Day* and Salman Rushdie's *Midnight's Children*." *World Literatures Written in English* 23, no. 1 (1984): 196–207.

Rushdie, Salman. *Midnight's Children.* New York: Alfred A. Knopf, 1980; paperback, New York: Avon Books, 1982.

Sangari, Kum Kum. "The Politics of the Possible." *Cultural Critique* 7 (Fall 1987): 157–86.

Indian Texts: Narrative

SAMSKARA:
THE PASSING OF THE
BRAHMAN TRADITION

Rajagopal Parthasarathy

U. R. Anantha Murthy (b. 1932) is the preeminent writer of his generation in Kannada, a Dravidian language spoken in Karnataka State in south-central India with an unbroken literary tradition of about fourteen hundred years. *Samskara* was first published in 1965. An English translation, by A. K. Ramanujan, followed in 1976.

Anantha Murthy himself explains the rather fortuitous circumstances by which he came to write the novel.[1] He was then a graduate student at Birmingham University, England, working on his Ph.D. dissertation, *Politics and the Novel in the 1930s*, under the supervision of Malcolm Bradbury, the English critic and novelist.

In writing *Samskara*, Anantha Murthy was coming to terms with the realities of his own oppressive Madhva Brahman past in a remote Karnataka village. The writing itself can be viewed as a samskara—a rite of expiation, *prāyaścita*—to atone for the oppressiveness of Brahmanism when its orthodoxies were being repeatedly questioned in the reformist climate of the 1930s and 40s. The novel, thus, is a serious contribution to the dialogue on the politics of religion in the Subcontinent.

Samskara calls into question the meaning of Hindu India, and of the institutions that help to define it. Foremost among the institutions is caste (*jāti*), a hierarchical ranking of social classes based on how pure or impure each is. Four social classes (varnas) are traditionally recognized: the Brahmans (priests), the Kshatriyas (warriors), the Vaishyas (merchants), and the Shudras (laborers). The classes were, according to the *Rig Veda* (10.90), formed at the creation of the universe. When Purusha, a primeval being, was sacrificed, the Brahman emerged from his mouth, the Kshatriya from his arms, the Vaishya from his thighs, and the Shudra from his feet.

The Brahman, as the highest in the social ranking, must at all times be ritually pure since he, as the spokesman for the community, intercedes with the gods. The Shudra, on the other hand, as the lowest of the four classes, performs most of the polluting tasks. Thus, labor among the social classes is divided on the basis of purity and impurity.

Caste governs social relationships, and confers a sense of identity on the individual. A man's relations, often even friends, are from the same caste. Intercaste marriage is taboo as it leads to pollution. Sexual relations across caste boundaries are considered equally polluting as they lead to confusion of classes (*varṇasaṃkara*). For this reason, a woman's sexual behavior is carefully guarded. It is the mother, and not the father, that determines a person's caste.

The Brahman is the keeper of the sacred traditions, the Vedas, which he has, for two thousand years, preserved, interpreted, and transmitted. His other occupation is the performance of sacrificial rituals. As makers of the Hindu tradition, Brahmans had enormous prestige. Indian civilization is unthinkable without their extraordinary presence. However, in the twentieth century, with the rise of non-Brahman movements, especially in Tamil Nadu and Maharashtra, they have finally seen the eclipse of their prestige. Few Brahmans today pursue their traditional occupation as priests. Their power has all but vanished. In village India today they live a hand-to-mouth existence.

Samskara, then, is also an elegy for the passing of the once resonant Brahman tradition. Perhaps the arrival of Islam in the twelfth century and of the Europeans in the sixteenth, together with the fall of Vijayanagara, the last great Hindu kingdom, in 1565 at the hands of the Muslims, hastened its untimely end.

Hindu tradition divides the life of an individual into four stages (*ashramas*). Following his investiture with the sacred thread, the novice (*brahmachari*) enters the home of his teacher to be instructed in the Vedas. On completing his studies, he returns home, marries, and becomes a householder (*grihastha*). Having raised a family and fulfilled his obligations as husband and father, he retires in middle age to the forest to become a hermit (*vanaprastha*). Finally, after a life of penance and meditation, he severs all his ties with the world and becomes a renouncer (*sann-yasi*). This scheme upholds the life of the householder, considered to be the greatest of the four stages, and the importance of the family. For it is the householder who practises the three ends of human life: he performs duties (*dharma*) appropriate to his status, earns a secure income (*artha*), and enjoys sensual pleasures (*kama*). By following them properly, he achieves salvation, release (*moksha*) from the endless cycle of birth and death (*samsāra-cakra*). Ascetic movements often omitted this important stage of the householder, emphasizing the virtue of homelessness for the renouncer.

In a Karnataka village, the street is a social unit, and generally comprises the households of a single caste. A street of Brahman houses is called an *agrahāram*. The houses are joined together to form two rows which face each other. The *agrahāram* in Durvasapura comprises nineteen Madhva Brahman households. The Madhvas are a Vaishnava sect founded by Madhva (13th c. C.E.) in the Tulu country in western Karnataka.

Samskara gives shape and breath to the experiences of the writer's Brahman childhood. It can be read as an initiation story focusing on an individual's movement from innocence to maturity through contact with experience.

Praneshacharya, a pillar of Durvasapura's Brahman society, has an illicit liaison with Chandri, an outcaste. Their unorthodox relationship enacts the familiar paradigm of the ascetic and the whore of which the locus classicus in the Indian tradition is the myth of Rṣyaśṛṅga, told in the *Mahābhārata*. Once, the sage Vibhāṇḍaka Kāśyapa was bathing in a lake. Seeing the *apsarā* Urvaśī there, he spilled his seed in the water. A thirsty doe stopped by the lake and drank the water. It became pregnant and gave birth to a boy, Rṣyaśṛṅga, "the deer-horned." Rṣyaśṛṅga was raised in the forest, and he saw no other human being apart from his father.

It so happened that the country of Aṅga was in the grip of a drought as its king, Lomapāda, had insulted the Brahmans. His ministers advised him to ask for their forgiveness, and to bring Rṣyaśṛṅga to his kingdom to rid the land of drought. The Brahmans returned. Lomapāda then sent one of his courtesans to the forest to lure Rṣyaśṛṅga.

She arrived near Kāśyapa's ashrama in a barge that resembled a hermitage. She sent her daughter, who was with her, to win Rṣyaśṛṅga over. He was delighted to see her and offered her fruits. She refused them and plied him with the choicest food and wines, while flirting with him at the same time. Ṛṣyaśṛṅga was overcome by passion. Noting the change in him, she retreated to her barge under a pretext.

When Vibhāṇḍaka returned, he questioned his son on his appearance. Ṛṣyaśṛṅga recounted in great detail the person of his unusual visitor: the full body adorned with ornaments, hair parted in the center and tied into braids with a thread of gold, eyes shaded with kohl, firm breasts, a thin waist, round hips protected by a girdle, and tinkling anklets at the feet. Ṛṣyaśṛṅga informed his father that he would like to seek out his visitor as he could not bear to be parted from "him." Vibhāṇḍaka counseled his son that it was the work of a demon, and he should therefore avoid "him." But Ṛṣyaśṛṅga turned a deaf ear to his father's words.

The young courtesan returned to the ashrama in Vibhāṇḍaka's absence, and Ṛṣyaśṛṅga eloped with her in her barge to Campāpuri, Lomapāda's capital. The rain fell in torrents soon after his arrival. This pleased Lomapāda, and he offered his daughter Śāntā in marriage to Ṛṣyaśṛṅga.

Ṛṣyaśṛṅga is initiated into the world of the flesh by the prostitute. Her body is the door he must enter in his passage from the sacred to the profane. She serves as a conduit for his spiritual powers which she successfully harnesses to ensure rain for the barren land. Likewise, Praneshacharya enters the real world after his baptism of passion with Chandri. Though a householder, he had denied himself the pleasures of the flesh: "By marrying an invalid, I get ripe and ready."[1][2] His self-denial is itself unbrahmanical, as Praneshacharya's ailing wife, Bhagirathi, is quick to point out. For kama is one of the legitimate human ends advocated by tradition. The novel, in fact, opens with her matter-of-fact admission of their unconnubial life together for twenty years. "Being married to me is no joy. A house needs a child. Why don't you just get married again?" To which Praneshacharya responds characteristically: "A wedding for an old man,"[1] though he isn't yet forty. His spiritual hubris prevents him from understanding the truth of her words. This opening scene at their home in the *agrahāram* foreshadows his liaison with Chandri later in the forest. Chandri fills him with the joy his invalid wife had never been able to give. The scene of their nocturnal encounter is rhapsodic in its simple acknowledgment of passion.

> Praneshacharya, full of compassion, bewildered by the tight hold of a young female not his own, bent forward to bless her with his

hands. His bending hand felt her hot breath, her warm tears; his hair rose in a thrill of tenderness and he caressed her loosened hair. The Sanskrit formula of blessing got stuck in his throat. As his hand played on her hair, Chandri's intensity doubled, she held his hands tightly and stood up and she pressed them to her breasts now beating away like a pair of doves.

Touching full breasts he had never touched, Praneshacharya felt faint. As in a dream he pressed them. The strength in his legs ebbing, Chandri sat the Acharya down, holding him close. [61.2]

In one version of the Ṛṣyaśṛṅga myth, quoted by Wendy Doniger O'Flaherty, the ascetic returns to the city with the prostitute mounted on his shoulders.[3] Heinrich Zimmer narrates a similar episode, in connection with Aristotle, based on the woodcuts of Hans Baldun Grien (1484–1545), the German Renaissance painter:

> . . . upon his naked back rides the naked courtesan Phyllis; with her whip she strikes his sunken flanks, guides him by a bridle attached to the bit in his mouth—that mouth which when young discoursed with the divine Plato, that mouth to whose words the world-conquering Alexander listened with veneration. The great sage, that noble model of *Homo sapiens*, the erect biped—here we see him creeping on all fours. Something in him impels him to renounce everything that had made him great and exemplary in his own eyes and those of the world, something he had never allowed to emerge, of which he had never become conscious—"Eros undefeated in battle," as the Theban maidens called it in Sophocles . . . .[4]

The abasement of the ascetic by the whore is complete.

Again, in Bernard Malamud's tale, "The Magic Barrel" (1958), the rabbi Leo Finkle falls in love with the prostitute Stella. By choosing a social outcaste for his bride, Leo asserts his humanity but also fails to uphold the Jewish tradition. And it is for the decline of this tradition that Malamud expresses concern. It is, however, obvious that he considers humanism important even though it conflicts with a person's religious beliefs. "The Magic Barrel" is symptomatic of the decline of the rabbinical tradition in as much as *Samskara* is that of the Brahman tradition. In their attempts to represent that decline both writers choose identical motifs: a priest (a figure of enormous prestige within the tradition) having or about to have a liaison with a prostitute (a disreputable figure outlawed by the tradition). However, the collapsing of boundaries between the pure and the impure is more easily accomplished in the fictional world than in the real. Tradition cannot be given up overnight, however desirable this may be. In traditional societies like India, the stroke of a pen, whether the writer's or the legislator's, accomplishes little. Caste is a fact of existence in secular India, and untouchability, though illegal, has not entirely disappeared in spite of Gandhi's Himalayan efforts to clean the brahmanical cowsheds. Durvasapura is a microcosm of Brahman India. The revolution that swept across the country was not the work of a Brahman, as was usually the case in traditional India, but that of a Vaishya of the Modhbaniya subcaste—Gandhi.

Naranappa is Praneshacharya's foil, the rival against whom he contends in the novel. Naranappa deliberately takes himself out of the pale of Brahmanism, and turns into a heretic, a Lokāyatika, in fact. Lokāyata is a materialist school which holds that sense experience is ultimately the only source of knowledge. It rejects the authority of the Vedas, is opposed to caste, treats Brahmans with contempt, and advocates a hedonist ethic. Naranappa sums up its position admirably: "All your Brahman respectability. I'll roll it up and throw it away for a little bit of pleasure with one female." [21] He defies every taboo, and turns the *agrahāram* upside down when he abandons his Brahman wife ("who in the world can live with a girl who gives no pleasure . . . " [20]) and sets up house with the outcaste Chandri whom he has brought from Kundapura. Naranappa represents, of course, the ultimate response to Brahman orthodoxy in the 1930s and 40s. On one occasion, he tells Praneshacharya, "Your texts and rites don't work anymore. The Congress Party is coming to power; you'll have to open up the temples to all outcastes. . . ." [20] His untimely death by plague, with which he is infected in Shivamogge, troubles the Brahmans. They are unsure whether he ought to be ritually cremated, and by whom, since he has no children.

Praneshacharya visits the temple of Maruti in search of an answer. In spite of being the Crest-Jewel of Vedic Learning, he is unable to come up with a solution to dispose of Naranappa's corpse. Neither the scriptures nor the temple offers an answer. In despair, he walks homeward, when he encounters Chandri in the forest, and succumbs to her charms. The liaison is a violation of all that Praneshacharya represents. For a Brahman, sexual intercourse with an outcaste is taboo. Besides, both Praneshacharya and Chandri are unfaithful to their spouses. Their infidelity is foregrounded by the legend of Arundhati, the paragon of the faithful wife. [65] After his liaison with Chandri, Praneshacharya forfeits his right to advise the Brahmans of Durvasapura about what to do with Naranappa's corpse. [66]

The *Baudhāyana-pitṛmedha-sūtra* (III.1.4) observes: "It is well known that through the *saṃskāras* after birth one conquers this earth; through the *saṃskāras* after death, the heaven." Orthodox Brahmans are, therefore, especially scrupulous to perform the funeral rites (*antyeṣṭi*), for death is the pollution feared most. Hence, Naranappa's death tears the *agrahāram* apart. He is not immediately cremated because his very status as a Brahman has now become questionable. In the eyes of the Brahmans, he is guilty of the following offenses: one, he abandons his Brahman wife, and takes up with an outcaste; two, he eats and drinks "forbidden things" [7]—meat, fish and liquor; three, he flings into the Tunga river the salagrama, holy stone, sacred to Vishnu and worshipped by the Madhva Brahmans, and spits after it; four, he fishes with his Muslim friends in the holy temple-pond. "Try and excommunicate me now," Naranappa had threatened, "I'll become a Muslim." [13] Had Naranappa become a Muslim, the Brahmans of Durvasapura would have had no option but to leave the *agrahāram* to escape pollution. "If he had really become a Muslim," observes Lakshmana, "no law could have thrown him out of the Brahman *agrahāram*. We would have to leave." [11] Hence, they endure his blasphemies in silence. Now, he returns to them in death, an even greater scourge. His plague-infected body poses a new threat that could wipe out the entire *agrahāram*. One after the other, the Brahmans of Durvasapura—Dasacharya, Gundacharya, Padmanabhacharya—are felled by the plague, and Durvasapura itself all but disappears from the map.

It is not uncommon for corpses to be disposed of in the sea or river if the person dies of an epidemic or has no survivors to perform the funeral rites. This is probably based on the superstition that the spirits who are responsible for epidemics would be infuriated if their victims are burned. This possibility for the disposal of Naranappa's corpse is not explored by the Brahmans.

Naranappa expresses what is repressed in Praneshacharya, whose own unbrahmanical behavior imitates the former's. If the pillar of Durvasapura Brahmans himself revels in pollution, what guidance and comfort can he offer to those who look up to him? Enmeshed in tradition, and unable to see their way, the Brahmans don't know what to do with Naranappa's corpse. On the other hand, Chandri, an outcaste, overrules tradition, and with the help of a Muslim, the fish merchant Ahmad Bari, arranges for Naranappa's cremation. In this too, she gets the better of Praneshacharya; she takes the burden off the Brahmans' hands, but exposes the inhumanity of orthodox Brahmanism that permitted itself to be trapped in ritual hairsplitting when faced with life-and-death issues. She exits from the story at this point, exactly in the middle of the novel. Long after her departure to Kundapura, the touch of her breasts is ripe in Praneshacharya's arms and memory:

> I was roused by the unexpected touch of her breasts, . . . in the darkness my hands fumbled urgently, searched for Chandri's thighs and buttocks—as I had never searched any dharma. [95–6]

Thus, in the unequal struggle between dharma and kama, the latter trounces the former and takes possession of Praneshacharya. It is Chandri's body that he pours over as if it were his beloved palmleaf scriptures. He is reborn, after this baptism of passion, as a *trija*, thrice-born.

After Chandri's departure to Kundapura, Praneshacharya's initiation is taken up by the irrepressible Putta, a half-caste Malera, who guides him through the labyrinth of the quotidian world. The car-festival at Melige is both the scene and the occasion. Putta unceremoniously eggs him on to break one taboo after another, and succeeds in desacralizing his ritual space. Praneshacharya accepts it as part of his rehabilitation.

Life spills over at the carnival, and Praneshacharya hungrily savors the experiences it has to offer. Of Putta he speaks gratefully, "Even my meeting him must have been destined. To fulfill my resolution I should be capable of his involvement in the living. Chandri's too is the same world. But I am neither here, nor there." [112] Putta leads him by the nose, as it were, through one polluting experience after another.

When Praneshacharya finishes his coffee at the Brahman restaurant, Putta urges him to go and eat in the temple where they serve festival meals for Brahmans. Praneshacharya remembers that he is still in mourning for his wife Bhagirathi's death, and he tells himself:

> One couldn't just enter a holy temple and eat there, one would pollute the temple; and as people say, the festival chariot will not move an inch. But didn't Naranappa manage even to eat the holy fish in the Ganapati tank and get away with it? He would never have the courage to defy Brahman practice as Naranappa did. His mind mocked: What price your resolve to join Chandri

and live with her? If you must, do it fully; if you let go, let go utterly. That's the only way to go beyond the play of opposites, that's the way of liberation from fear. [113]

Has Praneshacharya irrevocably cast the die in favor of living with Chandri, and turned his back on his Brahman past? A host of unanswered questions confronts the reader at the end of the novel. But does the novel really end? Or, does it stop abruptly with Praneshacharya's departure for Kundapura? What future would Praneshacharya, a Brahman, have with the outcaste Chandri? Will he, like Naranappa, set up house with her and begin life anew as a man of the world? Or, will he, like Mahabala, fade into obscurity in the arms of a prostitute? Praneshacharya's situation represents, in a microcosm, the erosion of the Brahman tradition, and its inability to preserve itself in the new India ushered in by Independence (1947)—the India of Gandhi's harijans, "God's people," a euphemism for the untouchables. Such questions keep surfacing throughout the novel.

The cockfight [113–15] is a potent motif that the writer introduces to enact the conflict within Praneshacharya, whose body is the space besieged by the powers of darkness he is unable to put to flight.

He had abruptly dropped into a demoniac world. He sat down in utter fear: if in that netherworld where he decided to live with Chandri, if in that depth of darkness, in that cave, the cruel engagement glinting in the eyes of these entranced creatures is just a part of that world, a Brahman like him will wilt. . . . It became clear that he didn't have the skills to live in this world of sharp and cruel feelings. [114]

A cockfight, like any other blood sport, offers the spectators an occasion to collectively get rid of evil forces that from time to time threaten them. By participating in it, albeit as a spectator and not as a player like Putta, Praneshacharya resumes his preparation for life in the real world.

The visit to Padmavati, a half-caste Malera woman living alone in a grove, is fraught with sexual implications. It parallels his earlier encounter with Chandri in the forest. Padmavati is one more prostitute figure who tempts the ascetic Brahman, stirring in him fires of passion.

Still in mourning and therefore unclean, Praneshacharya enters the temple and sits down to eat a meal with other Brahmans. This is the ultimate desecration. The old questions gnaw at his heart:

> Unless I shed brahmanhood altogether I cannot standaside, liberated from all this. If I shed it, I'll fall into the tigerish world of cockfights, I'll burn like a worm. How shall I escape this state of neither-here-nor-there, this ghostliness? [127–28]

He suddenly decides that the only way out of the present fear is to take upon himself to perform Naranappa's last rites, and to openly tell the Brahmans of Durvasapura about his lapses, "not a confession of wrongs done. Not a repentance for sins committed. Just the plain truth. My truth. The truth of my inner life." [129] When he is recognized as the great Praneshacharya himself, he flees the temple, and hurriedly leaves Melige for Durvasapura.

The novel ends abruptly without any resolution. The performance of Naranappa's funeral rites is no longer central to the story. Praneshacharya's spiritual regeneration is, and with it the regeneration of Brahman India with which we began this inquiry. The questions that Praneshacharya asks of himself are the questions Brahmans must ask of themselves if they expect to continue to preserve their identity. For the present at least, it is important to ask the questions, even if the answers to them are unsatisfactory or incomplete.

TOPICS FOR DISCUSSION

1. How does *Samskara* explore the Brahman's struggle between an orthodox way of life, as prescribed by the scriptures, and his own individual desires?

2. What are Chandri's and Putta's roles in Praneshacharya's rehabilitation as an individual?

3. Why does Naranappa's corpse pose such a formidable threat to the Brahman community of Durvasapura?

4. The novel as a form is not indigenous to the Indian literary tradition. How does Anantha Murthy exploit its conventions to narrate a hypnotic tale?

5. What do we learn about traditional India and its institutions from reading *Samskara?*

6. See Bergman's film, *The Seventh Seal.* Examine some of the affinities between the film and *Samskara.*

7. Bergman apart, do you see the influence of other Western writers on Anantha Murthy's style?

NOTES

1.   I had gone to see Bergman's film, *The Seventh Seal*, with Malcolm Bradbury. The film had no subtitles. And therefore,

fortunately for me, I understood it vaguely. It was a haunting experience. Such experiences can trigger off your creativity. The spiritual crisis of the hero came through, and I remember to have remarked to Professor Bradbury that a European has to create the medieval times from his reading and scholarship, but for an Indian writer it is an immediate experience, an aspect of living memory. Ever since then, it has been a pet theory of mine that different worldviews, which are the result of different historical epochs, coexist in the consciousness of the Indian writer, and therefore for him Chaucer, Langland, Shakespeare, Dickens, and Camus are contemporaries, however apart they stand historically for a European. Professor Bradbury said in reply to my remark that I should find a style and a theme which could embody such a coexistence. After two years [1963–65] in England I was getting tired, having had to always speak English. I had grown nostalgic. . . . I wrote my *Samskara* thus almost in a feverish speed.

Did the gypsy [Jof] of *The Seventh Seal* transform himself into my Putta? I remember putting down on paper that my hero Praneshacharya had turned back to see what was following him, and then came Putta, and wrote the rest of the novel for me. The beautiful pariah girl who escaped the plague in my *agrahāram* started the story which I could finish only twenty years later after Bergman moved me in a strange country far away in space and time.

From U. R. Anantha Murthy, "On Being an Indian Writer." Paper presented at the Center for Asian Studies, University of Texas, Austin, May 1, 1986.

Ingmar Bergman's existential film (1956) is set in fourteenth-century Sweden at the height of the Black Death. Although there are some obvious affinities between the film and the novel that could be usefully explored, they are not the subject of the present inquiry.

2. U. R. Anantha Murthy, *Samskara: A Rite for a Dead Man*, trans. A. K. Ramanujan (New Delhi: Oxford University Press [Three Crowns Books], 1976). All quotes with page numbers cited in text are from this same source.

3. Hsuan-tsang, *Si-yu-ki: Buddhist Records of the Western World*, trans. Samuel Beal (London: Kegan Paul, Trench, Trübner and Co., 1884). Quoted in Wendy Doniger O'Flaherty, *Śiva: The Erotic Ascetic* (Oxford: Oxford University Press, 1981), p. 46.

4. Heinrich Zimmer, "On the Significance of the Indian Tantric Yoga," in *Spiritual Disciplines: Papers from the Eranos Yearbooks*, trans. Ralph Manheim & R.F.C. Hull (Princeton: Princeton University Press, Bollingen Series XXX (4), 1985), p. 15.

REFERENCES

Anantha Murthy, U. R. *Samskara: A Rite for a Dead Man.* Translated, and with an afterword, by A. K. Ramanujan. New Delhi: Oxford University Press (Three Crown Books), 1976.

Anantha Murthy, U. R. "Search for an Identity: A Viewpoint of a Kannada Writer." In *Identity and Adulthood,* edited by Sudhir Kakar, 105-17. New Delhi: Oxford University Press, 1979.

Mukherjee, Meenakshi. "*Samskara.*" In her *Realism and Reality: The Novel and Society in India,* 207–07. New Delhi: Oxford University Press, 1985.

Naipaul, V. S. "A Defect of Vision." In his *India: A Wounded Civilization,* 110–22. New York: Alfred A. Knopf, 1977.

Nightingale, Margaret. "Anantha Murthy's *Samskara:* An Indian Journey to the End of Night." *New Literature Review* 4 (1978): 51–4.

TWO CLASSICAL INDIAN PLAYS: KĀLIDĀSA'S *ŚAKUNTALĀ* AND *ŚŪDRAKA'S LITTLE CLAY CART*

Barbara Stoler Miller

Among the genres of literature, drama is more concretely social than other forms by virtue of its performance before a live audience. Theater is a cultural institution that depends on patronage; the dramatist composes for an audience whom he imagines gathered into a tangible group. The Sanskrit term *dṛśya-kāvya*, which literally means "visual poetry," may be rendered "public literature" to contrast it with lyric and epic forms whose structure takes less direct notice of the audience.

Drama seems to have emerged as a sophisticated form of public literature in the city of Ujjain, in Northern India, during the height of the Gupta period (c. 390–470 C.E.). Evidence that the Gupta theater had antecedents comes from fragments of plays attributed to the Buddhist poet Aśvaghoṣa, who is said to have lived at the court of the Kushan ruler Kaniṣka in the first or second century C.E. Earlier playwrights are acknowledged in the prologues of Gupta plays, such as Kālidāsa's *Mālavikāgnimitra*; there are also references to a genre of early monologue plays and to popular theater. The best-known plays of the Gupta period are Kālidāsa's three dramatic romances, the *Śakuntalā*, the *Vikramorvaśīya*, and the *Mālavikāgnimitra*, as well as Śūdraka's satiric urban romance, the *Mṛcchakaṭikā* (Little

Clay Cart), and Viśākhadatta's political drama, the *Mudrārākṣasa* (The Minister's Signet Ring).

These plays represent different genres and give a good sense of what the theater of the time must have been like. The *Śakuntalā*, based on an episode from the epic *Mahābhārata*, is the model of the genre known as *nataka*, or "heroic romance." Dramatic romance in Western literature, represented by plays such as Euripides' *Alcestis* or Shakespeare's *The Tempest*, is comparable in many ways, though the mode of these plays may not be heroic. The *Little Clay Cart* is classed by critics as a *prakarana*, or "secular romance," on the basis of its invented story and the levity of its plot.

It is obvious from the plays that the conservative ideals of ancient brahmanical religion that were revived during the Gupta period only partially represented the cultural values of the society. Each of the plays is a complex, multilayered work that displays and explores conflicting social values. The formal and thematic complexity of the plays accords well with principles codified in the earliest extant Indian work on dramatic theory, the *Nāṭyaśāstra* attributed to Bharata. It was probably compiled during the Gupta period, based on a collection of older sources. Bharata's dramatic theory recognizes the emotional and ethical instruction afforded by the spectacle of drama, which is designed to mimic the conduct of people more closely than other forms of poetry. Like Aristotle, Bharata stresses emotional satisfaction through action. Although their modes of ordering experience are significantly different, Greek and Indian dramas were conceived and performed as sources of pleasure and insight for the audience. These two distinct understandings of drama crystallize our perceptions of classical Greek and classical Indian culture.

Greek tragedies present impossible heroic struggles against established orders in which the fate of every person in the story and, by extension, the whole human audience is implicated. When Aristotle discusses the emotional effect of a drama on an audience, he speaks both of the sympathy and of the excitement through which the play may bring about catharsis, that purgation of emotions which restores a balance of conflicting forces. In Greek tragedy the conflict is between the actors in the drama and a superior force, whether society or destiny. It involves a catastrophe that arouses fear and pity in such a way that these emotions are purged, and order is restored in the soul of the audience. Indian dramas represent human emotions in a theatrical universe of symbolically charged characters and events in order to lead the audience into a state of extraordinary pleasure and insight. The goal of a Sanskrit drama is to reestablish emotional harmony in the microcosm of the audience by exploring the deeper relations that bind apparent conflicts of existence. The manifestation of these relations produces the intense aesthetic experience called rasa. Indian dramas characteristically focus on the critical tension between duty and desire that is aesthetically manifest in the relation of the heroic sentiment (*virarasa*) to the romantic (*śṛṅgārarasa*), or the pathetic (*karuṇārasa*). The production of rasa is as basic to classical Indian theater as it is to lyric poetry. In contrast to the particularity of everyday emotion, rasa is an integration of emotions structured to give the spectator an experience of extraordinary universality.

In Bharata's mythic account, drama is a kind of holy presentation that the gods originated to offer ethical instruction through diversion when people were no longer listening to the scriptures. Bharata stresses the reward a king will gain if he presents dramatic performances as a gift to his subjects and an offering to the gods. For centuries, Indian dramas have been presented on the occasion of a seasonal festival, the birth of a son, a marriage, a royal consecration, a political victory, or any auspicious event. The ideal of education through dramatic spectacle is codified in Bharata's definition of drama: "Drama is a representation of the emotional states of the threefold universe. . . . It teaches duty to those who violate duty, desire to those addicted to love; it reprimands those who behave rudely, promotes restraint in those who are disciplined; it gives courage to cowards, energy to heroes; it enlightens fools and gives learning to learned men." Though the size of an audience in an Indian theater is limited by the necessity that the most subtle gestures of hand and eye be visible, the diversity of the audience is alluded to in Bharata's theory of theatrical success.

The techniques of performance used in the classical Indian theater were appropriate to the complicated verbal texts of the classical dramas. Drama belongs to a less academic tradition, in contrast to lyric poetry, which was composed in standardized, courtly Sanskrit and is rarely relieved by excursions into humor or lower registers of language and thought. The dramas are multilingual, composed in a mixture of Sanskrit and various Prakrits, which would be like a drama in Latin and various dialects of Italian. Sanskrit is the language of only one set of characters: kings and other men of high status. The brahman buffoon, the women of the court, hermitage, and city, as well as various minor characters, speak Prakrits. It seems reasonable to assume that the Prakrits used by the classical dramatists must have been drawn from current mediums of the day, stylized for purposes of characterization, musical sound, and emotive contrast. The Prakrits spoken by the buffoons and the women create verbal environments of comedy and love; phonetic ambiguities are both musical and conducive to comic punning or misinterpretation.

The characters in the plays are also diverse; drawn not only from divine and exalted human stations, but from every corner of society. By contrast, one does not find policemen, fishermen, dancing masters, buffoons, boorish royalty, masseurs-turned—monks, and the like in Sanskrit poems. The hero of the *Śakuntalā* is a king who enjoys varied society, indulges in all diversions, and has a brahman buffoon as his advisor. The hero of the *Little Clay Cart* is an impoverished brahman merchant whose buffoon is his loyal companion. The buffoon, called *vidūṣaka* in Sanskrit (a verbal parody on his role as "wise man") is an important aid in the heroes' adventures; he frequently commits the critical error that propels the plot to its conclusion. His words and actions invite comparison with Shakespearean clowns like Feste and Touchstone. He is usually in close contact with his counterparts in the realm of pleasure, the Prakrit-speaking females, and acts as a go-between with the audience too, thus sustaining relations at various levels in the theater. His gluttony and absurdity undermine the force of brahmanical authority. His literal interpretation of rasa as a feast of flavors makes the hero's erotic passion absurdly concrete. The heroine in each play is somewhat out of place: *Śakuntalā* is the daughter of a nymph and a royal sage, inappropriately living in an ascetic's grove; Vasantasenā is a wealthy courtesan in love with a brahman merchant too poor to afford her.

The range of social types represented in the plays' minor characters is often used only for comic effect, but it adds to one's sense that the plays were created for an audience that must have included people of varied taste and learning. Bharata refers to the medley of spectators who assembled to enjoy a dramatic performance. The theatrical occasion must have been shared by the patron, whether a king or rich merchant, with an audience who made demands on the playwright's ability to divert them.

The *Śakuntalā* and the *Little Clay Cart* both begin with benedictions, followed by prologues in which the playwright is named and the importance of the audience is explicitly discussed. The prologue in each play is a play-within-a-play that initiates a conventionalized pattern of structural oppositions. These include contrasts between prose and verse, Sanskrit and Prakrit, authority (in the person of the director) and spontaneity (in the person of the assistant or actress). The prologue to the Śakuntalā, on which Goethe is said to have modeled the prologue to *Faust*, gives a sense of how the actors and the audience are initiated into the dramatic action.

DIRECTOR (looking backstage): If you are in costume now, madam, please come on stage!

ACTRESS: I'm here, sir.

DIRECTOR: Our audience is learned. We shall play Kālidāsa's new drama called *Śakuntalā and the Ring of Recollection*. Let the players take their parts to heart!

ACTRESS: With you directing, sir, nothing will be lost.

DIRECTOR: Madam, the truth is:

I find no performance perfect
until the critics are pleased;
the better trained we are
the more we doubt ourselves.

ACTRESS: So true . . . now tell me what to do first!

DIRECTOR: What captures an audience better than a song? Sing about the new summer season and its pleasures:

To plunge in fresh waters
swept by scented forest winds
and dream in soft shadows
of the day's ripened charms.

ACTRESS (singing):

Sensuous women
in summer love
weave
flower earrings
from fragile petals
of mimosa
while wild bees
kiss them gently.

DIRECTOR: Well sung, madam! Your melody enchants the audience. The silent theater is like a painting. What drama should we play to please it?

ACTRESS: But didn't you just direct us to perform a new play called Śakuntalā and the Ring of Recollection?

DIRECTOR: Madam, I'm conscious again! For a moment I forgot.

The mood of your song's melody
carried me off by force,
just as the swift dark antelope
enchanted King Duṣyanta.

The actress' singing, like the beautiful movements of the magical antelope, or the art of poetry, makes the audience "forget" the everyday world and enter the fantastic realm of imagination that is latent within them. The mind of the poet, the hero, and the audience is symbolized by the director, who holds together the various strands of the theater so that the aesthetic experience (rasa) of the play can be realized and savored.

At the close of the prologue, the king enters, chasing a deer, armed with a bow and arrow. The chase continues and the movement builds in intensity until the king is about to kill the deer. At that moment, he is interrupted by two hermits who identify the deer with the sage Kaṇva's hermitage, which is the home of Śakuntalā. The scene shows the king abandoning himself to the passion of the hunt, a passion that threatens the calm of the forest and a creature of the hermitage it is his duty to protect. But the hermits remind him of this duty. The scenes of the hunt and the hermitage heighten the sense of interpenetration between the natural and social realms—nature is personified in Śakuntalā, society in King Duṣyanta. The passion of their encounter is so strong that the lovers have to undergo a trial of painful separation before order is restored and Duṣyanta is reunited with the chaste wife he rejected, now the mother of his son.

Consonant with the satiric undertone of the Little Clay Cart, the first character to appear after the prologue is the buffoon, who babbles about his empty belly and his master Carudatta's hard luck. The setting of the play is the city of Ujjain, populated by courtesans, burglars, spies, corrupt policemen, and other characters of the ancient urban demimonde. The main plot of the love affair of the poor merchant Carudatta and the grand courtesan Vasantasenā is complicated by an interwoven subplot of political conspiracy against the reigning king. Their love is frustrated by the brother-in-law of the king, a boorish hedonist, who pursues Vasantasenā, almost kills her, and accuses Carudatta of the crime. The clay cart of the play's title belongs to Carudatta's son and is a symbol of his father's poverty. Through a series of acts of generosity, including that of Carudatta's wife, Vasantasenā's jewels are deposited in the cart. They become crucial evidence in the case against Carudatta, which collapses only when the supposedly dead woman appears at the site of execution. The lovers are reunited, the conspiracy succeeds, and the new king rewards Carudatta and raises Vasantasenā's status so she can become Carudatta's second wife.

Here, as in the *Śakuntalā*, the hero unites with a heroine who embodies the mystery of erotic emotion, through her affinity with nature or her mastery of the arts of love, the ideal balance between duty and passion is restored. Within the context of their art, these plays offer insights into the frustration and fulfillment of human desire.

TOPICS FOR DISCUSSION

1. The plays can be compared with Greek or Shakespearean plays through analyses of structure, characters, and such themes and motifs as duty and desire, nature and culture, prophecies and curses, mortality and divinity, family, parents, children, recognition, or memory. Analysis should focus on the structure of each play, its beginning, especially the significance of the prologue in the Indian drama and its analogues elsewhere.

2. Seeing the stylization of characters in terms of symbolic gestures, actions, and speech is important for understanding the psychological content of the plays. One might ask, "Is female to male as desire is to duty?"—or is the relationship more complicated?

3. Examine the forms of love that are explored in the plays, e.g. erotic love, friendship, love between a parent and child, love of "home." How do these relate to the modes and meanings of separation?

REFERENCES

Baumer, Rachel van M., and James R. Brandon. *Sanskrit Drama in Performance.* Honolulu: The University Press of Hawaii, 1981.
Keith, A. B. *Sanskrit Drama.* London: Oxford University Press, 1924.

Miller, Barbara Stoler, ed. *Theater of Memory: The Plays of Kālidāsa.* New York: Columbia University Press, 1984.

van Buitenen, J.A.B. *Two Plays of Ancient India: The Little Clay Cart and the Minister's Seal.* New York: Columbia University Press, 1968.

III
Chinese Texts

THE BOOK OF SONGS

Pauline Yu

On first looking into *The Book of Songs* (*Shi jing* [*Shih ching*]), the Western reader might find it somewhat difficult to discover the grounds for the revered position it occupied in traditional China. To be sure, its very antiquity—it seems to have taken something close to its present form by the sixth century B.C.E.—would have assured it no small measure of respect, but the 305 poems in the collection do not offer any other immediately apparent reasons for their designation as a literal canon (*jing* [*ching*]) during the second century B.C.E. Those reasons exist, of course, but they cannot be located solely within the text itself. *The Book of Songs* thus illustrates a fundamental principle taken for granted by all traditional Chinese readers: that no literary text has meaning on its own but must rather be understood within its context, its background and sources—personal, social, political, and textual—its audience and reception, and its interpretive tradition. Indeed, the collection not only provides the first example of this principle, it establishes the precedent for the entire poetic tradition.

According to the Han dynasty historian Sima Qian [Ssu-ma Ch'ien], the compiler of *The Book of Songs* was none other than Confucius himself, who is said to have selected them from a larger group of some three thousand poems, edited their musical accompaniments (long since lost), and arranged them in their present order. Other Han dynasty texts state that this larger body of songs had been assembled by officials of the Zhou [Chou] dynasty who had been sent out to collect them as indices of the temper of the times and present them to the government—no doubt one of the earliest public opinion polls. Whereas there may be some truth to this second tradition, judging from the clearly pointed and political nature of complaint in many of the poems—the first is highly unlikely to have been the case. The several passages in the *Ana-*

lects in which Confucius mentions the *Songs*, praising their uses and effects, suggest that they already existed as a body by his lifetime. Yet however spurious, this attribution of editorship was never seriously questioned until modern times. It justified the conferral of canonical status (the other four original canons—the *Book of Documents* (*Shu jing* [*Shu ching*]), the *Book of Changes* (*Yi jing* [*I ching*]), the *Record of Ritual* (*Li ji* [*Li chi*]), and the *Spring and Autumn Annals* (*Chunqiu* [*Ch'un-ch'iu*])—were also said to have been traced in some way by Confucius and his writing brush); it ensured the text's inclusion in the educational curriculum of the elite and, more specifically, as an item on the civil service examination; and it obligated any scholar who wished to be taken seriously to make sure to indicate that an appropriate amount of time had been spent on the text—hence the volumes of commentary and scholarship produced over the centuries.

Up through the early Han at least four editions of the Songs are known to have circulated, which were associated with scholars from different geographical areas and perhaps with distinctive commentarial inclinations and emphases. However, only one emerged preeminent and essentially intact from the ongoing struggle to establish definitive versions of all classical texts during the dynasty. This is the so-called Mao edition which, with its own brief annotations and then two further sets of subcommentary appended by later exegetes, remained the standard text for several centuries. The great Song [Sung] philosopher Zhu Xi ([Chu Hsi] 1130–1200) disagreed with the interpretations of these earlier scholars and issued his own version of the *Songs* with *Collected Commentaries* (*Shi ji zhuan* [*Shih chi chuan*]), which did not, however, alter the basic configuration of the anthology. Although his readings of the poems became orthodox for the purpose of the civil service examination, they in turn came under fire during the Qing [Ch'ing] dynasty by scholars who questioned the accuracy of Zhu's glosses and often returned to the Mao annotations as philologically more sound. The Mao edition is standard today, although anyone working with the text in Chinese must consult the numerous Song and Qing commentaries as well.

The sheer volume of scholarship on the *Book of Songs* can be attributed not merely to its canonical status but quite simply to the fact that it is linguistically difficult. Almost every poem contains words or phrases that rarely appear in any other early text and whose meanings are therefore difficult to ascertain by the standard philological method of textual comparison and triangulation; hundreds of words are hapax legomena found in the *Book of Songs* alone. In addition, although the poems probably contain more personal pronouns than the poetry of later dynasties, their language still typically—like all classical Chinese writing—tends to suppress mention of grammatical subject and does not specify for tense, number, gender, or case. Moreover, most of them, like later Chinese poetry in general, are so brief that their basic situations are evocative at best. Titles assigned after the fact are singularly uninformative, generally consisting of two words drawn from the first line of the poem.

For the reader of the *Book of Songs* in translation, of course, many of these problems have necessarily already been addressed—whether happily or not—by the translator. Modern readers still confront, however, a heterogeneous and often perplexing text. The poems are almost all anonymous; six of them cite an author's name but that may have been merely formulaic. There is a great deal of rhyme, both internal and end, unlike most early poetry in other cultures, but some poems use none at all. The most common form employs three stanzas of four or six tetrasyllabic lines each, but again there is much variation from the norm. Natural imagery predominates but functions in a number of ways and, in general, the purposes of the songs as a whole—from simple expression of emotion to ritual ceremony—and their apparent intended audiences—fellow commoner or semi-divine ancestor—are obviously quite diverse.

Traditionally the 305 songs were grouped into four sections of varying size. The first 160 poems in the Mao edition are called the *feng*—a term which literally means wind, but can also denote custom or mores and is closely cognate with a word meaning to admonish or to criticize. However, because they are arranged into fifteen subsections loosely corresponding to different geographical areas, they are often referred to as the "Airs of the States." Many of the next seventy-four poems, the "Lesser Elegances" (*xiao ya* [*hsiao ya*]), treat similar subjects, drawn from daily life, as the "Airs" but place them in a more obviously aristocratic or "elegant" context. The thirty-one "Greater Elegances" (*da ya* [*ta ya*]) are similarly sometimes difficult to distinguish from the section preceding them but tend to include the longest poems in the collection, celebrating historical and legendary events and figures. Finally the forty "Hymns" (*song* or *sung*) of the last section are said to have been used by the Zhou dynastic house and two other feudal courts for ceremonial or ritual performances. Many of them evince no stanzaic divisions and are unrhymed, suggesting to some scholars that they were chanted rather than sung, or perhaps even accompanied by mime or dance. The terms *feng, ya,* and *song* were identified by early scholars as three of the "six principles" of the *Book of Songs,* the other three (*fu, bi* [*pi*], *xing* [*hsing*]) refer to different ways of employing imagery.

Of these subgenres in the collection, there is no doubt that the "Airs of the States" are the most accessible and easily appreciated by readers of any era. Whether or not the poems were polished by the literati, their subjects are those shared by folk songs and ballads in poetic traditions all over the world: friendship, courtship, elopement, marriage, abandonment; planting, harvesting, hunting, fishing; festivals, games, dances; government exactions, war, the sorrow of separation. Earlier in the twentieth century some Western sinologists attempted to use these songs as anthropological documents, mines of information on popular rituals and festivals of ancient China. Although this method ignored what must have been purely literary or musical factors in the composition of the pieces, there is no doubt that one can glean a good sense of the main concerns of Zhou dynasty culture, and in particular its focus on the importance of human bonds, loyalty, solidarity, and fertility. These pervasive themes, which more often focus on faithless desertion rather than joyful union, suggest in moving terms a society in which such bonds were not always maintained, where inconstancy, slander, rejection, and thus anxiety and insecurity, were the norm rather than the exception. To be sure, one can find several poems that appear to express a speaker's happiness, as in the following air from the state of Zheng [Cheng] (Karlgren 90, Waley 91):

> Wind and rain are chilly and cold;
> The cocks crow all together.
> Since I have seen my lord
> How could I not be pleased?
>
> Wind and rain sough and sigh,
> The cocks crow in one voice.
> Since I have seen my lord
> How could I not be healed?
>
> Wind and rain are dark as night;
> The cocks crow ceaselessly.
> Since I have seen my lord
> How could I not be glad?

This poem exemplifies many of the formal features of verse characteristic of the *Book of Songs* as a whole, and in particular the "Airs": a four-word line; three four-line stanzas; heavy use of reduplicative binomial phrases (in the first two stanzas' descriptions of the weather and the cocks); and much repetition with slight variations. The phrase, "since I have seen my lord" also recurs in several other songs, although more frequently one finds, "I have not yet seen my lord." The details of this scene are typically unclear: leaving aside the traditional political interpretation, one might read this (with Karlgren) as an aubade or (with Waley) as a wedding song that notes both the auspicious (cocks crowing in unison) and ill-omened (inclement weather) aspects of the day. Yet even though the poem rejoices in the pleasure or anticipation of past or future moments spent together, one cannot help noting that the rhetorical questions concluding each stanza—once again, a common feature of the "Airs"—leave as much in doubt as they confirm. Indeed, the frequent use of paired utterances—especially questions and suppositions, answered or denied ("Who says I am x; / I am in fact y"; "It is not that x; / It is rather y")—suggests an overriding concern centered on the relationship between appearance and reality, on fears of being misinterpreted, betrayed, or abandoned. In addition, of course, it may indicate that the songs were originally sung antiphonally, with two or more singers.

There are, of course, poems in which these fears are still relatively light-hearted, as in this well-known example of disarming directness (Karlgren 20, Waley 17):

> Drop go the plums—
> Of fruits there are seven.
> Seeking me are several men:
> May it be lucky soon!
>
> Drop go the plums—
> Of fruits there are three.
> Seeking me are several men:
> May it be the moment soon!
>
> Drop go the plums—
> In a short basket gather them.
> Seeking me are several men:
> May they speak up soon!

More common and ultimately more powerful, however, are poems in which anxieties have all too painfully been confirmed. In the following "Air" from the state of Pei [P'ei] (Karlgren 26, Waley 75), we do not know what precisely has occurred, but its effects are clear:

Floating is that cypress boat,
Floating in the current.
Wide awake, unsleeping,
As if in secret grief.
Not that I lack for wine
To gambol, to roam.

My heart is not a mirror,
It cannot be read.
Indeed I have brothers;
They cannot be leaned on.
When I go to complain,
I meet with their anger.

My heart is not a stone,
It cannot be turned.
My heart is not a mat,
It cannot be rolled.
My behavior is perfectly proper,
It cannot be measured.

My anxious heart is full of grief,
Despised by petty hordes.
Sufferings have been countless,
Insults not a few.
In quietude I ponder this;
Awake I strike my breast.

Oh sun, oh moon—
Why do you sometimes disappear?
The grief of my heart
Is like an unwashed dress.
In quietude I ponder this,
Unable to rise and fly away.

This mood of frustration and unrequited longing would come to pervade the later literary tradition as a whole.

Because the "Airs of the States" treat timeless themes in the most general, if laconic way, they are perhaps the section in the *Book of Songs* best suited for incorporation into a general educational curriculum. Many of the "Lesser Elegances" resemble the "Airs" to a great extent, although it has been noted that they seem to include more deliberately pointed songs of lament and censure, as in the following example (Karlgren 185, Waley 127), which opens:

Ministers of war—
You are the king's claws and teeth.
Why do you throw us in distress?
We have nowhere to stop and rest.

They are also more replete with details of aristocratic accoutrements, activities, and festivities, which may be of interest to someone wishing to flesh out a picture of Zhou dynasty upper-class daily life, but are obviously less lyrically appealing. Unlike the "Airs," many of these poems are demonstrably linked to actual historical events, and in some the authors identify themselves by name. Among the "Greater Elegances," the majority of which are quite long, the most interesting poems are those recounting the feats of the Zhou-dynasty culture heroes. Most notable among these heroes is Hou Ji ([Hou Chi] "Lord Millet"), the legendary progenitor of the ruling house, whose miraculous birth and equally miraculous subsequent rescues from certain death display remarkable similarities to those of figures in other cultures (Karlgren 245, Waley 238). The last section of "Hymns" is distinctive from the rest of the collection in its (appropriately) uniform mood of joyful praise and celebration—of harvests, victories, ancestors, and heroes.

As mentioned earlier, no matter how one chooses to approach the *Book of Songs* now, one should be aware of how they were read in premodern China, for those attitudes not only influenced the subsequent writing and reading of all later poetry but also reveal presumptions fundamental to the culture in general. The poems were obviously taken quite seriously by Confucius and his followers: the *Analects* contain several expressions of the Master's admiration for the collection, and the Warring States "commentary" on the *Spring and Autumn Annals*, the *Zuo zhuan* [*Tso chuan*], cites excerpts from over two hundred of the poems and indicates that quoting brief passages from the text was a common method of conveying political opinions obliquely but effectively. Such evidence of esteem for the didactic efficacy of the *Book of Songs*, as well as the fact that some pieces served indubitably as records of actual historical events and personages, seems to have led the early commentators to assume that the entire anthology could be shown to be performing such useful functions. Thus, for example, the first poem cited is said to have come from the state of Zheng [Cheng], which had a reputation for "disorderly" morals; and although it is not dated, many of the other songs in its section—as well as most in the anthology as a whole—are assigned to the reign of a particular ruler. The commentators explain that the song expresses, "a longing for a Gentleman (lord). It is a disorderly age, thus one longs for a Gentleman who will not alter his regulated behavior," just as the cocks maintain their punctual crowing despite the storms that keep the skies abnormally dark. Such interpretations as these have generally been castigated by modern scholars as far-fetched distortions of the original import of the poems, but their underlying assumptions should not be dismissed out of hand. Fundamental to such readings were the beliefs—articulated most fully in a "Preface" to the *Book of Songs*, which took its present shape by the first century C.E.—that poetry (or song, the two were interchangeable) expressed spontaneously what was in one's heart or mind; that this was an experience natural to anyone, not just some privileged (whether inspired or insane) group of "poets"; that this impulse arose from the world outside the singer; and that this world comprised nature, society, and the body politic, which were linked by resonating networks of correlations and correspondences. Any utterance on the part of an individual, therefore, could be assumed to implicate naturally something larger than a personal situation. At the same time, it would always be construed not as some abstract rumination but as a response to a particular set of circumstances that could be located in historical time. Such presuppositions and interpretive practices first developed around the *Book of Songs*; they served to dignify a text that might otherwise have been devalued or even lost (much as allegory served the Song of Songs) and continued to shape the later poetic and critical tradition.

TOPICS FOR DISCUSSION

1. In teaching the *Book of Songs*, one often encounters an initial bewilderment regarding poetic form itself. To a certain extent this is an inevitable, if lamentable, result of the relative deemphasis on poetry and its methods in the curriculum in general. To the same extent it is a problem that is, in the study of Chinese poetry, best addressed when considering the much later works of the Tang dynasty, when poetic forms became standardized. Nonetheless, the dictates of chronology place this text first in the syllabus, and there might be some use in presenting a poem from this early text in its word-for-word, transliterated shape, despite its relative irregularities.

Consider, for example, poem 23 in the Mao edition of the text (Karlgren 23, Waley 63):

> Wilds there-is dead doe
> White grass bind it
> There-is girl cherish spring
> Fine gentleman entice her

Forest there-is shrub tree
Wilds there-is dead deer
White grass wrap bind
There-is girl like jade

Slowly and gently gently [particle]
Do-not move my handkerchief [particle]
Do-not cause dog [particle] bark

The most immediate observation is likely to center on what happens to this poem in translation, and the versions available in English (see References) could be presented simultaneously and compared. Consideration could then move to "the poem itself." Seen in this word-for-word transliteration, the tetrasyllabic line becomes clear, as do the odd deviations from it. The spareness of the grammar is evident (although it is relatively more explicit than that of later poetry), and so is the richness of the rhyme scheme (*abab, cccc, ddd*) which also determines some of the choices in the incremental repetition. Students will also notice the juxtaposition of image and statement without intervening explanation and might be asked to consider the resultant role of the reader in putting them together. One useful exercise to make these methods come alive might be to ask them to compose something of their own using similar forms and content.

2. From a comparative perspective, the *Book of Songs* might most fruitfully be studied in at least three ways (in addition to the discussion about translation that is almost inevitable and certainly an issue at the heart of comparative literary studies). The first would be an essentially intrinsic approach focusing on the "Airs of the States" and comparing them to folk songs and ballads from other cultures. One might discuss the most prevalent themes and examine the literary features of the poems, such as stanzaic structure, repetition and variation, formulaic phrases and refrains, uses of natural imagery, and the attitudes these devices suggest.

3. A second, more broadly literary approach might consider the place of the *Book of Songs* within the Chinese tradition as compared with Western examples. Much ink has been spilled in the twentieth- century by scholars searching for some counterpart in early Chinese literature to the great epics of Europe and India. Instead one finds the *Book of Songs*, and rather than lament the lack of an extended fictional narrative, one might more usefully consider the implications for a literary culture of having its roots—as both China and Japan do—in the lyric. Some of these

might include, for instance, the valorization of brevity and suggestiveness; a concomitant faith in the ability of the reader to fathom "the meaning beyond the words"; a disinclination toward linear narrative sequentiality; and an assumption that literature is nonfiction, expressing unavoidably the experiences and responses of an identifiable individual.

4. Finally, a third, more sociological or anthropological approach would broaden the comparative scope to include myth and ritual, and would focus on the *Book of Songs* as a resource of information on rites, festivals, daily activities, beliefs, and values in pre-Confucian China. One might note, for example, the obsession with the centrifugal forces that constantly threaten to unglue human and social bonds—something Confucius would address in his emphasis on the family and filial piety. Another point of interest is the relative unconcern with death, which could be examined from the perspective of religious belief. Some integration of these three approaches would no doubt yield the fullest picture of a rich and diverse text.

REFERENCES

Three paperback translations of the *Book of Songs* are available, each with its particular merits and limitations. Bernhard Karlgren's *The Book of Odes* (Stockholm: Museum of Far Eastern Antiquity, 1964) offers the 305 poems in their standard Mao edition order in a reliable but uninspiring prose translation alongside the original Chinese text and occasional notes. Ezra Pound's *The Confucian Odes* (i.e., the *Shijing*) in *Classical Anthology Defined by Confucius* (Cambridge: Harvard University Press, 1954) also provides translations of the entire text; they are highly unreliable yet occasionally convey quite successfully—because of their skillful use of rhyme and imagery—the folk song "flavor" of the *Songs*. The compromise of choice is probably Arthur Waley's *The Book of Songs* (Boston & New York: Houghton Mifflin, 1937; recently reprinted with a new foreword by Stephen Owen), in which 290 poems are translated gracefully and accurately enough. Five brief essays on sometimes idiosyncratic topics of interest to Waley, as well as some additional textual notes, are appended. Like Karlgren, Waley also published separately a volume of notes addressing more philological, technical problems. The major drawback of Waley's volume is that he arranges the poems topically rather than in their original order, and since the topics of many poems are often quite vague, many arbitrary assignments are made. He does, however, provide a list for locating his versions in the Mao edition (and thus Karlgren's as well). Representative selections from the *Book of Songs* that would be adequate in range for use in a survey course are also available in two of the standard anthologies of Chinese literature. The *Anthology of Chinese Literature*, Vol. 1, edited by Cyril Birch (New York: Grove Press, 1965), contains thirty-three poems translated by either Pound or Waley, and provides examples of the various subgenres of the collection. In *The Columbia Book of Chinese Poetry* (New York: Columbia University Press, 1984) Burton Watson provides his own translations of thirty-five of the poems, most of them drawn from the "Airs of the States."

Chinese Texts: Lyric

THE POETRY OF RETREAT

Pauline Yu

As noted in the essay in this volume on "The Imaginative Universe of Chinese Literature," one of the most enduring assumptions in the Chinese tradition was that any consideration of the self inevitably implicated consideration of that self's relation to a larger, public sphere. In Chinese history, this issue focused on the nature of an individual's engagement in the running of the state—hence the centrality of retreat, which in this context was the most common means of signaling one's refusal to become politically involved (whether for reasons of lofty principle or mere expediency), as a literary theme. And indeed, in discussing the topic of retreat in classical Chinese poetry one could incorporate the works of virtually every major figure in the tradition, for it is a theme with a long, broad, and varied history. Even in the pre-Confucian *Book of Songs*, for example (compiled by the sixth century B.C.E.) one can find an anonymous poem (no. 206) whose first stanza reads:

> Don't take the big carriage:
> You'll just get dusty.
> Don't ponder a hundred worries:
> You'll just become ill.[1]

Although there is no clear evidence that the poem is in fact advocating a withdrawal from society, such an inference would not appear to be unwarranted; indeed, the subject was of prime concern to the major philosophers early in the tradition. Daoist [Taoist] texts like the *Zhuang Zi* [*Chuang Tzu*], of course, advocate retreat as a means of better attuning oneself to the fundamental principle underlying the universe (Dao [Tao]), and of maintaining one's philosophical, psychological, and physical peace and integrity. One famous anecdote recounts Zhuang Zi's refusal of a request to administer the kingdom of Chu [Ch'u] because he would rather be a tortoise alive and dragging its tail in the mud than a boxed-up, albeit highly revered, relic.[2] There are countless other passages in the text, as well, illustrating the grounds for such a position.

For Confucianism, the dominant ideology of the literati, the issue was considerably more problematic since one of its most important ideals prescribed the active participation in the public service of society for all individuals whose abilities, background, and education qualified them for it. At the same time, however, Confucius allowed that certain circumstances might dictate a contrary course of action: "Enter not a state that is in peril; stay not in a state that is in danger. Show yourself when the Way prevails in the Empire, but hide yourself when it does not. It is a shameful matter to be poor and humble when the Way prevails in the state. Equally, it is a shameful matter to be rich and noble when the Way falls into disuse in the state."[3]

Thus from an early stage in the literate culture a tradition of retreat was established, to be further reinforced following the introduction of Buddhism after the first century C.E. What is important to remember, however, is that it was conceived initially as a political gesture, as the renunciation of the bureaucratic life primarily on the grounds that to serve the existing government would compromise one's principles. It could therefore be disavowed: withdrawal was as often temporary (or repeated) as it was permanent. And unlike the eremitic traditions in Europe and India, renunciation usually did not assume the abnegation of all earthly contacts and pleasures—an ideal that would have been highly unlikely given the profoundly this-worldly emphasis of the indigenous philosophical schools of thought. Particularly as increasing governmental instability multiplied the dangers of political engagement and weakened the power of Confucian ideology, "reclusion"—while still ostensibly an act of protest—actually represented for many intellectuals a pleasant and fashionable opportunity to escape from irksome responsibilities and life-threatening intrigues, to enjoy the company of like-minded scholars at leisure, and to cultivate their gardens and their arts. Even in these cases, however, the instances of permanent retirement are rare. The most famous examples reveal how deeply entrenched was the ideal of service; typically one concept automatically invoked the other, and the thought of retreat would inevitably be balanced by the desire for engagement.

One of the earliest voices in the poetic tradition of retreat is that of the fourth-century B.C.E. figure Qu Yuan [Ch'ü Yüan], whose retirement from office was essentially involuntary. According to tradition he was slandered by rivals at court and consequently banished from his post as chief minister to the king of Chu [Ch'u] to wander in exile and eventually commit suicide in utter despair. The long poem, "Encountering Sorrow," is attributed to him. This poem was included in an anthology, the *Songs of Chu (Chu Ci [Ch'u Tz'u])*, that took its present form during the first century C.E. Whether actually of his hand or not, the poem provides an eloquent model of unswerving loyalty and devotion to service in the face of every deterrent. Its theme was echoed in countless later works expressing frustration of one's political aspirations. Another poem of later date in the same anthology, "Summons for the Gentleman in Reclusion," advocates in a different way the ethic of commitment by detailing the terrors of nature and urging its addressee to return to society. Both poems thus take the position that service to a worthy ruler is the avenue of choice. But whereas many of the poetic expositions (*fu*) of the Han dynasty celebrate in appropriately epideictic form the glories of the empire—its cities, parks, and festivities—the lyric poetry datable to its waning years reveals a mood of increasing pessimism and obsession with the transience of human life. Thus a recurrent refrain in the anonymous "Nineteen Ancient Poems," for example, laments the fact that human life "lacks the fixity of metal or stone," and, coupled with the collection's brooding on the apparent inevitability of separation and faithlessness, suggests an increasing wariness of, if not disenchantment with, commitments of any sort.

Such fears received an overtly political context and confirmation during the era following the downfall of the Han known as the Six Dynasties, when China not only experienced a series of power struggles and rocky successions but in fact lost half its territory to non-Chinese dominion for over two hundred years. As scholars have often noted, the Confucian ethic of official service grew as endangered as the governments it was meant to support, hence this is the period when retreat becomes an active issue. The considerable number of poets who died untimely deaths, often executed on trumped-up charges of treason; the obviously diminished size of the corpus that remains compared with its original state; as well as the burgeoning of such subgenres as "poems written on the way to execution" or "songs for coffin-pullers," all provide some index of the real precariousness of bureaucratic life. Interest in Daoism and then Buddhism flourished as the appeal of Confucian orthodoxy waned.

One of the earliest individuals to express the temper of these times was Ruan Ji ([Juan Chi] 210–63), whose eighty-two "Poems Singing My Thoughts"[4] argue clearly for neither service nor retreat, but rather articulate the anguish of insecurity and indecision and the difficulty of taking any action in perilous times. As someone who served under both the Wei rulers and the usurping Sima [Ssu-ma] family who established the Jin [Chin] dynasty, Ruan found his allegiances in conflict—as indeed were his fidelity to Confucian principles of service and his interest in Daoist mysticism. Although traditional Chinese commentators typically interpret his poems as referring to specific figures, issues, and incidents during his lifetime, in fact they rarely do so overtly enough to confirm such suppositions. The evocative generality of the first poem of the collection is characteristic of the group as a whole:

> Midnight and I cannot sleep:
> I sit up and pluck my singing zither.
> Through the thin curtain the bright moon shines;
> A cool wind blows my lapels.
> A lone goose cries beyond the wilds,
> Soaring birds sing in northern woods.
> I pace to and fro: what shall I see?
> Mournful thoughts alone wound my heart.[5]

Although Ruan Ji is reported, in an anecdote of dubious authenticity, to have employed such tactics as staying drunk for sixty days to avoid making a politically compromising decision (agreeing to marry his daughter to the scion of the Sima family), he never actually left the center of the political life around him. The most famous example of someone who did abandon government service, and who wrote extensively about it, is the figure Tao Qian [T'ao Ch'ien], or Tao Yuanming ([T'ao Yüan-ming] 365–427). Little is known for certain about his life, but anecdotes abound, largely because he created a vivid image of himself in his poetry and in other writings. The great-grandson of a noted statesman and general, Tao himself led a brief and undistinguished official career spanning thirteen years, which took him into and out of a number of posts, the final lasting fewer than three months. According to all of the official biographies, he left this position as magistrate of Pengze ([P'eng-tse], a small town some thirty miles from his home) in 405, because he refused to greet a visiting dignitary with the appropriate ceremony, having deemed him unworthy of the required protocol. Tao is thereby said to have refused "to bend his waist" for "five pecks of rice," a position echoed in the preface to his poetic exposition entitled "Returning Home," where he suggests that he has finally decided to reject the dictates of his "mouth and belly" and follow his true inclinations. Whatever the case, he renounced officialdom and its honors, returned to his family farm and a life of genteel poverty, and remained there until his death.

As a poet Tao was not particularly esteemed during his own lifetime and for generations thereafter; contemporary taste preferred an ornateness of imagery, parallelism, and allusion rarely found in the relatively simple, straightforward diction of his poetry. He was renowned rather for his character, for his apparent refusal—deemed excessive at times—to compromise personal principles for the sake of advancement, and his biography was included among the "Recluses" rather than the "Literati" in dynastic histories. The eighth century saw a revival of interest in Tao Qian led by the poet Wang Wei (701–61), who wrestled with many of the same issues in even more limpid language. The great Song [Sung] dynasty writer Su Shi ([Su Shih] 1037–1101) wrote poems following the rhyme schemes of all of Tao's lyric works; the latter's position as one of the greatest and best-loved poets has been secure ever since.

One of Tao's best-known works touching on the subject of retreat is actually not a poem but a prose composition (accompanied by an undistinguished poem of the same title), "The Record of Peach Blossom Spring." This short narrative, which is presented as an actual, dated, historical event, recounts a fisherman's accidental discovery of a settlement whose ancestors had escaped from political turmoil during the Qin [Ch'in] dynasty. The inhabitants live in peace, happiness, and oblivion of the outside world, their habits unchanged for the past five hundred years. They receive their visitor warmly but warn him when he leaves not to speak of them to people outside; instead he reports on his experience to the local prefect. However, when he is sent back to locate the community again, he fails to find it. Although it may have been inspired by popular stories of successful searches for immortality, Tao's account is distinctive by virtue of the fact that the author does not describe his recluses as Daoist immortals but as very human political refugees and thus—as the accompanying poem makes explicit—as models for himself. The "Peach Blossom Spring" was alluded to countless times in later works of literature and art as the image of the ideal of retreat.

As far as Tao Qian's own situation is concerned—judging from the account of himself he presents in a short and playful essay, the "Biography of the Master of Five Willows"—one might conclude that he made his decision to retire from official service with utter equanimity and led thereafter a carefree, wine-bibbing life unperturbed by hardships and second thoughts. Several of the one-hundred-thirty-odd poems in his corpus do present this image, one of the best known being the first of a series of five on "Returning to Live on the Farm":

> From youth not fitting with the common tune,
> My nature has always loved the hills and mountains.
> By mistake I fell into the dusty net—
> Gone at once for thirteen years.
> The fettered bird cherishes its old forest;
> Fish in a pond long for deeps of old.
> Clearing wastes at the edge of southern wilds,
> I hold to the simple, returning to the farm.
> My plot is one-odd acre square,
> A thatched hut eight or nine measures large.
> Elms and willows shade the back eaves;
> Peach and plum trees spread before the hall.
> Wreathed in clouds lies a distant town,
> Lingering thickly, the village's smoke.
> A dog barks deep within the lane;
> Cocks crow atop mulberry trees.
> My door and courtyard lack dust and confusion:
> In empty rooms there is peace to spare.
> So long confined within a cage,
> I've come back again to what is natural.

The images in this poem make clear the opposition around which Tao's decision is said to have centered: the dust, fetters, and confused complexity of a career engaged in by mistake, opposed to the freedom, tranquility, and naturalness of life on the farm. Much of the language evokes ideals associated with Daoism, such as holding to "the simple" (*zhuo* [*cho*], also sometimes translated as clumsy or stupid) and the notion of "what is natural" (*ziran* [*tzu-jan*], that which is so of itself). Tao is often described as a "nature poet," but it is clear that this concept of being able to act "naturally," in accord with one's inclinations, is of much greater interest to him than the details of Nature itself, although such possibilities, to be sure, are perhaps more easily realized away from the demands and trammels of courtly life. Hence traditional Chinese literary historians characterize him as the poet of "fields and gardens" (*tianyuan* [*t'ien-yüan*]), primarily, one sus-

pects, in order to be able to pair him with his contemporary Xie
Lingyun [Hsieh Ling-yün] 385–433), the poet of "mountains and
waters" (shanshui [shan-shui])—landscapes on a grander and
more rugged scale.

Tao Qian would have liked to have his readers accept the self-
image presented in "Returning to Live on the Farm," but the very
fact that he states his position so declaratively belies the artful-
ness behind the mask of artlessness, the self-consciousness behind the calm façade. Indeed, the other four poems in the series
do not maintain the transcendent peace of the first, dwelling instead on the very real difficulties of farming one's land and on the
grim reality of death, a theme that had been haunting Chinese
poets for centuries. And whereas one can find echoes of the first
poem's tranquil voice elsewhere in his collection, equally resonant
are more disquieting notes. Of his twenty-poem series on "Drinking Wine," for example, it is the fifth that is most commonly
anthologized and discussed because it confirms the self-image
Tao successfully convinced most readers to accept:

> I built my hut in the world of men,
> Yet there is no din of carriage and horse.
> You ask me how this could be so:
> With a distant heart one's place becomes remote.
> I pluck chrysanthemums beneath the eastern hedge
> And glimpse faraway the southern mountain.
> The mountain air at sunset is fine;
> Flying birds return with one another.
> Within this there is true meaning—
> About to discuss it I've already forgotten words.

Tao's preface to the series describes the poems as spontaneous
products of several pleasant, wine-filled evenings noted down by a
friend in a most casual fashion, but such claims to desultory
composition are difficult to accept. This poem in particular skillfully integrates paradox, internal dialogue, scenic imagery, allusion, and an open-ended conclusion; it suggests indirectly the
poet's ability to achieve a transcendent state of mind that accepts
the inevitability of human mortality (evoked by the references to
chrysanthemums, the southern mountain, and sunset) in a wordless apprehension of truth. Yet the remaining poems in the series
by and large do not share this somber calm: the poet instead
broods on the harsh reality of transience and returns over and
over again to the correctness of his decision to retire, as if to
convince himself. Indeed, when one considers Tao's poetry as a

whole it is difficult to avoid concluding that he was profoundly ambivalent about the choice he had made; that he could not relinquish the ideals of a Confucian scholar-official and could not easily reconcile himself to the life of a simple farmer. Yet this conflict is precisely what makes his work so representative of the theme of retreat in the Chinese tradition, in which poets are much more likely either to vacillate between or to embrace two alternatives, rather than to decide irrevocably for one or the other. This reflects not so much a fundamental inability to make a choice as a culturally deeply-rooted instinct to avoid taking extreme positions. These poets prefer to construe any situation as encompassing complementary aspects, each of which is necessary and inevitable. Thoughts of reclusion would thus typically invoke expressions of the desire for involvement in political life. In practice, of course, this meant that poets in office would long for the country and those in retreat would yearn after the court.

This penchant for complementary thinking dictates mention of Tao Qian's own match, the poet Xie Lingyun. As a poet Xie was better known to his contemporaries and more highly esteemed than Tao, not only because his more florid style gratified the tastes of the time, but also because he belonged to one of the two most powerful families of the Jin dynasty and in fact inherited the title of duke. His political career exemplifies the peripatetic and perilous path taken by all too many of his peers during the Six Dynasties: he held several offices but kept getting demoted and transferred from them, largely owing to his own indifference and ineptitude. His main love was the family estate in the mountains of southeastern China, on which he lavished considerable amounts of time and money landscaping and climbing—even inventing a pair of clogs with removable pegs to meet the different demands of uphill and downhill treks. He was also deeply involved with Buddhism and Buddhist monks, contributed to projects translating and publishing the sutras, and authored a key early document discussing the doctrine of instantaneous enlightenment. Falsely accused of sedition, he eventually fomented a rebellion in earnest and was executed in a marketplace in south China, to which he had previously been banished.

Xie Lingyun's poetry has been included less often in Western anthologies of Chinese poetry, no doubt because his frequent allusions are difficult to translate effectively. Together with Tao Qian, however, he played a key role in Chinese literary history. These two figures illustrate the centrality of politics for the Chinese intellectual—even as they reject it—as well as the varieties of withdrawal—to occasional penui y on a small farm or to an estate spanning two mountains in the company of an army of retainers. Their responses to "renunciation" were reenacted by countless scholar-officials after them. And it is equally important that in retreat they turned their attention to the natural world around them. Much has been written about the origins of "nature poetry" in China with various reasons typically adduced to explain its development during the Six Dynasties period. The phenomenon is certainly connected with the forced emigration of the Chinese nobility to the more lush, varied, and inspiring landscapes of the South following the loss of the North. The burgeoning interest in Daoism and Buddhism at this time (although Confucianism certainly recognized the beauties and moral values of nature) and the political insecurity that suggested the greater wisdom of retreat to the country also contributed to this development. Tao Qian and Xie Lingyun were certainly not the first poets to employ natural imagery, and they did so in different ways, but they did use it more frequently and extensively for its own sake, rather than as symbol for some abstract quality. Thus they set precedents that were fully realized during the Tang [T'ang] dynasty, when the greatest poets created sensuously vivid scenes whose images are imbued with, rather than merely ornament for, an emotional and intellectual content. The qualities for which Tang poetry is most admired—its concentrated vision and form; its precise yet evocative imagery; its preference for the concise and concrete as opposed to the discursive and abstract; its mode of presentation which places as much value, if not more, on what is implied as on what is stated directly—are all clearly adumbrated in the prior tradition.

TOPICS FOR DISCUSSION

1. Rather than comparing these Six Dynasties poets to specific texts, it is better to juxtapose them with broader traditions in other cultures. One possibility would be the topic of eremitism itself, which would compare the almost exclusively political context of retreat in China with the ascetic and monastic traditions in India and Western Europe (although one should certainly not overlook the politically charged nature of many Western pastorals).

2. The above topic could be fruitfully integrated with a discussion of larger philosophical trends: the resolutely this-worldly, monistic bent of Chinese thought, for example, can be contrasted with the dualism fundamental to both Greek and Judeo-Christian modes of thinking.

3. A third obvious choice for discussion is the topic of nature—attitudes toward nature, uses of imagery, and the relationship between the self and the landscape—that is perhaps best explored in conjunction with English romantic poetry. This juxtaposition suggests many immediate parallels that have been noted by scholars, but the dissimilarities are equally important; one might note, for example, the tendency of the Chinese poet to submerge the self in the landscape, as opposed to the way in which the romantic poet's self often expands to encompass, if not devour, the natural scene.

4. Finally, all of these themes could also be addressed if the poems were incorporated into a unit of study simply focused on the lyric tradition.

NOTES

1. Translation by Pauline Yu. The poem can be found in Bernhard Karlgren, *The Book of Odes* (Stockholm: Museum of Far Eastern Antiquities, 1964). See also Watson, listed in References.

2. Burton Watson, trans., *Chuang Tzu: Basic Writings* (New York: Columbia University Press, 1964), p. 109.

3. *Analects* VIII.13, trans. D. C. Lau (New York: Penguin Books, 1979), p. 94.

4. See Watson, listed in References.

5. Translation by Pauline Yu.

REFERENCES

There are problems with the English translations of these poets' work. The translations of Tao Qian's and Xie Lingyun's collected works, which also include extensive biographical information (James Robert Hightower, *The Poetry of Tao Ch'ien* [Oxford: Oxford University Press, 1970]; A. R. Davis, *T'ao Yüan-ming, A.D. 365–427, His Works and Their Meaning*, 2 vols. [New York: Cambridge University Press, 1983]; and J. D. Frodsham, *The Murmuring Stream: The Life and Works of Hsieh Ling-yün*, 2 vols. [Kuala Lumpur: University of Malaya Press, 1967]), are not available in paperback versions. H. C. Chang's *Chinese Literature 2: Nature Poetry* (New York: Columbia University Press, 1977) is available in an inexpensive edition and includes a representative selection of works. However, it presents many unsupported anecdotes as fact and injects considerable fustian into its translations. The best choice would probably be Burton Watson's anthology, *The Columbia Book of Chinese Poetry* (New York: Columbia University Press, 1984), which has an especially good selection from Tao Qian and also specifically addresses the issue of retreat.

TANG POETRY: A RETURN TO BASICS

Burton Watson

The history of Chinese poetry begins around 600 B.C.E. with the compilation of an anthology, the *Shi Jing* ([*Shih ching*] *Book of Odes* or *Book of Songs*), containing poems that probably date back several centuries earlier. The tradition continues with barely a break, down to the present day. Naturally, such an extended period of development saw the evolution of a number of different poetic forms and styles, and countless ebbs and flows in the tide of artistic inspiration.

It has generally been agreed by Chinese critics—and non-Chinese students of the language have found no reason to dissent— that the peak in literary achievement in this long process of growth was reached during the Tang [T'ang] dynasty, which ruled China from C.E. 618 to 907, particularly the middle years of this Period. This was the age of Li Bai [also Li Bo or Li Po], Du Fu [Tu Fu], Bai Juyi [also Bo Juyi or Po Chü-i], and numerous other figures renowned in Chinese literary history, when the art of poetry seemed to reach levels of expressive force and universality of statement it had hardly known in the past and was seldom to rival again. I would like here to try to convey some idea of the nature of this poetry and its appeal for English readers of today. Rather than attempting generalities, I will center the discussion around specific examples of Tang poetry, touching upon the qualities that can be effectively brought across in translation and those that must inevitably be lost.

Unlike the peoples of Europe and India, the Chinese did not develop a tradition of epic poetry. Though they had their internecine wars and campaigns against foreign invaders—Ezra Pound's "Song of the Bowmen of Shu" is a translation of an early work from the *Book of Odes* dealing with one such campaign—they seldom made feats of arms a theme of poetry. An overwhelmingly agricultural people, they preferred in their poetry to focus mainly upon the scenes and events of everyday life, which accounts for the generally low-key and ungrandiose tone of so much of Chinese poetry. It is also one reason why many of their works, even those written centuries ago, sound strikingly modern in translation.

The first work to be quoted is by the government official and poet Bai Juyi (772–846). Bai was one of the most prolific of the major Tang poets, and his works are particularly well preserved, in part because he took the trouble to compile and edit them himself, depositing copies in the libraries of several important Buddhist temples. The poem was written in 835 and is addressed to Bai's friend Liu Yuxi ([Liu Yü-hsi] 772–842), a fellow poet and bureaucrat who was the same age as Bai. The Chinese frequently exchanged poems with friends, often replying to one another's poems as one would reply to a letter; the practice constituted both an expression of friendship and an opportunity to exercise literary abilities and invite critical comment. When responding to a friend's poem, one customarily employed the same poetic form and sometimes the same rhymes or rhyme words as the original poem in order to add an element of challenge to the game.

"On Old Age, to Send to Meng-te (Liu Yü-hsi)"

The two of us both in old age now,
I ask myself what it means to be old.
Eyes bleary, evenings you're the first to bed;
hair a bother, mornings you leave it uncombed.
Sometimes you go out, a stick to prop you;
sometimes, gate shut, you stay indoors the whole day.
Neglecting to look into the newly polished mirror,
no longer reading books if the characters are very small,
your thoughts dwelling more and more on old friends,
your activities far removed from those of the young,
only idle chatter rouses your interest . . .
When we meet, we still have lots of that don't we!

(trans. Burton Watson)[1]

The subject of the poem is so universal an experience and the presentation so straightforward that comment seems almost superfluous. The poet, sixty-three at the time, begins by speaking directly to his friend Liu, but then quickly falls into a kind of private revery on the subject of old age and the changes it brings.

In the very last line he abruptly shakes himself out of his musings and addresses his friend once more. Unlike many traditional Chinese poems, this one employs no erudite allusions to earlier literature, though, as may readily be seen in the translation, it makes considerable use of verbal parallelism, a device common in both Chinese prose and poetry. The poem is in *shi* [*shih*] form, essentially the same form used in the *Book of Odes*. It employs a line that is five characters or five syllables in length, and is in the relatively free "old-style" form, which means there is no limit on the number of lines. A single rhyme is employed throughout, the rhymes occurring at the end of the even-numbered lines.

Bai Juyi is particularly remembered for his relaxed, warmly personal works such as that just quoted. He himself, however, placed a much higher value on his poems of social criticism. Confucius had emphasized the didactic function of poetry, citing the poems of the *Book of Odes* as examples, and Confucian-minded officials in later centuries often employed poetic forms to voice criticisms of the government or expose the ills of society. Bai Juyi, in his youthful years as an official, enthusiastically carried on this tradition, writing a number of outspoken works that he hoped would bring about changes in government policy. The following is a famous example.

The poem is entitled "Light Furs, Fat Horses," an allusion to a passage in the Confucian *Analects* (VI, 3) in which Confucius censures luxurious living among public officials. It was written in 810, when the poet held advisory posts in the capital, and the region south of the Yangtze River was plagued by drought. The poet had previously asked that the government take steps to aid the drought victims, but his pleas went unheeded. The poem depicts a banquet at a military encampment in or near the capital. It is in the same form as the poem previously quoted.

"Light Furs, Fat Horses"

A show of arrogant spirit fills the road;
a glitter of saddles and horses lights up the dust.
I ask who these people are—
trusted servants of the ruler, I'm told.
The vermilion sashes are all high-ranking courtiers;
the purple ribbons are probably generals.
Proudly they repair to the regimental feast,
their galloping horses passing like clouds.
Tankards and wine cups brim with nine kinds of spirits;
from water and land, an array of eight delicacies.

For fruit they break open Tung-t'ing oranges,
for fish salad, carve up scaly bounty from T'ien-chih.
Stuffed with food, they rest content in heart;
livened by wine, their mood grows merrier then ever.
This year there's a drought south of the Yangtze.
In Ch'ü-chou, people are eating people. (p. 246)

Tang poetry—at least, all that has come down to us—is almost entirely the product of a single group in society, the literati or scholar-bureaucrats, men who had received a firm grounding in the classical texts and had chosen to enter government service, often after passing the civil service examinations. For these men, the writing of poetry was no mere hobby or diversion, but an integral part of their lives as gentlemen and public servants, a means of airing their opinions, fulfilling their responsibilities to society, and furthering their spiritual cultivation.

The greatness of Tang poetry probably derives first of all from this tone of moral seriousness that pervades so much of it. There were other periods in Chinese literary history when poetry was mainly a pleasant pastime for members of the court or aristocracy, a vehicle for displacing verbal ingenuity or embroidering upon the patterns of the past. The Tang poets, though certainly not incapable of frivolous verse, generally had far more serious purposes in mind when they employed the medium, as we have seen in the example just quoted. They returned poetry to what they believed to be its original function, the addressing of important social and ethical issues.

At the same time, as evidenced in the first poem quoted above, they were not afraid to be frankly personal in their writing. Though this personal note was shunned in some periods of literary history, the best of the Tang poets such as Du Fu or Bai Juyi did not hesitate to record the experiences and emotional crises of their daily lives in their works, employing poetry much as the diary or autobiography forms are used in other cultures. To do so was for them a kind of literary and spiritual discipline.

The poet-official Wang Wei (699?–761), much of whose poetry describes the scenes of his daily life, purchased a country estate at a place called Wang River in the mountains south of Changan [Ch'ang-an], the Tang capital. The estate had formerly belonged to another well-known poet-official, Song Zhiwen ([Sung Chih-wen] d. 712?). In the following poem—the first in a famous series describing scenic spots on the estate—the poet muses on the passing of time, as graphically exemplified in the dying willows planted by the former owner, his own feelings of pity for Song Zhiwen, and the pity that owners of the estate in years to come will perhaps feel for him. This ability of the Tang poets, often within the span of a scant four lines, to open out huge vistas in time or space is one of the qualities that endows their poetry with its characteristic air of grandeur and mythic proportions.

> "Meng-ch'eng Hollow"
>
> A new home at the mouth of Meng-ch'eng;
> old trees—last of a stand of dying willows:
> years to come, who will be its owner,
> vainly pitying the one who had it before? (p. 200)

The Tang poets in their subject matter did not confine themselves to the autobiographical, however. Following a practice that is very old in Chinese poetry, they frequently adopted a persona from the folk song tradition in order to enlarge the breadth and social significance of their material, speaking through the voice of a peasant pressed into military service, a neglected wife, or a soldier on frontier duty. Here, for example,is such a work by Li Bai ([Li Pai [Li Bo/Li Po] 701–62), a poet particularly famed for his lyric gift and his works in folk song form. It is entitled "Ziye [Tzu-yeh] Song," Ziye being the name of a courtesan of earlier times who was noted for her brief and poignant songs. The poem is set in autumn—the time when women traditionally fulled cloth to make clothes to send to the soldiers at the border—and pictures a woman in the capital city of Changan (present day Xian [Sian]) dreaming of her husband at Jade Pass in Gansu [Kansu] far to the west.

> "Tzu-yeh Song"
>
> Ch'ang-an—one slip of moon;
> in ten thousand houses, the sound of fulling mallets.
> Autumn winds keep on blowing,
> all things make me think of Jade Pass!
> When will they put down the barbarians
> and my good man come home from his far campaign? (p. 207)

Before leaving the poem we may note that, according to some commentators, the first line should be interpreted to read "Ch'ang-an—one swath of moonlight." The question, in effect, is whether one chooses to imagine the women working under the thin crescent of a new moon, or under a full moon that floods the ground with light. Famous as these poems are and as often as they have been commented upon, the nature of the classical Chinese language is such that differences of interpretation of this kind continue to exist.

The poems quoted so far have all dealt with the world of human affairs, but this does not mean that Tang poets neglected the natural scenery around them. In very early times, nature was looked on as rather fearful, the abode of fierce beasts or malevolent spirits. But from around the fifth century on, Chinese printers and poets began to show a much greater appreciation of the beauties of the natural world, particularly the mist-filled mountain and river landscapes of southern China. The period was one of foreign invasion and political turmoil, and these mountain landscapes came to be seen as places of peace and safety, where one might escape from the perils of official life and perhaps even acquire the secrets of longevity.

This interest in natural beauty continued to be an important theme in Tang poetry, often bound up with religious overtones linking it to Buddhism or Daoism [Taoism]. The following poem, from a group of some three hundred poems attributed to a recluse known as Hanshan [Han-shan] or The Master of Cold Mountain, is an example. Hanshan was said to have lived at a place called Cold Mountain (Hanshan) in the Tiantai [T'ien-t'ai] mountains of Zhejiang [Chekiang] Province, the site of many Buddhist and Daoist temples. It is uncertain when he lived, though the late eighth and early ninth centuries are suggested as the most likely possibility. The poem is untitled.

> I climb the road to Cold Mountain,
> the road to Cold Mountain that never ends.
> The valleys are long and strewn with stones,
> the streams broad and banked with thick grass.
> Moss is slippery, though no rain has fallen;
> pines sigh but it isn't the wind.
> Who can break from the snares of the world
> and sit with me among the white clouds? (p. 263)

On the literal level the poem is a description of the scenery along the kind of mountain trail that I myself have climbed in the Tiantai range, with its rocky streambeds and pine-dotted slopes. At the same time the imagery of the ascent suggests a process of spiritual cultivation and the attainment of higher realms of understanding, while the white clouds of the last line—clouds that the Chinese believed were literally breathed forth by the mountain itself—are a frequently recurring symbol in Chinese literature for purity and detachment.

The next poem to be quoted, by a ninth-century writer named Gao Pian [Kao P'ien], also deals with the natural scene. But this is nature carefully cultivated and seen in close conjunction with human habitation. As the title "Mountain Pavilion, Summer Day" tells us, the setting is a pleasant country retreat in the hush of a long, hot summer's day. We are shown the masses of shade trees surrounding the house, the reflections of the building and terrace as they appear upside down in the pond that fronts them, and the trellis of roses whose fragrance is so strong in the courtyard. Beyond the courtyard, a curtain strung with crystal beads stirs gently in the cool breeze, but just who is napping behind the curtains we are not told. The poem is an example of the kind of mood piece at which the Tang poets excelled, deft sketches made up of a few artfully chosen details that serve to rouse the reader's curiosity and invite him to fill out the remainder of the scene from his own imagination.

"Mountain Pavilion, Summer Day"

Thick shade of green trees, long summer day,
lodge and terrace casting their images upside down in the pond.
Crystal-beaded curtains stir, a faint breeze rising;
one trellis of roses, the courtyard full of its scent.
(trans. Burton Watson)

This poem, along with the Wang Wei poem quoted earlier, is written in a form known as *jueju* [*chüeh-chü*] or "cut-off lines." The form is limited to four lines in length and usually employs a line of five or seven characters. Chinese is a tonal language and the *jueju* form, in addition to employing end rhyme, obeys elaborate rules governing the tonal pattern of the words. We do not know just how the four tones of Tang-period Chinese were pronounced, and even if we did, the effect of such tonal patterns could not be reproduced in a nontonal language such as English. But it is well to keep in mind that, though translations of Tang poetry may give an impression of relative freedom, the originals are often in highly controlled forms. The fact that the Tang poets not only complied with the exacting prosodic restrictions placed upon them, but even succeeded in dancing in their chains, is one of the wonders of their poetry.

One writer who seems to have welcomed the challenges presented by such demanding forms and who produced in them works of great power and originality was Du Fu (712–70), often referred to as China's greatest poet. He is particularly noted for the keen observations of nature recorded in his works, as well as for his tone of passionate sincerity and concern for the welfare of the nation. The following poem, entitled simply "Jueju," was written in his late years, when conditions of unrest in the country forced him to lead the life of a wanderer in the upper reaches of the Yangtze River, hoping always for an opportunity to return to his home in the northeast.

The poem begins with two lines in strict parallel form recording thoughtfully noted observations on the river scene: the river gulls appearing whiter when seen against the intense blue of the river, and the buds of spring blossoms—probably peach tree buds— seeming like so many flames about to burst into color. In the second couplet, however, the tense objectivity of the opening lines suddenly gives way to a rush of feeling as the poet realizes that yet another spring has come and is about to depart, while he is still far removed from his homeland.

> River cobalt-blue, birds whiter against it;
> mountains green, blossoms about to flame:
> I watch, this spring too passes—
> what day will I ever go home?
>
> (trans. Burton Watson)

The last poem in my selection, like the first one, is addressed to a friend, and deals with the theme of friendship and separation. It was the custom of Chinese gentlemen to write poems of commemoration when they gathered for a banquet, outing, or other social occasion, and this was particularly true when the purpose of the gathering was to see one of their number off on a journey. Official assignments kept the scholar-bureaucrats moving constantly about the empire, and there are numerous works by Tang poets bidding farewell to a friend or thanking friends for such a send-off. This poem is by Li Bai and addressed to his friend Meng Haoran ([Meng Hao-jan] 689–740), who was sailing east down the Yangtze to Yangzhou [Yang-chou] (previously Guangling [Kuang-ling]) in Jiangsu [Kiangsu]. The farewell party was held at a place called Yellow Crane Tower overlooking the river at Wuchang [Wu-ch'ang] in Hubei. All this information is carefully recorded in the heading of the poem, since the Chinese tend to feel that the circumstances that led to the writing of a poem are an important part of its meaning.

"At Yellow Crane Tower Taking Leave of Meng Hao-jan
   as He Sets off for Kuang-ling"

An old friend takes leave of the west at Yellow Crane Tower,
in misty third-month blossoms goes downstream to Yang-chou.
The far-off shape of his lone sail disappears
   in the blue-green void,
and all I see is the long river flowing to the edge of the sky.

                            (p. 211)

Like Wang Wei's poem quoted above on the successive owners of his country estate, this poem opens up vistas, here spatial ones that show us the sweeping mountain ranges and river systems of continental China. And unspoken but underlying it is the aching contrast between these vast, long-enduring features of the landscape and the frailty of human existence, as symbolized by the lone sail of Meng's boat fading from sight on the horizon.

Tang poetry, to sum up, stands out in the long history of Chinese poetic development because, eschewing the superficiality of an earlier age—the tendency toward bland impersonality and mannered manipulation of stock themes and images—it restored to Chinese poetry the lost note of personal concern. The Tang poets were not afraid to employ poetry to record their deepest and most intimate feelings, crying out for the alleviation of social ills, noting with wry candor the waning of their physical powers, longing for absent friends, or dreaming of the last journey home. And because they dealt with the basic impulses of the human being, their works easily survive the transition into another language and milieu. Tang poetry, as one who reads it will readily perceive, is not just the product of a particularly golden age in China's literary history, but a part of the universal human heritage.

Using the last poem quoted above as an example, I will illustrate the form of the original and give an indication of the pronunciation and literal meaning of the characters. The poem is in *jueju* form, one of the most popular forms in Tang times. As stated earlier, the *jueju* is limited to four lines and usually employs a line made up of five or seven characters (never a mixture of the two line lengths), though rarely a six-character line is used. There is usually a light caesura after the second character in a five-character line and after the fourth character in a seven-character line. Rhyme is required at the end of the second and fourth lines, with an optional rhyme at the end of the first line.

The example, Li Bai's farewell poem to Meng Haoran, uses a seven-character line. It has three rhyme words, *lou, zhou,* and *liu* in modern standard Chinese pronunciation, which all belong to the level tone rhyme category *you* [*yu*] and were rhymes in Tang-period pronunciation.

The *jueju* form requires observation of the rules of tonal regulation. For the purposes of such rules, the four tones of Tang-period Chinese were divided into two categories, level tones (indicated below by the sign -) and deflected tones (indicated by the sign +). The rules require that there be no more than two, or at most three, characters in succession belonging to the same tonal category in any line. (The first line, with four characters in a row in the level category, appears to be a violation of this rule, but the four characters include the third character in the line which, along with the first character in a seven-character line, is exempt from tonal requirements, and thus serves to break the series.) In addition, characters in key positions in the upper line of a couplet should be matched by characters belonging to the opposite tonal category in corresponding positions in the lower line of the couplet.

Below is the pronunciation of the poem according to modern standard Chinese and an indication of the literal meaning of each character. Nouns include no indication of number and verbs no indication of tense. Additional words may be used to make number and tense explicit (as in the case of "lone sail" below), but in most cases the translator must guess at number and tense on the basis of context. The title of the poem often plays a vital role in establishing the context of the poem.

+	-	-	-	-	+	-
gu	*ren*	*xi*	*ci*	*huang*	*he*	*lou*
old	friend	west	leave	Yellow	Crane	Tower

-	-	-	+	+	-	-
yan	*hua*	*san*	*yue*	*xia*	*Yang*	*zhou*
mist	blossom	three	month	descend	Yangzhou	

-	-	+	+	+	-	+
gu	*fan*	*yuan*	*ying*	*bi*	*kong*	*chin*
lone	sail	distant	image	blue (blue-green jade)	void	expire

-	+	-	-	-	+	-
wei	*jian*	*chang*	*jiang*	*tian*	*ji*	*liu*
only	see	long	river	heaven	edge	flow

TOPICS FOR DISCUSSION

1. What functions did poetry play in traditional Chinese society? What motives would lead an educated Chinese man or woman to compose poetry? What were looked on as the qualifications for writing poetry?

2. Why was poetry writing one of the requirements for persons taking the civil service exams? What good or bad effects might this have had on the development of poetry in Tang times? (Note that poetry was easy to grade on technical grounds. Also that making it a requirement on the exam meant that persons from all over the Chinese empire had to master the system of rhymes in use in the capital are, i.e., to learn the standard Chinese pronunciation of the time.)

3. What themes seem to be most important in Chinese poetry? What themes that are of major importance in other poetic traditions absent or of minor importance? What characteristics of Chinese society or thought does this reflect?

4. Most of the forms used for lyric poetry in Tang times prescribed the number of characters or syllables per line and often the total number of lines. This, coupled with the strong tendency to use end stopped lines, i.e., lines that constitute an independent syntactical unit, means that poets were greatly limited in the number of modifying words of phrases they could use. What good or bad results could come from the use of such highly restricted forms? In using such restricted forms, which also at times required verbal and tonal parallelism, was the poet saying what he wanted to say, or merely "filling in" the slots in the prosodic pattern? What recourse had the poet if he wanted greater freedom of form? (Note *fu* or rhyme-prose form, much freer in line length, length of poem, and syntax.)

5. What qualities of theme or treatment in traditional Chinese poetry have attracted the interest of Western poets in recent years? What influence has Chinese poetry in translation exerted on contemporary poetry in English? Does Chinese poetry appear to have been correctly or incorrectly understood by its admirers in the West?

6. Questions relating to translation: Is it possible or desirable to try to reproduce any of the formal characteristics of Chinese poetry when rendering it in English translation? Line form of the original? Rhyme? Verbal parallelism? How much explanation of historical or literary allusions is desirable? How should such explanatory material be presented?

NOTE

1. This poem and the others so indicated were translated for this essay and these translations are published here for the first time. Poems followed by page numbers in parentheses are included in Burton Watson, *The Columbia Book of Chinese Poetry* (New York: Columbia University Press, 1984). These poems retain the Wade-Giles system of transliteration.

REFERENCES

Graham, A. C. *Poems of the Late T'ang.* Baltimore: Penguin, 1965.

Liu, James J. Y. *The Art of Chinese Poetry.* Chicago: University of Chicago Press, 1962.

Owen, Stephen. *The Poetry of the Early T'ang.* New Haven: Yale University Press, 1977.

Owen, Stephen. *The Great Age of Chinese Poetry: The High T'ang.* New Haven: Yale University Press, 1981.

Watson, Burton. *The Columbia Book of Chinese Poetry.* New York: Columbia University Press, 1984.

Lyric Text: Chinese

SPRING GAZE (Chun wang)

by Du Fu

Translated by Pauline Yu

([Du Fu]杜甫(712-70): Spring Gaze [Chun wang]春望)

The country shattered, mountains and rivers remain.
Spring in the city—grasses and trees are dense.
Feeling the times, flowers draw forth tears.
Hating to part, birds alarm the heart.
Beacon fires for three months in a row;
A letter from home worth ten thousand in gold.
White hairs scratched grow even shorter—
Soon too few to hold a hairpin on.

國	破	山	河	在
nation	*broken*	*mountain*	*river*	*exist*
guo+	po+	shan-	he-	zai+
城	春	草	木	深
city-wall	*spring*	*grass*	*tree*	*deep*
cheng-	chun-	cao+	mu+	shen-
感	時	花	濺	淚
feel	*times*	*flower*	*sprinkle*	*tears*
gan+	shi-	hua-	jian+	lei+
恨	別	鳥	驚	心
hate	*parting*	*bird*	*alarm*	*heart*
hen+	bie+	niao+	jing-	xin-
烽	火	連	三	月
beacon	*fire*	*consecutive*	*three*	*month*
feng-	huo+	lian-	san-	yue+
家	書	抵	萬	金
family	*letter*	*worth*	*ten-thousand*	*gold-pieces*
jia-	shu-	di+	wan+	jin-
白	頭	搔	更	短
white	*hair*	*scratch*	*more*	*short*
bai+	tou-	sao-	geng+	duan+
渾	欲	不	勝	簪
quite	*about-to*	*not*	*bear*	*hairpin*
hun-	yu+	bu+	sheng-	zan-

Chinese Texts: Narrative

CHUANG TZU

Shuen-fu Lin

The *Chuang Tzu* (*Zhuang Zi*),[1] along with the *Tao te ching* (*Dao de jing*), is one of the principal texts in the philosophy of Taoism (Daoism). For more than two millennia it has had a profound and far-reaching influence on Chinese thought, literature, art, aesthetics, and religion. While one can think of other early philosophical texts which have exerted an equal or even greater influence on Chinese civilization, the *Chuang Tzu* is unique in being a book that appeals equally to reason and imagination. Since its compilation in the second century B.C.E., this text of philosophical mysticism has always been recognized as a literary monument in the Chinese tradition. Through translations, the *Chuang Tzu* has also attracted many admirers in the West during the last few decades. As one such admirer Arthur Waley has aptly described it, the *Chuang Tzu* is "one of the most entertaining as well as one of the profoundest books in the world."

It is now generally accepted that this text is not the collected works of Chuang Chou (Zhuang Zhou, better known as Chuang Tzu or Master Chuang), a philosopher and writer of astonishing brilliance and originality, who lived from about 369 to 286 B.C.E. Rather, it is a collection of philosophical writings of the fourth, third, and second centuries B.C.E. that generally belongs to the Taoist school of thought. This great book was supposed to contain fifty-two chapters originally. But our present *Chuang Tzu*, which is derived from the Kuo Hsiang edition completed around 300 C.E., contains only thirty-three chapters divided into three parts: the "Inner Chapters" (chapters 1–7), the "Outer Chapters" (chapters 8–22), and the "Mixed Chapters" (chapters 23–33). Recent scholarship has firmly established that the seven "Inner Chapters"—together with portions of a few "Mixed Chapters" (chapters 23–27)—are the earliest and the core segments of the book. The "Inner Chapters" are found to exhibit a remarkable unity and homogeneity in philosophy and style of writing. In both philosophy and literary style, only the "Inner Chapters" and those portions of the "Mixed Chapters" fully fit the descriptions of the works of Chuang Chou as provided in the last chapter of the book, titled "T'ien-hsia" ("Tianxia") or "Under Heaven" (see below). The rest of the book is regarded by modern scholars to be by multiple authors, by followers of Chuang Tzu's thought, and by other Taoist thinkers. These later chapters bear influence of the "Inner Chapters" in both thought and prose style but do not measure up to the magnificent command of language as seen in the writings of the man whose name has been used to designate the entire book. One can say that the value of the *Chuang Tzu* as a great work of literature in the Chinese tradition rests mainly on the most brilliant and original "Inner Chapters."

We know surprisingly little about the life of Chuang Tzu. In a brief biographical note in his *Shi Ji* [*Shih-chi*] or *Records of the Historian,* Sima Qian ([Ssu-ma Ch'ien] ca. 145-ca. 89 B.C.E.) says that Chuang Tzu was a native of Meng (which was probably in present-day Honan Province, south of the Yellow River) and once held a minor post in the "Lacquer Garden" there. He dates Chuang Tzu in the reigns of King Hui of Liang (370–319 B.C.E.) and King Xuan of Qi ([Hsüan of Ch'i] 319–301 B.C.E.), which were the height of the Golden Age of ancient Chinese philosophy. There are a number of stories about Chuang Tzu throughout the book that carries his name, but it is difficult to accept them as reliable biography. Nonetheless, these stories convey a consistent sense of a man who mocks logic, flails other philosophers who debate with him, shuns office and wealth, and looks upon death not as something to be feared but as part of the inevitable process of nature. In reading the "Inner Chapters," A.C. Graham has observed, one has the distinct impression of meeting the very same unusual individual.

One does not have to go far to look for a succinct description of Chuang Chou as a philosopher and writer. A passage about Chuang Tzu in the "Under Heaven" chapter reads:

> Boundless, vague, and without form; changing, transforming, never constant: is it death? or is it life? do I stand side by side with heaven and earth? do I set out with the divine and illumined? muddle-headed, where am I going? in a daze, where am I going to arrive? the ten thousand things all spread out around me, but not one of them is worthy to be my destination— some of the ancient "art of the Way" is to be found in this. When Chuang Chou got wind of it, he delighted in it. With his outland-

ish opinions, expansive discourses, and borderless words, he would often let himself go totally free without partisanship, not revealing things from one particular point of view. He thought that the world had sunken in the mud and could not be spoken to in serious language. So he used "goblet words" (zhiyan [chih-yen]) for endless, unfixed rambling, "words of those whom people respected" (zhongyan [chung-yen]) to give a ring of truth, and "imputed words" (yuyan [yü-yen]) to widen the range. Alone he came and went with the spirit of heaven and earth, without ever casting an arrogant eye upon the ten thousand things. He did not make demands with "right" and "wrong" in order to get along with the common people of the world. Although his writings are out of the ordinary, they are subtle and tactful and will do no one any harm. Although his words are at sixes and sevens, they are so crafty and cunning that they deserve to be appreciated. They are full of truths that never come to an end. Above he wandered with the "maker of things" and below he made friends with those who regard life and death as externals and know nothing of beginning and end. As for the Root, his understanding is broad and expansive, and profound, penetrating, and unbridled. As for the Ancestor, he may be said to have tuned himself and risen all the way up to it. Nonetheless, in responding to transformation and freeing himself from things, he set forth principles that are never exhaustive; but the principles being issued forth by him can never be shuffled off either. Alas! how abstruse! he was a man who had not succeeded in getting it all.

This is my adaptation of the magnificent translations of this startling passage done by A. C. Graham and Burton Watson. Before the twentieth century, together with other dubious chapters, "Under Heaven" was considered to have been written by Chuang Tzu himself. However, some recent scholars have convincingly demonstrated that this chapter was probably written by a Confucian scholar of the late third and early second centuries B.C.E. who was deeply influenced by the philosophy of Chuang Tzu. "Under Heaven" was the first general history of ancient Chinese thought, especially of the Warring States Period. It is an extremely important essay that documents the first "philosophic breakthrough" in Chinese civilization. It offers a synoptic view of the various schools of thought, largely in terse descriptive and discursive language combined with some direct quotations from the representative thinkers. The only exception to this approach is the passage quoted above—it should be noted that the passage does contain several sentences directly taken from the "Inner Chapters" also. Chuang Tzu is here portrayed not only as a profound mystical thinker but more importantly also as a poet of unbridled imagination. The shift from an essentially discursive to a highly literary, or even poetic, style of language (obviously in imitation of the language of Chuang Tzu's works) seems to be a deliberate attempt to do justice to the uniqueness of the life, thought, and writings of this thinker.

Chuang Tzu is without a doubt the greatest prose writer of the Golden Age of Chinese philosophy. His achievement as a writer is described in "Under Heaven" as embodied in the three interesting modes of using words—*zhiyan, zhongyan,* and *yuyan.* These three modes of language are intimately related to Chuang Tzu's ideas about life, language, and the world he lived in. Obviously, they have some broader implications in ancient Chinese culture and literature as well. Space does not permit me to address these important issues in any detail. I shall only provide a brief discussion of the three rhetorical devices since they are most directly relevant to the literary merit of the *Chuang Tzu.* Nevertheless, I should first mention that the terms *yuyan, zhongyan,* and *zhiyan* (in this order) come from chapter 27 entitled "Yuyan," or "Imputed Words" in the "Mixed Chapters" part of the book. Chapter 27 was probably written by someone directly influenced by Chuang Tzu's thought, and its date of composition was probably not long after that of chapter 2, "Qiwu Lun [Ch'i-wu Lun]" or "Discussion on Making All Things Equal," one of the "Inner Chapters." A discussion of the philosophical underpinnings for Chuang Tzu's three rhetorical devices are to be found in these two important chapters.

What do *yuyan, zhongyan,* and *zhiyan* mean? Although these three terms are not clearly defined, we can tell from the contexts in which they appear that they are conceived not as sharply distinct, but rather as overlapping categories. Moreover, each term also involves several possible meanings. The literal sense of *yuyan* is "words that contain an implied meaning." First and foremost, then, the term means something like "metaphorical or figurative writing" in English. It can be described as a device for expressing ideas or inner visions in imagistic and metaphorical language rather than in straightforward discursive language. Secondly, *yuyan* can also be taken to mean "fable, parable, exemplum, or allegory." In fact, in Modern Chinese, *yuyan* is still the term used to translate those concepts in English. This second interpretation is simply an extension of the basic meaning of "metaphor" to include a narrative element. The "Inner Chapters" of the *Chuang Tzu* abound with metaphors ranging from individual terms to extended symbolic anecdotes and stories. For example, "free and easy wandering" is metaphorical of "absolute spiritual freedom," the Great Thoroughfare of Tao (the Way); the "immortals" of the people of the highest spiritual attainment; the "gnarled tree"—and its variations, the "cripples or deformed people"—of the "great use of the useless"; the "boring of seven holes in Hundun [Hun-tun] (Chaos)" of the "destruction of primordial oneness and harmony"; and "butchering an ox" of the "secret to the nurture of life." It should be noted here that the *Tao te ching*, which is traditionally attributed to a certain Lao Tzu (Lao Zi), an older contemporary of Confucius (551–479 B.C.E.), relies on metaphor and paradox as the chief rhetorical devices in its eighty-one poem-like statements. But the use of metaphorical language in the *Chuang Tzu* is far more complex and sophisticated. Metaphors in the *Chuang Tzu* are usually extended ones and appear in larger narrative contexts. Through metaphorical language and symbolical stories, Chuang Tzu makes his otherwise abstract and mystical ideas more concrete for the reader to grasp. It is in this respect that Chuang Tzu can most readily be considered a "lyrical philosopher." The third sense of *yuyan* is "putting one's words into the mouths of other people." This brings to mind the notion of a "literary mask" so widely discussed in modern Western criticism. Not every story in the "Inner Chapters" involves the use of a "mask." Many stories are simply metaphorical of the author's particular philosophical ideas. The mask is found only in those stories in which specific characters are selected to serve as the author's mouthpieces. To illustrate, both the story about the enormous Peng [P'eng] bird (in chapter 1) and the one about Chuang Chou himself dreaming that he is a butterfly (in chapter 2) are metaphorical stories, while in "butchering an ox" (in chapter 3), Butcher Ding [Ting] is used as a mask.

Before we proceed to discuss *zhongyan*, let us ask this important question: Why does Chuang Tzu use metaphorical language, fable, parable, and masks rather than clear and straightforward discursive language to express his ideas and experiences? There are several reasons for this. First of all, the Taoists—including both Chuang Tzu and the author or authors of the *Tao te ching*—share with all mystics the same mistrust for the adequacy of language—especially discursive language—as a medium for the communication of a person's ideas, perceptions, and experiences. The ultimate goal of Taoism is to gain an understanding of Tao, the great Way of nature and the cosmos, in order to attain spiritual freedom, and to acquire a knack for living and a pristine perspective on the world. Tao is spontaneous, indivisible, unlimited, and unconditioned, but unfortunately, language chops things up by imposing on them artificial categories that destroy the clarity and oneness of the Taoist vision. Chuang Tzu's mistrust for language makes him even more aware of the need to use all the available resources of language and the literary art for pointing at least in the direction of Tao. The spirit of playfulness and the talent for variety in the use of language as displayed in the "Inner Chapters" are largely the result of Chuang Tzu's awareness of both the limitations and the powers of words. Second, the Taoist attitude toward language represents but an extreme expression of a common Chinese view. The ancient Chinese thinkers regard language essentially as a tool—and often an inadequate tool—for the communication of meaning, rather than as something that embodies truth and reality within it. This traditional Chinese view is tersely summed up in the remark attributed to Confucius: "Writing does not exhaust speech and speech does not exhaust meaning." To the Taoist, in addition to being inadequate, language itself can also become a trap. Therefore, in using words, one is advised always to maintain an attitude of freedom. This sense of freedom in using language has contributed to Chuang Tzu's creative use of metaphors, fables, parables, and fantasy for the expression of his philosophy. Third, the Taoists share with other major Chinese philosophical schools the same lack of interest in formal logic. Since the ancient Chinese thinkers were most concerned with living truth, and not abstract truth, analogy—rather than syllogism—was their usual tool for reasoning and verification. The fourth reason is connected to the Taoist perception that human beings are usually motivated by self-interest so that they tend to respond or accept more readily whatever agrees with their own views. Metaphorical language, fables, and parables all contain images of things or animal and human characters that exist in the external world. They direct the listener or reader toward a seemingly objective world that he can observe or associate with. Thus *yuyan* becomes a rhetorical device used by Chuang Tzu for the purpose of persuasion, for making his argument appear less motivated toward self-interest and hence more compelling.

The second rhetorical device *zhongyan*, or "words of those whom people respect," is related to the third sense of *yuyan*, namely, the idea of a literary mask. The term is sometimes read by scholars as *chongyan*, meaning "repeated words." Taken as such, *chongyan* would refer to passages quoted from other people.

But since most of the stories involving historical personages found in the "Inner Chapters" appear to be fictional rather than historical in nature, it seems safer to read the term as *zhongyan*, or "words put into the mouths of those whom people respect." *Zhongyan* is actually a subcategory of *yuyan*. It refers to stories in which wise men of the past or men who are venerable in years are used as the author's masks so that the words said may carry more authority. But the stories themselves are symbolic or metaphorical of certain ideas in Chuang Tzu's philosophy. The author of the "Imputed Words" chapter states that the purpose of *zhongyan* is "to put an end to argument." It should be noted that quotations from the wise men of the past and historical stories are also commonly used in the philosophical writings of other schools in the Warring States Period for the same rhetorical purpose. But Chuang Tzu's *zhongyan* also displays its special characteristics. Compared with such masks as plants, animals, mythical and legendary personages, or other fictitious characters, the wise men of the past are not as numerous in the "Inner Chapters." The Yellow Emperor, Yao, Xu You [Hsü Yu], Confucius, and his disciples Yan Hui [Yen Hui] and Zigong [Tzu-Kung] are the most important characters in the *zhongyan* stories. They are used sometimes as the author's masks and sometimes as contrasts to other idealized Taoist characters. In the stories involving Confucius and his disciples, Chuang Tzu shows himself to be an exceptionally shrewd critic of Confucianism because he uses these respected personages to perform two roles simultaneously, both as his masks and as his target of ridicule. By inventing conversations between Confucius and his disciples, he presents his own philosophy in a more persuasive fashion, while at the same time he undercuts the importance of the rival school by including a caricature of its founder and some of his most famous disciples. His stories thus accomplish a double-edged task.

A good example of Chuang Tzu's creative use of language in the *yuyan* and *zhongyan* modes is the following passage from "The Great and Venerable Teacher" chapter:

> Yan Hui said, "I've made progress."
> Confucius said, "What do you mean?"
> "I've forgotten benevolence and righteousness."
> "That's good. But you still have not attained your goal yet."
> Another day, the two met again and Yan Hui said, "I've made progress."
> "What do you mean?"
> "I've forgotten rites and music."

"That's good. But you still have not attained your goal yet."

Another day, the two met again and Yan Hui said, "I've made progress."

"What do you mean?"

"I'm able just to sit down and forget everything."

Greatly taken aback, Confucius said, "What do you mean by just sitting down and forgetting everything?"

Yan Hui said, "I let my limbs and organs drop away, expel my hearing and eyesight, detach from my physical form, cast off knowledge, and become identical with the Great Thoroughfare. This is what is called 'sitting down and forgetting everything.' "

Confucius said, "If you are identical with it, you have no more partiality; and if you let yourself transform, you have no more rigid norms. Are you really that worthy? May I, Qiu [Ch'iu], ask to follow behind you as your disciple?"

Even a cursory reading (especially of the paragraph in which Yan Hui talks about "letting his limbs and organs drop away") is sufficient to convince the reader that this story is not to be taken literally. It is only found in the *Chuang Tzu* and not in any text of the Confucian school of thought. There seems to be no doubt that the story was invented by Chuang Tzu in order to take advantage of Confucius as an effective voice for advocating his own philosophy. It illustrates metaphorically the process of attaining what Chuang Tzu regards as the highest level of spiritual development, which is so different from the process of self-cultivation advocated in Confucianism. In this general respect, it is an example of *yuyan*. At the same time, this brief parable is also the most complex and sophisticated example of the device of *zhongyan* found in the "Inner Chapters." It starts off as a parody of the standard situation of learning as recorded in the *Analects* of Confucius, in which students come to report to their teacher on their progress, to ask questions, and to seek further guidance from him. As the story proceeds, the tone becomes increasingly ironic. In Confucian self-cultivation, students are expected to internalize the ethical principles until they become part of their personality so that their actions will be automatically guided by them. In this story, however, Yan Hui, Confucius's most talented disciple, reports to his teacher that he has forgotten benevolence, righteousness, rites, and music, the four cardinal principles in Confucian ethics. The process of learning—one that originally emphasizes internalizing ethics and acquiring new knowledge—becomes a process of un-learning because the disciple is praised for being able to cast away what he has learned previously. This process of "un-learning" constitutes the fundamental aspect of Taoist spiritual cultivation. In Taoism, the touchstone of values is Nature and not people. Therefore, all man-made knowledge and values must be abandoned. The irony culminates in Yan Hui's attainment of Taoist sagehood, not by embodying all ethical principles in his very person, but by having forgotten everything and thereby transcending his limited human self, and becoming identical with Tao. In the story, "limbs and organs" refers to the physical body that is transformable, and "hearing and eyesight" refer to our sense perception that enables us to discriminate things. And, of course, knowledge is the sum of what is perceived and understood by the mind and the senses. Only by forgetting the bodily self, the opposition of this self to other things, and all knowledge is one able to enter the spiritual wholeness of the Way. But Chuang Tzu does not end his story here. It is true that the historical Confucius had very high regard for Yan Hui. Nonetheless, it would be totally ludicrous for him to ask Yan Hui to accept him as his disciple! Thus, in an entertaining parable, Chuang Tzu successfully uses Confucius and Yan Hui as both valuable masks and victims of his ridicule.

On the whole, examples of *yuyan* and *zhongyan* in the *Chuang Tzu* are quite different from those found in other philosophical and narrative texts of the Warring States Period. Before Chuang Tzu, fables and parables usually appear individually in prose and are used essentially as illustrative materials. In the "Inner Chapters" they begin to occupy the central positions in the artistic design of the prose. In suggestive power, aesthetic appeal, and comic exuberance, Chuang Tzu's *yuyan* and *zhongyan* stories far surpass those found in other ancient Chinese texts.

While *yuyan* and *zhongyan* seem to be primarily concerned with the practical aspects of expression of ideas and of winning an argument in debate or disputation, *zhiyan*, the third rhetorical device, is concerned with the more philosophical aspect of Chuang Tzu's theory of language and self-expression. Just like the other two terms, *zhiyan* has also been taken by scholars to mean a number of things. In my view, two widely used interpretations are particularly useful and relevant. First, as an object, *zhi* is known in the Taoist tradition as "a goblet for urging wine on a guest." It is apparently an unusual vessel which is designed to remain upright when empty and to overturn when full, thus illustrating the value of emptiness. The *zhi* vessel seems to have been chosen as a metaphor for the Taoist ideal use of the mind in making speech. As the seventeenth-century scholar Wang Fuzhi [Wang Fu-chih] has suggested, the Taoist advice is that one should keep his mind empty of all preconceived ideas and values until the occasion for speech arises and, at the end of a discourse, empty out the ideas and values which one has previously taken from outside. The point to be stressed here is that the goblet—a metaphor for the mind—is originally empty and gets filled with liquid, which comes from a larger container only when the occasion requires one to do so. *Zhiyan*, then, is speech that is natural, unpremeditated, always responding to the changing situations in the flow of discourse, and always returning the mind to its original state of emptiness as soon as a speech act is completed. In "Fit for Emperors and Kings" (chapter 7), it is said: "The Perfect Man uses his mind like a mirror—going after nothing, welcoming, responding, but not storing." *Zhiyan* refers to the kind of verbal act that is in keeping with this mystical way of functioning of the mind. If one can engage only in this sort of verbal act, one can keep his mind perpetually in a state of pristine naturalness, harmony, transparency, and emptiness. One can say that, in the story discussed in the previous section, when Yan Hui is able to "just sit down and forget everything," his mind is indeed like a *zhi* vessel.

Zhi has also been interpreted by scholars as a pun on another character pronounced *zhi*, meaning "uneven, irregular, and random." Understood as such, *zhiyan* means "irregular and random words." How do we relate this second sense of the term to Chuang Tzu's works? Each of the "Inner Chapters" is composed of a series of stories—largely fables, brief anecdotes, and parables—intermixed with passages of discursive prose. As discussed earlier, the fables, anecdotes, and parables constitute the *yuyan* and *zhongyan* modes of language in those chapters. The discursive passages, which represent the random comments made by the "implied author" (to borrow a term from Wayne Booth) on the stories, are the first and clearest examples of *zhiyan*. Discursive passages are also found within the stories and they are to be regarded as examples of "goblet words" as well. In other words, there is *zhiyan* in both *yuyan* and *zhongyan*. In the story from "The Great and Venerable Teacher" quoted earlier, Yan Hui's explanation of his experience of "sitting down and forgetting everything" and Confucius's subsequent comment on the philosophical implications of this experience are such examples. Since these passages do not follow any observably preset rule of structure, they do appear haphazard and irregular. The sense of randomness and irregularity actually goes beyond the individual discursive passages to permeate an entire chapter. Indeed, when we read each of the "Inner Chapters," we seem to be going through a sequence of rambling, disconnected stories and discursive passages that vividly reflect the mental activity or the process of thought and feeling of the "implied author." This highly lyrical feature of structure is the necessary result of the uniquely Taoist ideal way of speech as embodied in the metaphor of the "goblet words."

The "Inner Chapters" are not just seven long sequences of random jottings of Chuang Tzu's mystical thought, however. It is interesting to note that, despite some traces of textual corruption, the more carefully one reads these seemingly random pieces of prose, the more one feels that there is an intricate kind of unity within each of them. The internal harmony one feels in reading the "Inner Chapters" suggests that the form of each piece itself is a reflection of not only Chuang Tzu's own views of life and the world but also the ancient Chinese worldview. Most schools of ancient Chinese thought shared the same organismic conception of cosmos that is in sharp contrast to the causalistic or mechanistic conception characteristic of Western thought. But Chuang Tzu seems to be the first thinker to have attempted to render that conception in the very form of his prose. Indeed, the seemingly haphazard elements within each chapter relate to each other in a kind of "mysterious inductance." They are not organized in a causalistic or mechanistic manner; rather, they coordinate with each other in forming a "reticular" whole. The structure of each chapter may perhaps be described as "musical" because "variation on themes" is one important device that holds the elements together.

It is difficult, if not impossible, to find exact comparisons for the *Chuang Tzu* from Western literatures. To be sure, one can easily mention "philosophical essays" written by thinkers and authors in the Western traditions. But they would resemble more closely the rigorously structured argumentative essays written by ancient Chinese thinkers such as Hsün Tzu (Xun Zi, ca. 298–238 B.C.E.) and Han Fei Tzu (Han Fei Zi, 280?–233 B.C.E.) who came after Chuang Tzu. The "Inner Chapters" and many other portions in the *Chuang Tzu* are "philosophical essays" of a very special kind. Of the philosophical works before the *Chuang Tzu*, the *Analects* of Confucius (551–479 B.C.E.) and the *Mencius* (attributed to the Confucian thinker Mencius, ca. 372–289 B.C.E.) contain mainly recorded aphorisms, sayings, dialogues, and debates, the last of which are only found in the latter work. They are not two collections of "philosophical essays." With the earliest portions of the *Mo Tzu* (*Mo Zi*) which were written by the followers of Mo Ti (Mo Di, fl. 479–438 B.C.E.) possibly during the late fifth and the early fourth centuries B.C.E., there appeared the longer discursive "essays," each of which focused on a particular topic. Dialogues and anecdotes still figure importantly in these early examples of the ancient Chinese philosophical essay because philosophical discourse was still primarily oral. And the writers of these essays also began to pay attention to the logical method of developing an argument. In terms of the evolution of early Chinese philosophical prose, the *Chuang Tzu* represents a significant stage between these early works and the argumentative essays of Hsün Tzu. Beneath the surface randomness, humor, and fantasy, we can discern a more skillful "inner logic" in setting forth ideas than that found in the *Mo Tzu.* But in addition to the mysticism and humor, what make the *Chuang Tzu* a unique literary monument are the depth of imagination and lyric vision, the superb command of classical Chinese, and the artistic design that characterize many of the essays in the book.

TOPICS FOR DISCUSSION

1. How would you define Tao, the Way, as used in the *Chuang Tzu* and in the other principal Taoist text, the *Tao te ching*? (Interesting contrasts and comparisons can be made between the rhetorical devices used in the *Tao te ching* and those used in the *Chuang Tzu.* Unfortunately, space does not allow me to make any extensive comparison of the two texts here. Further, the problems of authorship and of the date of composition of the *Tao te ching* are too great to be adequately dealt with in a short essay. I therefore have purposely avoided an extensive discussion of the *Tao te ching* in this essay.) Are there any differences between the Tao in the *Chuang Tzu* and that in the *Tao te ching*? How does the Taoist concept of Tao differ from that used by the Confucians as seen in the *Analects* of Confucius, the *Mencius*, the "Great Learning," and the "Doctrine of the Mean"?

2. What is Chuang Tzu's attitude toward ethics, language, logic, and culture in general? Why does he take this attitude? Does he believe in the "perfectibility of man" as do the Confucian thinkers? How would you describe the Taoist sage (variously called the Sage, the Perfect Man, the Divine or Holy Man, and the True Man)? Why do the men in chapter 5 who have each displayed a "sign of virtue complete" all appear so ugly, strange, physically abnormal, deformed, and repulsive? How does this idea

of the sage differ from that found in the Confucian texts?

3. Discuss some of Chuang Tzu's literary devices used in the "Inner Chapters," devices such as metaphor, parody, metaphorical anecdote and parable, paradox, literary mask, humor.

4. Each of the "Inner Chapters" focuses on one central philosophical issue. What are they? How does Chuang Tzu set forth his ideas in discussing each central issue? How does he begin and end a chapter? What are the ways in which he organizes the ideas into one organic whole? Focusing on one chapter, discuss "rhetorical construct" as an integral part of his philosophy.

5. Would you consider Chuang Tzu a "lyrical philosopher"? Whom from other civilizations can you compare him to?

6. Certain ideas, images, characters, and themes recur throughout the "Inner Chapters": "flying," "immortals," and "the gnarled tree" are some examples. How and why are these elements described in different ways in different contexts?

7. How would you describe Chuang Tzu's approach to the issue of "enlightenment"? What are "clarity" (or "illumination" in chapter 2), "losing one's self" (in chapter 2), "the fasting of the mind" (in chapter 4), and "sitting down and forgetting everything"? In the conversation between Nanbo Zikui [Nan-po Tzu-k'uei] and Woman Crookback (in chapter 6), a detailed description of the path of spiritual growth for the Taoist is presented. Can you make sense out of it? Contrast the *Chuang Tzu* to the Christian mystical text *The Cloud of Unknowing*.

NOTE

1. At the author's request, certain names within this essay have been left in their Wade-Giles spelling with pinyin indicated in parentheses because these persons and titles are known universally in this form: these include Chuang Chou, *Chuang Tzu*, Han Fei Tzu, Hsün Tzu, Lao Tzu, *Mo Tzu*, *Tao te ching*, Tao.

REFERENCES

Feng, Gia-fu, and English, Jane, trans. *Chuang Tsu: Inner Chapters*. New York: Random House, 1974. This is a delightful book, richly illustrated with the Chinese text in elegant calligraphy and beautiful photographs. The translation is largely reliable and readable too.

Graham, A. C., trans. *Chuang-tzu: The Seven Inner Chapters and other writings from the book* Chuang-tzu. London: George Allen & Unwin, 1981. This is a must for everyone seriously interested in the *Chuang Tzu*. It offers an excellent introductory chapter about the life of Chuang Tzu and the various aspects of his thought. The translation is not easy to read but is philologically precise. Graham's introduction and notes throughout the book are full of brilliant insights.

Lin, Shuen-fu. "Confucius in the 'Inner Chapters' of the *Chuang Tzu*." *Tamkang Review* 18, nos. 1–4 (Autumn 1987-Summer 1988): 379–401. Portions of the material in the current essay also appear in more detail in this article.

Lin, Shuen-fu. "The Language of the 'Inner Chapters' of the *Chuang Tzu*." In *The Power of Culture: Studies in Chinese Cultural History*, edited by Willard J. Peterson. Hong Kong: The University of Hong Kong Press, 1991. Portions of the material in the current essay also appear in more detail in this article.

Mair, Victor H., ed. *Experimental Essays on Chuang-tzu*. Honolulu: University of Hawaii Press, 1983. This is a collection of nine interesting and valuable essays on the *Chuang Tzu*.

Mote, Frederick W. *Intellectual Foundations of China*. 2d ed. New York: Alfred A. Knopf, 1989. Read the chapters on "Early Confucianism" and "Early Taoism" for an excellent introduction to the ideas of these two schools of Chinese thought.

Watson, Burton, trans. *The Complete Works of Chuang Tzu*. New York: Columbia University Press, 1968. This is the only up-to-date translation of all thirty-three chapters of the *Chuang Tzu*. It contains an excellent short introduction. The translation is admirably readable and accurate. His shorter paperback edition, *Chuang Tzu: Basic Writings*, containing the "Introduction," the "Inner Chapters" and four other chapters, is an excellent choice for a textbook. A translation of the "Yuyan" chapter and the "Under Heaven" chapter discussed in this entry can be found in *The Complete Works of Chuang Tzu*.

RECORDS OF THE HISTORIAN

Joseph Roe Allen III

The *Records of the Historian* (*Shi ji* [*Shih chi*]) is the most important historiographic work in the Chinese tradition, which has always placed a great deal of value on such writing. But the
influence of this text is not merely historiographic: it is profoundly
literary and broadly cultural as well. The *Records* is arguably the
best-known and most revered prose work written in classical Chinese, an assessment that is modern as well as traditional. It is
also the primary text defining our understanding of classical and
early imperial China. Moreover, its author, Sima Qian ([Ssu-ma
Ch'ien] 145?–90? B.C.E.), is a major cultural hero, not only because of his authorship of the *Records*, but also because of the
personal strength that he displayed in bringing this text to completion. Sima Qian, in both his life and work, is central to the
Chinese definition of heroism. Quite simply, the *Records* is the
magnum opus of history and prose literature in China. While a
number of texts in the early Western tradition have roles that
parallel those of the *Records*, e.g., the Old Testament, and works
of Herodotus, Plutarch, and Tacitus, there is none that is as
inclusive or as definitive.

Judging from extant sources, Chinese historiographic writing
before Sima Qian was rather thin and fragmented. The earliest
historical work, and one that became a central Confucian classic,
is the *Book of Documents*, whose authentic chapters date from
around 1,000 B.C.E. The *Documents* is a group of heterogeneous
texts surrounding early cultural events and figures, both legendary and historical. Many of these texts are vivid displays of ora-
tory, but there are others that are closer to essays and simple
narratives. Perhaps the most prestigious early historical work is

the *Spring and Autumn Annals*, which is a chronology of political events surrounding the state of Lu (722–481 B.C.E.). The prestige of this text has little to do with its literary style, which is dry and telegraphic, or with any significant historiographic innovation (apparently all states had such records at that time); the *Annals* is important simply because it is attributed to Confucius, who is said to have claimed it as his most important work, a mind-boggling proposition for the work we now have. However, there is another work associated with the *Annals* (a relationship with problems of its own), the *Zuo [Tso] Commentary*, which is a very important literary and historical work. The *Zuo* is a collection of delightful narratives, often humorous and poignant, about political events of the Spring and Autumn period, some of which are referred to in the *Annals*. This so-called commentary is the most important pre-Sima Qian narrative text, and he drew on it extensively in his history. But Sima Qian also drew on the other parts of the early historiographic tradition represented by the *Documents*, the *Annals*, and other texts, not only as obvious historical sources, but also as models of types of discourse.

Following Sima Qian's *Records*, we have a continuous series of historiographic works that represent an unbroken chronicle of Chinese civilization down to the present day. The core works in that chronicle are the twenty-five official dynastic histories (*zheng shi [cheng shih]*) that represent, legitimize, and document power in various periods of imperial rule. While this legacy of historical writing contains a great deal of variation in quality and style, the form that each of those dynastic histories takes was dictated by Sima Qian's *Records*, especially as that form was codified in the second dynastic history by Ban Gu's [Pan Ku's] *History of the Han (Han shu)*. While no one dared to attempt the scope of the *Records*, almost every historian after Sima Qian, whether individual or committeed, freelance or imperially commissioned, looked to the *Records* as a model. Occasionally an important writer would work in a different historiographic format, such as Sima Guang's ([Ssu-ma Kuang] 1019–86) strictly chronological historical record of the period from 403 B.C.E. to C.E. 959 (a monumental work that is sometimes compared to the *Records*); but these were never allowed to stand as the "official" history of China. Thus, Sima Qian not only filtered the entire Chinese tradition that lay before him into a new format, that format then dictated the way the Chinese came to think about their world and their past. Sima Qian not only gave us the contents of early Chinese history, he gave us the vessel in which to carry them and which consequently shaped them.

Sima Qian was born just about the time Emperor Wu of the Han dynasty came to the throne, and Sima's life and career coincide chronologically and psychologically with the reign of that remarkable ruler (140–87 B.C.E.). This was a time when the glory of the Han was on the rise and China was first stretching itself across the Asian continent. Militarily, economically, and culturally it was the first golden age of Chinese imperialism. In the capital where Sima Qian grew up, Confucian orthodoxy was establishing itself, and there was a renewed interest in literature and the arts. With this vital atmosphere there also came a glorification and exploration of the classical and prehistoric past. This was the real beginning of imperial China.

As son of the imperial astronomer/historian, Sima Tan [Ssu-ma T'an], Sima Qian grew up inside the emperor's inner court, surrounded by its glory. The Sima family traced its lineage back to the royal record keepers of classical Zhou [Chou]. Sima Tan was the first, however, to hold the title Grand Historian (*Tai shi gong* [*T'ai shih kung*]), which became identified with the *Records*. Sima Qian's youth was spent in relative ease, filled with travel and learning, which were designed to prepare him for his father's position. In 110 B.C.E. Sima Tan lay on his death bed, whence he charged his son with the fateful and immense task of accepting not only his official position, but also his life's obsession, the completion of the first general history of China. In his autobiography Sima Qian describes his father's final plea; after a brief description of the astronomer's duties (which were themselves substantial), Tan says:

> When you become Grand Historian, you must not forget what I have desired to expound and write. Now filial piety begins with the serving of your parents; next you must serve your sovereign; and finally you must make something of yourself, that your name may go down through the ages for the glory of your father and mother. This is the most important part of filial piety. . . . [a review of the literary accomplishments of various classical sages follows] It has now been over four hundred years since the capture of the unicorn [the end of the *Spring and Autumn Annals*]. The various feudal states have merged together and the old records and chronicles have become scattered and lost. Now the house of Han has risen and all the world is united under one rule. I have been Grand Historian, and yet I have failed to set forth a record of all the enlightened rulers and wise lords, the faithful ministers and gentlemen who were ready to die for duty. I am fearful that the historical materials will be neglected and lost. You must remember and think of this!

In tears, Sima Qian replies:

> I, your son, am ignorant and unworthy, but shall endeavor to set forth in full the reports of antiquity which have come down from our ancestors. I shall not dare to be remiss![1]

Thus began the greatest historiographic work of China, if not of the ancient world. But this account is colored with hindsight (the autobiography appears as the postface to the *Records*), and can be read as an elaborate apologia for Sima Qian's life.

From the time of his father's charge to the completion of the *Records* in 90 B.C.E., Sima Qian was a busy man. He not only finished the history, he also performed his duties as court astronomer; most significantly, he recalculated the solar calendar into a highly accurate version that was inaugurated on December 25, 105 B.C.E., and which stood unchanged until the adoption of the Gregorian calendar in the twentieth century. As a high imperial official, Sima Qian was also in a position to offer counsel to the emperor on general affairs of state. That privilege led to the event most central to the definition of Sima Qian as a man and hero, an event that is inextricably bound up with the writing of the *Records*.

In 99 B.C.E. Sima Qian took it upon himself to defend General Li Ling, who had lost a battle and been captured by the Xiongnü [Hsiung-nü] enemy, a non-Chinese border tribe. Sima Qian's account of the incident argues that he did so not because of personal attachment to the general, but rather because of the nobility with which Li Ling served the Emperor. Unfortunately the defense of Li Ling implied the criticism of another general who was much in favor at the time, and thus brought Emperor Wu's wrath down upon Sima Qian. He was condemned to be castrated for his impunity, from which he could not afford to purchase his release (although castration itself may have been a reduced sentence for the crime of "defaming the emperor"). Suicide was the common alternative to the pain and disgrace of castration (which usually ended in death by infection anyway), but Sima Qian chose to live. He chose to live so he could write. In a letter that explains his actions in detail, Sima Qian concludes a review of the literary legacy of China's past with this evocation of his filial duty:

> I wished to examine into all that concerns heaven and man, to penetrate the changes of the past and present, completing all as the work of one family. But before I had finished my rough

manuscript, I met with this calamity. It is because I regretted that it had not been completed that I submitted to the extreme penalty without rancor. When I have truly completed this work, I shall deposit it in the Famous Mountain. If it may be handed down to men who will appreciate it, and penetrate to the villages and great cities, then though I should suffer a thousand mutilations, what regret should I have?[2]

Sima Qian chose to undergo this humiliation in order to carry out his father's charge, and that charge is interwoven with one of the greatest books in the Chinese tradition, which in turn increases his act of filial piety by linking his family's name with literary legacy of China. As seen in Sima Qian's review of the classical tradition with which he prefaces these remarks (not quoted), the greatest accomplishment of man in China has always been in the production of texts. With this decision Sima Qian both preserves and creates literature; thus is the magnitude of his heroism.

The text as we now have it is in 130 chapters, as Sima Qian records in his postface, but ten of these may be later reconstructions. Those 130 chapters are divided into five historiographic forms, which describe the workings of the Chinese world from remote antiquity down to the rule of Emperor Wu. While there are chronological sections and overlays in the *Records*, it is not a strict narrative of that world; it is rather a hierarchical description of its patterns of meaning.

At the top of that hierarchy are the twelve "Basic Annals" (*ben ji* [*ben chi*]), which describe in increasing detail the various ruling houses of early China, starting with the five mythical emperors and concluding with Emperor Wu of the Han. In between one has the royal houses, Xia [Hsia], Shang, and Zhou [Chou]; the Qin [Ch'in] state and its later manifestation as the first empire; all the Han emperors, the Empress Lu, and the primary challenger to the Han house, Xiang Yu [Hsiang Yü]. The form of these "Basic Annals" would seem to derive from the state annals of the classical period (such as the *Spring and Autumn Annals*), but Sima Qian has fleshed these out with considerable narrative detail. These houses are introduced in order and their stories are chronological as well, but they do not form a continual narrative, as one might expect (there are occasional cross-references). These twelve chapters represent the basic outline of political power of early China, which usually coincided with royal and imperial rulers, but not always (as Xiang Yu's inclusion suggests).

Second are the Chronological Tables (*biao* [*piao*]) in ten chapters, which are a macrovision of the political events occurring throughout China, viewed both chronologically and spatially. It has been suggested that here Sima Qian was inspired by earlier genealogical tables. Each *biao* is divided into columns and ranks. The columns mark the progression through time, while the ranks isolate the events of certain loci (usually geographic areas). For example, in the second table, "Year Table of the Twelve Feudal Lords," each column is designated a certain year (841–477 B.C.E.), under which there are the ranks for the twelve feudal houses containing brief notes regarding significant events in that feudal state. The Tables end with those associated with the Han dynasty, including the last that charts major events alongside the activities of the three primary imperial offices of the Han period. Needless to say the brevity of the entries negates any literary value, but taken together these tables provide a valuable two-dimensional overview of early Chinese historical developments.

The third section of the *Records* is composed of eight essays (*shu*) that review major institutions and areas of human endeavor in China over the centuries, but with an emphasis on the Han. These essays (which may derive from philosophic essays of the late classical period) are on rituals, music, law, calendars, astronomy, the imperial sacrifices, river systems, and weights and measures. This collection represents the major areas of concern for the imperial bureaucracy, and similar sets of essays (renamed *zhi* [*chih*]) come to form an important part of the later dynastic histories—they also contribute to the growth of the essay form in encyclopedia (*lei shu*). Such essays usually strive for comprehensiveness rather than evaluation, thus often containing conflicting citations from earlier materials, with little attempt to resolve them. Unfortunately the *Records* do not contain a bibliographic essay, but that is somewhat ameliorated by Ban Gu's inclusion of one in his *History of the Han*.

The next thirty chapters are devoted to the Hereditary Houses (*shi chia* [*shih jia*]), which are annals of the important, usually enfeoffed, families of the country (excluding those included in the Basic Annals). The Houses can be seen as the narrative versions of some of the Chronological Tables, with each rank expanded into a complete portrait of the feudal lineage, but isolated from the parallel narratives of the accompanying ranks. That is to say, while the Tables provide a view of these activities on a plane, the Houses provide a deep, but linear one. The most notable entry in this list is the "house" Confucius, who was never enfeoffed, nor even of political rank. This inclusion has been viewed as Sima Qian's editorial comment on the political importance of Confucius, whom elsewhere the historian calls an "uncrowned king." We do begin to see in this section more of the narrative strength that induced later writers to take Sima Qian's prose as their model.

The last section of the *Records* is not only the longest, in seventy chapters, it is universally acknowledged to be the best, especially in literary terms. Whenever we have a discussion of, or excerpts from, the *Records* they will almost always be from these seventy *liezhuan* [*lieh-chuan*]. The term *liezhuan*, usually translated as "biographies," is somewhat problematic. Burton Watson's rendering as "memoirs" is probably close to the original intent of the term, which literally might be translated as "arranged exegesis/traditions." Here we find the "lives" of early China (often those of individual men, but also of larger groups) told in Sima Qian's most engaging style. While the other sections of the *Records* seek to frame larger pictures of the Chinese world, either chronologically, spatially, politically, or topically, here we have the microcosm of that world seen in the tribulations, successes, and failures of particular men. The list of subjects includes not only the stories of political figures, writers, and military leaders, but also group portraits of assassins, scholars, knights errant, and clowns. Even entire peoples come under Sima Qian's descriptive spell, such as the Korean people, the southern barbarians, and the Xiongnü nomads who terrorized the Han from the northern steppes. In these last essays Sima Qian displays a breadth of vision and objectivity that can only be called "anthropological." The "Memoirs" are arranged chronologically where possible, the final being Sima Qian's autobiographical postface, the first of its kind in Chinese and worthy of consideration itself.

Both as history and as literature, Sima Qian's *Records* have cast a long shadow of influence over the Chinese tradition. He gave to Chinese historiography not only a form, but a style. Considering his time and circumstance, Sima Qian pursued his history with objectivity and thoroughness. Many of the sources upon which he drew are no longer extant, but where they are, his fidelity to the written record is notable. Moreover, Sima Qian was willing to question his sources when he felt they were suspect, sometimes directly, sometimes indirectly with the equivocation, "it is said that . . . " He points out inconsistencies and lapses in the record, trying to resolve and fill them. His quotation of sources (which are generally unmarked and sometimes adjusted to fit his impeccable prose style) include frequent verbatim citation of documents and literary texts, thereby preserving many otherwise lost historical materials and literary masterpieces. The historical accuracy of Sima Qian's *Records* has been attested to in recent times by archaeological finds that confirm his list of kings for the Shang dynasty, a list that previous to these finds was assumed to have been largely fictional. Of course Sima Qian did not operate with the supposed objectivity of the modern historian; his history clearly had a higher purpose. It was meant to instruct, to provide models, and to establish a cultural matrix for the China he knew. The Chinese viewed the past as the instructor of the present, both in specific examples (which they cited with abandon) and in general patterns. Certainly Sima Qian's purpose was to provide his age with model examples and instructive patterns. Moreover, he may have had a more personal objective in writing this history, not the least being the placement of his family name in the literary legacy of China. But those higher and personal purposes were integrated with his efforts to delve into his sources and construct a view of the world that was as accurate and consistent as possible.

Although they are not as self-conscious or elaborate as the Herodotean digression, throughout the *Records* we find Sima Qian's own evaluative comments are tucked into the narratives; these may be simply the choice of an adjective, or a more wordy aside. But his most authorial and authoritarian voice is found in the passages called Grand Historian Remarks (*Tai shi gong yue* [*T'ai shih kung yüeh*]) that close many of his chapters. Here Sima Qian consciously stands back and comments on the import of his story. These closing evaluations may be a confirmation of the truth of the narrative, they may comment on the lesson to be drawn from the narrative, and occasionally they will question the narrator's sources. This is where Sima Qian feels comfortable bringing his own, and perhaps his father's, personal views and experiences into the story. At the close of the composite portrait of several knights errant, Sima Qian has this comment:

> The Grand Historian remarks: I have seen Kuo Hsieh [one of the knights], and can report that in looks and bearing he hardly measured up to the average man, while nothing he said was worth remembering. Yet throughout the empire both worthy men and base men, those who knew him and those who did not, all admire his reputation, and whenever they talk about the knights, they always cite his name. There is a common saying, "The real looks of a man lie in his reputation, for that will never die." Alas that he met such an end![3]

Comments such as this are the clearest evidence in early Chinese literature of an author consciously commenting on the narrator's

work. This stance certainly derives from the evaluative interjec-
tions in Confucian philosophic discourse that are couched in the
formula "the master/gentleman says . . . ," and it leads to the
prolific interlocutor tradition in Chinese literary commentaries.

In addition to its contribution to the Chinese historiographic
tradition, Sima Qian's *Records* have left a legacy of narrative technique and literary style. Even in the early medieval period when
prose writing developed into a style of elaborate parallelism, the
simplicity and power of Sima Qian's style stood as the model for
historical writing. Then with the neoclassical (*fu gu* [*fu ku*]) movement of the Tang-Song [T'ang-Sung] period his style was resur-
rected as a model for almost all types of prose. Sima Qian's
narrative technique, which includes sophisticated use of characterization and plotting, was also a model for later writers of fiction. That fiction included not only the classical short stories of
middle and late medieval times (Tang-Ming [T'ang-Ming]), but
even, it is suggested, the vernacular novel that flourished in late
imperial times. And the *Records* still remain the standard of classical prose, having become a virtual textbook for modern courses
in classical Chinese, both in China and the West.

In the emulation of the *Records* as literature, it is the "Memoirs"
that are the object of attention. Here is found the narrative
strength of Sima Qian's prose. Often the most powerful portraits
are not those that trace an event or life through its chronological
progression, but rather those that describe the psychological or
cultural configurations of their subjects in a more "lyrical" fashion, one that dwells on the moments of significance. Thus, the
first "Memoir" of Bo Yi [Po Yi] (61), a symbol of personal rectitude
and strength, forms a reflective essay around a single event in his
life, rather than around his life as a biographical whole. But that
single act, refusing food from a usurper of the royal throne, is
what Bo Yi's life means—the rest is superfluous corporeal data.
Similarly the "life" of the famous, unorthodox General Li Guang
[Li Kuang] (110) is a pastiche of such moments, including some
that are suspect in terms of verifiable truth. But from this pastiche we come to understand Li, if not know him. One might argue
that only these fragments were available to Sima Qian, thereby
limiting the narrative development of these biographies. In the
case of Bo Yi that may be true (which would be significant in
itself), but in the second example, Sima Qian knew Li Guang
personally and thus could have easily presented a more straightforward narrative of his life (as he did for others). Sima Qian
chose to present this "partial portrait" of Li's life because it was

truer to the man than his "whole narrative." One of the shortcomings of later historians who sought to follow Sima Qian's example in the writing of "Memoirs" was the failure to see and portray the psychological, rather than biological, truth of their subjects. They became too chained to their historical data. With the passage of time such portrayals in China became more the domain of the fictional short story. So it should be, we might say, but Sima Qian would beg to differ.

Sima Qian felt that the history of man is the history of his mind as well as of his deeds, and the "Memoirs" were where he sought to capture the specific workings of that human mind. These chapters describe the soul that propelled the body of early China through its mundane world, a world that occupies the other sections of the *Records* to a greater extent. It is not coincidental that the "Memoirs" constitute more than half of this text; the mind of man is more than half of his life.

TOPICS FOR DISCUSSION

1. For the comparatist, the most important question raised in consideration of Sima Qian's *Records* is the role and configuration that historiography assumes within important civilizations of the world. Few, if any, traditions of historical writing are comparable to the Chinese in either breadth or length, both dimensions first attested to and promoted by the *Records*. On the one hand, the strength of this historiographic tradition results from the continuity of the Chinese language and script system, and on the other, the tradition contributes to that continuity. Since there was no other written language in East Asia at the time, the early sources upon which Sima Qian drew were all necessarily Chinese; and because he was writing after the great script reform of the Qin-Han [Ch'in-Han] period, the story he told was preserved in a language and script that is still readily accessible. In comparison, the Western historiographic tradition is a difficult amalgam of cultures, scripts, and languages (ancient Near Eastern, Greek, Roman, European), and its analogous "text" is similarly dispersed throughout those cultures.

Thus, the first thing the comparatist must address is the disparity between the Chinese historiographic tradition and those of other civilizations. What do these disparities tell us about the cultural and literary configurations of the traditions to which they belong? What is the role of the past, and its record, in the psychology of those peoples, either as individuals or as a cultural whole? What aspects of their pasts do the different civilizations choose to foreground in their historical writing (which is really to ask what is their past to them)? A fruitful area of comparison in this regard might be with the important historical texts of the Western tradition, such as the Old Testament, Herodotus, and Thucydides. This discussion could also address the question of the authorial intent in the writing of history; Herodotus and Sima Qian both paint a sweeping portrait of their known worlds, but their purposes as well as their methods are vastly different. The early Japanese historiographic tradition, as manifested in the *Kojiki* and the *Nihon shoki*, is derived from Chinese models, but comparison with them is also possible. This is especially so in the area of early myth, which is so rich in the Japanese texts and so lacking in the Chinese. A Western text that might be brought to bear here would be Hesiod's *Theogony*. This could lead to an interesting comparison of the relationship between myth and history in the separate traditions. Unlike the Greek and Japanese, the Chinese have tended to rewrite their myth into human history. In China, gods are transformed into men—a process diametrically opposed to Western "euhemerization."

2. A particular, and perhaps peculiar, topic that might be addressed in this regard is the position the *Records* holds within its own literary tradition when compared to the epic of the West (there being no epic in China) and the early narrative *monogatari* (especially the *Tale of Genji*) of Japan. Could one say, for example, that within its own cultural context, Sima Qian's *Records* held a position in the definition of narrative literature of China that is comparable to the "epic" in the West? Is the *Records* China's missing epic? Is it the Chinese equivalent of *monogatari*, or vice versa? Such consideration necessarily questions conventional definitions and discussions of the epic, history, and fiction, but such questioning is at the heart of the comparative method.

3. A related question that the comparatist can fruitfully pursue is that concerning the types of heroic and exemplary behavior the historians and/or biographers offer from their respective traditions. In Sima Qian's *Records* this will lead one into the heart of "Memoirs," which are certainly the most interesting in literary terms. In the West one will need to turn to the writers of "lives"; this will include the semidivine pagan pantheon and the Christian heroes, as well as the secular heroes of the tradition (e.g., the *Iliad*, the books of Moses [story of Noah, Job, etc.] Plutarch's *Parallel Lives*). The most revealing portraits will often be in those "unnecessary" biographies—i.e., those that the historian was not obliged

to include. In the *Records* these might be the lesser political figures (e.g. Wu Zuxu [Wu Tzu-hsü] (66) or the aides of the first Emperor of the Han [96]); poets (e.g., Qu Yuan [Ch'ü Yüan] (84) or Sima Xiangru [Ssu-ma Hsiang-ju] (117)); the Memoirs of various foreign peoples (110, 113–116, 123); or the composite biographies (121–129). These entries not only reflect Sima Qian's (and we assume his contemporaries') thoughts on exemplary personalities, in many cases they also define those personalities for the subsequent tradition. This is, for example, exactly the case for the writer/official Qu Yuan, who from this biography became one of the most important "types" in the Chinese literary and folk traditions.

4. Finally, the comparatist can focus on literary technique. These discussions will usually center on narrative styles (but one should not forget the nonnarrative sections of the *Records*); the four-part rubric discussed in *The Nature of Narrative*, by Robert E. Scholes and Robert Kellogg (New York: Oxford University Press, 1975) (meaning, character, plot, and point of view) is generally useful to begin discussing Sima Qian's style. In this regard, special attention should be paid to the following aspects of his narrative: use of symbolic signs and actions to "code" the lives of men; the use of dialogue and literary quotation (usually poems) in the penetration of thought; nonnarrative patterns of "plotting"; authorial and narratorial intrusions; the relationship between the narrative proper and the summary evaluation; and problems of irony and omniscience. Much of the beauty and power of Sima Qian's language is, of course, lost in translation, but within the tradition one can compare his narrative style with prose works that come both before and after the *Records*—such as the earlier *Zuo Commentary* or the philosophic anecdotes of *Zhuang Zi [Chuang Tzu]*, and the later medieval parallel prose and the Tang short story.

NOTES

1. Burton Watson, *Ssu-ma Ch'ien: Grand Historian of China* (New York: Columbia University Press, 1958), pp. 49–50.

2. Ibid., p. 66.

3. Burton Watson, trans., *Records of the Grand Historian of China: Translated from the Shih Chi of Ssu-ma Ch'ien* (Hong Kong: Commercial Press, 1974), 2:461.

REFERENCES

There are relatively few textual problems with the *Records*; the only major ones are the question of the reconstructed ten chapters and the uncertainty of the amount of text that might be attributed to Sima Qian's father—these questions are dealt with both by Watson and Chavannes.

Translation of a large part of the text is available in English (Watson; Yangs) and French (Chavannes), with a complete translation available in Japanese (Noguchi). Chavannes translates the first 47 chapters in order of their appearance (ending with the "Hereditary Life of Confucius"); Watson is more inclusive, and especially strong on the Memoirs themselves, but has rearranged their presentation. The introductory material in Chavannes's first volume is thorough and complete; Watson's separate study, *Ssu-ma Ch'ien*, is very valuable, not only on the life of Sima Qian but on other questions surrounding the text—it also includes translation of a number of pertinent documents. Several of the essays in Beasley and Pulleyblank are concerned with the *Records*; the introduction is an excellent comparison of Chinese and Japanese historiography. The entries for the text and author in the *Indiana Companion to Traditional Chinese Literature* will direct the reader toward the substantial secondary literature.

Beasley, W. G., and Pulleyblank, E. G. *Historians of China and Japan.* New York: Oxford University Press, 1961.

Chavannes, Édouard, trans. *Les Mémoires historique de Se-ma Ts'ien.* 5 vols. Leiden: E. J. Brill, 1967.

Noguchi Sadao, trans. *Shiki. Chugoku koten bungaku taikei.* Vols. 10–12. Tokyo: Heibonsha, 1968.

Watson, Burton, trans. *Records of the Grand Historian of China: Translated from the* Shih chi *of Ssu-ma Ch'ien.* 2 vols. New York: Columbia University Press, 1961.

Watson, Burton. *Ssu-ma Ch'ien: Grand Historian of China.* New York: Columbia University Press, 1958.

There are also translations available in Yang Hsien-yi and Gladys Yang, *Records of the Grand Historian* (Hong Kong: Commercial Press, 1974), but I have not seen the text.

THE JOURNEY TO THE WEST

Andrew H. Plaks

HISTORICAL AND CULTURAL CONTEXT

The title *The Journey to the West* (*Xiyou ji* [*Hsi-yu chi*]) refers not to a single literary work, but to an entire narrative tradition in China dealing with the legendary expedition of the Tang [T'ang] Buddhist master Xuanzang [Hsüan-tsang] to India in quest of Mahayana scriptures, in the company of a party of disciple/protectors including the "Monkey King" Sun Wukong [Sun Wu-k'ung]. The principal characters and episodes of this story-cycle have been treated in a variety of genres and literary forms from Tang times down to the present day, producing materials of great importance for the history of Chinese popular culture. For the purposes of literary analysis and comparative discussion, however, attention must be focused primarily on the hundred-chapter allegorical novel *Xiyou ji* that appeared in print during the late Ming period.

The chain of literary developments related to the Xuanzang cycles starts with the actual historical accounts of the original journey to the western regions. Almost immediately, the trek across uncharted mountains and deserts and the encounters with exotic peoples captured the popular imagination. Soon the stories were embellished with independent elements of pseudogeography, Buddhist demonology, even Chinese monkey lore—in which some see possible reflections of the Hanuman figure from the Indian epic *Rāmāyaṇa*—to yield the basic plot of the best-known episodes. These popular elements continue to be visible in a series of dramatic treatments of the pilgrimage, from the Yuan period down to the twentieth century, often emphasizing the supernatural transformations and stage acrobatics of the beloved monkey figure. By the Southern Song [Sung] period, several of the existing episodes had already been recombined to produce what is the earliest extant continuous narrative of the Xuanzang cycle, in the brief text entitled *Da Tang Sanzang qujing shihua* (*[Ta-T'ang San-tsang ch'ü-ching shih-hua] Master Tripitaka of the Tang Fetches the Scriptures, in Prose and Verse*). Slightly later, there appeared a full-length dramatic treatment known as *Xiyou ji zaju* [*Hsi-yu chi tsa-chü*], in which the dimensions of the cycle are expanded and some of the allegorical associations later applied to the story begin to surface. More recently, certain textual fragments have been discovered—one quoted in a mid-Ming encyclopedia, another given as a reading sample in a fifteenth-century Chinese-language textbook from Korea. These fragments attest to the existence of more or less complete colloquial prose narrative versions of the story in what is known as the *pinghua* [*p'ing-hua*] form well before the composition of the full-length novel.

At some point during the sixteenth century, these various types of antecedent narrative materials were brought together and recast as the hundred-chapter *Xiyou ji*. This text conforms in most respects to the conventions of the "literati novel," a genre that was taking shape by this period, following the appearance of the full recensions of *Sanguo zhi yanyi* (*[San-kuo chih yen-i] The Three Kingdoms*) and *Shuihu zhuan* (*[Shui-hu chuan] Water Margin*). Scholarly controversy continues to debate whether it is the 1592 edition printed by the Shide tang [Shih-te t'ang] publishing house, or one of two shorter versions published around the same time, that represents the "original" form of the novel. But from this point on, at any rate, the basic outlines of the novel were fixed, remaining essentially the same through a number of subsequent editions distinguished primarily by a series of marginal commentaries advocating varying interpretations of the allegorical message of the book. Over the years, a number of sequels and spin-off narratives were written, and in more recent times, the story has been adapted to other artistic media, such as film, television, and even comic books.

Exactly who was responsible for creating the hundred-chapter novel out of the various source materials and antecedent narratives remains a matter of considerable speculation. For a long time, the prevailing theory has assigned the authorship of the book to Wu Cheng'en ([Wu Ch'eng-en] ca. 1500–ca. 1582), a minor figure of some small renown within sixteenth-century literati circles. Wu Cheng'en had a reputation for wit and an interest in supernatural phenomena, and according to a laconic entry in one local history, he reportedly composed a work with this same title. Recently, however, a number of scholars have agreed that the evidence for this attribution is quite flimsy, thus leaving the question very much open, in spite of the fact that Wu's name continues to appear on all modern reprints of the book. This uncertainty has led to a more open-minded reappraisal of the earlier legends assigning the composition of the novel to the late-Song Taoist master Qiu Chuji ([Ch'iu Ch'u-chi] also known as Changchun zhenren [Ch'ang-ch'un chen-jen])—a theory that is quite dubious, but would nevertheless help to account for certain pieces of documentary evidence.

No matter who ultimately deserves the credit for this literary masterwork, there is no question but that the hundred-chapter novel represents more than simply the final stage of the expanding narrative cycles. Rather, it stands as an independent literary phenomenon distinct from the versions that preceded and followed it. This text is much fuller in its narrative detail and in its lively dialogue; it breaks new poetic ground in its use of incidental verse as well. In structural terms, it also reshapes the previous narrative versions by adding an extended prologue composed of the first twelve chapters (in keeping with a pattern established in the other three major Ming novels), as well as adding a number of key episodes that are apparently unique to the full recension of the novel. Most important is the manner in which the hundred-chapter novel superimposes on the text the intricate overlay of its allegorical apparatus: the story of a quest journey with a simple didactic framework of Buddhist salvation is effectively transformed into a complex and profound allegory of the process of spiritual cultivation, as reinterpreted within the broader context of late-Ming syncretic philosophy.

This new literary incarnation of the full-length *Xiyou ji* into a challenging allegorical composition was recognized by all of the traditional commentators. It is a bit ironic that the allegorical nature of the text has been obscured for Western readers by the very success of Arthur Waley's brilliant translation that appeared under the title *Monkey* in 1943. While Waley's English version established a lasting place for the novel in the eyes of European and American readers, his radical abridgment not only shortened the work, but through its selection of episodes, gave rise to a misleading impression that this is essentially a compendium of popular materials marked by folk wit and humor. This was no simple misreading on Waley's part. In taking this approach, he follows precisely the reading of the novel advocated by leading twentieth-century Chinese critics—especially by the influential scholar of the "May Fourth" generation, Hu Shi [Hu Shih], who rejected the various allegorical interpretations as fossils of an outmoded system of thought and values, and praised instead the comic exuberance of the story-cycles.

This view of *Xiyou ji* is not wrong as far as the Chinese popular tradition running before and parallel to the novel is concerned, but it fails to account for the serious level of meaning embedded in the allegorical framework of the book. Over the past ten years, literary scholars both inside and outside China have attempted to reassess the cultural significance of the serious allegorical dimension of the novel. A number of critical reinterpretations within the context of sixteenth-century intellectual history have appeared, a few Qing [Ch'ing] commentary editions have been reprinted, and at least three new Western translations, by virtue of their unabridged transmission of the text, now make the full dimensions of the allegory accessible to the Western reader.

SYNOPSIS

The main body of the novel is enclosed by the narrative frame of the journey that gets underway with the departure of the saintly monk Xuanzang in chapter 13, in quest of holy scriptures with which to save the souls of the Tang empire. Up to chapter 23, the initial episodes are devoted primarily to the gathering of the four "pilgrims": the simian Sun Wukong, the voracious pig Zhu Bajie [Chu Pa-chieh], the morose "Sand Monk" Sha Heshang [Sha Ho-shang], and the enigmatic dragon-horse. After this, the narrative settles into a regular rhythm of episodes continuing until the pilgrimage reaches its destination in India in chapter 98. This entire structural core is flanked on one side by the appended prologue not found in any of the antecedent narratives. The prologue relates the prior history of the monkey-pilgrim, from his spontaneous birth and emergence as the ruler of an enclosed earthly paradise, to his impatient search for enlightenment and immortality that takes him out into the world and ultimately puts him into a titanic struggle with the powers of Heaven. Much later, the narrative concludes with a somewhat anti-climatic fulfillment of the quest: the Master, still unable to see beyond the literal distinction between reality and emptiness, must be ferried across to the "other shore" of salvation in a bottomless boat, only to be rewarded, quite pointedly, with a set of "wordless scriptures." The book then closes on a somewhat incongruous note of triumphal return, apotheosis of the pilgrims, and closing hymns of praise and thanksgiving.

The sequence of episodes that makes up the body of the text is ordered according to the predetermined formula of the "eighty-one trials" required for fulfillment of the quest. But this total is actually reducible to a smaller number of self-contained episodes, typically spanning three or four chapters each. The paradigmatic form of these episodes can be schematized as follows: we begin with our pilgrims on the road, buoyant and satisfied with themselves for having come through their preceding trial, only to find their equanimity upset by cold, hunger, or discomforts of some other sort. Out of this ruffling of consciousness there emerges a demon. This demon, after one or repeated attempts, manages by stealth or sheer force to snatch from a protective enclosure the Master, and sometimes one or more of the pilgrims, and to entrap them in a secluded lair. Sun Wukong, who is usually not among those initially seized, employs either his own powers of vision or occasionally the help of others to locate the captives, but he fails in his initial attempts to break through the spell that keeps them bound. In most cases it is only after he seeks external aid—the bestowal of either a secret formula or a magic weapon, or else the direct intervention of a Buddhist savior—that the demon is finally subdued. The demon's true form is then revealed, and the thralldom is dispelled, leaving the pilgrims free to continue on their way until the quick emergence of the next peril. Within this predictable outline the separate episodes each present variations on the pattern, often with bizarre or whimsical forms of demons, obstacles, and saviors. Among the most memorable episodes are those running from chapters 24 to 26 (the premature seizure of the "fruit of perfection" in the Temple of Five Estates), 27 to 31 (the "exile" of the monkey-pilgrim, which leads to a perilous state of disequilibrium marked by his own replication with a false double), 37 to 39 (the Hamlet-like usurpation of a conjugal bed and a kingdom in the Black Cock Realm), 44 to 46 (a contest of occult powers with a trio of heterodox Taoist wizards in the "Cart-slow" Kingdom), 53 to 55 (the topsy-turvy inversion of sexual hierarchies in the Kingdom of Women at Xiliang [Hsi-liang]), 56 to 58 (the restaging of the "exile" and false doubling of the Mind Monkey), 59 to 61 (the eruption of desire and wrath at the Mountain of Flames), 72 to 73 (entanglement in the web of the "Seven Passions" in the guise of seductive spider demonesses), 80 to 83 (an assault on the Master's primal purity by the Lady of the Earthly Wellsprings), and 93 to 95 (the near capitulation of the Master to the sexual designs of the Jade Hare demoness).

LITERARY ANALYSIS

A critical analysis of the full hundred-chapter recension of *Xiyou ji* must focus on at least two principal aspects: the formal features of structure and rhetoric that mark it as an example of what has been called the sixteenth-century "literati novel," and various attempts at unraveling its allegorical code to arrive at a meaningful interpretation.

From the first of these two perspectives, *Xiyou ji* presents in many ways an example of striking adherence to the aesthetic conventions of the mature Ming novel genre—in spite of the fact that its subject matter diverges so sharply from the other three "classic" examples. For one thing, the hundred-chapter length in itself constitutes a generic feature, with the earliest editions of the novel divided, according to the Ming practice, into twenty "volumes" of five chapters each. However, the use of the resulting structural divisions as a grid for significant narrative rhythms is not as neatly articulated here as in the other major examples. This is most likely a result of the author's interest in certain other numerological patterns that he uses in plotting his work, most noticeably cycles of nines (for example, the water crossings in chapters 9, 49, and 99; or the fulfillment of the quest of eighty-one trials in chapter 99). In addition, he plays with certain more whimsical numerological schemes, such as the symmetrical placement of parallel motifs in chapters at the two ends of the hundred-chapter span. For example, he restages the attainment of dubious enlightenment in chapters 2 and 98, and the crossing of the margins of civilization in chapters 13 and 88; and he reserves special focus for unusual single-chapter episodes that happen to fall in chapters numbered with perfect squares (36, 49, and 64). At the same time, the author follows the structural model of the other Ming masterworks in his use of the device of dividing his long text into two equal halves, demarcated by a significant midpoint—in this case the crossing of the "River of Communion with Heaven" ("Tongtian he" ["T'ung-t'ien ho"]) on the back of a mystical giant tortoise. The appending of a prologue section set outside of the central world of the narrative in the hundred-chapter recension also matches a pattern clearly observed in *Jin Ping Mei* [*Chin P'ing Mei*]. The author provides an initial structural model for his book according to this pattern, while also raising some of the central issues to be taken up in the body of the text. Here, we get a suggestive parable of the idea of the "stilling of the monkey of the mind," and a structural model for the quest whose end is its own beginning. The parallel to *Jin Ping Mei* is even more striking in that this initial section is itself prefaced by a "prologue to the prologue," taking the form of a philosophical disquisition on the concept of cyclical non-finality. At the other end of the book, the final point of the structural arrangement again conforms to the common pattern of finishing with an open-ended conclusion: in this case a superficial grand-reunion scene that is patently "empty," and pointedly withholds the expected final synthesis of the allegorical message.

A second area in which the *Xiyou ji* conforms to the conventions of the late-Ming literati novel is in its use of a range of rhetorical devices. As in the other major examples of classic Ming fiction, the narrator of this work also maintains the pose of a streetside oral storyteller spinning his yarn out of a variety of formulaic rhetoric and tag expressions. On the surface these stock devices link the novel to its various antecedent versions in the popular tradition. But in actuality, these are subordinated to the sophisticated allegorical design of the work. The same is true of the use of descriptive and narrative verse within the text, a throwback to various genres of mixed prose and verse storytelling (including the *shihua* [*shih-hua*] version of the narrative noted above) that here provides the occasion for certain innovative forms of mock-heroic verse, frequently displaying considerable poetic virtuosity.

The primary rhetorical feature of the novel is its use of a prevailing tone of irony to deflate the pretensions of the pilgrims and demons alike, while also undercutting the simplistic didacticism of the surface message of the quest. The many puns and word games that spice up the text no doubt contribute to its humorous quality, but at the same time these elements direct the reader to look beyond the amusing literal level of the story. The primary thrust of this ironic discrepancy between the surface and the underlying meaning suggests the reading of the text as allegory. One of the early commentators describes the allegorical function as follows:

> What is said refers to Xuan-zang, but what is meant is actually not about Xuan-zang. What is recorded refers to the fetching of scriptures, but what is intended is not about the fetching of scriptures. It just deliberately borrows this to allegorize the great Tao.[1]

These words are strikingly reminiscent of various classical definitions of Medieval Western allegory as *alienoloquium*, or "saying one thing and meaning another."

The author himself signals to the reader the need for an allegorical deciphering of his text by providing several episodes in which the intended significance is all but transparent: for example in the subdual of the bandits of the "six senses" in chapter 14, the suppression of the temptress labeled the "seven passions" in chapter 73, or the taming of tigers and dragons (conventional symbols for unbridled consciousness) at several points.

The specific hints used to set up the allegorical framework occur in a number of predictable locations, chiefly in the names and iconographic details applied to individual figures, in the parallel couplets that serve as chapter titles, and in many lines of verse interspersed throughout the narrative. These labels draw upon a broad range of philosophical terminology from the three major schools of thought: Buddhism, Taoism, and Confucianism. First, we have the many Buddhist figures who appear in the text and the frequent echo of conventional Mahayana expressions about "crossing over" to the "other shore" of salvation, or other symbols of Zen [Ch'an] enlightenment. To these is added another set of terms derived from Taoist occult lore, particularly that related to the pursuit of immortality through the practice of "refining the inner cinnabar." These include references to certain types of alchemical paraphernalia, metaphors of the gestation of a "newborn" transcendent self, the notion of an optimum firing time (huohou [huo-hou]) for incubating the refined essence of the self, and the application of terminology associated with the so-called "five elements": wood, fire, earth, metal, and water, whose never-ending processes of combination and dissolution symbolize the cycles of change at the heart of the cosmic order. These associations also leave room for a considerable overlapping with various terms of Confucian provenance, especially the hexagram lore of the Yi Jing ([I Ching] Book of Changes). What is most important about these different sets of philosophical, or pseudophilosophical, terms is the fact that they do not cancel one another out, but rather join forces to form interlocking networks of symbols. This synthesis results from the syncretic intellectual currents at the time of the novel's composition in the sixteenth century, which brought together the Confucian cultivation of moral perfection, the Buddhist cultivation of transcendent enlightenment, and the Taoist cultivation of physical immortality under the banner of the "unity of the three teachings" (sanjiao heyi [san-chiao ho-i]).

The key to the interpretation of the allegorical structure of Xiyou ji, in short, lies in the confluence in the late-Ming intellectual milieu of Buddhist, Taoist, and Confucian ideas, specifically

in the strain of all three schools commonly referred to as "philosophy of mind" (*xinxue* [*hsin-hsüeh*]). Various expressions based on
the terms *xin* ([*hsin*] translated as "mind," "heart," or "consciousness," according to the context) recur throughout the text of the
novel. From the very start, the author explicitly labels the mon-
key-figure brought to the center stage in the unprecedented prologue section as a "monkey of the mind" (*xinyuan* [*hsin-yüan*]).
This common expression, used to describe the unchained force of
ego, begins to develop its special allegorical implications as soon
as the unruly monkey is subdued and caged under "Five-elements
Mountain" in chapter 7, an event glossed for us in the chapter
title as the "stilling of the mind-monkey" (*ding xinyuan* [*ting hsin-
yüan*]). From this point on, the author misses no chance to emphasize the notion that the entire "Journey to the West" is
essentially a pilgrimage of the mind, an idea brought forward in a
number of allegorical hints and explicit statements. For example,
the book opens with a mini-pilgrimage by the Monkey-king to "the
Cave of the Crescent Moon with Three Stars (an anagram for the
character *xin*, which in its written form, looks like a hooked curve
with three dots), and near the journey's end in chapter 85 we are
told, "the Holy Mountain is nowhere but in your mind."

On the basis of such passages, the allegorical significance of
the quest begins to fall into place. First, although the course of
the narrative pits our heroes against external obstacles and hostile forces, these are to be understood as manifestations of an
internal process. Thus, we are warned early on that "the bodhi-
sattvas of salvation and the demons of self-destruction are all
manifestations of a single concept," and elsewhere, "with the
emergence of consciousness, all types of demons come forth; with
the extinction of consciousness, all the demons are extinguished."

The allegorical progress of the journey therefore becomes a
matter of coming through a series of spiritual trials unscathed. In
some cases the "problem" at issue is simply one of carelessness or
negligence (for example, the Master and the pilgrims are incapable
of remaining within a protective circle drawn by Sun Wukong in
chapter 50, or it may be one of impatience for the moment of
fulfillment (as in the Master's premature bid for enlightenment
atop a moonlit pagoda in chapter 36). At other points more abstract issues are at stake, including the problem of disunity, as
allegorized in the two exiles of the mind-monkey, with the resulting state of destructive multiplicity in the guise of false doubles.
In such cases, the principal obstacle is a blockage of vision, typically the failure to discern the false masquerading as the true.

One of the most interesting of these allegorical obstacles appears in a number of scenes in which the pilgrims are confronted with demonic weapons taking the form of a variety of enveloping objects (bags, bottles, bells, or bowls) that threaten to destroy them by swallowing them within the confining bounds of their own self-consciousness. The allegorical significance of all of these impediments to enlightenment helps to explain why so many of the "trials" involve instances of sexual temptation, since the disequilibrium of sexual desire, perhaps more than anything else, brings together all the other problems of consciouness already discussed. Thus, the allegorical labels attached to the scenes of sexual confrontation suggestively gloss them as "straying from the true nature," "disordering of the mind," or "forgetting the source," in order to stress the philosophical problem that is really at issue.

This identification of the obstacles of the pilgrimage as primarily symptoms of excessive self-consciousness provides a key to interpreting the sequential degrees of attainment that mark out the path to enlightenment. Inthe familiar terms used in the "philosophy of mind," what is required to attain true enlightenment is what is called "recovering the lost mind" set adrift in psychic diffusion (*qiu qi fangxin* [*ch'iu ch'i fang-hsin*]), "cleansing the mind" (*xixin* [*hsi-hsin*]) of its blockages caused by the strivings of ego or reducing a destabilizing multiplicity of consciousness to a stable oneness of the primal self (*yixin* [*i-hsin*]).

One way in which this process is worked out in the course of the allegorical narrative is through the progressive integration of the five-member pilgrim band into what is described in Buddhist terminology as a single harmonious body (*yiti* [*i-t'i*]). Through the course of the journey we can observe a certain gradual improvement on this point. But at the same time, the author continues to deny the simplistic notion of steady progress by taking pains to deflate each of the individual pilgrims in turn, and to undermine the final fulfillment of the quest as a whole, thus leaving many questions unresolved regarding the precise sequence of the quest, chief among them the perennial issue of gradual versus sudden enlightenment. Ultimately, the allegory comes to rest on the illusory nature of the pursuit of enlightenment itself, a sense that adds further significance to the allegorical imagery of destructive self-containment described earlier. This understanding conforms to the central teaching of the Mahayana Buddhist text entitled *Prajnaparamita Xinjing* ([*Hsin-ching*] *Heart Sutra of Transcendent Wisdom*), which is actually quoted in full at the start of the journey and then recalled at several points later on. This doctrine of the ultimate identity of reality and emptiness seems to be behind the conclusion that the conscious pursuit of emptiness, as in the pseudoenlightenment in chapter 36, is itself a symptom of incomplete cultivation. This idea is apparently what is intended in the use of the monastic name of Sun Wukong, whose literal meaning, "enlightened about emptiness," implies a retreat from a literal-minded pursuit of the Void. In this sense, the attainment of the "fruit" of the quest (*chengguo* [*ch'eng-kuo*]), which appeared to be self-destructive in chapter 25, is eventually redefined as a return to the original starting point (*fanben* [*fan-pen*]) of concrete existence.

The profound allegorical content of the *Journey to the West* lends itself to comparative treatment in the light of some of the greatest examples of allegory in the Medieval and Renaissance Western tradition. Beyond occasional critical comments drawing simplistic parallels to Bunyan's *Pilgrim's Progress*, somewhat more compelling arguments have compared the book to Rabelais's *Gargantua and Pantagruel*. The comparison is usually drawn in terms of their exuberant humor and the celebration of life-force shared by Garantua and the pig and monkey pilgrims, rather than with respect to the anticlerical ideological content of Rabelais's work. This sort of East-West comparison becomes more fruitful when the quest-journey in this Chinese work is brought into focus with Dante's spiritual pilgrimage, or with other examples of *psychomachia*, especially with Spenser's exactly contemporaneous allegorical romance, the *Faerie Queene*. Within the corpus of the classic Chinese novel itself, the issue of reality and emptiness (*sekong* [*se-k'ung*]) is also taken up in a quasi-allegorical manner in the *Jin Ping Mei* and *Hongloumeng* ([*Hung-lou meng*] *Story of the Stone* or *Dream of the Red Chamber*). But nowhere else is this worked out with such profundity as in *Xiyou ji*, with the possible exception of one seventeenth-century dream-vision entitled *Xiyou bu* ([*Hsi-yu pu*] *A Supplement to Journey to the West*) by Dong Yue [Tung Yüeh].

TOPICS FOR DISCUSSION

1. How are the humorous elements of the popular Xuanzang story-cycle and stage performances transformed in the hundred-chapter novel into a profoundly serious allegorical structure? At what points do the various puns and word-games, and the slap-stick episodes involving Sun Wukong and Zhu Bajie end, and the injection of serious ideas begin? How does the author use ironic

rhetoric to undermine the literal level of the story and direct the reader toward his allegorical message?

2. How should one interpret the sequence of episodes along the path of the allegorical quest? Within the overall framework of the narrative structure, what does the author seem to be saying about the issue of gradual spiritual progress versus sudden enlightenment? Is every episode a necessary step toward the final goal, or does the pilgrimage go nowhere and end up at the beginning?

3. What is the significance of the bestowal of wordless scriptures at the moment of the attainment of the quest? Why does the author continue to undercut the spiritual attainment of the pilgrims even as they near their goal?

4. The various sets of philosophical terms in which the allegory is couched, including Buddhist devotional expressions, Taoist alchemical terms, and hexagram lore from the *Book of Changes*, seem to work at cross purposes. How are these conflicting sets of terms brought together in the novel's allegorical exploration of the process of self-cultivation?

NOTE

1. Anonymous preface (attributed to Yu Ji [Yü Chi]) in a 1662 woodblock commentary edition entitled *Hsi-yu cheng-tao shu* (author's translation).

REFERENCES

Translations

Jenner, William. *The Journey to the West*. Beijing: Foreign Languages Press, 1983. Complete, readable translation, without scholarly apparatus.

Lévy, André. *Pélérinage vers l'Ouest*. Paris: Gallimard, forthcoming. Complete French translation.

Lin Shuen-fu and Larry Schulz. *Tower of Myriad Mirrors*. Berkeley, CA: Asian Humanities Press, 1978. Translation of *Xiyou bu*.

Waley, Arthur. *Monkey*. London: 1943; reprint, New York: Grove Press, 1958. Abridged translation of approximately one-fourth the original text.

Yu, Anthony C. *The Journey to the West*. Chicago: University of Chicago Press, 1977–83. Complete translation with extensive scholarly introduction and notes.

Critical Studies

Fu, James S. *Mythic and Comic Aspects of the Quest*. Singapore: Singapore University Press, 1977.

Hsia, C.T. "The Journey to the West." In *The Classic Chinese Novel*, pp. 115-64. New York: Columbia University Press, 1968.

Kao, Karl S.Y. "An Archetypal Approach to *Hsi-yu chi.*" *Tamkang Review* 5, no. 2 (October 1974): 63–98.

Plaks, Andrew. *The Four Masterworks of the Ming Novel.* Princeton: Princeton University Press, 1987, pp. 183–276.

Yu, Anthony. "Two Literary Examples of Religious Pilgrimage: The *Commedia* and the *Journey to the West.*" *History of Religions* 22, no. 3 (February 1983): 202–30.

CAO XUEQIN'S *HONGLOUMENG*

(*Story of the Stone* or *Dream of the Red Chamber*)

Anthony C. Yu

The most popular and most widely acclaimed work of traditional Chinese prose fiction had several names given to it even as it had existed in many manuscript versions (none containing more than eighty chapters) prior to its formal publication, in movable type, in 1791–92 as a novel of 120 chapters. The variety of its titles and the vicissitudes of its textual history constitute part of what continues to intrigue the readers of this unusual narrative.

According to Cao Xueqin (1715–63; or alternately, 1724–64), putative author who conceived the work and might have completed it substantially, the novel was first titled *Shitouji* (*Story of the Stone*). If the account in the first chapter is to be believed, suggestions were then made by his first readers to change it to *Qingsenglu* (*Record of Brother Amor*), or *Hongloumeng* (*Dream of the Red Chamber*), or *Fengyue baojian* (*Bejeweled Mirror of Romance*), or finally, *Jinling shier chai* (*Twelve Beauties of Nanking*). An early edition of the work was printed with the title *Jinyu yuan* (*The Marital Affinity of Gold and Jade*). Each name for the narrative, we may say, emphasizes a certain aspect or theme of this vast and complex work.

The first title patently picks up the pervasive stone motif and imagery in the novel: the names of many of its characters, including that of the male protagonist Baoyu (precious jade) and one of the females, Daiyu (black jade), are associated with rock, stone, or nephrite. Baoyu is not only said to have been born with a piece of unusually carved jade in his mouth, but his identity in a previous incarnation, according to the novel's initial mythic frame, is as a piece of stone—one rejected as unfit by the goddess Nüwa in her legendary task of repairing the sky. This stone, however, befriends a plant—the Crimson Pearl Flower—which, out of gratitude for the nurture of faithful watering, vows to repay such kindness with a lifetime of tears. The love story between Baoyu and Daiyu, his teenage cousin and the plant's mortal incarnation, thus unfolds in the action as "predestined," with a strong hint of tragedy from the beginning. This experience of passion is designed to continue to test the stone's worth, to determine whether the stone is comprehending (*tongling*) or unknowing and unteachable (*huanshi*).

Knowledge is indeed a major theme of the novel: social, moral, artistic, psychological, and sexual. Chinese works of fiction traditionally are none too ambiguous on what they seek to convey, and in this respect, Cao Xueqin seems rather unique in his achievement. Not only is his composition a masterfully woven tapestry of intricate figurations and thematic motifs; it is as well a highly reflexive document that constantly prods and provokes its readers to consider the content and medium of fictive knowledge. Although *A Bejeweled Mirror of Romance* and *The Record of Brother Amor* continue ostensibly to highlight the amatory aspects of the plot, the two titles also provide different emphases.

The former title, of course, refers to both the reflective and fictive nature of art. Our author often takes enormous delight in reminding his readers, subtly but repeatedly, that his engaging and apparently real depiction of life and love ("All that my story narrates, the meetings and partings, the joys and sorrows, the ups and downs of fortune, are recorded exactly as they happened. I have not dared to add the tiniest bit of touching-up, for fear of losing the true picture"[1]) is paradoxically no more real than the image in the mirror. The addition of the description, bejeweled or precious (*bao*), to the mirror, however, broadens its allusive significance. On the one hand, the term, *baojian*, can in secular usage often point to an inscribed maxim, carved or written for its beholder's constant admonition. So to name the tale thus is to add an aura of caution to its engrossing content (cf. the frequent use of the word *jing* in the narrative, translated as "disenchantment" or "warning"). On the other hand, a bejeweled or precious mirror in Buddhist literature can betoken either the unsullied mind of the faithful or the great round mirror wisdom (*adarsana-jñana*) which, in reflecting all things, can provide true knowledge.[2] The play of rhetoric throughout the novel on real (*zhen*) and unreal (jia), the homophones of which are used also as the family names of major characters, accentuates the authorial preoccupation with the paradox of truth in fiction.

A more explicitly religious note is struck in the latter title, for the oxymoronic predicament inherent in the name *Brother Amor* (qingseng) suggests the ironic clash of vocation and nature. A Buddhist monk is supposed to renounce all ties to world and kin, but Baoyu, the young protagonist, is driven to seek enlightenment in the very experience of attachment. Unable to forget his beloved Daiyu long after her death, Baoyu flies into the Gate of Emptiness for refuge at the end of the one-hundred-twenty-chapter novel. However, real question remains as to whether even his assumption of a reclusive, monastic existence can alleviate an obsessive and afflicted memory. Perhaps the most remarkable aspect of this use of Buddhist elements in the novel is the way in which Baoyu's entire venture has been made deliberately suggestive of an ironic parallel to the experience of reading the work itself. Much as the young man has been led to a grudging acknowledgment of life's impermanence through the most intense entanglements in the human world, so the reader must work through a contemplation of Form (itself equivalent to Illusion) and the Passion it engenders to reach a kind of truth, which is knowledge of the Void.[3] In this kind of juxtaposition, the Buddhist advocacy of detachment from an unreal and ephemeral world is subtly undermined and subverted by an aesthetics of engagement with the reality of fictive illusion.

Although the narrative thus concerns a young man's growth and enlightenment, it is also nonetheless a story preeminently about women, because the young man's initiatory experience is seen to be largely shaped by his changing relationships with a group of attractive young women, the cousins and maids celebrated as The Twelve Beauties of Nanking. The naming of that famous city (Jinling has been the capital of several imperial dynasties) may seem to locate the novel in the southeastern part of China, which probably was familiar to the author in his own youth. Students of the work, however, are quick to point out that its exact geography defies determination, for the imaginary space of the great mansion and the spectacular Prospect Garden in which Baoyu and his female companions reside incorporates distinct features of northern and southern China.

More significant than its locative and topographical peculiarities is the novel's sympathetic, exalted, and relentless focus on women in an aristocratic household. Together with the boy

Baoyu's articulate preference ("Girls are made of water and boys are made of mud. When I am with girls I feel fresh and clean, but when I am with boys I feel stupid and nasty"), such depiction registers an astonishing challenge to the traditional norms of patriarchal Confucianism. Cao Xueqin's treatment of the women's beauty, their sartorial resplendence, their literary talents, their political sagacity, and their "revolutionary or antifuedal" behavior has been frequently noted and justly praised. What has yet to receive thorough investigation is how the world and action of the "beauties" both mirror and parody the male society of the time. The women's activities in forming poetry clubs and competing in poetic contests, for example, dramatize the politics of literary art by miming and mocking the experience of male candidates in imperial examinations. (At the same time, they reflect the clandestine nature and ambiguous status of actual poetry clubs (shishe), which were alternately forbidden and encouraged in the Ming-Qing periods.) The managerial skills of Phoenix (Wang Xifeng), Baoyu's cousin-in-law, and the benign resourcefulness of Grandmother Jia provide direct rebuke for the inept and often immoral shenanigans of the male members of the household.

The final title of the novel, Hongloumeng (Dream of the Red Chamber or Mansions), is probably the best-known to Chinese and foreign readers alike. Most translations, with perhaps but one exception, have used this denomination, for undoubtedly it appears to many as a succinct epitome of the work. Whether the color red refers obliquely to the Buddhist notion of the phenomenal world as "red dust" is subject to debate. There is little doubt, however, that coupled with the towered buildings (literal meaning of lou) it describes, red chamber or mansion conjures at once an image of power, wealth, and baronial opulence for most readers. After all, gates and pillars of the rich were painted bright red in traditional China, and vermilion steps fronted royal palaces. Varying shades of red are employed in countless ways throughout the narrative to evoke the baroque splendor of the Jia mansion and the plutocratic existence of its inhabitants.

To this picture of power and prosperity is joined, however, the jarring phenomenon of dream, with all its suggestiveness of transience and unreality. The word is an apposite synecdoche for both the tale's content and its total vision. Not only are there more than twenty episodes of dream in the novel—several of which are crucial to the plot's structure and development—but the protracted histories of the narrative's main characters, particularly that of the protagonist, are portrayed as dreamlike. The "golden days" of youth, affluence, dominion, insouciant love, and exuberant festivities seem to be no more permanent or substantial than oneiric blossoms, vividly wrought and intensely moving in their instants of flowering, but they then vanish as inevitable victims of human folly and implacable time.

The several names of the narrative, and their allusive resonance relative to its content, may not indicate indecisiveness of authorial intent, but they surely help explain why scholars find it difficult to arrive at a consensus on the novel's main theme or meaning. Although most readers since its first publication have been impressed by the realistic account of family fortunes and love's tragic vicissitudes, allegorists of the so-called *suoyin* school (literally, exploring obscurities) in the early twentieth century have sought to interpret the work as a veiled romance of the early Qing court or a disguised tract of Han nationalism calling for the revival of the Ming. Since the philosopher Hu Shih's essay of 1911, in which he argues forcefully for the identification of the fictive Baoyu with the author Cao Xueqin and the interpretation of the novel as autobiography, scholars have concentrated for decades on the Cao family and its history in order to search for possible signifying keys for cracking whatever code of character or plot they perceive in the work. Others have interpreted the tale as a superb novel of manners, meticulous in its chronicling of social details and riveting in its charting of an aristocratic family's prosperity and decline. Some have seen in the novel a uniquely Chinese exemplum of the Bildungsroman, wherein the education and enlightenment of the adolescent Baoyu[4] take on moral, psychological, and religious overtones. However it may be finally conceived, the book's richness of content and originality of design invite reading and rereading.

The opening mythical sequence already alluded to reveals the pre-existent identity of the principal lovers as the Luminescent Stone-in-waiting and the Crimson Pearl Flower, respectively. Such designations recall a conventional technique in Chinese fiction, wherein characters appearing as reincarnations of figures (divine, human, and sometimes even animal) of a different time must work out the karmic consequences of their previous fate. What is remarkable in the present novel is that a plant and a stone, objects noted by the Chinese for their proverbial lack of sentiency and feeling (*mushi wuqing*), are made veterans of the most passionate attachments.

The earthly story begins with the arrival of Lin Daiyu at the Jia mansion after the decease of her mother. A year younger than her cousin, Jia Baoyu, she gains the immediate affection of the family matriarch, Grandmother Jia. She impresses her new acquaintances, kin and servants alike, as well with her learning, sharp wit, delicate health, and exquisite beauty. When Daiyu and Baoyu first meet, the two cousins both express the feeling—out loud or in silence—that they seem to have seen each other before (chapter 3). This dramatic encounter thus constitutes the narrative enactment of their karmic origin and destiny, for the shock of recognition is but a confirmation of their common memory in this human stage of their rebirth.

The stage is swiftly set for further development of their relation when Yuanchun, an imperial concubine and Baoyu's older sister, returns to pay her parents a ceremonial visit (chapters 17–18). To do proper homage to the royal guest, the family spares no expense in erecting a vast pleasure garden, meticulously landscaped and elaborately linked with a system of walkways, waterways, groves of bamboos, miniature rock mountains, and refined studios and residences. Appropriately named Daguanyuan (The Prospect Garden or The Garden of Complete Vision), the garden in its scenic grandeur and symbolic resonance seems to mirror the sweeping totality of imperial Chinese civilization.[5]

After her brief visit the royal consort decrees that each girl of the family is to be given a residence in the garden, and Baoyu, as the only male member, joins the entourage by special permission. Within such an idyllic setting, so artfully constructed and virtually unsullied by the mundane concerns of commerce or officialdom, the young cousins pass their days in exciting, and seemingly endless, rounds of seasonal festivity, games, and poetic contests. In such a conducive setting the love between Baoyu and Daiyu blossoms.

The path of the lovers, however, is anything but straight or tranquil. The narrative in the central portion of the novel (chapters 23–80) progressively makes it clear that for Lin Daiyu especially, the journey through pubescence toward young adulthood is fraught with increasing anxiety over her marital prospect. That she finds herself drawn more and more to her cousin Baoyu only exacerbates her worry over her plight as an orphan (her father died shortly after her entrance into the Jia household) lodging in a borrowed home, her declining health that a physician would eventually attribute to consumption, and the possibility of rivalry for her cousin's affections among their kin in the household.[6] The last threat is most keenly posed by Xue Baochai, another cousin whose beauty, intelligence, and literacy obviously have Baoyu's attention, but whose disciplined taciturnity and cultivated tactfulness in the management of houshold affairs provide the sharpest contrast to Daiyu's personality. What renders Baochai most dangerous in Daiyu's eyes is the fact that the former was given at her birth a golden locket by a mysterious monk, with the instruction that she was to marry only someone with a corresponding piece of jade (chapter 28). The peculiar possessions of both the girl and Baoyu thus unwittingly literalize the phrase, "the goodly affinity of gold and jade" (*jinyu liangyuan*), a common euphemism for marriage.

The enigma confronting Baoyu, an only child (an elder brother died years before) spoiled and doted upon by his grandmother, mother, and virtually all senior female relatives, concerns how to hold on to this comfortable and ostensibly carefree existence. As the sole heir of the familial line, his inviolable responsibility consists in working hard to master certain Confucian classics and the prescribed style of the "eight-legged essay" in hopes of passing the examinations leading to civil service. However, he has a deep distaste for such "orthodox" learning requisite for officialdom, and his lethargy is perhaps a sign of his latent rebellion against an incompetent but self-righteous father (whose name Jia Zheng is homophonous with False Rectitude or Governance). Baoyu enjoys no other delight than unbridled commerce with his female companions, indulging incessantly in flirtatious play and literary games. The conflict between duty and desire that focalizes the contradiction of his existence is further complicated by his enjoyment of human community on the one hand, and his struggle on the other for some liberating insight into the disappointment, the frustration, and all other kinds of emotional tumult such relations necessarily entail.

The love that flourishes between the two cousins and eventually consumes them is extraordinary on several counts. Within the traditional culture of imperial China, where parents are invested with the absolute authority of all marital arrangements, premarital affection between the sexes seldom exists precisely because they have so little opportunity to meet, let alone to enjoy any form of acquaintance and courtship. The two most prominent literary antecedents to the novel that may be considered exceptions to this custom nonetheless resort to depicting the unmarried lovers either as engaging in furtive intercouse that ends eventually in disaster (*The Romance of the Western Chamber*) or as establishing contact through the mysterious medium of premonitory dreams (*The Peony Pavilion*). Cao Xueqin is unique in constructing a tale

in which his hero and heroine are permitted prolonged and intimate association in a hospitable setting. The unbreakable bond
that unites the two assumes a natural course of development,
proceeding from intuitive childhood attraction, through shared
periods of camaraderie, banter, communication, and growth, to
poignant moments of heated dispute and passionate disclosure.

Their relation is erected upon a genial friendship that deepens
into a quest for mutual understanding, belying the common opinion that the experience of the two teens does not move much
beyond infatuation and romantic longing. Baoyu's gift of two used
silk handkerchiefs causes Daiyu to realize that his is an affection
that truly discerns the nature of her devotion (chapter 34). Similarly, his accidental revelation, which Daiyu inadvertently overhears, of why he appreciates her more than all other female
companions (because she is the only girl who has never tried to
persuade him to "establish himself and acquire a name"—chapter
32) indicates how much he cherishes that sentiment which un-
conditionally affirms his individuality. In portraying a love of such
magnitude and fierce independence with such psychological depth
and expressive detail of incident and character, the author intends to show us not only how he would harrow the fixities of
certain cultural ideals, but also what cruel loss we suffer when
that love is denied its legitimate consummation.

That denial materializes as both the fortune of the Jia family
and the health of Daiyu markedly decline. Continuous abuses of
power, dereliction of duty, and profligacy on the part of the Jia
clan have progressively confirmed the initial announcement of
doom by the Goddess Disenchantment to an uncomprehending
Baoyu in a dream (chapter 5), that his family's "stock of good
fortune has run out, and nothing can be done to replenish it."[7] As
the years advance, marriage and other causes force the young
residents of the Prospect Garden to leave, an unavoidable event
dreaded by Baoyu and by many of the cousins and the maids.

Although Baoyu by this time seems to have settled on Daiyu to
be his spouse, his choice is overruled by the grandmother by
reason of Daiyu's failing health, and the resultant unlikelihood of
her providing him an heir. At a critical juncture, Baoyu loses his
jade and, momentarily deranged, is deceived by his grandmother,
mother, and sister-in-law into marrying Baochai. The time of their
ceremony also marks the lonely, agonizing death of Daiyu (chapters 97–98). Not long thereafter, the two great mansions of the Jia
family abutting each other on Two Dukes Street in the capital are
raided and their worst offenders receive imperial punishment

(chapter 105). Although Baoyu's father, Jia Zheng, is eventually restored to favor, the last part of the novel makes it clear "that the Jias had come down in the world"[8] never to regain their former glory.

Throughout the plight of his family, Baoyu is preoccupied with his personal, inconsolable grief for his beloved Daiyu. When he finally resolves to end his struggles, his departure for the civil service examination becomes the appropriate—for it is the most ironic—occasion for him to leave Baochai (now pregnant with his child) and his family permanently and vanish as a Buddhist monk.

Although this sketch of the plot apparently focuses on a "triangular" love story, many readers would argue that this theme alone hardly conveys the sense of panoramic drama and voluminous descriptiveness suggestive of a Tolstoi or a Proust encompassed in this Chinese novel. The capacious intricacy of the plot and the several hundred characters display the full range of Qing society: royalty, officials, merchants, artisans, male and female clerics, farmers, servants of all grades and varieties, actors and actresses, prostitutes and catamites. The verve and élan of the vernacular have never been more eloquently caught by a writer with a superb ear, so much so that whole speeches and dialogues not only solicit memorization by devoted readers but also find felicitous adaptation on the modern stage or screen. The cultural activities dear to the literate elite—chess, music, opera, painting, calligraphy, gardening, architecture, domestic appointments, and verbal games of all kinds—receive the most lively presentation. The art of traditional lyric poetry, as it is utilized in narrative for scenic enhancement, character definition, and structural delimitation, attains unprecedented heights of subtlety and effectiveness.

Precisely because the novel has made extensive use of so many aspects of traditional culture, twentieth-century Chinese criticism, Marxist and non-Marxist alike, has tended to concentrate on reconstructing in minute detail the economic, social, intellectual, and cultural settings of the story. The range of divergent topics treated in books, monographs, and articles encompasses land holdings, monetary practice, agricultural and horticultural customs, architecture and garden design, textile production, pharmaceutical items and medical prescriptions, and such imported artifacts as mechanical clocks, port wine, and medicinal ointment for colds and nasal congestion. Combined with the interest in the author's family (the autobiographical approach) and the determination to penetrate the glyphic rhetoric of the author (one framing character was named Zhen Shiyin or literally, true-events-concealed), Chinese critical scholarship unwittingly has regarded the narrative more as a historical document than as a masterpiece of fiction. What is urgently needed is a more systematic examination of the novel's art of making fiction, of the various ingredients that join to draw up for its readers its particular "fictional contract." If the novel's message is that life is illusory like a dream or fiction, why is fiction about life such an engaging illusion? In a work that has the word dream so prominently in one of its titles and that has deployed more than twenty such episodes throughout its length, what is the peculiar significance of the oneiric image and phenomenon? And, in a culture noted for "happy endings" and poetic justice in its literary history, how are we to respond to this exceptional narrative with its emphasis on the impotence of love and virtue, the ironic perversion of purposive action, and the finality of suffering, separation, and death? Is tragedy compatible with Taoist resignation or Buddhist detachment? These are some of the questions still awaiting detailed exploration.

The novel's rather elaborate textual history also complicates its interpretation. Apparently prior to the novel's completion, it was already circulated in manually transcribed manuscripts among a group of the author's friends and kinsmen. At least eleven versions of these manuscripts (the earliest dating back to 1754, nine years before the death of Cao Xueqin, the author) have come down to us, all bearing commentary by a person with the sobriquet of Zhiyanzhai (Red Inkstone) and additional remarks by one Jihusou (Odd Tablet) and several other named and unnamed readers. The composite commentary draws the picture that the manuscript was discussed jointly at times by these readers and one person then wrote down the specific remarks.

The importance of the Red Inkstone commentary is to be defined by the obvious knowledge of the author and his family enjoyed by the commentators, by the revelation of how a work like *Hongloumeng* was read by a group of traditional Chinese readers, and by the degree to which the commentary illumines the process of artistic creation and textual formation peculiar to this novel. Notwithstanding their value, the Red Inkstone manuscripts also present us with enormous problems.

For one thing, none of the surviving versions of the Red Inkstone manuscript contains more than eighty chapters, and this raises the inevitable question of how we are to understand the author's self-declaration in the 1754 version of the novel:

Cao Xueqin in the Nostalgia Studio worked on it for ten years, in the course of which he rewrote it no less than five times, dividing it into chapters, composing chapter headings, renaming it *The Twelve Beauties of Jinling* and adding an introductory quatrain.[9]

If Cao's statement clearly implies that he has finished his novel, what has happened to the last forty chapters?

The answer to this question is further complicated by the fact that when the novel was published in 1791–92 in its one-hundred-twenty-chapter form, it bore the prefaces of two men, Cheng Weiyuan (c. 1742-c. 1818) and Gao E (c. 1740-c. 1815), who claimed:

> The text of the last forty chapters represents a patchwork of different fragments collected over the years. It is a unique text: we have no other text to collate it with. For this reason our editing has been confined to making a continuous narrative and removing the inconsistencies. We have not ventured to tamper with the text beyond those minimal requirements. Until some better text comes along which would justify a thoroughgoing revision, we are unwilling that any of its original features should be obscured.[10]

The ongoing debate among textual specialists, therefore, concerns whether Cheng and Gao were telling the truth. Those scholars skeptical of these remarks tend to regard the last forty chapters as a product of inferior editing or even forgery. Others, however, believe that the long version may indeed have preserved the authentic vision of Cao.

The other problem posed by the Red Inkstone commentary stems from the very intimate relation the scholiast enjoys with the author. Red Inkstone views himself as the privileged witness of many events and personages presented in the novel. In that sense, he is not only a special reader but a unique one. Text, reader, and author in his instance are linked not so much by imaginative and empathetic understanding as they are by actual participation in allegedly the same experience. Though the drift of his remarks does not amount to a total disavowal of *Hongloumeng* as a work of fiction, Red Inkstone certainly tends to single out certain parts of the novel for praise because "there was really such a person" or "this was what actually happened." The commentary, valuable as it is, thus also serves to convert fiction to history, and the modern student should use it with discretion.

TOPICS FOR DISCUSSION

1. *Hongloumeng* is a work replete with all varieties of symbolism: color (red), natural objects (rock, stone, jade), cultural artifacts (garden), human behavior (dream). How are these symbols used in the structuring of plot, shaping of character, and definition of place?

2. Compare the effects of the vicissitudes of family fortunes and social change depicted in *Hongloumeng* with those portrayed in such Western works as Thomas Mann's *Buddenbrooks*, and Anthony Trollope's *Palliser Novels*.

3. The "fatefulness of love" plays an important role in *Hongloumeng*. How does this theme compare with its treatment in such works as *Tale of Genji*, Alessandro Manzoni's *I Promessi Sposi*, Leo Tolstoy's *Anna Karenina*, and Henry James' *Princess Casamassima*?

4. Is *Hongloumeng* a Bildungsroman? A tragic novel?

5. Does *Hongloumeng* contribute toward "the poetics of Gender"? In what way?

6. What is truth in fiction?

NOTES

1. *The Story of the Stone: A Novel in Five Volumes by Cao Xueqin*, trans. David Hawkes and John Minford, 5 vols. (Harmondsworth, England: Penguin Books Ltd., 1973–1986), 1:50.

2. The best discussion of the Buddhist use of the mirror metaphor is Paul Demiéville, "Le miroir spirituel," in *Choix d'etudes bouddhiques (1929–1970)*, 131–56 (Leiden: E. J. Brill, 1973). Cf. also Alex Wayman, "The Mirror-Like Knowledge in Mahayana Buddhist Literature," *Asiatische Studien* 25 (1971): 353–63; and "The Mirror as Pan-Buddhist Metaphor-Simile," *History of Religions* 13/4 (1974): 251–69.

3. *The Story of the Stone*, 1:51.

4. C. T. Hsia has likened Baoyu to Holden Caulfield of J. D. Salinger's *The Catcher in the Rye* and Prince Myshkin of Dostoevski's *The Idiot*. See *The Classic Chinese Novel: A Critical Introduction* (New York: Columbia University Press, 1968), pp. 245–98.

5. See Andrew H. Plaks, *Archetype and Allegory in the "Dream of the Red Chamber"* (Princeton: Princeton University Press, 1976), especially chapters 7–8. The garden so vividly described and realized in the narrative has been a favorite for illustrators and painters for generations. In contemporary China, two life-size replicas, one in Shanghai and one in Beijing, have been constructed by the Chinese government for popular enjoyment. The one in the capital has also been used to film the widely acclaimed television series (in 50 episodes) of the novel that began in 1985.

6. For a study of the triple causes of Daiyu's tragedy (her ill health,

her orphanhood, and her mythic beliefs) see my "Self and Family in the *Hung-lou Meng: A New Look at Lin Tai-yü as Tragic Heroine," Chinese Literature: Essays, Articles Reviews* 2 (1980): 199–223.

7. *The Story of the Stone,* 1:137
8. Ibid., 5:193–4.
9. Ibid., 1:51.
10. Ibid., 3:15.

REFERENCES

Translations

Dream of the Red Chamber. Translated by Chi-chen Wang. New York: Doubleday, 1958. Abridged version.
A Dream of Red Mansions. Translated by Yang Xianyi and Gladys Yang. 3 vols. Peking: Foreign Language Press, 1978–80. Complete and reliable.
The Story of the Stone. Translated by David Hawkes and John Minford. 5 vols. Harmondsworth, England: Penguin Books Ltd., 1973–86. A careful, highly literate rendition. Hardback edition with larger print available by Indiana University Press.
Le Rêve dans le pavillon rouge. Translated by Li Tche-houa and Jacqueline Alézaïs, revised by André d'Hormon. 2 vols. Paris: Gallimard, 1981. Good notes, introduction, and glossary. Complete and accurate.

Critical Studies

Chan, Hing-ho. *Le Hongloumeng et les commentaires de Zhiyanzhai, Mémoires de l'Institut des Hautes Etudes Chinoises.* Paris: Presses Universitaires de France, 1982.
Hawkes, David. "The Translator, the Mirror and the Dream—Some Observations on a New Theory." *Renditions* 13 (1980): 5–20.
Hawkes, David. "The Story of the Stone: A Symbolist Novel." *Renditions* 25 (1986): 6–17.
Hsia, C. T. *The Classic Chinese Novel: A Critical Introduction.* New York: Columbia University Press, 1968.
Li, Wai-yee. *Enchantment and Disenchantment: Love and Illusion in Chinese Literature.* Princeton: Princeton University Press, 1993.
Lu, Tonglin. *Rose and Lotus: Narrative of Desire in France and China.* Albany: State University of New York, 1991.
Miller, Lucien. "Masks of Fiction in *Dream of the Red Chamber." Monographs of The Association for Asian Studies* 28. Tucson: The University of Arizona Press, 1975.
Minford, John, and Robert E. Hegel. *"Hung-lou meng."* In *The Indiana Companion to Traditional Chinese Literature,* edited by William H. Nienhauser, Jr., pp. 452–56. Bloomington: Indiana University Press, 1986.
Plaks, Andrew H. *Archetype and Allegory in the* Dream of the Red Chamber. Princeton: Princeton University Press, 1976.

Plaks, Andrew H., ed. *Chinese Narrative: Critical and Theoretical Essays.* Princeton: Princeton University Press, 1977.

Spence, Jonathan. *Ts'ao Yin and the K'ang-hsi Emperor, Bondservant and Master.* New Haven: Yale University Press, 1966.

Wang, John C. Y. "The Chih-yen chai Commentary and the *Dream of the Red Chamber.*" In *Chinese Approaches to Literature,* edited by Adele Rickett, pp. 189–220. Princeton: Princeton University Press, 1978.

Wu, Shih-ch'ang. *On the Red Chamber Dream.* Oxford: Clarendon Press, 1961.

Yu, Anthony C. "Self and Family in the *Hung-lou Mêng:* A New Look at Lin Tai-yü as Tragic Heroine." *Chinese Literature: Essays, Articles Reviews* 2 (1980): 199–223.

Yu, Anthony C. "The Quest of Brother Amor: Buddhist Intimations in *The Story of the Stone.*" *Harvard Journal of Asiatic Studies* 49/1 (June, 1989): 55–92.

Yu, Anthony C. "The Stone of Fiction and the Fiction of Stone: Reflexivity and Religious Symbolism in *Hongloumeng.*" *Studies in Language and Literature* 4 (October, 1990): 1–30.

Social and Cultural Background

Fairbank, John K. "Introduction: The Old Order." In *The Cambridge History of China,* edited by Denis Twitchett and John K. Fairbank. Vol. 10, pt. 1, pp. 1–34. Cambridge: Cambridge University Press, 1978.

Goodrich, Luther Carrington. *The Literary Inquisition of Ch'ien-lung,* 2d ed. New York: Paragon Book Reprint Corp., 1966.

Ho, Ping-ti. "The Significance of the Ch'ing Period in Chinese History." *Journal of Asian Studies* 26 (February, 1967): 189–95.

Kahn, Harold L. "The Education of a Prince: The Emperor Learns His Roles," in *Approaches to Modern Chinese History,* edited by Albert Feuerwerker, Rhoads Murphy, and Mary C. Wright, pp. 15–44. Berkeley: University of California Press, 1967.

Liu, Kwang-Ching, ed. *Orthodoxy in Late Imperial China.* Berkeley: University of California Press, 1990.

Naquin, Susan, and Evelyn S. Rawski. *Chinese Society in the Eighteenth Century.* New Haven: Yale University Press, 1987.

Plaks, Andrew H. "The Literati Novel: Historical Background." In *The Four Masterworks of the Ming Novel,* pp. 3–54. Princeton: Princeton University Press, 1987.

Waley, Arthur. *Yuan Mei: Eighteenth Century Chinese Poet.* 1957; reprint, Stanford: Stanford University Press, 1970.

"Women in Qing Period China—A Symposium." *Journal of Asian Studies* 46/1 (February, 1987): 7–70. Informative and current research on the subject in three articles by Charlotte Furth, Susan Mann, and Vivien W. Ng.

LIU E'S *THE TRAVELS OF LAO CAN*

C. T. Hsia

By the end of the eighteenth century, China had produced six major novels that are now generally regarded as classics of world literature. These six are *The Romance of the Three Kingdoms* (*Sanguo zhi yanyi* [*San-kuo chih yen-i*]), *Outlaws of the Marsh* (*Shuihu zhuan* [*Shui-hu chuan*]), *The Journey to the West* (*Xiyou ji* [*Hsi-yu chi*]), *Jin Ping Mei* [*Chin P'ing Mei*], *The Scholars* (*Rulin waishi* [*Ju-lin wai-shih*]), and *A Dream of Red Mansions* (*Honglou-meng* [*Hung-lou meng*], also known in translation as *The Story of the Stone*). The last two were written during the Qianlong [Ch'ien-lung] period (1736–1796), when the Qing [Ch'ing] dynasty was enjoying its last period of prosperity before its military weakness was exposed by the encroaching European powers. As is well known, starting with the disastrous Opium War (1839–1842) with Great Britain, China suffered a long series of defeats from the European powers and Japan during the remainder of the nineteenth century. These national humiliations, in turn, accounted for the rising numbers, in some Northern provinces, of the so-called Boxers, who hated the foreigners in their midst and believed that with their fists and swords they could remain invincible even against the guns of the West. Incredibly, Empress Dowager Cixi [Tz'u-hsi] welcomed the Boxers in June 1900 to the capital city of Beijing [Peking] where they began a prolonged assault on the legation quarters of the foreign diplomats and their families. This event led eight affected powers, including Great Britain, Germany, Russia, Japan, and the United States, to send an expeditionary force to punish China. Upon the fall of Beijing in August, the Empress Dowager, the puppet emperor, and his court fled in precipitate haste for the ancient city of Xian [Sian] in Shaanxi [Shensi] Province, somehow hoping that the more enlightened Chinese officials left behind would be able to negotiate another face-saving treaty with their conquerors. But for the American insistence on preserving the territorial and governmental integrity of China, the eight Allied Powers might have partitioned the country forthwith.

Though the Qing dynasty was not overthrown until 1912, even its most loyal supporters among the Chinese elite began to sense the approaching end of an era when the capital fell into foreign hands, and feared for the future of their country. At the same time, the more enlightened patriots and journalists sought to awaken the nation by launching newspapers and magazines in Japan and in the treaty ports where they could enjoy better protection from the imperial authorities. Particularly in Shanghai, the treaty port par excellence, novelists and translators were kept busy meeting the public's insatiable demand for new reading matter. During the last dozen years of the dynasty, over a thousand book-length titles of original and translated fiction were published, a larger number than all the extant pre-1900 novels and story collections published during the Ming and Qing.

Four late-Qing novelists attained a permanent place in Chinese literary history. Of the four, two—Li Baojia ([Li Pao-chia] 1867–1906) and Wu Wo-yao (1867–1910)—were prolific novelists and journalists. The other two each wrote only one novel during the late Qing, though Zeng Pu ([Tseng P'u] 1872–1935) continued to be active as a translator and publisher in the Republican years and Liu E (courtesy name Tieyun [T'ieh-yün], 1857–1909) wrote treatises on a variety of topics, in addition to a small volume of poems belatedly published in 1980. His best-known work, of course, is the twenty-chapter *Travels of Lao Can* (*Laocan youji* [*Lau-ts'an yu-chi*]), which remains to this day the best-liked of late-Qing novels among the Chinese, and has proved to be quite popular as well with Western readers interested in China.

Liu E, a native of Jiangsu [Kiangsu] Province, was the son of a *jinshi* ([*chin-shih*] someone who had passed the metropolitan and palace examinations), who served only in provincial posts. Liu E himself did not seriously prepare for the examinations, but read widely and took an early interest in such subjects as music, mathematics, astronomy, and medicine. His concern for the Yellow River prompted him to specialize in the prevention and control of floods. In 1888–89, as an assistant to the director of Yellow River conservancy, he gained a good reputation helping to repair the dikes in Henan [Honan]. In 1890, he was invited by Governor Zhang Yao [Chang Yao] of Shandong [Shantung] to be one of his advisers on flood control, and continued to serve in the province until 1893 even though the Governor had died in 1891.

Liu E resigned from his post in Shandong because of his mother's death, but soon after the mourning period, he began to promote various schemes as an industrial entrepreneur, trying to build railways and develop mines with foreign help. Most of his plans came to nothing, however, because of the apathy or enmity of the imperial court or the provincial officials involved. In the fall of 1900, Liu E went from Shanghai to Beijing and with the help of his Russian friends purchased large quantities of rice stored in the Imperial Granary, then under the control of the Russian troops. Liu E distributed this rice at a nominal price to the hungry in the capital, and yet for this philanthropic deed he was later accused by his enemies at court of the treasonous crime of misappropriating imperial property. In 1908 Liu E was banished to Xinjiang [Sinkiang] partly for this crime, and he died in Tihwa the next year at the age of fifty-three.

Written in 1903–04, *The Travels of Lao Can* was serialized initially in a Shanghai fiction magazine edited by Li Baojia, and subsequently in a Tianjin [Tientsin] daily. The hero Tie Ying ([T'ieh Ying] meaning "iron heroic"), nicknamed Lao Can ("old and decrepit"), is clearly autobiographical. He shares not only the author's many-sided interests, but also some of his experiences as a new arrival in Shandong in the fall and winter of 1890.

But *The Travels of Lao Can* is implicitly a novel about the Boxer catastrophe as well, which reflects the author's gloomier view of China after the events of 1900, illustrated in the concluding statement of his preface: "The game of chess is finished. We are getting old. How can we not weep?" Since *The Travels of Lao Can* takes place in the year 1890, when Liu E was only thirty-four, he refers to the Boxer Incident and its calamitous consequences by way of the prophetic recluse Yellow Dragon (Huanglong Zi [Huang-lung Tzu]). The whole novel, like the preface, is permeated with the author's deep sorrow over China's senility and impotence, which became all the more apparent after the occupation of Beijing by the Allied Powers. Like so many scholars of the time, Liu E searched for the cause of China's debilitation, and found the answer in the basic inhumanity of Chinese society for the last thousand years, as seen in the submissive apathy of the people despite their perpetual maltreatment by the officials. Though he cannot address the Boxer Incident directly in the novel, he does indict two Manchu officials easily identifiable as Yuxian [Yü-hsien] and Gangyi [Kang-i]—both fanatic supporters of the Boxers—describing their earlier misdeeds as blind but self-righteous officials who torture and kill the innocent in callous disregard of mercy and justice. The novel effectively suggests that such cruel officials, if entrusted with high posts at court, will hasten the collapse of an empire. Though Yuxian never rose above the rank of governor, Gangyi was a Grand Councillor and Associate Grand Secretary enjoying the trust of the Empress Dowager.

Soon after Liu E arrived in Shandong in 1890, he must have heard of the misdeeds of Yuxian, then Prefect of Caozhou [Ts'ao-chou] (as is the fictitious Yu Xian [Yü Hsien]), as mentioned in chapters 4–6. Subsequently, as governor of Shandong, Yuxian was the first official of his importance to abet the antiforeign activities of the Boxers and legitimize their status. (The villainy of one such Boxer, Wang the Third, is described in chapter 6.) In 1900, as Governor of Shansi, Yuxian killed Chinese Christians, and personally supervised the massacre in Taiyuan of foreign missionaries and their families. He was subsequently decapitated as a war criminal at the insistence of the Allied Powers.

Gangyi was perhaps the most fervent spokesman at court for the Boxer cause, and it was probably upon his recommendation that the Empress Dowager opened the city gates to the Boxers to usher in a reign of terror. As an antiforeign reactionary, Gangyi could not have approved of the industrial schemes of Liu E, and did accuse him of treason in 1897, but there is little reason to believe that the two knew each other personally. Liu E, therefore, must have assigned the similar-sounding name Gang Bi ([Kang Pi] meaning "obstinate, stubborn") to a judge who quite wrongly holds an innocent woman, Mrs. Jia Wei [Chia Wei], responsible for the death of a whole household of people, and accordingly applies torture to prove his point. This murder case dominates the last six chapters of the novel.

The atrocities of Yu Xian and Gang Bi largely determine the hero's movements in an otherwise plotless novel. But Lao Can is not a knight-errant able to right wrongs with his sword; even the backing of Governor Zhuang [Chuang] does not assure of success in his attempts to rectify cases of official injustice. In chapters 16–17, he challenges Gang Bi's right to place Mrs. Jia under torture, and secures her and her equally pitiable father's release from prison. But earlier, though Lao Can is even more profoundly shocked by Yu Xian's unbelievable cruelty, he can do little other than compose a poem to vent his anger and submit a report to Governor Zhuang. In chapter 19, the Governor finally informs Lao Can of his decision on Yu Xian, "I shall certainly do something about it. But at the moment I dare not 'recommend a man and then cashier him'; it would appear disrespectful of the Emperor."

Governor Zhuang then, though a conscientious administrator of evident good will, is too much of a career bureaucrat to risk incurring the Emperor's displeasure over his contradictory recommendations. And with even less excuse, he had earlier adopted a scholar's plan to let the Yellow River flood over its banks, thus causing the death of several hundred thousand people. In the novel, this heart-rending tale of official folly is effectively retold by Cuihua [Ts'ui-hua] and Cuihuan [Ts'ui-huan], two young prostitutes entertaining Lao Can and his friend Huang Renrui [Huang Jen-jui] at an inn for the night. Both girls are survivors of the flood, and Cuihuan suffers especially as the daughter from a well-off family, now regularly beaten by her bawd and customers alike for her unwillingness to serve. But the two kind-hearted men soon redeem the girls, and ensure them a better future as their concubines.

The girls' better fate, however, is of no benefit to their already drowned fathers, and the hundreds of thousands of hapless victims of the man-made deluge. In Cuihua's version of the story, Governor Zhuang did "shed a few tears" upon giving his reluctant consent to the scholar's inhumane plan. These are perhaps also the tears of commiseration that are praised in the preface, but the governor's uneasy conscience on this momentous occasion as on the later occasion, when he declines to reprimand or cashier Yu Xian, seems to say that it is unavoidable for a man of his importance to make or agree to wrong decisions. For all its chivalrous fervor, *The Travels of Lao Can* is a novel grounded in political reality: the success the hero enjoys in delivering a few individuals from the clutches of injustice and misery only renders the more poignant the plight of multitudes oppressed by bad officials and victimized by misguided policies.

But in form this political novel remains—except for the middle section (chapters 8-11)—a record of Lao Can's travels. The significance of that section—where one Shen Ziping [Shen Tzu-p'ing] (instead of the hero) visits the Peach Blossom Mountain and talks with the girl philosopher Yugu [Yü-ku] and the prophet Yellow Dragon will be discussed shortly; for the present, we may observe that, in the chapters where Lao Can is a dominant figure, we invariably watch him at close range. The author's skill enables us to share his moods, observations, and innermost reflections. No heroes of earlier Chinese fiction have achieved this degree of auto-biographical intimacy, and but for the adoption of a third-person narrative, *The Travels of Lao Can* could have been the earliest

Chinese lyrical novel in the first person. Even as it stands, its rambling narrative structure and its fascination with seemingly inconsequential events would suggest the author's greater indebtedness to the Chinese nature poets and familiar essayists than to the novelists. Whereas the latter are by and large content to use stock imagery in their descriptions of people and scenery, Liu E astonishingly renders sensory impressions, and some of his elaborate passages depicting landscape or music are justly celebrated. Take, for example, the passage in chapter 12 where the restless hero, detained in the city of Dongchang [Tung-ch'ang] because the Yellow River has partially frozen, leaves the inn after supper to enjoy the nocturnal view from the dike:

> He raised his head and looked up at the hills to the south. The snow-white line reflected the light of the moon; it was extraordinarily beautiful. The mountain ranges rose tier on tier, but they could not be clearly distinguished. A few white clouds lay in the folds of the hills so that you could hardly tell cloud from hill unless you looked intently. The clouds were white, and the hills were white; the clouds were luminous, and the hills were luminous too. Yet because the moon was above the clouds and the clouds beneath the moon, the clouds were luminous with a light which had penetrated from behind. This was not true, however, of the hills; the light there flowed directly from the moon and was then reflected by the snow, so that the light was of two kinds. But only the nearer parts were like this. The hills stretched away to the east farther and farther until gradually the sky was white, the hills were white, and the clouds were white, and nothing could be distinguished from anything else. (pp. 131–32)

But what is equally impressive though less often cited by critics is the meditative passage immediately following. As it is too long to quote in its entirety, only the central portion is given:

> By this time the moonlight was making the whole earth bright. Lao Can looked up. Not one star appeared in the sky except for the seven stars of the Dipper which could be seen clearly, gleaming and twinkling like several pale points. The Dipper was resting slantwise on the west side of the "Imperial Enclosure," the handle on top, the bowl below. He thought to himself, "Months and years pass like a stream; the eye sees the handle of the Dipper pointing to the east again; another year is added to man's life. So year after year rolls along blindly. Where is an end to be found?" Then, remembering the words of the *Book of Odes*,

> In the North there is a Dipper
> But it cannot scoop wine or sauce,

he mused, "Now indeed is a time when many things are happening to our country; the nobles and officials are only afraid of bringing punishment on themselves; they think it is better to do nothing than to risk doing something, and therefore everything is allowed to go to ruin. What will the final result be? If this is the state of the country how can an honest man devote himself to his family?" When he reached this point in his thinking, unconsciously the tears began to trickle down his face, and he had no heart left for the enjoyment of the scenery. (p. 132)

This passage faithfully follows the workings of the hero's consciousness as it juxtaposes freshly received impressions with lines of poetry suddenly retrieved from memory, and reverts to melancholy thoughts in contemplation of the signs in the sky. The experience depicted here is nothing unusual: any serious-minded Chinese scholar well-read in poetry and conerned about the times could have such thoughts while pacing under a bright moon. But whereas such poignant ruminations are frequently caught in Chinese verse, the concept of the subjective hero was so alien to the tradition of Chinese fiction that it was nothing short of extraordinary for Liu E to grope toward the stream-of-consciousness technique not only here but in many other passages as well.

To justify the structural peculiarity of the novel, we could say that to counterbalance the melancholy thoughts of Lao Can, expressed here and in many other places, the author excludes him from the idyllic gathering at the Peach Blossom Mountain and allows the Yellow Dragon to discourse at some length on cosmic philosophy and the future of China. If Lao Can is often angry and despondent in his contemplation of China, then the Yellow Dragon may be regarded as a portrait of the author's ideal self predisposed to an optimistic reading of Chinese history. Thus, if in the allegorical dream of the first chapter, Lao Can is denounced as a traitor and almost drowned for offering Western nautical instruments to save the ship of China, the serene recluse Yellow Dragon envisions a period of cultural florescence following the revolutionary turmoil of the present, when Chinese civilization shall have assimilated European culture and become even more glorious. In the perspective of recent Chinese history, his predictions are much too sanguine, and his methods of calculation too arcane for some tastes. But Liu E, after all, is a scholar of the late Qing: despite his Western connections as an industrial entrepreneur, he had in his youth studied with a religious leader of the so-called Taigu [T'ai-ku] school, which stressed the essential moral identity of Confucianism, Buddhism, and Daoism [Taoism]. Liu E valued this teaching highly, and maintained a lifelong friendship with his fellow disciples. Thus he is quite incapable of admitting the general inferiority of traditional Chinese culture, as Hu Shi [Hu Shih], Lu Xun [Lu Hsün], and other champions of the New Culture were able to do in the early Republican period.

But the author's other spokesman in the idyllic interlude, the girl philosopher Yugu, has already anticipated these thinkers in her acute analysis of the Chinese situation during the last thousand years. She appears rather conventional in reiterating the main tenet of the Taigu school that the three teachings are alike in "encouraging man to be good, leading man to be disinterested," and she speaks with a clearly Confucian emphasis. Yet she is brave and discerning enough to blame the decadence of China since at least the late Tang [T'ang] on Neo-Confucianism with its moral intolerance and repression of natural impulses. The sadism of the bad offiials in the novel, then, would seem to stem directly from this tradition of moral inflexibility and obsessive concern with evil. With his manifest sympathy for Chinese women, whose lot had become much worse under Neo-Confucianism, it is little wonder that Liu E should have presented most of his female characters as victims of official oppression while assigning a utopian beauty, living far from the madding crowd of ordinary Chinese, the key task of exposing Neo-Confucian hypocrisy and inhumanity.

In chapter 18, a colleague jokingly calls Lao Can Sherlock Holmes, and in the next chapter, he does assume the role of a detective in trying to get to the bottom of the case. During the first decade of this century, Sherlock Holmes had enthralled even Chinese readers of Western detective fiction, so it was not strange for Liu E to be tempted to write a detective story to conclude his novel. But when Gang Bi is beaten at court in chapters 16–17, the murder case that had wrongly implicated Mrs. Jia Wei has served its purpose in exposing yet another official's shocking incompetence and cruelty. Though the subsequent story of trapping the real instigator of the multiple murders is quite interesting in itself, it is just a tale of domestic crime that has nothing to do with the main thrust of the novel. Liu E himself is apparently aware of the problem, and so resurrects all the victims of poisoning in order to nullify the crime and end the novel on a happy note.

Despite the thematic irrelevance of its final episode, *The Travels of Lao Can* remains a very moving novel both for its personal lyricism and its impassioned pondering of the fate of China following the Boxer catastrophe. For today's readers, what is most endearing about the novel, and what makes it so much closer to us in feeling than the six major novels produced before the nineteenth century, is the author's strong humanitarian regard for all his fellow Chinese, which reinforces his love of China in an especially poignant fashion. The most beloved of all late Qing novelists, Liu E is thus also the very first of the moderns on account of his obsession with China and his helpless compassion for all suffering Chinese.

TOPICS FOR DISCUSSION

1. *The Travels of Lao Can* is of special interest when seen in relation to the Chinese literary tradition as a whole. In his preface, Liu E places himself in the company of Zhuang Zi [Chuang Tzu], Sima Qian [Ssu-ma Ch'ien], the Tang poet Du Fu [Tu Fu], Cao Xueqin [Ts'ao Hsueh-ch'in], and Wang Shifu [Wang Shih-fu], the author of the play *Romance of the Western Chamber*. According to Liu, what does he have in common with these great writers of the past? Can he be seriously regarded as a latter-day Du Fu?

2. Discuss Liu E's almost revolutionary achievement in transforming the traditional type of Chinese novel into a lyrical vehicle capable of rendering a character's innermost feelings and thoughts. Compare his novel in this regard with Western lyrical novels of the early twentieth century, and further compare Lao Can as a subjective hero with his Western counterparts and with Jia Baoyu [Chia Pao-yu].

3. Explore *The Travels of Lao Can* as a political novel, particularly with reference to its dual concern with the Yellow River and the Boxer catastrophe. In what significant ways does the work differ from political novels of the Western tradition, such as those by Stendhal, Dostoevsky, Conrad, and Henry James discussed in Irving Howe, *Politics and the Novel* (New York: Horizon Press, 1957)?

4. Chinese scholars have taken *The Travels of Lao Can* most seriously as a critique of Chinese bureaucracy and Neo-Confucianism. Compare in this regard Wm. Theodore de Bary's defense of Neo-Confucianism in *The Liberal Tradition in China* (New York: Columbia University Press, 1983) and *East Asian Civilizations: A Dialogue in Five Stages* (Cambridge: Harvard University Press, 1988).

REFERENCES

The Travels of Lao Can, Harold Shadick's complete translation of the twenty-chapter *Laocan youji* (Cornell University Press, 1952), has superseded all earlier English versions. It is quite readable, and has a useful introduction and many explanatory notes. A new edition, in paperback, was issued in 1990 by Columbia University Press, New York. The page numbers for sections quoted in this essay refer to this paperback edition. Liu E wrote at least nine chapters of a sequel, generally known as *Laocan youji erji* [*Lao-ts'an yu-chi erh-chi*]. The first six chapters, about the infatuation and awakening of a nun named Yiyun [I-yün], are fully comparable to the best of the early chapters. Under the title "A Nun of Taishan," they are available in Lin Yutang, trans., *Widow, Nun and Courtesan* (John Day, 1950; Westport, CT: Greenwood Press, 1971).

The present writer has written extensively on traditional and modern Chinese fiction in a manner that would appeal to students of Western and comparative literature. Thus a fuller guide than this chapter is C. T. Hsia, "The Travels of Lao Ts'an: An Exploration of Its Art and Meaning," in *Tsing Hua Journal of Chinese Studies*, N. S., vol. 7, no. 2 (Taipei, 1969). To those who have found *The Classic Chinese Novel: A Critical Introduction* (New York: Columbia University Press, 1968; Bloomington: Indiana University Press, 1980) helpful in their reading of *Journey to the West* and *The Story of the Stone*, a quartet of essays is further recommended for a fuller understanding of *The Travels of Lao Can:*

Hsia, C. T. "Chinese Novels and American Critics: Reflections on Structure, Tradition, and Satire." In *Critical Issues in East Asian Literature*, edited by Peter H. Lee. Seoul International Cultural Society of Korea, 1983.

Hsia, C. T. "Obsession with China: The Moral Burden of Modern Chinese Literature." Appendix I in *A History of Modern Chinese Fiction.* 2d ed. New Haven: Yale University Press, 1971.

Hsia, C. T. "The Scholar-Novelist and Chinese Culture: A Reappraisal of *Ching-hua Yuan.*" In *Chinese Narrative: Critical and Theoretical Essays*, edited by Andrew H. Plaks. Princeton: Princeton University Press, 1977.

Hsia, C. T. "Yen Fu and Liang Ch'i-ch'ao as Advocates of New Fiction." In *Chinese Approaches to Literature from Confucius to Liang Ch'i-ch'ao*, edited by Adele A. Rickett. Princeton: Princeton University Press, 1978.

THE STORIES OF LU XUN

Theodore Huters

Generally considered to be modern China's finest writer, Lu Xun ([Lu Hsun] pen name of Zhou Shuren, 1881–1936) wrote 25 stories between 1918 and 1925 that were published in two volumes, *Nahan* (generally translated as *Call to Arms*) in 1923 and *Panghuang* (*Wandering*) in 1926. These stories capture the pathos and agonizing complexity of a traditional world passing from the scene while a new world stuggles to be born. If Lu Xun consciously regarded himself as one thoroughly in favor of the new, the hidden difficulties of that position are revealed in close examination of his stories. They give full vent to the violations of the human spirit that their author felt to be inscribed within the ideology and social structures of traditional culture, but they are even more obsessed with the problems of creating something new out of that order, which paradoxically still possessed a profound hold over Chinese mental life while itself being in utter disarray. While Lu Xun also wrote poetry, essays both touchingly personal and sharply polemical, as well as path-breaking scholarship, it is these few stories that leave the most vivid imprint on the imagination.

Lu Xun was born to a prominent family in a district on the Southeast coast of China, famous for producing careful scholars. His grandfather was a holder of the "presented scholar" degree and, as such, was one of but a few thousand men in the whole empire eligible for the very highest governmental posts. Lu Xun's father was, however, a ne'er-do-well, and when the grandfather was imprisoned because of his involvement in an abuse of the imperial examination system—a very high crime indeed—at a time when Lu Xun was still quite young, the family fortunes went into abrupt decline. Lu Xun's father died during this period and the young man and his brother were eventually sent off to one of the new schools set up in the course of the "self-strengthening" movement in late nineteenth-century China to teach Western technical subjects. According to Lu Xun's own account of this affair, for someone from a family as firmly committed to traditional scholarship as his own to be sent off to such an institution was regarded as a great disgrace.

By the early years of the new century Lu Xun was in Japan, part of a mass migration of Chinese students in search of the new (i.e., Western) learning that Japan had decided to pursue some decades before China did. Partly owing to the feeling that his father's illness had been aggravated by the traditional methods used to treat him, Lu Xun had decided to study Western medicine. However, when he saw pictures of how helpless even quite physically healthy Chinese were in the face of the foreign armies fighting on Chinese soil during the Russo-Japanese War of 1904–05, Lu Xun suddenly realized that his country required spiritual rather than physical healing. He quit the provincial medical school where he had been studying and returned to Tokyo to take up literature—a move, as has been pointed out many times, quite in concert with the traditional Chinese view that universal concepts were more important than piecemeal concerns of utility.

Lu Xun later noted bitterly that his concern for spiritual enlightenment through literature was quite at odds with the utilitarian concerns of the vast majority of Chinese students in Japan at that time. His various literary enterprises, which included an aborted attempt to found a literary journal and publishing two volumes of translations of stories of mostly Eastern European origin with his brother, came to nothing. He returned to China in 1909 a disillusioned young man. For the next sixteen years he held positions as a teacher and educational bureaucrat, working in the Ministry of Education in Beijing after 1912. During the years before 1918 he wrote little, immersing himself instead in detailed antiquarian studies, something for which his fine childhood education had prepared him well. The years after 1915 in China also witnessed the beginning of an iconoclastic intellectual movement that considered far more than the questions of material advantage that had so dominated Chinese thought in the first decade of the century. This current, which initially centered around the journal *New Youth*, eventually came to be called the New Culture Movement. One of the principal issues that came to dominate the ensuing discussion of culture was the revitalization of literature, regarded by the young radicals as having been up until then either too genteel or too didactic in its complicity with the old society. After 1917, calls for a new literature in the vernacular encapsulated these concerns. The new literature would replace that which had theretofore usually been written in a classical language that had not changed significantly for two thousand years.

Given that Lu Xun's literary eareer in Japan has all the marks of a premature awareness of the dominant concerns of the New Culture Movement (with the significant exception of advocacy of the vernacular), it is perhaps inevitable that Lu Xun and the radicals found one another. The account Lu Xun leaves of what he retrospectively regarded as the founding meeting, however, makes it clear that he, at least, had profoundly mixed feelings about signing on. Lu Xun begins his recollection by describing how his friend Qian Xuantong (one of the most resolute of the iconoclasts) used to visit him at his hostel in Peking. On one visit, Qian found Lu Xun copying out ancient inscriptions:

> "What's the use of copying these?" One night, while leafing through the inscriptions I had copied, he asked for enlightenment on this point.
> "There isn't any use."
> "What's the point, then, of copying them?"
> "There isn't any point."
> "Why don't you write something? . . . "
> I understood. They were bringing out *New Youth*, but since there did not seem to have been any reaction, favorable or otherwise, no doubt they felt lonely. However, I said:
> "Imagine an iron house having not a single window and virtually indestructible, with all its inmates sound asleep and about to die of suffocation. Dying in their sleep, they won't feel the pain of death. Now if you raise a shout to wake a few of the lighter sleepers, making these unfortunate few suffer the agony of irrevocable death, do you really think you are doing them a good turn?"
> "But if a few wake up, you can't say there is no hope of destroying the iron house."
> True, in spite of my own conviction, I could not blot out hope, for hope belongs in the future. I simply could not use my inevitable lack of evidence to refute his affirmation of faith. So I finally agreed to write, and the result was my first story "A Madman's Diary." From that time on, once started I could not stop writing, and I would compose a short story-like piece of writing to dispose of the entreaties of my friends until after a while I had more than a dozen.[1]

More than anything else, perhaps, this passage illustrates the skeptical distance from utopian enthusiasms an embittered thirty-six-year-old brings with him when called to the arena of conflict by enthusiastic youths who have not yet lost any battles. The reference to the loneliness that the young publishers of the magazine must have felt surely is an echo of Lu Xun's devastating solitude ten years earlier in Japan when his translated collections of stories received almost no response. Moreover, the unhappy consequences of the revolution of 1911—in which the overthrow of the empire brought about worse problems—probably accounts for his belief that bringing about a higher awareness of China's problems, since it could not affect any real change, would only result in greater subjective pain. Although he fears any efforts toward change may do more harm than good, he is unwilling to resign himself to the bleakness of his own vision. His contradictory attitude toward writing itself shows up starkly in the final paragraph: he writes only to put off his friends, but once he begins he cannot stop. There is clearly a highly uncomfortable moral burden at work here that forces itself out in various ways, which come to be represented in the range of narrative forms that he produced over the following years to express his convoluted feelings.

Lu Xun's dilemma—essentially whether he should write or not—also reflects the weight of a Chinese intellectual heritage that had become highly fragmented even by 1917. Within the Confucian tradition there had always been great stress on the idea that careful intellectual self-cultivation led to profound comprehension and even control over external phenomena. The simultaneous collapse of the authority of Confucianism and the growth of an increasingly dominant Western presence in urban Chinese life after 1900 brought about a real crisis of consciousness in those years. For the educated elite in general and for writers in particular, the whole notion of intellectual agency became frought with unprecedented problems. On the one hand, sudden release from the strictures of old custom combined with a surviving sense of the vast potential of the mind to bring about a genuine sense of utopian possibility. At the same time, however, the splintering of the old Chinese worldview combined with the manifest loss of prestige of a traditional education to amplify suspicion that even the most finely trained mind was in fact cut off from the workings of the world.

To Lu Xun's evident consternation, the juxtaposition of these two contrary tendencies contributed to a remarkably mercurial intellectual environment. While it seems clear that Lu Xun leaned toward the pessimistic side of this dichotomy, it is also perhaps true that his predisposition to caution resulted not so much from hard experience as from his fears about the hazards implicit in the utopian position. Caution about the risks of self-delusion involved in any too-hasty embrace of visionary schemes was to be a hallmark of his literary career. On first glance it may seem paradoxical that the thoroughly iconoclastic Lu Xun appeared to base his understanding of the world on a deeply conservative notion of human behavior. He had understood, however, that the disregard for the past embodied in the new beliefs would cause modern China only to repeat the worst mistakes of the traditional way of doing things. This convinced him that true radicalism lay solely in the painstaking evaluation and reevaluation of actions and the multiplicity of motives behind them.

The story he refers to, "A Madman's Diary," was published in the spring of 1918 and profoundly affected the emerging oppositional discourse of the New Culture Movement. Although evidently inspired by the Gogol story of the same name, Lu Xun's story places his "madman" in the center of an epistemological allegory distinctly at odds with the import of its namesake. The dominant theme that emerges in the "Diary" concerns the difficulty of gaining and using real knowledge, something that had obsessesed Lu Xun for years and that lies at the center of many of his stories about Chinese intellectuals. The story is told in two parts: there is a short introduction by an "external" narrator who reveals to the reader the circumstances of the diary that he is about to present. The introduction is written in formal classical Chinese and contains vital information: that the Madman has since recovered and gone on to await an official posting. The diary that follows shows the Madman gradually realizing a paranoid version of the social and personal torment that faced any modern Chinese intellectual committed to cultural transformation. The opening entry, "Tonight the moonlight is fine; it has been more than thirty years already since I have seen it," signals the beginning of a process of tortured enlightenment: he has been in the dark, but is finally going to be able to see. The light coming to him, however, while undeniably brighter than darkness, is of a peculiarly spectral and mediated sort. It is both real and unreal; like moonlight, it is a reflected image of the real thing. The twin associations of lunacy and the clarity of mind associated with moonlight in the Buddhist tradition reinforce this dichotomy.

As the diary entries proceed, the protagonist gains increasing knowledge about the truth of his circumstance. His central realization, which comes in the third of thirteen sections, is that

Chinese society is "cannibalistic," that it is, in other words, not only a polity in which everyone's core motivation is to survive at the expense of others, but that individual survival depends precisely upon victimizing others. The Madman also understands that he is as much a candidate for "consumption" as anyone else, more so, in fact, since he has discovered the secret. Furthermore, the Madman comprehends this only after he has painstakingly studied the canonical texts of his heritage. This not only testifies to a hypocrisy even more damaging that the stark fact of cannibalism, but to the iconoclastic notion that any further perusal of the canon—the dominant intellectual activity of the Chinese tradition, particularly of the years after 1700—will only reveal its utter bankruptcy. The cental irony of the text, however, lies in the painful realization that this knowledge is gained in inverse proportion to his ability to communicate it to those who surround him. His "enlightenment" therefore becomes a paradox: to the extent that he subjectively validates himself, the Madman cuts himself off from the community that formed him. Even more to the point, it is just this community that must be made aware of its own abuses of rationality if the poor man's plight is to have hope of remedy. If the impossible situation of the Madman is taken as emblematic of the difficulty of communicating the truth of the intellectual revolution, then the theme, which appears in many of the stories, becomes the problematic of the act of writing itself, a powerful subtext that mirrors Lu Xun's own contradictory assertions to Qian Xuantong.

The process of learning the truth continues its wrenching progress throughout the course of the story, with each realization coming closer to the Madman personally and shattering a fragile equilibrium that he has just painfully rebuilt over the shocks received from his earlier insights. His second realization, that his brother is also a man-eater, is particularly difficult to recover from, but it eventually determines him to embark on a program of reform. He finally succumbs to despair, however, when he realizes that the label of "madman," by putting him so resolutely in the category of victim, will make it easier for the others to eat him. His ultimate act of recognition comes in the final three sections, in which the protagonist first realizes that the little sister who died as a child had been devoured by his brother and then, crushingly, that the sister's flesh had probably also been mixed into his own food. The possibility that the Madman has also eaten human flesh is too much for him, and the diary closes within a few lines of his becoming aware of this possibility. It ends with the plaintive appeal to "Save the children . . . "

The end of the diary is not, however, the end of the story. At this point the reader must recall the introduction's laconic account that the protagonist has gone on to await a government post. The knowledge the Madman has so painfully gained during the course of the story, then, becomes even more problematic. Did he simply think better of his predicament, or, more likely, was the final insight concerning the universality of the corruption—and that his own complicity was as great as anyone else's—too overwhelming to sustain? The gruesome conclusion based on the latter hypothesis is that there is no way to stand outside society and gain intellectual leverage over it. All knowledge beyond a narrow band of solipsistic perception is social, and society resists to the utmost any attempts to teach it new things. Any efforts made in spite of society quickly and inevitably return to solipsistic futility. Balancing the social and moral dimensions of knowledge would appear to be the answer tantalizingly held out, but it is portrayed as a solution that continually slips over the horizon of reasonable expectation.

Another theme that dominates Lu Xun's stories is the issue of communication between intellectuals and the common people. In a sense this is an extension of the question of social knowledge and is already adumbrated in the relationship between the Madman and the crowd of people who fear him much more than the evil social system that has victimized them for so long. However, in some of his later stories Lu Xun succeeds in putting this matter on a more personal footing in which the issue of individual responsibility becomes the principal focus. The story that probably best poses the dilemma of individual moral choice is generally referred to as "The New-Year Sacrifice," although the original title, "Zhufu," means something more like "benediction." This story contains three distinct levels of narration: the first, and most complex, being the contemporary account of a modern intellectual's return to his ancestral home during the new year holiday. From the beginning his account stresses his alienation from the place and from his old-fashioned relatives. The closest relative he can find to stay with, for instance, is Fourth Uncle Lu, a man so distant from the narrator's modern sensibilities that he still finds it obligatory to blame the reformists of the late 1890s, apparently oblivious of the fact that these men have since become the most staunch conservatives in the land. The narrator thus does his best to draw a sharp contrast between himself as a modern man and the benighted rural town—a town that is, incidently, the location for several of the other stories.

The narrator's complacent sense of himself, however, had been thoroughly disturbed by his encounter the previous day with Xianglin's Wife, a twice-widowed woman from the rural hinterland of the town, who had on several occasions worked for Fourth Uncle's household and had since been reduced to outright beggary. Whereas everything else in town has seemed to change very little since the narrator's last visit, Xianglin's Wife has undergone a real transformation and looks like a hag far older than her presumed forty years. When she sees the narrator on the street, she eagerly seizes upon the opportunity to ask him a question, reasoning that he should know the answer because he is scholarly. Taken aback by this, the narrator tries to prepare himself, but is completely nonplussed when the question she asks him turns out to concern whether ghosts exist or not. Trying to calculate what it is she wishes to hear, he replies that there may well be, at which point she rejoins that this implies there must be a hell, too. He attempts to hedge, but she immediately proceeds to the conclusion that all members of a family must meet again after death, thereby finally revealing her panic at the prospect of being sawed in half in hell and split between her two husbands.

Once the narrator belatedly realizes Xianglin's Wife had an agenda behind her questions, he tries his best to get out of the commitment implicit in having allowed himself to make an affirmative reply. By finally retreating to the position that he "was not sure" about the answers to her questions, he consoles himself: "Besides, I had distinctly declared, 'I'm not sure,' contradicting the whole of my answer. That meant that even if something did happen, it would have nothing at all to do with me. 'I'm not sure' is a most useful phrase." The next day the narrator hears that Xianglin's Wife has died and he has the following exhange with his uncle's servant:

> "When did she die?"
> "When? Last night or today—I'm not sure."
> "How did she die?"
> "How? Of poverty of course." After this stolid answer he withdrew, still without having raised his head to look at me.
> My agitation was only short-lived, however. For now that my premonition had come to pass, I no longer had to seek comfort in my own "I'm not sure," or his "dying of poverty," and my heart was growing lighter. Only from time to time did I still feel a little guilty.

Some time later, the narrator concludes his meditations on Xianglin's Wife's condition with the consolation that: "Whether spirits existed or not I did not know; but in this world of ours the end of a futile existence, the removal of someone whom others are tired of seeing, was just as well both for them and for the individual concerned." He then switches to the second mode of narration, an omniscient, historical voice that relates Xianglin's Wife's life history.

The confident image of the modern man fully in control of himself and his environment is carefully eroded during the short course of the narrator's exchanges with Xianglin's Wife. His utter inadequacy in coping with the desperation of the dying peasant woman reveals the gap between the utopian aspirations of the new intelligentsia and the resistance of an intractible reality. And the "I'm not sure" of which he is so proud turns out to be the same refuge as taken by his uncle's superstitious servant. The final syllogism the narrator reaches—that his own peace of mind is more important than the wretched woman's claims to life—demonstrates the horrifying extent of the narrator's solipsism and the resulting moral incapacity. This moral deficiency is ultimately also a product of the situation of the "in-between" intellectual in post-traditional China. Denied traditional authority by rapid social change, his confidence in his ability to choose the correct course of action has been eroded along with it. As a result, while the intellectual may understand the desperate plight of victims of mass cruelty, a fatally weak sense of his own capacity to stand apart from conventional opinion causes him to be able only to vacillate fecklessly on the sidelines of the acts of casual brutality that are the stuff of everyday life.

The third level of narration, a segment imbedded in the omniscient account of the widow's life, moves the issue of solipsism decisively from the individual to the social plane. In this short passage, Xianglin's Wife repeatedly tells the tale of her son having been eaten by a wolf. The initial response to her story on the part of the townspeople is sympathetic, but her constant repetition of the tale soon causes her audience to harden their hearts and laugh at her every time she begins. The townspeople thus mirror the earlier response of the narrator to his exchange with the unfortunate woman: at first moved and disturbed by what she has to say, everyone soon learns to live with it by finding ways to minimize its shocking effect.

The message that emerges is that no story can truly communicate the panic-stricken desperation of real experience. In the world of "The New-Year Sacrifice," all stories are infuriatingly instransitive, and even the best of intentions to tell and to hear will ineluctably go awry.

The same sense of the ultimate hollowness of storytelling is one that haunts all of Lu Xun's narratives and takes an ever larger role in his second collection of stories. It is perhaps this sense of futility and stony intransivity that caused Lu Xun to stop writing fiction in 1926. His own sense of desperation seemed to demand some surer vehicle of communication, and it was thus that, after a period of intellectual uncertainty during the politically tumultuous years of the late 1920s, he turned gradually to Marxism as a means of gaining the leverage over reality he had sought for so long in vain. His Marxism was always to be one of epistemological inquiry, however, rather than of the hard dogmatism that eventually came to dominate the literary policies of the Communist Party. The Party's treatment of Lu Xun contains a grand irony greater than that found in any of his stories. For not only has his legacy been treated by the cultural authorities of that Party as one of commitment to a rigid set of postulates, but his stories have been subjected to a series of state-sanctioned interpretations designed to freeze all the ambiguity and soul-searching out of them. In a sense, perhaps, this is conclusive testimony to the power of his vision.

TOPICS FOR DISCUSSION

1. Lu Xun's writing—with its stress on the formal means of expressing authorial subjectivity, its deliberate undermining of techniques associated with more naive forms, and its sense of itself as being a new and separate discourse—seems to significantly resemble that of European modernism. Yet the historical context in which Lu Xun worked was quite different from that of modern Europe. How, then, to anatomize Lu Xun within the discourse of modernism? Was European influence decisive, in spite of Lu Xun's own despair that China could never really appropriate anything from the West? How does European modernism's sense of itself as autonomous of both politics and popular culture square with Lu Xun's turn to a more accessible vernacular and commitment to political engagement?

2. Lu Xun had read a certain amount of Nietzsche. Are their nihilisms comparable? Lu Xun's stories continually seem to bump up against meaninglessness almost in spite of themselves, as opposed to Nietsche's defiant stance. Lu Xun's position as an intellectual in a culture threatened from the outside by a domi-

nant world culture able and willing to back up its claims to superiority by force of arms is clearly a significant variable here. Is there any sense in which Lu Xun finds his own freedom of epistemological inquiry limited by concerns of national survival? Or do these concerns simply push him in an even more radical direction?

3. Does Lu Xun's political engagement raise the old question about the relationship between the literary canon and social concern? Given the generally different conception of this relationship within Chinese culture, do Lu Xun's stories shed any new light on this vexing issue? Beyond this, the highly politicized nature of the Chinese cultural sphere in this century has contributed mightily both to the environment in which Lu Xun worked and in which he has been read. What is the relevance of such a context in our own, and quite exotic, judgment of his texts?

4. Lu Xun, educated in a completely different tradition, eventually came to write his stories in forms inspired by attempts at appropriating foreign influence. Does the confluence of these two traditions suggest ways toward a universal poetics? Certainly almost all modern Chinese writers have devoutly aspired to writing with universal appeal. What issues in bringing these hopes to fruition are pointed toward in Lu Xun's work?

NOTE

1. Translation by Theodore Huters, based on Preface to *Call to Arms, The Complete Stories of Lu Xun* (Bloomington: Indiana University Press, 1982), p. ix.

REFERENCES

For the historical context for twentieth-century Chinese literature, readers may wish to consult "Timeline of Significant Events in China, 1911-1987," pp. 345-46.

The only complete translation of Lu Xun's stories—*The Complete Stories of Lu Xun*—is that of Yang Xianyi and Gladys Yang for the Foreign Languages Press (FLP) in Beijing. The FLP edition is available in this country, as is a reprint in paperback from Indiana University Press. The four volume *Lu Xun: Selected Works*, also translated by the Yangs, is available in two editions from FLP, the second one revised in pinyin and published in 1980. It does not contain translations of all the stories, but has the important ones, as well as many of Lu Xun's essays, his prose-poems, and his many historically important polemical writings from the 1930s. Leo Ou-fan Lee's *Voices from the Iron House: A Study of Lu Xun*, published in 1987, is the best monographic treatment of Lu Xun's writing and contains a complete bibliography of scholarship on Lu Xun published in English through 1986. Two essays not included in Lee's bibliography—both by literary scholars not in the China field—are worth consulting, since they both touch on issues of Western methods of interpreting non-Western texts. They are, Frederic Jameson, "Third World Literature in the Era of Multinational Capitalism," *Social Text* 15 (Fall 1986): 65–80, and Margery Sabin, "On Lu Xun," *Raritan* IX:1 (Summer 1989): 41–67.

Chinese Texts: Narrative

CAMEL XIANGZI
(Rickshaw)
BY LAO SHE

David D. W. Wang

One of the most important Chinese novelists of the 1930s, Lao She (pseudonym of Shu Qingchun, 1899–1966) presents us with a double image. While we now remember him best as the writer of *Camel Xiangzi* (1937), a heartrending portrait of a rickshaw puller's degradation in a society devoid of justice and rationality, his fame was first built on a series of farcical novels like *The Philosophy of Lao Zhang* (1925) and *Divorce* (1933), which won him the nickname "king of laughter." To regard Lao She as a humanitarian realist is certainly justified, but in so doing we overlook his comic talents and make him merely a good practitioner of the kind of "orthodox" realism initiated by writers like Lu Xun. In fact, what truly distinguishes Lao She from other modern Chinese writers is not so much his mimetic exposure of social abuses as his exaggeration of them in terms of both farcical and melodramatic discourses—discourses deriving their powers from excessive display of laughter or tears, dramatic reversal or parade of moral/intellectual values, and, most importantly, compulsion to defy the sanctioned mode of representation.

Lao She was born into a Manchu family of limited means in 1899, a time when the Manchu name ensured neither social privilege nor a secure future. His father, a guard of the Imperial Palace, died protecting the forbidden city in the Boxer Rebellion, while the Emperor and Imperial Dowager had fled to the west. Lao She and his mother survived the bayonets of looting soldiers only by miraculous luck. But these early traumas bring not so much sadness as muffled laughter to Lao She's recollections. One discerns a sense of absurdity when he relates his father's sacrifice for an "empty" cause, or his own survival in a most unlikely manner.

This sense of absurdity provides the basic tone of Lao She's humor in fiction: his laughter is directed not only at a world full of irrationalities, but also at Lao She himself trapped in such a world; not only at funny subjects, but also at subjects that could have elicited indignation or tears. The ambiguous laughter can be heard when Lao She describes, in a self-mocking tone, his marginal identity as a Manchu growing up in the Republican period, his poor family situation, his lonely overseas experiences as a language teacher (1924–29), and his untimely "absence" from two of the most important scenes in modern Chinese history—the post-May Fourth days and the Chinese Communist takeover of the mainland—due respectively to his teaching commission in England and to his tour in the United States.

But Lao She might have burst out with his most outrageous laughter in the Great Cultural Revolution (1966–76), a historical event he would have been happy he missed. Years after being designated as a People's Artist, Lao She found himself the enemy of the "People" in the heyday of the revolution. When things are suddenly deprived of meaning, nothing but infinite chaos punctuated by a peal of demonic laughter is left. That Lao She chose to end his own life by drowning should be no surprise. For the "King of Laughter," suicide may well painfully recapitulate the ironic telos of his philosophy of laughter, in that it carries out to the extreme the auto-destructive tendency embedded in his mockery and self-mockery, while indicating a final scorn at absurdities he had experienced all his life.

Camel Xiangzi has been lauded not only as a milestone of Lao She's career, but also as a climax of "hard-core" realism in modern Chinese fiction. Chronicling the process whereby an honest young rickshaw boy in Beijing is degraded to the level of a social misfit, the novel is as much a powerful indictment of social injustice as a sympathetic exposé of the desire and despair of lower-class people in quest of fortune. Rife with passages about the manners and customs of Beijing, the novel represents yet another of Lao She's accounts of his hometown. Compared with his other full-length fiction, *Camel Xiangzi* constitutes a drastic turn in stylistic strategies. One finds in it neither a hilarious parade of clowns nor slapstick action, but a display of the overwhelming environments against which people fight their ever-losing war. Lao She's pessimistic representation of reality and his conviction in deterministic mechanism are so emphatically pronounced in the novel that it demands a reading in the light of Zolaesque naturalism. But behind the novel's grim, tearful facade lurks an ambiguous laughter. As Lao She puts it, "laughter and tears [evoked in his fiction] are but two sides of one coin."[1]

An orphan growing up in the slums of Beijing, Xiangzi is an honest young man with very limited ambitions—to own a rick-shaw—and he does have the ability to achieve this goal. Xiangzi works hard toward this dream and his self-esteem keeps him from indulging in various forms of self-debasement—opium smoking, whoring around—unlike his peers. But no sooner has Xiangzi fulfilled his dream than he is inadvertently drafted into the army as a coolie and his rickshaw is taken away. Although he later manages to escape from the barracks (taking with him three army camels that he sells for a cheap price and thereby gets his nick-name, "Camel"), the theft nevertheless represents the first step in his downfall, because his integrity has suffered.

This event is just the beginning of Xiangzi's bad luck. Lao She seems determined to let his hero experience all sorts of troubles before meeting the final blow. Xiangzi's marriage to his boss's ugly, domineering daughter, Tigress, is another disaster. He never likes Tigress, but she manages to seduce him one night while he is drunk. Later he is forced to marry her when she pretends to be pregnant and is driven, as a result, out of the family by her father. Nor does Xiangzi's hard work bring any reward. All his money is confiscated by an unscrupulous detective when his new employer, Professor Cao, a kindhearted socialist, is accused of conspiratorial activities and his home is raided by the police. In low spirits, Xiangzi begins to smoke and drink, and to associate with those rickshaw pullers he formerly despised. He even contracts gonor-rhea from the mistress of the house where he is temporarily hired. This, however, does not complete Xiangzi's misfortune. He is fi-nally driven to despair by his wife's death from a difficult child-birth and by the suicide of his neighbor Fortune, a girl who supports her family through prostitution, and who is the only person with whom Xiangzi can find spiritual communion.

Much has been said about the novel's humanitarian concern for social underdogs, and its naturalist depiction of the down-and-out life. However, little attention has been paid to its formal structure, and next to nothing has been said of its "genealogical" link with Lao She's comic works. Seeing that Lao She's funniest writings have in fact always implied the grimmest vision of the human condition, one wonders if *Camel Xiangzi* is governed by the converse of this strategy—if a force intervenes in the novel's naturalist presentation of life "as it is," a force that can express itself only in suppressed laughter.

Lao She writes about Xiangzi's degradation according to a classical comic convention: the incrustation of something living with something mechanical. The novel, to begin with, is about the "love affair" between a rickshaw puller and his rickshaw. While there is nothing wrong with Xiangzi's humble wish to own a rickshaw, the way he expresses his desire must be understood in romantic terms, which gives rise to amusement about their relation. One can even discuss the comic routine of mistaken identity on Xiangzi's romantic gesture (rickshaw mistaken for woman). In Lao She's comic fiction, we come across a long list of good or bad characters obsessed with things or ideas including money, painting, matchmaking, patriotism, and "modern wives." Xiangzi is but one more character on the list, though his is a long, sad entry.

Xiangzi's first downfall is, of course, full of melodramatic power. Though we do not agree with Xiangzi's theft, we are somehow willing to forgive his misdeed because of his lovable personality and the external environment he is put in. Nevertheless, as the novel goes on, we come to realize that Xiangzi's loss of his rickshaw and subsequent theft of the camels are only the overture of his troubles. His bad luck proliferates at an amazing speed in the rest of the book, to the point that there arises a rhythm of mechanical repetition of misfortune. Three times chance seems to favor his hope to possess a rickshaw, money, and a beloved woman, and three times he ends up losing everything. In the course of the novel, Xiangzi is robbed by the army, harassed by secret police, maltreated by his clients, seduced and fooled by Tigress and another woman, cheated by his boss, addicted to gambling, afflicted with venereal disease, and finally rejected by the business he once loved. Not only does he lose his rickshaw twice, he also loses his wife, his son, his benefactor, his confidante, his fortune, and finally, his self-respect.

Alongside his unbelievably bad luck, a new image of Xiangzi surfaces—Xiangzi the unlikely loser, whose touch on anything or anyone causes immediate disaster. While the "parade" of catastrophes highlights the melodramatic essence of the novel, indicting a society short on justice and sympathy, it also unexpectedly evokes a tacit humor: like the predictable Chaplinesque victim, Camel Xiangzi finally enacts farce. At the outset, we keep our fingers crossed, hoping that something good will turn up to drive away Xiangzi's bad luck. But when suspense becomes routine, anticipating only a worsening situation, and a deus ex machina is but a familiar device precipitating another downfall, the magic of melodrama wears off. We are left with a growing ironic curiosity to wait and see how "bad" things can become. So much misfortune calls attention to itself; Camel Xiangzi, the loser, joins Candide and Schlemiel in the march of ridiculously unrelenting persecutions.

Our changing attitude toward the "spectacle" of Xiangzi's misfortune not only reveals our psychological self-defense mechanism in operation, but also points to Lao She's own ambiguous outlook on the irrationalities of the human condition. If Lao She's comic/farcical vision involves subsuming objects to inappropriate concepts or turning upside down social norms and ethics, this is equally true of his most pathetic view of life. The novel's obsessive exhibition of human suffering, its indiscriminate conversion of the lively to the living-dead, is bound to be amusing, however tragic the actual outlook.

Whereas Lao She's early novels exaggerate social abuses by means of a Dickensian parade of grotesques and buffoonery inherent in late Qing exposé fiction, *Camel Xiangzi* reverses the comic/farcical discourse and substitutes surface tears for surface laughter. Beneath both laughter and tears, however, lurks a similar outrageous impulse, amounting to a flirtation with chaos and self-negation. Melodrama lavishes emotion in the name of probing the most moral and behavioral norms in the world, while farce celebrates the excess of emotions resulting from the loss of moral and behavioral norms. *Camel Xiangzi* lies at the juncture of the modes of melodrama and farce; it is as excessively pathetic as *The Philosophy of Lao Zhang* is radically hilarious. Both kinds of novels derive their theatrical absurdity (and horror) from Lao She's skepticism about the meaning of reality and his cynical response to any effort to better the status quo.

Insofar as he is a romantic trapped in an unfeeling environment, Xiangzi is a more humble and wretched version of Lao She's intellectual heroes like Ma Wei of *The Two Mas* (1929) and Lao Li of *Divorce*. Like his counterparts, Xiangzi fails to understand that in a society full of injustice and unexpected exploitation, any effort to accomplish an idealistic goal will become a meaningless joke—and as a result he will be the victim of his own great expectations which are "laughable" from a cynical point of view. Driven on by a desire to idealize, Xiangzi's character is less tragic than obtuse. In the end, it is obvious to the reader that the world is an unfathomable black hole, and any project to make sense out of it was doomed from the start. Only romantic self-delusion could keep one from that laughably self-evident truth.

Xiangzi's wife Tigress is one of the most unforgettable characters in Lao She's fiction. A petulant, extra-large-size "princess" of the slums, Tigress's persona is imbued with farcical potential. Lao She seems to despise this character to the extent that he develops a fascination with her. Kept as an old maid by her selfish father to run the rickshaw rental, Tigress finally revolts by seducing Xiangzi and marrying him. Life has made her "another strange object, old yet new, girl yet woman, female yet male, human yet beast-like."[2] Her complexion changes from grayish-green to reddish-black according to her cosmetic skill, and her appetite for food and sex is insatiable. A shrew, Tigress's literary predecessor is the character in "The Woman from the Liu Village," a female farcical trickster who beats her husband and father-in-law, maltreats the women of the family, and rules the village in the name of Christianity. In both cases, the shrews are grotesques that intimidate and amuse us at the same time. But the comic dimension of Tigress is not fully expressed until she is opposed to the weak and pale Fortune. By physique and personality, the two are already in sharp contrast. Put side by side, they act out both a naturalist interlude about the persecution of the good by the bad, and a black comedy of the triumph of the victimizer over the victim.

The overtones of black comedy can be detected even in Lao She's treatment of Tigress's death. Due to her age and to over-nutrition during her pregnancy, Tigress has a hard time delivering the huge baby. Similarly, in the short story "Grandson," Lao She describes the outrageous result of a woman overfeeding her pregnant daughter-in-law with goodies. Here, with just as much comic malice, he narrates how much Tigress eats and how little she exercises, which promise the same disastrous result. Yet the pain Tigress suffers becomes all too real. Tigress, true to her personality, dies one of the most noisy deaths in Lao She's fiction. For two weeks, she rolls in bed, her groans and cries horrifying all the neighbors. Even so, Tigress has time to order everybody around. When her personal deities fail to come to the rescue, Tigress sends for the "Toad Spirit" medium and her "acolyte"—a middle-aged pimp with a yellow face. The two frauds fake trances, while they enjoy hot sesame-paste biscuits and braised pigfoot bought by Fortune. When they find Tigress is dying, they run away. These two imposters make the death scene even busier and noisier. However, they best demonstrate what in Lao She's mind human suffering and death are all about: "Folly and cruelty are part of the natural order of this world, for reasons beyond our understanding."[3]

Tigress's and Fortune's deaths serve only as preludes to Lao

She's climactic celebration of death and decay at the end of *Camel Xiangzi.* The last chapter of the novel, which was suppressed by Lao She for the 1955 edition, presents a macabre carnival in the most grandiose and grotesque style seen in Chinese since the execution scene in Lu Xun's "True Story of Ah Q." The chapter does not add anything to the sum of miseries already in the plot, offering instead a general look at the vivacious and prosperous life in Beijing when spring returns. But exactly because it seems to be describing "nothing," it becomes an empty coda, questioning the formal and thematic closure of a novel overloaded with miseries, deaths, and misfortunes. The final chapter culminates in the execution of Ruan Ming, a radical student who had once betrayed Xiangzi's benefactor Professor Cao, and who now is in turn betrayed by Xiangzi. Lao She plainly reinvokes Lu Xun's indignation over the Chinese "crowd" syndrome with the callous and curious onlookers of this scene of bloodshed. But even as he criticizes the bloody carnival scene, Lao She seems carried away by his own exuberant language, to the point that the now-familiar critique sounds just as ostentatious as the Beijing manners and morals it criticizes.

We find Xiangzi far away from these crowds. Totally emptied of any meaning in life, Xiangzi now appears a walking dead man, a mean-spirited loafer parading for small pittances in Beijing's endless wedding and funeral processions. He has become a living prop, furnishing the last spectacle rich and elegant people can still afford. We last see Xiangzi amid a funeral parade. To yield to parading in homage to the dead has become an irresistible "temptation" to Xiangzi, not only because it assumes a spurious grandeur, but also because everything outside the parade has begun to look lifeless, meaningless, and unreal. Both Xiangzi's gruesome gestures and the pomp of the processions give us a strong sense of decadent theatricality, a deadly sensation. Nowhere else can we find a more emphatic example of Lao She's farcical strategy than in watching Xiangzi turned into a human robot, mechanically carrying banners in a funeral parade.

The end of the novel, accordingly, is not so much about Xiangzi's realization of self-delusion as about his degradation to an inanimate living dead, merely a thing. The blows of life deprive him of his rickshaw, making him part of the majority he used to look down upon, and practically changing him into a machine. In other words, the comic machinery runs full circle in the novel, and turns its human agent into an automation. Thus we return to the first chapter in which Lao She generalizes the life of Beijing rickshaw pullers as one dominated by the mechanical run of Fate. It is within this narratorial frame that Xiangzi's story is singled out as representative, since his ups and downs are just like a "specific screw in the machine."[4]

Whether a cannibalistic[5] society, a naturalist "machine without a god," or a "big wheel of fortune," the "machine" runs in its monotonous, unchanging way, threatening to devour anyone's effort or desire to escape it, and moulding different lives into one identical type. Xiangzi's ghastly "comedy" lies in that he never realizes that he is dealing with such an infamous machine until it is too late. It is only now apparent that the main body of the text has become congruent with this empty and mechanical man-prop and with the empty and mechanical city-prop around him, due to the cumulative and insidious rewriting of the naturalistic formulas into their own deconstructions. It is only now that we acutely sense the carnivalesque impulse that has always existed in Lao She's novels.

TOPICS FOR DISCUSSION

1. Lao She exaggerates the abuses and absurdities of Chinese society via the modes of melodrama and farce. The laughter and tears evoked are theatrical yet poignantly "real" with regard to the social malaise in question, thereby exposing the limitations of realistic conventions. In what sense can we read *Camel Xiangzi* as a realist/naturalist novel in the vein of nineteenth-century Western canons? And in what way can we detect the novel's attempt at modernism, especially in its exploration of the boundary of representation and in its play with the concept of the absurd?

2. Lao She has admitted that he was much influenced by Dickens, in terms of exuberant rhetoric, melodramatic plotting, galleries of grotesques, and a vision of a world that is not only monstrous but also absurd. Given the fact that *Camel Xiangzi* has most often been read in terms of Zolaesque naturalism, can one still discern Dickensian influences in its plot and characterization? Does Dickens's London bear any resemblance to Lao She's Beijing? Does Dickensian tragicomedy shed any light on Lao She's philosophy of laughter?

3. Xiangzi's pathetic downfall comes not only from the environment he is situated in but also from his obsession with owning a rickshaw. Discuss the rickshaw "character" in *Camel Xiangzi* in a social as well as a romantic context. How can we define the quadruple relation between Xiangzi, Tigress, Fortune, and the rickshaw?

4. For years, the conclusion of *Camel Xiangzi* has been a focus of controversy. Discuss the three "endings" of the novel now available in different Chinese and English editions—Xiangzi reunited with Fortune; Xiangzi in total despair; and Xiangzi parading amid a funeral procession, against the background of a happy Beijing—and the aesthetic and ideological motivations behind each of them.

NOTES

1. Lao She, "Wo zenyang xie *Lihun*" (How I wrote *Divorce*), in *Lao She shenghuo yu chuangzuo zishu* (Lao She's accounts of his life and works), ed. Hu Jieqing (Hong Kong: Sanlian shudia, 1980), pp. 44–5.
2. Lao She, *Luotuo Xiangzi* (*Camel Xiangzi*) (Hong Kong: Nanhua shudian, 1979), p. 147.
3. Ibid., p. 243.
4. Ibid., p. 4.
5. Lu Xun uses the term cannibalistic in his famous story, "A Madman's Diary," referring to a callous, bloodthirsty Chinese society operating in the guise of good manners.

REFERENCES

For the historical context for twentieth-century Chinese literature, readers may wish to consult "Timeline of Significant Events in China, 1911-1987, in Relation to Contemporary Chinese Lettres" pp. 345-46.

Camel Xiangzi has three translations: *Rickshaw Boy*, trans. Evan King (New York: Reynal & Hitchcock, 1945); *Rickshaw*, trans. Jean James (Honolulu: University of Hawaii Press, 1979); *Camel Xiangzi*, trans. Shi Xiaoqing (Bloomington: Indiana University Press in association with Foreign Language Press, 1981). Evan King's version "rewrites" the pathetic ending into a happy reunion between Xiangzi and Fortune; Shi Xiaoqing's edition eliminates the last chapter and half of the penultimate chapter.

CONTEMPORARY CHINESE LETTRES

Theodore Huters

Close examination of modern and contemporary Chinese literature reveals an internal paradox that the almost uniformly didactic face it presents to the world seeks to mask. On its surface, this literature seems to have little of the painful scrutiny of the problematic nature of its own working that is the very hallmark of modernist literary movements elsewhere in the world. One finds instead that twentieth-century Chinese writers focused intensely on the matter of how ostensibly agreed-upon ideas were to be disseminated. If writing's didactic exterior reflects a conscious wish to communicate positive information about society, however, the question about what that information should be, while rarely allowed overt thematic expression, can be seen as a subtext that haunts almost all writing throughout the years since 1917. Questions of how to communicate rather than the problematics of the message itself form the center of modern literature's explorations of itself; thus the issue of how to get that message across has of necessity expanded to crowd out other issues. The question of how, or even if, ideas can propagate, having by and large taken the place of even such basic issues as whether literature should be so manifestly didactic, has, however, assumed a highly wrought complexity. And it is within this complexity that one can discern the anxieties about literature's role and literature's limits that rarely emerge to the level of conscious discussion.

Many of the reasons for the initial shying away from overt questioning of the nature of literature can be found by examining the effects of the disintegration of the traditional intellectual order in the years after 1895. As other essays in this volume demonstrate, Chinese literature prior to that time can be roughly characterized as being an expression of a perceived unity between man, society, and the cosmos. As Western social organization in the late nineteenth century was proving itself by force of arms so competent in producing the wealth and power necessary to national survival, educated Chinese increasingly came to doubt that their own social order and ideology could maintain the equilibrium that had existed in the past. To the extent that the old terms of agreement on the relationship between humans and society became dubious, it became urgent to find something to replace them.

In trying to reformulate a stable intellectual and social order, however, Chinese thinkers kept running up against the stubborn fact that history lay at the heart of traditional ideology. The unity between self and society, and past and present, that had anchored the Chinese worldview was made possible only by a sense that historical practice had demonstrated the existence of this harmony in the past and guaranteed it in the future. But the long process of political turmoil in the nineteenth century, which ended only by invalidating the traditional system in the eyes of many prominent thinkers, brought a disabling uncertainty to the old way of conceiving history. Without the adhesive power of a positive concept of the past, the relationship of self and society was put on a new and uncertain footing, something virtually unprecedented within the tradition and profoundly disturbing to the traditional notion of how things should be.

For reasons quite independent of the coming of the West, writing had been growing in stature as a key component in intellectual discourse throughout the nineteenth century. After 1895, a perception about the power of literature as a tool in social reform was imported into China from Japan. When these two factors were combined with the old idea that writing was a moral exercise that improved the author even as it affected the reader, literature seemed to provide the natural, if not the only, vehicle to restore a sense that the subjective and objective realms of cognition could remain in balance. With the revelations of history now suspect, the literary tradition remained the only tangible evidence of the continuity of Chinese civilization. The literary tradition was also perceived as unique to the Chinese people, and as something that could not be taken away, whatever else might happen in these unprecedentedly hazardous times. A newly dynamic concept of literature (now defined more strictly in the belletristic sense) thus emerged after 1895. It was charged with the monumental tasks not only of providing a sense of national continuity, but with restoring the old balance between self and society.

As part of the convulsive intellectual change that accompanied the volatile political environment of the waning years of the Qing dynasty, literature plunged enthusiastically into its role as a key constituent of a society in transformation. Because of the powerful sense of crisis and the demand for rapid solutions, however, the augmented role in insuring social cohesion that writing now came to play was defined in a way that was strikingly political even by the most stringent of Confucian standards. What this political solution called for most vociferously was the creation of a new context that would guarantee significance to the scattered phenomena of a newly conceived world. The initial upshot of this pressure for social cohesion was that commentators on the new mission of literature could agree much more readily on how urgent it was that a new message be sent than on the specific content of the message itself. Most of the literary theories that grew out of this crisis thus tended to focus quite specifically on the necessity of expanding the audience that the new writing would reach, with the precise nature of the message to be conveyed receiving much less attention.

Behind a superficial congruence on the question of enlarging the readership, however, lay a substantial area of potential discord. The difficulty was presented by the inevitable gap between a literature seen primarily as a means of attacking the flaws of the old society and one regarded as offering practical solutions to social problems. Literature was thus torn between viewing itself as a positive contributor to social order through the propagation of a somewhat premature agreement on what that order should be, and a divisive agent continuing to explore the reasons for Chinese failure. But the focus on external orientation that these two contradictory master themes shared allowed little room for the literary introspection that came with modernism in the West. In other words, the prospect of writing that explored its own complicity in the furtherance of a moribund but still dominant tradition represented a real threat to the positivist outlook that provided modern Chinese literature with its raison d'être.

A literature that put the validity of the transmission of ideas into radical question thus violated the very terms by which the enterprise had come to constitute itself, not to mention running counter to the main trends in the long history of writing in China. Furthermore, such questioning ran the risk of further atomizing an order already knocked asunder by the horrible realization that the traditional system could no longer meet the dual tasks it had set for itself of both making sense of the world and providing information about how it should be run. Narrative literature of the last decade of the dynasty soon found itself in a classic double bind. Charged with the contradictory tasks of criticizing the existing order and spreading the word about a new social structure, the very pressure of combining the two often led writers to represent a social chaos so profound that remedy seemed almost beyond conceiving. Despair over the terrible responsibility involved in trying to bring representation, a new context, and rhetorical suasion within the same sphere may account for the devastating pessimism of what Lu Xun pejoratively called "novels of exposure" that dominated the literary scene in the last decade of the Qing. From its very inception, then, the redefined concept of literature created a series of powerful subtexts of radical uncertainty even as it aspired in its theoretical pronouncements to present affirmative news of a new social order.

Much of Lu Xun's unique brilliance lay in his determination to directly face the contradictions between the need to transmit positive information and the underlying instability of any such formulations. The tension in "Diary of a Madman," for instance, runs between the "Madman's" sense that he has figured out the problem and his plain inability to communicate it. What is most provocative about the story, however, is that his very frustrations in transmitting his painfully acquired information lead him back again and again to reexamine earlier assumptions about which he had been quite secure. The intransitivity of his "truths," in other words, brings about the process that leads to their eventual undermining. The story also provides a clear picture of how self and society have become alienated from one another in post-traditional times. The Madman's utter inability to get his message across causes him to voice it in ever shriller tones and leads directly to what his interlocuters must regard as indulgence in the purest subjectivity. Lu Xun, as someone trained in the more secure years before 1898, and by that token perhaps more sensitive to the epistemological crisis of later years, brings to his stories his despair over whether or not writing can perform the tasks it has taken upon itself.

Writers that came after Lu Xun, however much they admired him, rarely seemed to pursue his lead, remaining for the most part content to devote themselves to denunciations of the old ways without pausing to consider the ways in which their own discourse was related to traditional patterns of cultural interaction. The urgent desire to assume a positive point of view from which to speak would seem to be largely responsible for this. As so clearly represented by the Madman, the very iconoclasm of the May Fourth period weakened the pressure that the traditional social context exerted on literary representation to keep subject and object in balance. With all but social atomization reduced to a matter of memory, the younger writers of the 1920s and 1930s could now rail freely against society without giving conscious voice to Lu Xun's concern about keeping personal and social concern on the same horizon.

Wu Zuxiang [Wu Tsu-hsiang], writing in the early 1930s, a period of great political activism, clearly represents the various facets of this freedom in his story, "Young Master Gets His Tonic." In this work the eponymous Young Master is as secure in his ignorance as the implied author standing behind him is sure of his own moral perspective on that ignorance: no doubts are entertained on either side. From the perspective of the transmission of the attitudes that Wu so clearly intends to project, however, the problem with this story lies in the very starkness of its vision. The knowledge the peasants gain leads to action that brings about only death, while Young Master remains impervious to transformation. Only the obtrusive intervention of the ironic voice of the writer can provide any mediation between the two worlds. In this sense, it is only the confidence of the authorial voice, a presence quite abstract from the protagonists within the story—and completely confident of its ability to tell the reader exactly how reality should be read—that gives any moral vector to the events that take place within it. At the same time this is a story of utter atomization: the resolute exteriority of the narratorial voice from the events of the story, and the vast distance between the author and both points of view represented within it, signify a complete breakdown of communication. The failures end up—even as the tale ostensibly ignores all these issues—pointing to the same problems that Lu Xun had been concerned with, transmitting knowledge from those who know and those who must learn, albeit in a much cruder fashion.

With Ding Ling's "When I Was in Hsia Village," however, the abrupt distances that had been so confidently ignored in "Young Master" become the theme of the story. What makes this piece compelling is the dilemma faced by the narrator in her position as representative of the Communist Party. As can be seen from "Young Master" and some of the other stories discussed in this chapter, hopes engendered by communist ideology provide ready answers to the uncertainties forced upon other writers by the collapse of the traditional order: communism answers the question of just what it is that is to be propagated with resounding certainty. But in "Hsia Village" the narrator opens the story with a journey from the known quantity of the Political Department (filled with "turmoil" though it may be) to the alien confines of the village. The change in cognitive terrain is indicated best by the transformation of the relationship between the narrator and Ah Kuei, a local woman who betrays her rather lowly origins by her taciturn manner and the fact that she has feet that had once been bound. At first the narrator seems confident and in charge and Ah Kuei remains silent, but this is reversed once they reach the village. Ah Kuei suddenly becomes lively and the narrator can neither understand what the villagers are talking about nor how to get around. This, then, is essentially the same territory first identified by Lu Xun as becoming more alien to the intellectual the closer he or she looks at it.

What eventually emerges in the text is a story of individual self-sacrifice of the type so often rehearsed in patriotic melodrama. But in "Hsia Village" the motif has been turned upside down. Instead of a straightforward account of noble actions bravely undertaken, the actions are first framed in a miasma of gossip, uncertainty, and pettiness. Clearly Ding Ling means to contrast the confident assertions made in propaganda concernin the interpretation of individual action with a bleaker reading informed by assumptions about the tenacity of traditional prejudices. The response the state asks for and that society actually provides are shown to be at odds. Indeed, in this respect the story provides the perfect feminist riposte to the male playwrights who affirmed the national unity of wartime China by writing historical dramas around heroines from past dynasties who almost invariably had terrible punishments inflicted upon them as tests of their loyalty to the idea of the state. For all the author's evident intention to give the story an affirmative ending, one gets the feeling, if only from the pervasive uncertainty with which the tale is told, that state, society, and the individual will have great problems in ever accommodating one another with the harmony that both Marxism and Confucianism aspire to.

In a social environment in which membership in a greater context was by far the most pressing determinant of individual behavior, the possibility of permanent disharmony between the individual and society raises serious problems. In "Hsia Village," the narrator hints broadly at her own alienation from her context, but for the heroic village girl Chen-chen, her distance from the society around her is more than subjective impulse; it is forced upon her by her fellow villagers' determination to regard her bad luck, rebelliousness, and lack of penance as evidence of profound moral deficiency. Perhaps the most ominous thing about her predicament is the extent to which it grows out of traditional prejudices on the part of the villagers. Instead of seeing her behavior as part of a modern narrative of patriotic self-sacrifice, they see it as a culpable failure to respond to the initial violation in the fashion sanctioned by tradition. To them, only suicide would have demonstrated her commitment to the only ideal of female integrity that held any meaning under the old code of ethics.

In the case of the story as a whole, however, the patriotic background provided by the war effort provides enough immanent meaning to allow a sense that the healthy impulses—by which is often meant willingness to follow the Party line—of the new generation will create the kind of environment where rational action is possible. But the specter of social meaninglessness that often breaks through the surface is overtly present in a wide range of other stories from many periods of modern Chinese history—from the early 1920s on to the post-Cultural Revolution period after 1979. In such stories, individual actors, set free from the mooring of an authentic context in which to act, slide easily into the most extreme kind of subjective indulgence, where the external world becomes merely a projection of internal desire. It is symptomatic of the Party's view of the nature of literary expression that it has systematically confused such personal fantasies with more carefully worked-out representations of individual points of view. The opprobrium heaped upon stories like "Hsia Village" in 1942 is a case in point.

In May of 1942, Mao Zedong summarily banished the possibility of an introspective mode of inquiry from literature in the by then substantial territories controlled by the Communist Party. The central message of his "Talks at the Yan'an Forum on Literature and Art" concerns itself with the overwhelming need to transmit positive knowledge about the revolution to those lacking substantial education. This new line not only represents the desire of the Party to consolidate and spread its control, but also reflects the sense that the new political community had by then generated a body of practical and theoretical behavior sufficient to require transmission. But it also must be recalled that the wish to propagate positive knowledge rather than critical awareness of the problem of knowing goes back to the initial impulses of the post-1895 reform and to the preponderance of literary voices in the 1930s. The "Talks" spend so much time addressing the twin questions of why and how ordinary people are to be written to, incidently, that they hardly even raise the question of what specific forms are to be used in the enterprise. Given that it became the key text in Chinese literary policy for thirty-five years after its promulgation, the "Talks" barely discuss any literary question other than issues concerned with getting the message across and making that message an affirmative one.

Zhao Shuli's "The Rhymes of Li Youcai" is one of the first stories produced in the communist-controlled area after Mao Zedong laid down the literary line at Yan'an in 1942. The position of the eponymous hero is emblematic of the contract made between the nascent state and the majority of writers who chose to play by its rules. This is true in both affirmative and negative senses, in what is addressed and what must be ignored. Both sides agree that literature and art are vital tools in the mobilization and "creation" (to use Mao's term) of public opinion. The notion of public opinion is, in turn, the key to the Marxian concept of "worldview," the perspective through which people see the way society is constructed, and their own position and possibilities within it. By embodying the correct worldview, Li Youcai is able to awaken people to the realities of their situation and thus bring about a climate of opinion conducive to the Party's exercise of its policy line. Since the line itself is never at issue, the proper focus of such a story can only be on the question of how its transmission is best affected. In effect, this often entails neglect of the more literarily fruitful questions of what the impediments are to gaining a proper perspective and how blockages to implementation can be removed. In this sense, Li Youcai represents the ideal picture of the Party's view of the new artist.

The world within the story is presented as being transparent to the reader, but its characters are trapped within it by a combination of fear and subjugation to traditional perceptions. It takes the gnomic power of Li Youcai's rhymes to sum up each situation and character he encounters and thus allow his audience to concentrate their diffuse feelings of discontent. For all the clarity of the narrated situation, however, the extent to which ignorance and impotence pervades the story is remarkable. Without Li Youcai's effective oppositional discourse (effective primarily because its audience can be so precisely delineated), resistance to the traditional sources of power dries up almost immediately. Even the representative of the Party has the wool pulled over his eyes, and people considered politically reliable by virtue of their class background prove to be embarrassingly easy to buy off. The responsibility of the artist in maintaining a proper perspective, in other words, could not be greater. But a perception of the artist as having so much power, while no doubt highly flattering to the writer in the heat of wartime cooperation, could not but be a double-edged sword. If the Party is so dependent on the writer to create the proper climate of opinion, the obverse is that it must take extreme measures to guard against that power being used improperly.

As if emblematic of the writer's vulnerable position vis-à-vis the exercise of political power, Li Youcai's own existence in the village is highly precarious. For all his ability to move the masses, when the forces of reaction realize the full extent of the threat he poses to them, they simply chase him out. It takes the restoration of proper Party authority to allow him to return. Li's situation, moreover, is parallel to that of the political activity of the villagers: their common denominator is an inability to act on their own. It requires the intervention of higher and wiser powers both to formulate their discontents in practical fashion and then to motivate them to take action. The world created within this story thus contains a chasm between knowledge and action so wide that only political authority can fill it.

The rather insubstantial little story "Star" by Lu Yanglie illustrates the same point, but by the time it was written, even the process of gaining wisdom is represented as being utterly dependent upon the Party—the Tibetan protagonist is obtrusively shown to have been incapable of learning anything on his own. This story, published in 1965, marks the closure of the tension in "Li Youcai" between the power of literary figures to represent reality and the Party's monopoly on action. In the years between the two stories, writers had used their theoretical position of authority to mount a series of challenges to the Party in efforts to gain greater autonomy for the literary voice. By the late 1950s, Party literary authorities had responded furiously to these demands for autonomy by setting the requirement that the Party be the exclusive inspiration for knowledge rather than sharing that responsibility with writers. Given the Party's stress on unity between thought and action, the division of labor illustrated in "Li Youcai" was perhaps too fraught with ambiguity to survive long.

The Cultural Revolution, beginning in 1966, represented the high point of Party control. During this period, all earlier writing was carefully reviewed with an eye toward gauging the extent of its utility to the Maoist line, with the predictable result that very little was allowed to continue in circulation. Ironically enough, Lu Xun was virtually the only modern writer whose work was not banished from the shelves. Such new writing as appeared during the period also stressed loyalty to Mao and to communist ideals, but it did so by combining extravagant depiction of the subjective feelings of ideal characters with stress on how correct those feelings were. The old literary ideal of harmony between self and society was thus fulfilled by ideological decree, brought about only, as it were, at gunpoint. There was, as a result, a profound long-term cost to the status of literature as an effective didactic device. Since the goals of the Cultural Revolution were so far removed from people's actual experience of the time, literature's long enlistment in its cause—coerced though it may have been— appears to have finally brought to the surface certain doubts about literature's powers to affect social practice.

The first works to appear after the event consisted largely of attacks on Cultural Revolution policy and political figures sponsored by those in the new leadership who stood most to gain from discrediting their predecessors. Very soon, however, the range of political attack extended itself. In Wang Meng's "The Barber's Tale," for instance, if one takes the barber as standing for the writer/intellectual voice, a new dimension of disillusion can be seen. Wang wistfully contrasts the years of openness and harmony immediately following 1949 with the bitter period that followed. The depiction of the behavior of Tang Jiuyuan, the cadre denounced in the Cultural Revolution and rehabilitated later, provides most of the story's resonance. In the first place, Tang's apparent failure to have learned any real lesson in human sympathy following his restoration to power sounds a new note of pessimism in literature of the communist period. In the second place, the narrator's frank awareness of his own marginality points to a new willingness on the part of writers to acknowledge the reality of their position vis-à-vis Party authority. The illusion of the writer as an equal partner in the propagation of socialism is finally held up to convincing scrutiny, providing a thematic core not only to this story but to much other post-1979 literature as well.

This recognition that literature's sense of itself had become vulnerable brought a sort of existential crisis to Chinese letters in the 1980s. This crisis caused the old idea that literary realism effected the most secure link between representation, moral instruction, and people's sense of how their own lives were lived to be thrown into doubt. As Liu Binyan—the writer eventually to be expelled from the Party in the mini-purge of early 1987—said in January of 1979: "There are some intermediate stages between life and a literary work; couldn't one put some of those materials, semi-finished products, some thoughts and depictions before the readers's eyes before they are finished?"[1] Perhaps Liu here gives voice to the principal anxiety of "The Barber's Tale": construction of a new literary context can only result from the reconstruction of a social context; and the reconstruction of context runs the risk of reproducing past patterns of behavior. Liu's choice in "Between People and Monsters" to write reportage that constantly signifies an awareness of its own status as literary artifact represents his wish to step back from an authoritarian tone of his own: if he tells his readers in no uncertain terms that such things as this should not occur, he also self-consciously refrains from offering an even implicit solution to the more vexing problems both of how such things arose in the first place and how to prevent them in the future. The deliberate jumping of authorial focus and discordant language found throughout the text constitute the formal signs of his reluctance to render the sort of flat, comprehensive judgment that the Party had always been so free in dispensing.

The younger generation of writers that has begun to write only after the Cultural Revolution continues Liu's skepticism. Ah Cheng (b. 1948), for instance, in his story "The Chess Master" ponders the question of where meaning comes from in a period in which the confident certainty of earlier years has been rudely effaced. The rather casual way that Wang Yisheng and the narrator agree to disagree about the significance of the stories they tell each other on the train during their journey to the country in the first part of "Chess Master" represents a call for pluralism on the part of both authors and readers of narratives. The almost complete relegation of political issues to the background of the story suggests the continuing literary recognition that state and society are not necessarily the same entity.

The way in which chess comes to stand for existential significance, however, does point to the void left by the realization that the relationship between self, society, and the state is merely arbitrary, if not brought about by outright coercion. Chess becomes the vehicle by which meaning is salvaged from the nihilism that follows the exposure of the Cultural Revolution as a massive fraud. Thus chess is much more than simple amusement; it is obliged to stand for significant aspects of the Chinese tradition—at first as an anti-political Daoism and later as a sign that Wang Yisheng comports himself in accordance with Confucian morality as well. The story's rather melodramatic ending illustrates the difficulty of combining open-ended narratives with the need to affirm strong intellectual closure. Is the reader meant to take the early freedom of action or the affirmation of traditional values at the end as the import of the story?

Characterization has been an enduring problem in modern Chinese literature. Reflecting the dissolution of the old harmony between self and society, authors have tended either to over-dramatize their characters, most often as projections of ideal selves, or, if social concern predominates, to make them rigidly schematic. Given the feelings about the state following the Cultural Revolution, it is no surprise that the narratives of the past ten years are filled with confessional writings that project and greatly magnify their authorial persona. Breaking away from this overly emotional connection to their characters can, in fact, be seen as one of modern and contemporary Chinese literature's most enduring challenges. Zhang Xinxin was already a remarkably sophisticated narrative artist in the period before she was sharply criticized in the "Spiritual Pollution" campaign of late 1983. In the wake of the attacks on her, she and her collaborator Sang Ye conceived of a series of interviews that were first published in New York's *China Daily News* in 1984–85. These interviews, given the collective title of *Beijing ren* (*Beijing's people*—with overtones of "Peking man") and eventually published in a single volume (*Chinese Lives*), proffer a radically new approach to the vexatios problems involved in the representation of character.

The interview form accords with Liu Binyan's wish to present less than fully finished characters before his readers. While Zhang herself credits Studs Terkel for the idea of interview literature, she and Sang Ye have achieved a breakthrough of sorts in Chinese narrative practice with this new style. Perhaps more than anything else, the depiction of the characters responding to questions that are left out of the text represents the authorial persona in a new and highly ambiguous fashion: the authors are shown to be giving shape to the text with their questions, but the failure to include the questions themselves signifies their intentional modesty in allowing people to tell their own stories. The authors, in other words, remind us of the inevitability of their presence even as they point to the inevitability of the limitations to what they can know. Zhang and Sang Ye thereby inscribe within the structure of their text an implied critique of the two extremes of earlier Chinese narrative. The reader is constantly reminded that the characters are held at a far enough distance to avoid the sentimental involvement that writers have tended to invest in their creations. At the same time, however, the vivid sense that the characters are speaking directly to us prevents their being used as ideological emblems and to appear thereby to be little more than figures in a distant landscape of political allegory.

The collection of these stories that resulted allows a sense of character individuality and diversity virtually unprecedented in modern Chinese letters. The concerns that Confucian or Marxist didacticism had always injected into literary representation are shown here to be merely a few among many. The variety of opinions and activities represented in the collection also puts the political authority that has always been such a large part of Chinese life into new perspective. If the state has for most of its existence established ideal modes of behavior for its subjects, *Chinese Lives* demonstrates the extent to which the potential for political coercion is diminished when people become able, at least to some extent, simply to ignore the state's ideological demands. The political critique the book presents, then, is neither a direct challenge to Party hegemony nor a more moderate opposition to policy line coupled with theoretical acceptance of Party legitimacy. It is instead the simple affirmation, actually far more revolutionary in the Chinese context, that the current political dispensation neither can nor does speak to the questions that most people put at the center of their lives.

TOPICS FOR DISCUSSION

1. The profound ideologizing of contemporary Chinese literature has deep roots within Chinese culture, but it would also seem to mark a profound inability to achieve social consensus. Looking at the question of the literary canon from such a perspective, is there not an implicit challenge to the very concept of canon (from those who see the process of making literature contingent as an opportunity to meet new cognitive and aesthetic needs), or perhaps its ultimate valorization (from those who see primarily the costs of such intellectual instability)? The real question behind all this, however, is whether literature must be seen as epiphenomenal to other and more powerful discourse—the historical, the political, the economic. Is it valid to look at our canon in this light? What are the varieties of the relationship of literature to society? For all its flaws, contemporary Chinese literature raises these questions.

2. Perhaps more than any other set of readings in this series, contemporary Chinese literature raises the question of aesthetic universals. The reception of the literature within China has been marked by its vicissitudes, many of which are not simply the

result of partisan political struggle. Does the highly uneven quality of most modern Chinese literature speak for or against the idea of universals of literary response?

3. The Western reader seems to have difficulties accepting the representation of character in most Chinese literature, a situation that reaches an extreme with modern texts. Is it possible to analyze Chinese narrative in such a way as to be able to explain some of the differences between the Western and Chinese concepts of character?

4. Most traditional theories of literature in both China and the West see literature as a reflection of social practice. It is possible that in some sense modern and contemporary Chinese literature shows how the reverse might be true? Could the model of epistemological uncertainty evident in much of this literature have inspired any of the political thinking in twentieth-century China?

NOTE

1. Rudolf Wagner, "Liu Binyan and the *Texie*," *Modern Chinese Literature* 2.1 (Spring 1986): 69.

REFERENCES

For the historical context of twentieth-century Chinese literature, readers may wish to consult the "Timeline of Significant Events in China, 1911–1987, in Relation to Contemporary Chinese Lettres," pp. 345–46.

Ah Cheng. "The Chess Master" (1984). *Chinese Literature*, Summer 1985, pp. 84–131.
Duke, Michael S. *Blooming and Contending: Chinese Literature in the Post-Mao Era.* Bloomington: Indiana University Press, 1985.
Kinkley, Jeffrey C., ed. *After Mao: Literature and Society, 1978–1981.* Cambridge, MA: The Council on East Asian Studies, Harvard University, 1985.
Lau, Joseph S. M., C. T. Hsia, and Leo Ou-Fan Lee, eds. *Modern Chinese Stories and Novellas 1919–1949.* New York: Columbia University Press, 1981. Contains both Ding Ling [Ting Ling], "When I Was In Hsia Village" (1940), and Wu Zuxiang [Wu Tsu-hsiang], "Young Master Gets His Tonic."
Link, Perry, ed. *Roses and Thorns: The Second Blooming of the Hundred Flowers in Chinese Fiction, 1979–80.* Berkeley: University of California Press, 1984.
Link, Perry, ed. *Stubborn Weeds: Popular and Controversial Chinese Literature after the Cultural Revolution.* Bloomington: Indiana University Press, 1983. Both the Link collections have excellent introductions discussing the immediate post-Mao period in some detail.
Liu Binyan. *People or Monsters? And Other Stories and Reportage from*

China After Mao. Edited by Perry Link. Bloomington: Indiana University Press, 1983.

Lu Xun. "Diary of a Madman." In *The Complete Stories of Lu Xun,* translated by Yang Xianyi and Gladys Yang. Beijing: Foreign Languages Press, 1981; Bloomington: Indiana University Press, 1981.

Lu Yanglie [Lu Yang-Lieh]. "Star" (1963?). In *Literature of the People's Republic of China,* edited by Kai-yu Hsu, 813–23. Bloomington: Indiana University Press, 1980.

Mao Zedong. *"Talks at the Yan'an Conference on Literature and Art": A Translation of the 1943 Text with Commentary.* Translated by Bonnie McDougall. Ann Arbor: Center for Chinese Studies, University of Michigan, 1980.

Wagner, Rudolf G. "The Chinese Writer in His Own Mirror: Writer, State and Society—The Literary Evidence." In *China's Intellectuals and the State: In Search of A New Relationship,* edited by M. Goldman, T. Cheek, and C. L. Hamrin, pp. 183–231. Cambridge: The Council on East Asian Studies, Harvard University, 1987.

Wang Meng. "The Barber's Tale" (1979). *Chinese Literature,* no. 7 (1980): 22–40.

Widmer, Ellen and David Der-Wei Wang, eds. *From May Fourth to June Fourth: Fiction and Film in Twentieth-Century China.* Cambridge: Harvard Contemporary China Series, no. 9, Harvard University Press, forthcoming 1993.

Zhang Xinxin and Sang Ye. *Chinese Lives: An Oral History of Contemporary China.* Edited by W.J.F. Jenner and Delia Davin. Translated by the editors and Cheng Lingang, et al. New York: Pantheon Books, 1987.

Zhao Shuli. "The Rhymes of Li Youcai." In *Rhymes of Li Youcai and Other Stories,* translated by Sidney Shapiro. 1950; Beijing: Foreign Languages Press, 1980.

Timeline of Significant Events in China, 1911–1987, in Relation to Contemporary Chinese Lettres

October 1911	Rebellion begins that leads to overthrow of Manchu Qing dynasty and the foundation of the Republic of China in 1912.
1918	Publication of Lu Xun's first story, "Diary of a Madman."
May 4, 1919	Student demonstration against concessions made by Chinese government in signing of Treaty of Versailles. Known subsequently as the May Fourth Movement, it has been used ever since to symbolize the various reform initiatives of the New Culture Movement, including the widespread adoption of Western political ideas, opposition to various Chinese customs, and advocacy of the use of the vernacular language for all literary and discursive purposes.
1921	Founding of Chinese Communist Party (CCP) in Shanghai.
1922–23	Sun Yat-sen reorganizes Nationalist Party along Leninist lines, leading to eventual political alliance with the CCP.
April 1927	Chiang Kai-shek breaks alliance with CCP, gains control of central China for Nationalist government. Chiang establishes government at Nanking.
1930	Founding of the League of Left-wing Writers, marking effective domination of contemporary literary discourse by Marxism.
September 1931– February 1932	Conquest of Manchuria by Japan in September followed by short invasion by Japanese forces of Shanghai and the surrounding territory.

October 1936	Death of Lu Xun; December, Nationalist and Communists renew "united front," this time against Japan.
July 7, 1937	Full-scale invasion by Japan results in loss of much of urban China for the next eight years.
May 1942	Mao Zedong's "Talks at the Yan'an Forum on Literature and Art."
1945	Japan surrenders. Civil war between Nationalists and Communists begins almost immediately.
October 1, 1949	Proclamation of the founding of the People's Republic of China in Beijing, now restored as national capital.
1957	Suppression of the "Hundred Flowers" policy that had briefly encouraged critical speech. Beginning of "Anti-rightist movement."
1966	Beginning of "Great Proletarian Cultural Revolution."
September 1976	Death of Mao Zedong.
July 1977	Deng Xiaoping reinstated as vice-chairman of the CCP.
1983–84	Campaign against "spiritual pollution."
December 1986	Demonstrations in cities lead to campaign against "bourgeois liberalization" in 1987.

STORY OF THE WESTERN WING (*XIXIANG JI*)

(*Romance of the Western Chamber*)

Stephen H. West and Wilt L. Idema

In chapter 23 of the *Dream of the Red Chamber* the hero of the novel, Jia Baoyu, is surprised by the sickly Lin Daiyu while he is reading the *Story of the Western Wing*. He at first tries to hide the book from her, but relents and lets her read it. She becomes so swept up in the book that she sits entranced and silent after finishing it. But, when Baoyu starts to tease her with a quotation from the play, she calls it "a horrid work," and threatens to denounce him to his parents for reading it. This is fitting comment on the *Xixiang ji*, a play that has been, since its opening performance, the most popular love-comedy in China. It provided the vernacular model of stories of the "brilliant student and talented young lady" that would later inform such works as the *Dream of the Red Chamber*, and it was happily devoured by innumerable young men and women who easily recognized themselves in the protagonists of the play. The play, in fact, came to have attached to it the notorious status of a lover's bible, and many eager champions of morality censured this masterpiece as a "book that teaches lechery" (*huiyin zhi shu*) and damned the author to a life in hell—an opprobrium that only further increased the appeal of the work.

The work is one play of several written by Wang Shifu (ca. 1250–1300), about whom we have practically no information. According to the *Register of Ghosts* (*Lugui bu*), he was a citizen of the capital of China, which was then called Dadu, "Grand Metropolis" (near modern Beijing), and his activities may be dated to the middle or second half of the thirteenth century. He is credited in the same register with fourteen plays; of the original fourteen only three, including the *Story of the Western Wing*, are wholly extant. One of the other two, *The Story of the Dilapidated Kiln (Poyao ji)*, dramatizes the tale of the spectacular rise to fame and fortune of the poor student Lü Mengzheng. This play, which still exists in a text from the eunuch agency for theatricals from the Ming court, relates the tale of a young student who overcomes poverty and prejudice to win his degree and his young lady. The other complete extant work is the *Hall of the Beautiful Spring (Lichun tang)*. This work, which is collected in an anthology dating from the seventeenth century, is an unremarkable tale of conflict between two high officials of the court of the Jürchen emperor Zhangzong (r. 1190–1208) of the Jin. Both plays, in fact, are rather mediocre and have been largely neglected by historical scholarship. One other play, *The Tea-Trading Boat*, exists in fragmentary form. It relates the story of a courtesan, Su Xiaoqing, who falls in love with a young student, Shuang Jian, but who is forced by her madam to marry an ugly merchant, who takes her away in his trading craft. Shuang Jian pursues the couple and eventually wins the woman back by invoking his privileges as a newly minted magistrate, and the ugly merchant's claim to the woman is curtly dismissed. The theme of this play, the love triangle of Shuang Jian, Su Xiaoqing, and the merchant was perhaps the most popular love story in China between the twelfth and fourteenth centuries, until supplanted by the *Story of the Western Wing*. Of the other nine plays attributed to Wang not a single vestige remains, although judging by the titles, their thematic range was broad. There were love tragedies, historical plays, courtroom dramas, and deliverance plays treating the conversion of famous figures to Taoism. All of these factors—the paucity of biographical information, the wide variety of subject matter, and the remarkable preference for materials that circulated in the writings of other playwrights and in other vernacular forms—suggest that Wang Shifu was probably a professional playwright who wrote commercial plays for the capital theater. He was, however, anything but a hack. The *Story of the Western Wing* shows him to have undergone a sound traditional education in the classics, the histories, and the philosophers and demonstrates as well that he had wide-ranging knowledge of the lighter branches of literature like classical tales and lyrics.

The *Story of the Western Wing*, actually a cycle of five separate *zaju* (the Chinese term for northern drama written between the twelfth and fifteenth centuries) is perhaps the single most popular piece of oral performing literature ever written in China. It has passed through nearly 150 separate editions since the time of its publication in the early Ming period and has spawned numerous recensions in other regional forms of drama and in other forms of performing literature, including ballads, *chantefable*, drum songs, etc. Unfortunately, with the exception of one translation, the play is known in the West only through translations of an edition of the seventeenth century compiled and bowdlerized by Jin Shengtan, the famous Ming critic. He saw fit to excise some of the bawdier parts of the play in an attempt to control the explicit expression of sexuality and to vouchsafe the conventional purity of Oriole, the main female lead. Furthermore, he cut away the fifth of the plays. He was following what had become a tradition in criticism to assign the last play to the noted playwright Guan Hanqing, an unfortunate trend that began in the early sixteenth century by a playwright-critic who attempted to prove that a hearsay legend to that effect was wrong! The disputed authorship of the fifth play has led to unfortunate consequences for Western audiences, who are often left translations that omit that play or severely truncate it.

The *Story of the Western Wing* was not an original composition but a play that borrowed heavily and directly from previous sources, including Tang literary short stories (*chuanqi*) and ballads, Song dynasty "drum songs" (*guzi ci*), and Jin and Yuan ballads (*zhugongdiao*). The ultimate source for Wang Shifu's play was "Tale of Oriole" (*Yingying zhuan*), a short story in the classical language by the Tang dynasty statesman and poet Yuan Zhen (779–831). His "Tale of Oriole" is rightly considered as one of the finest examples of the classical tale of the Tang dynasty.

The tale narrates how a certain student Zhang, at the age of twenty-three and still very proudly a virgin, travels from the Capital, across the Yellow River, to Puzhou, where he stays outside town at the Monastery of Universal Salvation. When local troops mutiny, he is able to save the monastery from looting through his connections with some of the officers. A distant aunt, a widow who is also staying at the monastery, expresses her thanks by inviting him for a meal, at which she also introduces her daughter Oriole to him. Our student Zhang immediately falls in love with Oriole and tries to contact her through her girlservant. By a poem, Oriole invites him to her room at night, but when he shows up, she rebukes him sternly for his immoral designs. Only a few nights later, however, she comes to his room of her own volition. For a few months they have an affair (in which her mother apparently acquiesces, hoping for a marriage) until he returns to the Capital. When he comes back, they resume their affair until the examinations once again summon him to Chang'an. On the eve of his departure, he asks her to play the zither for him, but, overcome by grief, she has to stop in the middle of the melody. In the Capital, student Zhang, despite a very touching letter from Oriole, decides to break with her for good because, he claims, her beauty would destroy him. A year later, both of them are married to someone else, and when he asks to see her, she refuses.

Within its genre, the "Tale of Oriole" is remarkable for its absence of supernatural elements and its insistence on psychological realism. The characterization is not without irony. The author stresses both student Zhang's lack of experience in matters of love and sex and his total infatuation which initially make him such an easy victim to the wiles of women and from which he, despite his protestations, only slowly, and never completely, recovers. In the case of Oriole, we only catch glimpses of a contradictory behavior that results from a continuing inner conflict between desire and shame. The resulting enigma of her personality greatly adds to the appeal of this story.

By the eleventh century, the "Tale of Oriole" not only circulated in written form but had also entered the realm of oral literature. When the poet Zhao Lingzhi (1051–1134) adapted the "Tale of Oriole" as a drum song (guzi ci), he stated in his preface that scholars liked to talk about this romance and that entertainers knew to narrate its outline. He also suggested that these versions departed considerably from the original tale. In his own version, he provided an extensive excerpt of Yuan Zhen's work. The tale proper is further followed by a short discussion on the propriety of student Zhang and Oriole's behavior that is concluded by a final lyric. The two final songs clearly censure Student Zhang for his lack of love and his betrayal of Oriole.

In the twelfth century adaptation of the "Tale of Oriole" into the ballad form known as "All Keys and Modes" (zhugongdiao), the author, a certain "Scholar Dong" (Dong jieyuan, c. 1190–1208), departed radically from the tale in the beginning and ending of the story. These changes were not made out of ignorance of the original tale, but from a desire to change forever the focus and direction of the story. In his adaptation, Dong Jieyuan greatly expanded the material provided by the "Tale of Oriole." If Yuan Zhen's work in English translation runs to about ten pages, Dong

Jieyuan's composition takes up over two-hundred! This expansion is achieved both by a far more detailed narration and by the addition of many new episodes, for which Dong Jieyuan often found his inspiration in other Tang dynasty tales and in popular lore. Unfortunately, it is impossible to determine to what extent Dong Jieyuan in his expansion of the story drew on the pre-existent treatment of the romance of Student Zhang and Oriole in the oral tradition. He expanded some scenes to which only allusion is made in the tale. For instance, the siege of the monastery, barely mentioned by Yuan Zhen, is given a complete book in the ballad. But it is in the final three books of the ballad that Dong Jieyuan turns the story in a completely different direction from his source, even as he continues to quote from it. In the ballad, when the widow finds out about the affair of her daughter, she summons Oriole's servant, Crimson, in order to scold her. But she is soon persuaded by the latter's arguments that it would be a folly to expose the affair and much wiser to agree to the marriage. Oriole happily consents and, with the help of a monk, Student Zhang is able to present an engagement gift. The next day the widow, the abbot, and Oriole see him off to the Capitol, to take part in the examinations.

After passing his examinations, Zhang Gong falls ill, delaying his return to Oriole. In the meantime, Zheng Heng, Oriole's original fiancé, arrives with the story that the new graduate Zhang has been forced to marry the daughter of a minister. The widow therefore decides to have her daughter marry Zheng Heng, and at the banquet that night a tearful Oriole is positioned between her lover and her fiance. Zhang Gong, at a loss what to do, shares the monk Dharma Wit's room for the night and the latter offers to kill the widow. At that moment, they are joined by Oriole and Crimson. When our protagonists have become so desperate that they want to commit suicide together, Dharma Wit suggests that they seek the help of the governor, Du Que. The couple (accompanied by Crimson) elopes that very night and is welcomed by Du Que. When Zheng Heng appears in court on the following morning to claim his bride, Du Que shames him into killing himself, and Zhang Gong and Oriole happily celebrate their marriage.

Dong Jieyuan, spurred on by the dictates of his genre, changed the "Tale of Oriole" almost beyond recognition as he turned a story of a young man's recovery from infatuation into a rich and varied love comedy. His main character is Zhang Gong, and the ironic portrayal of our student verges at times on caricature: as soon as the prime example of Chinese manhood is struck by love he becomes a babbling fool who is wax in the hands of admiring women. The characterization of Oriole is greatly developed. She is portrayed as a passionate and intelligent, but well-educated maiden, torn between her emotions and her equally strong sense of morality. Her mother is shown as outwardly stern but inwardly weak and doting, a condition that causes all of her clever schemes to backfire. Crimson, who scarcely has any identity at all in Yuan Zhen's tale, now becomes, in the time-honored and apparently universal tradition of love comedy, one of the most important characters—the clever servant girl, whose stratagems are essential in bringing the high-born but ineffectual lovers together. The holy abbot is shown to be only too eager to meddle in worldly affairs but turns out to be of little practical use. The only monk in the monastery who shows himself to be capable of daring self-sacrifice is Dharma Wit, who can barely recite a sutra! Du Que is portrayed as the ideal official, but his appearances are kept to a minimum. On the other hand, the characterization of Zheng Heng, the suitor who relies on his connections and riches instead of his looks and talents, is purely grotesque and developed in loving detail.

If Wang Shifu followed this source closely when penning the drama, he did not follow it slavishly. The dramatic, as opposed to narrative, form posited different requirements, to which were added the specific formal features of *zaju*. What were narration and description in the ballad had to be recast as dialogue or monologue; repetition of action was to be avoided, and flashbacks were impracticable—for dreams the traditional Chinese stage had evolved appropriate conventions. Moreover, Wang Shifu had to deal with the typical *zaju* convention that, within each act, all the songs had to be assigned to a single character. In this way, over half of the text of any act may be assigned to only one of the many characters in it, and it is his or her perception of the situation and reaction to it that is most vividly impressed upon the audience.

In his *Story of the Western Wing*, Wang Shifu considerably tightened up the plot of our story. From the first appearance on stage of Oriole's mother, we know that her daughter has a fiancé who is supposed to be on his way to Puzhou, and Zhang Gong informs us that his primary motive for coming to Puzhou is to visit Du Que. During the siege of the monastery, the widow promises her daughter in marriage to anyone capable of repulsing the rebels, so that when she subsequently refuses to accept our student as a son-in-law she commits a clear breach of promise. A young son, Happy, is given a role in her discovery of the affair between his sister and the student. In the play, moreover, it is not Zhang Gong who wants to leave to take part in the examinations, but it is the widow who demands that he succeed in the examinations as a precondition to her consent to the couple's marriage. In this way, Wang Shifu also considerably accentuated the characterization of the widow who, while remaining a doting parent, now becomes much more status-conscious, stern and devious.

However, she more than fully has her match in Crimson, who has most benefitted from the convention to assign all the songs within a single act to one performer. Her role has been much expanded as she has the singing role in six separate acts. She continues to play an important part in the plot but now quite often serves as an ironic commentator on the behavior of her social betters. In his characterization of Zhang Gong and Oriole, Wang Shifu adhered closely to the *Story of the Western Wing in All Keys and Modes*, but our student emerges as a somewhat more positive, if less central, character, and some of the elements of caricature that are found in Dong Jieyuan's handling are toned down (probably because they conflicted with the role type playing our student). The stage apparently neither allowed for the ribaldry of the all-keys-and-modes nor required the frequent fits of suicidal desperation so conducive to a high point of suspense. Some characters fared less well at the hands of Wang Shifu—Zheng Heng's role was much reduced. Dong Jieyuan's Dharma Wit was split into two figures: his diminished fighting role was taken over by Benevolent Perception and the original character of Dharma Wit shrunk to a minor subsidiary role. The most convenient explanation for this operation would be that the "martial role of Benevolent Perception in performance required a different type of actor, but such good stage logic left us with two rather dull characters.

Roughly, the play is set in two spheres, one within and one outside of the monastery walls. These two domains, which reflect the ancient cosmological division in China between the binary principles of Yin and Yang, also represent two distinct sides of the personality of the main character, Student Zhang. In one realm he is the promising student, enroute to the civil service examinations and eventually to success as an official. His career would normally involve a marriage to the daughter of a successful bureaucrat and the creation of his own family. He is a master in this world, dependent on his skills as a scholar, and a budding Confucian.

The other realm is that of Yin, represented in the play by the cloister—the monastery removed from the public world of Yang. Within that compass Student Zhang's life is literally dominated by women. In this domain he relinquishes control of his own destiny and life to women who assume control of his mental and physical well-being. This change is wrought primarily from the influence of unrestrained female sexual attraction. The monastery, because of age-old associations with deviant sexual practices in the mind of non-Buddhist Chinese, also provides the perfect background for a witty and sometimes bawdy commentary on sex and carnal appetite.

The major plot of the drama is set in motion when the student, visiting the monastery to while away some time, encounters Oriole. When he espies her, she is dressed in the white robes of mourning for her father, but she is twirling a sprig of radiant blossoms—a daunting image of sexual congress to come. The student moves into the monastery, where he rents a room in a devious effort to get nearer the girl. He first attempts to meet her while she goes about her accustomed vigil of nocturnal sacrifices in the garden. He waits expectantly for her arrival and then intones across the wall a poem to which she responds. At first mutually attracted by looks, they are now drawn to each other by poetic talents. This is the first episode of one of two themes that begin to take form through the rest of the drama. They are, respectively, that of the relationship between divine maidens and earthly lovers and that of the *caizi jiaren* or "beautiful young maiden and talented young scholar." The first, that of divine goddesses, is provoked by the white clothes Oriole wears. She reminds Student Zhang first of Kuan Yin, the compassionate Bodhisattava who is associated with the white moon. His first impression of a descending goddess is carried forward by his rare glimpses of the girl, who disappears before he can get a good look at her. Eventually, other comparisons are drawn between Oriole and Kuan Yin, as well as other celestial females, most notably Chang E, goddess of the moon. This comparison is tied literally to the moon, a dominant image within the play and a symbol, as well, of Oriole's constancy. However, the moon also suggests a legendary figure, who stole the elixir of life from her husband only to flee to the moon, where she lives in eternal and cold loneliness. It is this later figure that Oriole herself adopts as a persona to give expression to her own sense of isolation. These constant references to stellar women lend to the drama an element of the ethereal and of the other-worldly quality of a woman who is quite unattainable on earth.

The structure of the "talented scholar and beautiful maiden" gains specificity as the play focuses on the model provided by the tale of Sima Xiangru, the talented Han poet-scholar, and Zhuo Wenjun, the beautiful widow who eloped with him. This story not only provided the prototype for the love of Student Zhang and Oriole, but it set once and for all the parameters of the treatment of that story in later vernacular fiction. The constituents of the story as found in early sources may be summarized as follows: Sima Xiangru (179–17 B.C.E.), the son of a rich family of Chengdu, after failing despite his literary talents in his first attempt to make a career at court, returns home to find his family estate in ruins. However, a certain Zhuo Wangsun is impressed with Sima and invites him to party at his house. There the poet plays a zither, and Zhuo's recently widowed daughter, Wenjun, falls in love with the talented young man. They elope that night, and ultimately Sima Xiangru's fame as a writer spreads to court. After being employed as an envoy to the southwestern barbarians by the emperor, he is accorded the highest honors by the officials in Shu (modern Sichuan), and Zhuo Wangsun gives Zhuo Wenjun her full dowry inheritance. Sima returns to the capital where he is appointed keeper of the funerary park of emperor Wen and retires to Mouling. From the many anecdotes about Sima Xiangru in the miscellany from the later Han, *Xijing zaji*, one account is added concerning a dalliance between Sima Xiangru and the concubine of another man in Mouling. When Zhuo Wenjun heard about it, she purportedly wrote a rather famous poem entitled the "Lament of the White Hairs" (*Baitou yin*), in which she bemoaned her rejection because she had grown older and in which she longed for a true and lasting relationship. The important point of this spurious addition to the story (both of the transmitted texts of the "Lament of the White Hairs" are written in a poetic form that was not extant at the time of her life) is that it changes the direction of the story from its original focus. It henceforth provided a literary model for tales about women of good family who had been courted and seduced by a talented young scholar, and who then had to suffer the fear or actual ignominy of him selecting another young bride when away at a capital post.

The adaptation of this model for the *Xixiang ji* has allowed the playwright to retain Dong Jieyuan's version of the story in which Oriole, who had originally played the zither in the "Tale of Oriole," is replaced by Student Zhang, who plays it to win her heart. This allows for the use in act 5 of play 2 of this famous scene of stringed seduction, but through the associations with the tradition of the "Lament of the White Hairs," the story also allows the playwright to exploit the dramatic potential of Oriole's rejection, which concludes the Tang dynasty tale. These stories of scholars and beauties have two distinct possibilities as endings: either a happy reunion where lovers are united forever or a dissolution of the romance and rejection of the woman as the man moves on into the public world of Confucian society. In such a way, the story of Sima Xiangru and Zhuo Wenjun provides background dramatic tension as the play moves into the fifth act, and accounts partially for the quick acceptance of Zheng Heng's lie about Student Zhang taking another wife.

While these two themes provide partial structuring of the text, the play is also a witty examination of human relations. And it is in the realm of human interaction that Crimson and Widow Cui emerge as central characters. It is this feature of the play—the relationship between Oriole and her mother in particular—upon which modern Chinese critics have seized. As early as the May Fourth movement, the *Western Wing* was heralded as a popular masterpiece, one that thoroughly rejected the traditional values of authoritarian "feudal" society, a play that, as Guo Moruo states, was a victory of "living human nature over dead morality." While the post-1949 critics in China were wont to see the conflict between mother and daughter as an example of feudal repression, it is in fact a deep exploration of the abuse of human relationships as dictated by traditional Confucian society. In the hierarchical relationships of Confucianism, there is an idealized set of superior-inferior relationships in which responsibility and goodness operate in a reciprocal symbiosis. Those in inferior positions have a responsibility to act as filial and obedient children, ministers, wives, or younger brothers, and those who are in a superior capacity are supposed to reciprocate with kindness and compassion. Thus, a crisis can develop when a child such as Oriole finds herself drawn into a conflict between love and desire on the one hand and filial respect and duty on the other. Moreover, in a society in which marriages were arranged according to family alliances and were based on a calculus of social and political values, love—as an expression of individual desire—had no sanctioned outlet. Therefore, for Oriole to love a poor student like Zhang was an act that both violated her responsibility to the family to maintain a chaste reputation and was in direct contradiction to a prescribed marriage based on the precepts of maintaining or strengthening family status.

Obligations within these relationships could be abused from above, as well, since the power lay with the superiors and the only sanction on their behavior was a belief in the moral perfectibility of humanity—that they would act only out of goodness. The widow's reneging on the marriage, coupled with her obsession with status, reveal her to Oriole as a pathological liar who will sacrifice the emotional welfare of her own daughter to support the outward facade of a family in control of its own destiny. It is true that, at one level, Widow Cui is trying to abide by her dead husband's wishes to consummate the marriage alliance with Zheng Heng and thereby also bring her family safely under the protection of a highly placed male. But to Oriole this appears as heartlessness and the simple commodification of her own being. As she remarks to her mother she feels she is a "piece of goods to be sold at a loss," something that can be offered, withdrawn, and then offered again as a transaction on the marriage market.

Crimson, too, operates within the realm of human interaction, emanating as a force of resolution, ferreting out deception and guile on the part of other characters. For instance, she accuses Oriole and the student Zhang of adopting the roles of *caizi* and *jiaren* as self-conscious personae with which to interact with each other. She manages to coerce them eventually to drop these posturings and interact with each other honestly—stripped of the poses into which the student-beauty model forces them. And, when the affair is discovered by the widow, she also confronts the old woman and accuses her outright of dishonesty, pointing out that it was the widow's own failure to keep her promise of marriage that led directly to the affair. Crimson's arguments bring Madam Cui to the realization that her obsession with status and name is nothing but a hollow self-deception; she realizes that her daughter's behavior stemmed directly from her inability to maintain control in a household stripped of male guidance by death.

In a way, Crimson, as the color red suggests, is the symbol of real and vibrant life in a society of poseurs, a world in which self-conscious roles are adopted for human interaction. As such, she represents the exploration of the age-old Chinese dichotomy between actualizing internal human values (*ren*) and abiding by a strong but external, stipulated, and customary code of behavior (*li*). Crimson has other functions in the play that are related to the etymology of her name. She acts as an informant in the techniques and behavior of romance and sex—advising the prudish young man on proper techniques and pushing Oriole toward the liaison with straightforward advice ("just close your eyes"). She is ever ready with a sexual quip—accusing the student of impotence or suggesting masturbation as an alternative to intercourse, for instance. Her speech is peppered with sexual innuendo and double entendre.

This leavening of sexuality makes for good comedy—just as in other dramas of the world theater. It is coupled, however, with a darker side of the sexual discourse: the fear and repression of female sexuality. Oriole's beauty fills up and spills out of the monastery. She causes havoc among the monks, she entices the student from his proper responsibilities, and her comeliness calls down the siege by the bandit leader. This last result, in particular, speaks to the power of uncontrolled female sexuality. While she is rescued from the predicament by the student, at one point she believes that her only options are forced marriage to the bandit—a form of rape—or her suicide. This message, that uncontrolled female sexuality calls down a curiously symmetrical form of punishment, seems a clearly didactic message of a text that is vaguely reminiscent of Chinese theories of sexual therapy. One should also note that while the student is completely enthusiastic and open about his enjoyment of the romance and of the sexual act itself, Oriole is practically silent.

These are only a few remarks on the complex world of the *Western Wing*, which provides a rich and varied matrix of action, characterization, and plot from which to mine a multitude of interpretative possibilities. Wang Shifu had at his disposal a long and complicated textual history, and he combined elements from all of them in creating his own work. By combining conventional elements of the theatrical and literary tradition with his own deep learning and unique imagination, he created a drama that has strong ties to other forms and stories from the corpus of performing literature, but in its uniqueness transcends them all.

TOPICS FOR DISCUSSION

1. Trace the development of the characterization of Oriole, Student Zhang, and especially Crimson from the "Tale of Oriole" to the *Story of the Western Wing*. How are they altered by the formal requirements of each genre?

2. What is the significance of the name Crimson (*Hongniang*, literally "the red maiden")?

3. One of the interesting features of the *Story of the Western Wing* is that it deals so much with written communication and the misunderstanding of that communication. When an understanding is finally reached between Oriole and the student, it is relayed through the music of the zither. What does this say about the

trustworthiness of language in the text? Or about the relationship between language and feeling?

4. While Student Zhang is completely expressive of his feelings and pleasure in the text, Oriole is practically silent until a marriage contract is created. What does this say about the expression of female pleasure? How does one account for the fact that Oriole's physical existence occupies central narrative space while there is complete silence about that body's gratification? Is silence itself a structuring element in the text?

5. Eating and illness are two major themes in the play. What are their relationships to each other and to the progress of the love story?

6. Compare the lovers of the *Story of the Western Wing* and the *Dream of the Red Chamber*. How does the relationship of Jia Baoyu, Lin Daiyu, and the various maids of the novel compare with that of Student Zhang, Oriole, and Crimson?

REFERENCES

For a fine study and translation of "The Tale of Yingying," see James R. Hightower, "Yüan Chen and 'The Story of Ying-ying,' " in *Harvard Journal of Asiatic Studies* 32 (1973): 90–123. This translation has been reprinted in *Traditional Chinese Stories, Themes and Variations*, edited by Y. W. Ma and Joseph S. M. Lau, 139-45 (New York: Columbia University Press, 1978).

"The Story of the Western Wing in All Keys and Modes" has been translated into English by Li-li Ch'en as *Master Tung's Western Chamber Romance (Tung Hsi-hsiang chu-kung-tiao), A Chinese Chantefable* (Cambridge: Cambridge University Press, 1976).

The earliest translation of Wang Shifu's *Story of the Western Wing* into a European language dates to the French version of the eminent sinologue Stanislas Julien, which first appeared in 1872 in the pages of a periodical and was reissued in book form in 1880 as *Si-siang-ki ou l'Histoire du pavillon d'occident, Comédie en seize actes* (Geneve: H. Georg, Th. Mueller). From the very start of his career, Julien had been a student and translator of Yuan drama. He attempted to redress the eighteenth century prejudices against Chinese drama that stemmed from Prémare's early rendition of Ji Junxiang's *Orphan of Zhao (Zhaoshi guer)* with a new translation in 1839 and his translation of Li Xingdao's *The Chalk Circle (Huilan ji)* indirectly influenced Bertolt Brecht in his conception of *Der Kaukasische Kreidekreis*. The translation of the *Story of the Western Wing* was the crowning achievement of his lifelong involvement with Chinese vernacular literature. As in the case of all other western translators so far, Julien based himself on the Jin Shengtan edition of the text and accordingly only translated the four "authentic" plays of the cycle. His translation was primarily intended as a crib for students and was accompanied by extensive notes and even reprinted the Chinese text of the arias. The next western language translation to appear was the German rendition of all five plays by Vincenz Hundhausen in 1926, which was entitled *Das Westzimmer, Ein Chinesisches Singspiel aus dem dreizehnten Jahrhundert* (Eisenach: Erich Roth Verlag). This is a very free adaptation in the German tradition of *Nachdichtung* or "recreation" which allows the translator a very wide leeway in superimposing his own thoughts and fancies on the text of his choice. (His work created quite a scandal upon its appearance, and Hundhausen was accused by one of his reviewers of having plagiarized Julien's translation. Hundhausen sued the reviewer for libel and many members of the German sinological community one way or another became involved in the imbroglio. See the review of Hundhausen's translation by E. Haenisch in Asia Minor 8 [1932]: 278–82.)

In the mid-thirties, two English-language versions of the *Story of the Western Wing* appeared almost simultaneously. In 1936, Stanford University Press published Henry H. Hart's *The West Chamber, A Medieval Drama.* Hart also limited himself to a translation of the first four plays and even omitted the final act of the fourth play as in his opinion "it is an anticlimax and adds nothing to the interest of the play." In his preface, Hart chided Hundhausen for casting his rendition of the arias into rhymed couplets and called it "an effort which more often than not distorts the sense of the original." Accordingly, Hart presented the arias in his translation as free verse. Ironically, Hart's version has been "poeticized" by Henry W. Wells, who in 1972 published an adaptation of Hart's translation in which all prose passages had been recast into blank verse and all arias had been rhymed! ("*The West Chamber [Hsi-hsiang chi]*, Attributed to Wang Shih-fu, Rendered into English Verse by Henry W. Wells," in *Four Classical Asian Plays in Modern Translation*, comp. and ed. Vera Rushforth Irwin, pp. 95–230 [Baltimore: Penguin Books, 1972].)

The publication of Hart's rendition was preceded by one year by the publication of another, soon-to-become-standard, English language version by S.I. Hsiung, *The Romance of the Western Chamber (Hsi-hsiang chi)* (London: Methuen and Co., 1935), in which Hsiung translated all five plays. This edition was reissued in 1968 by Columbia University Press with a new introduction by C.T. Hsia, who regretted that the translator based himself on the Jin Shengtan edition instead of using one of the earlier Ming editions.

A new translation of the *Hongzhi* edition appeared in 1991: Stephen H. West and Wilt L. Idema, *The Moon and the Zither: A Study and Translation of the Hongzhi Edition of the Story of the Western Wing* (Berkeley: University of California Press, 1991). This is a translation of the complete and unbowdlerized text with extensive textual and historical notes.

IV
Japanese Texts

Japanese Texts: Lyric

THE *MAN'YŌSHŪ* AND *KOKINSHŪ* COLLECTIONS

Donald Keene

THE *MAN'YŌSHŪ*

The *Man'yōshū* is the first, and in the opinion of most scholars of Japanese literature, the greatest collection of Japanese poetry. The exact period of the compilation is unknown, but the last dated poem was composed in 759, and the final selection of poems probably took place soon afterwards. The name of the compiler is not given, but there is strong reason to believe that Ōtomo no Yakamochi (718?–85), an important poet and sometime governor, edited the bulk of the *Man'yōshū* and possibly the entire work. The last four of the twenty books of the collection are given over so largely to his poetry that they have even been called his "poem diary."

The three characters used to write the name of the collection, *man*, *yō*, and *shū*, mean literally "Ten Thousand Leaves Collection," and it has been generally supposed that this was a figurative way of referring to the large number of poems contained in the collection, 4,516 in all; "ten thousand" (*man*), like the English word "myriad," was often used to express any large number. According to the theory first advanced by scholars of Chinese literature, however, "ten thousand leaves" was a poetic way of saying "ten thousand ages," and was so used in numerous Chinese texts. Even if we accept this emendation, it does not entirely clear up the ambiguity: should "ten thousand ages" be interpreted as an exaggerated description of the perhaps 400 years of poetry included in the *Man'yōshū*, or should it be interpreted as signifying that the collection was destined to last for ten thousand years? The meaning of the title remains to be determined.

The vast majority of the poems in the *Man'yōshū* are in the form of the tanka—a poem in five lines consisting respectively of

5, 7, 5, 7, and 7 syllables. (The lack of a stress accent in Japanese and the excessive ease of rhyming caused poets to depend on syllabics as a means of distinguishing poetry from prose.) The masterpieces of the collection, however, are the *chōka* (long poems), of which there are 265 examples. A *chōka* was written in alternating lines of 5 and 7 syllables with an additional line of 7 syllables at the end. The longest examples run to over 150 lines. There are also sixty-two poems in non-traditional forms, including four in Chinese. The oldest poem of the collection, if we can accept the traditional attribution, is the first, said to have been composed by the Emperor Yūryaku (reigned 457–79). Many poems bear prefaces composed in classical Chinese giving the circumstances of composition, which are usually not otherwise apparent because of the brevity of the tanka.

The poems were recorded in an extraordinarily complicated script. Chinese characters were used sometimes for their meaning, sometimes merely to transcribe Japanese sounds. The problems encountered when reading texts that combine two entirely different systems of writing, neither suited to the Japanese language, are enormous, and some poems have not yet been given definitive pronunciations. When a new system of writing, the *kana*, was invented in the ninth century it was so much more suited to writing Japanese than the earlier systems that people forgot how to read the *Man'yōshū*, and the collection as a whole was not rediscovered until the seventeenth century, though poems known as songs had survived.

The absorption of Chinese learning, originally undertaken mainly in the hopes of strengthening the country politically in face of the vastly more evolved continental culture, greatly enriched Japanese poetry, as we can tell by comparing the poems in the *Man'yōshū* with those in the even earlier *Kojiki* (*Record of Ancient Matters*), an account of Japan from the creation until the sixth century, which is virtually free of Chinese influence. New themes and new modes of expression were quickly adopted by the Japanese poets almost as soon as they came into contact with books of poetry from the continent. This influence is most readily apparent in the poems composed in Chinese by members of the court. In contrast, the *Man'yōshū* on first reading may seem almost untouched by this influence, but it is nonetheless present, and helps to account for the superiority of *Man'yōshū* poems to those in the *Kojiki*.

Although the Japanese were eager to improve their poetry by incorporating Chinese poetic techniques, they remained reluctant to use borrowed Chinese words in their poetry. This reluctance was maintained by tanka poets until the late nineteenth century. It is as if English poets after the Norman conquest had absorbed the techniques and subject matter of French poetry but had refused until the twentieth century to use any words not of pure Anglo-Saxon origin. Of the 6,343 different words in the *Man'yōshū*, all those of Chinese origin (with two exceptions only) are found in the heavily Buddhist Book XVI. Such words as *hōshi* (priest) and *dan'ochi* (parishioner) were probably used because no "pure" Japanese equivalents existed. A few words such as *ume* (plum; Chinese *mei*) and *yanagi* (willow; Chinese *yang*) were earlier borrowings that by this time had been assimilated into the Japanese language.

The *Man'yōshū* is unique among anthologies of Japanese poetry in the variety of its poetic forms, its subject matter, and its authors. Although the great majority of the poems are the short tanka, there are also dialogues and various other unusual poetic forms. However, the *chōka* are the glory of the collection. The *chōka* survived vestigially in some later collections, but the masters of this form were all *Man'yōshū* poets.

The content of the poetry is also exceptional. In most later anthologies the tanka are generally about the seasons or about love, but in the *Man'yōshū* many tanka describe travel, and there are also tanka of both humorous and deeply religious meaning. The *chōka* include elegies for deceased princes and princesses, poems commemorating events of national significance, and expressions of grief over the departure of soldiers for the frontier. Some poems reveal specific Chinese or Buddhist influence, such as those that praise liquor in the manner of the Taoists or those that insist in Buddhist fashion on the transitoriness of life.

The authorship of the poems is also exceptional in that poems by persons of humble status, in no way associated with the court, were included. It may be that some poems attributed to soldiers on the frontier or to rustics were in fact composed by courtiers assuming these roles, but many were surely by plebeian authors. In the *Kokinshū* and later imperial collections such poems were usually said to be "anonymous."

Perhaps the quality of the *Man'yōshū* that most clearly distinguishes it from later Japanese poetry, however, is the directness of the expression of the poets' emotions. Later poets, largely because the tanka form was so short, tended to rely on suggestion to fill out what was actually stated, but the *Man'yōshū* poets, free to extend their poems beyond the five lines of a tanka, could give full vent to their feelings in a *chōka*. Eighteenth-century scholars of national learning referred to the "masculinity" (*masuraoburi*) of such expression and contrasted it with the "femininity" (*tawayameburi*) found in the later imperial collections. This is an oversimplification, but it accounts for the popularity of the *Man'yōshū* during the war years of 1941–45, when the "feminine" indirectness of the *Kokinshū* fell into disfavor, and innumerable studies of the "spirit" (*seishin*) of the *Man'yōshū* appeared.

The particular strength of the *Man'yōshū* poets was their ability to treat truly tragic, as opposed to merely sad emotions, and to confront harshly dramatic, as opposed to merely touching human experiences. For example, a fair number of poems describe the poet's reflections on seeing a dead body by the side of the road or on the shore. Dead bodies do not appear in the *Kokinshū*; the rules of good taste had come to dominate poetic composition, and the poets believed that the falling of the cherry blossoms, no less than the sight of a corpse, could stir in the beholder an awareness of the impermanence of this world. Some poems on cherry blossoms do indeed convey so poignant a sense of the passing of time as to bring tears to the reader's eyes, but the dramatic impact of falling cherry blossoms is obviously not as strong as that of the sight of a corpse washed by the waves.

The poems in the *Man'yōshū* fall into three main groups: love poems (*sōmon*), elegies (*banka*) and miscellaneous poems (*zōka*). Over half the poems in the collection are about love, most often described in terms of unhappy or frustrated love affairs; this is true also of the love poetry in later anthologies. The elegies are usually public poems that treat the deaths of members of the court and were probably written by court poets in response to commands of emperors or high officials, but some elegies are private, mourning the death of the wife or child of the poet. The public elegies were apparently composed in keeping with funerary practices observed during the seventh century. It was customary to place the body of a deceased member of the imperial family in a temporary shrine for an indeterminate period of time, during which the person was considered to be not dead but in a kind of limbo where he could hear words addressed to him. After 700, when the first recorded cremation occurred, poets were no longer called on to compose elegies in which they assured the dead that they would never be forgotten, thereby inducing them not to return to this world as malevolent spirits. The miscellaneous poems of the *Man'yōshū* are those that do not fit into either of the above two categories.

The greatest of the *Man'yōshū* poets, Kakinomoto no Hitomaro, composed all of his datable works during a period of some ten years at the end of the seventh century. This corresponds to the reign of the Empress Jitō, who ascended the throne in 686 after the death of her husband, the Emperor Temmu, and who continued to rule until her death in 702 even after she formally yielded the throne to a young emperor. Little is known about Hitomaro's life, but we know from his poetry that he served Jitō as a poet laureate, accompanying her on her visits to Yoshino and elsewhere, and composing poetry commemorating such occasions. Hitomaro's devotion to Jitō and the rest of the imperial family was absolute; it can hardly be doubted that he believed in the divinity of the empress he served.

Hitomaro has been called a "professional court poet." This should not suggest that he received payment for his poems; probably he depended financially on his stipend as an official, and wrote poetry because people at the court recognized his skill. In his elegies he expressed a grief that seems wholly appropriate and believable, though he may never have met the dead prince or princess he mourns. He certainly did not employ the conventional language one expects of a poet laureate who is obliged to produce a poem on state occasions even if they do not interest him. Ironically, Hitomaro is so convincing in his poems that describe matters he could not have known from personal experience that doubts have been expressed about the truthfulness of poems in which he narrates personal grief.

Regardless of the degree of literal truth in Hitomaro's poems, their poetic truth is incontestable. One theme runs through his poetry, a yearning for the past, and regret over what has disappeared. A sense of contrast between eternal nature and the transience of man gives poignancy to his observations and universality to his sorrow.

It was long customary to say that Yamabe no Akahito was the second most important poet of the *Man'yōshū*, but today at least two other *Man'yōshū* poets—Yamanoue no Okura and Ōtomo no Yakamochi—are ranked higher than Akahito. His reputation in the past owed much to his special mastery of the tanka, which became the standard verse form for a thousand years. Although thirteen of the fifty poems of Akahito in the *Man'yōshū* are *chōka*, they have not been praised nearly so much as the tanka—some, "envoys" (*hanka*), appended to his longer poems. His *chōka* on Yoshino, for example, is pleasant but unmemorable, and his mentions of the mountains and clear streams, lacking the specificity that Hitomaro would have given them, seem to have been chosen mainly to suggest the peace and prosperity of the reign. However, in the envoys Akahito beautifully evoked the atmosphere of

Yoshino. He was especially admired by later poets because of his skill in conveying with the few words of a tanka the beauty of nature, the subject that most appealed to them; the grandeur of Hitomaro lay beyond their field of vision.

In contrast to the diminished reputation of Akahito, that of Yamanoue no Okura (660?–733?) has sharply risen in the twentieth century, and he now ranks second only to Hitomaro in the esteem he enjoys among general readers. His poems include examples (rare in Japanese literature of the past) with social and intellectual concerns. They are often introduced by prefaces in Chinese that explain the underlying philosophical truths, whether Confucian, Buddhist, or Taoist. This distinctiveness in Okura's poetry has been attributed to his birth in Korea. According to proponents of this theory, Okura and his father fled to Japan from the Korean kingdom of Paekche in 663, the year of the disastrous defeat of the Japanese army in Korea at Hakusukinoe. The main literary significance of this discovery, assuming it is true, is that Okura would have obtained from his father a better education in the Confucian classics and possibly in Buddhism than most Japanese of that time.

We possess almost no information about Okura before he was appointed in 701 as a member of an embassy to China. He was only a minor official, but probably his superior knowledge of Chinese earned him a position within the embassy. After his return to Japan, he rose slowly within the official hierarchy, finally becoming governor of Chikuzen in 725 or 726.

Okura's reputation is based mainly on three or four *chōka* that are unique among the poems of the *Man'yōshū*. The prefaces to the poems often state a didactic purpose that might not be apparent from the poems themselves. For example, the poem entitled "Poem to Set a Confused Heart Straight" bears this preface:

> There is a certain type of man who knows he should honor his father and mother, but forgets to discharge his filial duties with devotion. He does not concern himself with his wife and children, but treats them more lightly than a pair of discarded shoes. . . . Though his spirit may soar free among the blue clouds, his body still remains among the dust of this world.

The poem contains an attack on the indifference to worldly obligations taught by the Taoists. It insists on both the family relationships dear to Confucianists and the ascetic discipline of the Buddhists.

Other poems by Okura treat such subjects as the impermanence of human life and the suffering that comes with old age. These themes were not unique to him, but Okura's expression is so powerful that any similarity in material to other poems in the *Man'yōshū* is quickly forgotten. His poem on the "difficulty of living in this world" contains this memorable passage:

> Few are the nights they keep.
> When, sliding back the plank doors,
> They reach their beloved ones,
> And sleep, arms intertwined,
> Before, with staffs at their waists,
> They totter along the road,
> Laughed at here, and hated there.

The most celebrated of Okura's poems is his "Dialogue on Poverty." The dialogue is between two men, the first a poor but proud man who wonders how people worse off than himself manage to survive, the second a destitute man who indirectly answers the first man's questions by describing his misery. During the next thousand years not another such poem would be composed in Japanese. Okura's ability to enter into the feelings of two persons who live under conditions he probably never himself experienced may have been fostered by observations he made when serving as the governor of a remote province. It is remarkable all the same that he should have thought two such unpoetic figures worthy of being described in a *chōka*.

The final period of the *Man'yōshū* was dominated by Ōtomo no Yakamochi. His poetry lacks the grandeur of Hitomaro's and the social concern of Okura's, but his voice is distinctive and the range of his poetry is exceptional. One of Yakamochi's best-known poems, favored especially during periods of nationalism, is the one he composed in 749 after the discovery of gold in the province of Mutsu. This was the first time gold had been found in Japan, and it could not have come at a more opportune time: the great statue of Buddha, erected in Nara by command of the Emperor Shōmu, could now be given a coating of gold. The emperor declared at the ceremonies during which the statue was consecrated that he was the "servant of the Three Treasures" of Buddhism. He also issued at this time a proclamation in which he quoted the oath of loyalty to the throne made centuries earlier by the Ōtomo family. Yakamochi was overcome by this recognition of the services rendered by his family, which despite its ancient lineage had suffered an eclipse, and in his *chōka* celebrating the discovery of gold he referred to his family's maxim of loyalty.

With the rise of the Fujiwara, a rival clan, the Ōtomo family once more fell into disfavor. Yakamochi did not suffer the severe punishment meted out to leaders of his family (on the grounds that they had forgotten their traditional obligation to defend the court), but in 758 he was appointed governor of Inaba, a remote and unimportant province. This was tantamount to exile; being an Ōtomo, even one uninvolved in politics, was a crime in the eyes of the Fujiwara. On New Year's Day of 759, at his post in Inaba, Yakamochi composed the tanka that is the last datable poem in the *Man'yōshū*. Yakamochi was in his forty-second year when he composed it, and lived twenty-six years longer, but no poems from this period of his life are known to survive.

His most appealing poems are three tanka composed in 753. Here is the third:

uraraka ni	In the tranquil sun of spring
tereru haruhi ni	A lark soars singing;
hibari agari	Sad is my burdened heart,
kokoroganashi mo	Thoughtful and alone.
hitori shi omoeba	

This note is appended to the poem: "In the languid rays of the spring sun, a lark is singing. This mood of melancholy cannot be removed except by poetry: hence I have composed this poem in order to dispel my gloom." Yakamochi is most attractive when he writes in this sort of private situation, rather than in response to a public occasion. His melancholy, stemming from vague sentiments of frustration and isolation, colors his best-known tanka, which are closer in tone to the poems of the *Kokinshū* than to the early *Man'yōshū* poetry.

THE *KOKINSHŪ*

The *Kokin Waka Shū* (*Collection of Waka, Old and New*) is usually referred to by the shortened form of the title, *Kokinshū*. It was the first imperially sponsored collection of poetry in Japanese. The date of the presentation of the completed text to the Emperor Daigo is usually stated to be 905, though some scholars disagree. The circumstances of compilation are not known, but the four editors apparently chose works for inclusion from existing collections of poetry by both known and unknown authors. Poems by 127 poets were included. Not surprisingly, the best represented poets were the compilers themselves. Ki no Tsurayuki (868?–946), the best-known *Kokinshū* poet and the author of the Japanese preface, was represented by 102 poems out of a total of 1,111 poems, and the other three compilers contributed a total of 141 poems.

The *Kokinshū*, following the example of the *Man'yōshū*, is in twenty books, but the divisions into books was far more systematic. The first six books are devoted to poems about the seasons, two books each of spring and autumn poems, and one book each of summer and winter poems. The beauties of the seasons, especially the flowers and birds associated with each, came to be considered the most typical subjects of Japanese poetry, though they had not figured prominently in the Man'yōshū. A large proportion of the poems composed during the next millennium would describe the seasons, either directly or by referring to such characteristic phenomena of the different seasons as haze, mist, fog, sleet, and so on. Some seasonal words became arbitrary: the moon, unless qualified by another seasonal word, was always the autumn moon, the moon whose light was most appreciated. In the haiku, a much later development in Japanese poetry, the presence of a seasonal word was not merely desirable but absolutely essential. Japanese sometimes explain this insistence in terms of the distinctiveness of the four seasons in Japan, but probably it is safest to content oneself with noting that as far back as the *Kokinshū*, poets were unusually sensitive to the seasons.

Summer and winter were given only half the number of books received by spring and autumn poems. This marked preference among the seasons seems to reflect the climate of Kyōto, where springs and autumns are delectable, but the summers stifling and the winters bitterly cold. The choice of birds and flowers celebrated in the *Kokinshū* poems were also typical of Kyōto, and even poets who lived in regions where the *hototogisu* (a kind of cuckoo) was never heard would dutifully mention it in their summer poems.

The six books of seasonal poems are followed by one each of congratulatory, parting, travel, and "hidden names" poems.[1] Then follow five books of love poetry. The prominence of love poetry (some 360 poems) reflects its importance during the ninth century, the "dark age" of poetry in the Japanese language, when men of the court wrote their compositions in Chinese, and only the circumstance that women normally did not learn Chinese obliged them to compose *waka* as a part of courtship. Love continued to rank as an important, indeed essential subject of Japanese poetry, although in China the major poets seldom described their loves.

The remaining books of the *Kokinshū* are relatively unimportant; the last two in particular give the impression of having been appended mainly to fill up the assigned twenty books. Once the selected poems were assigned to the various books, the compilers had to arrange the poems within each book. They could have followed the example of *Kaifūsō*, the first collection of poems written in Chinese by members of the Japanese court, and arranged the poems in descending order by rank of the author. Or, they could have followed the *Man'yōshū* and clustered together poems by the same authors. Instead, the compilers arranged the poems in terms of temporal progression. In the case of spring poems, those that described the first haze headed the section, followed by poems on the early blooming plum blossoms, then by cherry blossoms in the bud, in full glory, and finally scattered. In the love poems the first tremors were followed by hidden love, the anguish of unrequited love, and finally resignation, tracing the course of a typically unhappy love affair.

Many poems are preceded by brief introductions in prose that describe the circumstances of composition, but far more valuable to the understanding of the work as a whole is the preface in Japanese by Ki no Tsurayuki, the first statement on the special qualities of Japanese poetry. He attributed to poetry the power to "move heaven and earth, smooth the relations between men and women, and calm the hearts of fierce warriors." Of these three powers, the ability to "smooth relations between men and women" is given by far the greatest prominence in the *Kokinshū*. In contrast to a common justification for poetry found in the prefaces to collections of poetry in Chinese, there is no suggestion that poetry may be of use in promoting good government. Tsurayuki listed instead the occasions that inspired Japanese poets of the past to write poetry:

> . . . when seeing the blossoms fall on a spring morn, hearing the leaves fall on an autumn evening, they sighed to see the drifts of snow and ripples in the mirror increase with each passing year; when they were startled to realize the brevity of life on seeing dew on the grass or the foam on the waters; when those who yesterday were prosperous had now lost their influence; or when falling in the world, they had become estranged from those they had loved.[2]

These occasions for poetry can be resumed under one general theme, sorrow over the passage of time, whether in the sights of nature or in one's looking glass that shows the snow (white hair) and ripples (wrinkles) of old age. A painful awareness of the passage of time is typical of the *Kokinshū* and distinguishes it most conspicuously from the anthologies of Chinese poetry with which the Japanese were familiar. Nostalgia for the past is one of the keys of understanding Japanese lyricism.

Although Japanese poetry was credited in Tsurayuki's preface with the ability to move the gods and demons, its tone was subdued. A blunt statement, no matter how powerfully expressed, would have seemed crude to the *Kokinshū* poets who sought perfection in the language, the order of the words, and the music of successive syllables even more than in the meanings of the poems. Many subjects could not be treated because they were considered to be vulgar or, at any rate, unattractive. This kept the poets from treating large areas of human experience, but they did not feel frustrated. It was only when in the moods described in the preface that they felt impelled to express themselves in Japanese (as opposed to Chinese) poetry, and they gladly obeyed the rules of taste established by the court though this tended to favor artificiality and even insincerity. Poems were often composed in connection with competitions during which participants were divided into two teams and were required to compose *waka* on assigned themes, regardless whether or not these themes reflected the poets' actual feelings.

Perhaps none of the poems composed by Ki no Tsurayuki and his generation are sincere in the manner that *Man'yōshū* poetry is sincere. The love poetry, for example, almost never describes the joys of love but, rather, the impossibility of enjoying happiness with the beloved, a more "poetic" theme. The language of the love poems tends to be lachrymose, and the pathetic fallacy is much in evidence: birds, deer, insects and even plants join in the poet's suffering. The narrowness of court society provided yet another theme, the fear of hostile gossip.

The imagery of *Kokinshū* poetry, whether seasonal, amorous, or miscellaneous, tends to be repeated. Many poems describe cherry blossoms at all stages of their flowering, but there are few or none on such familiar flowers as the chrysanthemum. Poets usually reacted more to other poets than to their own personal experiences. Even if a poet happened to have been struck by the beauty of peach blossoms, for example, he would not have been so daring as to write about blossoms that had been ignored by his predecessors but would have dutifully described instead the scent of plum blossoms or the clouds of cherry blossoms. Perhaps the compilers rejected poems that employed unusual imagery, but whatever the reason, the *Kokinshū* established a poetic diction—some 2,000 words in all—that would be observed with only minor additions by poets of the next thousand years. Not only was the vocabulary restricted, but the associations of flowers, trees, and birds were established. Japanese poets did not fret over these limitations on their expression; all the *Kokinshū* poets wanted to say could be said clearly and beautifully with the vocabulary at their disposal.

The success of the *Kokinshū* is to be measured not only in terms of its intrinsic merits but also in the influence it exerted on later poetry and prose. One might argue that it is the central work of Japanese literature, providing the basic poetic knowledge expected of every educated person until recent times. It was quoted again and again, and variations on its themes were made by countless poets of later date. Tsurayuki wrote in the preface:

> We rejoice that we were born in this generation and that we were able to live in the era when this event [the compilation of the *Kokinshū*] occurred. Hitomaro is dead, but poetry is still with us. Times may change, joy and sorrow come and go, but the words of these poems are eternal, long as the trailing vines, permanent as birds' tracks. Those who know poetry and who understand the heart of things will look up to the old and admire the new as they look up to and admire the moon in the broad sky.[3]

It was unusual for a Japanese not to have wished to have been born in some golden age in the past, but Tsurayuki's confidence in the lasting value of the collection that he and his associates had compiled was fully merited. Perhaps the compilers were overly successful. The poetic vocabulary that they handled so brilliantly was not merely a legacy to poets of future generations but tended to restrict what they could say, and its conventions— such as a feigned perplexity over whether they saw cherry blossoms or snow—were repeated long after they lost their freshness. Many poets of later generations incorporated one or more lines from the *Kokinshū* in their poems, not by way of plagiarism, and certainly not to parody, but as part of an attempt to come even slightly closer than their predecessors to the heart of a perception.

Tsurayuki declared in his preface that Japanese poetry had its "seeds in the human heart." The artifice of some poems in the *Kokinshū*, especially when compared to those in the *Man'yōshū*, may make us question this statement, but Tsurayuki intended no deceit. These poems, written in Japanese at a time when the prestige of Chinese was much greater, were ultimately based not on artifice but on the emotions of the poets; their sensitivity, whether in response to nature or to the vicissitudes of love affairs, was genuine. A poem in thirty-one syllables is limited in what it can state, but the *Kokinshū* poets were able to transcend the limitations of the form and express under the flawlessly finished exteriors sentiments that can still move us.

TOPICS FOR DISCUSSION

1. Similarities between *Man'yōshū* poetry and that in other literatures: What makes the poems affecting even to someone unfamiliar with Japanese culture? It has often been stated that the poetry of the *Man'yōshū* is prevailingly masculine. Does this seem a meaningful judgment?

2. Does the list given in the Preface to the *Kokinshū* of the circumstances under which poetry is most likely to be composed accord with the poetry itself? In what ways does the *Kokinshū* poetry seem most unlike that of the *Man'yōshū*? Do the *Kokinshū* poets succeed in overcoming the limitation they imposed on themselves by restricting their poetic expression to one form, the tanka?

3. The *Kokinshū* has often been said to be a "feminine" collection. Does this opinion seem justified? Can you find antecedents in the *Man'yōshū* for the most characteristic *Kokinshū* poetry?

4. Both the *Man'yōshū* and the *Kokinshū* were for the most part the work of court poets. Compare and contrast this with the poetry composed in other countries.

NOTES

1. By "hidden names" (*butsumei*) was meant poems that contain puns on place-names and other proper nouns artfully concealed in the text.
2. Translation by Laurel Rasplica Rodd in *Kokinshū*, p. 41.
3. Ibid., p. 47.

REFERENCES

Levy, Ian Hideo, trans. *Man'yōshū*. 4 vols. Princeton: Princeton University Press, 1981.

McCullough, Helen Craig. *Kokin Wakashū*. Stanford: Stanford University Press, 1985.

Nippon Gakujutsu Shinkōkai, trans. *The Manyōshū*. New York: Columbia University Press, 1969.

Rodd, Laurel Rasplica, et al., trans. *Kokinshū*. Princeton: Princeton University Press, 1984.

Lyric Text: Japanese

A Japanese *Waka*

by Ono no Komachi (mid-9th c.)
from the *Kokinshu*, no. 1030, msc. volume

Translated by Haruo Shirane

人　　　に　　　あはむ

hito　　　　　ni　　　　　　　　awamu
("person")　(indirect object　("meet")
("him")　　　particle)

月　　　　の　　　なき　　　よ　　　は

tsuki　　　　no　　　　　　naki　　　　yo　　　　wa
("moon")　　(possessive　("not have")　("night")　(subject marker)
("opportunity")　particle)

[On this night of no moon when there is no opporunity to meet him]

思ひをきて

omoiokite
("rise up in longing")
(the i or hi in omoi also means "fire")
(oki means "embers, live charcoal")

むね　　はしり火　　に

mune　　　　　hashiribi　　　　　ni
("breast")　　("flying flames")　　(particle indicating place)
(mune hashiri means: "the breast heaves, pounds")

心　やけをり

kokoro　yakeori
("heart")　("burns")
　　　　　(yake also means "fret," "fume")

[I rise up in longing, my breast heaving, my heart burning in the flying flames.]

Waka are thirty-one syllable Japanese poems.

Kakekotoba ("pivot-word") creates two or more words out of a single word. For example, *tsuki* means both "moon" and "opportunity," *omoi* means "to long for" and the *i* in *omoi* means "fire," *okite* means "to wake up" and *oki* means "embers."

Engo ("associate words") are words linked by imagistic association. "Fire" (*hi*), "embers" (*oki*), "flying flames" (*hashiribi*), and "burn" (*yake*) are all *engo*.

The condensed nature of the poems, particularly the multiplicity of meanings for each word or phrase, as well as the wealth of implied meaning or significance, leads to a wide range of translations, as the following examples show.

> Hito ni awamu
> Tsuki no naki yo wa
> Omoiokite
> Mune hashiribi ni
> Kokoro yakeori

———

This night of no moon
There is no way to meet him.
I rise in longing—
My breast pounds, a leaping flame,
My heart consumed in flame.

> Translated by Donald Keene.
> *Anthology of Japanese Literature*, Grove Press, 1955.

On such a night as this
When the lack of moonlight shades your way to me,
I wake from sleep my passion blazing,
My breast a fire raging, exploding flame
While within me my heart chars.

> Translated by Robert Brower and Earl Miner.
> *Japanese Court Poetry*, Stanford University Press, 1961.

On those moonless night
when I long in vain for him,
   love robs me of sleep
and my agitated heart
burns like a crackling fire.

> Translated by Helen Craig McCullough.
> *Kokin Wakashū*, Stanford University Press, 1985.

THE POETRY OF MATSUO BASHŌ

Haruo Shirane

The modern haiku derives from the seventeen-syllable *hokku* (opening verse) of a *haikai no renga*, or comic linked-verse sequence. These usually consisted of from thirty-six to one hundred links composed in alternate verses of seventeen (5/7/5) and fourteen (7/7) syllables by one or more poets. In the seventeenth century (or early Edo period [1600–1867]), when Matsuo Bashō (1644–94) began his career as a *haikai* poet, the *hokku* was regarded primarily as the beginning of a linked-verse (*renga*) sequence. Bashō considered himself to be, first and foremost, a comic linked-verse poet and was a *haikai* teacher by profession, but he often composed independent *hokku*—commonly referred to by modern readers as haiku—for which he is primarily known today and which lie at the heart of his prose narratives.

In a linked-verse session, the author of the *hokku* was required to include a *kigo* (seasonal word), which functioned as a greeting to the gathered poets and established a special line of communication between the poet and the audience—a connection that proved crucial to the independent *hokku*. In the course of poetic history, the seasonal words used in classical poetry (the thirty-one-syllable *waka* and later orthodox-linked verse, or *renga*) had come to embody particular emotions, moods, and images. Thus, "spring rain" (*harusame*), which always meant a soft, steady drizzle, brought sweet thoughts; the endless, oppressive "summer rain" (*samidare*) connoted depression; and the cold and sporadic "early winter showers" (*shigure*) were associated with the uncertainty and impermanence of life. The importance of seasonal words in the *hokku* is evident in the following poems from the beginning and end of Bashō's *The Narrow Road to the Deep North*

(*Oku no hosomichi*), which describes his journey of 1689:

yuku haru ya	The passing spring:
tori naki uo no	Birds cry, and in the eyes
me wa namida	Of fish are tears.
hamaguri no	A clam being parted
futami ni wakare	From its shell at Futami—
yuku aki zo	The passing autumn.[1]

The two respective seasonal references, "the passing spring" (*yuku haru*) and "the passing autumn" (*yuku aki*), indicate more than the temporal dimensions of the poems; in the classical tradition they are strongly associated with the sorrow of separation, particularly that caused by a journey. In the opening poem, nature at large—here represented by birds and fish—connotations of the seasonal word, the poem also expresses Bashō's sorrow at leaving behind his friends. In the final poem, the departure of autumn (and implicitly that of Bashō) becomes as difficult and as painful as prying apart the shell of a clam. On the surface, the two poems appear to depict only nature, but the seasonal words, coupled with the larger context, underscore a recurrent theme of *The Narrow Road to the Deep North*: the sorrow of the eternal traveler.

Haikai, or comic linked verse, deliberately employs contemporary language and subject matter, which was forbidden in classical poetry. The sense of the comic that informs *haikai* usually derives from humorous subject matter, from verbal play, and from parody of traditional poetry and literature. Ichū, a *haikai* theorist of the Danrin school, once stated that "a poem that draws on the literary tradition and at the same time parodies it is *haikai*." The same is true of much of Bashō's poetry, though in a more subtle manner than in earlier *haikai*. A good example is Bashō's famous frog poem, which marks the beginning of his mature poetry, in the so-called Bashō-style:

furu ike ya	An ancient pond—
kawazu tobikomu	A frog leaps in,
mizu no oto	The sound of water.
	(1686)

Kawazu (frog), a seasonal word for spring, was a popular poetic topic, appearing as early as the *Manyōshū* (*Collection of Ten Thousand Leaves*, 759), the first major anthology of Japanese poetry.

The following *waka* (vol. 10, no. 2165) appears in a section on frogs:

kami tsu se ni	On the upper rapids
kawazu tsuma yobu	A frog calls for his lover.
yū sareba	Is it because,
koromode sasumimi	His sleeves chilled by the evening,
tsuma makamu toka	He wants to share his pillow?

By the Heian period (late eighth to late twelfth c.), the *kawazu* was almost exclusively associated with the blossoms of the *yamabuki* (kerria), the bright yellow mountain rose, and with limpid mountain streams, as in the following anonymous spring poem from the *Kokinshū* (*Collection of Old and New Poems*, 908):

kawazu naku	At Ide, where the frogs cry,
Ide no yamabuki	The yellow rose
chirinikeri	Has already scattered.
hana no sakari ni	If only I had come when
awamashi mono o	The flowers were in full bloom!

In the medieval period, the poet was often required to compose on the poetic essence (*hon'i*) of a given topic. By then, the *hon'i* of the *kawazu* had become its beautiful voice. In a fashion typical of *haikai*, Bashō's poem on the frog works against these traditional associations. In place of the plaintive voice of the frog singing in the rapids or calling out for his lover, Bashō gives us the plop of the frog jumping into the water. And instead of the elegant image of a frog in a fresh mountain stream beneath the bright yellow rose, the *hokku* presents a stagnant pond. One of Bashō's disciples suggested that the first line be "A yellow rose—" (*yamabuki ya*), an image that would have remained within the associative bounds of traditional poetry. Bashō's version, by contrast, provides a surprising and witty twist on the classical perception of frogs.

This is not to say that Bashō rejects the seasonal association of the frog with spring. The *kawazu* appears in spring, summer, and autumn, but in the seasonal handbooks used by both Bashō and his readers, the frog is listed in the category of mid-spring, along with insects and reptiles that emerge from underground hibernation during that season. As a seasonal word, the frog thus deepens the contrast or tension between the first half of the poem, the image of an old pond—the atmosphere of long silence and rest—and the second part, a moment in spring, when life and vitality have suddenly (with a surprising plop) returned to the world.

In Bashō's time, the seasonal words in *haikai* formed a vast pyramid, capped at the top by the key seasonal topics (*kidai*) of the classical tradition—cherry blossoms (spring), the cuckoo (summer), the moon (autumn), and the snow (winter)—that remained the most popular subjects even for early Edo *haikai* poets. Spreading out from this narrow peak were the other seasonal topics derived from classical poetry. Occupying the bottom and the widest area were the *kigo*, which by Bashō's day literally numbered in the thousands. In contrast to the seasonal topics at the peak, which were highly conventional and conceptual, those that formed the base were drawn from and directly reflected contemporary life. Unlike the elegant diction of the words at the top of the pyramid, the new words at the ever-expanding base were earthy, sometimes vulgar, and drawn from a variety of "tongues," particularly those of popular Edo culture and society.

Bashō's place in *haikai* history can be defined by his attempt to tread the "narrow road" between the complex, rigidly defined, aesthetic order centered on traditional seasonal topics and a strongly antitraditional movement that sought to break out and explore new topics, new subject matter, and new poetic language. As the frog poem suggests, Bashō draws on the classical tradition, not in order to return to it, but to infuse it with new life. Indeed, for those aware of the cluster of associations that had accumulated around the seasonal words, the beauty of Bashō's poetry often lies, as it does in the frog poem, in the subtle and ironic tension between the traditional associations and the new presentation.

It has often been noted that the effect of the frog poem derives from the intersection of the momentary and the eternal, of movement and stillness. The two parts of the poem interpenetrate: the sound of the frog accentuating the stillness of the ancient pond and the quiet atmosphere highlighting the momentary. A similar effect can be found in the following poem, also from *The Narrow Road to the Deep North*:

shizukasa ya	How still it is!
iwa ni shimiiru	Penetrating the rocks,
semi no koe	The cicada's shrill.
	(1689)

In this summer poem, the cries of the cicada, which seem to sink into the surrounding rocks, intensify the profound feeling of silence. According to Ogata Tsutomu, a modern commentator, the spirit of the speaker becomes one with the voice of the cicada and penetrates the rock, arriving at a deep, inner silence.[2] In a number of *hokku* written by Bashō at this time, a small, vulnerable, or fragile creature—a cicada, a frog, a cricket, etc.—is cast against a temporally or spatially unbound setting, creating a feeling of loneliness (*sabishisa*). This poignant and tender mood is savored and appreciated for the inner peace and quiet communion with nature that it brings.

In early Edo *haikai*, the comic element derived almost entirely from parody of classical poetry (*waka* and orthodox linked verse), from the playful destruction of the aesthetic world created by classical tradition. Many of Bashō's earlier poems are in fact clever displays of wit that make light of the conventions of classical poetry. However, Matsuo Bashō's mature poetry, which begins from the period of the frog poem, transformed *haikai* into a serious form that embraced larger human and worldly concerns even as it retained its comic roots. The comic element in Bashō's mature poems usually derives from a sense of "newness" (*atarashimi*) or the unexpected, which brings a wry smile rather than the laughter typical of earlier *haikai*. In the frog poem, it is the unexpected, sudden plop of the frog that provides the comic overtone. The solemn opening line, "An ancient pond—" (*furuike ya*), however, tempers and internalizes this comic aspect, making it part of a highly meditative poem. This ironical movement or tension, which is both serious and light, profound and minor, is sometimes called *sabi*, a hallmark of Bashō's mature style.

Bashō and his disciples speak broadly of two fundamental kinds of *hokku*: the "single-topic" (*ichimotsu shitate*) *hokku* and the "combination" (*toriawase*) *hokku*. Examples of "single-topic" *hokku* by Bashō are:

kegoromo ni	In fur robes,
tsutsumite nukushi	They are warmly wrapped—
kamo no ashi	The feet of the wild duck.
	(1693)

bii to naku	Crying "Bee—,"
shirigoe kanashi	The sadness of the trailing voice—
yoru no shika	A deer at night.
	(1694)

Each poem describes a single topic, the feet of a wild duck and the voice of the deer, albeit in a surprising and fresh manner.

The "combination" (*toriawase*), by contrast, combines two or more different images in one *hokku*. Bashō's disciples further divide the "combination" into two types: those "outside the circumference," which bring together two (and sometimes more) images that traditionally are not found together, and those "inside the circumference," which combine images that are associated with each other in the classical tradition. Bashō once said that "combinations that emerge from within the circumference are rarely superior, and all of them are old-fashioned." As we have seen, in classical poetry the frog usually appeared in combination with fresh water and the yellow rose to form an elegant and bright image. Bashō's poem effectively goes outside that "circumference," but had Bashō used "A yellow rose—" (*yamabuki ya*) instead of "An ancient pond—," as one of his disciples suggested, he would have stayed within the "circumference."

Sometimes a "combination" of distant, "extra-circumference" images are held together by an intermediary image, as in the following poem by Bashō.

aoyagi no	Branches of the willow
doro ni shidaruru	Drooping down into the mud—
shiohi kana	The tide is out.
	(*Sumidawara*, 1694)

The gap between the two elements of the "combination," the willow (*aoyagi*) and low tide (*shiohi*), two classical images never associated in the poetic tradition, is bridged by the earthy, non-classical image of mud (*doro*). The *haikai* element derives from the vernal, feminine image of the elegant willow, admired for its gracefully drooping branches, being unexpectedly soiled by the mud on the bay bottom.

Bashō's distant "combinations" are closely associated with the "links by scent" (*nioi-zuke*) that he regarded as an aesthetic and literary ideal in *haikai* linked verse. The following example is from a thirty-six-link verse sequence in *Sarumino* (*The Monkey's Straw Raincoat*, 1691).

sō yaya samuku	A priest returning to a
tera ni kaeru ka	Temple as he grows cold?
	(Bonchō)

saruhiki no	A monkey trainer,
saru to yo o furu	Passing through life with a monkey—
aki no tsuki	The moon of autumn.
	(Bashō)

In the first verse a priest has come back from a chilly day of begging for alms, and in the second verse a monkey trainer, fated to pass his days with a monkey, is juxtaposed with the autumn moon, an image of loneliness. The two scenes are linked by a common mood, by the solitary and humble sadness of two individuals who stand outside the warm embrace of society. The second verse (by Bashō) probes the chilly atmosphere and loneliness of the previous verse (by Bonchō) even as it stands apart. To use *haikai* terminology, the new verse "lets go" (*tsukihanasu*) of the previous verse even as it catches its "scent" (*nioi*).

The same kind of "link by scent" can be found within the confines of a single *hokku*, as in the following verse by Bashō,

kiku no ka ya	Chrysanthemums scent—
Nara ni wa furuki	In old Nara the ancient
hotoketachi	Statues of Buddha.
	(1694)

The chrysanthemum, which blooms amidst the bright colors and leaves of autumn, possesses an old-fashioned but refined fragrance. The dignified and elegant buddha statues that fill the temples in the old capital of Nara have no overt connection to the scent of chrysanthemums—the statues are not surrounded by flowers—and yet the two images share overtones: both evoke a quaint, elegant atmosphere.

The "distant combination" can take the form of a question and an answer, one of the formats from which Japanese linked verse first arose. The following poem was written shortly after Bashō fell ill on a journey:

kono aki wa	Why have I aged
nande toshi yoru	This autumn?
kumo ni tori	A bird in the clouds.
	(1694)

According to one of Bashō's disciples, the speaker, hampered by the vicissitudes of old age, looks enviously at the bird in the floating clouds, symbolic of eternal travel. The bird in the clouds also reflects the speaker's loneliness. Whatever connection the readers finally draw, they must leap from one mode or state to another (in this instance, from a subjective, lyrical statement to an objective description).

The "combinations" found in Bashō's *hokku* do not usually employ simile or metaphor proper, in which a direct transference is made between one image and another. Instead, Bashō relies on selective juxtaposition, in which the connections are only suggested. The *hokku* usually juxtaposes either two antithetical items or two similar elements. In either case, the combination is usually unexpected and "new"—that is to say, it works against traditional associations, shedding new light on both sides of the "combination" and often joining a classical topic with a nonclassical image or phrase.

The notion of "scent" (*nioi*) also applies to the relationship between Bashō's prose and the embedded poetry. Like the two parts of the *hokku*, the poem and the surrounding prose often highlight each other even as they can be read and appreciated independently. The linking by "scent" also occurs between poetry and painting. Instead of the poem simply reflecting the content of the painting or sketch on which it appears, we often find the two juxtaposed, creating a montage effect, in which the poetry and the painting are joined only by shared overtones.

The *toriwase* (combination) is usually made possible by the *kireji* (cutting word), one of the formal requirements of the *hokku*, which severs the semantic, grammatical, or rhythmic flow of the poem. The cutting word frequently takes the form of the exclamatory particle *ya* at the end of the first or second line, or the exclamatory particle *kana* at the end of the poem. According to Bashō, any of the seventeen syllables of the *hokku* can function as a cutting word as long as it "severs" the poem. In the frog poem, the *ya* (translated by a dash) at the end of the first line splits the poem into two parts, causing the two halves to reverberate against each other. In typical Bashō fashion, the cutting word sets up an opposition or parallel between a visual image and an auditory sensation.

The cutting word, like the seasonal word, vastly increases the complexity and power of the seventeen-syllable *hokku*, commonly recognized as the shortest poetic form in world literature. It can only be effective, however, if the reader makes it so. In linked verse, the *hokku*, or opening verse, was followed by a second verse, which drew on or emerged out of the overtones of the first voice. In the independent *hokku*, or haiku, the reader must perform the same task in his or her imagination. To "cut" a verse is to entrust the final meaning to the reader, to allow the audience to participate actively—an aesthetic process similar to the cadenza in pre-Romantic music, in which the composer leaves part of the musical notation blank for completion by the performer. It is no accident that Matsuo Bashō once said, "those verses that reveal seventy or eighty percent of the subject are good. Those that reveal fifty to sixty percent, we never tire of."

Many of the literary characteristics of Bashō's *hokku* are also to be found in his travel journals, where much of his best poetry appears. In addition to hundreds of *haibun* (poetic prose) vignettes and essays, Bashō wrote a series of more extended works (all available in English translation), *Nozarashi kikō* (*Record of a Weather-Exposed Skeleton*), *Kashima mōde* (*A Visit to Sarashina Village*), *Oku no hosomichi* (*The Narrow Road to the Deep North*), and *Saga nikki* (*The Saga Diary*), all of which are based on journeys to various parts of Japan. Most of these journeys, particularly that which is described in *The Narrow Road to the Deep North*, Bashō's masterpiece, involve a search for or visit to *utamakura*, famous places in Japanese poetry.

Like seasonal words, *utamakura* (poetic places) were aesthetic clusters, which, as a result of their appearance in famous poems, possessed rich overtones. When mentioned in a poem (or, as Bashō often did, in prose), the established associations radiated out from the *hokku*, providing depth to the seventeen-syllable verse. From as early as the classical period, *utamakura* became popular poetic topics, and like seasonal topics, they assumed fixed associations that the *waka* poet was required to employ. Relying on poetry handbooks, classical poets could easily write about places that they had never seen, just as they composed poems about aspects of nature that they had never encountered. Bashō broke from this tradition, and in a manner that deliberately recalled certain poet-priests of the classical and medieval past— Nōin, Saigyō, and Sōgi—he journeyed to numerous *utamakura*, where the present met, sometimes in ironic and violent disjunction, with the literary past. If, for most classical poets, the *utamakura* represented a beauty that transcended time and place, Bashō's travels brought him face to face with the impermanence of all things. This tension between the unchanging and the changing, between literary tradition and intense personal experience, between classical diction and contemporary language lies at the heart of both Bashō's prose and poetry.

The following is from *Record of a Weather-Exposed Skeleton*.

akikaze ya	The autumn wind!
yabu mo hatake mo	Nothing but thicket and fields
Fuwa no seki	At Fuwa Barrier.

Fuwa Barrier (in present-day Gifu Prefecture), originally one of the three main checking stations in Japan, was abandoned in the late eighth century. However, it continued to exist in literature as an *utamakura*, immortalized by the following poem by Fujiwara no Yoshitsune in *Shinkokinshū* (*New Collection of Old and New Poems*, 1205):

hito sumanu	The shingled eaves
Fuwa no sekiya no	Of the guard post at Fuwa
itabishashi	Where no one lives,
arenishi nochi wa	Have collapsed, leaving only
tada aki no kaze	The winds of autumn.

Coming upon the guard post at Fuwa (which literally means "unbreakable"), the speaker in Bashō's poem finds that even the building has disappeared, leaving only thickets and open fields swept by autumn winds. The *hokku* follows the "poetic essence" (*hon'i*) of Fuwa Barrier (the pathos of decay) as well as that of the "autumn wind" (loneliness). But these classical associations, which are embodied in Yoshitsune's *waka*, are presented anew in a striking manner, using nonclassical diction: "nothing but thickets and fields," a phrase which subtly contrasts the present with the poetic past.

Bashō repeatedly told his disciples that they "should awaken to the high and return to the low" (*takaku kokoro o satorite, zoku ni kaerubeshi*). Matsunaga Teitoku, who established Edo *haikai*, defined *haikai* as linked verse with *haigon*, vocabulary that classical poetry had excluded as being vulgar and "low" (*zoku*). The use of *haigon* (literally *"haikai words"*) transformed the verse into a popular form that could be enjoyed by all classes. At the same time, however, *haikai*'s poetic "liberation"—particularly its free use of *haigon*—seriously threatened the literary nature of *haikai*, often making it more a form of amusement or vulgarity than a serious literary genre. Bashō was the first major poet to bring a heightened spiritual and literary awareness to *haikai*. He infused the "high" (*ga*) into the "low" (*zoku*) of *haikai*, or rather, sought the "high" in the "low," a pursuit that ultimately transformed the *hokku* into a powerful poetic form. As the frog poem suggests, Bashō sought the new in the old, the profound in the trivial, the serious in the comic.

"Awakening to the high" also meant exploring and sharing in the spirit of the "ancients," the superior poets of the past. The long and difficult journeys to *utamakura* were a means of communing with the spirits of the great poets of the past, of sharing in their poetic experience. For Bashō, the great figures were Li Bai, Hanshan, Du Fu, and Bo Juyi in the Chinese tradition, and Saigyō, Sōgi, Rikyū, and Sesshū in the Japanese tradition—most of whom, significantly, had been recluse poets or artists. The work of these "ancients" was bound together, in Bashō's mind, by a common literary spirit, of which the best of *haikai* should partake. It was not enough, however, simply to imitate and borrow from the "ancients," whose "high" art—particularly Chinese poetry, *waka*, and *renga*—had become aristocratic, refined, and exclusive by Bashō's day. The poet must also—and here Bashō parts company with his medieval predecessors—return to the "low," to the everyday life, to immediate personal experience, and to the popular language and "tongues," all of which change from day to day. It was only by "returning to the low" that one could create poetry with "newness" and lightness, which were critical to the life of *haikai.* For Bashō, it was ultimately the harshness of travel on foot, which combined the associations of *utamakura* with the vicissitudes of everyday life, that became the quintessential means of "awakening to the high and returning to the low" and that led to much of his finest poetry.

TOPICS FOR DISCUSSION

1. What are the formal characteristics of haiku? What functions do the cutting word and the seasonal word have? What kind of techniques are commonly used in haiku? What is the difference between haiku and the thirty-one syllable *waka*, or classical lyric? What are the strengths of this particular form? Its weaknesses?

2. In what ways can Bashō be considered a nature poet? What kind of imagery does he use? What kind of relationship does his poetry and travel accounts have to the literary tradition (including Chinese poetry)? What role does the theme of impermanence play in Bashō's poetry and travel accounts?

3. What significance does the notion of a journey have in *Narrow Road to the Deep North*? In what ways is it a journey into the past? A religious journey? In what ways does *Narrow Road to the Deep North* resemble a Noh play? What is the relationship between travel and poetry? Between the prose and the poetry in *Narrow Road to the Deep North*?

NOTES

1. All translations are by Haruo Shirane.
2. Ogata Tsutomu, in Ogata Tsutomu, ed., *Haiku no kaishaku to kanshō jiten* (Tokyo: Ōbunsha, 1979), p. 82.

REFERENCES

Bashō. *Oku no hosomichi.* There are a number of English translations.

Bashō. *Back Roads to Far Towns.* Translated by Cid Corman. Fredonia, NY: White Pine, 1986. Notes by Kamaike Susumu. An elegant translation that attempts to suggest the elliptical qualities of the original.

Bashō. *The Narrow Road to the Deep North.* Translated by Nobuyuki Yuasa. Middlesex, England: Penguin Books, 1966. The style, particularly that of the poetry, is inferior to other translations, but it is available in low-cost paperback and includes a number of other key travel works by Bashō: *The Records of a Weather-Exposed Skeleton, A Visit to Kashima Shrine, The Records of a Travel-worn Satchel,* and *A Visit to Sarashina Village.*

Bashō. *A Haiku Journey: Bashō's Narrow Road to a Far Province.* Translated by Dorothy Britton. Accurate prose translation (though the poetry translations are somewhat old-fashioned) with Japanese original. Available in paperback.

Keene, Donald, ed. *Anthology of Japanese Literature from the Earliest Era to the Mid-Nineteenth Century.* New York: Grove Press, 1955. Contains extended excerpts from *The Narrow Road to the Deep North* and other writings by Bashō and his disciples. The haiku is well translated. Available in paperback.

McCullough, Helen, comp. and ed. *Classical Japanese Prose.* Stanford: Stanford University Press, 1990. Contains complete and accurate translations of *The Journey of 1684* and *The Narrow Road of the Interior.* Available in paperback.

For more information on Matsuo Bashō or an introduction to traditional haiku in general, see:

Keene, Donald. *World Within Walls.* New York: Holt, Rinehart and Winston, 1976. See Chapters 1–5.

Henderson, Harold. *An Introduction to Haiku.* Garden City, NY: Doubleday and Company, 1958.

Nippon Gakujutsu Shinkokai, ed. and trans. *Haikai and haiku.* Tokyo: Nippon Gakujutsu Shinkokai, 1958.

Ueda, Makoto. *Matsuo Bashō.* Tokyo: Kodansha International, 1982. Reprint edition.

Japanese Texts: Narrative

THE TALE OF GENJI

*Edward G. Seidensticker and
Haruo Shirane*

THE TALE OF GENJI: AN HISTORICAL OVERVIEW
by Edward G. Seidensticker

INTRODUCTION

The Tale of Genji, or *Genji monogatari,* was written early in the
eleventh century by a lady of the Fujiwara clan known as
Murasaki Shikibu. (This is not her real name, which is unknown,
but a traditional epithet or sobriquet.) Among the scant known
facts about her life, which extended from the late tenth century
into the early eleventh, is that she saw court service, beginning in
the first decade of the eleventh century and ending we do not
know when. The *Genji* was probably begun during that same
decade. We do not know when it was finished, and indeed we
cannot be sure that it is in fact finished.

The title comes from the family name of the hero, Genji or
Minamoto. He is the son of the emperor regnant at the beginning
of the story. His death is not described, but it occurs between the
forty-first and forty-second of the fifty-four chapters into which
the story is divided. The remaining chapters have to do largely
with the affairs of Kaoru, a young man thought by the world to be
Genji's son but in fact the illegitimate son of one of his wives.

The action covers upwards of seventy years. There are hundreds of characters, perhaps fifty of them important. Yet the plot
is essentially simple. The *Genji* is a love story, of a sort dissimilar
to that commonly found in European literature. The latter, when
it is about love, tends to be about courtship, with marriage either
occurring or being frustrated at the very end. The *Genji* is about
the maturing of love after marriage. In the fifth chapter Genji finds

the young girl who is to be the great love of his life. Their marriage takes place in the ninth chapter. The lady, who, like the author, is known as Murasaki (we are never told her real name), dies in the fortieth chapter, a third of a century later. The forty-first chapter sees Genji through the first full year of his bereavement, and he too is gone from the scene. Most of the story, then, centers upon a complex relationship that is deepened by tribulations—especially polygamous rivalries—and the passage of time. The concluding chapters have to do with the altogether less successful and satisfying affairs, largely amorous, of Kaoru.

CHARACTERIZATION

The standard English translation of the title includes the word "tale." It renders a common but ambiguous Japanese word, *monogatari,* which carries strong connotations of the old-fashioned and pre-modern. "Romance" might do as well. Both terms stand in contrast to "novel," which covers most important European and American fiction since the eighteenth century and most Japanese fiction of the last hundred years.

To many Western readers, the most striking thing about the *Genji* is that it does in fact seem so modern. For the past fifty years or so the idea has had considerable currency that it should be called a novel, and that it is the first great novel in the literature of the world. Objections to the idea have also become fairly commonplace, and they have to do largely with the possibility that Murasaki Shikibu's aims were not those of the modern novelist and the fact that "novel" is so European a term and concept. In effect they argue that Western cultural imperialism has found a non-Western work interesting and is trying to appropriate it into a Western mode.

If, however, the romance and the tale are understood to be forms of narrative fiction in which the chief interest is in plot and the novel the narrative form in which the chief interest is in character, then the grounds for considering the *Genji* a novel are not at all weak. It seems modern and holds the attention of the modern reader because the characterization is so subtle and skillful. If it were a tale or a romance and the characterization were as flat as it usually is in such a work, then remarkable incident would have to be relied upon to hold the attention of the reader through the very great length (more than a thousand closely printed pages in English translation) of the work. Yet the *Genji* contains no violence and few really dramatic events. Genji himself may seem a bit too good and talented, at least at the outset, but saints and villains do not abound, as they tend to do in romances. The events, though of that world so far above most of us, tend to be ordinary, not beyond the common experience. It holds the interest of many a reader all the same, and the explanation must be in the characterization. The fifty or so important characters are kept apart from one another with remarkable skill. The achievement is all the more remarkable in that it has no precedents in the literature of the East and probably none in the literature of the world. So, if we know what we mean by the term, we may indeed call the *Genji* a novel.

Many who see the *Genji* as a novel also see it as a psychological novel, a novel of states of mind, and compare it in this regard to Proust's *Remembrance of Things Past*. Whether or not the comparison is apt, a psychological theme runs through it that also runs through some masterpieces of modern fiction: the quest for a parent. Genji is still an infant when his mother dies. Mothers are very important in a polygamous society, in which fathers are shared with so many others. The pursuit of his mother's image leads Genji first to the stepmother with whom he has the guilty love affair and then to Murasaki. The stepmother came to court and gained the emperor's love because of a close resemblance to an earlier and much-loved wife, Genji's mother. Murasaki is her niece, and again the resemblance is close. The theme, in attenuated form—life itself seems attenuated after Genji's disappearance from the scene—persists through the concluding chapters. Kaoru sets forth uncertainly on an uncertain love affair because he is looking not for a mother figure but a father figure. He senses that there is something peculiar about his paternity, though he does not know what it is.

The characterization becomes more subtle and successful as the long narrative progresses. In this fact is the best argument that it is essentially by a single author, even though the text we read may not in all its details be the text that emerged from that one author's hand. There have long been theories of dual or multiple authorship, having to do in large measure with the clear break that occurs with Genji's death. It is impossible to believe, however, that one writer could have brought the story and the characterization to so high a level and another writer, without preparation or warning, could have taken over and brought it to yet higher levels.

If it were possible to read the *Genji* as a series of related but independent novels, like the Barchester novels of Trollope, then it might be recommended that the reader begin with one of the stronger pieces, and return to the first and weakest after the sense of the pleasures that lie ahead is secure. The *Genji* is a single, continuing story, however, and so a beginning must be made at the beginning, where Murasaki Shikibu's powers are least apparent. One may add quickly, however, that even these earliest chapters are better than anything the Japanese or their mentors, the Chinese, had produced earlier, and better, too, than Japanese fiction of the millennium since.

The earliest chapters have about them more of the romance or the tale than any other part of the work. Although Murasaki Shikibu already outdoes her predecessors, the romancers of the tenth century, she is still under their influence. The hero is too gifted a man to be quite true, and the story is of his brilliantly successful public career. There is a setback, a time when he must live in exile, but that may be seen as a conventional initiation rite, and one does not for a moment doubt that he will emerge from it prepared for yet greater successes. This first or romantic stage goes through the exile and return, or the first score or so of chapters.

There follows what may be called the comic stage, through the thirty-third chapter, a stage largely concerned with the generation of Genji's children. The characterization is more realistic. Genji, so nearly perfect in the early chapters that one almost comes to dislike him, is an altogether more believable and sympathetic human being.

The thirty-fourth and thirty-fifth chapters are the longest of the book, accounting for about a sixth of the text. Through them and the half dozen following chapters darkness gathers over Genji's private life as his public career reaches a glorious climax. This third section may be called the tragic phase. Genji's great love, Murasaki, falls ill and dies, and the little princess whom he marries late in life is caught in adultery.

Then, suddenly, comes the announcement that Genji is dead. Three uncertain chapters follow, one of them quite possibly spurious, and the remarkable last section begins. The main action departs the court and the capital, character and incident are on a smaller scale, society falls away layer by layer, and in the end one last sad heroine is left in the solitude of a nunnery. It may be called the abstract or meditative phase of the story, and Kaoru may be called the first non-hero or anti-hero in the literature of the world. Only a very sure and skillful writer could have undertaken anything so daring. The last stages of *Genji* are fiction of the highest order.

The *Genji* stands in isolation. Only in the twentieth century has characterization emerged once more as a principal concern for Japanese fiction writers. The new concern is a result of Western influence. With it has come recognition of the fact that a Japanese writer was very good at characterization almost ten centuries ago. The *Genji* did not cease to be read through those centuries. Not all generations have attached the same significance to it, and doubtless our modern reading will presently give way to others. This remarkable writer and her large and complex work lend themselves to modern concerns and will lend themselves to post-modern ones as well.

In this century, evidence has accumulated in such quantities that it seems unanswerable to establish that the *Genji* is a sort of historical novel. If it were a carefully planned and executed historical novel, such as Scott and Thackeray wrote, then of course the action would have to begin at least three-quarters of a century before the narrative present and proceed methodically through the years. The *Genji* is not an elaborately contrived historical novel of this sort. Yet the first readers or hearers of the early chapters (probably the original manuscript was sent out to its earliest audience chapter by chapter) must immediately have been aware that Murasaki Shikibu was writing of a time perhaps a century before her own. This immediate awareness was soon lost, and evidence has been painstakingly assembled to bring it back to us. In it must surely be one of the "meanings" Murasaki wished to convey.

BUDDHIST NARRATIVE

The first sentence of the forty-second chapter announces Genji's death and continues with the sad statement that no one now alive is his equal. The implication is that no one ever again will be. The principal characters of the last chapters, after Genji's death, are but fractions of the man he was. The great ones and the great day are in the past. Social decline is irreversible. This social decline may be seen as concrete manifestation of absolute, existential decline. *Mappō*, a popular idea of the day, held that the Buddhist creed itself must decline, passing through three stages, in the last of which form would remain but substance be lost. One chronology had the final stage beginning in the eleventh century. So the *Genji* seems to tell us that even the tenets of "the Good Law" are not immutable. All that is immutable is decline.

There is another sense in which the *Genji* may be seen as a grand Buddhist parable. The great sin of Genji's life is an act of adultery with his father's best-loved wife. Shadows gather over his late years even as his public career moves from triumph to triumph, and among them is the knowledge that a young wife of his late years has had the adulterous affair that results in the birth of Kaoru. So the workings of karma, the Buddhist concept of cause and effect, are apparent. The effects of our deeds, good and bad, will work themselves out, in this life or in future lives. What Genji did he now has done to him.

If the awareness of karma is fairly explicit in the sequence of events, another Buddhist awareness, of the transience and the illusory nature of the world and all its material surfaces, is implicit throughout the story. Time as the great ravager and destroyer is a constant presence. The knowledge that time moves relentlessly on and levels everything before it does not, however, lead to nihilism and despair. Quite the opposite: the very fact that beauty and pleasure must vanish asks that the whole of the sensible being concentrate upon them. The *Genji* is a work of exquisite sensibility, and it is a strongly lyrical work.

The consciousness of nature and its beauties might suffuse certain masterpieces of European lyric poetry, especially since the early nineteenth century, but one would be hard put to find a major work of fiction in which nature is the continuing presence it is in the *Genji*. On virtually every page we are aware of the seasons and their trees and flowers, and even the phases of the moon; and when, rarely, we are not informed of them, the omission is so conspicuous as to take on a significance it could not have in a Western novel. Natural imagery and the passage of the seasons are tightly interwoven with the characterization, and even offer hints by way of solving one of the great mysteries, whether or not the *Genji* is finished. It begins and ends in high summer, an unlikely season; and so two summer scenes form parentheses around a work that is predominantly vernal and autumnal.

THE TALE OF GENJI: CRITICAL APPROACHES
by Haruo Shirane

One of the obvious attractions that the *Genji* holds for modern readers is the fact that it is a major classic by a woman. In this regard it lends itself to comparison with other works by women in the classical period—*The Gossamer Years (Kagerō nikki)*, by the mother of Michitsuna, *As I Crossed a Bridge of Dreams (Sarashina nikki)*, by the daughter of Takasue, etc.—as well as more modern or Western narratives by women. In Murasaki Shikibu's day, as in previous centuries, men devoted themselves to writing prose in Chinese, the official language of religion and government. (The only prose writing that was taken seriously was historical and philosophical writing, all of which was done in Chinese and little of which is read today.) One consequence was that women, who were not obligated to write in a foreign language and who were in fact discouraged from doing so, were the first to create a substantial body of prose texts in the vernacular. If Virginia Woolf lamented the silence of Shakespeare's sister, Japan's Shakespeare was a woman who had many literary sisters. In the tenth century, vernacular prose, particularly literary diaries, belonged to women to the extent that the leading male poet of the day, Ki no Tsurayuki, pretended to be a woman in order to write a literary diary in Japanese—a reversal of the George Eliot phenomenon. Of particular interest here is the striking evolution in the point of view to one that is almost exclusively that of the female protagonist.

Reading and interpretation of the *Tale of Genji* are greatly enhanced by an understanding of contemporary narrative conventions which *The Tale of Genji* both follows and works against. It was a plot convention of the vernacular tale that the heroine, whose family has declined or disappeared, is discovered and loved by an illustrious noble. This association of love and inferior social status appears from the opening line of the *Genji.*

> Which imperial reign was it? Of the many consorts who were in the service of the emperor, there was one who was not of particularly high status but who received the special favor of the Emperor. (Translation: Haruo Shirane)

In the opening chapter, the emperor regnant, like all Heian emperors, was expected to devote himself to his principal consort (the Kokiden lady), the lady of the highest rank, and yet he dotes on a woman of considerably lower status, a social and political violation that eventually results in the woman's death. Like his father, Genji pursues love where it is forbidden and most unlikely to be found or attained. In the fifth chapter, Genji discovers his future wife, the young Murasaki, who has lost her mother and is in danger of losing her only guardian when Genji takes her into his own home.

Narrative conventions often invert social and political realities. In Murasaki Shikibu's day, it would have been unheard of for a man of Genji's high rank to take a girl of Murasaki's low position into his own residence and marry her. In Heian aristocratic society, the man usually lived in his wife's residence, either in the house of her parents or in a dwelling nearby. The prospective groom had high stakes in marriage, for the bride's family provided not only a residence but other forms of support as well. When Genji takes a girl with absolutely no political backing or social support into his house and marries her, he openly flouts the conventions of marriage as they were known to Murasaki Shikibu's audience. In the *monogatari* tradition, however, this action becomes a sign of excessive, romantic love.

A number of other sequences in the *Genji*—those of Yūgao, Suetsumuhana, Tamakazura, the Akashi lady, Oigimi (Agemaki), and Ukifune—start on a similar note. All of these women come from upper or middle-rank aristocratic families that have, for various reasons, fallen into social obscurity and must struggle to survive. The appearance of the highborn hero signifies, at least for those surrounding the woman, an opportunity for social redemption, an expectation that is usually fulfilled in the earlier *monogatari.* Murasaki Shikibu, however, focuses on the difficulties that the woman subsequently encounters, either in dealing with the man, or in making, or failing to make, the social transition between her own class and that of the highborn hero. The woman may, for example, be torn between pride and material need, or between emotional dependence on the man and a desire to be more independent, or she may feel abandoned and betrayed—all conflicts explored in the *Genji.* In classical Japanese poetry, which had a profound influence on the *Genji,* love has a similar fate: it is never about happiness or the blissful union of souls. Instead, it dwells on unfulfilled hopes, fear of abandonment, deep regrets, and lingering resentment.

The *Genji* can be read and appreciated as Murasaki Shikibu's oeuvre, or corpus, as a closely interrelated series of texts that can be read either individually or as a whole and that is the product of an author whose attitudes, interests, and techniques evolved significantly with time and experience. For example, the reader of the Ukifune story (the last five chapters, devoted to Ukifune) can appreciate this sequence both independently and as an integral part of the previous narrative. Murasaki Shikibu altered the significance of her existing text, or body of texts, not by rewriting it, but by adding and interlacing new sequences. To take a larger example, love, glory, and *miyabi* ("courtliness"), the secular ideals assumed in the earlier volumes, are placed in relative and ironic perspective in the latter chapters by the emergence of their opposite: a deep-rooted desire to renounce the world and achieve detachment. It is thus fruitful to compare and contrast sequences and chapters that have strong parallels—for example, the "Evening Faces" (*Yūgao*) chapter with the Ukifune sequence, or the "Lavender" (*Wakamurasaki*) chapter with the *Tamakazura* sequence.

Indeed, the *Genji* calls out for constant comparison of its many distinctive female characters. The author links many of the women by blood or physical appearance, in the form of surrogate figures. For example, in the opening chapter, after losing the Kiritsubo consort (Genji's mother), the emperor finds consolation in Fujitsubo, a lady of similar countenance. Genji, longing for his deceased mother, is likewise drawn to his father's new consort. Frustrated by Fujitsubo's stiff resistance and the barriers that separate them, he eventually finds a substitute and a wife in the young Murasaki, who is Fujitsubo's niece and almost identical in appearance. In each case, the loss of a woman leads the man to find a surrogate, who is similar in appearance, or closely related, or both. But while the women may appear similar in the eyes of the men who pursue them, they are strikingly different in character and social status.

An equally significant form of linkage exists among characters who are not associated by blood or appearance but who bear common social, spiritual, and emotional burdens. Perhaps the most revealing of these analogous relationships involves Asagao, Princess Ochiba, and Oigimi, three royal daughters who appear in three different parts of the *Genji*. Owing to an unfortunate turn in family circumstances, all three women have been placed in difficult positions. But despite the obvious rewards of marriage, each one rejects the advances and generous aid of a highborn, attractive noble: Genji, Yūgiri, and Kaoru, respectively. None of these women is directly related to the other. Nevertheless, each successive sequence explores, with increasing intensity, the problem of honor, pride, and shame in regard to the spiritual independence of a highborn but disadvantaged lady.

The *Genji* can also be discussed as a kind of Bildungsroman, in which the author reveals the development of the protagonist's spirit and character through time and experience. In the *Genji*, this growth occurs not only in the life of a single hero or heroine but over different generations and sequences, with two or more successive characters. Genji, for example, gradually attains an awareness of death, mutability, and the illusory nature of the world through repeated suffering. By contrast, Kaoru, his putative son, begins his life, or rather his narrative, with a profound grasp and acceptance of these darker aspects of life.

The same is true of the mature Murasaki, the heroine of the first half, and Oigimi, the primary figure of the last part. By the beginning of the middle chapters, Murasaki has long assumed that she can monopolize Genji's affections and act as his principal wife. Genji's unexpected marriage to the high-ranking Third Princess (Waley: Nyosan), however, crushes these assumptions, causing Murasaki to fall mortally ill. Though Oigimi never suffers the way Murasaki does, she quickly comes to a similar awareness of the inconstancy of men, love, and marriage, and rejects Kaoru even though he appears to be the perfect companion. Building on the earlier chapter, Murasaki Shikibu makes a significant leap, moving from a narrative about the tribulations of love and marriage to one that explores a world without men.

Another topic of discussion is aesthetics, which manifests itself in every facet of the narrative. In the *Genji*, beauty is found in the fleeting, in the uncertain, in the fragmentary, and in the inherently sorrowful aspects of the world. The cherry blossoms—the quintessential image of Japanese aesthetics even today—were loved by Heian poets not only because the delicate, multi-petaled flowers reminded them of the glories of this world but because the same blossoms, in a matter of days, turned color, faded, and scattered in the wind like snowflakes, a sorrowful reminder not only of the brevity of life and fortune but of the uncertainly and fickleness of the human heart. In the *Genji*, the essence of nature and human life tends to be grasped in terms of their end, in their dying moments rather than in their birth or creation. The dominant season of the *Genji* is autumn, when nature, in all its melancholy hues, seems to wither and fade away.

This aesthetics extends to the characters. In one of the opening chapters of the *Genji* the young hero discovers the fragile Yūgao, or the Evening Faces, who is seized by an evil spirit (presumably that of the Rokujo lady) and expires in the hero's hands. Genji comes, as he does elsewhere, to an understanding of his love, not in its fulfillment, but in its all-too-sudden and incomprehensible loss. Indicative of the symbolism that permeates the *Genji* is the woman's name, Yūgao, a gourd-like plant (suggesting her lowly origins) whose beautiful white flowers, at the height of summer, bloom in the dusk and fade before the sunrise.

Perhaps the most important critical concept in Japanese poetry from the classical period onward was the notion of *yojō* or *yosei*, which has two broad meanings. On the one hand, *yojō* refers to poetry or art as an expression or product of excess, irrepressible emotions. When we compare Genji to the heroes of the Western classics, to Achilles and Odysseus, a strikingly different set of human values emerges. Genji does not triumph through strength and courage, by cunning and intelligence, by resisting temptation, or through acts of benevolence and insight. In fact, he fails in almost every one of these categories (his successor Kaoru even more so). Instead, heroism lies in his capacity to express that inner weakness and deep emotion through aesthetic means, through poetry, painting, music, and other artistic forms.

Yojō also means overtones, what is beyond the referential meaning of words, what is implied rather than stated. Visually, this implies that the shadows—for example, the dusk and early dawn—have more allure and depth than light or darkness. Musically, it suggests that the faint echoes, the reverberations that linger in the ear, are often more moving than the melodic notes themselves. It also implies that the fragrance, wafting on a gentle breeze, is often more memorable than the flower itself. Such is Kaoru, The Fragrant One, whose bodily scent reaches into the houses of unsuspecting women. The name borne by Oborozukiyo, the daughter of the Minister of the Right, with whom Genji is caught sleeping in the early chapters, literally means "The Evening of the Misty Moon." As in Japanese poetry, the softly enshrouded moon is more erotic and seductive than a brightly shining crescent.

Yojō also implies an intertextual fabric. *The Tale of the Genji* is interwoven with elaborate allusions to Chinese poetry and literature, to Buddhist scriptures, and to *waka.* Many of the places in the *Genji*—Suma, where Genji is exiled, or Uji, where Kaoru discovers the two beautiful sisters—are *utamakura,* famous placenames in Japanese poetry, with rich clusters of associations that are woven into the drama. *The Tale of Genji* unfolds over seventy-five years, three generations, four imperial reigns, and presents over five hundred characters, and yet it gravitates toward intensely emotional and meditative scenes in which the language, rhetoric, and themes of poetry are foregrounded and in which the primary reference is not to an "external" world so much as to other literary and poetic texts.

The aesthetics of overtones also extends to the structure of the *Genji,* in which the aftermath, the lingering echoes, and the memories are often more central to the narrative than the event or action itself. The opening chapter, for example, describes the tragic love affair between the emperor and Genji's mother. The greater part of the chapter, however, is an extended meditation on the death of the lover, climaxed by poetry and allusions to Yang Guifei [Yang Kuei-fei] and "The Song of Sorrow" by Bo Juyi [Po Chü-i], Japan's favorite Chinese poet. In the manner of lyrical narratives, the tone is elegant, poetic, and uplifting even though the subject matter is tragic. These scenes belong to a familiar poetic topos, the lament, and share much with the literary diaries by women which often ruminate on the consequences and significance of the past.

In *The Tale of Genji*, as in much of Japanese literature, the fragment or the part is often more aesthetically important than the whole. It is revealing that we do not know if the *Genji* is in fact finished. The last chapter, "The Floating Bridge of Dreams," suggests both an end and a new beginning, and is no more closed than a number of other earlier chapters. The ending, or a lack of it, has disturbed some Western scholars, but Japanese critics have never made it an issue, for the notion of an open, unbound text is a given, just as is the poetics of overtones, fragmentation, and uncertainty.

TEXTS, AUTHORSHIP, AND TRANSLATIONS
by Edward G. Seidensticker

Much Japanese scholarship has gone into conflation of early texts towards establishing a definitive one, a text that closely approximates the original. Unless a much earlier text is found than the earliest surviving ones, and it is most unlikely that this will ever happen, a completely acceptable recension is impossible. The main lines of texts vary from each other in thousands of details, and there are numerous variant texts that seem to belong to neither line.

Through the Kamakura Period, the preferred line was the Kawachi one, a thirteenth-century conflation. Since about the fifteenth century what is called the "blue-book" line has emerged dominant. It derives from the work of Fujiwara Teika, the great poet, critic, and scholar of the late twelfth and early thirteenth centuries. Most modern printed editions are based on "blue-book" manuscripts. A very large proportion of the variations has to do with niceties of verbal and adjectival conjugation that cannot in any event be rendered into English. They are therefore more of a trial for the translator into modern Japanese than for the translator into English. The most extreme variations do not in any event change character or story in large measure.

The last chapter is in some respects different from the other chapters. The title, for instance, is different, having no specific reference to a word or incident in the chapter itself. A careful reading of it—and the reader need not be a specialized student of the work—is our best if not our only way of deciding whether or not the *Genji* is complete. So it is too with questions of single, dual, or perhaps multiple authorship: is the break between the forty-first and frty-second chapters so radical that only a change in authors can explain it; or is the argument above acceptable, that no second author can have taken over without preparation and produced the remarkable last chapters? The nearest thing we will ever have to an answer must come from careful reading of the text.

There have long been theories that the chapters were not written in the order in which we now have them. In the decades since the Second World War, the matter has held the interest and attention of Japanese scholars as has no other. The view has been persuasively argued that the earlier chapters telling the main story of Genji, his great love, and his political career were written first, and that certain "short stories" by which the main narrative is unaffected were inserted later. Of the two Seidensticker translations to be mentioned below, one consisting of excerpts from the other, the shorter one, with a single major exception accounted for in the introduction, follows the main narrative and leaves out the supposed insertions. Comparison between the two should help the reader to decide whether to accept the theory, still supported by many Japanese scholars, that the chapters were written in the order in which we have them, or to choose the opposite theory—or perhaps some ingenious theory of the reader's own contriving. The exercise is not merely pedantic. To have the chapters in the order in which Murasaki Shikibu wrote them is to have invaluable evidence as to how she grew and matured—and in turn upon the problem of authorship.

There are two English translations, complete or nearly so. That by Arthur Waley appeared in installments more than a half century ago, and is available in Modern Library. That by Edward Seidensticker was published by Alfred Knopf in 1976. A selection of early chapters from the latter translation, about a fifth of the whole, was published by Vintage in 1985. As has been noted above, these translations do not include elaborate commentary. They do, however, have brief introductions. The illustrations in the Seidensticker translations, though they date from the seventeenth century, are the product of a remarkable tradition of antiquarian scholarship, and should convey a notion of the surroundings in which Genji and the rest did what they did.

TOPICS FOR DISCUSSION

1. *The Tale of Genji* (*Genji monogatari*) is often said to be the world's first novel. The word *monogatari*, however, is usually translated as "tale" or "romance." In what ways are these terms relevant or not relevant for discussing the *Genji*? Why?

2. What kinds of social, psychological, or political difficulties do the women in *The Tale of Genji* encounter? What parallels and differences do you see? Select two or three major female characters that are involved with Genji and compare them in terms of character, physical surroundings, social background, connection to power, and relationship to the hero.

3. In what ways can Genji be called a hero? What makes him so appealing to some Western readers and so offensive to others? In what ways does the nature of the hero change as *The Tale of Genji* unfolds? Is it appropriate to call Kaoru an anti-hero?

4. Discuss the role of aesthetics in *The Tale of Genji*. How is it related to the lives, thought, and relationships of the characters? To politics and religion?

5. What kind of worldview and religious concerns do the characters have? How do their religious ideals conflict with their secular involvements and attachments? Discuss the difference between taking the tonsure and achieving salvation. Do you think that *The Tale of Genji* is a narrative of karmic retribution?

6. Discuss the evolution of *The Tale of Genji*. In what ways do the later parts differ from the earlier parts in regard to the perspectives that the female characters have on society and men?

REFERENCES

The major translations are the following:

Waley, Arthur, trans. *The Tale of Genji*. London: George Allen and Unwin. 1935. Reprint. New York: Random House, 1960. An abridged edition is also available in Anchor paperback.

Seidensticker, Edward G., trans. *The Tale of Genji*. New York: Alfred A. Knopf, 1976. An abridged edition is also available from Vintage.

For those interested in literary criticism and scholarship on *The Tale of Genji*, see the following. All are available in paperback.

Shirane, Haruo. *The Bridge of Dreams: A Poetics of The Tale of Genji*. Stanford: Stanford University Press, 1987.

Field, Norma. *The Splendour of Longing in The Tale of Genji*. Princeton: Princeton University Press, 1987.

Bowring, Richard. *The Tale of Genji*. In *Landmarks of World Literature*. Cambridge: Cambridge University Press, 1988.

A BOOK OF ONE'S OWN: *THE GOSSAMER YEARS*; *THE PILLOW BOOK*; AND *THE CONFESSIONS OF LADY NIJŌ*

Barbara Ruch

INTRODUCTION

The early Japanese literary tradition of poetry, fiction, and nonfiction narrative is based on the language of women and written in an orthography used by women or by men communicating with women. It was this vernacular Japanese of the aristocratic class with its special script, as opposed to Chinese (the Latin of East Asia) used in official writing by men, that lies at the foundation of the Japanese literary consciousness. In no other culture can we find extant a major and early written literature that is a woman's literature. This alone excites the imagination.

Three of the most extraordinary nonfiction narratives in the early Japanese literary tradition are *The Gossamer Years*, *The Pillow Book*, and *The Confessions of Lady Nijō*. Although genre issues are complex, not wholly resolvable, and often of questionable significance, it should be said at the outset that these three works are not normally considered members of the same genre. For the purposes of the present exercise, however, they will be treated together as representative of the best of autobiographical narratives by women in pre-modern Japan.

THE GOSSAMER YEARS

The author of *The Gossamer Years*, known to us only as the Mother of Michitsuna, lived during the last half of the tenth century (935?–95) in the imperial capital, Heian-kyō (present-day Kyoto). She was born into a minor branch of the powerful Fujiwara family, her father reaching the rank of provincial governor. She is the only eminent representative of this golden age of women writers who never served in the palace. However, she was courted by—and while still quite young—became the secondary wife of the high-ranking and powerfully connected Fujiwara no Kaneie, who in later years became the head of the Fujiwara family and the highest-ranking statesman in Japan. This difference in their status had a marked impact on their married life. She bore Kaneie a son, Michitsuna. Ironically, since it was not as a mother that she seems to have sought existential value, the parental role was apparently the only one, in terms of human relations, that in the end gave her life satisfaction and sustenance. In *The Gossamer Years*, she refers to her son as "the one who keeps me alive."

Reportedly one of the most beautiful women of her time, she was, as well, an extremely gifted poet. In her thirties, her stature as a *waka* poet led to her being commissioned to write a verse for a poetry screen for the Minister of the Left. Thirty-six of her poems are contained in imperially-commissioned poetry anthologies (the *Shūishū*, etc.), and her poems were also selected for various private anthologies.

Her most profound influence on Japanese literary history, however, has been through her autobiographical prose account of her stormy marriage to Kaneie, the *Kagerō nikki* (literally, the *Gossamer Diary*). It is the prototype of the journal style that would be typical of women writers. These "diaries" were not, however, written day by day; they took a narrative prose form wholly compatible with fiction yet devoid of fantasy and grounded firmly in autobiography.

In the history of Japanese vernacular literature, her act of taking up the brush to compose in narrative form her personal real-life drama in an outspoken, wholly secular, confessional fashion was, as far as we can tell, unprecedented. Her obsession for divulging, with raw candor, her own emotions of jealousy, bitter hatred, and outrage over betrayal and rejection—and the particular events in her life she chooses to divulge—appear to spring from internal necessity, not poetic impulse. The work therefore seems unrelated to its only prose-diary predecessor, *The Tosa Diary*, written by the famous male poet Ki no Tsurayuki (ca.

868–945), a work we have no evidence she ever saw. If a rudimentary prose-diary genre existed in her time, all evidence of it is now lost, and her work is certainly the first example of the genre that may be considered a literary art.

Michitsuna's Mother, at some point in composing *The Gossamer Years*, goes back and appends an introductory preface in which she briefly assumes a third-person stance that she makes little attempt to sustain. In it she attempts to explain and justify her bold new literary form.

> Yet, as the days went by in monotonous succession, she had occasion to look at the old romances, and found them masses of the rankest fabrication. Perhaps, she said to herself, even the story of her own dreary life set down in a journal, might be of interest; and it might also answer a question: had that life been one befitting a well-born lady? But they must all be recounted, events of long ago, events of but yesterday. She was by no means certain that she could bring them to order.[1]

The title *Kagerō nikki* is taken from a passage at the end of Book I where the author comments on the insubstantial nature of all things in her life:

> Indeed, as I think of the unsatisfying events I have recorded here, I wonder whether I have been describing anything of substance. Call it, this journal of mine, a shimmering of the summer sky.[2]

Scholars to this day are divided as to whether *kagerō* refers to a short-lived, translucently hued summer insect like a mayfly, or to the summer phenomenon of shimmering heat waves rising in the air with a watery miragelike effect. Arthur Waley chose to translate the word as "gossamer," in the original sense of a film of cobweb floating in the still air—a word that, though lacking in accuracy, is both beautiful and metaphorically appropriate.

The Gossamer Years is divided into three books, the first, covering a fifteen-year period, is in memoir fashion, apparently written long after the events described. The narrative proceeds as the author's memory is prodded by a record she has clearly kept of her own poems and those she has received from others at important moments in the evolving story. Books II and III, covering roughly three years each, become increasingly like records of day-to-day developments. The great detail lavished on the year 971 near the close of Book II leads one to suspect that was the year she was moved not only to reexamine her life but to begin this literary attempt to record its most significant pain. How had she come to this? How had it begun? Had her life been a loss? The account is of beginnings, passion, and marriage; it describes her uncertain and painful position as secondary wife in a system of polygamy coded to benefit family and male prestige.

Her emotions range from joy to frustration to lonely pain and bitterness to, finally, an unsettled state of partial resignation as middle age sets in. As hope fades she suffers less. Book III ends inconclusively with a tentative and apparently abortive exchange of love poems between her son and a prospective bride, as well as an unexpected scattering of poetic exchanges between the author and Kaneie, which is brought to an end when Kaneie has an underling send her a reply: "The Prince is very busy today."

The tone of *The Gossamer Years* is radically personal and its focus startlingly self-enclosed. Nothing exists beyond the events in which the author has directly participated; she has no access at all to public life. No one has an identity or an existence except in relationship to the author. The narrative is so egocentric that the people central to her life are never named, not even, as would have been customary, by rank or residence. They are referred to only by privately coded adjectival circumlocutions that have meaning only in relation to the author: Kaneie is "that unreasonable person," "the one at the center [of my concern]," or "the person from whom I have heard nothing for some time," and so forth; her father is "the person who seems to care for me." Even hated rivals high and low are "the person in the main house," "the lucky one," or "the insolent one," and so on (an aspect of the original work abandoned by translators as impossible to convey).[3] The reader, therefore, is totally shut out of the inner life or state of mind of all characters except that of the author. The world is a projection of the light from her eyes.

Needless to say, all her techniques combine to create one of the most prejudiced autobiographical narratives in Japanese literature. The strong sense of realism comes not from any attempt at objective chronicling, but from the startling openness with which she confesses such socially unacceptable emotions as jealousy and hatred and from the palpable reality of her obsessive emotions. As she strives to justify her sense of outrage and to win our pity, she projects a less-than-winning personality. Unlike the self-created heroines of later autobiographical narratives, such as Izumi Shikibu or the Daughter of Takasue, who charm or enthrall us, Michitsuna's Mother leaves few readers fond of her. Yet the power of her work has survived centuries and fed a long literary tradition. Once read, she remains indelibly in mind.

Although she was absent from the palace, the Mother of Michitsuna was, nonetheless, the aunt of the author of the *Sarashina nikki* (*As I Crossed the Bridge of Dreams*, translated by Ivan Morris), and her elder half-brother was married to the sister of Sei Shōnagon, author of *The Pillow Book*, who was a literary rival of Lady Murasaki. We have no proof that Murasaki Shikibu read *The Gossamer Years*, but it seems virtually impossible for her to have missed it. In the geographically small and almost incestuously interrelated Heian aristocratic world, with its passion for literature and its openness to anything new and amusing, manuscripts were readily borrowed, copied, and passed from hand to hand. Writers were eager to have their works appreciated, and readers were hungry to enjoy them. Murasaki began her great novel, *The Tale of Genji*, during the decade following the death of Michitsuna's Mother. *The Gossamer Years* had surely demonstrated for the first time that real life was more engrossing and more moving than old fairy-tale fantasies. The attack made by the Mother of Michitsuna on "old romances" consisting of the "rankest fabrication" surely helped to open the way for Murasaki to conceive of writing vernacular prose fiction based wholly on the real world of men and women.

THE PILLOW BOOK

The Pillow Book by Sei Shōnagon was written when the author was a lady-in-waiting in the entourage of Empress Sadako (also known as Teishi) during the last decade of the tenth century. A brilliantly talented daughter of a noted scholar and poet of the Kiyohara family, Sei Shōnagon is one of the greatest prose writers in all of Japanese history, yet most of her life story remains a mystery. Even her name and her dates are unknown. "Sei Shōnagon" was the sobriquet by which she was known at court, "Sei" being the Sino-Japanese reading of the first character *kiyo*, in her surname, and Shōnagon (lesser counselor) was one of several typical court ranks derived from that of a male relative and bestowed on court ladies. The Kiyoharas had produced generation after generation of fine scholar-poets, and Sei as a child clearly received an unusually fine education in Japanese and Chinese letters. It is clear from *The Pillow Book* that she not only held her own in the company of literary men but enjoyed besting them with her quick, erudite wit and apt bons mots drawn from an enormous store of memorized classics from both the Chinese and Japanese tradition.

Although it is believed she had been married briefly and bore a son before she entered court and that she remarried and had a daughter later in life after the death of Empress Sadako, virtually none of this can be documented. That she became a Buddhist nun at the death of her husband and died in lonely poverty also belongs to the realm of legend.

Despite this dearth of verifiable biographical fact, however, Sei Shōnagon, the woman, comes vividly to life through *The Pillow Book* itself. Clearly, in writing this work, she was not keeping a diary, nor trying to sum up her life. But it is so close an observation of the world in which she lived that in many ways we can visualize her and her surroundings even more clearly than we can in the case of Michitsuna's Mother. Sei Shōnagon's book of seemingly (yet surely not wholly) random entries is so outrageously self-assured, so charged with opinion, so pointedly sarcastic, so abundantly witty, so intensely full of delight and wonder at the world of man and nature, the author, like a well-rounded character in a novel, becomes strikingly real to us.

The origins of her *Pillow Book* are described by Sei Shōnagon herself. One day, she explains, the empress was presented with a quantity of blank notebooks. Paper of this nature was a luxury item in short supply, and the empress asked Sei Shōnagon's advice as to how best to use the gift. The emperor had decided to use a similar gift to have a copy of the famous and voluminous Chinese history *Records of the Historian* (*Shiji*) made for him. Sei's reply to the empress, "let me make them into a pillow," seems inordinately flip. Clearly her answer cannot be taken literally. Could this perhaps be an erudite allusion to a line from a poem by the Chinese poet Bo Juyi (Po Chü-i), as some scholars suggest, in which he describes himself napping with his head pillowed on books? More likely, her words refer to some type of memo book in which to jot down poetic ideas and record examples of *uta-makura* (poetic pillow words) which provide the opening words or lines upon which the poems "rest." The meaning of Sei's reply remains obscure, yet, far from flip, it was clearly the right thing to say.

> "Very well," said Her Majesty. "You may have them." I now had a vast quantity of paper at my disposal, and I set about filling the notebooks with odd facts, stories from the past, and all sorts of other things, often including the most trivial material. On the

whole I concentrated on things and people that I found charming and splendid; my notes are also full of poems and observations on trees and plants, birds and insects. I was sure that when people saw my book they would say, "It's even worse than I expected. Now one can really tell what she is like." After all, it is written entirely for my own amusement and I put things down exactly as they came to me. How could my casual jottings possibly bear comparison with the many impressive books that exist in our time? Readers have declared, however, that I can be proud of my work. This has surprised me greatly; yet I suppose it is not strange that people should like it, for, as will be gathered from these notes of mine, I am the sort of person who approves what others abhor and detests the things they like.[4]

She was also the sort of person whose astute observation and keen insight turned even her most random of jottings into not only an expression of beauty but also an instrument of revelation. *The Pillow Book* contains eyewitness descriptions of events and ceremonies, anecdotes about the author herself and people she knows, small experimental fictions invented in her imagination, impressions, casual essays, and lists of things that interest her. This last category, the list or litany, was not invented by Sei, but was a favorite traditional Korean form and had its origins in the Chinese *fu.* Songs based on puns, topographical catalogs, lists of opulent clothing, architecture, foods, and the seasons provided opportunity for intricate sonorous word games in all three cultures of North East Asia. But Sei's lists are more than clever, they are penetrating, and startle the reader into reflection.

THINGS THAT CANNOT BE COMPARED

Summer and Winter. Night and day. Rain and sunshine. Youth and age. A person's laughter and his anger. Black and white. Love and hatred.[5]

THINGS THAT HAVE LOST THEIR POWER

A large boat which is high and dry in a creek at ebbtide.

A woman who has taken off her false locks to comb the short hair that remains.

A large tree that has been blown down in a gale and lies on its side with its roots in the air . . .

A man of no importance reprimanding an attendant.[6]

THINGS THAT ARE DISTANT THOUGH NEAR

Festivals celebrated near the Palace.

Relations between brothers, sisters, and other members of a family who do not love each other.[7]

THINGS THAT ARE NEAR THOUGH DISTANT

Paradise.
The course of a boat.
Relations between a man and a woman.[8]

These passages of *The Pillow Book* make it the clear predecessor of the *zuihitsu*, or miscellaneous essay, genre to which such later masterpieces as Kamo no Chōmei's *An Account of My Hut* and Yoshida Kenkō's *Essays in Idleness* belong. Zuihitsu (following the brush) is a less structured form than the "essay" in the Western tradition; central to the idea of "following one's brush" is the implicit absence of author-directed intent, a leisurely perambulation through a mental landscape as varied and unstructured as natural scenery.

Sei Shōnagon's *Pillow Book*, however, does more than merely ruminate out loud. In the best tradition of the Western essay, she is self relevatory and articulates herself aggressively, confident in her authority to speak in her own voice. The basic stance is not unlike autobiography: that is, the essayist's "I" speaks only for herself, claims a right to her opinions and biases, and hopes to enunciate them so cunningly that the reader cannot fail to agree. And we, the readers, often disagreeing, sometimes even horrified, with deep pleasure watch her brilliant mind at work. The essayist's prose style and personal ruminations are often every bit as revealing as a direct autobiographical account.

Sei Shōnagon's social attitude toward those outside court circles is elitist to the extreme, and sometimes startles the modern reader. Her contact with anyone outside the highly refined circles to which she belonged was limited only to occasional glimpses and her prejudices, fed by ignorance, are blatant. She looks upon the lower classes, working people, and the poor as if they were curious species of animals (see the section called *THE WAY IN WHICH CARPENTERS EAT*, p. 255), and she finds an incongruous waste in the beauty of moonlit snow on the hovels of the poor (see *UNSUITABLE THINGS*, p. 71)—lessons in how isolation and lack of intercourse cultivates prejudice.

Although Sei Shōnagon was also a prolific poet, relatively few of her poems survive: a few in imperially sponsored anthologies and private collections; the rest in *The Pillow Book* and in the *Sei Shōnagon-shu*, a private collection of her own poems. Like the Mother of Michitsuna, it was for that special "book of her own" in prose—self-expressive, grounded in her real life experience—for which she is remembered and admired. *The Pillow Book* is second only to *The Tale of Genji* among the works of the Heian court at that golden age around the year 1,000. It is one of the pure jewels in the Japanese vernacular language.

THE CONFESSIONS OF LADY NIJŌ

Two and a half centuries after the age of Sei Shōnagon and Murasaki Shikibu, Japanese court culture had become an elaborately attempted replica of the world idealized in Murasaki's masterpiece, *The Tale of Genji*. In the thirteenth-century *Confessions of Lady Nijō*, therefore, Nijō's own real-life story, her upbringing, her relationships, her preoccupations, and, most of all, her literary allusions resonate with *Genji* analogies and sensibilities. At the same time her considerably broader horizons bespeak the new age in which reduced aristocratic power led directly to an increased awareness of, and indeed lively encounters with, those living outside the mansions of the great.

The original Japanese title of Lady Nijō's book, *Towazugatari*, means literally "an unsolicited account." In the aristocratic literary tradition, the writing of poetry and fiction was more often than not undertaken at someone's request, or required by some occasion. A talented lady-in-waiting would be asked to produce a new tale for her empress or entourage much as Mozart was asked to compose a new opera or symphony for his patron and associates. Lady Nijō makes it clear, however, that no one has asked her for this story; she has written it out of deeply personal motivations. In this regard, no matter how different her personality, the life she led, or the manner in which she recounts it, she shares with Michitsuna's Mother and Sei Shōnagon a compelling need for a "book of her own."

Lady Nijō was born in 1258 to a high-ranking minister of state from the Koga family. Her poetically talented and socially prominent mother, who died while she was still an infant, had been in service at the court of ex-Emperor Go Fukakusa, and because of this connection the young Nijō was taken into his court when she was four and brought up there. When Nijō reached puberty, the twenty-seven-year-old Go Fukakusa took her, with her father's consent, as his concubine. Thus began a life-long relationship of love, trust, and affection between them that could not be extinguished even by his relations with his primary and secondary wives or by her several spectacular affairs with prominent statesmen, a high priest, and even Go Fukakusa's brother and bitter rival. Had her father not died when she was only fifteen, leaving her without the indispensable parental advocate in the marriage politics of the day, she might well have become an imperial wife.

Our knowledge of Lady Nijō is based almost entirely upon the one book she penned. This highly sophisticated autobiographical narrative seasoned with moving poetry is divided into five books and covers thirty-six years of her life. The narrative begins in 1271, when Go Fukakusa first takes her as a lover. It proceeds through her rise, her scandal-ridden fall, and her ultimate expulsion from the palace, and then follows her fascinating experiences and thoughts during her seventeen years wandering the land as a Buddhist nun.

The opening pages depict a New Year drinking party in which Go Fukakusa, well in his cups, informs Nijō's father that the time has come to permit his young daughter to come to him as a lover. Nijō's father accepts the proposal and formal cups of sake are exchanged. Over the next two weeks the retired emperor makes formal gifts to the young girl of clothing accompanied by love notes intended to woo her and prepare her for the liaison. Her father and his household staff prepare for Go Fukakusa's first night visit with careful attention to the furnishings and so on. The child, however, is so innocent of what is supposed to happen, so reticent and so tearfully frightened, Go Fukakusa ultimately gives up. With some embarrassment he hopes that she will not betray to the household his failure to consummate what was sanctioned and expected by all but the child to be their first night of a formal sexual liaison, as she joins the network of women under Go Fukakusa's protection. The second night, when she remains obstinately opposed, Go Fukakusa takes her against her will. Though the event is traumatic, it is clear that much like the outcome of initially forced consummation on the wedding night in many virgin marriages, she grows to care for him, suffer jealousy over his other liaisons, and in general is disposed toward him as no victim of rape in current parlance would be.

In looking back over her childhood in Book I, she shares with us an early longing for the freedom that comes with taking religious vows and for the enviable literary life lived by the peripatetic twelfth-century poet-priest, Saigyō:

> I remember looking at a scroll when I was only nine years old called "Records of the Travels of Saigyō" . . . I had envied

Saigyō's life ever since, and although I could never endure a life of ascetic hardship, I wished I could at least renounce this life and wander wherever my feet might lead me . . . and make out of this a record of my travels that might live on after my death.[9]

Not only does she, indeed, take vows and set out in the footsteps of Saigyō, but more and more she feels an inner pressure to write and thereby to restore her family's waning literary prestige. The inner imperative intensifies until, as she grows older, the fear sets in that she will fail. The book that will have made her life worthwhile and restore her family's fame may never be completed. She may not be sufficiently blessed by the spirits of past literary greats to empower her to write well enough. She is in her mid-forties; she begins to have nightmares and to expend her few treasures at shrines and temples for prayers that she may succeed.

This year marked the thirty-third anniversary of Father's death. . . . I looked at the stone markers, lingering reminders of the dead. I was saddened by the knowledge that none of my father's poems had been included in the most recent imperial anthology. Had I still been serving at court, perhaps I might have been able to appeal, for one of his poems had appeared in every anthology since the *Shokukokinshū*. The thought that my heritage—a poetic tradition upheld by our family for eight generations—had come to such a hollow end upset me.[10]

She returned home and that night had a dream in which her father appears speaking words intended to comfort her:

"No one on either side of our family has ever forsaken poetry. . . . The waves of our influence have always been felt in the Bay of Poetry." As he stood to leave, Father gazed upon me and recited:

Sow all the words you can
For in a better age
Men shall judge the harvest
By its intrinsic worth.

I awoke with a start. His shadow lingered in the tears on my sleeves.[11]

She begins pilgrimages to shrines and temples making pledges, bargaining for divine strength. She spends seven days in prayer before the grave of the great *Man'yōshū* poet, Hitomaro.

Born in a grove
Of luxuriant bamboo,
Am I fated to be
But an empty stalk?[12]

Lady Nijō's book ends in 1306 when religious services, held on the third anniversary of ex-Emperor Go Fukakusa's death, rekindle her grief at the loss of the one person who had been dear to her for most of her life.

She seems weary and fearful that her life, which produced but a single book and a few poems, has been in vain.

> That all my dreams might not prove empty, I have been writing this useless account—though I doubt it will long survive me.[13]

Having had no one upon whom she could rely to circulate her book to the world, her fears were well-founded. Her book lay neglected, largely unknown over the centuries. Miraculously, however, it did survive her—in a single copy rediscovered only in 1940 in the Imperial Household Library in Tokyo, mis-stored (for how many centuries?) among geographic manuscripts.

Lady Nijō, who had been inspired to become a nun and to devote her life to literature by the poet-priest Saigyō's example, would be amazed to learn that her own work, when it emerged from its long hibernation, had a similar radical effect on a twentieth-century novelist. Setouchi Harumi (b. 1922), upon reading Nijō's story, was so moved that she, too, became a Buddhist nun in order to pursue single-mindedly her artistic and personal freedom. She is active today as a writer, critic, and lecturer on women's issues.

TOPICS FOR DISCUSSION

1. All three of these very personal books, *The Gossamer Years*, *The Pillow Book*, and *The Confessions of Lady Nijō*, are based on what Thomas Mallon calls "the private fingering of ordinary experience."[14] Yet all three authors have a vivid awareness of audience and a strong sense of the self that each wants posterity to remember and appreciate. "I write for myself and strangers," said Gertrude Stein.

This clear wish on the part of Lady Nijō, and seemingly Sei Shōnagon as well (despite her protests of embarrassment), reminds one of Madame de Sévigné's view of her own letters. Then too, Gide and Claudel went so far as to have their diaries printed during their own lifetimes. Little comparative work has been done on autobiographical writing by women in Japan and the West. The earliest woman writer of English, Dame Julian of Norwich (1342?-?) lived centuries after that golden age of women writers in

Japan, and she wrote about the goodness of God rather than the life of men and women.

Lady Nijō's book might be used together with *The Book of Margery Kempe* (translated by Barry Windeatt. Penguin Books, 1987), the earliest surviving example of autobiographical writing in English (c. 1373-c. 1440), which was lost for centuries until one manuscript was found in 1934. After twenty years of marriage and fourteen children, Margery Kempe enters a religious life of pilgrimage and travels widely. In sharp contrast to Nijō, however, Margery could neither read nor write, but as an aging woman dictated her recollections to a priestly scribe. True to Western tradition, her book is written for the glory of God and to magnify the name of her Savior, Jesus Christ. Nonetheless her candor in recounting her madness after childbirth, her economic failures in the brewery trade, and her difficulties with her husband, make it a moving and remarkably revealing work.

2. Among the issues such literary juxtapositions raise is that of the religious vs. the secular. Whereas Japanese autobiographical narratives were thoroughly secular, and gave form to publicly confided private emotions in an encapsulated world of like-minded people, the history of the genre is markedly different in the West. The aim of St. Augustine's *Confessions* was "to praise God," and down through the ages to Rousseau, who consciously broke the tradition, "confessions" were fundamentally religious; Christian autobiography predominated. Where the Western writer viewed the "self" in relation to God, the Japanese perceived the "self" in relation to social peers who judged her life and her right to a posterity.

3. Margaret Cavendish (1623?-1673?), in her book *The True Relation of My Birth, Breeding, and Life* sounds a bit like Michitsuna's Mother when she says:

> I verily believe some censuring readers will scornfully say, why hath this Lady writ her own life? since none cares to know. . . . I answer that it is true, that 'tis to no purpose to the readers, but is to the authoress, because I write it for my own sake, not theirs.

But if we are going to consider these Japanese works with others separated so far in time, a more interesting exercise might be to view them together with the intimate journals of George Sand or Lord Byron's short jottings. Considerably more modern comparisons are surely possible as well, and are recommended.

4. Another related topic is the contract of trust that a culture permits (or disallows) between its writers and readers. The Japanese have traditionally distrusted fiction. It was fabricated, false, a deception that verged on sin. To them the autobiographical impulse was the most sincere form of writing; it was the essence of veracity. In the West was not the reverse, until recently at least, true? Take, for instance, the following example from Dostoyevsky:

> Every man has reminiscences . . . he would not reveal even to his friends . . . other things . . . a man is afraid to tell even himself. . . . A true autobiography is almost an impossibility . . . man is bound to lie about himself.

Sigmund Freud is also suspicious of the biographical impulse: "Whoever undertakes to write a biography binds himself to lying, to concealment."

5. In conclusion, our three books surely provide a basis for a new look at gender theory. In "Daughters Writing: Toward a Theory of Women's Biography," Bell Gale Chevigny postulates that women's autobiographical writings emerge as

> strategies by which the author seeks to explain or justify her current sense of herself, a need which might be especially strong in a woman who feels herself moving into uncharted waters and whose sense of herself is subject to sharp shifts in direction.[15]

One thousand years ago the Mother of Michitsuna would surely have said, "That's why I wrote!" And seven hundred years ago, expelled from court, newly tonsured and garbed as a nun, heading in that new, uncharted direction, Nijō dreamed of those strategies, to justify her worth, restore her family's literary name, and no doubt thereby redefine her own sense of herself.

But Sei Shōnagon would have given Bell Gale Chevigny an argument. What a delight it would have been to hear.

NOTES

1. Mother of Michitsuna, *The Gossamer Years: A Diary by a Noblewoman of Heian Japan*, trans. Edward Seidensticker (Rutland, VT and Tokyo: Charles E. Tuttle and Co., 1964; paperback, 1974), p. 33.
2. Ibid., p. 69
3. English requires a stated subject for every verb. Classical Japanese on the other hand is comprised essentially of modified verbs whose implied subject becomes clear primarily through the use of intricate verbal levels of reverence, politeness, or neutrality totally absent in the

English language. Requiring a grammatical subject, the English translation therefore normally chooses names for characters as a convenience.

4. Sei Shōnagon, *The Pillow Book of Sei Shōnagon*, trans. Ivan Morris (Middlesex, England: Penguin Books, 1971), pp. 263–264.

5. Ibid., p. 88.

6. Ibid., p. 145.

7. Ibid., p. 181.

8. Ibid.

9. Daughter of Koga no Masatada, *The Confessions of Lady Nijō*, trans. Karen Brazell (Garden City, NY: Doubleday Anchor Books [paperback], 1973), p. 52.

10. Ibid., p. 250–51.

11. Ibid., p. 251–52.

12. Ibid., p. 252.

13. Ibid., p. 264.

14. See Thomas Mallon's study of diarists, *A Book of One's Own* (New York: Tickman & Fields, 1989).

15. Bell Gale Chevigny, "Daughters Writing: Toward a Theory of Women's Biography," *Feminist Studies*, vol. 9, no.1 (Spring 1983): 79–102.

REFERENCES

General Background

Morris, Ivan. *The World of the Shining Prince: Court Life in Ancient Japan.* New York: Alfred A. Knopf, 1964. (Also Penguin paperback and Peregrine paperback, 1969.) The best overall introduction to Japanese Court life during the golden age of women writers. Commentary is sometimes patronizing, however, and tends to pronounce customs "bizarre" if they differ from Western practice.

Wakita Haruko. "Marriage and Property in Pre-modern Japan from the Perspective of Women's History." *Journal of Japanese Studies*, vol. 10, no. 1 (Winter, 1984): 73–99.

Translations

Daughter of Koga no Masatada (1258–1306?). *Towazugatari.* Translated by Karen Brazell as *The Confessions of Lady Nijō*. Garden City, NY: Doubleday Anchor Books, 1973; Stanford: Stanford University Press, 1976 [hardcover and paperback]. This translation, based mainly on the 1966 Tsugita annotations and interpretations and which won a National Book Award for Translation, includes a twenty-one page introduction concerning the author's life, the content of the work, the history of the manuscript, and the author's intent in writing such a work.

Towazugatari is also translated by Wilfred Whitehouse and Eizo Yanagisawa as *Lady Nijō's Own Story: Towazugatari: The Candid Diary of a 13th Century Japanese Imperial Concubine*. Rutland, VT and Tokyo: Charles E. Tuttle and Co., 1974. This translation, based primarily on the 1969 Tomikura annotations and commentary, includes twenty-two pages of appendices on the historical background of the court in Lady Nijō's day, and her life story with an explanation of key events.

Mother of Michitsuna (active 954–93). *Kagerō Nikki.* Translated by Edward Seidensticker as *The Gossamer Years: A Diary by a Noblewoman of Heian Japan.* Rutland, VT and Tokyo: Charles E. Tuttle and Co., 1964; paperback, 1974. Seidensticker's translation includes a twenty-two-page introduction which describes the author, her work, textual history, and literary context, with what today may be considered a somewhat controversial and dated interpretation of men and women's views of each other.

Sei Shōnagon (965?-?). *Makura no sōshi.* Translated by Ivan Morris as *The Pillow Book of Sei Shōnagon.* New York: Columbia University Press, 1967, 2 vols.; Middlesex: Penguin Books, 1971, reprinted 1974, 1 vol. paperback. Volume 2 of the hardback version is devoted entirely to copious notes on the text which is translated in full in volume 1, and also includes more than seventy pages of Appendices on Annual Observations and Ceremonies, People, the Zodiac, Genealogies, Governmental hierarchies, as well as maps and illustrations designed for specialists. The paperback edition is approximately a two-thirds abbreviation of the hardback version, and the notes and appendices have been prepared for nonspecialists.

To date no works of literary criticism on these three books have been published in English.

"AN ACCOUNT OF MY HUT"

Paul Anderer

Kamo no Chomei was born in 1153, and at the age of fifty, he tells us, he renounced the world and became a Buddhist monk. He was of a hereditary line of Shinto priests, and in better times, may well have succeeded his father as a priest at the Kamo Shrine in Kyoto. But the late twelfth century was among the most strife-torn and transforming of all periods in Japan, and this was not to be.

In 1212, ten years after he took the tonsure and assumed a Buddhist name, after he adopted to the life of a recluse in the mountains, Chomei wrote a brief essay. "An Account of My Hut" seems a simple, almost a fragile, literary structure, yet has proven to be among the most resilient and enduring of Japanese texts. Indeed, when we recall how frequently Japanese writing—whether a thirty-one-syllable lyric, a Noh play, or a narrative of over a thousand pages—coheres around the site of a hut or a small sequestered dwelling, located in the mountains or on a strand of desolate beach, at a discrete remove from the pressures of politics and society, we begin to understand the range and importance of Chomei's account. We might also adjust our sense of a literary "monument," of a "classic" work of canonical stature, to accommodate other understandings of how literary strength or spiritual value can be recognized or measured.

"An Account of My Hut" has been variously described, but to begin simply we can say that it is written in two parts. The first is an illustration of suffering in the world. Here the writing is reminiscent of the apocalyptic Buddhist commentary and parables popular at the time, and finds a visual analogue in those medieval picture scrolls depicting a desiccated world haunted by hungry ghosts. The second part, though nostalgic and often brooding in tone, is yet a celebratory record of how the author recovered, under specific conditions, at a particular place, what he calls "peace," or more minimally, "absence of grief." It is an account, finally, of a cultural survivor, who had witnessed changes as dramatic and abrupt as any in Japanese history. No modern Tokyo writer, sipping coffee under a naked light bulb, recollecting the glow of fireflies, had greater material cause for nostalgia than did Chomei.

Plainly, this short, diary-like rendering we know as "An Account of My Hut" offers no thorough historical record of occurrences in the second half of the twelfth century. (In brief, a ruling family was ousted, bringing to an end a four-hundred-year era of "Peace and Tranquility," while rival military clans fought it out, intermittently attacking, pillaging, or occupying the capital city of Kyoto.) But neither does Chomei ignore completely the sights and the consequences of that history, as does much later medieval writing—where concrete reference to worldly distress seems but a lapse of concentration, so strong is the meditative urge. The "Account," to be sure, is the work of a cleric, whose adopted faith teaches most fundamentally that the world is a place of suffering, that the things of the world are illusory, inconstant, and impermanent. It is a work moreover that, from beginning to end, means to be instructive (when Chomei claims that he is writing to please himself, as though he has no audience, he is affecting a familiar stance taken, among others, by Sei Shonagon when she wrote her *Pillow Book*[1] ca. 996). Yet the didactic tone is modulated, where it does not break off altogether. The will to transmit abstract religious truth fades away, and in its place we find another impulse: to speak in a personal, lyrical way of suffering and of a path toward tranquility. In this sense, the "Account" is no mere tract which heaps scorn on this "cracked husk of a world," but rather a guide directing us to a remote mountain hut, where in solitude Chomei reveals affection for all that the world has torn and scattered—for a whole culture uprooted, unhoused, in need of shelter, however fragile or temporary.

For many, it seemed, religion itself was to provide that shelter. In fact, a number of popular Buddhist revival movements had emerged and were enthusiastically embraced in Chomei's day. Their popularity sprang, no doubt, from the sheer scale of violent change, wherein people of every place in society were daily brought face to face with uncertainty. This historical predicament was given heightened significance in the notion of *mappo*, or the "last days of the Law." According to Buddhist chronology, in this phase the world would lapse into degeneracy, laws and rites would be imperfectly observed, and ordinary suffering would yield to chaos. This age was to have begun three thousand years after the Buddha's birth (1052 by a numerical estimate) and was to continue for an indefinite period. This put Chomei and his culture squarely within a sick, decadent cycle, and gives a distinctly religious aura to that litany of disasters with which the "Account" begins.

And so the Fire that sweeps the capital, which was a fire in fact and can be documented, assumes figural significance as an inevitable inferno brought on by the vanity of city-dwellers. The Whirlwind, given realistic detail as "roofs of bark or thatch were driven like winter leaves in the wind," also reminds the author of "the blasts of Hell," and is of such uncommon force that "it must be a presage of terrible things to come." The Moving of the Capital, which was a historical occurrence, seems a pure sign of instability and the unexpected, provoking both anxiety and a painful comparison between these days and the past—when rulers were wise and forebearing, and people presumably did not "all feel uncertain as drifting clouds." With the Famine there is the graphic scene of bodies decomposing along the banks of the Kamo River, and of an infant, unaware its mother is dead, still sucking at her breast; yet it also totalizes the author's vision, as he sees that the world is one of "foulness and evil." Finally, the Earthquake seems to signal the end, as "mountains crumbled and rivers were buried, the sea tilted over and immersed the land"; as for damage throughout the capital, "not a single mansion, pagoda, or shrine was left whole." Considered the most benign of the four elements, the earth itself had thus broken apart to afflict the people. With this, Chomei concludes his litany of disaster and extraordinary suffering, drawing out the ultimate lesson "of the vanity and meaninglessness of the world." As mentioned earlier, Chomei's language in this section has parallels in other religious or secular writings of this general period. In the monk Genshin's *Essentials of Salvation*,[2] for example, a catechetical text and a medieval best-seller, the Hell which awaits karmic evildoers is described as horrifyingly as is Chomei's Kyoto-Hellfire (even as the heavenly rewards awaiting those who attain salvation, in Genshin's portrayal, assume a certain this-worldly form in the pleasures of his hut, in the way Chomei will describe them as he continues his "Account"). Also, in the warrior tales, and notably in *The Tale of the Heike*,[3] which grew from oral stories that had begun to circulate in Chomei's day, we find episodes of fire, earthquake, and moving capitals, as well as examples of unnatural disaster and disease, with the reiteration that clearly "the world was fixed on the path of chaos," or again, that "for men of sensitive souls, the world now seemed a hopeless place." Also noticeable in the *Heike*—whose theme is that of impermanence and the fall of the mighty and whose subject is the historical struggle between the Heike and the Genji clans—is that the reach toward a certain epical breadth is often interdicted by lyrical intensity ("the blood stained the sand like dark maple leaves"). Here, as in Chomei's "Account," a way out, a path toward salvation, follows the path of the exile, haunted by the loss of past glory. Here, too, tranquility is recovered in the quiet of a mountain retreat, where the former Empress, now a Buddhist nun, waits for death "on a velvety green carpet of moss."

When Chomei concludes his opening section with a reflective passage on "Hardships of Life in the World," and when he tells us that in his fiftieth year he renounced the world and took Buddhist orders, we are given both certain biographical facts, as well as the sketch of a literary archetype. Even in better times, indeed, in some of the memorable writing of the lost Heian golden age, we regularly come across the figure of an emperor abdicating or a love-stricken courtier withdrawing to outlying hills and the contemplative life, even though many such world-weary figures never finally take their vows, or continue to return at intervals to the colorful complications of the city.

In that sense, just when he seems most "original"—setting off on his own solitary road, leaving the vanities of culture and society behind—Chomei moves modestly but with grim, focused determination, along a well-traveled literary path. He then fashions a hut "where, perhaps, a traveler might spend a single night." It is this kind of path and dwelling that will carry and shelter Saigyo and later Bashō along their own protracted period of exile and wandering. Here too we identify the traveling priest who, in some out of the way but culturally resonant place in Nature, will discover the heroes and heroines of many Noh plays. The hut which Chomei builds is of materials, wood and thatch. But it assumes shape because of certain cultural materials which Chomei knew and used, and sought to rescue.

Like other influential medieval literati, Chomei was a writer (essayist, compiler of miracle stories, travel diarist, but primarily a poet) and a monk. Literature, and especially poetry, came thus to be practiced and preserved as a religion. And the poet's life, like the monk's life, was one of seclusion or exile. It was spare, unadorned in any practical sense, marginal, and precarious. Yet it did have formidable precedents. Genji himself was exiled to a forlorn dwelling on Suma beach, a dark but crucial chapter in

Murasaki's great narrative—one of its several illustrations of karma leading even the brightest of lives into darkness. And beside the figure of Genji in this scene is that of Po Chü-i [Bo Juyi], the most influential of all Chinese poets for classical writers in Japan, who himself built a hut on Mt. Lu (just as beyond Po Chü-i [Bo Juyi] emerges the figure of the Indian recluse-sage, Vimalakīrti).

This is exile, then, but an enabling deprivation. Lacking color, variety, action, its very blandness (a trait widely celebrated in Taoist [Daoist] and later Ch'an [Chan] or Zen texts) generates other insights, other tastes. These Chomei attempted to identify in his *Mumyosho* (*Notes Without a Name*), one of the most famous of all medieval treatises on poetry and aesthetics. Chomei himself had written poetry in a so-called new style, notable for its "mystery and depth," or *yugen*, an aesthetic category of crucial importance to medieval culture. But here, in the question and answer form typical of such discussion, Chomei feigns ignorance, and asks what "new style" poetry, and its alleged "mystery and depth," might possibly mean. The answer (his own of course, but deferentially attributed to his master, the priest-poet Shunei) gives no definition, but a series of metonymical illustrations:

> on an autumn evening, for example, there is no color in the sky nor any sound, yet although we cannot give any reason for it, we are somehow moved to tears. . . .
>
> again, when one gazes upon the autumn hills half-concealed by a curtain of mist, what one sees is veiled yet profoundly beautiful; such a shadowy scene, which permits free exercise of the imagination in picturing how lovely the whole panoply of scarlet leaves must be, is far better than to see them spread with dazzling clarity before our eyes. . . .
>
> it is only when many meanings are compressed into a single word, when the depths of feeling are exhausted yet not expressed, when an unseen world hovers in the atmosphere of the poem, when the near and common are used to express the elegant, when a poetic conception of rare beauty is developed to the fullest extent in a style of surface simplicity—only then, when the conception is exalted to the highest degree and the words are too few, will the poem, by expressing one's feelings in this way, have the power of moving Heaven and Earth within the brief confines of a mere thirty-one syllables, and be capable of softening the hearts of gods and demons.[4]

In the atmosphere of all that Chomei writes, in the contours of his fragile hut and the misty views of autumn twilight it provides, what if not the old lost world of the Heian court "yet hovers like an unseen world," waiting to be apprehended? Nature immediately and clearly surrounds Chomei in the mountains, but it is the distant world of a fading culture which he consciously gathers about him:

> On mornings when I feel short-lived as the white wake behind a boat, I go to the banks of the river and, gazing at the boats plying to and fro, compose verses in the style of the Priest Mansei. Or if of an evening the wind in the maples rustles the leaves, I recall the river at Jinyo, and play the lute in the manner of Minamoto no Tsunenobu. If still my mood does not desert me, I often tune my lute to the echoes in the pines, or pluck the notes of the Melody of the Flowering Stream, modulating the pitch to the sound of the water.[5]

What Chomei sees in Nature are not "unmediated visions," generated by the force of the poet's free imagination. Setting out on an "ambitious journey," Chomei passes through the fields of Awazu, there to "pay my respects to the remains of Semimaru's hut"; crossing the Tanagami River, he visits the tomb of still another Heian poet, Sarumaru. These are lyrical movements in prose, through sights and sounds recorded by other wanderers. Even "the hooting of owls," a startling sound suggestive of the stark isolation of the mountain, contributes to Chomei's "endless pleasure," since Saigyo had also heard and sung of the owl's "eerie cries." Far beyond Chomei's hut, in the city, the world rages and people fall victim to a dizzying flux. But inside the hut (where on a shelf rests his books of poetry and music and extracts from the sacred writings, and beside them a folding koto and a lute) or in the Nature which immediately surrounds it, Chomei lives both in solitude, and in the company of a tradition he willfully places in all he hears and sees.

Throughout the medieval period, it is the poet who most movingly illuminates this forlorn, tumble-down, autumnal scene. But it is in the prose-poetry of Chomei's "Account" that within this scene, if dimly and in monochrome, emerges a human figure—a medieval portrait of the artist, though here an old man. The "Account" warns us of disaster and hardship in the world. And it reveals the path of renunciation, which leads into Nature and the crude but comforting arrangement of a hut ten feet square. Still, it is Chomei himself, the aging poet-priest, who is the hidden—and so in the terms of medieval aesthetics—the truly valuable subject of this "Account."

Chomei is "hidden" insofar as he does not stand forward in this work and present his life for our scrutiny and judgment, which seems to be the dramatic burden St. Augustine or Rousseau bear. His are modest claims: "I seek only tranquility. I rejoice in the absence of grief." When he tells us simply what he knows of the world, of human dwellings, and finally of attachment, Chomei reveals himself as an all-too-human monk. He is weak by the standards of the world he has renounced, and weak before his religion's imperative, since he remains attached to what is, after all, illusory.

But Chomei is strong in a way that is comprehensible, given the history he experienced. He knew that much of the past was gone and much else would not last. He mourned what was lost and gathered about him what was left. In a hut on Toyama in 1212, he recorded the exact site, the day to day moments, where he eked out his own and his tradition's survival.

TOPICS FOR DISCUSSION

1. Explore the uses of landscape in Chomei's "An Account of My Hut." What values are ascribed to the city and its buildings? to the country? To what extent is religious feeling a product of the environment?

2. Like the Book of Job, Chomei's "Account" is one of unnatural suffering. To whom (or to what) does Chomei turn in his need? Does he accept his fate as a sufferer? Does he protest against it? What does he learn for having suffered?

3. What role does culture—the arts of music and poetry in particular—play in the "Account?" Does Chomei renounce culture or does he preserve it? Is the hut which he builds a product of culture, or an extension of life in nature?

NOTES

1. Ivan Morris, trans., *The Pillow Book of Sei Shōnagon* (New York: Columbia University Press, 1967, 2 vols.; Middlesex, England: Penguin Books, 1971, reprinted 1974, 1 vol. paperback).

2. Tsunoda Ryūsaku, Wm. Theodore de Bary, and Donald Keene, eds., *Sources of the Japanese Tradition* (New York: Columbia Unversity Press, 1958).

3. Helen Craig McCullough, trans., *The Tale of the Heike* (Stanford: Stanford University Press, 1988).

4. Robert H. Brower and Earl Miner, *Japanese Court Poetry* (Stanford: Stanford University Press, 1961), p. 269.

5. Donald Keene, ed., *Anthology of Japanese Literature: From the Earliest Era to the Mid-Nineteenth Century* (New York: Grove Press, 1955; paperback, 1960), p. 208.

REFERENCES

Keene, Donald, ed. *Anthology of Japanese Literature: From the Earliest Era to the Mid-Nineteenth Century.* New York: Grove Press, 1955; paperback, 1960. Includes a complete translation of *An Account of My Hut (Hōjōki),* as well as selections from other medieval prose works.

SEVEN JAPANESE TALES BY TANIZAKI JUN'ICHIRŌ

Ken K. Ito

Over the course of a career that spanned more than half a century, Tanizaki Jun'ichirō (1886–1965), possibly Japan's greatest modern writer, explored man's yearning for ideal worlds and for images of femininity that stood for all that was beautiful, sensual, and seductive in these imagined realms. The stories in *Seven Japanese Tales* provide an introduction to a body of work, comprising some twenty-eight weighty volumes in the standard edition, that records the writer's lifelong pursuit of worlds charged with desire. In the first part of his career, the writer was drawn to an imagined "West," endowed with a freedom unavailable in a repressive Japan and adorned with beautiful, spirited women. Later, he professed an attraction to the burnished beauty of the past, the measured order of tradition, and the warm sensuality of the "mother." But Tanizaki refuses to fit into the convenient pattern of native identity rediscovered, for in the fiction written in the final decade of his life he again explored desires unbound by traditional restrictions, intoxications associated with the new and the foreign. The shifts and reversals in Tanizaki's preferences call attention to an important facet of his cultural sensibilities: the ideals he pursued were, for all the seeming contrasts they exhibited, connected by powerful, interwoven currents of feeling. Both his "West" and his "past" are products of the imagination, alternatives to a mundane reality. They are realms of desire that existed within the mind of a writer endlessly sensitive to the cultural fantasies and yearnings spawned by a society in flux.

Born in the middle of the Meiji era (1868–1912), Tanizaki was a son of the *shitamachi*, the merchants' quarter of Tokyo, which then still retained traces of the Edo period (1600–1867), when the townsman had been at the center of a vigorous urban culture. Much remained, in Tanizaki's youth, of the old neighborhoods of Edo (the previous name for the modern city of Tokyo) and the traditions that had evolved there over the years. As the young child of a prosperous merchant family, Jun'ichirō enjoyed the pleasures of *shitamachi* life—visits to the Kabuki theater, which he loved, and such seasonal observances as trips to view the cherry blossoms and the fall foliage. So deeply rooted was Tanizaki in the milieu of his youth that he later characterized himself as "a townsman's son, born in the *shitamachi* of Tokyo during the second decade of Meiji, reared amidst the various cultural features, the manners and the practices of the era, who later became a novelist using these as the foundation of his work."

Yet the young Jun'ichirō's happy years in the *shitamachi* were relatively short. His father, an utter failure as a merchant, suffered one business reversal after another until the Tanizakis were reduced to a hand-to-mouth existence. The gritty realities of life in rented back-alley lodgings quickly replaced all that was satisfying about Jun'ichirō's childhood in the *shitamachi.* Jun'ichirō was able to continue his education beyond middle school only by working as a live-in houseboy for a well-to-do family. A gifted student, he eventually gained entrance to the prestigious Tokyo Imperial University, but he passed from adolescence to young manhood learning the indignities of domestic service.

The world of the *shitamachi,* stolen from Tanizaki by poverty, was meanwhile being gradually destroyed by history. The *shitamachi* was the site of many early industrialization schemes, and it was swamped by massive in-migration from rural areas. For a writer who later wrote that "the native of Tokyo has no home," the *shitamachi* was the first of many lost worlds, luminous and out of reach.

The *shitamachi* of the Edo period provides the setting for the work that launched Tanizaki's career, "The Tattooer" (1910), a polished gem of a story about an artist who transforms a young girl by embellishing her skin with a giant spider. From the opening lines, it is clear that the Edo of this work belongs not to any actual past but to a past transfigured by the imagination:

> It was an age when men honored the noble virtue of frivolity, when life was not such a harsh struggle as it is today. . . . In the illustrated romantic novels of the day, in the Kabuki theater . . . everywhere beauty and strength were one. People did all they could to beautify themselves, some even having pigments

injected into their precious skins. Gaudy patterns of line and color danced over men's bodies.

The fictional world portrayed here owes much to Tanizaki's enthusiastic reading of Western literature, particularly Poe and Wilde; the stance of aestheticism, the Romantic idea of the Artist, and the images of the Eternal Woman and the femme fatale lie heavily over "The Tattooer." But perhaps less evident is how skillfully Tanizaki integrates these imported concepts with materials from his native environment. The portrayal of the single-minded tattooer draws upon an earlier genre of "artisan stories," which glorified demonically dedicated craftsmen, and the apprentice geisha who discovers the fatal power of her sexuality is a descendant of the numerous "poisonous women" who inhabited the late-Edo and early-Meiji popular consciousness.

"The Tattooer" contains the seeds of much that would bloom forth in Tanizaki's later writing. Aside from showing his powerful syncretic urge, it also presages his lifelong fascination with sadomasochism and foot fetishism. But perhaps the story's most important feature is that it displays the paradigm of a man's attempt to transform a woman to match his vision of the ideal. This paradigm was to become Tanizaki's major vehicle for exploring the tense struggle between the inner phenomenon of desire and the outer world, a struggle always shaped, in the writer's fiction, by the dynamics of power. "The Tattooer" appears, on the surface, to be built around a power reversal. At the beginning of the story, all authority rests with the tattooer, who drugs the timid young geisha and injects her unconscious body with his pigments. The tattoo, however, makes the girl beautiful beyond compare in a world where beauty equals power. It turns her into a femme fatale who claims the artist for her first victim. This seemingly simple reversal contains many of the elements of Tanizaki's later examinations of the paradoxes of power, for it shows the writer's concern with the connection between power and fantasy. When the tattooer surrenders to the girl's beauty, he bows before a projection of his own desires. His subservience validates the omnipotence of his own imagination.

In the decade following the publication of "The Tattooer," Tanizaki delved further into aestheticism and sadomasochism, and he wrote mysteries that became precursors of the genre in Japanese fiction. He also produced numerous examinations of abnormal psychology, such as "The Thief" (1921), in which a narrator who initially seems reliable gradually reveals his identity as a kleptomaniac, and "Terror" (1913), which portrays the emotions of a man with a phobia of trains who is forced to board the object of his worst nightmares.

Though these stories are never less than entertaining, the real breakthrough in Tanizaki's work came when he began to realize that some fantasies belong not only to the individual but to culture. Specifically, Tanizaki turned his attention to the Japanese obsession with the West. In works such as "Aguri" (1922), a story about a man experiencing a strange physical erosion as he pours his energies into transforming his mistress into a westernized woman, he explored the longing for a "West" that had little to do with any actual foreign land, a "West" that had arisen in a national consciousness dominated by a desire for modernity. Tanizaki's examination of this cultural obsession culminated in *Naomi* (1924–25), a comic novel whose narrator pursues the "West" by trying to turn a Japanese barmaid into his own version of Mary Pickford.

Tanizaki was never content with simply setting down fantasies on paper, and in the early twenties he immersed himself in the "West." He moved with his family to the foreigners' quarter of Yokohama, a port city that was a point of entry for everything new from abroad. There, he lived as westernized a life as a Japanese could live, occupying a Western-style house with tables and chairs, and taking ballroom dancing lessons. However, he was violently torn from this city that he loved, for Yokohama was destroyed, along with Tokyo, in the massive earthquake of 1923.

Tanizaki and his family fled to Kansai, the area comprising the cities of Kobe, Osaka, and Kyoto. Initially, the writer had planned to take refuge in the region only temporarily, but his stay there lengthened as his sensibilities underwent a gradual change. He rediscovered the urban landscape of the *shitamachi* in Osaka's older neighborhoods, whose preservation he credited to the survival of the Osaka merchant class. As Tanizaki recognized the opportunity to recover the roots of his own class identity, Kansai began to represent for him the order and the harmony of the past, the traditions of the East that had been lost in Tokyo's mad embrace of westernization. The writer would eventually come to call the area his "second homeland." Yet he never felt completely at home. In one of his essays he says that his observations of Kansai were made "from beginning to end . . . through the eyes of an immigrant from Tokyo." The Kansai that Tanizaki describes always seems as distant as it is familiar.

The attractions of Kansai soon began to appear in Tanizaki's

fiction. He chose to render the entire narrative of *The Whirlpool*
(1928–30) in an exotic variant of the Osaka dialect. And in *Some
Prefer Nettles* (1928–29), he probed the contradictory yearnings of
a westernized Tokyo man who feels the pull of tradition during
trips to various parts of the Kansai region. When radical nationalism took root in the thirties and many writers and artists embraced a "return to Japan," Tanizaki displayed his own highly
personal responses to these cultural currents. He wrote "In Praise
of Shadows" (1933), an idiosyncratic yet elegant redefinition of
traditional aesthetics. And he produced a series of works set in
the past such as "A Blind Man's Tale" (1931). In this story, the
sixteenth-century struggles that led to the unification of Japan
under the Tokugawa shogunate are recounted by a blind masseur
who served the ladies of the warring feudal lords. This choice of a
narrator allows Tanizaki to reinsert women into a segment of
history dominated by men, and to reexamine the deeds of the
mighty from the point of view of a lowly yet opinionated servant.
Though such stories as "A Blind Man's Tale" seemingly embody
an act of homage to the past, they are actually appropriations of
history with little regard for the past's integrity. An older, and
franker, Tanizaki would admit as much:

> No matter how attractive a certain subject seems, I can muster
> neither desire nor ability to write about it unless it is a fantasy
> born of my own mind. I have written a work or two that resem-
> bles historical fiction, but by and large these are things I made
> up. Such pieces as "A Blind Man's Tale," "The Secret History of
> the Lord of Musashi" . . . and "The Mother of Captain
> Shigemoto" are all of this ilk.[1]

Of Tanizaki's works set in the past, the most brilliant achievement is "A Portrait of Shunkin" (1933). On the surface, this account of a beautiful blind musician of the Edo period and her
manservant is a story of perfect devotion. From his boyhood, the
servant Sasuke waits upon his mistress Shunkin, worshipfully
ministering to her every need. Though the two eventually become
lovers, this side of the relationship goes unacknowledged as they
continue to behave toward each other as mistress and servant.
When Shunkin's beauty is destroyed by an unnamed attacker
who pours boiling water on her face, Sasuke makes a frightening
self-sacrifice. He destroys his own eyes with a needle so that he
can serve his mistress without seeing her disfigurement. With the
image of her past beauty locked securely in his mind, Sasuke
continues to tend to Shunkin until her death many years later.

A more stable hierarchy would be hard to imagine, yet there are indications of deeper dynamics in the relationship. The balance of power becomes less clear when it is taken into account that the blind Shunkin is totally helpless without Sasuke. A relationship defined on his side by devotion is for her a matter of survival. Moreover, Shunkin's domineering attitude owes a great deal to Sasuke, for he molds her behavior through the subtle formative powers of acquiescence. Even the manservant's act of self-mutilation turns out to be less sacrificial than it initially seems; the loss of his sight allows Sasuke to "see" in his mind's eye a Shunkin severed from corporeal limitations and transformed into an image of unchanging beauty. There is every indication that this "Shunkin" becomes more important to Sasuke than the Shunkin who exists in person:

> Apparently the blind Sasuke had given himself up to his imperishable ideal. To him, there was only the world of his old memories. If Shunkin had actually changed in character because of her misfortune she would no longer have been Shunkin. He wanted to think of her as the proud, haughty girl of the past; otherwise, the beautiful Shunkin of his imagination would have been destroyed.

For all that it does to emphasize Sasuke's devotion, "A Portrait of Shunkin" is also the story of a man's effort to possess an ideal, an effort that reduces a woman to an object subordinate to the fantasy she inspires.

Tanizaki uses two rhetorical strategies to persuasively present "A Portrait of Shunkin." The first involves his manipulation of the historical and geographical settings. Through frequent comparisons with Tokyo and with the present, he creates a fictional world of the Osaka past ripe with possibilities unavailable elsewhere, a world capable of supporting the unique relationship described in the work. The other strategy involves the construction of a complex, multilayered narrative. Tanizaki employs as his narrator a man with antiquarian tastes who claims to have learned about Sasuke and Shunkin in the course of his researches. This narrator tells the story in his own voice, as well as by quoting from such "sources" as a biography of Shunkin, which he presumes was written by Sasuke after his mistress's death, and an interview with an old woman who served the blind couple in their later years. Initially, the narrator is careful to specify the limits of his knowledge and to sift through his "sources" for accuracy. He even questions some of the information provided by his unavoidably biased "sources." Through such actions he achieves a mantle of reliability so complete that he can later put forward his own interpretations and speculations with impunity.

During the late thirties and the war years, Tanizaki continued to be drawn to the Japanese tradition. He produced the first of his three complete translations into modern Japanese of the eleventh-century classic, *The Tale of Genji*. And he wrote *The Makioka Sisters* (1943–48), his elegy to a graceful Kansai way of life destroyed by the war. Both endeavors were marked by the times in which they were undertaken. Because of fears that the militarist authorities would object to any portrayal of improprieties in the imperial line, even a fictional one, Tanizaki had to remove from his translation all references to Genji's affair with his father's concubine Fujitsubo and the subsequent ascension of their son to the throne. He also revised his original plan for *The Makioka Sisters*, substituting a lyrical and nostalgic treatment for the depiction of "depravity and decadence" among Osaka's privileged classes that he had first hoped to write. Even so, the censors found the novel's celebration of comfortable prewar life a threat to the austere morals of a nation at war. The serialization of the work was stopped after the first few chapters were published in 1943.

When peace came, Tanizaki finished *The Makioka Sisters* and then proceeded to take advantage of the freedom of postwar Japan. He plunged into portrayals of desires unfettered by traditional expectations, fantasies that belonged to the chaotic present. The two major novels of this final phase of his career, *The Key* (1956) and *Diary of a Mad Old Man* (1961–62), focus upon aging protagonists whose relentless desires drive them to an insupportable level of sexual excitement. In these last works, Tanizaki explores the losses and the opportunities of old age, the waning of sexual prowess, the ties between passion and mortality, and the gratification of manipulating others. He uses the diary-novel form in both works to probe such issues as the isolation of human subjectivity and the convenience of writing as a means of shaping experience.

These concerns are seen in the masterful "The Bridge of Dreams" (1959), which takes up a recurring theme in Tanizaki's fiction, that of a man's yearning for the maternal. This work, written shortly after Tanizaki moved away from the Kansai region and settled in the seaside resort of Atami, shows that the preoccupations of the writer's last years could be integrated with his interest in Japanese tradition. Though "The Bridge of Dreams" is set in modern times, Tanizaki uses frequent allusions to classical literature to endow it with an atmosphere suffused with the mystery and the sense of distance of the past. The work borrows its title from the final chapter of *The Tale of Genji*, with which it shares the motif of a man's pursuit of the memory of one woman in another. The narrator of "The Bridge of Dreams," who tells the story in the form of a personal memoir, describes how his father had acquired a substitute for his dead first wife by marrying a woman resembling her, and by making this second wife imitate the first in all ways, even taking her name. The father's efforts succeed so well that the two women blend together in the son's mind. When the father falls ill, he engineers another substitution by instructing his son to take his place in caring for his wife. Becoming an inheritor of his father's obsession, the son ministers to his stepmother until she meets an untimely death under suspicious circumstances. His love for her continues undimmed even as he writes his account years after her death.

"The Bridge of Dreams" addresses Tanizaki's concern with the plasticity of truth in writing, for the memoirist himself calls attention to his selectivity:

> Of course, all that I record here is true: I do not allow myself the slightest falsehood or distortion. But there are limits even to telling the truth; there is a line one ought not to cross. And so, although I certainly never write anything untrue, neither do I write the whole of the truth. Perhaps I leave part of it unwritten out of consideration for my father, for my mother, for myself. . . . If anyone says that not to tell the whole truth is in fact to lie, that is his own interpretation. I shall not venture to deny it.

The reference here is to the incestuous relationship between the memoirist and his stepmother, which is hinted at throughout the work but never confirmed. The narrator records the birth of a half-brother in the year of his father's death, leaving it to the reader to gather that the child was conceived at a time when illness made it difficult for his father to engage in sexual intercourse. Though there is no way to verify this, it seems highly likely that the narrator has duplicated Genji's feat of fathering a son who is outwardly his brother. If "The Bridge of Dreams" focuses on a father's success in moling his second wife to accord with his desires and in bending his son to his will, it also shows the son's union with his mother, and his power to set down a story as he sees fit.

Tanizaki once said that only "lies" interested him, and he expressed an admiration for works that "set down lies as though they were the truth." The memoirist of "The Bridge of Dreams," who sets down his account of the fulfillment of a deathless desire, is the creation of an author who reveled in the power of fantasy, an author who understood that illusion lay at the heart of fiction.

TOPICS FOR DISCUSSION

1. Tanizaki knew English and was an avid reader of Poe and Wilde during the early years of his career. How are the influences of these Western authors expressed in works such as "The Tattooer," "Terror," and "The Thief"?

2. Okada, the protagonist of "Aguri," thinks to himself: "Really, shopping to enhance the beauty of the woman you love ought to be like a dream come true." What views about women underlie such thoughts? What does Okada value about Aguri, and what does he gain through his fetisistic preoccupation with her clothing?

3. Tanizaki is a master of first-person narration; in the stories collected in *Seven Japanese Tales*, his first-person narrators include the researcher of "A Portrait of Shunkin," the memoirist of "The Bridge of Dreams," the increasingly suspect student of "The Thief," and the blind masseur of "A Blind Man's Tale." What do these stories gain from being told in the first person? How are the points-of-view of these narrators limited or biased?

4. Both "A Blind Man's Tale" and "A Portrait of Shunkin" feature sightless characters. How does blindness affect the fates of Yaichi, Shunkin, and Sasuke? What restrictions and what opportunities does blindness place before these characters?

5. Tanizaki's contemporary, Satō Haruo, wrote that "The Portrait of Shunkin" was actually a "portrait of Sasuke." How much do we learn about Shunkin's feelings and motives, and how is this information conveyed? How does our knowledge of Shunkin compare with what we learn about Sasuke?

6. After he wrote "A Portrait of Shunkin," Tanizaki remarked: "The one concern uppermost in my mind was to find the form that would best convey the greatest feeling of reality. In the end I settled on the laziest, easiest, method for a writer." Is Tanizaki's narrative style in this story lazy or easy? What are its components and how is it structured? How does it seek to "convey the greatest feeling of reality"? Some Japanese scholars argue that Stendhal's Abbess of Castro influenced the narrative strategy of "A Portrait of Shunkin." What similarities and differences are there between the two texts?

7. The one Western work that Tanizaki himself acknowledged as a source for "A Portrait of Shunkin" was Hardy's "Barbara of the House of Grebe" (from *Wessex Tales*), which he translated into Japanese shortly before beginning to work on his story. He later

said that "A Portrait of Shunkin" evolved as he took the situation of "Barbara of the House of Grebe," in which a woman ceases to love a handsome husband when his physical beauty is destroyed, and hypothesized about what a Japanese would do in the same situation, what would happen if the male and female roles were reversed. How did Tanizaki make use of his source material from Hardy? Does the relationship between these two texts constitute a case of what we generally think of as "influence"?

8. "The Bridge of Dreams" borrows its title from the final chapter of *The Tale of Genji*. What thematic concerns does it share with the eleventh-century classic? How does Tadasu's love for his stepmother compare with Genji's fixation upon Fujitsubo or Kaoru's pursuit of Ukifune? How does Tanizaki's portrayal of this particular kind of male desire differ from that of the female author of *The Tale of Genji*?

9. In "The Bridge of Dreams" and "A Portrait of Shunkin" elements of the stories are deliberately left ambiguous or mysterious. Why does Tanizaki not reveal exactly who destroyed Shunkin's beauty, who fathered Takeshi, or how Tadasu's stepmother died? What do these texts gain from their author's reticence? How are these deliberate obfuscations tied to the interests of the narrators of these stories?

10. What sort of woman is Tadasu's stepmother in "The Bridge of Dreams"? How fully is she depicted as a character? What are the essential features of the image of "mother" that Tanizaki draws in this story?

NOTE

1. Tanizaki Jun'ichirō, *Tanizaki Jun'ichirō zenshū* [The Complete Works of Tanizaki Jun'ichirō], vol. 19 (Tokyo: Chūō Kōronsha, 1968), p. 418. Translation of this passage is by Ken K. Ito.

REFERENCES

Critical Introductions

Ito, Ken K. *Visions of Desire: Tanizaki's Fictional Worlds*. Stanford: Stanford University Press, 1991.

Keene, Donald. *Dawn to the West: Japanese Literature in the Modern Era—Fiction*. New York: Holt, Rinehart and Winston, 1984, pp. 720–85.

Petersen, Gwenn Boardman. *The Moon in the Water: Understanding Tanizaki, Kawabata, and Mishima*. Honolulu: University Press of Hawaii, 1979, pp. 44–120.

Seidensticker, Edward. "Tanizaki Jun'ichirō, 1886–1965." *Monumenta Nipponica* 21, no. 3–4 (Autumn 1966): 249–65.

Translations

Tanizaki Jun'ichirō. *Diary of a Mad Old Man.* Translated by Howard Hibbett. New York: Perigee Books, 1981.

Tanizaki Jun'ichirō. *In Praise of Shadows.* Translated by Thomas J. Harper and Edward G. Seidensticker. New Haven: Leete's Island Books, 1977.

Tanizaki Jun'ichirō. *The Key.* Translated by Howard Hibbett. New York: Perigee Books, 1981.

Tanizaki Jun'ichirō. *The Makioka Sisters.* Translated by Edward Seidensticker. New York: Perigee Books, 1981.

Tanizaki Jun'ichirō. *Naomi.* Translated by Anthony H. Chambers. New York: Alfred A. Knopf, 1985.

Tanizaki Jun'ichirō. *Seven Japanese Tales.* Translated by Howard Hibbett. New York: Perigee Books, 1963. The seven tales are: "A Portrait of Shunkin," "Terror," "The Bridge of Dreams," "The Tattooer," "The Thief," "Aguri," and "A Blind Man's Tale."

Tanizaki Jun'ichirō. *Some Prefer Nettles.* Translated by Edward Seidensticker. New York: Perigee Books, 1981.

BEYOND ABSOLUTION: ENCHI FUMIKO'S *THE WAITING YEARS AND MASKS*

Barbara Ruch

> Just as there is an archetype of woman as the object of men's eternal love, so there must be an archetype of her as the object of his eternal fear, representing, perhaps, the shadow of his own evil actions.
>
> Mieko, *Masks*[1]

INTRODUCTION

During the last two decades of her life, Enchi Fumiko was heralded by critics as the most important living woman writer in Japan. Gender specificity is an integral part of the vocabulary of the Japanese literary world; since the tenth century it has recognized the special voice, concerns, and, in a highly gendered language of the modern world, the particular rhetoric of female writers. Yet, while often described as the "towering peak" among contemporary women writers "the likes of which we may never see again,"[2] the power of Enchi's writing—voluminous, erudite, rich in variety and scale—made her indisputably one of the very few giants of postwar Japanese literature, irrespective of gender. It was on these grounds that she was elected to the Japan Academy of Arts in 1970, was awarded the Bunka Kōrōshō or Distinguished Cultural Achievement Award in 1979, and in 1985 was decorated by the Emperor with the Bunka Kunshō or Order of Cultural Merit, the highest award a Japanese citizen can receive.

This eighty-one-year-old "giant" was tiny, plain, ladylike, willful, and spoiled. While innocent of the ordinary daily-life skills that had always been performed by servants, she was nonetheless tough, unpretentious, and private. She had no use for Western-style logic or argument and no head for business. Voracious for knowledge and insight, she was a constant study. And she wrote all the time. "Write and then die, that's all there is," she'd say. "I never knew any other writer who worked so tirelessly and relentlessly," said the novelist Niwa Fumio.

It is no mere hyperbole to say that her likes may never be seen again. Born in the Meiji Period (Oct. 2, 1905), Ueda Fumi, as she was then named, was the third child of the eminent linguist, Ueda Kazutoshi (Mannen), nationally famous Professor of the Japanese language at the Tokyo Imperial University, and his wife Tsuruko (née Murakami), descended from the wealthy Hosokawa clan. Raised in an affluent and privileged academic household, surrounded by her father's magnificent library of classics, and exposed to a constantly renewed stream of modern literary and popular journals, she grew up an avid reader. Her paternal grandmother, Ine, also a member of the household, read to young Fumi from such late-eighteenth-century writers as Bakin, Akinari, and Tanehiko. She developed a passion for the Kabuki theater, which the family frequented with much pleasure throughout her childhood.

Her distinguished father was clearly a dominant presence in the formation of her interest in classical Japanese literature and was a support to her in all her undertakings until he died when she was thirty-two years old. She wore a jade ring he gave her throughout her lifetime until it broke a few months before she died. It became the subject of one of her last writings.

At age thirteen Fumi[3] entered the girls high school affiliated with Japan Women's University, and by the time she was sixteen she had read the complete works of Tanizaki Jun'ichirō, and had almost finished reading through the hundred-some volumes of the *Yūhōdō Library of Classical Japanese Literature*. At the Ueno Public Library she poured over books on Western drama and Kabuki and became thoroughly absorbed in the world of theater. Precocious, dissatisfied with school, and wanting to study drama, with parental consent she left high school. Her father employed as her private tutors four professors from various Tokyo universities to teach her French and English language and literature as well as Sino-Japanese (*kambun*) literature, and a British missionary woman taught the young girl Biblical literature.

It was a heady time in the theater world of Tokyo. Osanai Kaoru (1881–1928), the playwright and drama critic, pioneered in establishing modern Western-style theater in Japan. He trained Kabuki actors to work outside their own tradition and to stage, in his newly-designed theater, adaptations of Western novels and plays. As early as 1904, when still a student, he had assisted in producing an adaptation of Alphonse Daudet's 1884 novel, *Sapho*, and went on to produce plays by Ibsen, Chekhov, and Gorky, as well as Chikamatsu. He had traveled to Russia, Germany, England and France to study their theater productions first hand.

One day in May, 1924, nineteen-year-old Fumi attended a public lecture by Osanai on the subject of modern drama and his soon-to-be opened Tsukiji Little Theater. Enthralled, she began to frequent the Little Theater, notebook in hand, and at home, determined to become a dramatist, she began secretly to write plays. When the magazine *Kabuki* solicited new plays for publication in 1926, she submitted a one-act play entitled *Furusato* (*Native Place*); it became her first published work. Emboldened, she gained permission in 1927 to become an auditor (and the only woman) in Osanai's drama seminar at Keiō Gijuku University. Impressed by the plays she had written, Osanai published several of them in his journal *Drama and Criticism*.

By Christmas Day of 1928, Ueda Fumi's career as a talented young playwright had been launched: her play *Banshun sōya* (*A Turbulent Night in Late Spring*) had not only been published, it had been produced and was just completing a successful run at the Tsukiji Little Theater. The Ueda family hosted a celebration party for their twenty-three-year-old daughter at a famous downtown restaurant, but there amidst the flowers and rustling silks, celebratory toasts and happy laughter, Osanai, only forty-seven, suffered a heart attack and died before her eyes.

Fumi's next months were markedly changed. She spent her time in the company of writers who were associated with the new proletarian magazine *Nyonin geijutsu* (*Women's Arts*) to which Osanai had recently introduced her, and which had published *A Turbulent Night*. Among them, the writer-activist Hirabayashi Taiko (1905–1972), the same age as Fumi, became her life-long friend; the novelist Kataoka Teppei (1894–1944), the most dynamic and politically active of the group, a married man with children, eleven years her senior, became the object of her passion.

It was an unsettling and exciting time. Socialism was in the air; Marxist thought represented for them a direct and hope-filled attack on all the authoritarian, hierarchical Confucian beliefs and feudal practices that had destroyed people's freedom and aspirations over the centuries, particularly those of women. Yet, like her own heroine in *A Turbulent Night*, she was uneasy, feeling herself being swept into the emotionalism of the proletarian movement less from pure conviction than for love of Kataoka. And she could see the same happening to other women. But she reasoned that those who could easily abandon their parents' homes and lead a life of revolution must have little of value to leave behind. She could not easily shed her own heritage, which had much about it that was still dear to her. She felt herself feigning passion for Kataoka's politics when her real passion was for him, and she hated this falseness in herself. Further, adultery, in the case of a woman, was then a criminal act in Japan. Constantly aware that her own conduct could rebound to ill effect upon her father's distinguished reputation, bewildered and insecure, she made a calculation. She would accept an arranged marriage proposal. Marriage would set her life on an even keel; it would be a mooring from which she could protect herself from being swept into the activities of anarchistic movements. At the same time marriage would provide her with the quiet freedom to pursue her career and to go on loving Kataoka in a state of composed equilibrium. In short, as she recalled it, in "cowardice," in marriage, she decided to throw herself away.

On March 27, 1930, she married thirty-four-year-old Enchi Yoshimatsu, chief of the research section of the *Tōkyō Nichinichi* newspaper. Although she gave birth to a daughter two years later and she remained married to Yoshimatsu until his death at age seventy-seven in 1972, she realized at once that her move had been a great miscalculation, and she regretted the marriage, for everyone's sake, all her life.

Nonetheless, the greatest nonliterary influence on "Enchi literature" was her married life. It changed her from a playwright into a novelist. And in her loveless union she dealt with the phenomenon of marriage itself—one man and one woman under one roof for life—constantly over the years. It is startling, in Ibsen, to hear young Hedda Gabler say of her new marriage: "And then the most unbearable thing of all . . . everlastingly having to be together with—the self same person." But it is sobering and revealing to watch Enchi in later years, dedicated to almost brutal self-knowledge and to resolute truth, examine such a wife in middle age. In "Enchantress" (1957) Chigako faces old age under the same roof with a husband for whom she has come to feel only contempt and yet to whom she has grown accustomed. Seated next to each other on a train on the way home from seeing their daughter off to America, the aging couple, as usual, talk past each other; he is oblivious to her sense of loss. As they talked "it gave Chigako the same feeling of impatience as when two foreigners ill-versed in each other's languages try to converse."[4]

For the next twenty years, married life sapped Enchi's energy and self-esteem as well as her dedication to literature; she all but ceased to write. Instead she joined study groups devoted to reading the ancient Japanese classics such as the *Kojiki*, *Nihongi*, and *Heike monogatari*. When she did write she turned to short stories and essays but found the shift from dialogue-dependent plays to descriptive and explicative prose excruciatingly difficult. Although a book of short stories, *Kaze no gotoki kotoba* (*Words like the Wind*), was published in 1939, it made no impression on the literary world.

Throughout the late 1930s and 40s, she endured the war, lost her breasts to surgery for tubercular mastitis, developed uterine cancer and nearly died of complications after a radical hysterectomy. During that period when penicillin was not available, she was hospitalized for many months in and out of critical condition. In the May 25, 1945, air raids, her home was burnt to the ground and she lost everything, including the entire treasured Ueda-Enchi library. Though in her heart a writer, she still wrote little, mostly juvenile literature and journal articles for the money she and her family needed simply to survive the war years.

When the war ended Enchi Fumiko, the writer, was born. In 1949, at age the age of forty-four, she began work on a long novel that was based on the adult life of her maternal grandmother—a story she had tried to write many times over the years but had been too close to its dilemma and the real people involved to turn it into fiction. Now slowly, bit by bit, in serial form she composed *The Waiting Years*. The original Japanese title *Onnazaka* means literally "women's-slope," a term that sounds somewhat like a place name but which implies the long uphill life journey of women.

In 1953, while still at work on *The Waiting Years*, Enchi published a collection of stories called *Himojii tsukihi* (*Days of Hunger*) that became her breakthrough in the postwar literary world. Vastly different from the somewhat sentimental, cloying style then associated with much of women's writing, it was greeted with acclaim.

The title story features Saku, who is considered unmarriageable due to an unsightly birthmark on her back. However, she is married off to Naokichi, a contemptible miser and lecher who makes her life a living hell. When he ultimately becomes bed-ridden, their son proposes that they murder him to relieve her of this burden of a man. Instead of seizing the opportunity, Saku is shocked into realizing that now she alone is capable of protecting the life of this miserable man. In a kind of epiphany her long-lived hatred is transformed into "a kind of love" that transcends the helpless Naokichi and represents something of deep value inside her. The moment transforms her own opinion of herself and the meaning of her own life. She dreams that a black crow has become a phoenix.

"Stark realism," "gruesome," "superb depiction of human tenacity," were the adjectives critics used. *Days of Hunger* received the 1954 Women Writer's Prize. That same year Enchi was elected to the board of the Japan Writer's Association.

THE WAITING YEARS

Her first unquestionable masterpiece, however, which had taken decades to germinate and eight years to write, was *The Waiting Years*. Hardly noticed as it appeared piece by piece in a small journal, *The Waiting Years* was completed and published in book form in 1957. It was immediately acclaimed and received one of Japan's most prestigious awards for literature, the Noma Literary Prize. "A rare jewel among masterpieces of modern literature," wrote the novelist-critic Takami Jun.[5]

As a child, little by little, Enchi had learned the story of her maternal grandparents from adult whispers and comments. She was fourteen when her grandmother, Murakami Kin, died; the family's recollections of her grandmother's suffering voiced on that occasion made an indelible impression upon her. Her grandfather, Murakami Tatetomo, died ten years later, but it took her years to gain the objectivity and the perspective of age that she would need to create a masterwork of fiction from their lives.

Whatever occurred in her grandparents' household will never be known, but Enchi's fictional transformation of her grandmother's painful life goes far beyond a narrative of one woman's existential dilemma. *The Waiting Years* is a brilliant recreation of a Meiji period household between the 1880s and 1920s. It is a portrait of marriage and of all the devastating effects that this institution had on the women of that age.

The character Shirakawa Yukitomo is a wealthy bureaucrat in a prefectural office—arrogant, sexually self-indulgent—who lives "like a feudal lord in the prefecture where he worked." He gives money to his wife, Tomo, and sends her to Tokyo to select for him a mistress—one whom, he wants to be sure, Tomo will find appropriate as a maid in their household and of whom she will approve. Having a mistress was an institution that had just been outlawed in 1882. The person Tomo consults privately in Tokyo tries nonetheless to be sensitive to the young wife's agonizing task, and comments kindly: "I suppose that when a man reaches his position—that kind of thing becomes a necessity, doesn't it?" Tomo, her smile "elusive as the smile on a Noh mask" replies, "It does seem so. People come to expect it, you see."[6] Young Tomo, in love with her husband and dedicated to serving him, begins her long climb up the woman's slope.

It is not long before a second mistress is required, and as the years pass Yukitomo turns even to his daughter-in-law. She is flirtatious and seductive and, repelled by her own boorish husband, enjoys her father-in-law's bed. During this time Tomo changes from a young wife eager to please to, first, a horrified sacrificial victim to his ego and will and, finally, to a perpetrator herself, of the crime of oppression. Tomo's pity is burned away by jealousy and humiliation, and she takes on a fearsome authority over all these women, including her own daughter.

She has no code of life conduct to guide her but the same Neo-Confucian one under which both she and her husband have been raised. This code required a woman to submit completely to the men in her family—and a wife, the complete submission of her "self" to her master's. Tomo spends her life proudly, and to her mind, successfully suppressing her natural wishes and passions. The idea of protest or rebellion never enters her mind.

Only on her deathbed does the seal of endurance rupture and her perceptions transcend the confines of family, society, and time. What has lain in her dormant all these years she utters aloud, half delirious. Her husband has treated her as non-human, as worse than refuse. How dare he now bury her with the ceremony and honor that implies she was a valued human being. In her dying words to her niece she discharges her one and only verbal volley against him:

> . . . tell him that when I die I want no funeral. Tell him that all he needs to do is take my body out to sea at Shinagawa and dump it in the water. . . . Tell him to dump my body in the sea. Dump it . . .

The message has a powerful effect upon Yukitomo:

> . . . his expression went blank . . . fear stirred as though he had seen a ghost. . . . His body had suffered the full force of the

emotions that his wife had struggled to repress for forty years past. The shock was enough to split his arrogant ego in two.[7]

The power of this work lies less in the tale than in the mature mastery of language and of human psychology Enchi demonstrates in her depiction of character. She has the ability to see her own culture as if free of the shackles that immobilize her characters. As in drama, everything is vested here in human relations; each of Yukitomo's women is clearly differentiated with distinct personalities, motivations, and pain. The subtle interaction among them is one of the notable achievements of this novel.

Like Euripides, Enchi is sometimes considered so severe in her depiction of even the female victims who are her heroines that she is accused of being a misogynist, yet this is clearly not the case. Moses Hadas's defense of Euripides may be applied fruitfully to Enchi as well:

> The alleged misogyny, as anyone who reads the plays can see, is the reverse of the truth. . . . His sympathy [is] for all victims of society, including womankind. . . . The main object . . . is to criticize the antiquated conventions of a constrictive social order which hamper and oppress contemporary life.[8]

In Enchi's novel *Masks*, Dr. Mikamé speaks a line that no misogynist could write. He says, "Even the sadistic misogyny of Buddha and Christ was nothing but an attempt to gain the better of a vastly superior opponent."[9]

Misogyny aside, Enchi has on the other hand also been accused of misanthropy or specifically of a contempt for men. Certainly in her most representative works the husbands she depicts are a sorry lot, and in most cases are abominable. Yet her stance is not anti-male. Love between men and women is of the greatest importance and is of the highest good.

Ibsen's women lived during the very same years depicted in *The Waiting Years*. Had he been alive (he died the year after Enchi was born) to read her works as she so avidly read his, he would have appreciated that their subjects were the same: "a married woman, trapped" in roles that are both devoid of meaning and demeaning. Both authors explore the nature of wife and mother, husband, and marriage, and the impact of social custom on these fundamental elements of human life. Ibsen would have profoundly agreed with the underlying premise of *The Waiting Years*. As he said in his notebooks:

> A woman cannot be herself in contemporary society; it is an exclusively male society with laws drafted by men. . . . These

women of the modern age, mistreated as daughters, as mothers, as wives, not educated in accordance with their talents, debarred from following their real mission, deprived of their inheritance, embittered of mind . . . what will result from this?[10]

The partial victory and yet ultimate defeat of Helene Alving in Ibsen's *Ghosts* is not unlike that of Tomo in *The Waiting Years*. Both women wasted their lives protecting their debauched husbands; both had in the end a small vindication but a large defeat. Both are shackled by outmoded and unjust laws and mores. As we see in *Ghosts*:

> PASTOR MANDERS: Nobody can be held responsible for the way things turn out. But nevertheless one thing is clear: your marriage was arranged in strict accord with law and order.
>
> MRS. ALVING: Oh, all this law and order! I often think **that's** the cause of all the trouble in the world . . . I should never have kept it a secret, the kind of life Alving led. But at the time I didn't dare do anything else . . . what a coward I was!
>
> PASTOR MANDERS: Do you call it cowardice, to do what is quite plainly your duty?
>
> MRS. ALVING: The reason I'm so timid and afraid is that I can never get properly rid of the ghosts that haunt me. . . old defunct theories, all sorts of old defunct beliefs . . . . They are simply lodged there, and we cannot get rid of them.[11]

What is cowardice in a woman? This is an existential question. Enchi knew from personal experience the severe ramifications of cowardice. She also knew that its dimensions were different for a woman than for a man. Helene Alving accuses herself of cowardice, but after partially escaping, she sinks back into a sublimated life. Helene, however, is unusual among Ibsen's heroines. Tomo cannot find the answer to what cowardice is. Or rather, she proudly chooses a path she believes takes the greatest courage and strength, only to sense in the end, her energies spent, that it has been a useless choice.

By and large the heroines that attracted Euripides, Ibsen, Tolstoy, and other male writers were women who displayed the daring strength that united their emotions with definitive, often spectacular, action: Electra, Medea, Nora, Hedda, Anna. Brilliant though such writers' insights into the female psyche may seem, for Enchi, such women were more the products of men's romantic, ill-informed fantasies, than real.

An exchange such as Nora and her husband's in *A Doll's House* would have been unthinkable in Tomo's day, and undoubtedly still is beyond the approbation of most in Japan today:

HELMER: Don't you care what people will say?

NORA: That's no concern of mine. All I know is that this is necessary for **me** . . .

HELMER: Isn't it your duty to your husband and children?

NORA: My duty [is] to myself.

HELMER: First and foremost, you are a wife and mother.

NORA: I believe that first and foremost I am an individual.[12]

A Japanese woman who walked out would step not into the fresh air and onto a path to freedom, but off the edge of the human world into an empty abyss.[13]

Enchi's characters are instead women of endless, prideful endurance who would not take socially suicidal action no matter how unpardonably provoked. They are everyone's wife or sister or neighbor to whom overt rebellion seems not so much impossible as foolish. Had they merely resigned themselves to their "proper" roles, however, they would have seemed admirable to men and become merely secondary characters. Far from resignation, for Enchi's women it is a steel-like resolution to endure, and to endure at the center of things, that is the foundation of their lives. With careful design they never marginalize themselves by fighting back or fleeing. But neither do they ever absolve the men responsible for their oppression and pain. Behind elusive smiles like Tomo's, "enigmatic as a Noh mask," implacable rancor brews. Beneath the sheen of beautiful grooming, behind the light laughter, the flattering gestures, deep wells of pain, terror, and festering malice brew toxins that cause their psyches to split and take on a secret inner life.

Such Enchi heroines terrified male readers who were unaccustomed to encountering Japanese women who burned with secret and implacable hatred of male conduct. The outraged cries, noisy harangues, and definitive counter-action of women in Western literature were fascinating and made for enjoyable reading; they were after all a far distant species of humankind. Here was Enchi, however, steeped in the language and mores of Japan's own great classical literature, herself, through and through, a "lady," with never a rebellious act or word, describing in elegant, rich prose, well-mannered, desirable, quiet Japanese women who silently nurtured their wrath against their oppressors and wordlessly plotted vengeance. It was chilling.[14]

MASKS

Representative of this type of Enchi heroine is Mieko, the central character in her 1958 novel *Onna-men* (literally Woman-masks; translated in 1983 as *Masks*). Whereas *The Waiting Years* is historical fiction, *Masks* is an extremely complex multi-layered novel about contemporary women. As if in double or triple exposure, they seem to reverberate with motivations, perceptions, and witch-like powers created out of some collective unconscious—characteristics which they share with the women in Lady Murasaki's eleventh-century *Tale of Genji*, particularly the character Rokujō.

In *Masks*, Mieko, the quiet, yet charismatic, middle-aged poetess of the *Shinkokinshū* school, "secretive as a garden of flowers at night,"[15] is a woman who "has a peculiar power to move events in whatever direction she pleases, while she stays motionless. She's like a quiet mountain lake whose waters are rushing beneath the surface toward a waterfall. She's like the face on a Noh mask, wrapped in her own secrets."[16]

Mishima Yukio, in his review of this brilliant novel, wrote:

> *Woman-Masks* is unique among all postwar novels; Mrs. Enchi's flawless blend of classical erudition and aesthetic consciousness create a fragrant, heady wine of superb quality. . . . To the theme of woman's deep resentment she adds a new terror that transcends time.[17]

Masks is divided into three parts, each named for a category of female mask used in the performance of Noh plays. Japan's oldest surviving form of choreographed and intoned drama, Noh had its roots in verbal, instrumental and choreographed rites involving the placation of demonic forces—often the restless vengeful spirits of those who had died full of rage or grief. Performed exclusively by male actors, Noh reached its perfection in the fifteenth century under the great playwright-actor, Zeami, many of whose plays have female characters in central roles.

In *Masks* we see one of the several archetypical Enchi heroines that male critics found most chilling. Nineteen-year-old Mieko marries Toganō Masatsugu, only to discover that in his powerful, wealthy, provincial family, the old tradition of supplying male family members with housemaid-mistresses has been preserved, and that Masatsugu's mistress, Agui, is already ensconced in the bride's new home. Her idealistic hopes for her marriage dashed, Mieko nonetheless grows to feel pity for Agui, who she learns has already been forced by Masatsugu to abort two of his (and of course her) children. Her pity turns to hatred, however, when Agui's own jealousy leads her to cause Mieko to miscarry her first child. Silently Mieko plots revenge upon her husband and the family that made him what he was. She secretly takes a lover and bears twins believed by the Toganōs to carry their own blood. The girl, Harumé, is brain-damaged at birth and, mentally retarded, is sent away. The boy, Akio, in adulthood marries Yasuko but dies in a mountain climbing accident before producing an heir.

The novel begins at this point with Mieko and Yasuko, like two beautiful witches, both widows, inseparable companions, manipulating those around them to their own ends. Mieko, a silent force behind Yasuko, proceeds to use Yasuko (half-willing, half-afraid) to commit "a crime that only women can commit"[18]—to eradicate the Toganō family without their knowledge by breeding through Harumé a descendant free of their blood.

There is ample room for comparison between *Masks* and Ibsen's *The Master Builder*, both of which involve a woman's manipulation of others, and death. From *The Master Builder*:

> SOLNESS: Don't you believe too, Hilde, that you find certain people have been singled out, specially chosen, gifted with the power and the ability to **want** something, to **desire** something, to **will** something—so insistently—and so ruthlessly—that they inevitably get it in the end?
>
> HILDE (with an inscrutable expression in her eyes): If that is so, we'll see someday—if I am one of the chosen.
>
> SOLNESS: One doesn't achieve such great things alone. Oh, no. One has to have—helpers and servants—if anything's to come of it . . . One has to summon them, imperiously, inwardly, you understand.[19]

Mieko, as we learn through her essay on the *Tale of Genji* incorporated within the novel, is deeply influenced by the character Lady Rokujō from that tale (as undoubtedly Enchi herself was). Rokujō, the woman whose jealousy was so great it walked the earth apart from her body and without her knowledge to wreak vengeance on other women, is seen by Mieko (and Enchi, as she later wrote in essays) not so much the victimizer, as the victim of Genji's ego and society's moral code. In the case of both Rokujō and Mieko, a demonic force to control others bursts forth from one whose existence had been at the pleasure of others, who had been deprived of all means of such control over others.

Ibsen understood this demonic archetype too. In his notes about *Hedda Gabler* he says: "The demonic thing about Hedda is that she wants to exert an influence over another person."[20] Hedda herself says, "I want to feel that once in my life I control a human destiny."[21] The point should not be lost that men's influence over women, overt and authoritarian, was considered normal, but the reverse (women's covert manipulation of men), from a male perspective, was seen so abnormal as to be demonic.

Enchi, like Jung, saw the spiritual realm as possessing a psychological reality that cannot be explained away. "We are so accustomed to the apparent rational nature of our world," wrote Jung, "that we can scarcely imagine anything that cannot be explained by common sense."[22] Enchi's use of this dimension goes far beyond the spirits and ghosts in Bakin, Akinari, or the Kabuki theater that influenced her. Nor was hers a Freudian world of suppressed subconscious desires.

Can two people actually be one dual personality? She explores this hypothesis in the relationships of Mieko and Yasuko and of the twins Harumé and Akio, as well as in other works. On the other hand, can one person really be two? For Jung this was not only possible, it was by no means pathological: the split occurs "spontaneously, without one's knowledge or consent and even against one's intention."[23] In *Masks* Yasuko confesses to this experience, of which Lady Rokujō in *Genji* is of course the prototype in Japanese literature.

There is as well considerable discussion in *Masks* about spirit possession and shamanism, which provides a rich source of comparison with shamanism as described in such Western classic studies as that of Mircea Eliade. Several of the characters in *Masks* are engaged in research on the subject. Professor Ibuki, who lusts after Yasuko, expresses views on shamanism that are merely stereotypical—no doubt set out by Enchi so as to give the reader an opportunity to see his naiveté and look deeper. He sees shamanistic activity as the average modern male might, as sexually fueled; the line between shamanistic practice and prostitution is blurred.[24] "The state of inspiration itself is intensely physical, heightening a person's sexuality to the furthest degree (unlike intellectual labor which diminishes sexuality), so that the body of a medium in a trance comes to seem the very incarnation of sex."[25]

A true shaman however is merely a medium for the spirit that possesses her. Yasuko may act as medium but it is Mieko's spirit that mobilizes her, and the ultimate sexual act is relegated by their combined wills to their instruments, Harumé and Ibuki. The novel is an exploration of the ability of one's psyche to appropriate the will of another and affect the course of his or her actions. It is simplistic to interpret Enchi's works such as *Masks*, "Enchantress," "Bond for Two Lifetimes—Gleanings," and others as "shamanistic works," as some do. Her interest is less in the shaman or *miko* than in the demonic force of the human psyche or spirit in its attempt to control its own and other's lives.

CONCLUSION

Enchi Fumiko's interest in the Japanese classics was life-long, and she devoted years to translating many of them into modern Japanese. In 1967, despite illness and failing eyesight, she embarked on the modern translation of the *Tale of Genji*. It was published in ten volumes in 1972–73 and remains the most easily understood and enjoyed of several modern translations in Japan today. She is also the author of extensive essays devoted to character analyses of the women created by Lady Murasaki in *Genji*.

In a book introducing young people to the works of the great seventeenth-century playwright Chikamatsu Monzaemon, Enchi translates into modern Japanese two of his plays that deal with the love suicide of a timid young husband and wife who are unable to endure the pressures exerted on them by their parents and society and who lack the ability or "courage" to flee and lead thereby a life of certain ostracism. In her introduction she writes:

> It is only the poet who can scale the wall of time and see such a state of human oppression as unnatural. Chikamatsu was one such genius. In his works about men and women whose freedom has been stolen from them and who are hounded to death, he offers not one word of refutation against that social order, but even these some hundreds of years later he succeeds in inspiring in the modern reader a deep empathy for these victims, these men and women mired in their unhappy fates. I believe that is what literature, indeed, what the classics are all about.[26]

Enchi's words about Chikamatsu may unequivocally be applied to the masterpieces of Enchi Fumiko herself. They contain no debates, no harangues, no pamphleteering. Only the brilliantly beautiful, terrifying depiction of social custom that crushes women and the chilling truth about what that does to humankind.

The great bulk of Enchi literature remains untranslated—most of her prize-winning fiction, notably her great trilogy *Ake o ubau mono* (The Thing Which Purloins Red), which draws heavily on her own life, and which won the Tanizaki Jun'ichirō Prize for Literature in 1969; *Yūkon* (Frolicking Spirits), a collection of three novellas that received the Grand Literary Prize of Japan in 1972; and *Shokutaku no nai ie* (The Family with No Dining Table; 1979), a stunning fiction based on the highly publicized arrest for murder of a radical, militant student and the response of his father, a high-ranking employee of one of Japan's foremost corporations who refuses, despite custom, to take any responsibility for his son's actions. None of her plays has yet been translated.

TOPICS FOR DISCUSSION

1. A familiarity with Lady Murasaki's masterpiece *Tale of Genji* and with the great tradition of Noh drama will enrich the reader's appreciation of Enchi's novel *Masks*, which resonates both substantively and visually with allusions, associations, and images from both *Genji* and the Noh repertory and staging. Under no circumstances, however, does a lack of such knowledge render her works inaccessible to the Western reader. It is no more necessary for the reader of Enchi to have seen a Noh play than for the reader of *Medea* to have seen Greek drama performed. It is of great interest, nonetheless, and adds to one's appreciation if, in conjunction with the novel, one looks at a book of photographs[27] of Noh masks with special attention to the masks after which Enchi has named her three chapters: *Ryō no onna*,[28] the face of the vengeful spirit of an older woman, her energies turned inward, associated with Mieko at the beginning of the novel; *Masugami*,[29] a young woman, blank of mind but frenzied in passion, the face associated with the beautiful, retarded Harumé in bed with Ibuki; and *Fukai*[30] or "Deep Well," the face of an older woman who knows the bitter taste of revenge and loss—Mieko at the close of the book. Other masks such as *Magojirō*,[31] a young woman at her peak of feminine beauty, and *Zō no onna*,[32] cold, cruel, and disdainful, also play key roles in the novel.

2. Interesting discussions arise from comparing Mieko to Lady Rokujō's vengeful spirit that punishes Genji by possessing and destroying his wife Aoi and one of his lovers, Yugao. Lady Rokujō became an archetype in the Japanese literary tradition, which is explored in the Noh play *Aoi no Ue* (Lady Aoi)[33] and in Yukio Mishima's modern theater adaptation, "The Lady Aoi."[34] The *Tale of Genji* is discussed elsewhere in this volume.[35]

3. Dreams play an important role in *Masks*. In an entirely personal, Jungian fashion Yasuko interprets her own dreams, and through this process attempts to individuate herself from her late husband Akio and his mother Mieko. There is no glossary of symbolic meanings to be decoded; rather, Yasuko's symbols have meaning only to herself and are her key to the restoration of balance in her own life.

4. One of the most difficult yet important aspects to a discussion of Enchi literature will lie in her relation to feminism. Her themes and her characters seem the obvious subject for such an examination. Enchi, however, had little or no interest in feminist theory. She was concerned that women writers be encouraged to write, that women be restored to the pages of Japanese history, and that there be amelioration, or at least greater awareness, of the wrongs which society, and in particular the family (its central symbol) perpetrate in discriminating between the rights and privileges of women and men. But she was not a feminist in any current Western sense of that word.

As we can see from the quote that opens this essay, her women define themselves always in obsessional preoccupation with the men who cause them pain. Questions may be raised as to whether Enchi's women conduct their lives as strategies for dealing with the sins of men or whether she saw in some women an autonomous agenda. Perhaps "Boxcar of Chrysanthemums" most clearly provides food for thought in this regard.

NOTES

1. Enchi Fumiko, *Masks*, trans. Juliet Winters Carpenter (New York: Adventura, Vintage Books, 1983), p. 57.

2. Takenishi Hiroko, "Enchi Fumiko," *Buritanika kokusai nenkan* 1986 (1987): 93.

3. The writer is called by her given name, Fumi, in the sections of the paper discussing her childhood, then by her married name, Enchi, which was the name she used as a novelist.

4. Enchi Fumiko, "Enchantress," trans. John Bester, in *Modern Japanese Short Stories*, ed. Edward G. Seidensticker, John Bester, and Ivan

Morris (Tokyo: Japan Publications Trading Co., Ltd., 1961), p. 92.

5. Kamei Hideo and Ogasawara Yoshiko, *Enchi Fumiko no sekai* (Tokyo: Sōrinsha, 1981), p. 39.

6. Enchi Fumiko, *The Waiting Years*, trans. John Bester (Tokyo: Kodansha International Ltd., 1971), pp. 13–14.

7. Ibid., pp. 202–03.

8. Euripides, *Ten Plays by Euripides*, trans. Moses Hadas and John McLean (New York: Bantam Classics paperback, 1981), p. viii.

9. Enchi Fumiko, *Masks*, p. 133.

10. Henrik Ibsen, *Four Major Plays*, trans. James McFarlane and Jens Arup (New York: Oxford University Press, The World's Classics paperback, 1981), pp. viii–ix.

11. Ibid., pp. 123–26.

12. Ibid., p. 82.

13. In 1912 the leading women's literary magazine *Seitō* (*Bluestocking*) had published an open letter written by Hiratsuka Raichō, the magazine's founder, and addressed directly to Ibsen's Nora. The letter expressed admiration for the power of Nora's intuitive act of leaving but focussed on concern for Nora's low level of self-awareness. It expressed doubt that her act could lead to any real kind of freedom or independence. In general the staff of the magazine viewed Nora with disdain as unreal and ignorant of reality. Cf. Sharon L. Sievers, *Flowers in Salt: The Beginnings of Feminist Consciousness in Modern Japan* (Stanford: Stanford University Press, 1983), p. 170 ff.

14. Virtually all male critics in Japan responded with admiration for her literary powers while using adjectives that revealed their sense of discomfort over the women characters she depicts. For examples see note 5, p. 50 passim.

15. Enchi Fumiko, *Masks*, p. 92.

16. Ibid., p. 30.

17. Kamei Hideo and Ogasawara Yoshiko, op. cit., p. 61.

18. Enchi Fumiko, *Masks*, p. 126.

19. Henrik Ibsen, op cit., p. 321.

20. Ibid., p. xi.

21. Ibid., p. 226.

22. Carl G. Jung et al., *Man and His Symbols* (New York: Dell Publishing Co., 1964 [Aldus Books]), p. 31.

23. Ibid., p. 8.

24. Enchi Fumiko, *Masks*, p. 78.

25. Ibid., p. 77.

26. Enchi Fumiko, *Enchi Fumiko ga kataru—"Chikamatsu monogatari"* (Tokyo: Heibonsha, *Kataribe-zōshi* books, vol. 8 [originally published in 1980 under the title *Kokusenya gassen—Chikamatsu monogatari*]).

27. One such book is Toru Nakanishi, *Noh Masks*, trans. Don Kenny (Tokyo: Hoikusha, 1983). For a short history of the Noh theater, with photographs, see Donald Keene, *Nō, The Classical Theatre of Japan* (Palo Alto and Tokyo: Kodansha International Ltd., 1973).

28. Enchi Fumiko, *Masks*, p. 25.

29. Ibid., p. 61.

30. Ibid., p. 141.

31. Ibid., p. 22.

32. Ibid., p. 23, 40.
33. *Japanese Noh Drama*, vol. 2 (Tokyo: Nippon Gakujutsu Shinkōkai, 1959). This volume also contains a photograph of a Fukai mask.
34. Donald Keene, trans., *Five Modern Nō Plays by Yukio Mishima* (New York: Alfred A. Knopf, 1957).
35. For quick and useful access to the *Tale of Genji* plus a summary of each chapter see William J. Puette, *Guide to the Tale of Genji by Murasaki Shikibu* (Rutland, VT: Charles E. Tuttle Co., 1983) and Richard Bowring, *Murasaki Shikibu, The Tale of Genji*, in *Landmarks of World Literature* (Cambridge: Cambridge University Press, 1988). The chapter about Yugao's death can be found translated in Donald Keene, *Anthology of Japanese Literature* (New York: Grove Press, 1955).

REFERENCES

Enchi Fumiko. *Masks* (*Onna-men*, 1958). Translated by Juliet Winters Carpenter. New York: Adventura, Vintage Books, 1983.
Enchi Fumiko. *The Waiting Years* (*Onnazaka*, 1949–1957). Translated by John Bester. Tokyo: Kodansha International Ltd., 1971; paperback, 1984.
Enchi Fumiko. "Blind Man's Bluff" ("Mekura oni," 1962). Translated by Beth Cary, in *The Mother of Dreams and Other Short Stories: Portrayals of Women in Modern Japanese Fiction*, edited by Makoto Ueda, pp. 165–77. New York: Kodansha International, 1986.
Enchi Fumiko. "A Bond for Two Lifetimes—Gleanings" ("Nisei no en shui," 1957). Translated by Phyllis Birnbaum, in *Rabbits, Crabs, Etc.: Stories by Japanese Women*, pp. 25–47. Honolulu: University of Hawaii Press, 1982. (See also the next item for another translation of the same work. The Birnbaum translation is recommended, but both translations are usable.)
Enchi Fumiko. "Boxcar of Chrysanthemums" ("Kikuguruma," 1967). Translated by Yukiko Tanaka and Elizabeth Hanson, in *This Kind of Woman: Ten Stories by Japanese Women Writers, 1960–1976*, edited by Yukiko Tanaka and Elizabeth Hanson, pp. 69–86. Stanford: Stanford University Press, 1982.
Enchi Fumiko. "Enchantress" ("Yo," 1956). Translated by John Bester, in *Modern Japanese Short Stories*, edited by Edward G. Seidensticker, John Bester, and Ivan Morris, pp. 90–117. Tokyo: Japan Publications Trading Co., Ltd., 1961.
Enchi Fumiko. "Love in Two Lives: The Remnant" ("Nisei no en shui, 1957). Translated by Noriko Mizuta Lippit and Kyoko Iriye Selden, in *Japanese Women Writers: Twentieth Century Short Fiction*, pp. 97–111. Armonk, NY: M. E. Sharpe, 1991.

NOTE: As of this writing no critical work on Enchi Fumiko's writing has yet appeared in English.

THE WOMAN IN THE DUNES

John Whittier Treat

Abe Kōbō's 1962 novel *Suna no onna*—the story of a vacationing schoolteacher kept captive in a sand pit—created a literary sensation in Japan, earning its author not just that year's Yomiuri Prize but a secure place among the half-dozen most critically noted novelists to appear there since 1945. Ōe Kenzaburō, the Japanese writer with whom he is most often paired, has lauded Abe as "the most important postwar writer." Mishima Yukio, who never allowed his politics to interfere with his recognition of talent, praised Abe just as highly. Abe attracted attention outside of Japan with the 1964 translation of this novel, *The Woman in the Dunes*, and he briefly enjoyed near-celebrity status when the film version was awarded the Special Jury Prize at Cannes that same year. *The Woman in the Dunes*, like the six other of his novels subsequently translated, was reviewed widely, especially in the American press. Abe was enthusiastically welcomed as a Japanese novelist recognizably avant-garde and thus, perhaps somewhat oddly, readily fathomable. Abe was interested in such issues as freedom and existence, appropriating an idiom that seemed no more peculiarly Japanese than that of Poe, Kafka, or Beckett; and New York critics were pleased to discover a Japanese writer whose work demanded no extravagant exegesis, no Oriental hermeneutics. Niki Jumpei, that hapless thirty-one-year-old high-school teacher who disappears into the sand pit of an unnamed village, is familiar enough to readers acquainted with the biographies of Gregor Samsa or Nagg and Nell to dispense with the need for explanatory, intercultural footnoting. *The Woman in the Dunes* was fashioned plainly enough in the discourses of our modern crises that reading it could be a pleasant pastime rather than grueling schoolwork.

Indeed, one of the more attractive features of the book is the simplicity of its desert setting and its focus on the single relationship between the captive, Niki, and his widow captor. Unlike other Japanese novels, there is no surplus of inscrutable cultural practices to distract or confuse the reader. *The Woman in the Dunes* borders on pure allegory, so easily paraphrased is its story and so straightforward is its movement toward the inevitable conclusion. For just that reason Stanley Kauffmann dismissed the work as too "schematic": once he grasped Abe's design he was impatient with the languor of the work's pace. But what irked Kauffmann is, for other readers, inseparable from the book's appeal. The novel so nicely stands on its own. One needs to know nothing of either Abe or his other works, or perhaps of Japanese literature or culture at all, to appreciate it. When asked which Japanese writers had influenced him, Abe tersely replied none, though that can hardly be true. Perhaps Abe meant that his work should be taken as both original and portable. By and large, Abe's work has been accepted that way, which is to say as part of modern culture's—not solely Japanese culture's—obsession with the problematic of alienation in contemporary society. One American scholar has referred to this obsession, a bit euphemistically, as Abe's "avowedly international style."

At the same time Abe has been termed, in Brad Leithauser's words, a "vexatious author." There is frequently the suspicion that Abe's work is only deceptively uncomplicated, that perhaps it is informed by actually dense ideas discreetly interred among plot and characters. In fact there are traces of philosophical intent bared in a literary vocabulary that includes "freedom," "existence," and "morality." These traces lead back to the details of Abe's own life that suggest—in their particularly twentieth-century character—the nature of Abe's attraction to philosophical and political systems equally the product of modern times.

Certainly biographical facts about Abe are well known and nearly always mentioned in Western accounts of his work. The jackets of his novels tell us he was born in Tokyo in 1924, and that he was a medical doctor by training though not by profession. We learn that he lived until his death in early 1993 with his wife, the artist Abe Machi, in a Tokyo suburb. Only rarely do we read, however, that "Kobo Abe was raised in China." Even in its inaccuracy (in point of fact Abe grew up in Manshūkoku, the "Manchu Nation," Japan's puppet state from 1932 to 1945 in present-day northeast China) this statement points to a history with which he, as a boy and young man, was inextricably bound: the history of Japan's empire and a war that failed miserably, the resulting populations thrown into disarray by the turmoil of defeat. For the adolescent Abe, thrust into adulthood, the collapse of the Japanese state in 1945 was an abject lesson in the real extent of the modern absurd.

Japanese critics often note in Abe's work the problem of the *kokyō*, a term only awkwardly translated into English as "one's birthplace" or "native village." Most everyone in Japan will tell you they have one; even if they have lived all their life in a high-rise apartment building in some Orwellian Tokyo or Osaka housing tract, more likely than not there is a rural village somewhere that retains a status as their ancestral point of origin. But it is precisely that fixed point of origin which Abe's fiction lacks, or rather, possesses only in an ironic sense, a sense which his literary characters inevitably appropriate. He once wrote in an essay:

> I was born in Tokyo, and raised in what was called Manchuria. My family comes from Hokkaido, however, and I lived for a number of years there, too. In other words, my place of birth, place of origin, and place of family registry are each different. I find it very difficult to write a biographical statement. In essence I believe myself to be a person without a native home [*kokyō*]. Perhaps this is the real reason why there is a certain hatred of that very idea among my feelings. Any and every thing that makes a value out of permanency inflicts damage upon me.[1]

Abe's profound distrust of notions of the fixed, of determinacy, does not derive so much from the "crisis of metaphysics" or "crisis of language" we might speak of in European literature. But like a Czech Jew in Vienna, or an Irishman in Paris, Abe, upon reflection, was surprised to find himself where he was. Originally taken to Manchuria by his father, a doctor at the Japanese medical school there, Abe stayed on in the colony after his father died in early 1945—supporting himself and his mother by hawking cider—until being repatriated the following year. It was in that interim that Abe witnessed the collapse of Manshūkoku: the near instantaneous evaporation of a political fiction, the descent into genuine anarchy of a "nation" that, as Abe noted, never amounted to anything more real than a sign hung out to view but which "became meaningless each night when darkness fell." Perhaps this is why there is in every typical Abe novel, including *The Woman in the Dunes*, a map or blueprint that utterly fails to lead its owner to his destination. For maps to work one has to believe places are not only real, but reachable. Abe's acquaintance with recent history made such belief hopelessly ironic. One of his major early novels, as yet untranslated, is *The Beasts Head for*

Home [*Kemono-tachi wa kokyō mezasu*]. An adolescent Japanese, left parentless in Manchuria at the end of the war, roams the alien countryside searching for fellow countrymen and ultimately a way back to Japan. *The Beasts Head For Home* is the one Abe work that both has the closest autobiographical parallels and establishes the pattern for the more fantastic works that followed. It is a work that clearly expresses how slippery and ultimately treacherous the fiction of "nation" or "home" can be. Its narrator muses to himself on just this point at the end of the novel:

> Hell, it seems like I just keep going in circles over the same ground . . . no matter how far I go, I don't get a single step beyond the wilderness . . . maybe there's no such thing as "Japan" after all . . . where I go, the wilderness goes with me . . . Japan keeps running away from me.[2]

Manchuria, together with other Japanese colonies such as Korea and Taiwan, collectively constituted what was commonly referred to as the *gaichi*, the "outer lands," a term opposed to the *naichi*, the "inner lands," by which was meant the home islands. Abe Kōbō, both literally and figuratively, is a *gaichi* writer; a writer from a place with no real name—no real meaning—but only a provisional, relative, and oppositional usage. Perhaps this is why the critic Isoda Kōichi termed Abe "psychically a stateless person." The discourse of place, rightly seen as so important in the work of many Japanese writers, is a discourse that Abe alternatively yearns for and mocks. One senses in Abe's fiction that he, insofar as he identified with his characters, would nostalgically like to have found home, but that he also learned to distrust the ideology implied in the notion of people "belonging," essentially, to a particular place. Indeed he found suspect the idea of culture establishing any enabling basis as fixed or permanent. Abe once explained to another critic, Honda Shūgo, why he told the stories he did:

> It's all because of my experiences at the end of the war. I spent a year and a half in Shenyang [in Manchuria]. I was struck by how all the standards of society completely fell apart. I totally lost any faith in anything constant or everlasting.[3]

Given the disillusionment that Abe experienced with the defeat of the Japanese empire, it is not surprising that once back in occupied Japan he would have been drawn to radical solutions addressing the history of imperialism and colonialism that he was himself part of. As for many Japanese intellectuals, the most persuasive of those proposed solutions was Marxism. Abe was selected to travel to Eastern Europe in 1956 as one of the Japan Communist Party's more prominent young members. His account of what he saw there later resulted in his expulsion from the Party; however, a Marxist influence continued to inflect Abe's fiction. The social identity of his characters, including that of Niki Jumpei, is usually that of alienated worker in an advanced capitalist economy. Their alienation is necessarily linked with a contradiction between life as it is led and life as it is expected to be, the nature of which they only gradually, if ever, grasp; and when they do, it is usually as an "absurdity." Niki Jumpei, for example, initially finds it quite ridiculous that anyone would choose to live as his captors do; it is only later that he comprehends the irrefutable businesslike logic that keeps them in their pits. The question that remains for Niki to answer is whether he will subscribe to that logic, whether he will rethink the absurd as in fact reasonable.

It is a question asked by many of Abe's other characters. In the early 1950s he wrote *The Wall: The Crime of S. Karuma* (the first part in a series of works now collectively known as *The Wall* [*Kabe—S Karuma-shi no hanzai*]), which deals with another ordinary white-collar worker—Mr. Karuma—who wakes up one morning only to realize he has forgotten who he is. This Kafkaesque story, which won Abe the prestigious Akutagawa Prize, was followed by a steady production of novels and plays (he is at least as well known in Japan as a playwright as he is a novelist). Most of his books share common themes. In each of them, for instance, someone is apt to disappear: fetuses used by scientists to develop an amphibian race in *Inter Ice Age Four* [*Daiyon kanpyōki*]; a husband who uses a mask to hide his identity from his wife in *The Face of Another* [*Tanin no kao*]. *The Ruined Map* [*Moetsukita chizu*] describes a detective on the trail of a vanished fugitive. *The Box Man* [*Hakootoko*] refers to a misanthrope who has retreated into, well, a box. In *Secret Rendezvous* [*Mikkai*], a man searches for his wife who was spirited away by an ambulance; and in *The Ark Sakura* [*Hakobune sakura maru*] the novel's entire list of characters have disappeared into an abandoned quarry turned into a bomb shelter (the "ark") to last out the coming nuclear war.

But *The Woman in the Dunes* is Abe's most famous and most skillfully executed account of estranged characters who disappear or seek those who have. The novel takes place entirely amid sand, a severe setting reminiscent of the barren Manchurian wilderness in the earlier *The Beasts Head For Home*. But unlike that more solid ground, the sand of this novel is fluid, plastic, formally indeterminate: like the medium of modern fiction, the dunes that entrap Niki Jumpei are all the more difficult to grasp for their amorphousness. The story of *The Woman in the Dunes* succinctly matches the theme, making it his most readable novel as well as the most technically complete, sustaining the highest degree of tension. It is the summer of 1955, and Niki Jumpei, an amateur entomologist, heads for the arid desert coastline in search of new species. Stranded after missing the last bus back to town, he accepts the offer of local villagers to spend the night in one of their homes, homes built at the bottom of sixty-foot sand pits accessible only by rope ladders. He is put up in a particularly dilapidated pit inhabited solely by a woman, roughly his own age, who recently lost her husband and daughter in a sand storm. The next morning he discovers it is he who has been "collected": the rope ladder has been withdrawn. This is only the first of the many ironies and paradoxes with which the novel is constructed. For most of the novel Niki schemes various escapes, some of which involve deceiving the same woman to whom he is progressively drawn and all of which culminate with humiliating failure; but why, after all, should he be so eager to return to the conventional world he earlier scorned? Was he any less trapped in his marriage and his job than he is here? Why does he sexually desire the woman who, in order to secure his help in her Sisyphean work of shoveling the sand that incessantly encroaches upon her home, keeps him prisoner? And, finally, months later, when the rope ladder, inadvertently left in place, suddenly provides Niki with a means of escape, why does he hesitate and conclude that really there's no rush; he might as well flee tomorrow as today? These are the incongruities that, so implausible but so plausibly told, make the novel absurd. The purposelessness, lack of harmony, and sense of futility that particularly characterized post-World War II French theater characterizes this Japanese novel as well. The nihilism of an Ionesco or Beckett antihero finds a counterpart in that of Abe's kidnapped Niki Jumpei, for whom no action seems efficacious: every escape comes to naught.

What lies behind this absurdism, however, is a profound cynicism: a distrust of transcendence, a disbelief in value. This is a cynicism that Lionel Trilling termed the modern "disenchantment of our culture with culture itself." Finally, life in the dunes strikes Niki Jumpei as no less logical than life anywhere else. Presumably not too many readers would agree—one reason why Abe is a "vexatious" author—despite the apparent accessibility of his settings and characters. How, one is tempted to ask of this novel, does it make sense? One response, and a response engendered by historical events paralleling those which are in part responsible for the character of Abe's work, is found in an observation Hannah Arendt makes in *The Origins of Totalitarianism*: "To yield to the process of disintegration has become an irresistible temptation, not only because it has assumed the spurious grandeur of 'historical necessity' but also because everything outside it has begun to appear lifeless, bloodless, meaningless, and unreal." Arendt is talking about Western literature in the wake of Hitler and Stalin, but her insight applies to Abe, too. On the one hand, disenchantment implies (with no small measure of self flattery) that he who is disenchanted has freed himself from an earlier enchantment. Yet for many modern readers, everything outside does appear "lifeless, bloodless, meaningless, and unreal." Abe's world, no less than that of any Western intellectual inclined to draw similar conclusions, is one in which values are ridiculed by history.

This sense of recent history rendering life so absurd led Abe to use an existential technique to portray life. Thinking of occupied France during World War II, Walter Kaufmann called existentialism the result of contemplating philosophy from an "extreme situation"; occupied Manchuria during the same war provided Abe with a similar opportunity. Niki Jumpei, in escaping to what he has escaped from, realizes not only his absurdity but the inevitability of locked struggle with the Other, represented in the pit by the person of the woman. Niki and the woman are mutually dependent on each other even as they would psychically wear each other down. This is the same sort of circular battle that characterizes the confrontation of the existential Self with the Other. *The Woman in the Dunes* can be described as a story of flight from the Other: at the beginning Niki tells us he has come to the village to flee, if even for a moment, the "tedium and irksomeness of responsibility," responsibility (*gimu*) being the diffuse social ties that bind him. But once in the pit, that diffuseness does not disappear, it becomes acutely immediate, concrete, and inescapable. Now the woman is his clear opponent, his Other from which he cannot flee.

The release from responsibility that Niki seeks in flight is tantamount to a life outside of civilization. However, on the remote coastline he does not find the Arcadia he seeks, only more tedious struggle. The sand of *The Woman in the Dunes*, because it is so fluid and unfixed, is death; as Niki concludes when he notes the decaying wood of the woman's shack, "the sand rots everything."

The pit is the perfect Sartrean extreme condition, and its sole other inhabitant is one whom Sartre would call the "In-itself": her infuriating acceptance of the apparently pointless life she leads there undermines Niki's resolve to escape, and her sexual overtures are a dangerous invitation to complicity. "First she would sow the seeds of scandal by bringing him to an act of passion, and then the chains of blackmail would bind him hand and foot." Later, as he succumbs to her seduction, she appears as the Other characteristically seeks to appear: natural. Here "natural" means the sexual object, towards which Niki is irresistibly attracted despite his knowledge of the dangers. The woman remains nameless, but is otherwise described in astonishingly intimate detail—the omnipresent sand makes the wearing of clothes usually too abrasive. She is described more by her genitals than by any other feature: like the sand (the title in fact may be translated as "The Woman of Sand") she is both fascinating and treacherous.

Niki's existential claustrophobia is reiterated by the omnipresent sand, the sand they shovel nightly, that falls into their food, that worms its way into the beams of the house, that even intervenes between their skins while copulating. Gritty and smooth at the same time, the sand symbolizes their full gamut of relations: simultaneously hostile and alluring, threatening and comforting, murderous and seductive. Those relations, like the sand (collected by the villagers and sold to construction companies), have a telos: both Niki and the widow seek to exact from each other their own respective liberty. For Niki that would be freedom from the pit; for the woman freedom from the unshared burden of her labors and her loneliness. Perhaps the author Abe seeks his own freedom in release from escape—which Niki may have achieved at the conclusion of the novel. That sort of freedom could only be found in the establishment of a community through an existentialist transformation that makes "escape" moot. These lines close to the end of the novel suggest Niki believes he has found that community:

> There was no particular need to hurry about escaping. On the two-way ticket he held in his hand now, the destination and time of departure were blanks for him to fill in as he wished. In addition, he realized that he was bursting to talk to someone about the water trap [he had just devised]. And if he wanted to talk about it, there wouldn't be better listeners than the villagers.

The possibility of those "better listeners" makes Niki's situation in the sand pit somewhat less extreme; this perhaps distinguishes *The Woman in the Dunes* from novels by others of Abe's generation. Much of postwar Japanese literature describes extreme situations: it is full of references to war, hunger, and moral degeneration. But by and large these scenarios do not provide their characters with the opportunity to change themselves. Rather, they remain merely the backdrops against which essentially conventional people play out conventional melodramas. *The Woman in the Dunes* is different; the possibility of change exists—in such a way that suggests the novel makes a political statement as well as an absurdist or existential one.

This is an interpretation likely to be resisted. While it is well known that Abe was once a Party member, most people would doubtlessly agree with Edward Seidensticker when he says that a reader of *The Woman in the Dunes* "is more likely to think of Kafka or Beckett long before he thinks of Mao or Stalin."[4] True, but that is not to say the novel rejects issues of power. *The Woman in the Dunes* is political because Niki is granted a partisan choice: to accept the "society" devised by the villagers or to return to the society he left. Moreover, the novel is political in a particularly personal way. Abe's work in general has been called oblivious to history. In Leithauser's words, the "unlocalized Anywhere" of his settings eschews historical specificity. However, "historical" is loosely defined here; "history" can be used in many contending senses, which certainly include that of "a tradition of ideas" as well as that of "a record of experiences." Abe Kōbō's adoption of existentialist and absurdist techniques is often traced, along with those of his Western colleagues, to common philosophical sources, Nietzsche and Heidegger among them. Like Nietzsche, Abe's appears to dismiss all ethical impulses in his conception of the foundation of social order. Instead he locates the basis of modern society in the rationalization of cruelty. With Heidegger he shares the radical critique of civilization as rootless—*heimatlos*, or without unassailable foundations. However, alongside his leftist sympathies, and his Nietzschean or Heideggerian impulses to, as some might claim, deconstruct, there are traces of the other kind of history—that of lived experience. Intellectual parallels between East and West risk obscuring the tumultuous historical circumstances amid which Abe Kōbō grew to young adulthood.

Abe's desire to address the contradictions that lead to absurdity makes *The Woman in the Dunes* political. The sand that both threatens and enables the life—the economic life—of the villagers is one example of such a contradiction. A source of revenue, at the same time the sand is a treacherous nuisance; it imprisons them while it provides them, through its exchange, with sustenance. The sand constitutes both a strategy of containment and a place of business, the basis of a material production. When Niki discovers that the sand lifted out of the pits is sold, despite its substandard quality, to construction firms, suddenly he understands not only the logic, the rationale, of the village's enforced division of labor, but even their indifferent attitude to those people who may dwell in buildings made with unsafe concrete. The villagers represent an ultimate in alienation and so seem more like himself; they are people with no deep attachment to any particular moral value other than mere survival.

The penultimate turning point in the novel comes when Niki accidentally stumbles upon a means of production from which he is not so resignedly estranged. The water trap mentioned in the passage above was the accidental result of a hole dug in the sand originally intended to catch crows but which, instead, accumulated water through capillary action. Niki is ecstatic at his find; he has produced something very useful of his own. At this point thoughts of a new kind of freedom enter Niki's consciousness:

> As long as he had this device the villagers would not be able to interfere with him so easily. No matter how much they cut off his supply, he would be able to get along very well. . . . He was still in the hole, but it seemed as if he were already outside.

In a sense Niki is already outside. Although some villagers are still above the pits, and others below them, the dependency of the latter on the former is now less than total and the work demanded of Niki less humiliating. Marx writes in *Capital* that "the realm of freedom actually begins only where labor which is in fact determined by necessity and mundane considerations ceases." The struggle is to wrest a realm of freedom from a realm of necessity, and Niki is tempted to believe he is on the verge of winning. His life in the pit, where until now his labor was the requisite exchange for food and water, is transformed with the technology of the water trap into one where his labor might be offered freely. It may be another of Abe's ironies that Niki "wrests a realm of freedom" from this. After all, his dull life as a high-school teacher is to be replaced by his dull life as tender of the water trap. Once he ignores the rope ladder dangling before him, he has clearly chosen that variety of monotony over the other, and the exercise of his choice is political insofar as he has recognized his new power over how his labor is to be disbursed. For him the appeal of remaining in the pit can be taken in one of at least two ways:

either the work in the pit is now so less alienating than that of a teacher that he embraces it wholeheartedly, or that same work, while just as ruthless, is so less cloaked in ideology than that in conventional society that he elects to stay for the sheer, strange probity of it.

Abe's novels invariably contain passages that divide experiences, insects, or people, etc., into often bizarre categories. E. Dale Saunders, the translator of *The Woman in the Dunes*, suggests it is Abe's training as a physician that made him so attentive to taxonomy; perhaps, alternatively, it is a fascination with the essentially arbitrary nature of how we organize ourselves and the world around us. Some of us are teachers, others shovel sand; but Abe leaves which is more absurd a profession—if either—an open question. This and the other unresolved paradoxes one encounters in Abe's work are less attributable to his being Japanese, than they are to the insights he gained from his lived experiences in a wartime "nation" and a postwar economic "miracle." These are experiences which, though perhaps not quite our own in all their individual details, nonetheless made Abe Kōbō a Japanese writer very much at home anywhere ideologies totter and crumble into absurdity.

TOPICS FOR DISCUSSION

1. Japanese literature has been traditionally viewed as particularly attentive to setting: one thinks of Kawabata and Tanizaki, for example, as two modern novelists who have brought unique places (such as Asakusa or Ashiya) to life in their works. This alleged hallmark of the Japanese literary sensibility—we are told it stretches back to the beginnings of writing in Japan—seems conspicuously lacking in Abe. Or is it? What is the status of the sand pit as a "place" in this novel? Does it even matter that the story unfolds in Japan? Does Abe have a particular purpose in mind when he so generalizes his locations?

2. Abe is often compared to Kafka and Beckett. The absurd and surrealistic elements of his works suggest a shared cynicism, a common disillusionment. What, if anything, do works such as Kafka's *The Trial*, *The Metamorphosis*, and Beckett's *Malone* share with *The Woman in the Dunes*? What might have produced any similarities? Are they meaningful similarities?

3. The comparison of Abe with absurdist playwrights often leads to the further comparison with Sartre. Take Sartre's *Nausea* as an example: does Abe argue a philosophy, an ontology, as

forcefully as Sartre does? If so, how akin is it to French existentialism? Why might Sartre and Abe share a common, or different, approach to postwar society?

4. Is calling *The Woman in the Dunes* a political novel supportable? What makes a novel political in the first place? Does Abe reveal any of his social views in the work? What are they, and what would make some of those opinions "political" and others not? Take a work by another Marxist postwar novelist—Pier Paolo Pasolini, for instance—and compare the subtlety of their politics. Do novels have to be about revolutions or elections to be political?

5. It has been said of Abe's works that history is present by its absence. Do you agree? Does the fact that we learn Niki Jumpei disappears in 1955, and is declared legally dead in 1962, mean anything special? Or is history something more than a matter of dates? What would "history" mean to Abe the absurdist, Abe the existentialist, Abe the Marxist? Are the World War II experiences of Abe's youth irrelevant to our interpretation of this novel?

6. Much of the novel concerns the sexual, and often brutal, relations between Niki and the woman. Why? What particular role do those relations play in the novel? How does Abe use eroticism to tell his story? What purpose does sex serve for Niki? The woman? Does Niki strike you as a misogynist? Is Abe a feminist?

7. What are we to make of the novel's conclusion? Has Niki assimilated into the village? Is he still a prisoner? If so, then of what, or whom? Or has he attained some sort of freedom? How would we define that freedom? What is its relationship to freedom in a liberal, existentialist, or Marxist context?

NOTES

1. Abe Kōbō, quoted in Osada Hiroshi, "Abe Kōbō o yomu," in Nihon bungaku kenkyū shiryō kankō kai, ed., *Abe Kōbō—Ōe Kenzaburō* (Tokyo: Yuseido, 1974), p. 78.

2. Abe Kōbō, quoted in Osada Hiroshi, p. 78. Translated for this essay by John Whittier Treat.

3. From a volume of critical essays edited by the Nihon Bungaku Kenkyu Shiryo Sosho and published by Yuseido.

4. Edward G. Seidensticker, "The Japanese Novel and Disengagement," *Journal of Contemporary History*, vol. 2, no. 2 (1967): 177–94.

REFERENCES

Suna no onna has been translated into many languages, but only once into English: *The Woman in the Dunes*. Translated by E. Dale Saunders.

New York: Alfred A. Knopf, 1964; reprint, New York: Random House, 1972.

Abe Kōbō. *The Ark Sakura*. Translated by Juliet W. Carpenter. New York: Alfred A. Knopf, 1988.

Abe Kōbō. *The Box Man*. Translated by E. Dale Saunders. New York: Alfred A. Knopf, 1974.

Abe Kōbō. *The Face of Another*. Translated by E. Dale Saunders. New York: Alfred A. Knopf, 1966.

Abe Kōbō. *Inter Ice Age Four*. Translated by E. Dale Saunders. New York: Alfred A. Knopf, 1974.

Abe Kōbō. *The Ruined Map*. Translated by E. Dale Saunders. New York: Alfred A. Knopf, 1969.

Abe Kōbō. *Secret Rendezvous*. Translated by Juliet W. Carpenter. New York: Alfred A. Knopf: distributed by Random House, 1979.

MISHIMA YUKIO, THE ALLEGORIST

Richard Torrance

More has been written in English on Mishima Yukio than on any other modern Japanese writer. The number of his major novels, plays, and critical writings translated into English exceeds those translated of any other Japanese literary figure, including his mentor, the Nobel laureate for literature, Kawabata Yasunari, and Natsume Sōseki, the novelist whose image graces Japan's most widely circulating denomination of paper currency. Mishima Yukio's fame abroad owes something to his tireless self-promotion. He was also well received by those seeking to understand Japan when he spoke forcefully in English about Japanese culture. However, it was his spectacular suicide on November 25, 1970, that gave his name instant international notoriety.

Mishima Yukio committed *seppuku*, or ritual disembowelment. This very painful ceremony of self-destruction was institutionalized in the late twelfth century in Japan and came to be respected as a means for a warrior to atone for a mistake, crime, or an indiscretion, or as the ultimate expression, one beyond words, of a warrior's love for and loyalty to his lord. The act also became a powerful symbol of loyal protest. The ostensible motive for Mishima's seppuku and subsequent beheading by a confederate was his failure to arouse the Japanese Self-Defense Force to stage a coup d'état to reform the constitution and restore the emperor's position as the embodiment of the nation. It is doubtful, however, that he ever had any real hope of succeeding in his conspiracy to overthrow Japan's democratically elected government. His deepest desire and most terrible fear was to die the glorious, heroic death he had fantasized about since his childhood and had acted out again and again in his literature.

Mishima Yukio (a pen name) was born Hiraoka Kimitake in 1925. Both his mother and father were from families whose members were often a part of or closely associated with the state bureaucratic elite, and his father continued his family's tradition of governmental service to the emperor. Mishima obeyed his strict, overbearing father's wishes and proceeded along an elite educational path headed for a position in the upper echelons of the government. In the prewar educational system normally reserved for the aristocracy, he consistently passed examinations that qualified him for one of the few places open to commoners. He was a brilliant student. On graduating from the Peers' School in 1944 at the head of his class, his scholastic achievement earned him the singular honor of a silver watch sent by the emperor. He entered Tokyo Imperial University and studied law in preparation for the high position in the bureaucracy that he would take up in 1947 when he received formal appointment to the Ministry of Finance. He soon resigned, however, to pursue a literary career. By his twenty-third birthday, having divided his energies between his writing and his studies, he had managed to have two collections of short stories and a novel published under the extremely difficult circumstances of war and defeat. When he was free to devote his immense energy and intellect solely to literature, he produced a remarkably prolific flow of novels, plays, and criticism.

Mishima Yukio had been raised to serve a metaphysical concept of the nation as embodied by a divine emperor. When the emperor renounced his divinity—acquiescing to the demands of U.S. Occupation authorities that he not embody but symbolize the nation—the central coordinates of Mishima's moral and legal education were displaced. Service to the nation no longer meant advancing the cause of a powerful empire, living for a rich mythology, and being prepared to sacrifice one's life to protect the imperial institution. Instead, Mishima—who with some justification probably saw himself as one of the brightest young men of his generation—became a mere functionary in an administration under foreign control. The war was not supposed to have ended so anticlimactically.

The writings of Yasuda Yojūrō and other intellectuals associated with wartime Japanese Romanticism, a literary movement that glorified irony, death, and self-destruction, probably had a decisive influence on the young Mishima. Yasuda had undertaken the task of fashioning an aesthetic that would support Japan's total mobilization for war. He discovered the source of Japanese beauty in the poetry of lamentation in the *Man'yōshū*, Japan's first collection of poetry compiled ca. 759. He then argued that at the moment of death or killing in battle, this spirit of lamentation was invoked, and the Japanese individual found ultimate happiness in the dissolution of the self into the beauty of his or her origin. Death was aesthetic victory. If the defeat of Japan resulted in sincere and beautiful slaughter on an enormous scale, it was aesthetically preferable to an undramatic victory. These kinds of orgiastic celebrations of annihilation fascinated Mishima in his last years at Peers' School.

We know from Mishima's autobiographical novel *Confessions of a Mask* (which in 1949 launched his postwar literary career) and from other accounts as well that many of Japan's young intellectuals were united in and intoxicated by a "community of death" during World War II. Perhaps the last years of the war constituted the most liberating experience of Mishima's life. In the face of the potential destruction of the homeland, the educational system ceased operating, and students were drafted or sent to work in factories or government offices. It was summer vacation the whole year round. All was permitted the brave young men who would certainly die beautifully in repelling the coming American invasion. As boys often do, the child Mishima dreamed of a glorious, exquisitely painful death, and during his late adolescence the purity of violence seemed to cover the earth. Perhaps 90,000 people died in the firebombings of Tokyo alone. Mishima certainly did not expect to survive. He wrote of this period in *Confessions of a Mask*: "even more than before, I found myself immersed in a desire for death. It was in death that I had discovered my real 'life's aim.'"

But Mishima did not die. At his physical examination for the military draft, the frail, effeminate youth was disqualified by a less-than-competent doctor who made an incorrect diagnosis that Mishima had tuberculosis. Mishima and his father let this diagnosis stand. Then, on August 15, 1945, Emperor Hirohito announced Japan's surrender. Mishima had more than enough reason to believe that his "final aim" would be accomplished despite the end of the war. In his words, a "civil war" continued. Occupied by foreign powers (primarily the United States) its industrial capacity destroyed, and threatened by massive food shortages, the Japanese nation—and Mishima and the emperor with it—seemed headed for the beautiful annihilation Yasuda Yojūrō had envisioned. Once again, the cataclysm did not come. Mishima's fellow citizens went about the ugly, petty business of survival and reconstruction. In the midst of innumerable struggles to survive, he remained committed, or perhaps addicted, to the romantic quest for a metaphysical unity worthy of the sacrifice of his life. He was thus innoculated against that creeping epidemic of the postwar era, the quotidian.

He resisted participation in the everyday life of the postwar period by adopting a variety of personas. He went through a "Greek phase" and built up the muscles of his weak torso by lifting weights. Playing at being a samurai, he posed almost nude with a sword for a fashion photographer. Mishima appeared in the movies as a gangster and starred in the film adaptation of his short story "Patriotism" (1961) as the idealistic young officer in the Imperial Army who commits suicide after the failure of a prewar coup d'état. The literary prankster in the Japanese media, he played with members of the fashion, political, and theatrical elites. As Hashikawa Bunzō, one of Japan's most perceptive thinkers on the nature of modern Japanese nationalism, concluded in 1964, "Mishima Yukio has brought a terrible humor to the literary world . . . but from behind the mask of a clown peer the eyes of the god of death."[1] Mishima's romantic nihilism was not an imported idea or an act. He brought immense discipline, force of will, and linguistic genius to the creation of allegories whose stylistic brilliance addresses the meaninglessness of language in the postwar period. His allegories are about absence.

Mishima's literary career can be divided broadly into three phases: his early Japanese Romanticism of the war years, the apolitical period that began with the success of *Confessions of a Mask* in 1949, and the period during which he gradually returned to active political support of the emperor as the embodiment of the nation in the early 1960s and which saw the publication of his four-volume novel, *The Sea of Fertility* (1965–70). *The Sailor Who Fell from Grace with the Sea* (henceforth abbreviated as *The Sailor*) was written over a five-month period from January to May of 1963. John Nathan's translation is admirable and responsible, but it should be noted that the title of Mishima's original (*Gogo no eikō*) means literally *A Ship in Tow in the Afternoon* or *Glory in the Afternoon*, the title pivoting on a pun on the word "*eikō*" (towing a ship to glory). The title probably refers most directly to the fact that the protagonist, Tsukazaki Ryūji, is pulled to his ultimate destination, the glory of death, by the boys who plan to murder him in dry dock.

The Japan portrayed in *The Sailor* is quite different from present-day Japan. Color televisions, air conditioners, mink coats, personal automobiles, brass beds, and stylish imported clothing are rather commonplace symbols of an affluent consumer culture

in contemporary Japanese society, but, in the Japan of the early
sixties, such items signified the substantial wealth of a privileged
bourgeois family. At this point in his career, Mishima may well
have been trying to "tow" his island nation away from aspirations
to possess the western luxuries owned by Ryūji's lover Kuroda
Fusako. If such was the case, he failed. Even in 1970, he probably
could not have imagined how thoroughly Japanese society would
be seduced by "crass consumerism."

Setting the novel in Yokohama, traditionally Japan's most important port city and gateway to the west, allowed Mishima to
portray Japan as an unsullied abstract unity that is always just
out of reach (something like the imperial household); by avoiding
realistic descriptions of a postwar Japanese street, for example,
Mishima could project a prewar conception of the state onto the
sea, the source of ultimate power and authority. Thus the streets
of Yokohama are "simplified and abstracted" by the sea. In the
scant information provided about Tsukazaki's past, Tokyo
emerges as a void, a barren land laid waste by firebombs. As
Kuroda Fusako's bedroom is described from her son Noboru's
vantage point at the peephole, it is soon clear, in lovingly fetishis-
tic detail, that this is not a Japanese but a foreign space, once
profaned by "a blond hairy body." The terrestrial realm in *The
Sailor*—"There wasn't a single Japanese room in Fusako's
house"—is allegorical emptiness.

The sea in *The Sailor* performs much the same symbolic function as the temple in Mishima Yukio's 1956 novel *The Temple of
the Golden Pavilion*. The protagonist in *The Temple of the Golden
Pavilion*, a Buddhist acolyte named Mizoguchi, is a slave to the
beauty of the temple. Mizoguchi undergoes a process of nihilistic
radicalization until he reaches the point where he understands
that the perfect and ultimate beauty of the temple will only become manifest at the moment of its destruction in flames. Determined to die with the beautiful, he sets fire to the temple. His
nerve fails at the last moment, however, and he flees from the
object of desire that dominates him. In *The Sailor*, Ryūji is likewise a slave to the power of the sea. Ryūji first appears in *The
Sailor* as a nihilistic hero who desires to sacrifice himself to the
sea and thus make glory manifest. However, he undergoes a process of growth that is the reverse of that experienced by
Mizoguchi. Ryūji becomes domesticated, less nihilistic, and betrays the object of his desire; his jealous lover, the sea, takes
revenge through the agency of the boys. Both heroes long to
annihilate themselves and merge with the object of fear and desire

that dominates them. The conclusions of both novels—destruction of the object, the temple, and destruction of the subject, Ryūji—are reached through the mediation of radically nihilistic secondary characters: Kashiwagi in *The Temple of the Golden Pavilion*, the Chief of the gang of boys in *The Sailor*. These literary artifices—essentially speech-making abstractions—expose all of society's conventions as hollow fictions, and the way is thus cleared for a metaphysical truth that transcends everyday life. Beauty, Glory, Temple, Sea, and Emperor are interchangeable concepts that stand for an inexplicable desire that dominates and demands self-immolation.

Taken together, *The Temple of the Golden Pavilion* and *The Sailor* epitomize what is commonly called the "Mishima aesthetic," which remained remarkably consistent from the start of Mishima's literary career to its end. The sea was a leitmotiv in this aesthetic. In his first sustained novel, *A Forest in Full Flower* (1944), Mishima wrote, "Upon reflection, I wonder if my fear of the sea is not a different aspect of my longing for it." In Mishima's world, forces attract precisely because they are dangerous. When the sea in *The Sailor* lacks the potential to obliterate the subject, the seascape becomes "a shiny log floating on the dirty water." On the other hand, when the sea is linked to death, it takes on a power that is inexpressible, as we see when Ryūji considers leaving behind his life as a sailor: "The secret yearning for death. The glory beyond and the death beyond. Everything was 'beyond'; wrong or right, had always been 'beyond.' *Are you going to give that up?*"

So powerful is the sea as a transcendental abstraction that it erases all class, generational, and educational boundaries. The thirteen-year-old, bourgeois "genius," Noboru, may look down on the sailor as a "beast," but he comes to share Tsukazaki's essential vision of the sea. It is not "psychology" or "sociological background" that determines how the sea is perceived, but rather the sea defines itself beyond human experience.

For Tsukazaki, sexual desire is "pure abstraction" and becomes "consubstantial" with "glory" and "death" in the sea. Erotic ecstasy is linked to death and glory by the poetic lamentations of the woman left to wait for the sailor who will never return. This association pervades *The Sailor*:

> *I* [Ryūji] *could have been a man sailing away forever.* He had been fed up with all of it, glutted, and yet now, slowly, he was awakening to the immensity of what he had abandoned.

> The dark passions of the tides, the shriek of a tidal wave, the avalanching break of surf upon a shoal . . . an unknown glory calling for him endlessly from the dark offing, glory merged in death and in a woman, glory to fashion of his destiny something special, something rare.

Noboru's voyeuristic vision of the sea differs from the sailor's only in its specific inflections. On the night he first witnesses Tsukazaki and his mother engaged in the sexual act, the "full long wail of a ship's horn," a lament "demanding grief," a "scream from the sea" provides Noboru with the metaphysical unity (the sea) he requires to comprehend ecstasy. "The universal order at last achieved, thanks to the sudden, screaming horn, had revealed an ineluctable circle of life—the cards had paired: Noboru and mother—mother and man—man and sea—sea and Noboru"; only the association of death with the sea and Eros is missing from Noboru's initial apprehension of the Mishima aesthetic. Noboru's perception fully coincides with Tsukazaki's after Noboru learns to kill:

> He [Noboru] saw them as marvelous gold embroideries leaping off a flat black fabric: the naked sailor twisting in the moonlight to confront a horn—the kitten's death mask, grave and fang-bared—its ruby heart . . . gorgeous entities all and absolutely authentic: then Ryūji too was an authentic hero . . . all incidents on the sea, in the sea, under the sea—Noboru felt himself drowning in deep "Happiness," he thought, "Happiness that defies description. . . ."

Offering no clear purpose or glorious end for which the individual subject can legitimately kill or die, postwar Japanese society, when compared to the sea, is banal, empty, and lacking reality. (One suspects that for Mishima the allegorist reality was the function of a unifying idea.) What the Mishima aesthetic demands is a revolution of sorts, or as the thirteen-year-old Chief proclaims:

> "We must have blood! Human blood! If we don't get it this empty world will go pale and shrivel up. We must drain that sailor's fresh lifeblood and transfuse it to the dying universe, the dying sky, the dying forests, and the drawn, dying land."

The Mishima aesthetic favors images of cataclysm, but its revolution is a fake. This vanguard of "boys from good families" is not interested in transforming the world by the violent overthrow of the existing social order. In the context of a Japan that was being "towed" by a foreign power, a Japan that had been forced to renounce its sovereign right to wage aggressive war and had been deprived of an emperor who could legitimate violence, vast expanses of the prewar literary vocabulary—"glory," "death," "blood"—had become perverted or meaningless. It was this kind of postwar linguistic dislocation, of which Mishima was surely aware and which he exploited to the full, that gives his best work a shimmering, hallucinatory brilliance. The Mishima aesthetic was formed during total mobilization for war from dreams of the ecstasy experienced at the moment of obliteration in ultimate sacrifice for a higher metaphysical unity. His rhetoric remained the rhetoric of war, but, without the higher cause, his allegories lacked purpose. In a world in which only fiction reigned, he returned to perhaps a forced faith in the imperial institution. Perhaps he finally found his utopia of lamentation for fallen heroes.

At about the time *The Sailor* was published, during a period when Mishima was gaining recognition in the United States and Europe, the Mishima aesthetic was falling into disfavor among many critics and readers in Japan. His increasingly radical right-wing politics and public displays of bisexual machismo probably alienated many readers. But one suspects that, in the end, people were growing tired of his obsessive themes. As was shown, with some inversions, *The Temple of the Golden Pavilion* and *The Sailor* are similar stories. This is not to suggest that Mishima was a limited writer. *The Sound of Waves* (1954), a touching love story centering on a platonic romance between a young fisherman and an innocent girl diver, and *After the Banquet* (1960), a persuasive political novel about a naive, elderly statesman who runs for the mayoralty of Tokyo on the Socialist ticket and is defeated by corrupt rightist political interests, are two very different works. They indicate that Mishima was capable of intelligently portraying a range of experiences. Though he appears, at times, to have been tone-deaf to the language diversity of everyday life, he had an enormous command of the classical literary language, and, almost single-handedly, he revitalized the creation of Noh and Kabuki plays in the classical manner. Still, when Mishima really invested himself in his writing—and it is a sign of his artistic integrity that he continued to do so—the result was most often a beautiful eroticization of death. His brilliantly metaphorical and difficult telling and retelling of the desire for a glorious death in a decadent age probably exhausted many readers.

Mishima Yukio's reputation in Japan relative to other writers may not be what it is in the United States and Europe. What other Japanese writer has had a movie made out of his or her life by a prominent American director? Nonetheless, he continues to command respect from Japanese intellectuals, writers, and the reading public, quite apart from the political and religious cult that celebrates him. A prestigious literary award has recently been established in his name and his best novels continue to sell well. His plays are received enthusiastically at the Japanese National Theater, a state institution staging only works canonically regarded as the best of the Japanese theatrical tradition. In the debate over what was lost and what was gained by Japan's surrender on August 15, 1945, Mishima Yukio's voice will most certainly continue to be heard, providing powerful testimony as to the enormity of the loss.

TOPICS FOR DISCUSSION

1. In the process of providing a literary and historical context for *The Sailor*, the work was read here as allegory. Are there other ways to read the work? Do Mishima's gorgeous rhetoric and striking metaphors, which confound certain stereotypes about class and age, preclude reading the work as a realistic novel. Is it likely that a sailor from Ryūji's impoverished background would develop such an articulate aesthetic and philosophy of nihilism? Even among elite families, is there a thirteen-year-old boy who could speechify as pompously as the Chief without provoking laughter? On the other hand, Mishima's use of narrative perspective—utilizing the boy to define the man and woman, contrasting the boy's view with the sailor's view of himself, and incorporating the detective's report to bolster Kuroda Fusako's judgement of the sailor—is clearly a realistic technique for erasing authorial presence. Can some other genre—novel of abnormal psychology, surrealism, magic realism—be proposed to account for the unrealistic aspects of the novel?

2. The early influence of Yasuda Yojūrō and Japanese Romanticism on Mishima Yukio was stressed above. Comparatists have identified a number of other influences: Raymond Radiguet, Rainer Maria Rilke, Oscar Wilde, Proust, Cocteau, Yeats, Goethe, Thomas Mann, D'Annunzio, Gide, Francois Mauriac, and perhaps most importantly Nietzsche. Mishima was comparatively well read in European literature. Does Mishima's popularity in Western Europe and the United States owe something to the fact that readers feel at home with a Western literary tradition they perceive in his writing? Can one identify foreign literary influences in *The Sailor*?

3. Article Nine of the postwar Japanese Constitution states, "The people renounce war as a sovereign right of the Nation," and, "land, sea, and air forces, as well as other war potential, will never be maintained." Japan, of course, maintains a military force, but the vocabulary of aggression has been purged: it is called the Self-Defense Force. This unique, and given Japan's long, venerated military tradition, odd situation enabled Mishima to adopt the pretense that he was the sole personification of Japan's martial spirit in the field of serious literature. In this capacity, he raised issues that have universal implications. His theory of aggression was projected not on the individual but on the communality. He was, after all, trained in the law. Can a nation, a people, survive without sadomasochistic mythologies sanctifying murder and glorifying the self-sacrifice of death for a higher cause? Can a literature prosper without such mythologies, without "good guys" and "bad guys" formally designated by death and killing for the benefit of the common good? Can the individual exist without some agent, in the case of Japan the emperor, who channels the undercurrent of the death wish in legitimate directions? Mishima's career and ritual suicide answers all of these questions with a thunderously dramatic "No." Was he right? Are these questions universal, or are they produced by a Eurocentric way of thinking?

NOTE

1. Hashikawa Bunzō, *Hashikawa Bunzō chosakushū,* 8 vols. (Tokyo: Chikuma Shobō, 1985), 1:272.

REFERENCES

As was noted above, a great deal has been written in the United States and Western Europe on Mishima Yukio, and the following list of materials in English by or about Mishima is certainly not a comprehensive bibliography. Dates in parentheses refer to years the works appeared in English.

Novels and short stories by Mishima Yukio which have been translated into English include *The Sound of the Waves* (1956), translated by Meredith Weatherby; *Confessions of a Mask* (1958), translated by Meredith Weatherby; *The Temple of the Golden Pavilion* (1959), translated by Ivan Morris; *After the Banquet* (1963), translated by Donald Keene; *The Sailor Who Fell from Grace with the Sea* (1965), translated by John Nathan. Mishima's "Patriotism," translated by Geoffrey Sargent, is found in a collection of his short stories, *Death in Midsummer and Other Stories* (1966). *Forbidden Colors* (1968) and *Thirst for Love* (1969) were translated by Alfred Marks. Mishima's four-volume epic of transmigration, *The Sea of Fertility*, is available as *Spring Snow* (1972), translated by Michael Gallagher; *Runaway Horses* (1973), translated by Michael Gallagher; *The Temple of Dawn* (1973), translated by E. Dale Saunders and Cecilia Seigle; and *The Decay of the Angel* (1974), translated by Edward G. Seidensticker. One of Mishima's seminal postwar short stories, "The Boy Who Wrote Poetry," translated by Ian Levy, is found in Howard Hibbet, ed., *Contemporary Japanese Literature* (New York: Alfred A. Knopf, 1977).

The following plays by Mishima have been published in English translation: *Five Modern Nō Plays* (1957), translated by Donald Keene; *Twilight Sunflower* (1958), translated by Shigeho Shinozaki and Virgil Warren; *Madame de Sade* (1967), translated by Donald Keene.

Sun and Steel (1970), translated by John Bester, and *The Way of the Samurai: Yukio Mishima on "Hagakure" in Modern Life* (1977), translated by Kathryn Sparling, are autobiographical and political essays which offer Mishima's perspectives on the personal nature of Japanese culture.

Two biographies have been written in English on Mishima: John Nathan, *Mishima: A Biography* (1974) and Henry Scott-Stokes, *The Life and Death of Yukio Mishima* (1974). The former provides the more detailed study of the complicated circumstances of Mishima's upbringing, and the latter contains more personal reminiscence and information concerning Mishima's final years. Important critical essays on Mishima's life and works are found in Donald Keene, *Landscapes and Portraits* (1971), Masao Miyoshi, *Accomplices of Silence* (1974), Ivan Morris, *The Nobility of Failure* (1975), Ueda Makoto, *Modern Japanese Writers and the Nature of Literature* (1976), and Donald Keene, *Dawn to the West* (1984). Marguerite Yourcenar has written an insightful, book-length essay on Mishima's literature, entitled *Mishima ou la vision du vide* (1981), translated with the collaboration of Alberto Manguel as *Mishima: A Vision of the Void* (1986).

The motion picture based on Mishima's life is *Mishima*, Paul Schrader, director, Lucas and Coppola, executive producers (Warner Brothers, 1985).

Japanese Texts: Narrative

KAWABATA YASUNARI'S
SNOW COUNTRY

Michael C. Brownstein

In 1968 Kawabata Yasunari became the first Japanese to win the Nobel Prize for literature. The award coincided with the centennial of the Meiji Restoration, which ushered Japan into the modern era after centuries of feudalism and self-imposed isolation. Apart from the well-deserved recognition for Kawabata, therefore, the Nobel Prize also signified the growing international appreciation of Japanese literature, especially modern fiction.

If Western readers were only vaguely aware of Japan's rich literary tradition, Japanese have, at least since the Restoration, been far more conscious of Western writing as the discourse of the Other. This consciousness of the Other through writing was (and still is) a central factor in the history of Japanese culture. For a thousand years or more before 1868, the Other was Chinese civilization. Few Japanese knew China firsthand, but Chinese writing provided Japanese with a basis for their own and served as the medium through which Chinese literature, philosophy, and religion, not to mention knowledge of the rest of Asia, reached Japanese shores. But this consciousness of the Other entailed an acute self-consciousness, a constant questioning of the nature and value of what is essentially Japanese. The discourse of the Other has thus served as a mirror through which Japanese have periodically rediscovered and redefined themselves. When the West replaced China as the principal foreign influence, Western literature presented a new challenge to this self-image. Kawabata's long career exemplifies those of many other modern writers who experimented with these influences in an effort to create a modern Japanese literature, one that would transcend the literature of the past without losing touch with it.

Born in Osaka in 1899, Kawabata became a "Master of Funerals" at an early age. He lost both parents by the age of two, his grandmother at seven, and his sister at nine. He was then left with his ailing grandfather, who died when Kawabata was fifteen. These and the deaths of more distant relatives are thought to account not only for the melancholy tone that pervades his best-known writings but also his lifelong devotion to Murasaki Shikibu's *Tale of Genji* and other classics, with their aesthetics of *mono no aware*, or "the pathos of things" and *mujō*, or "impermanence." In *Snow Country* (*Yukiguni*), as in his other works, the beauty of the world appears tinged with sadness; indeed, sadness or loneliness is for Kawabata, as for Lady Murasaki, the essential quality or condition of beauty, the affective response to immanent loss.

In 1920 Kawabata entered Tokyo University, first as a student in the English department. The following year he switched to Japanese literature and graduated three years later in 1924. By that time, he had already published his first story "Shōkonsai Ikkei" ("A View of the Yasukuni Festival," 1921) and attracted the attention of Kikuchi Kan, the preeminent literary figure of the day. Kawabata also joined a group of writers who called themselves the *Shin Kankaku-ha*, the "Neo-perceptionists" or "Neo-sensationalists." Such groups were a characteristic feature of the literary landscape; collectively they made up the *bundan*, or "literary circles." They typically published their own literary magazines (often short-lived) in which they would present their critical manifestos and publish their fiction or poetry—though it is often difficult to find in the latter a programmatic implementation of the former. Their theories usually reflected the latest European ideas, which were used to criticize prevailing literary trends, and the Neo-perceptionists were no exception. Drawing on Dadaism, Futurism, Expressionism, and other post-World War I modernist movements in Europe, Kawabata and his associates tried to situate themselves between the Naturalists on the one side, with their self-absorbed confessional novels, and the Marxist-inspired proletarian writers on the other. Regardless of their philosophical orientations, the Naturalists and the Proletarians both stood for an uncompromising objectivity in literature, whether in depicting the sordid details of the author's own life or the tragic circumstances of the downtrodden. The Neo-perceptionists, on the other hand, brought into question the presumed "objectivity" of reality and the role of language in its representation. More than anything else, their movement called for a revolution in literary language, emphasizing the subjectivity of "reality"—how the world was perceived and ultimately transformed aesthetically by the mind through language.

Their concern with language was accompanied by experiments in form as well. Postwar aesthetic movements in Europe stood against the coherent picture of reality found in the nineteenth-century novel, but whereas earlier Japanese writers had despaired at ever seeing a Japanese Hugo, Dickens, or Dostoevski, the new wave of European influence proved much more congenial. This suggests a basic affinity between classical Japanese aesthetics and twentieth century modernism, and explains why elements of both can be detected in a novelist like Kawabata or a poet like Ezra Pound. As a group, the Neo-perceptionists ceased to exist by 1928, but the influence of Kawabata and other members on the development of Japanese fiction count it as one of the important movements of the modern era.

In 1926 Kawabata published the work that first brought him fame and that remains one of his most popular works: *Izu no Odoriko* (*The Izu Dancer*). The story belongs to a long tradition of Japanese travel narratives written over the centuries by court nobles, samurai officials, poets, and others for whom the romance of "the road" had religious and aesthetic associations. Many Noh plays too open with a Buddhist priest on a journey during which he encounters the ghost of some famous person, now suffering the torments of hell for past sins. In *The Izu Dancer*, the youthful narrator recounts his trip on foot down the Izu Peninsula in the autumn of his twentieth year. Along the way he joins up with a group of traveling entertainers and falls in love with the youngest, a girl who turns out to be too young for him. Although his illusions are shattered when he accidentally catches sight of the girl emerging naked from a hot spring, the reality seems to come as a relief. Even so, when he leaves the troop to return by boat to Tokyo, he breaks down in tears.

The story is based on a trip Kawabata himself made while still in college after the woman he was engaged to suddenly broke off the affair. Written at the height of his Neo-perceptionist period, *The Izu Dancer* is more heartfelt and direct than experimental. In his depiction of Kaoru the dancer, moreover, we find the prototype of the idealized child-woman who appears in later works, including of course, *Snow Country*.

With the success of *The Izu Dancer* behind him, Kawabata nonetheless continued to explore new approaches to fiction. *Asakusa Kurenai Dan* (*The Asakusa Scarlet Gang*, 1929–30), and *Suishō Gensō* (*Crystal Fantasies*, 1931), for example, are two rather different experiments with the various influences at work on Japanese writers during this period: Joycean stream of consciousness, naturalistic description, and nostalgia for the ethos of old Edo following the Great Earthquake of 1923, to name a few. Even if Kawabata was not as prolific as other writers, his openness to these influences partly explains why he was able to write for as long as he did, and in such variety: children's stories, popular fiction, critical essays, and even the screenplay for *Kurutta Ippeiji* (*A Page of Madness*, 1926), now an avant-garde film classic.

Other notable works from this early period include the first of his "palm of the hand" stories, which he continued to write throughout his career. Widely divergent in theme and content, most of these are only a page or two long and strike the reader as fragments or scenes from some larger work. For that matter, many of his longer works seem unfinished or incomplete works-in-progress that Kawabata added to even after they were published as "complete." Such is the case with *Snow Country*. Between 1935 and 1937, Kawabata published seven chapters in different journals. He then collected and revised them for a book that won a literary prize and was adapted as a play. Over the next ten years, however, he made further additions and revisions, publishing the novel in its present form in 1948. Even so, Kawabata wrote a "palm-sized" version just before his death in 1972.

In the 1930s, the usually shy and diffident Kawabata emerged as a prominent figure in the *bundan*. He was a member of the editorial staffs of important magazines and counted among the judges for the prestigious Akutagawa Prize, which is awarded each year to outstanding new writers. Kawabata himself received an array of literary prizes for his novels, but he is also remembered for his role in discovering fresh talent. As an established figure whose opinion was much sought after, Kawabata was instrumental in promoting the careers of Mishima Yukio and others. After World War II, Kawabata began to attract attention from abroad. He became president of the Japan P.E.N. Club in 1948, a position he held for seventeen years. He also continued to write, publishing such widely admired works as *Sembazuru* (*A Thousand Cranes*, 1949–51), *Yama no Oto* (*The Sound of the Mountain*, 1954), and *Nemureru Bijō* (*The House of Sleeping Beauties*, 1960–61). Equally important, he was one of a handful of modern novelists whose works first gained an audience outside Japan through the efforts of Western scholars, beginning with Edward Seidensticker's translation of *Snow Country* in 1956. *Snow Coun-*

try concerns a love affair between Shimamura, a urbane Tokyo dilettante with a wife and children, and Komako, a geisha at a mountain hot springs resort. Another female character, Yoko, appears in the opening pages and later emerges as the third person in their love triangle. The book is divided into two parts that recount Shimamura's second and third visits to the resort, but the first part contains a long description, as well, of his first encounter with Komako. The title refers to an area on the northern part of the main island that faces the Sea of Japan. As the name suggests, the locale receives the full brunt of the cold that sweeps down from Siberia in winter to bury the mountains in snow.

The resort towns that dot the landscape lure mountain climbers in spring and summer, and skiers in winter. Shimamura, however, is no sportsman. Some critics have described him as a man of the senses, but Shimamura lives and has his being not in nature or his own body but in his mind. In Tokyo he is a drama critic with a modest reputation for his expertise in Western ballet, though he has never actually seen one. Indeed, for Shimamura, an evening at the ballet would rob it of its appeal:

> Nothing could be more comfortable than writing about the ballet from books. A ballet he had never seen was an art in another world. It was an unrivaled armchair reverie, a lyric from some paradise. He called his work research, but it was actually free, uncontrolled fantasy. He preferred not to savor the ballet in the flesh; rather he savored the phantasms of his own dancing imagination, called up by Western books and pictures. It was like being in love with someone he had never seen.[1]

The central tension in the story is between the "phantasms" of Shimamura's idealizing imagination and a reality that, though vital and dynamic, is subject to decay and death. Shimamura cannot bear too much reality, and so cleaves to a world of fantasy because it is "like being in love with someone he had never seen." In this respect, Shimamura may be compared to the protagonist in Shelley's *Alastor*, the poet who "drinks deep of the fountains of knowledge, and is still insatiate," and whose desires "point towards objects thus infinite and unmeasured." When these objects cease to suffice, "he images to himself a being whom he loves" in a dream or a vision.[2]

The first chapter of *Snow Country*, for example, suggests that Yoko is Shimamura's "veiled maid," for he first sees her "as rather like a character out of an old, romantic tale" on the train taking him to the snow country and his reunion with Komako. Musing over the fact that only the forefinger of his left hand seems to recall Komako,

> he brought the hand to his face, then quickly drew a line across the misted-over window. A woman's eye floated up before him. He almost called out in his astonishment. But he had been dreaming, and when he came to himself he saw that it was only the reflection in the window of the girl opposite. Outside it was growing dark, and the lights had been turned on in the train, transforming the window into a mirror.[3]

Shimamura is fascinated by the "unreal, otherworldly power" of the window, which simultaneously reflects the lighted interior of the train while permitting him to see the dim outlines of the passing countryside as darkness falls. This is the central metaphor of the novel, for the semitransparent "mirror" is an image of reality mediated by the imagination, what Wordsworth calls "the mighty world / Of eye, and ear,—both what they half create, / And what perceive."[4] Riding in the same coach as Shimamura, Yoko watches over a sick man while Shimamura gazes at her reflection in the train window. Nevertheless,

> it was as if he were watching a tableau in a dream—and that was no doubt the working of his strange mirror.
> In the depths of the mirror the evening landscape moved by, the mirror and the reflected figures like motion pictures superimposed one on the other. The figures and the background were unrelated, and yet the figures, transparent and intangible, and the background, dim in the gathering darkness, melted together into a sort of symbolic world not of this world. Particularly when a light out in the mountains shone in the center of the girl's face, Shimamura felt his chest rise at the inexpressible beauty of it.[5]

Shimamura's perceptions thus mediate the distance between his imagination and the world, leading at times to epiphanic moments of beauty when the two seem fused, as in the passage above. The image of Yoko's face floating over and through the darkening landscape outside is more vivid, more enchanting than the memory of Komako. When he later recalls how Yoko called out to the station master at one of the stops, it was with "a voice so beautiful it was almost lonely, calling out as if to someone who could not hear, on a ship far away."[6] It was, perhaps, in Shelley's words, "like the voice of his own soul / Heard in the calm of thought."[7] And just as the poet in Shelley's *Alastor* pursues his vision of the veiled maid to the ends of the earth, so Shimamura follows his to the remoteness of snow country.

Shimamura's name, though common enough, means "island hamlet," and his movements seem to be shadowed by his own "Alastor," or "Spirit of Solitude." Whenever he attempts to grasp his ideal within the context of the real, he too is often disappointed at what he finds. An example of this is the excursion he makes to an area near the resort where *Chijimi,* a special cloth, was once woven. A collector of this cloth and something of an expert on its manufacture, Shimamura is naturally curious about the locale. However, it turns out to be depressingly empty of any life, and the end of his visit finds him waiting on the train platform for two hours with cold feet. Perception itself thus plays an ambiguous role: it is the source that feeds the enchanting fantasies of his imagination, but also destroys them by revealing too much of the real.

Incapable of passion and commitment, self-indulgent and narcissistic, Shimamura is hardly a sympathetic character. As the story unfolds, Shimamura begins to appear less like Shelley's "youth of uncorrupted feelings" than one of those "meaner spirits" whom Shelley criticizes in his preface, those who are "morally dead" and doomed to "a slow and poisonous decay," because they are "deluded by no generous error, instigated by no sacred thirst of doubtful knowledge, duped by no illustrious superstition, loving nothing on this earth, and cherishing no hopes beyond, yet keep aloof from sympathies with their kind."[8] Shimamura's is a "sad little dream world" circumscribed by what he cannot see, whether it is the distances beyond the Border Range or the depths of his own inner emptiness. Nevertheless, he serves as the consciousness through which the events of the story are related, and it is his sensibility that transforms those events into moments of remarkable beauty or poignant sadness. By restricting his point of view to Shimamura, Kawabata makes it seem as if only he is capable of registering such moments. There is no indication that for Komako the snow country is anything but a remote backwater, a place from which few escape to a better life or to which some return to die, where she seems fated to lead a pointless life at the beck and call of transient visitors.

The tension between imagination and reality in Shimamura is brought out most fully in his relationship with Komako. She is the novel's triumph and perhaps the most memorable of Kawabata's female characters. Just prior to starting *Snow Country,* he wrote in another work:

> I am in general attracted by the danger present in a girl who has had the misfortune to grow to maturity separated from her flesh and blood but who herself dislikes being thought of as unfortunate, who has fought with her misfortune and won, but who because she has won this victory can see the precipitous abyss before her, yet has never feared it because of her high spirits. By ascribing the qualities of such a girl to her "child's heart," I too return to the heart of a child; that is the kind of love I experience. For this reason, I always fall in love with women who are in between a child and an adult in age.[9]

These lines seem to describe the character of Komako fairly closely. She was nineteen when Shimamura first met her, perhaps more an adult than a child, but in their encounters she alternates between the passionate sensuality of a mature woman and an engaging girlishness. Against her better judgment she falls in love with Shimamura. Quick-tempered and proud, Komako is also plagued by a degree of self-loathing that, when she suspects Shimamura is mocking her, precipitates her emotional outbursts. The intensity of her attraction toward him stems from more than her loneliness or his sophisticated ways. Her compulsion to show Shimamura her diary or the dreary rooms where she lives is fueled by her need to have him see her, not as a fantasy of his imagination, but as a complex and very real young woman. She almost achieves this near the end of the first part, when she plays the shamisen for him and sings:

> By the time she had begun her third song—the voluptuous softness of the music itself may have been responsible—the chill and the goose flesh had disappeared, and Shimamura, relaxed and warm, was gazing into Komako's face. A feeling of intense physical nearness came over him. The high, thin nose was usually a little lonely, a little sad, but today, with the healthy, vital flush on her cheeks, it was rather whispering: I am here too. The smooth lips seemed to reflect back a dancing light even when they were drawn into a tight bud; and when for a moment they were stretched wide, as the singing demanded, they were quick to contract again into that engaging little bud. Their charm was exactly like the charm of her body itself. Her eyes, moist and shining, made her look like a very young girl. She wore no powder, and the polish of the city geisha had over it a layer of mountain color. Her skin, suggesting the newness of a freshly peeled onion or perhaps a lily bulb, was flushed faintly, even to the throat. More than anything, it was clean.
> Seated rigidly upright, she seemed more demure and maidenly than usual.[10]

Even here Shimamura's defenses are at work: in an effort to neutralize the "feeling of intense physical nearness," his perceptions break down the experience into its parts so that they can be idealized and distanced, rendering her "more demure and maidenly than usual."

In the second part of the novel, images of decay and death become more prominent, coloring Shimamura's perceptions of the changes in Komako's life. Although less than a year has passed since his previous visit, she has in the meantime become a real geisha with a contract. Her fate is adumbrated by that of Kikuyu, the geisha seen briefly as she retires to an uncertain future. The worst thing Komako can say of Kikuyu is that she is weak, and weakness in herself seems to be Komako's worst fear. In the climactic scene that signals the end of their affair, Shimamura calls Komako "a good girl," and then, moments later, "a good woman." She has become too much a woman, too real in Shimamura's mind, and so his interest shifts to Yoko.

Yoko is the least developed character, as mysterious at the end of the novel as at the beginning. She is described in images that are maternal, as in the first chapter where Shimamura watches her tending the sick man on the train, or later, after their only substantial conversation, when he hears her singing as she bathes the innkeeper's daughter. But she is also described as "the girl" whose voice is "so high and clear that it was almost lonely." Yoko embodies the ideal of virginal purity, childlike yet also maternal, that so fascinated Kawabata. The precise relationship between Komako and Yoko is never revealed, but one interpretation is to see Yoko as an aspect of Komako. For Shimamura, Yoko is an objectification of the idealized girl-in-the-woman he first sees in Komako, but who also prevents him from seeing Komako as she really is. It is just this side of herself that Komako finds burdensome, the girl-in-the-woman who must die or go insane as Komako struggles to come to terms with her life.

At the end of the novel, Yoko is among the crowd of people who are watching a movie in an old cocoon warehouse when the film catches fire and destroys the warehouse. This is a distinctly modern image of the Buddhist truth that the realm of the senses is not merely an enchanting if deceptive illusion, but rather, in the words of the *Lotus Sutra*, it is a "burning house," where human beings are "scorched by birth, old age, sickness, death, care, grief, woe, and anguish."[11] As Shimamura and Komako approach the inferno, he mentally detaches himself, his gaze distracted by the "cold fire" and "limitless depths" of the Milky Way. When they see

Yoko fall through the burning structure, moreover, each responds in ways that say much about their personalities. Komako breaks away from him and rushes into the fiery structure to retrieve Yoko's limp body, in a horizontal movement toward the "burning house" of reality. Shimamura, on the other hand,

> felt a rising in his chest again as the memory came to him of the night he had been on his way to visit Komako, and he had seen that mountain light shine in Yoko's face. The years and months with Komako seemed to be lighted up in that instant; and there, he knew, was the anguish.[12]

Shimamura's anguish is at the death of another illusion. Knocked off balance by the crowd, his head falls back in a vertical movement to gaze up at the Milky Way, realm of the unattainable, which seems to flow down inside him "with a roar."

TOPICS FOR DISCUSSION

1. Shimamura first visits the resort in early spring, while his two later trips are in winter. What role do the seasons play in the narrative? Compare Kawabata's use of nature imagery with that of the English romantics.

2. When Shimamura first sees Yoko in the train, she is looking after a sick man (the music teacher's son), who later dies. What is his function in the story? What Western novelists employ secondary characters to objectify aspects of the primary characters?

3. Shimamura sees Komako's interest in literature as rather like his own interest in the Western ballet, "a complete waste of effort." How do different Western novelists view the relationship between life and art?

4. The "Palm-of-the-Hand" version of Snow Country, "Yukigun-ishō" ("Gleanings from Snow Country"), contains only selections from the first third of the novel. Apart from the opening scene, where Shimamura watches Yoko's reflection in the train window, all the others are of Shimamura's moments with Komako during his first and second trips to the resort. As a series of loosely connected vignettes from their affair, can it stand on its own by Western definitions of a "short story"? Is Snow Country only a long short story?

5. Apart from its function as a setting for the novel, does the snow country play a metaphorical role? What Western writers use a particular place to signify a state of mind, an idea, or a moment in time?

6. *Snow Country* offers some intriguing parallels with Shelley's *Alastor*, as suggested in the essay. If Shimamura reminds us in some ways of *Alastor*'s poet-protagonist and Yoko of the "veiled maid," does Komako's function in the narrative compare with that of the "Arab maiden"? The *Alastor* poet's encounter with her is described as follows:

> Meanwhile an Arab maiden brought his food,
> Her daily portion from her father's tent,
> And spread her matting for his couch, and stole
> From duties and repose to tend his steps:—
> Enamoured, yet not daring for deep awe
> To speak her love:—and watched his nightly sleep,
> Sleepless herself, to gaze upon his lips
> Parted in slumber, whence the regular breath
> Of innocent dreams arose: then, when red morn
> Made paler the pale moon, to her cold home
> Wildered, and wan, and panting, she returned.[13]

NOTES

1. Kawabata Yasunari, *Snow Country and Thousand Cranes*, translated by Edward G. Seidensticker (New York: Knopf, 1958), p. 25.
2. Percy Bysshe Shelley, Preface to *Alastor, or The Spirit of Solitude*, in Thomas Hutchinson, ed., *Shelley: Poetical Works* (London: Oxford University Press, 1970), p. 14.
3. Kawabata, *Snow Country*, p. 7.
4. William Wordsworth, *Tintern Abbey*, pp. 105–07, in John O. Hayden, ed., *William Wordsworth: The Poems*, 2 vols. (New Haven and London: Yale University Press, 1977) I:360.
5. Kawabata, *Snow Country*, p. 9.
6. Ibid., p. 119.
7. Shelley, *Alastor*, 153–54, p. 18.
8. Shelley, Preface to *Alastor*, p. 14.
9. Kawabata, *Fubo e no tegami* (*Letters to My Parents*, 1932–34), cited in Donald Keene, *Dawn to the West: Japanese Literature of the Modern Era, Fiction* (New York: Holt, Rinehart and Winston, 1984), pp. 804–05.
10. Kawabata, *Snow Country*, pp. 73–4.
11. *Scripture of the Lotus Blossom of the Fine Dharma*, trans. Leon Hurvitz, in *Records of Civilization: Sources and Studies* 94 (New York: Columbia University Press, 1976), p. 61.
12. Kawabata, *Snow Country*, p. 174.
13. Shelley, *Alastor*, 129–39, p. 18.

REFERENCES

Kawabata Yasunari. *Beauty and Sadness*. Translated by Howard Hibbet. New York: Alfred A. Knopf, 1975.

Kawabata Yasunari. *The House of the Sleeping Beauties and Other Stories*. Translated by Edward G. Seidensticker. Tokyo: Kodansha, 1969.

Kawabata Yasunari. *Japan the Beautiful and Myself*. Translated by Edward G. Seidensticker. Tokyo: Kodansha, 1969.

Kawabata Yasunari. *The Lake*. Translated by Reiko Tsukimura. Tokyo: Kodansha, 1978.

Kawabata Yasunari. *The Master of Go*. Translated by Edward G. Seidensticker. New York: Alfred A. Knopf, 1972.

Kawabata Yasunari. *The Old Capital*. Translated by J. Martin Holman. San Francisco: North Point Press, 1987.

Kawabata Yasunari. *Palm-of-the-Hand Stories*. Translated by Lane Dunlop and J. Martin Holman. New York: Alfred A. Knopf, 1988.

Kawabata Yasunari. *The Sound of the Mountain*. Translated by Edward G. Seidensticker. New York: Alfred A. Knopf, 1970.

Kawabata Yasunari. *Snow Country and Thousand Cranes*. Translated by Edward G. Seidensticker. New York: Alfred A. Knopf, 1958.

Keene, Donald. *Dawn to the West: Japanese Literature of the Modern Era, Fiction*. New York: Holt, Rinehart and Winston, 1984, pp. 786–845.

Masao, Miyoshi. *Accomplices of Silence: The Modern Japanese Novel*. Berkeley: University of California Press, 1974, pp. 95–121.

Ueda, Makoto. *Modern Japanese Writers and the Nature of Literature*. Stanford: Stanford University Press, 1976, pp. 173–218.

SŌSEKI'S *KOKORO*

Paul Anderer

When Natsume Sōseki (1867–1916) completed *Kokoro*, he was
seriously ill and near the end of his life. Illness, to be sure, figures
as metaphor in much of his writing. He is often perceived as a
novelist of victims, especially self-victimizers—those Japanese intellectuals who had serious, prolonged exposure to the West and
were showing resultant pathological signs. Sōseki's life spanned,
and was strongly identified with, the Meiji period (1868–1912). If
any modern writer can be said to speak for his time, it is Sōseki.
Though he did not begin writing in earnest until his middle years,
in little more than a decade he produced more than a dozen books
on a very few themes—betrayal, loss, and a certain "sickness unto
death" are chief among them. His work reveals a scrutiny and an
intelligence lacerating enough to expose both the inner turmoil
and the dislocations this transformative age produced.

Like the shadows which fall over the characters in *Kokoro*,
Sōseki has cast his shadow over much Japanese writing, of his
own and later generations. When critics say he has no rightful
successor, they signal respect for the integrity and force of
Sōseki's fiction, which has not diminished over time. Certainly
there have been detractors. Tanizaki, for one, took him to task for
a priggish portrayal of love and a brooding moralism that left no
room for sensuality. In his late writing (i.e., from the trilogy of
Sanshiro, And Then, and *The Gate*, begun in 1908, through *Light
and Darkness*, his last uncompleted work, in 1916) Sōseki does
seem to have severed connections with the richly comic, parodis-
tic fictional style of the Tokugawa period (1600–1868), which his
early work had put to good use. Yet in grappling with his own
increasingly depressive self, Sōseki found a method to inscribe a
cultural crisis. Nowhere does this method show forth, with greater
simplicity and dramatic power, than in *Kokoro*.

Kokoro was not conceived as a long novel, but as a story, and then a set of stories on a related theme. This is characteristic, not only of most post-Restoration fiction and the exigencies of serial publication in newspapers and magazines, but of much fine or influential Japanese prose of preceding eras. There are generic affinities as well, with the traditional diary and memoir, since *Kokoro* in all its parts is told by a personal narrator. Indeed, established terms like "novel" or "fiction," based on particular narrative or epistemological premises, may be inadequate to describe the type of story even Sōseki—an avowedly modern, experimental writer—has produced.

In *Kokoro*, as in *Grass on the Wayside* (1915), the work which followed it and is cited by critics as his only "autobiographical novel," Sōseki seems to be writing confessional prose, revealing traces of the older diary and epistolary styles, yet charging it with a heightened awareness: that a personal story might be dramatically revealing, both of individual consciousness and a wider, social world. Too dense and circumstantial to be allegory, *Kokoro* might be called a tale of moral disorder. If the tone and quality of the writing seems reminiscent of Conrad, so too is the critique of cultural adventurism, the criss-crossing ambitions of modern individuals, driven by a historical imperative to overreach old boundaries and definitions. Sōseki pushed Japanese prose toward new, if isolating limits. With skill and exercise of will, he traced in his fiction the shape of ideas and beliefs, old and new, even as the characters who held them were about to vanish.

Natsume Kinnosuke (Sōseki is a pen name) was born in Tokyo in 1867, the eighth child of elderly parents. By general account, he was unwanted. He was let out for care to one couple who neglected the infant, then for adoption to another couple who eventually divorced. At the age of nine, Sōseki was shunted back to his parents. Later he would claim, credibly, that his childhood memories were cast over by "a cold and sad shadow."

Sōseki's early immersion in the Chinese classics is conspicuous in his schooling. Throughout his life—even toward the end when he was feverishly turning out his modern novels—Sōseki wrote *kanshi* (Chinese poetry), which specialists judge among the finest composed by a Japanese of any period, much less one as distracting as the Meiji. From his Chinese studies Sōseki would have gleaned a Neo-Confucian sense of an ordered universe, which was subject to violation by selfish excess. The moral urgency of his fiction, the fear it generates in the face of transgression, no doubt derives from this classical, ethical background.

Yet to enter college in the mid-1880s, Sōseki proposed to study English, either by choice or in acquiescence to the powerful current of the time (many advanced textbooks, in a variety of disciplines, were still in the English language). Sōseki complained incessantly about the dull instruction, yet acquired a stunning fluency in the written language, attested to both by his superb English translation (ca. 1891) of Chomei's twelfth-century parable, *The Account of my Hut*, and later by his trenchant criticism, based on wide and careful reading, ranging from Arthurian legend to Swift, *Tristram Shandy* to George Meredith.

In college Sōseki expressed a career wish to become a writer—in the 1890s still a suspect, if not a demeaning, profession for someone with a degree—or to become an architect, for which he was wholly untrained. Instead, on graduating, he accepted a middle-school teaching post on the island of Shikoku, then moved even further west to Kumamoto in Kyushu, where he taught at the Fifth National College. It was a bizarre path for a brilliant graduate of Tokyo Imperial University to follow. There is evidence he wished to inflict a certain austerity on himself and left Tokyo for the provinces "in the spirit of renouncing everything." The experience shows up in his fiction, from the early comic *Botchan*, actually set in a remote provincial town, to the late *Kokoro*, set between Tokyo and the provinces. Throughout his career, Sōseki proved himself to be a keen observer of the multiple tensions, misrecognitions, and hostilities that separated the country and the city.

Then, in 1900, at the age of thirty-three, already married and a father, Sōseki accepted a government grant to study in England for two years. Alone, he set sail from Yokohama in what has often been described as the most fateful move of his life.

His London sojourn, personally harrowing for Sōseki, has assumed over the course of this century in Japan, a paradigmatic significance. The misery and humiliation Sōseki encountered—skimping on a meager stipend in a shabby flat; passing up meals to purchase books; spending days on end in isolation; handing over an extortionary fee to a diffident tutor (W. J. Craig, an editor of the Arden Shakespeare); being eyed in a crowd like some exotic, helpless prey ("a lost dog in a pack of wolves"), imagining in his despair detectives at his heels—all this has been passed on as a cautionary tale about deception and betrayal of the outside, by the Western "other." Sōseki did arrive in England with great expectations, believing he would leave his mark on English letters, and returned a profoundly disillusioned man. He had studied the

West, to the point of adulation, and the West ignored him. Sōseki in London has in this way come to symbolize not only Meiji Japan, struggling against unequal treaties and the full force of nineteenth-century colonialist prejudice to "arrive" in the modern world, but also twentieth-century Japan which, by so many technological and economic indices, has indeed "arrived," yet with a schizophrenic cultural identity, and a morbid concern about its image in the "world outside."

It is then remarkable that upon his return in 1903, Sōseki should have been such an outspoken critic of that Japanese nationalism which was prevalent between the Sino-Japanese and Russo-Japanese wars. Cries of "yamato damashi" (Japanese spirit) were a cover, he claimed, to hide a real fear that no such spirit, no cultural confidence, still existed. In eloquent essays and public lectures, Sōseki sought to reach and warn an often youthful audience that civilization meant more than a materialist accumulation of labor-saving devices, or that rote and random copying of Western ways would lead eventually to superficiality or mental collapse. Yet he was no reactionary, and was equally stoic in saying there was no turning back. Sōseki's many physical ailments—the gastric ulcers of which he was to die—have been well documented, as have signs of mental disorder during and following his stay abroad. It is fair to suggest that Sōseki himself became a casualty of that unbridled competition he would warn others against. That he was in no sense superficial is clear from all he wrote.

Back in Japan, Sōseki took up residence in Tokyo and a position of prestige at the Imperial University. He succeeded Lafcadio Hearn as lecturer in English, an act he ruefully felt would be hard to follow. It was while teaching that he began to write fiction, beginning with *I Am a Cat* (1905), a ranging and exuberant social satire, skewing both Meiji commercialism and academic pomposity. But by 1907, exhausted in his attempt to be a teacher in what was, after all, a government bureaucracy, Sōseki accepted an offer to join the editorial staff of the *Asahi Shimbun*, a mass circulation daily. By the existing standards of social respectability, Sōseki again had taken a puzzling downward step. Yet it also gave him more time to devote to his fiction, and a more visible, public presence. Over the years he conscientiously used his position at the newspaper to discover and advance promising young writers, even those from literary "schools" he perhaps despised.

Trained as a classical scholar, prodigious too in his knowledge of Western literatures, Sōseki, when he came to write his own fiction, was acutely aware of the relativity of narrative forms. He approached literature, if not quite scientifically, at least with an experimental bias and seemed eager to generate hybrid stories, mixing, for example, a "fictive" Western strain of allegory or romance with Japanese prose, grounded, as it often was, in the lyric, as well as in the certainties, shared by Japanese writers and readers alike, that literary art was a concrete and imitable activity. No modern author, except perhaps Mishima, tried to write prose in so many different styles. For all his acknowledged greatness as a Meiji culture hero, Sōseki has thus appeared, to some Japanese readers, to be unpredictable and in a strict sense, inimitable.

A line which seems crucial to Kokoro—"You see I am lost. I have become a puzzle even to himself"—is a declaration identical to St. Augustine's, and we might conclude that this book is a species of literary confession. Yet Sōseki was a fierce critic of the prevailing literary school of his day, the Japanese Naturalists—writers who advertised their goal as a plain, unvarnished depiction of objective reality, yet whose work in practice was grim, salacious, and self-relevatory, the details of which were regularly traced back to the author's real life. However unpalatable, this writing claimed the virtue of being sincere, "true to the self." Sōseki reviled much of this "confessional" work as a self-serving sham. He had little faith that a "modern self" even existed, let alone possessed a capacity to be sincere. (His doubts were most intricately laid out in The Miner, where, under the pretext of exploring life "underground" in a copper mine, Sōseki really explores the various narrative tricks behind the construction of a fictional "character.") By this light, the confessional Naturalists appeared to Sōseki both ethically misconceived and stylistically narrow. To the end Sōseki believed that as a writer he bore a moral responsibility, which transcended devotion either to his own suffering self or to an aloof and decadent art.

We can trace in Sōseki's fiction, then, a wide range of influence—from Edo raconteur to William James, Zen koan to Jane Austen—but what identifies his various fictional experiments as a corpus is a will to illuminate, but not glorify, the condition of outsiders, even exiles. In this way, Sōseki has emerged not just as a spokesman for Meiji culture, but as the dominant presence in modern fiction down to our own day. This is because in book after book he engages the various ways Japanese have become—or been made—strangers in their own land. This represents a crisis of spirit, a sickness of sorts, and though other writers have styled themselves "doctors of the soul," Sōseki only traces the affliction, offering no quick cures.

"I should never have noticed him had he not been accompanied by a Westerner," the youthful narrator of *Kokoro* explains how he discovered on a crowded beach the stranger who would change his life. The youth gravitates toward this stranger, whom he calls Sensei, or teacher. Sensei lives in the city, an intellectual who holds no position and is unrecognized by the world. Yet he grows in stature in the youth's eyes, until by the end of the first section, he has become a presence to rival the youth's real father, who lies ill and dying of a kidney disease in the provinces. Finally, prior to his suicide, Sensei writes a long letter to the youth, confiding the secret of his past, heretofore revealed to no one, not even his wife.

Few other characters appear in *Kokoro*, and none of the major characters have personal names. The prose is spare, almost stark. For a Japanese book of reminiscence (the "events" have all occurred, we know, before the story begins) there is scant lyrical detail. More to the point, such details do not float free, unhinged from the drive of the narrative. "Sensei's hat, which had hung on top of a slender cedar sapling, was blown off by the breeze," we read, at the close of one episode, then read, at the opening of the next: "I picked up the hat immediately." Edwin McClellan, who translated the book, has remarked on the beauty of *Kokoro*'s simplicity, especially in the last section. This has less to do with the influence of classical poetry on the prose (as we find regularly, for example, in Kawabata's fiction), than with the austere beauty of medieval prose, as in Chomei's *An Account of My Hut* or the exile chapters in the *Tale of the Heike*—writing that, like Sōseki's, traces hesitant, ambivalent movements across a barren, monochromatic terrain.

The three part structure of the book seems endlessly replicated internally, by an array of triangular relationships. It is as though no character, no element of the world, reacts directly with any other. Between the youth and his father stands Sensei; between Sensei and his wife, the shadow of K; between even flowers and their natural appreciation, the grave at Zoshigaya. Finally, shuttling between country and city, belonging nowhere, the youth reads Sensei's "testament" in isolation on a train.

It is a still, impotent, deadlocked world, in which no one goes anywhere, or wants anything, unless someone else has already been there (recall the Westerner at the beach) or wanted the same thing too. Sensei, we come to know, feels love for Ojosan, but does not profess love and marry her until after his friend has made his own feeling known. After betraying oneself by not expressing one's deepest desires, any other betrayal seems not only possible but likely. "Can a man change so because of the death of one friend?" Sensei's wife asks the youth early on in the book. "That is what I want you to tell me." But he will never tell her, even after he learns the answer, because by then he has himself become a betrayer, a modern self, baptized, as it were, in the blood of his Sensei, and so incapable of having direct, human contact.

As the narrative unfolds, the heroes disappear, as if procession-ally, each one smaller, more diminished, than the one gone by. The Meiji Emperor, General Nogi, K, and last Sensei, putatively, the truest hero of the book, who could not in life say to those who loved him what he will confess, on paper, at his death. And even this "truth" he leaves as a legacy to the youth, and no other.

"I would rather be truly ill than suffering from a trifling cold like this," Sensei once tells the youth. "If I must be ill, then I should like to be mortally ill." This "higher illness," a mental suffering, becomes a token of value for Sensei and for the youth. Similarly, K's high-mindedness—a rectitude that had him live according to the Koran, the Bible, and Buddhist doctrine simultaneously, and that killed him as surely as any shock at being betrayed by a friend—comes to appear in retrospect a positive spiritual ideal. But it is an ideal, like Sensei's and the youth's, that is bound up in secrecy and ultimately, silence.

On one hand, then, we encounter the language of the "hero," the isolated modern self—that monster which Sōseki relentlessly tracked throughout his career and captured most fully in this book. It is language veering toward silence. But there are other languages in *Kokoro*. We hear, for example, the wife speaking plainly of her concern and fear for her husband, and the voice of the youth's father, dying of an ordinary illness, expressing a sim-ple joy in his son's accomplishments. And there is this:

> I believe that words uttered in passion contain a greater living truth than do those words which express thoughts rationally conceived. It is blood that moves the body. Words are not meant to stir the air only; they are capable of moving greater things.

Here surely is Sōseki's own voice, condemning every secrecy and silence, of his heroes, or of any merely self-referring art. It is the voice of a writer who, almost in defiance of actual experience, clung to a belief that literature is language shared, and that such language could heal hearts and reorder the world.

TOPICS FOR DISCUSSION

1. Sōseki's late novels, including *Kokoro*, are often described as being dark and tragic. In what sense do K, Sensei, and the narrator lead tragic lives? Does the book present theirs as an alterable fate?

2. Compare *Kokoro* to a confessional work from the Western tradition (Augustine, Rousseau, *The Sorrows of Young Werther*). Explore the conditions under which an "I" makes itself present in literature, and what burdens this "I" bears, to express itself or to speak for a society or a culture.

3. How does the past, or tradition, function in *Kokoro?* Are distinctions drawn between a personal, individual past and a more general, cultural past?

REFERENCES

Translations

Natsume Sōseki. *Grass on the Wayside*. Translated by Edwin McClellan. Chicago: University of Chicago Press, 1968.
Natsume Sōseki. *Mon.* Translated by Francis Mathy. London: Peter Owen, 1972.
Natsume Sōseki. *Sanshiro*. Translated by Jay Rubin. Seattle: University of Washington Press, 1977.
Natsume Sōseki. *Sorekara*. Translated by Norma Field. Baton Rouge: Louisiana State University Press, 1978.

Criticism

Keene, Donald. "Natsume Sōseki" in *Dawn to the West*, 305–54. New York: Holt, Rinehart and Winston, 1984.
McClellan, Edwin. *Two Japanese Novelists*. Chicago: University of Chicago Press, 1969.
Miyoshi, Masao. *Accomplices of Silence*. Berkeley: University of California Press, 1974.

THREE PLAYS OF THE NOH THEATER

Thomas Blenman Hare

The plays *Izutsu*, *Atsumori*, and *Ataka* are mainstays of the classic repertory of Noh with a consistent popularity and continuous performance tradition of five to six centuries. The first two were written by Zeami Motokiyo (1363–1443) and exemplify his ideas about the classic formal structure of Noh. They also display thematic characteristics that are common to many plays of the repertory, but rarely realized with such skill and grace. The third play, *Ataka*, was probably written by Zeami's grand-nephew, Kanze Kojiro Nobumitsu (1435–1516). It contrasts both formally and thematically with the other two and exemplifies a strain of Noh that has been equally popular in performance even though it has attracted less scholarly attention. All three works are performed a number of times each year, by both professionals and amateurs, on the Noh stages of contemporary Japan. *Atsumori*, in particular, has found an appreciative reading audience in the West as well, thanks to Arthur Waley's fine translation.

Noh attained a recognizable form as an independent performance art in the latter decades of the fourteenth century and was molded into what we have come to consider its "classic" formal structure early in the fifteenth. The individual whose name is most intimately associated with this accomplishment is Zeami, but other Noh masters, including his father, Kannami (or Kan'ami) Kiyotsugu (1333–1384), also played important roles in the early development of Noh.

Zeami was born into a provincial family of Noh performers just as Noh was beginning to attract the attention of rich patrons in the capital Kyoto. At the time, Kannami was the talented leader of a small provincial troupe whose performances relied on the mainstays of the regional style of Yamato. That style emphasized dramatic imitation (*monomane*), and found particular success in the imitation of demons and women who, through some emotional trauma such as the loss of a child, have fallen prey to states of emotional disorder.

Rival troupes of performers had already begun to establish a base of patronage in the capital. The Ōmi troupes (named for a region near the capital) had attracted the attention of the most powerful men in the land, including the shogun Yoshimitsu (1358–1408). They were famous for a more abstract performing style of particular visual beauty, characterized by the term *yūgen*, which, in the context of Noh, means something like "elegant mystery."

Kannami's successes in Kyoto eventually brought his troupe to the attention of the young shogun, and his talent (as well as Zeami's youthful beauty) gained for the troupe the generous patronage of wealthy aristocrats. Perhaps even more importantly, performance in the capital gave Zeami access to elements of the elite literary tradition, which he was quick to incorporate into his plays and dramaturgy. His own successes during his lifetime were mixed. He seems to have maintained a wide following among the common people of Kyoto and nearby provinces, but aristocratic patronage was more erratic. Near the end of his life, he and his troupe were persecuted by the shogun Yoshinori (1394–1441) for reasons which remain unclear but may have been in some part politically motivated. All the same, the innovations Zeami effected upon Noh were far-reaching, and his influence is clearly recognizable in the work of subsequent actors and playwrights such as his son Motomasa (d. 1432), his son-in-law, Komparu Zenchiku (1405–68), and even Nobumitsu.

Zeami produced, in addition to at least thirty to forty of the most famous plays in the repertory, a body of related dramaturgical work that ranges in character from detailed technical essays on how to construct plays to quite abstract and in some sense philosophical writings on the aesthetics of performance and the spiritual vocation of the actor. He left, as well, an extensive body of anecdotes, critiques, and miscellaneous information in notes recorded by one of his sons, Motoyoshi. These "treatises," as they have often been termed, give us a valuable perspective from which to examine the plays. They reveal some of Zeami's and his contemporaries' artistic aims and offer an intimate view of the contexts and problems inherent in performing Noh in its earliest days. We will refer to some of this material in preparing for a discussion of *Izutsu* and *Atsumori.*

Zeami identifies three basic dramatic modes in his discussions of playwriting: those of the old man, the woman, and the warrior. The most formally orthodox plays comprise five sections and take old men as their central figure. It will be worth our while to consider one of these plays to get a general idea of the formal characteristics of a "typical" Noh play.

Just before such a play begins, the chorus (usually eight voices) takes its seat along the right side of the square Noh stage. (Stage directions will be given from the point of view of someone in a good seat near the front of the stage.) Meanwhile the instrumental ensemble, consisting of a flute player and two or three drummers, assumes its position near the back of the stage.

The first section of the play begins with the entrance of a secondary character, called the *waki*, who is likely to be accompanied by one or more subordinates. The *waki* is very often a wandering priest, either Buddhist or Shinto, and he comes on stage to the accompaniment provided by the instrumental ensemble. He sings a short song as he makes his entrance along an open passageway to the back left side of the stage. Once he and his retinue have entered the stage proper, he delivers a self-introduction, then sings a song of travel before assuming his seat near the front right corner of the stage.

The ensemble begins another instrumental piece at the opening of the second section, and now the primary character of the play, the *shite* (pronounced "sh'tay"), emerges from behind a curtain at the end of the aforementioned passageway. The *shite* may be accompanied by one, or sometimes two, subordinates. As the *shite* comes on stage, he sings a series of three songs, generally in the form of expressive monologues, relating in some way to the natural surroundings or legendary associations of the setting of the play.

The third section opens with a series of questions posed by the *waki* to the *shite*. The *shite*, in answering these questions, usually provokes yet further suspicion, which leads, after some continued dialogue, to a narrative in which the *shite* reveals that he has some special relation to the setting, to the *waki*, or both. This narrative provides the central interest of the fourth section of the play, and at its end, the *shite* disappears—or perhaps we are to understand rather that the *waki* has fallen asleep and begun to dream. In any case, the *shite* leaves the stage to change costume. During the intermission another character, called the *kyōgen* or *ai-kyōgen*, appears to discuss the preceding events with the *waki*. When the *shite* has changed costume, and the discussion between the *kyōgen* and *waki* has reached its conclusion, the fifth and final section of the play opens. Now, the *shite* reappears in a truer manifestation of his nature, and brings the play to its visual and kinetic high point, be it with a highly elegant and abstract dance, a rehearsal of some lifetime adventure, or the enactment of a miracle. This last section provides a formal climax to the previous sections of the play and achieves a kind of aesthetic closure through a principle of cyclical development which Zeami calls *jo-ha-kyū*.

Jo means "preface" or "inception"; thus the entrance of the *waki* becomes the preface to the play in that it identifies a setting and sets a general mood. *Ha* means "break" or "rupture" and constitutes a change in the pace and trajectory of the *jo*; it does this through the *shite*'s monologue, the introduction of questions, doubts, suspicions about her or his identity, a shift of focus, and usually a narrative about the *shite*'s identity. The *kyū* (fast finale), then brings about the climax of the play. Zeami, having borrowed the word *jo-ha-kyū* from an earlier, more technical and constricted performative context (in the dance and concert music of the imperial court), discovered in it a wonderfully malleable structuring figure to inform a variety of his plays. He also went on to apply it to a full day's cycle of plays, and indeed, to the world at large— finding in it a universal principle of transformation—from seasons and the ages of a life to the smallest gesture in dancing or coming to speak a word. It became for him in some ways a measure of truth, as did "action" for Aristotle, when he spoke of Greek tragedy as the imitation of an action.

If Aristotle, in his discussion of Sophocles' *Oedipus Rex* can inscribe the abstract notion of a completed action into the practical expedient of plot, then Zeami gives *jo-ha-kyū* a more concrete instantiation in his characters by means of the aesthetic ideals *monomane* and *yūgen*. *Monomane*, "dramatic imitation," is, in Zeami's own words, the "presentation of a comprehensive likeness of the object portrayed, . . . but adjusted according to the social quality of the object portrayed."[1] This *monomane* was apparently the strong suit of the Yamato troupes, and Kannami was renowned for being able to carry off this kind of imitation with extraordinary success.

Yūgen, or "elegant mystery," was a term borrowed from twelfth- to thirteenth-century poetics, where it seems to describe a rich mysterious beauty only vaguely suggested on the surface of the phenomenon in question, which itself may appear quite plain and monochromatic. There are plays in the Noh repertory that seem to express this kind of *yūgen*, but what Zeami intends seems a rather more conspicuously visual beauty. His ideal exemplar of *yūgen* is a high-born court lady of the ancient days of the imperial court.

Any discussion of *monomane* and *yūgen* remains frustratingly vague without reference to specific plays, however, so we will now turn our attention to *Atsumori* and *Izutsu*, which will perhaps give us a better idea not only of these aesthetic ideals, but also of formal characteristics and some of the thematic concerns of Noh.

Atsumori is based on the legend of the valiant young Taira warrior who gives his name to the piece. In *Heike monogatari* (*The Tales of Heike*), we find the first full account of the story: The once powerful Heike clan has been chased out of the imperial capital by the forces of the Genji, and has suffered a string of defeats. They have encamped on the beach at Suma, facing the sea, with their backs to high cliffs, in the hope that they will be safe for a while. On the night before the story takes place, they have passed their time in elegant courtly pursuits, and the sixteen-year-old boy Atsumori has dazzled the Heike assembly with his flute playing. In fact, the strains of his flute even reach the enemy encampment over the cliffs high above.

Early the next day, the Genji ambush the Heike by storming down the cliffs which they had thought their security. In the confusion, the Heike race toward shore to embark on warships and escape to sea. Atsumori himself is among the crowd rushing away from the enemy attack when he remembers that he has left his flute behind. It is an imperial treasure and cannot be allowed to fall into the hands of the Genji, so Atsumori makes his way back to the Heike camp, finds it, and then tries to catch up with his clan who have already put out to sea. He swims his horse out into the offing, only to be sighted by a rough warrior from the Genji forces. Accused of cowardice in showing his back to the enemy, Atsumori returns to shore to do battle with the warrior, Kumagae no Jiro Naozane. He is no match for the latter and is quickly unhorsed. Kumagae tears off the Heike warrior's helmet and is about to behead him when he realizes Atsumori is but a boy, elegantly powdered and made up to the height of court fashion. He orders the boy to announce his name, but Atsumori demurs, revealing only that he is a prize catch for a Genji warrior. Kumagae, impressed by his bravery and struck with pity at his youth, offers to let him go, but in the meanwhile, other Genji warriors have appeared on shore, and Kumagae realizes that Atsumori will be killed by one of them if not by his own hand, so he promises to pray for the repose of Atsumori's soul and strikes off his head.

In approaching this source material, it was Zeami's concern to remain faithful to the original story, but to emphasize its more elegant or beautiful aspects. He says that in taking a famous character from the Genji or the Heike, one should "bring out the connection between him and poetry and music, then . . . [the play] will be more interesting than anything else. It should contain some particularly colorful places. . . . The character should carry a sword and wear a quiver, and these weapons should lend the role dignity." He cautions his actors to "inquire into the way to hold [these implements] and use them so that you can manipulate them correctly."[2] These last words express some concern for the actor's accurate imitation of a warrior, or *monomane* in other words, but the emphasis on poetry and music already indicates a certain specificity of intent on Zeami's part, a desire to focus on only certain aspects of the original story.

So, in the second section of the play, when the *shite* and his fellows come on stage, the first lines they sing read "To the music of the reaper's flute/No song is sung/But the sighing of wind in the fields."[3] The reaper's flute music is so elegant that it astonishes the *waki*, who happens to be the priest Rensei (formerly the warrior Kumagae, Waley calls him "Kumagai"). This unexpected elegance, then, provides the suspicion around which the *shite-waki* dialogue of the third section develops. The *waki* says he would not expect to hear such fine music among peasants like these reapers, and they respond that he should not despise those of lower social class, pointing out that the flute playing of rustics is renowned in poetry throughout the world. The *shite*'s companions leave the stage and he alone remains behind, further deepening the *waki*'s suspicions. Now, on being asked to reveal his name, the *shite* begs in return ten recitations of the *nenbutsu*, "Praise to Amida Buddha," whereupon he reveals that he is "one of the family of Lord Atsumori." He disappears from stage after a short song and changes costume while the *kyōgen* delivers an account of how Atsumori met his end. Notice here that the narrative of the fourth section of the play is postponed until after the costume change. This is different from the orthodox format we discussed earlier, but is in keeping with Zeami's remarks about the plays of the warrior mode. In such plays, he says, the narrative is to be set in the latter half of the play, thereby pushing the *ha* closer to the *kyū*, perhaps to bring the kinetic potential of a martial narrative closer to the kinetic performance of the fifth section of the play.

When the *shite* reappears, he is Atsumori himself in young

warrior's dress. Kumagae is amazed, and he and Atsumori recite in alternating phrases a line about the resolution of their erstwhile enmity: "Once enemies . . . /But now . . . /In truth may we be named . . . /Friends in Buddha's Law."[4] The important narrative of the fourth section yet remains to be delivered, however. It too begins with strains of reconciliation and praise of Buddha, but then Atsumori turns to general observations about the transcience of Heike glory, and eventually he comes to the night before that fateful day on the Suma shore. "My father Tsunemori gathered us together./'Tomorrow,' he said, 'we shall fight our last fight./Tonight is all that is left us.' "[5]

Kumagae recalls having heard the Heike that night, "Many voices/Singing to one measure."[6] And with these lines, Atsumori begins a relatively slow, elegant dance comprised of abstract movements. We are well into the fifth section of the play now and come to its climax with a brief reference to the battle between Kumagae and Atsumori: "Atsumori turns his horse/Knee-deep in the lashing waves,/And draws his sword./Twice, three times he strikes; then still saddled,/In close fight they twine; roll headlong together/Among the surf of the shore./So Atsumori fell and was slain, but now the Wheel of Fate/Has turned and brought him back."[7]

Atsumori, sword raised and advancing on Kumagae, seems poised to exact revenge for his own death, but when he cries "There is my enemy, . . . the other is grown gentle/And calling on Buddha's name/Has obtained salvation for his foe;/So that they shall be reborn together/On one lotus seat. 'No, Rensei is not my enemy. Pray for me again, oh pray for me again.' "[8] The play comes to its end with this full resolution of enmity.

Atsumori is an unusual play in that the *waki* and *shite* are so closely related. In most of Zeami's Noh, the *waki* is a far less identifiable individual with only the vaguest, if any, connection to the *shite*. It also breaks with the pattern of most warrior plays in the abstract dance that Atsumori does near the end. In most other warrior plays, this dance is replaced by a vigorous mimetic exercise accompanying the narrative of a battle. In this regard, *Atsumori* may be less obvious an example of *monomane* than some of the other warrior plays, but it shares many other characteristics with them, and even in this atypicality exemplifies Zeami's dictum about "bring[ing] out the connection between [the *shite*] and poetry and music." The Buddhism of the play is not Zen, but rather the popular religion that calls on believers to chant the *nenbutsu* and rely on the grace of Amida.

Although one may detect strains of Zen in Zeami's "treatises," it is much more common to find this kind of devotionalism in his plays.

Atsumori was written by 1423 at the latest, probably several years earlier. It is a relatively early play for Zeami and seems to reflect a stronger interest in *monomane* than *Izutsu*, which probably was not written until near 1430. The latter play finds its source in *Ise Monogatari* (*The Tales of Ise*), a tenth-century collection of short narratives explaining the circumstances behind, and framing, certain exchanges of love poetry in the classical style. Two poems from the collection become particularly important in the Noh play *Izutsu*. They are part of a courtship exchange between the young Narihira, a famous lover of the ninth century, and the otherwise unnamed daughter of Aritsune. Narihira's poem reads:

Tsutsu izutsu	Well curb, on the well curb,
Izutsu ni kakeshi	On the well curb once
Maro ga take	We marked our height,
Oinikerashi na	But I've grown taller since I saw you last,
Imo mizaru ma ni	Well past those marks we left upon the well.

The woman's response is:

Kurabe koshi	Side by side we stood
Furiwakegami mo	Comparing our locks then,
Kata suginu	But now my hair hangs far below my shoulders.
Kimi narazu shite	If not for you,
Tare ka agu beki	For whom shall I tie it up one day.

In *Ise monogatari*, these poems look both back on a past in which two childhood playmates marked their height upon the enclosure of a well, and forward to a future in which the same playmates, now grown to adulthood, will be married. Already, then, there was a concern with time in the circumstances from which the Noh was created, but Zeami expands this concern beyond the death of the two characters in question to create an intricate, multilayered exposition of the *shite*'s psychology. In the second section of the play, she comes on stage to recite the following lines:

The autumn night is lonely as it is, but more so here,
For no one comes to this old temple garden where the wind
    blows, deepening night.
In whispers through the pines, the moon inclines to slanting
    eaves
Covered with forgetful grass: The now forgotten past
I once again recall in ferns of recollection;
But how long will I live on in ivied remembrance, with
    nothing to await?
All things lead to memories and
Memories alone remain to me
In this world remaining on though he is gone.[9]

Thereafter, the theme of recollection appears again and again in the play. The brief third section emphasizes the temporal separation of the play's present from the events in the *Ise monogatari* story by developing the *waki*'s suspicion that a beautiful young woman should come there to offer flowers at the grave of Narihira, who has been dead so long. This leads to the narrative of section four, where the *shite* eventually reveals that she is the ghost of Narihira's lover. In the course of her narrative, she quotes the poems mentioned earlier as well as part of another poem from the same story,

Kaze fukeba	The wailing wind,
Okitsu shiranami	Strong enough to raise white waves out upon the sea
Tatsutayama	Blows down now
Yowa ni ya kimi ga	From Tatsuta. Will you cross the mountains
Hitori yukuran	All alone in dark of night?

A few words of this poem had already appeared in the first section, and it will appear again later as well, as will the exchange quoted earlier. These three poems, indeed, become the kernel around which the entire play is constructed. Each time the poems are quoted, in part, or entirely, they engender new associations from the surrounding context, so that the play becomes a meditation on the range of meanings they can suggest and the rich ironies thereby created.

At the end of the fourth section, the *shite* disappears. The *kyōgen* comes on stage to give a more detailed account of the original story in *Ise monogatari*. When he leaves, the *shite* reappears, no longer disguised as a young village woman, but now wearing the keepsakes Narihira left her, a court robe and hat. Quoting fragments of famous poems from *Ise monogatari* (including those mentioned earlier), she performs a very slow and elegant dance, at the end of which she gazes down into the temple well to see her reflection in the clothes her lover gave her:

> Reflected there, his image reawakens all my love,
> I see myself, his image reawakens all my love.
> The spirit dressed in robes her lover wore
> Fades from sight, the wilted flower's color gone.
> Its fragrance lingers on.
> The temple bell tolls,
> Night fades with the dawn,
> The morning wind plays around rustling pines,
> Here before the ancient cloister, ripped like plantain leaves,
> My dreams are torn away, I wake,
> My dreams are torn away, dawn breaks.

For all its simplicity, *Izutsu* was one of Zeami's favorite plays, and it is thought by many to be one of the finest works in the repertory. If we consider it in the light of *monomane* and *yūgen*, the former element seems diminished in importance. There is little emphasis on the imitative portrayal of a woman's actions—there is little action in the play at all. What seems to have been imitated is rather a state of mind, a profound attachment to a lover long since dead, through the ironic recollection of his poems. This poetic element must have something to do with *yūgen*, partially because it gives mysterious access to a fragile and beautiful world far removed in time, under the surface of a very simple story line, and little action. The mystery of it all is perhaps best encapsulated in those last lines, in which the entire experience of the *shite*'s appearance evaporates into the dawning day.

Although the formal conventions and aesthetic ideals that Zeami imparted to Noh were enormously influential in its development, they do not by any means represent all that is interesting or even characteristic of the art. There are many fine works of a very different sort in the current repertory. Few of them are likely to date from Zeami's time without also having passed through his hands and undergone his revision to some degree, but even after Zeami put his stamp on Noh, these other types of plays continued to be written and performed. Some have even argued that there was a reaction against plays in the "Zeami-style" during the last decade of his life. This may overstate the case, but in all events, there remains a broad variety of Noh that do not follow the patterns we have just outlined. There are, for example, plays that take a sort of variety-show format. Although short on poetry and dramatic cohesiveness, these works can be both entertaining in performance and fascinating historically. (The best example of such a play is probably *Jinen Koji* by Kannami.)

There are also many plays with a stronger element of conflict than is usual in Zeami's Noh. Some are stories of jealous love, some are vendetta plays. Dramatized myths and legends form yet another group. One of the best of these is entitled *Ataka.* It treats the successful passage of the general Yoshitsune and his band of retainers through the barrier gate at Ataka, on the northwest coast of the island of Honshu.

Yoshitsune was the general of the Genji forces who defeated Atsumori's clan. Not long after his glorious victory he was slandered by retainers of his elder brother, the shogun Yoritomo, and a warrant was issued for his arrest. Yoshitsune and his band of loyal samurai thereupon made their escape to northern Japan where they found refuge for a few short years under the protection of an old and powerful local aristocrat. When the aristocrat died, his son betrayed Yoshitsune to Yoritomo, and the Genji hero par excellence was forced to commit suicide.

Ataka is centered on an incident along the escape route north. As the hero in the play, Yoshitsune is far overshadowed by his stalwart retainer Benkei, a whopping-great warrior priest with cunning intelligence and unfailing courage. Benkei is the *shite* and Yoshitsune's part is always played by a child. There are nine other samurai in Yoshitsune's band, as well as a mountain guide (the *kyōgen*). The *waki* is Benkei's opponent, the chief barrier guard, Togashi, who is accompanied by a subordinate. From the beginning, then, with such a large cast of characters, this play has a very different look from the plays by Zeami we have examined.

As Benkei and his party approach the barrier of Ataka, they are afraid they will be recognized and arrested unless they can disguise Yoshitsune. They decide that their only option is to pass off their cherished lord as a humble coolie. Having taken this course, they warily approach the barrier gate. Despite their precautions, the barrier guards find them suspect, even as they explain that they are simply an innocent group of priests collecting alms for the reconstruction of a great temple lost in the previous wars. The ruse seems dangerously close to failure, and the priests begin to perform their own last rites because Togashi has threatened to execute them. In the recitation of those rites they make reference execute them. In the recitation of those rites they make reference to the divine retribution to be visited upon any who harm them, something which gives Togashi reason to pause.

He interrupts them with the offer of reprieve if they can produce a subscription list, proof that they are indeed a group of priests collecting alms. This is one of the high points of the play: Benkei's spontaneous invention and extemporal recitation of the text of the supposed subscription list, while he holds before him an unrelated scroll hastily retrieved from the luggage on Yoshitsune's back. The final lines of Benkei's recitation resound to the heavens, and the barrier guards are struck to the heart with fear. They open the gates and allow Benkei's party to pass, but as the last low coolie (actually Yoshitsune) is about to go through, Togashi stops him. The samurai all turn back, hands on the hilts of their swords, but Benkei manages to restrain them even as he demands to know why the "coolie" has been detained:

> TOGASHI: I myself gave the order to stop him.
> BENKEI: And why is that!
> TOGASHI: I stopped him because he looks like a certain person.
> BENKEI: What! Why, there's nothing unusual in one person looking like another. Who does he look like?
> TOGASHI: Somebody says he looks like Lord Yoshitsune, so I stopped him till we've settled the matter.
> BENKEI: How's that! You think this coolie looks like Lord Yoshitsune!
> TOGASHI: Exactly.
> BENKEI: Why, I've never heard such a thing, this miserable coolie looking like Lord Yoshitsune . . . this must be the finest moment in his life! Well, damn it all, I thought we'd get as far as Noto before sunset tonight, (he turns to Yoshitsune), and here you are straggling behind with your measly baggage . . . of course you attract suspicion! Well, I'd been thinking all along how useless you were. I'll show you a thing or two (and grabbing the coolie's walking staff he beats him soundly). Get yourself through that gate!
> TOGASHI: Scold him as you may, we will not let him pass.
> BENKEI: They've got their eyes on the baggage, damned thieves.

At this point the samurai line up in a wall behind Benkei, swords ready to defend their "coolie," and the sight is so intimidating to Togashi and his man that they claim they were mistaken and allow the party to pass through the barrier.

The scene changes to a spot down the road safely removed from the threat of the barrier guards, and the mood turns from the excitement of imminent battle to the sadness and humiliation of Benkei's abject apology to Yoshitsune for having raised his hand against him. Yoshitsune responds with grateful acknowledgment that Benkei's tactics have saved his life, and the party now reflect on the past few years, their army's success over the Heike, and their sad change in fortunes since.

They are now interrupted by Togashi who has come with sake to apologize for "his previous rudeness." The play concludes with a reconciliation between Togashi's party and Benkei's warrior-priests. Benkei drinks a prodigious amount of sake and dances, Togashi wishes them well and they continue on their journey north, "feeling as though they'd stepped on a tiger's tail, and slipped through the jaws of a poisonous snake."

Ataka was written more than a half century after *Atsumori* and *Izutsu*, and reflects numerous changes in the social context of Noh as well as the taste of its patrons. The presumed author, Nobumitsu, was the seventh son of Zeami's nephew Onnami. As a junior child in a family of Noh actors, Nobumitsu would not normally have been entitled to perform *shite* roles, but would have acted as *waki* or perhaps played in the instrumental ensemble. The heir to the troupe, Nobumitsu's elder brother, died young, however, so Nobumitsu became acting head for his underage nephew, later performing the same function for his grandnephew as well. In these circumstances, Nobumitsu occasionally played *shite* roles, and moreover, in writing, he allotted greater dramatic responsibility to the *waki* than was the case in Zeami's plays. He follows Zeami's lead in certain parts of his plays, notably in the travel songs, and he adopts some of the same dances in his plays, but a kernel of dramatic conflict animates most of his extant work. Trivial though it may at first seem, the fact that the texts of Nobumitsu's compositions tend to be longer than Zeami's while in performance the plays are often shorter, illustrates their differing aesthetic aims.

In several ways, the plays of Nobumitsu (and his son Nagatoshi, 1488–1541, and contemporary Komparu Zempo, 1454–1520) provide transitions to the dramatic forms of later ages, in particular to Kabuki. Indeed, Ataka itself is a favorite play of the Kabuki repertory, retitled *Kanjinchō* (*The Subscription List*).

For at least three centuries, Noh has been a highly self-conscious and refined art. It is expensive to produce, access to its professional ranks is strictly limited, and it can hardly be called popular. But it is generously patronized, mostly by older people who themselves chant and dance Noh plays as amateurs. Noh has, moreover, been an inspiration for the work of several twentieth-century masters. Yeats thought he found in it an aristocratic drama, "distinguised, indirect and symbolic," and several of his Cuchulain plays bear a distinct if distant resemblance to Noh. Benjamin Britten's opera *Curlew River* has its source in a beautiful and tragic Noh called *Sumidagawa,* written by Zeami's son Motomasa. Kurosawa Akira, the great Japanese cinematic director, has borrowed extensively from Noh in his films. These borrowings range from the visual effect of, say, the witch in his version of *Macbeth,* to the characterization of Tsurumaru in *Ran,* who is taken almost fully formed from the Noh *Semimaru.* In a more general sense, Kurosawa makes extensive use of the Noh music and its vocabulary of movement, and one might even go so far as to discuss the dramatic evolution of certain of his films in terms of *jo, ha,* and *kyū.*

Translations and studies of Noh have appeared in the past decade or so in increasing numbers. As videotapes and recordings of the six-hundred-year-old art also begin to appear, Noh may have a yet greater influence on the arts of our own times.

TOPICS FOR DISCUSSION

1. Someone once said that in "Western" drama, something happens, whereas in Noh, someone appears. How does this conform to your own understanding of the plays *Atsumori, Izutsu,* and *Ataka?* If some of these plays seem to leave little room for conflict and action (the mainstays of many famous plays in Western languages) what do they have instead to provide a concrete experience on the stage? How might an actor approach the roles of *shite* in these plays?

2. Critics have often discussed the use of imagery in Noh. Do you perceive anything noteworthy about the imagery of these plays? Are particular images recurrent? What might be their significance? How do images of the natural world interact with the internal world of the *shite?*

3. Many Noh plays are set in the country, in famous places or old temples and shrines. What significance do you see in this? How does the setting of the play determine its nature? Do you think the setting might itself be termed a character in the play, as the setting of certain novels becomes a kind of character in the

interactions of those novels? Do you find anything in the plays you have read to remind you of pastoralism?

4. Noh shares certain important characteristics with Greek tragedy. It had its origins in religious festivals; it is performed by characters wearing masks, it is largely serious in nature, and it is highly formalized structurally. But how do these plays compare with tragedies you have read? What differences immediately come to mind? What do you learn about tragedy from its contrast with Noh?

5. What sort of potential do you see for these plays outside the context of traditional Japanese performance? Do they offer any potential for production on a Western stage? How might you go about presenting them to a Western audience?

NOTES

1. Author's translation from Omote Akira and Katō Shūichi, eds., *Zeami, Zenchiku*, Nihon shisō taikei, vol. 24 (Tokyo: Iwanami shoten, 1974), p. 20. Another English translation can be found in Thomas Rimer and Yamazaki Masakazu, *On the Art of the Nō Drama: The Major Treatises of Zeami* (Princeton: Princeton University Press, 1984), p. 10. See also Thomas Blenman Hare, *Zeami's Style* (Stanford: Stanford University Press, 1986), pp. 227–28.

2. Quoted in Hare, *Zeami's Style*, pp. 185–86.

3. Zeami Motokiyo, *Atsumori*, trans. Arthur Waley, in *The Noh Plays of Japan* (New York: Grove Press, 1957), p. 64.

4. Ibid.

5. Ibid.

6. Ibid.

7. Ibid.

8. Ibid., p. 73.

9. All translations from this point on in the essay are by Thomas Blenman Hare.

REFERENCES

Translations

Atsumori has been translated (with additional background material) by Arthur Waley and is available in his book *The Noh Plays of Japan* (New York: Grove Press, 1957), pp. 63–73. The translation alone has also been included in the widely available *Anthology of Japanese Literature From the Earliest Era to the Mid-Nineteenth Century*, edited by Donald Keene (New York: Grove Press, 1955), pp. 286–293.

A translation of *Izutsu* can be found among those commissioned by Nippon Gakujutsu Shinkōkai, *Japanese Noh Drama*, vol. 1 (Tokyo: Kenkyūsha, 1955), pp. 91–105. Another version with detailed analysis and background material is found in the book *Zeami's Style* listed below, pp. 135–153.

Ataka is to be found among the plays in *Japanese Noh Drama*, vol. 3, pp. 149–171.

General

Bethe, Monica, and Karen Brazell. "Nō as Performance: An Analysis of the Kuse Scene from Yamaba." *Cornell University East Asia Papers*, no. 16 (1978).

Hare, Thomas. *Zeami's Style: The Noh Plays of Zeami Motokiyo.* Stanford: Stanford University Press, 1986.

Keene, Donald, ed. "Twenty Plays of the Nō Theater." *Records of Civilization: Sources and Studies*, no. 85 (1970).

Rimer, Thomas, and Yamazaki Masakazu, trans. *On the Art of the Nō Drama: The Major Treatises of Zeami.* Princeton: Princeton University Press, 1984.

THE LOVE SUICIDES AT SONEZAKI

Donald Keene

In the 1880s, when the Japanese first began to examine their own literary heritage in light of their newly acquired knowledge of Western literature, the fame of Shakespeare in England, Goethe in Germany, and Racine in France induced them to search their own dramatic literature for a Japanese equivalent. The Japanese possessed a rich tradition of theater: the Noh drama, perfected in the fourteenth century, had enjoyed the patronage of the shoguns for almost 500 years, and the Kabuki theater of actors and the Bunraku theater of puppets, both developed in the seventeenth century, had enjoyed the favor not only of the commoners but of many members of the samurai class. However, even though the plays, especially those written for the Noh theater, contain magnificent poetry, no one had ever thought of the dramatists as poets, and the plays themselves had not been elevated to the rank of "literature." The task of the playwright had traditionally been to provide suitable vehicles for the talents of the actors at his disposal, and it was usual to rewrite plays when they were revived so as to meet the demands of new actors and new audiences. The authorship of many of the best-known plays was uncertain; virtually every superior Noh play—about half of the repertory of some 240 plays—was for centuries attributed to Zeami (1363–1443), though modern scholars grudgingly give him credit for no more than 25. The authorship of Kabuki and Bunraku plays, a matter of small interest to the audiences, was complicated by the practice of having three or more dramatists collaborate in writing a single long play, each man composing several acts. There was certainly no Japanese dramatist who occupied the place of importance in his countrymen's esteem comparable to that enjoyed by Shakespeare, Goethe, or Racine.

The dramatist eventually chosen as the "Japanese Shakes-peare" was Chikamatsu Monzaemon (1653–1725).[1] Chikamatsu was born to a samurai family of some distinction, though his father, for reasons we do not know, lost his position as a retainer of the daimyo of Echizen and, becoming a *rōnin* or masterless samurai, moved to the capital. As a boy Chikamatsu served as a page in a noble household in Kyoto. At the time the puppet the-ater was patronized by members of the nobility, and this may be how Chikamatsu was first introduced to this art. Eventually, he decided to make his career in the theater. It was most unusual for anyone of Chikamatsu's background to become associated with a profession that was generally despised, but he may have had no choice: his father had lost his position and income as a samurai, and Chikamatsu's service in a noble household was unlikely to lead into a means of earning a living.

Chikamatsu's first play for the puppet theater seems to have been *Yotsugi Soga* (*The Soga Heir*), written in 1683. Although the work is immature and contains some scenes that are so ludi-crously exaggerated in sentiment and action as to suggest bur-lesque, it also contains some passages of poetic beauty that presage the masterpieces of later years. His first major play was *Shusse Kagekiyo* (*Kagekiyo Victorious*), written in 1686 for Takemoto Gidayū (1651–1714), the most celebrated chanter of the puppet theater. The function of the chanter was to declaim or sing the lines of the text, sometimes describing the scene or comment-ing on the action, sometimes speaking for the different characters, modulating his voice to suggest a young woman, an old woman, a fierce warrior, a child, and so on. The musical accompaniment for the chanter's declamation and singing was provided by the sami-sen, an instrument somewhat resembling the guitar but with a much stronger and harsher tone, which had been introduced to Japan from China by way of the Ryūkyū Islands in the sixteenth century. The puppets in Chikamatsu's day were each operated by one man, but shortly after his death the three-man puppet was introduced and is today the most conspicuous feature of the Bun-raku theater. Of the three elements in a performance—the texts chanted by the narrator, the musical accompaniment, and the puppets—the most important has traditionally been the text, though the ideal is an equal balance of interest among the three.

Chikamatsu's decision to write for the puppet theater was an event of significance in the history of the drama of the world. Playwrights in other countries have sometimes written for pup-pets, rather than actors, but Chikamatsu was the only major dramatist who devoted himself primarily to the puppet theater. He also wrote plays for Kabuki actors, especially for Sakata Tōjūrō. His Kabuki plays written between 1688 and 1703 were for the most part intended to serve as vehicles for Tōjūrō's particular talents. In 1703, however, Chikamatsu shifted his main efforts back to the puppet theater, and although he continued to write Kabuki plays from time to time in the following years, all the works for which he is celebrated today were written for Takemoto Gidayū and his successors.

A serious dramatist faces special problems when writing plays to be performed by puppets. An actor can alter his expression at will, and if the part requires him to seem affable in one scene and menacing in another he should possess the ability to effect this change. A puppet, on the other hand, retains throughout a play the fixed expression carved into the wood of his face. Moreover, the heads are restricted to a limited number of types—good young man, bad young man, good middle-aged man, bad middle-aged man and so on—and this means that there is not much possibility of a character developing during the course of a play. As soon as the audience sees a puppet with, say, the head of a bad young man, it recognizes his basic character, and no matter what friendly words he may utter, there is never any doubt but that he is a bad man. There is reason to think that Chikamatsu found this limitation of the puppets a hindrance to the composition of his plays. One can imagine how Shakespeare would have felt if he had to choose a puppet head for his Macbeth: would it be the apparently good man of his first appearance, the bad man of Duncan's murder, or the frightened man at the banquet? Obviously, no one expression would suit all of the moods encompassed by the role of Macbeth, and in several of Chikamatsu's plays there are complex characters who cannot be pinned down as simply good, bad, frightened, or whatever. These characters demand actors, rather than puppets.

Why then did Chikamatsu shift his main efforts back to puppets in 1703? Various theories, none conclusive, have been advanced. The first and most plausible is that Chikamatsu, unlike dramatists who wrote for Kabuki actors, took pride in his texts and disliked the liberties that actors took (and still take!). The actors felt it was their privilege to change the text in any way that would improve the performance in the eyes of the spectators, even if this meant drastically changing the play. Whole acts were omitted, speeches assigned to one character were given to another, and entirely unrelated scenes were sometimes borrowed from other plays and interpolated in the work. Chikamatsu anticipated such behavior on the part of the actors; in some of his Kabuki plays he left the climactic scene a blank for the actor to improvise according to his fancy and his particular talents. But it must have been maddening, all the same, when a play to which he had devoted great care was torn to pieces by temperamental or self-indulgent actors. The puppets, on the other hand, had no egos to satisfy. Moreover, if the chanter arbitrarily changed the text he would hopelessly confuse the samisen accompanist and the puppet operators; the chanter therefore had no choice but to deliver the text as written. Today, before a chanter begins his recitation of a section of a puppet play he lifts the text reverently to his forehead and, even though he probably knows every syllable by heart, he turns the pages of the text at the appropriate places, pretending to be reading. Even if a chanter is blind he keeps up the same pretense in deference to the authority of the text. Chikamatsu may have left the Kabuki theater for the puppets because he wanted to have his plays performed as written.

It has also been suggested that the shift may have been dictated by economic reasons: the puppet theater was (and is) associated with the city of Osaka, unlike Kabuki, first performed in Kyoto. During the late seventeenth and early eighteenth centuries Osaka became the commercial capital of Japan, the city of the greatest wealth, and Chikamatsu may have supposed that the theater would prosper in such surroundings. Or, as other critics have suggested, Chikamatsu may have left Kabuki because his favorite actor, Sakata Tōjūrō, had retired from the stage. In short, we do not know the reasons, but the success of the plays he wrote for the puppet theater, despite the problems that such a theater imposes, testifies to his extraordinary ability.

The play that Chikamatsu wrote for Takemoto Gidayū's puppet theater in 1703 was *Sonezaki Shinjū* (*The Love Suicides at Sonezaki*). It scored such a success that Gidayū's theater, which had been threatened with bankruptcy, entered its period of greatest prosperity, and it created a vogue for plays about lovers' suicides. The word *shinjū*, which I have translated as "love suicides," means literally "within the heart." It was used from the late seventeenth century to designate pledges of love, especially between a prostitute and a customer. The prostitute was compelled by her profession to pretend to be in love with every regular customer, but sometimes the man would demand proof that she really loved him, some objective evidence of what was "within her heart." Initially this proof took the form of oaths, or of tearing out a fingernail or of tattooing the customer's name somewhere on her body; but oaths can be broken, fingernails grow back, and even tattoos can be removed. Increasingly painful proofs were demanded, such as cutting off the tip of a finger; but the supreme proof was a willingness to die with the man. This practice gave rise to a whole genre of plays written by Chikamatsu and his imitators.

In the fourth moon of 1703, the love suicides of Tokubei, a shop assistant, and Ohatsu, a prostitute, became the subject of gossip in Osaka. Chikamatsu, learning of the circumstances, decided to write a play about the unhappy lovers. He worked quickly, and within three weeks of the event the first performance of *The Love Suicides at Sonezaki* was presented by Gidayū's company. Chikamatsu's play faithfully evoked the atmosphere of the Osaka of his day, especially the licensed quarters, where men went not only for sexual pleasure but for a freedom of which they were deprived by the rigidly organized society. His hero is an ordinary young man who works in a shop that sells soy sauce, his heroine a prostitute of the lower ranks, not a grand courtesan. Chikamatsu apparently invented the villain, Kuheiji, in order to make more plausible the decision of the unhappy lovers to commit suicide; surviving accounts of the actual event indicate that Tokubei and Ohatsu committed suicide not because of the machinations of some other person but because they were tired of living. When their bodies were discovered, broadsheets were issued with the details. There was nothing edifying about the event; indeed, one account sternly ended with the words "they polluted the wood of Sonezaki," referring to the disrespect shown by the lovers who committed suicide within the precincts of a Shinto shrine.

Chikamatsu probably possessed no special knowledge of what had impelled the lovers to die. He started with the fact of their bodies being discovered and proceeded to imagine in reverse order the sequence of events that had led to the tragedy. For most people of the time the deaths of Tokubei and Ohatsu were no more than the subject of gossip for a couple of days, until the next love suicide claimed their attention. There was nothing heroic about either Tokubei or Ohatsu, but Chikamatsu decided that their story had the makings of tragedy. Aristotle in his *Poetics* wrote that the hero of a tragedy must be a person better than ourselves, and this belief was passed on to the dramatists of later centuries. Shakespeare's tragic heroes are kings, princes, and generals, and if a character of a social status similar to Tokubei's had appeared he would probably have been comic, perhaps speaking a dialect or in some other way rendering himself foolish in our eyes; he definitely would not have enjoyed the privilege of dying with the woman he loved. Chikamatsu obviously knew nothing of Aristotle's theories of drama, but he was aware that he had to give tragic stature to Tokubei and Ohatsu if their deaths were not to seem merely sordid. Tokubei and Ohatsu are elevated not by their social positions but by the purity and strength of their love.

Chikamatsu created in Tokubei a hero of a kind not found in Western drama before the twentieth century. Practically the first thing we learn about him is that he has entrusted a large sum of money that he desperately needs to his friend Kuheiji. But as soon as Kuheiji appears the audience knows from the puppet head that this young man is not to be trusted, and every word Kuheiji speaks is so disagreeable that one can only marvel that Tokubei believes this man is his friend. When he confronts Kuheiji with the promissory note to which Kuheiji has affixed his seal, Kuheiji declares that he lost his seal before the date of the note and could not possibly have affixed it. We know Kuheiji is lying; worse, it is clear that he carefully planned to swindle Tokubei out of his money by falsely reporting the loss of the seal. Tokubei, frustrated and enraged, attempts to take back the money with his fists, but he is no match for Kuheiji and his cronies. In a standard Japanese historical film if a hero is set upon by twenty armed adversaries we can always be sure that he will defeat them single-handedly, but Tokubei is soundly thrashed. At the end of the act he tearfully informs bystanders that within three days he will demonstrate to the people of Osaka that he was telling the truth. It is not clear what he intends, but probably the only course of action he could imagine was suicide.

The second scene is set in the brothel where Ohatsu works. The other prostitutes are gossiping about Tokubei, and soon Kuheiji arrives, much to Ohatsu's distress. She catches a glimpse of Tokubei outside the gate and goes to him, only to be summoned back to the house. She tells him to conceal himself under the train of her outer robe, and Tokubei, obeying, crawls to the house and hides under the porch. Surely no hero of a tragedy has ever made a less dignified entrance! Ohatsu, after exchanging sarcastic remarks with Kuheiji, asks (as if to herself) if Tokubei is willing to die with her. Tokubei takes her foot, which is hanging over the edge of the porch, and passes it across his throat as a sign of his willingness. His gesture is resolute, but it is in response to

Ohatsu's question; he is not leading but following. All the same, he has taken the first step towards achieving tragic stature.

Up until this point nothing about Tokubei had even remotely suggested the hero of a tragedy. Chikamatsu was surely aware that Tokubei would have to be made a more impressive figure if his love suicide was to excite the admiration of the audience. The means he chose were appropriate to the puppet drama though not possible in a conventional theater of actors: he had the chanter describe in extraordinarily beautiful poetry the journey of the lovers to the place where they will die. The journey description (*michiyuki*) is a feature not only of all varieties of traditional Japanese theater but is prominent in other kinds of literature as well.[2] The *michiyuki* of *The Love Suicides at Sonezaki*, the most beautiful Chikamatsu ever wrote, uses every resource of the Japanese language to convey the tragedy of the impending deaths and thereby to impart grandeur to the two people before us. Tokubei, as he walks his last journey, grows taller before our eyes. His character has not been transformed; rather, the purity and strength that have always been within him are for the first time exposed. He is no longer a pathetic figure but a man who can kill the woman he loves and then himself. Finally, Chikamatsu assures us that the lovers will without doubt attain Buddhahood. Their suicides have become the means of salvation.

It might seem that the lovers' suicides snuffed out the lives of two people just when their most admirable qualities had been revealed, but Chikamatsu believed that lovers who died together would be reborn together in Paradise. This promise of salvation may seem like a throwback to medieval tales, but the atmosphere is entirely in keeping with the times. The tragedy is caused by Kuheiji's cheating Tokubei out of his money. It would be inconceivable in a Noh play (or even a tragedy by Shakespeare) that money would control the destinies of the characters, but this is literally true of both Tokubei and Ohatsu. He cannot return the dowry money he accepted from his uncle because he has been swindled by Kuheiji. If he had the money, he could buy up Ohatsu's contract and free her from the brothel, but without money he is powerless to keep her from the arms of other men. Ohatsu presumably became a prostitute because her family needed the money, and she cannot escape the brothel unless a customer "ransoms" her. The one free act, the one act that requires no money, is to die, and the lovers die, confident that after death they will be together in Amida's paradise.

The Love Suicides at Sonezaki created a new genre of Japanese theater, the *sewamono*, or plays about contemporary life. The Noh plays invariably dealt with the distant past, and Kabuki plays that in fact treated recent events always masked them by pretending that the story was set in the world of some centuries earlier. It goes without saying that the authorities would not tolerate criticism of the regime, but even if the treatment was favorable, no person of consequence could be represented on the stage. Tokubei and Ohatsu, however, were so insignificant in the eyes of the authorities that their stories could be enacted without censorship. Chikamatsu insisted on the contemporaneity of the *sewamono* plays by mentioning currently fashionable articles of clothing, the names of shops, and even the names of his own plays (rather in the manner of an excerpt from *The Marriage of Figaro* being played in the last scene of *Don Giovanni*). He seems to have been insisting that tragedy was possible even in such peaceful, humdrum times, and he emphasizes his point by choosing quite ordinary people for the heroes and heroines of various plays. The first tragedy composed in English with a common man for its hero, *The London Merchant* (1731) by George Lillo, has a preface in which the author argues that plays treating people of the middle class can be just as tragic as those that deal with people of superior rank. This was the discovery that Chikamatsu made some thirty years earlier.

The success of *The Love Suicides at Sonezaki* did not induce Chikamatsu to abandon the variety of drama on which his reputation had been founded, plays that treated, often in exaggerated terms, the heroes of Japanese history. Indeed, his greatest triumph came with *Kokusenya Kassen* (*The Battles of Coxinga*, 1715), a play abounding in spectacular effects. But Chikamatsu is remembered today especially for a half-dozen or so *sewamono*, beginning with *The Love Suicides at Sonezaki*. Not surprisingly, the later examples of *sewamono* show advances over the simple plot of the first one; audiences came to expect a greater diversity of incidents and characters than those represented by the hero, heroine, and villain of *The Love Suicides at Sonezaki*. Chikamatsu revised the play for its revival of 1719, adding a scene in which the wicked Kuheiji is apprehended, too late to save the death-bound couple. The play was apparently not performed even once between 1719 and 1955, presumably because the producers of Bunraku and Kabuki plays thought that it was too uncomplicated for modern tastes; but since its revival of 1955 it has been performed almost every year, abroad as well as in Japan, and it is now recognized as a masterpiece of Japanese theater.

TOPICS FOR DISCUSSION

1. Chikamatsu was dubbed "the Japanese Shakespeare" by Japanese scholars of the late nineteenth century. Do you find any justification for such an association?

2. The characters who appear in *The Love Suicides at Sonezaki* are all commoners of humble station. Does this prevent the play from attaining tragic stature?

3. Do you find individuality in the characters? If not, would you attribute this to the fact that it was a puppet play? Or to the fact that the characters lack the financial means to live as they please? Or to the demands of the society in which they lived? If you find individuality, explain in what way this is achieved by Chikamatsu in his portraiture.

NOTES

1. The date of Chikamatsu's death is often given as 1724, but he died towards the end of the eleventh lunar month on what was January 6, 1725, according to the solar calendar.

2. There is an important study of the language and functions of the *michiyuki* in French, *Michiyuki-bun* by Jacqueline Pigeot (Maisonneuve, 1982).

REFERENCES

Keene, Donald. *Major Plays of Chikamatsu*. New York: Columbia University Press, 1961.

Keene, Donald. *Nō and Bunraku*. New York: Columbia University Press, 1990.

Keene, Donald. *World Within Walls*. New York: Holt, Rinehart and Winston, 1976.

Postscript

East-West Literary Relations: The "Wisdom" of the "East"

Lucien Miller

INTRODUCTION

One of the more promising ways to go about comparing the literatures of Asia and the West is to focus on the phenomenon of wisdom literature. The Western view that Asia is the repository of a special wisdom may occasionally be found from the earliest imaginative and historical encounters between the "West" and the "East." Thanks to Jesuit missionaries, the French Philosophies, Schopenhauer, and Max Müller, "the wisdom of the East" receives growing attention from the sixteenth through the nineteenth centuries, and reappears under various guises during the twentieth. Before discussing what is meant by wisdom, and what is behind this Western habit of reading Asian texts as wisdom literature, we need to recognize that words such as "East" and "West" ought to be placed in quotation marks, as a first step in contemporary wisdom, if you will. Distinctions between "East" and "West" are partly whimsical, depending quite literally on where one is when the sun rises or sets, and partly matters of adoption and convenience, whereby the extra-European world has borrowed "Orient" and "Occident" from European vocabulary, where these words originate and properly belong. In fact, anachronistic language such as "East" and "West," "Orient" and "Occident" is both arbitrary and revealing, belonging to what Edward Said has called "imaginative geography," which differentiates between familiar and unfamiliar space that is considered "ours" or "theirs."[1] My "East," determined by historical precedent and academic interests, includes those Far Eastern and South Asian cultures whose literatures are the subject of this volume, namely, China, India, and Japan, while "West" signifies countries where the major language is English or a European language. The discourse on wisdom in this essay is that of Western authors, scholars, travelers, and missionaries who write about this "East," as well as that of some Asian commentators.

There are a host of twentieth century imaginative literary works which exemplify or play with the notion of "the wisdom of the East." Starting around the turn of the century, one thinks of Rudyard Kipling's *The Jungle Book*, *The Second Jungle Book*, or *Kim*, Hermann Hesse's *Siddhartha*, André Malraux's *Man's Fate*, E. M. Forster's *A Passage to India*, Jack Kerouac's *Dharma Bums*, Robert Pirsig's *Zen and the Art of Motorcycle Maintenance*, Maxine Hong Kingston's *Woman Warrior*, Italo Calvino's *Invisible Cities*, and more recently, Salman Rushdie's *Satanic Verses*. Before this century, our list might range from Aeschylus' *The Persians*, to Johann Wolfgang von Goethe's *Westöstlicher Divan*, Richard Burton's *The Book of the Thousand and One Nights*, Gustave Flaubert's *Salammbo*, and Victor Hugo's *Les Orientales*.

How are we to understand this Western imaging whereby the "East" is sometimes exoticized or eroticized, to be sure, but is also projected as a source of wisdom? And how do native readings of Asian texts compare to Western views of Asian "wisdom"? Of the many theories for this turning "East," I should like to single out two. One has to do with the biblical concept of wisdom, and the second with alterity, or otherness.

There are a cluster of images which surround the word "wisdom" among the biblical texts associated with that name—*Job*, *Psalms*, *Proverbs*, *Ecclesiastes*, *Canticle of Canticles*, *Wisdom*, and *Sirach*. Biblical wisdom may be characterized as teachings about conduct in family, tribe, and nation, which are passed from father to son, mother to daughter, and which deal with ultimate questions of a moral or ethical nature about life and death. In the later wisdom texts, wisdom is predicated of God, and has an inaccessible, transcendent character.[2] Eastern wisdom may be viewed as a supplement, or as a filling of a void in biblical wisdom. The biblical notion of an ultimate, transcendent knowledge creates an appetite for its discovery in diverse cultures and times. Conversely, a feeling or experience of the inadequacy of one's native, biblical wisdom impels one to search for it abroad.

In this movement, the dynamics of alterity are significant. Whether the relation is between individuals or cultures, the encounter between self and other informs, challenges, or shocks. The potential for alteration through difference is pervasive. The self may assimilate the other, as did many of the Spanish conquistadors who obliterated Meso-American peoples and cultures, or try to become the other, as did some members of the American Beat generation who interiorized selected Asian philosophies. The question is always what to do with the awareness of difference in the encounter with otherness. The temptation among Western seekers of wisdom may be one of seeing the other as different and superior, or sometimes as different and inferior, but more rarely as both different and equal.[3]

To explore some of the theoretical and methodological possibilities of our topic, "the 'wisdom' of the 'East,' " let me juxtapose a few major literary texts from China, India, and Japan against representations of the Far East in Anglo-American and European literatures. I shall focus on the conceptualization of wisdom, the assumption that there is a "real East," and the question of canonicity. Such an approach uncovers cross-cultural readings of "wisdom" which are mutually illuminating.

DISCOURSE ON WISDOM LITERATURE

As suggested previously, one dominant Western image of Asian classics is that they are "sacred books" containing an eternal wisdom either missing from, or complementary to, the Western canon. Interestingly, if we contrast Asian classics to Asian and Western discourse about them, "the wisdom of the East" becomes a chameleon of changing colors. As illustrations, let us consider introductions to the Indian epic, the *Mahābhārata* and three Chinese classics—the *Dao De Jing* [*Tao Te Ching*], the *Zhuang Zi* [*Chuang Tzu*], and the *Yi Jing* [*I Ching*].

Each of these "wisdom" texts exemplifies some aspect of the problem of representation. A case in point is the edition of the *Mahābhārata* produced by Ananda K. Coomaraswamy and Sister Nivedita.[4] In attempting to present the *Mahābhārata* to Westerners, Coomaraswamy and Sister Nivedita take an Occidentalist perspective, reconstructing the Indian classic along the lines of what they take to be Western notions of the "wisdom of the East." They themselves are two persons whom the Western reader might readily consider to be Hindu authorities on Indian literature, for in their prose and their names one finds the voice of authoritative spokespersons for Indian wisdom. In fact both are in some sense outsiders, one an Asian westernized by education, faith, and career, the other a Westerner devoted to Indian spirituality. Coomaraswamy was born to a Christian family of mixed Ceylonese and British parentage, held a Ph.D in geology, and was widely read in Western philosophy and religion, as well as in Indian culture. He lived for many years in the United States, working as the curator of the Boston Museum of Fine Arts. Sister Nivedita (Margaret Noble, also a Christian) was an Irishwoman who became a disciple of Swami Vivekananda. She found in India models of transcendence and androgyny, as well as alternative political and social roles for women, and a means to dissent against British society.[5] Are Coomaraswamy and Nivedita representatives of the "East" or the "West," or else the ideal mediators between cultures? How we respond to the wisdom of the East is determined by our assumptions about those who represent it.

Regarding native versus foreign views of the *Mahābhārata*, an Indian reader might not think of the epic primarily as a source of "wisdom," but rather as a treasure house of tales. Within the Indian tradition, the *Mahābhārata* is technically not considered a revealed text containing sacred or religious matter. In the West, on the other hand, the most appealing part of the *Mahābhārata* is the *Bhagavad Gītā*, a kernel of Indian philosophy and metaphysics which, as Barbara Stoler Miller tells us, Henry David Thoreau took to Walden Pond because Asian ideas supported his critique of eighteenth century rationalism and nineteenth century materialism.[6]

Another twist in the yarn of representation of Asian wisdom is found in the psychologist Carl Jung's reading of the *Yi Jing* (*Book of Changes*), which is among the all-time bestsellers of Chinese literature. At the time he wrote his foreword to the book, Jung was in his eighties; he stated that his age made him daring. He was so daring, in fact, that he risked appearing unscientific, claiming that the Chinese text had a voice which spoke to him: "The *I Ching* tells me of its religious significance, of the fact that at present it is unknown and misjudged, of its hope of being restored to a place of honor—this last obviously with a sidelong glance at my as yet unwritten foreword."[7] Again, this time in the figure of a Western authority on psychology, we see the importance of the spokesperson in determining the Asian object as wisdom.

Among the many Western renderings of "the wisdom of the East," Thomas Merton's *The Way of Chuang Tzu* is one of the more compelling. It is an intuitive version of the fourth century

B.C.E. Chinese Daoist [Taoist] classic by the celebrated Catholic Trappist monk and writer, who felt an affinity with a Chinese contemplative. In "A Note to the Reader," he remarked that if Augustine could read Plotinus, if St. Thomas Aquinas could adapt Aristotle, and if Teilhard de Chardin could use Marx and Engels, "I think I may be pardoned for consorting with a Chinese recluse who shares the climate and peace of my own kind of solitude, and who is my own kind of person."[8] Author of numerous works on Western and Eastern spirituality, and a leader in the American peace movement of the 1960s, Merton said he would not have dared to write *The Way of Chuang Tzu* without the encouragement of John C. H. Wu, a specialist in Chinese literature and culture. Merton read various translations of *Zhuang Zi* in French, German, and English, and meditated upon them for five years, before doing what he called his "interpretations," clearly stating that he was not a translator knowledgeable in Chinese. His creative reading is immediately appealing and accessible, opening up Zhuang Zi's philosophy of intuition and his concept of "no-self" and "no-action" to Western readers, and communicating an essential grasp of the elusive dao [tao].

To my mind the result is one of Merton's best books. However, *The Way of Chuang Tzu* raises an interesting question about Western discourse on Eastern philosophy: To what extent can an intuitive insight based on lifestyle and personal affinity as poet and recluse lead to meaningful representation of a Daoist classic? Should Merton's renditions be read as translations, rather than as creative interpretations, his attempt to represent the "East" to the "West" may be viewed as a distortion or projection. The absolute, impersonal dao, for instance, is occasionally (one has to look hard for examples) personified as "He," or the "Maker," or even "God." It seems to me that a more fruitful approach to Merton's text is to see it as a creative rereading of the Western self in the context of the Zhuang Zi other, and as such, a source for a deepening understanding of aspects of Western culture, as well as Chinese. This in fact would be a useful way of reading the majority of Western translations and interpretations of Asian texts, that is, as revelations of self. Merton's introduction and his commentary on this "wisdom" text is a concrete example of representation of self and other, East and West. Reading him, one may begin to understand topics as diverse as Western metaphysics, the "kingdom of heaven" of the Gospels, Franciscan simplicity, human connaturality with animals, or modern American poetics. East-West parallels and contrasts are clarified through intriguing analogies: the Jewish *Torah* is to the Christian *New Testament* as the Confucian *Analects* are to the *Zhuang Zi.* Thus, he surmounted the foreignness of the *Zhuang Zi* by providing Western intertexts, allowing Christian readers, for example, to feel comfortable finding parables in the *Zhuang Zi,* analogous to the Gospels, just as Merton himself did. Thus, in Thomas Merton's hands, *The Way of Chuang Tzu* becomes a work of East-West "wisdom."

The sixth century B.C.E. Chinese Daoist classic, the *Dao De Jing,* presents Western readers with a more fundamental problem about wisdom literature: Is there a text? *A Translation of Lao Tzu's Tao Te Ching and Wang Pi's Commentary* by a Western-trained Chinese scholar, Paul J. Lin, lists the many factors which make the *Dao De Jing* a questionable text: oral transmission, unidentified author(s), uncertain order prior to the invention of paper and printing (early texts written on wood or bamboo strips were bound with hemp which rotted), the intermixing of text and commentaries and the confusion over both (there are 5000-, 13,000-, and 16,000-word texts, and some 600 commentaries), and the proliferation of translations (there are around eighty to date, more than forty in English alone, and new versions have appeared every other year for the past twenty years).[9] Thus, whether they know it or not, readers of the *Dao De Jing* in Chinese or in translation are entirely dependent on the scholarly or imaginative interpretations of Orientalists and Occidentalists. As Holmes Welch has remarked: "To read [the *Dao De Jing*] is an act of creation."[10] In a certain sense, there is no *Dao De Jing* text—an important discovery for seekers of Daoist "wisdom."

THE "REAL" EAST

A reading of the previously considered group of Asian texts, and the discourse they engender, suggests ways in which wisdom is imagined or invented by specialists and aficionados both native and foreign. While interpreters, whether writers or readers, would agree there is no "East" or "West," geographically speaking, they commonly assume there is a "real" East in Asian wisdom literature, one which has to be sought after, or otherwise invented.

The myths of Kālī and Krishna in India and those contained in Marco Polo's accounts of China are examples of how problematic the question of the "real" East is.

In Hindu mythology, Kālī is a female god, the divine destroyer. Her fearsome, insane appearance—lips dripping blood, matted hair, necklace and earrings made of human heads, four arms holding a severed head, snakes writhing about her waist and feet—is viewed within Indian traditions as a stimulus to realizing the ephemeral nature of the phenomenal world. Krishna, by contrast, is the divine lover, the embodiment of youthful beauty, who makes endless love with the many milkmaids who surround him.[11] This identification of erotic and divine love in Krishna is not unfamiliar in the West to a reader of the *Song of Songs*, commentaries by Bernard of Clairvaux, or mystical poetry by St. John of the Cross, but it appears to be far more developed and celebrated in India, especially in Bengali literature and culture.[12] For our purposes, what is revealing is the response to such terrifying or erotic images of the divine. Tracing Western historical images of Shakto-Tantrism over the past two hundred years, for example, David Kopf has noted the constant need to create a discourse to explain the relation between sexuality and religion, a discourse which has never been satisfactory. "Because Shakto-Tantrism seems to express something alarming, or liberating, to each new generation of Westerners, it could never achieve even a modicum of objectivity in scholarship."[13] The eighteenth century British Orientalists were biased in favor of classical Hinduism, and therefore were disdainful of medieval Hinduism, such as Shakto-Tantrism, or popular, regional religion. They considered the cult of Kālī orgiastic religion and witchcraft. This negative view was not reversed until the early twentieth century, when the British High Court Justice in Calcutta, John Woodroffe, assumed an alias (Arthur Avalon) and wrote several treatises defeminizing and desexualizing Shakto-Tantrism. Discovering the importance of their own anti-establishment art and literature, Western-trained Bengali scholars turned to allegorizing the erotic. With the sexual revolution in the West, medieval Hinduism became eroticized, especially within the counterculture. (One is reminded here of Jack Kerouac's *Dharma Bums* in which Buddhism becomes a rationalization for womanizing). Lastly, Marxists and feminists have seen in Shakto-Tantrism a protest of the anti-Aryan Hindu masses, or simply a fertility religion.[14]

Echoes of this ambivalence over sexuality, divine and erotic love, and the "real" East may be found in E. M. Forster's *A Passage to India*. Its female protagonist, Adela Quested, declares "I want to see the real India," only to experience the shattering of her prosaic sense of reality. There are hints of Kālī and of sexual violence in the novel in the attempt "to ravish the unknown" at a temple festival, and in the sheer terror of the Marabar Caves where Adela imagines she has been raped.[15] "Do you know anything about this Krishna business?" the headmaster, Fielding, asks Aziz, his Muslim friend, at the end of the novel, reminding us of the enigmatic Hindu god of love who is always being asked to come to his devotees, but who never seems to do so.[16] Forster's novel appears to admit to the impossibility of representing the "real" India, yet there is sufficient stereotyping on the part of both the narrator and Asian and Western characters to enforce the view that there is a "real East" and a "real West." The narrator speaks of "a hundred Indias," where nothing is definable, yet informs the reader that "most Orientals" overrate hospitality, thinking it signifies intimacy, and all tend to generalize from their disappointments. There is such an entity as "Oriental pathology," claims Mr. McBryde, the Superintendent of Police. Mrs. Moore's son, Ronny, tells his mother that behind every remark an "Oriental" makes, something is hidden. Aziz likes Mrs. Moore, finding her "Oriental." Conversely, in an "Occidental moment," Aziz hangs English paintings on his wall.[17]

In *The Travels of Marco Polo* we have an attempt both to record and to imagine the "real" East. At the beginning of *The Travels* (authentic title, *Description of the World*, Italian title, *Il Milione*), the narrator claims the book is free of fabrication, stating that Marco has recounted "all the great wonders seen, or heard of as true" during his journeys through Asia (Armenia, Persia, Tartary [China], and India) in the last decades of the thirteenth century. In fact, Leonardo Olschki has noted, the book combines realism and romance, being "both a guidebook and a doctrinal work, fused into a literary combination so successful that it is impossible to tell the one from the other."[18] There are several reasons for considering *The Travels* an imaginative work, besides the fact that it mixes genres. Marco never kept a diary during his twenty-five years in Asia, and the book is a reconstruction by Rustichello of Pisa, "a professional writer of chivalric romances," to whom Marco told his story while they were cellmates (the exact nature of their collaboration is unclear).[19] While there are critical editions of various Marco Polo manuscripts, no orginal text is extant.[20] A host of names and places in *The Travels* are identifiable, arguing for its historical reliability, but the work is also full of fantasy. European documents attest to Marco's existence and travels, but no corresponding evidence has been found in China. Lastly, from the perspective of oral art and storytelling techniques, *The Travels* is full of repetition, formulaic statements and narrative patterns, exaggeration and bombast, reminding us of folk literature and fairy tales.

In *The Travels*, while Marco is passionately interested in Asian flora and fauna, customs, foods, geography, and personages, he frequently imagines "the East" in terms of the more familiar "West." A marvelous and mysterious fish migration is understood when its timespan is found to correspond with the Christian calendar of Lent.[21] When each of the three Magi (Marco says they are from Persia) goes to adore the infant Jesus, he discovers that the Christ child is exactly like himself in age and appearance—a case of the other being a reflection of the self, and of "the East" (Persian Magi) being known in terms of "the West" (infant Christ).[22] As Mary B. Campbell has written, the East is envisioned as a complement to the West. "The being Marco has given it, by means of his bald declarations and copious lists, is the body of the West's desire."[23]

As a book which represents "China," *The Travels of Marco Polo* enjoys contemporary imitators of its discourse—most notably, Italo Calvino's *Invisible Cities* (*Le città invisibili*), an imaginative work in which Marco Polo one day explains to Kublai Khan that all the cities of China he describes are variant readings of Venice.[24] Aside from structural parallels—both Marco Polo and Calvino are fond of catalogues of things and repetition—*Invisible Cities* is a work of fiction which endlessly plays with perspectives on notions of the "real." The "cities" of "China" are not representations of reality, but images which are themselves reality, created by the act of writing and reading. Through the play of differences between cities, word puzzles, and lovely or startling twists in perspective, the reader realizes that each city is a landscape of a former, or possible, self. The book imagines the "real" East so that the Western self might discover itself, but it also intimates that the Asian self needs the Western other to realize its self—"only through foreign eyes and ears [Marco Polo's] could the empire manifest its existence to Kublai."[25]

DISCOURSE ON CANON: HIGH AND LOW LITERATURE

In "the East"—China, India, and Japan—notions of canonicity vary considerably, even when there is a widely shared sense of what is an authorized or accepted text within a particular tradition. These differences illuminate our understanding of Asian views of what the West may term the "wisdom of the East."

The ancient Chinese classic, the *Shi jing* [*Shih ching*] (*Book of Songs*, sixth century B.C.E.), enjoys canonical status because Confucius praised it, and because commentators read it as political allegory and "the voice of the people." The Chinese ideograph for "classic," *jing* [*ching*], as found in the title, refers to the *woof* (the threads running lengthwise) upon which a fabric is woven, and thus stands for that which is foundational, or upon which everything is built. In contemporary Communist China, one encounters a quite different sense of wisdom and canon, a respect for "the wisdom of the people" in the oral folk literature of Chinese minorities. Here we have forgotten or ignored literature becoming contemporary classics, partly because of the aesthetic appeal of oral art and partly because of political reasons—the minorities are found in sensitive border areas and good relations with them are important to Chinese security.[26]

Lady Murasaki's *Tale of Genji* (early eleventh century, C.E.) epitomizes traditional Japanese aesthetics of the Heian era—especially the idea of sensitivity to things (*mono no aware*), and the notion that beauty and the ephemeral are synonymous.[27] Such concepts seem compatible with the novel's depiction of the amorous intrigues of its hero, Genji. What is unfamiliar to the Western reader is Buddhist discourse on *Genji*. For example, the president of a popular contemporary Buddhist movement, Soka Gakkai, and Professor Makoto Nemoto have spoken of Genji, the Shining Prince, as an embodiment of the light which emanates from the body of Buddha, and have speculated that Lady Murasaki may have been thinking of the thirty marks and eighty physical features said to adorn the body of Buddha when she created her central character. Genji, viewed as the seeker of truth, is the religious man who moves from romantic relations to a longing for transcendence and salvation.[28] Such a reading "stretches" the significance of *Genji* for Western readers, for it locates a book of wisdom where we might least expect to find it, among the romantic classics of Japanese literature.

This stretching may go in different directions, of course—an Asian reading of an Asian text can alter Western understanding, but conversely, a Western reading of an Asian text may produce a new model of "the wisdom of the East." A case in point might be a feminist reading of another Japanese classic of the Heian era by a woman writer, Sei Shōnagon's *The Pillow Book* (*Makura no sōshi*). This work suggests the possibility of a Japanese feminist poetics.[29] Written in then-acceptable feminine diary form by a lady-in-waiting to the Empress Sadako, *The Pillow Book* exhibits an astonishing aggressiveness, a self-confidence, and an arrogance which are surprisingly modern. Here is a woman who is more than merely allowed to speak. Her superior sophistication in matters of poetry, taste, and style seem to locate her at the head of an anonymous community of women. The diary form, filled with the fragments and details of the world of an aristocrat, brilliantly expresses Sei Shōnagon's person. And yet, while we celebrate the wisdom behind the survival of the work of a woman writer, she is too subordinate and apolitical to be considered a tenth-century feminist. Ever the precious observer, what matters to her is aesthetics and style—the right poem written by the right lover using the right ink on the right paper—and not with the position of women, with whom she is a competitor. The "wisdom" of the West cannot be stretched too far.

CONCLUSION

In our approaches to East-West literary relations through discourse, the "real," and canonicity, we see that the "wisdom of the East," while perhaps largely a Western idea, depends as much on its interpreters as it does on its creators. Wisdom is attractive because it is other and different, an alternative to the self's own self-perception. Not really concerned with biblical notions of conduct or the transcendent, the awareness of difference focuses on the discourse surrounding a text—who represents it, and to whom, what are their intentions, explicit or implicit, or their authority? Whether the authority is a religious devotee, psychologist, recluse, or feminist, the context of "turning East" may be a reflection of Western privation, desire, or need. In any case, once we find "the wisdom of the East," we encounter a revelation of the Western self, a discourse which reflects a need for Asian intertexts to interpret that self. Another discovery comes with the search for the "real." When facing the exotic, the horrible, or the weird in another culture, both scholarly and creative imaginations have difficulty being objective. The East may be stereotyped, or become the object of the West's desire. With the question of canonicity, perspectives on wisdom shift dramatically—the folksy replaces literariness, romantic intrigue becomes a Buddhist salvation story, and a woman's diary is seen as feminist poetics.

What seems to me most revealing about this inquiry into the "wisdom of the East" is that it discloses our own discourse to ourselves as we cast about in the sea of scholarship and the imagination, following the spirit of the *Dao De Jing*, "naming the unnameable."

NOTES

With thanks to Mahasweta Sengupta for comments on Ananda K. Coomaraswamy, Sister Nivedita, and the *Bhagavad Gītā*, and Wendy West for insights on *Invisible Cities* and *The Pillow Book of Sei Shōnagon*.

1. Edward Said, *Orientalism* (New York: Pantheon Books, 1978), p. 54.
2. Roland E. Murphy, "Introduction to Wisdom Literature," in *The Jerome Biblical Commentary*, ed. Raymond E. Brown, Joseph A. Fitzmyer, and Roland E. Murphy (Englewood Cliffs, NJ: Prentice-Hall, Inc., 1968), pp. 487–494.
3. For patterns of alterity and New World genocide, see Tzvetan Todorov, *The Conquest of America: The Question of the Other*, trans. Richard Howard (New York: Harper & Row, 1982), pp. 42–49, 133.
4. Ananda K. Coomaraswamy and The Sister Nivedita (Margaret E. Noble), "The Mahabharata," in *Myths of the Hindus and Buddhists* (1913; New York: Dover Publications, 1967), pp. 118–216.
5. Ashis Nandy, *The Intimate Enemy: Loss and Recovery of Self under Colonialism* (Delhi: Oxford University Press, 1983), p. 36.
6. See Afterword, "Why Did Henry David Thoreau Take the *Bhagavad-Gītā* to Walden Pond?" in *The Bhagavad-Gītā*, trans. Barbara Stoler Miller (New York: Columbia University Press, 1986), pp. 155–161.
7. See Jung's Preface to *The I Ching or Book of Changes*, trans. Richard Wilhelm and Cary F. Baynes, Bollingen Series XIX (Princeton: Princeton University Press, 1967); Carl Jung, *Synchronicity: An Acausal Connecting Principle*, trans. F. R. C. Hull (New York: Bollingen Foundation Inc., Pantheon Books, 1955).
8. Thomas Merton, *The Way of Chuang Tzu* (New York: New Directions, 1965), p. 11.
9. Paul J. Lin, *A Translation of Lao Tzu's Tao Te Ching and Wang Pi's Commentary* (Ann Arbor: Center for Chinese Studies, University of Michigan, 1977), pp. ix-xxiv.
10. Holmes Welch, *Taoism: The Parting of the Way* (Boston: Beacon Press, 1965).
11. See David R. Kinsley, *The Sword and the Flute: Kali and Krishna, Dark Visions of the Terrible and the Sublime in Hindu Mythology* (Berkeley: University of California Press, 1975).
12. Edward D. Dimock, Jr. and Denise Levertov, trans., *In Praise of Krishna: Songs from the Bengali* (Garden City, NY: Anchor Books, Doubleday & Company, 1967).
13. David Kopf, "Sexual Ambivalence in Western Scholarship on Hindu India: A History of Historical Images of Shakto-Tantrism, 1800–1970," in *As Others See Us: Mutual Perceptions, East and West*, ed. Bernard Lewis, Edmund Leites, and Margaret Case (New York: International Society for the Comparative Study of Civilizations, 1985), p. 143.
14. Ibid., pp. 143–155.
15. E. M. Forster, *A Passage to India* (1924; New York: Harcourt, Brace & World, 1953), p. 288, and ch. 12, "Caves."
16. Ibid., p. 319. For the call to Krishna theme, see pp. 80, 246. Ronny, to whom Adela is engaged to be married, is ironically linked

to Lord Krishna with the phrase, "He comes." The Brahman, Godpole, is still calling for Krishna to come late in the novel, p. 319.

17. Ibid., pp. 13, 23, 33, 70, 86, 142, 218.

18. Leonardo Olschki, *Marco Polo's Asia: An Introduction to his "Description of the World" called "Il Milione,"* trans. John A. Scott (Berkeley: University of California Press, 1960), p. 14. Other important studies include: Henry Yule, additions by Henri Cordier, *The Book of Ser Marco Polo*, 2 vols., 3d ed. (London: John Murray, 1903); A. C. Moule and Paul Pelliot, eds. and trans., *Marco Polo: The Description of the World* (London: G. Routledge and Sons, 1938); *The Travels of Marco Polo*, trans. Ronald Latham (Harmondsworth, England: Penguin Books, 1958).

19. Ibid., p. 12.

20. Ibid., p. 3.

21. L. F. Benedetto, *The Travels of Marco Polo*, trans. Aldo Ricci, intro. Sir E. Denison Ross (New York: Viking Press, 1931), p. 23.

22. Ibid., p. 34.

23. Mary B. Campbell, *The Witness and the Other World: Exotic European Travel Writing, 400–1600* (Ithaca: Cornell University Press, 1988), p. 112.

24. Italo Calvino, *Invisible Cities*, trans. William Weaver (New York: Harcourt Brace Jovanovich, 1972).

25. Ibid., p. 21.

26. See forthcoming volume, *Folktales of Chinese Minorities from Yunnan*, ed. Lucien Miller, trans. Guo Xu, Lucien Miller, and Xu Kun (Seattle: University of Washington Press). For the folk culture movement in modern China, see Chang-tai Hung, *Going to the People: Chinese Intellectuals and Folk Literature, 1918–1937* (Cambridge: Harvard University Press, 1985).

27. *Genji* is considered a classic for other reasons—its antiquity, its female authorship, its psychological realism, its portrait of daily life among Heian era (794–1185) aristocracy, and the artful role of its author-narrator. See chapter 3 section on *Tale of Genji* in Shuichi Kato, *A History of Japanese Literature: The First Thousand Years*, trans. David Chibbett (Tokyo: Kodansha International Ltd., 1979).

28. Daisaku Ikeda and Makoto Nemoto, *On the Japanese Classics: Conversations and Appreciations*, trans. Burton Watson (New York: Weatherhill, 1974), pp. 9–10 (idea of classic), 129–132 (Buddhist reading).

29. Ivan Morris, trans., *The Pillow Book of Sei Shōnagon* (New York: Columbia University Press, 1967; Penguin Classics, 1986). For the feminist poetics used here, see Laurence Lipking, "Aristotle's Sister: A Poetics of Abandonment," in *Canons*, ed. Robert von Hallberg (Chicago: University of Chicago Press, 1984), pp. 85–105.

Summaries of the Masterworks

*Compiled by Nadine Berardi**
Columbia University

INDIAN TEXTS

Classical Sanskrit Lyric:
Kālidāsa (c. 400 C.E.), Bhartṛhari (fifth century C.E.),
and Jayadeva (twelfth century C.E.)

Sanskritic culture, whose preoccupation with language goes back to an early concern with faultless oral transmission of scripture, produced a magnificent corpus of lyric poetry and prose called kavya. Kavya literature is characterized by a careful representation of emotion through intensely stylized and figurative language. The *Meghadūta*, Kālidāsa's exquisite monologue poem of love's separation (c. 400 C.E.), the cynically desirous verses of the poet Bhartṛhari (fifth century C.E.), and Jayadeva's *Gītagovinda*, an erotic poem about the god Krishna, are representative of the Sanskrit lyric. The *Gītagovinda*, unique because it incorporated elements of narrative and dramatic lyric (the two other kavya genres) and because it associated the aesthetic of erotic love with profound religious surrender, served as a model for some of the later devotional poetry in regional languages.

---

*In consultation with Barbara Stoler Miller, Paul Anderer, Theodore Huters, Haruo Shirane, and Pauline Yu.

539

Classical Tamil Poetry and Poetics
(first century B.C.E.–third century C.E.)

The *Eight Anthologies* and the *Ten Songs* which form the corpus of classical Tamil poetry were written between the first century B.C.E. and the third century C.E. The poems, ranging from short lyrical stanzas of three lines to long narrative works, were produced for the Tamil aristocracy and are entirely secular. There was an elaborate poetic "grammar," shared by five or six generations of poets, in which landscape, flora, and fauna, observed with a naturalist's precision, became codes for the phases of activity and feeling associated with either the themes of inner life and love in the *akam* genre, or the representation of public activities and strife in the *puram* genre. Women preside in *akam* poems, where nuances of love are captured in the speech of universalized characters and overheard by the audience. In *puram* poems, on the other hand, the poet speaks directly to the audience about the relationship of predominantly male characters to the world around them.

Devotional Poetry of Medieval North India
(fifteenth–seventeenth century C.E.)

The saint-poets of North India—Kabir, Ravidas, Nanak, Mirabai, Surdas and Tulsidas—lived between the fifteenth and seventeenth centuries C.E. and wrote in dialects of medieval Hindi. Their poems are inspired by bhakti, an intense, often reciprocal love between God and devotee. Bhakti may be expressed either lyrically, toward a visible, personal God, or philosophically in the case of a more abstract devotion which debunks the mediacy of religious institutions. Because of their beauty, their accessibility in comparison to Sanskrit literature, and their immediacy of feeling, the devotional poetry of the saints continues to transcend social boundaries and has become a widely popular vehicle of traditional culture.

Lyric Poetry in Urdu: *The Ghazal*
(sixteenth century until the present)

The ghazal, a thriving genre of Urdu poetry, was adopted from Persian in the sixteenth century, though it traces its origins to the preludes of seventh century Arabic odes. Its rich legacy of poetic convention and literary tradition allows extreme condensation of meaning, often including homage to great predecessors. Literally "conversation with women," the ghazal sensitively represents feelings heightened by desire for an elusive ideal, whether erotic or mystical. While the component couplets are independent of one another in meaning, there is a formal unity in the ghazal, resting on a common meter, rhyme, scheme, and the frequent use of an end-refrain.

The Poems and Stories of Rabindranath Tagore
(1861–1941)

Rabindranath Tagore (1861–1941) was not only the most prolific figure of modern Indian literature—in poetry, novels, short stories, dramas, and non-fiction—but a painter, composer, educator, reformer, and philosopher as well. He contributed to the creation of a new literary Bengali: vigorous, musical, highly Sanskritized language evokes, in his best poems, both spiritual joy shadowed by darkness and creative energy balanced by peaceful surrender; the rich, flexible language of his short stories gives shape to close observations of Bengali life. For Tagore, sensitively portrayed landscapes and the ambiguity of human feelings were more meaningful than blunt philosophical statement; he considered real joy to be the attainment of the infinite within the finite. Unfortunately, Tagore's reputation has suffered from translations (including his own) which inadequately reflect the complex musicality of his poetry and descriptive prose.

Mahābhārata including the *Bhagavad Gītā*
(400 B.C.E.–400 C.E.)

The longer of the two Sanskrit epics, the *Mahābhārata*, consisting of over 100,000 verses, is a martial saga of the successionary feud for an ancient North Indian kingdom. Transmitted orally for centuries, it was expanded during the period of its composition (400 B.C.E.–400 C.E.) into an encyclopedic repository of Hindu myth, legend, genealogy, morality, and speculative thought. The epic is traditionally attributed to the sage Vyāsa, who as an ancestor of the Pāṇḍava heroes is himself a vital part of the narrative and its context, ensuring both dynastic lineage and textual transmission. Within the tradition the work is not considered scripture, but a case may be made for its role, along with the *Rāmāyaṇa*, as a foundation text of popular Hinduism. The theme of transcendent peace through detachment which unites the main narrative with numerous subsidiary episodes is epitomized in the *Bhagavad Gītā*. The *Gītā*, a first century C.E. addition to the epic, is a poetic dialogue of Hindu devotionalism which proposes surrender to the god Krishna as a solution to the conflicts of cosmic order and a highly relative code of social ethics.

Rāmāyaṇa (500–300 B.C.E.)

The shorter and more popular of the two major Indian epics, the *Rāmāyaṇa*, is a poem of family loyalties, adventure, love, loss, and mythic renewal. While legends surrounding Rāma, a king of the solar dynasty, form the core of the epic, later additions provide sectarian frames for Rāma as an incarnation of the god Vishnu and as a royal model of moral behavior. The nucleus of the work is sufficiently homogeneous to be assigned to a period between 500 and 300 B.C.E. and to be attributed to a single author, traditionally accepted as the sage Vālmīki. Consisting of 24,000 verses, it is considerably shorter than the *Mahābhārata*. It is probable that literary redaction of oral tradition accounts for its stylistic and structural unity as well as its acceptance as the first work of Sanskrit lyric poetry. The influence of the *Rāmāyaṇa* in South and Southeast Asia has been unparalleled. For over two millennia it has been retold in the literary and performative idioms, both classical and folk, of nearly all languages and religions of the region.

Anita Desai: *Fire on the Mountain* (1977) and *Games at Twilight* (1978)

The novels and short stories of Anita Desai (1937–), one of the most internationally acclaimed Indian writers, have been an inspiration for other Indian women writing in English during the 1960s and 1970s. While most important modern Indian writers have depicted adult males whose dilemmas mirror those of emergent India, Desai's work focuses on characters previously marginalized in Indian fiction—women, children, adolescents, and the elderly. Desai's superb novel *Fire on the Mountain* views without sentimentality the role of women in Indian society. It shares with her contemporaneous short story collection *Games at Twilight* an emphasis on characters who seek escape from a powerful complex of social, religious, and familial obligations that hinder their search for individuality.

R. K. Narayan: *The Financial Expert* (1952)

R. K. Narayan (1906–), first published in the 1930s, is a major Indo-Anglian novelist who enlarged the way English was used in Indian fiction. In his novels the small dramas of middle-class life are played out in Malgudi, a fictitious South Indian town. Narayan's style, keenly observant and gently ironic, has a dryness and distance which mediate between the everyday life of Malgudi and an extraordinary, timeless realm revealed by outside forces. While Margayya, the hero of the novel *The Financial Expert*, temporarily achieves glory from Laksmi, goddess of fortune, through the agency of the eccentric Dr. Pal, his fall from illusory wealth grants him a new spiritual perspective.

The Short Stories of Premchand (1880–1936)

Premchand, the first important writer to use modern Hindi for prose fiction, created a panoramic portrait of North Indian society in approximately 300 short stories and 14 novels. Though his statement that the short story should "solve life's problems" reflects an early didacticism, Premchand's mature works are powerfully realistic and psychologically complex. As they are depicted in his later stories, the social values of village life do not change. The powerful exploit the weak, either by deliberately taking advantage of the inequities of Hindu caste rules, or else by mindlessly accepting them. The humble rarely transcend these illusory yet dehumanizing distinctions and the grinding poverty to which they are condemned.

Salman Rushdie: *Midnight's Children* (1980)

Salman Rushdie (1947–) published *Midnight's Children* in 1980. It is a novel luxuriant with recent history, cultural vocabulary, and myth. It is also an exuberant use of the English language to express Indian realities. The family history and life events of Saleem Sinai, narrator and central figure, parallel developments on the subcontinent. Illuminating the focal Indian question of identity is a complicated allegory in which the lives of a pair of changelings, one Hindu and the other Muslim, belie any clearcut opposition. Instead, the ragged duality of an inseparable jumble is reflected in a structure and style which cleverly shade the borders between fiction, history, and myth.

U. R. Anantha Murthy: *Samskara*

(1965)
The Passing of the Brahman Tradition

U. R. Anantha Murthy (1932–) is the preeminent writer of his generation in the Kannada language. His acclaimed novel *Samskara* was written in 1965 after his study of Indian reformist politics of the thirties and forties prompted him to explore his own Karnataka Brahman background. Central to the novel's plot are three characters, clearly outside the pale of orthodox Brahmanism, who force Praneshacharya, a pillar of his Brahman community, to realize that orthodoxy has become a convenient way to repress his passion and retreat from life. When Praneshacharya determines to live with the outcaste woman, Chandri, he reveals his transgressions to the village. His spiritual power, and by extension that of Brahman India, is channeled to the real world by his rejecting the inhumanity of orthodox Brahmanism.

Two Classical Indian Plays:
Kālidāsa's *Śakuntalā* (c. 400 C.E.) and
Śūdraka's *Little Clay Cart* (c. 400 C.E.)

Sanskrit drama appears to have emerged as a sophisticated form of public literary activity during the height of the Gupta reign (390–470 C.E.). While *Śakuntalā*, its material drawn from mythological sources, is the model for the heroic romance, *Little Clay Cart* is a secular romance with an invented story. In both plays the exploration of conflicting social and personal values in the plot, realized through classical India's consummate theatrical arts, provided the audience with an emotionally integrated experience of extraordinary universality. The union of hero and heroine, Duśyanta and Śakuntalā in Kālidāsa's play, and Carudatta and Vasantasenā in *Little Clay Cart*, restores the balance between duty and passion; the romance and heroism of the dramatic context are enjoyed imaginatively, offering both pleasure and insight. Sanskrit drama, which reached a wider audience than lyric poetry, balanced its rarefied aesthetic with comedic material, picaresque characters, and the use of dialects.

CHINESE TEXTS

The Book of Songs (sixth century B.C.E.)

The Book of Songs (*Shi jing*), containing 305 poems, was anthologized in its present form by the sixth century B.C.E. Intended for very diverse purposes and audiences, the poems may be simple emotional expressions, adjuncts to ritual and ceremony, or celebrations of historical and legendary figures and events. It is interesting to note that while the foundations for the Indian and Western literary traditions are epic, the position held by *The Book of Songs* in the canon implies that Chinese literary culture is rooted in the lyric.

The Poetry of Retreat
(important poets Tao Qian and Xie Lingyun, fourth–fifth century C.E.)

The theme of retreat, of compelling concern throughout Chinese literary history, was usually a response to social and political instability. Frequently a result of dangerously conflicting political allegiances, the desire to retreat could also be seen as a tension between the Confucian principle of service to society and Taoist mysticism. Two of the important poets who lived during the chaotic times of the Six Dynasties and explored eremitic impulses were Tao Qian (365–427) and Xie Lingyun (385–433).

Tang Poetry: A Return to the Basics
(eighth–ninth century C.E.)

Wang Wei (699–761), Li Bai (701–762), Du Fu (712–770), Bo Juyi (772–846), and Hanshan (eighth-ninth century) were among the great Chinese poets whose work represents the peak of literary achievement reached during the Tang dynasty (618–907). Tang poems, written almost entirely by bureaucrat-scholars for whom poetry was an integral element of life, were great, in part, for their tone of moral seriousness. While these poets addressed social and ethical issues of far-reaching importance, they also brought to their poetry a note of personal concern and intimate experience.

Zhuang Zi [Chuang Tzu] (second century B.C.E.)

The *Zhuang Zi*, compiled in the second century B.C.E., is both a work of philosophical mysticism and a literary monument. Although the text is a collection of philosophical writings by different authors who lived between the fourth and second centuries B.C.E., its reputation as a great work of literature rests on the brilliant and original earlier chapters of Zhuang Zhou ([Chuang Chou] 369–286 B.C.E.). Zhuang Zhou has been called a great lyrical philosopher because of his playful use of metaphorical language, allegory, and other rhetorical devices.

Records of the Historian (second-first century B.C.E.)

Sima Qian was the greatest historian of ancient China. He survived severe imperial punishment to complete *The Records of the Historian* (Shi Ji), a work which was both an encyclopedic history and description of the Chinese world and the standard for classical prose. While it has long been clear that Sima Qian was at once respectful of his written sources and critical of their inconsistencies, the accuracy of some of his previously uncorroborated material has recently been confirmed by archaeological finds. In addition to chronicling the political history of dynasties, the *Shi ji* is also a document of culture and society, containing treatises on astronomy, geography, calendrical studies, rites, and music.

The Journey to the West (sixteenth century C.E.)

The 100-chapter sixteenth-century literati novel *Xiyou ji* (*The Journey to the West*) is the culmination of a millennium-long narrative tradition that had featured the same characters and episodes in a variety of genres. *The Journey to the West* is, on the surface, a folk tale of fantastic adventures in which the Buddhist master, Xuanzang, is helped by a rebellious and supernaturally resourceful monkey king in his quest journey to India for the Mahayana scriptures. At the same time, however, an intricate allegory of spiritual quest is maintained throughout the narrative.

Cao Xueqin's *Hongloumeng* (eighteenth century C.E.)
(*Story of the Stone* or *Dream of the Red Chamber*)

There are many ways in which *Hongloumeng*, written by Cao Xueqin (1715–64), merits its place as the best-loved Chinese novel. It is a tender and tragic love story set within a panoramic chronicle of Qing society that centers on the decline of the wealthy and powerful Jia family. *Hongloumeng* is also a work of poetic genius, versatile in its creative use of genres from China's long literary tradition.

Liu E's *The Travels of Lao Can* (1903–04)

Liu E's (1857–1909) tour de force, *The Travels of Lao Can* (1903–04), is still the most popular of the late Qing novels. Written in the wake of the Boxer incident, the novel is permeated by the author's deep sorrow over China's debilitation. For all the chivalrous fervor its eponymous hero demonstrates in the course of his journeys, *Laocan youji* is a novel grounded in political reality; the success of the hero in rescuing a few individuals from misery only renders more poignant the plight of oppressed multitudes. Meditative passages using an incipient stream-of-consciousness technique achieve an autobiographical intimacy extraordinary in light of the scarcity of subjective heroes in Chinese fiction.

The Stories of Lu Xun (1918–1925)

Because of the power of his work, and his creation of a new literary style in the vernacular, Lu Xun (1881–1936) is considered to be the founder of modern Chinese literature. Though he produced poetry, essays, and literary scholarship, twenty-five stories written between the years 1918 and 1925 remain his best-known work. The futility of action in Lu Xun's stories captures the pathos of a society in transition and complements a powerful subtext on the hollowness of storytelling.

Camel Xiangzi (Rickshaw) (1937)
by Lao She (1899–1966)

Lao She (1899–1966), one of the most important Chinese novelists of the 1930s, is best remembered for *Camel Xiangzi*, the exposé of an honest young Beijing rickshaw puller's degradation by a cruel and unjust society. Though lauded as a milestone of naturalistic representation in modern Chinese fiction, certain of Lao She's stylistic strategies give the novel overtones of black comedy.

Contemporary Chinese Lettres

Literature seemed to be the natural vehicle for providing a sense of intellectual significance once the role of history was undermined along with the traditional intellectual order. When a new, strikingly political concept of literature emerged in China after 1895, it was enmeshed in the conflict between the directive to transmit positive information and the need to critique the system. The tension between the need for radical critique and the equally pressing need to construct something new has haunted Chinese literature since that time.

Story of the Western Wing (Romance of the Western Chamber) (thirteenth century C.E.)

Xixiang ji (*Story of the Western Wing*), one of three extant plays by Wang Shifu (thirteenth century C.E.), is perhaps the single most popular drama ever written in China. The material, based on a twelfth-century ballad which in turn borrowed from previous stories, found its artistic culmination in the masterly construction and unconventional characterization of Wang's play. An example of *zaju*, a highly stylized musical drama written between the twelfth and fifteenth centuries, *Story of the Western Wing* took on the status of a love manual and became the vernacular model for later works with the highly popular "brilliant student-talented lady" theme.

JAPANESE TEXTS

The Man'yōshū (seventh–eighth century C.E.) and Kokinshū (eighth–tenth century C.E.) Collections

The *Man'yōshū*, consisting of 4,516 poems, is the earliest extant anthology of Japanese poetry and is noted both for the expansive *chōka* verse form and the short *waka* (or *tanka*).

The *Kokinshū* (eighth-tenth century C.E.), containing 1,111 poems by 127 poets, was the first imperially sponsored collection of *waka*, the thirty-one syllable classical poetic form. The

Kokinshū not only provided the standard of poetic knowledge that every educated person was expected to meet, but became the model of poetic diction for the next 1,000 years.

The Poetry of Matsuo Bashō (1644–94 C.E.)

Matsuo Bashō was a *haikai* (comic linked verse) poet, who introduced traditional aesthetic values into *haikai* and who transformed the opening verse of *haikai*, or the *hokku* (17-syllable verse form, known in the twentieth century as *haiku*), into high art.

The Tale of Genji (eleventh century C.E.)

The Tale of Genji, an extraordinary work of fiction written in the early eleventh century by Murasaki Shikibu, an attendant at the imperial court, is noted both for its subtle psychological drama and its panoramic depiction of a remarkably refined and aesthetically oriented civilization.

A Book of One's Own: *The Gossamer Years* (tenth century C.E.); *The Pillow Book* (tenth–eleventh century C.E.), and *The Confessions of Lady Nijō* (thirteenth–fourteenth century C.E.)

These autobiographical and poetic narratives (including diaries and miscellaneous essays) were written in vernacular Japanese by court women. *The Gossamer Years* is an autobiographical narrative that describes the tribulations of a woman married to a high-ranking aristocrat.

The Pillow Book, the first example of the miscellaneous essay genre (*zuihitsu*), describes the experience of Sei Shōnagon, an attendant at the imperial court.

The Confessions of Lady Nijō which describes the author's love affairs at court and her subsequent peregrinations as a nun, comes toward the end of this tradition of women's autobiographical writing.

"An Account of My Hut" (1212 C.E.)

"An Account of My Hut," written by Kamo no Chōmei, a poet who became a recluse during the turbulent years of the early thirteenth century, is a two-part autobiographical essay on (1) the destruction of civilization and his Buddhistic vision of the impermanence of the world, and (2) his life and meditations in a solitary hut outside the capital.

Seven Japanese Tales (1910–1959)

The stories in *Seven Japanese Tales*, written by Tanizaki Jun'ichirō (1886–1965), possibly Japan's greatest modern writer, are representative of the author's ability to apprehend the fantasies of his culture.

Beyond Absolution: Enchi Fumiko's
The Waiting Years (1957) and *Masks* (1958)

The first masterpiece by Enchi Fumiko (1905–1986), heir to the special legacy of the Japanese female writer, is *The Waiting Years*, which portrays, through brilliant recreation of a Meiji-period household, the devastating effects of marriage on the women of that age. Enchi's flawless blend of classical allusion and aesthetic consciousness produced the chilling beauty of *Masks*, resonant with images from both *The Tale of Genji* and the Noh repertory.

The Women in the Dunes (1962)

Abe Kōbō's (1924–1993) novel *The Woman in the Dunes*, which created a literary sensation in Japan, expresses how treacherous Abe feels the fiction of "nation" or "home" can be. In the novel a vacationing school teacher, Niki Jumpei, held captive in a sand pit by a recently widowed woman, is progressively drawn to his captor and wonders if he was any less trapped by his marriage and job.

Mishima Yukio, The Allegorist (1925–1970)

Haunted by postwar emptiness and the banality of daily survival during economic recovery, Mishima Yukio sought to recapture a prewar conception of the state as an unsullied, abstract unity for which the individual could give his life. In his novel *The Sailor Who Fell from Grace with the Sea* (1963), the protagonist is a slave to the sea, the source of ultimate power and authority identified with beauty, metaphysical truth, and the emperor.

Kawabata Yasunari's *Snow Country* (1948)

Kawabata Yasunari (1899–1972), the first Japanese to win the Nobel Prize for literature, attempted to create a form of modern Japanese literature that would transcend the past without losing touch with it. *Snow Country* fuses both elements of twentieth century modernism and classical Japanese aesthetics.

Sōseki's *Kokoro* (1914)

Natsume Sōseki (1867–1916), whose life spanned the Meiji period (1868–1912), wrote a number of novels, perhaps the best of which is *Kokoro*, which reveals the inner turmoil and cultural crisis caused by the shifting values of the modern age.

Three Plays of the Noh Theater
(fifteenth–sixteenth century C.E.)

Noh, one of Japan's oldest theatrical forms, attained its status as an independent performing art in the fourteenth century. The great actor-playwright-aesthetician, Zeami (1363–1443 C.E.), and before him his father, Kan'ami (1358–1408 C.E.), gave Noh its classic formal structure. The plays *Atsumori* (1423) and *Izutsu* (1430) by Zeami, and *Ataka* by Nobumitsu (1435–1516 C.E.) are mainstays of Noh repertory with a five-century history of continuous popularity and performance. In *Atsumori*, a slain warrior and his killer are reborn as reaper and priest to resolve their enmity. By contrast, *Izutsu* portrays the love of a lady's ghost for her long-dead lover. *Ataka*, a play with many characters and abundant dramatic conflict, can be seen as a transition between Noh and later forms such as Kabuki.

The Love Suicides at Sonezaki (1703 C.E.)

Chikamatsu Monzaemon (1653–1725 C.E.), one of the great dramatists of the puppet theater, wrote *The Love Suicides at Sonezaki*, a tragedy inspired by an actual incident in Osaka in which a shop assistant and a prostitute, unable to achieve freedom together, commit suicide. It created a genre of lovers' suicide plays (*sewamono*) which, unlike Noh, dealt with contemporary life and ordinary people.

Historical Timelines

INDIAN HISTORY

Dates	Periods	Events
B.C.E. 3000		
2300	**PREHISTORY** **Indus River Civilization** **(ca. 2300–1750)**	Development of urban grain-growing civilization on the Indus River; two main cities are Harappa and Mohenjo Daro; undeciphered proto-Dravidian script; destroyed by environmental pressures, migrations.
1750	**Aryan Migration** **(ca. 1750–1000)**	Migration into Northwest of India of nomadic herding tribes from Iranian plateau; Indo-European language development; oral religious traditions preserved in *Vedas*, oldest of which, the *Rig Veda*, predates migration.
1000	**Brahmanism** **(ca. 900)**	Early Hinduism characterized by sacrificial rituals, belief in karma and reincarnation, and division of society into four classes (*varnas*).
500	*Buddhism* *Jainism*	
326	**Invasion of Alexander the Great** **Mauryan Empire** **(324–200)**	Domination of North India by Chandra-gupta, extended to South by grandson, Ashoka.
250	**Development/Diffusion of Sanskrit Culture**	Major texts of Hindu tradition take shape: *Mahābhārata*, *Rāmāyaṇa*, codification of laws, grammar, science, arts; gods Shiva, Vishnu are major figures; spread of Sanskritic culture to South India.
200	**Invasions of North India**	Invasians by Central Asian tribes: Bactrian Greeks; Sakas; Kushans (establish dynasty ca. 78–200 C.E.).
C.E. 300	**CLASSICAL HINDU CULTURES**	Classical Hindu tradition expressed in poetry, drama (Kalidasa); art, temple architecture; philosophy (Vedanta); and new forms of devotional (*bhakti*) worship.
320	**Gupta Dynasty** **(320–550)**	Guptas dominate North India at beginning of "classical" period.

Dates	Periods	Events
455	**Invasions of Huns** (ca. 455–528)	Successive invasions of Huns; other Central Asian tribes destroy Gupta empire.
650	**Rajput Dynasties**	Warlike clans appear in Rajasthan.
	South Indian Dynasties (ca. 650–1336)	Pallava dynasty dominates the south; continuing conflict with Cholas, Cheras, Pandyas.
711	**Arabs Take Sind (711)**	
1000	**Raids of Mahmud of Ghazni (997-1027)**	
	MUSLIM DOMINANCE	Invasions of Muslims from Central Asia lead to political dominance of Muslims in North India and introduction of Persian culture and Islamic religion into South Asia.
1192	**Delhi Sultanate** (1192–1526)	Turko-Afghan chieftains establish sultanate at Delhi; dominate North India.
	Vijayangar (1336–1646)	Rise of Hindu kingdom in South India; independent of Muslim rulers until destruction of capital city in 1565.
	Portugese traders in India (1498)	
1526	**Mughal Empire** (1526–1858)	Mughal Empire unifies North and parts of South India under its rule; amalgam of Persian and Indian culture created in its courts and territories.
	European traders in India	Establishment of trading outposts in India: Dutch (1609); English (1612); French (1674).
1700	**Rise of Regional Powers**	Weakening of Mughal authority frees local Muslim rulers; rise of indigenous regional powers: Sikhs (Punjab), Rajputs (Rajasthan), and Marathas (West India).
1757	**Battle of Plassey**	Victory over Nawab of Bengal gives East India company control of Bengal and begins expansion of British power in India.
1800	**BRITISH RULE**	Political dominance of Britain introduces Western culture, language, methods of government, and technology into urban administrative centers.

Dates	Periods	Events
1947	**MODERN SOUTH ASIA** **India (1947)** **Pakistan (1947)**	Independence from British rule; partition of British India into modern countries of India and Pakistan (East and West).
1971	**Bangladesh (1971)**	War between East and West Pakistan results in separation of Pakistan into two states: Pakistan and Bangladesh.

Prepared by Judith Walsh, associate professor, Comparative Humanities Program, State University of New York, Old Westbury.

CHINESE HISTORY

Dates	Periods	Events
B.C.E. 5000		Neolithic cultures
3000	**XIA/HSIA DYNASTY (ca. 2200–1750)**	
1800	**SHANG DYNASTY (ca. 1750–1100)**	One of the Three Dynasties, or San Dai (Xia, Shang, and Zhou), thought to mark the beginning of Chinese civilization; characterized by its writing system, practice of divination, walled cities, bronze technology, and use of horse-drawn chariots.
1200	**ZHOU/CHOU DYNASTY** **Western Zhou (ca. 1100–771)** **Eastern Zhou (771–256)**	A hierarchical political and social system with the Zhou royal house at its apex; power was bestowed upon aristocratic families as lords of their domains or principalities. Although often compared to European "feudalism," what actually gave the system cohesion was a hierarchical order of ancestral cults. The system eventually broke down into a competition for power between rival semi-autonomous states in what became
600		known as the Spring and Autumn period (722–481) and the Warring States period (403–221). It was during these tumultuous times that Confucius (551–479) lived.
	QIN/CH'IN DYNASTY (221–206)	Created a unitary state by imposing a centralized administration and by standardizing the writing script, weights, and measures. Known for its harsh methods of rule, including the suppression of dissenting thought.
C.E.	**HAN DYNASTY** **Western Han (202 B.C.E.–9 C.E.)** **Eastern Han (25 C.E.–220 C.E.)**	Modified and consolidated the foundation of the imperial order. Confucianism was established as orthodoxy and open civil service examinations were introduced. Han power reached Korea and Vietnam. *Records of the Historian*, which became the model for subsequent official histories, was completed.

558

Dates	Periods	Events
	PERIOD OF DISUNITY (220–581)	The empire was fragmented. The North was dominated by invaders from the borderland and the steppes. The South was ruled by successive "Chinese" dynasties. Buddhism spread.
600	**SUI DYNASTY (581–618)**	China is reunified.
	TANG/T'ANG DYNASTY (618–906)	A time of cosmopolitanism and cultural flowering occurred. This period was the height of Buddhist influence in China until its repression around 845. Active territorial expansion occurred until defeat by the Arabs at Talas in 751.
1200	**SONG/SUNG DYNASTY Northern Song (960–1126)** **Southern Song (1127–1279)**	An era of significant economic and social changes: the monetization of the economy; growth in commerce and maritime trade; urban expansion and technological innovations. The examination system for bureaucratic recruitment of neo-Confucianism was to provide the intellectual underpinning for the political and social order of the late imperial period.
	YUAN DYNASTY (1271–1368)	Founded by the Mongols as part of their conquest of much of the world. Beijing was made the capital. Dramas, such as the famous *Story of the Western Wing*, flourished.
	MING DYNASTY (1368–1644)	The first Ming emperor, Hongwu, laid the basis of an authoritarian political culture. Despite early expansion, it was an inward-looking state with an emphasis on its agrarian base. Gradual burgeoning of the commercial sector; important changes in the economy and social relations in the latter part of the dynasty; also a vibrant literary scene as represented by publication of the novel *Journey to the West*.
1800	**QING/CH'ING (1644–1912)**	A Manchu dynasty. Continued the economic developments of the late Ming, leading to prosperity but also complacency and a dramatic increase in population. The acclaimed novel *Dream of the Red Chamber* was written in this period. Strains on the polity were intensified by a rapid incorporation of substantial new territories. Its authoritarian structure was subsequently unable to meet the military and cultural challenge of an expansive West.
1900		

Dates	Periods	Events
	REPUBLIC (1912–1949)	Weak central government following the collapse of the dynastic system in 1911–12; Western influence was shown by the promotion of "science" and "democracy" during the New Culture Movement. The attempt of the Nationalist government (est. 1928) to bring the entire country under its control was thwarted by both domestic revolts and the Japanese occupation (1937–45). The Nationalists fled to Taiwan after defeat by the Communists.
	PEOPLE'S REPUBLIC (1949–)	Communist government. The drive for remaking society ended in disasters such as the Great Leap Forward and the Cultural Revolution. Economic reform and political retrenchment since around 1978.

Prepared by Michael Tsin, assistant professor of Chinese history, Department of East Asian Languages and Cultures, Columbia University.

JAPANESE HISTORY

Dates	Periods	Events
B.C.E. c.4000	**JŌMON CULTURE**	Prehistoric culture characterized by hand-made pottery with rope pattern design.
500	**YAYOI CULTURE (ca. 300)**	More advanced agricultural society, using metals and wheel-turned pottery.
C.E. 200	**Tomb Period (ca. 300)**	Great earthen grave mounds and their funery objects, such as clay *haniwa*—terra-cotta figurines of people and animals, models of buildings and boats—attest to emergence of powerful clan rulers. Among these was the Yamato clan, whose rulers began the imperial dynasty that has continued to the present.
400	**Introduction of Buddhism (552)**	
600	**Taika Reform (645)**	Reorganization and reform based largely on learning imported from China: Buddhism, writing system, bureaucratic organization, legal theories.
	NARA (710–784)	Establishment of first permanent capital at Nara; emergence of Japanese patterns of administration and institutions. Beginning of classical period.
800	**HEIAN (794–1185) (Late Heian: FUJIWARA)**	Great flowering of classical Japanese culture in new capital of Heian-kyō (Kyoto). Court aristocracy, especially women, produced a great body of literature—poetry, diaries, the novel *The Tale of Genji*—and made refined aesthetic sensibility their society's hallmark.
1000 1200	**KAMAKURA (1185–1333)**	Beginning of military rule, as samurai (warriors) replaced nobles as actual rulers of Japan. Imperial court remained in Kyoto but shogun's governing organization was based in Kamakura, which is south of modern Tokyo.
	Kemmu Restoration (1333–1336)	

Dates	Periods	Events
1400	**ASHIKAGA (1336–1573) (MUROMACHI)**	New warrior government in Kyoto retained marginal control of the country, but from its base in Kyoto's Muromachi district became patron of newly flourishing artistic tradition, influenced by Zen Buddhist culture as well as samurai and court society.
	Country at War	Warring factions engaged in lengthy, destructive civil wars.
	Unification (1568–1598)	
1600	**TOKUGAWA (EDO) (1600–1867)**	Country unified under military government which maintained 250 years of secluded peace, leading to development of vibrant urban "middle-class" culture with innovations in economic organization, literature, and the arts.
1800		
1900	**MEIJI RESTORATION (1868) Meiji Period (1868–1912) Taisho (1912–1926) Shōwa (1926–1989)**	Emergence, through Western stimulus, into modern international world marked by dramatic alterations in institutions, traditional social organization, and culture.
	CONTEMPORARY JAPAN 1945–PRESENT Heisei (1989–)	Japan as a world power in the twentieth century.

Prepared by Amy Vladeck Heinrich, director, C.V. Starr East Asian Library, Columbia University.

Index

Contributors

Joseph Roe Allen III is associate professor of Chinese language and literature at Washington University in St. Louis. His publications include *In the Voice of Others: Chinese Music Bureau Poetry* (1991) and *Forbidden Games and Video Poems: The Poetry of Yang Mu and Lo Ch'ing*, forthcoming.

Paul Anderer is professor of modern Japanese literature in the Department of East Asian Languages and Cultures, and director of the Donald Keene Center of Japanese Culture at Columbia University. He is author of *Other Worlds: Arishima Takeo and the Bounds of Modern Japanese Fiction* (1984), and general editor of a forthcoming, five volume series: *Japanese Criticism 1885–1990*. His primary fields of interest are modern Japanese fiction, film, and criticism, as well as comparative literary history and theory.

Michael C. Brownstein is associate professor of literature at the University of Notre Dame. He has published translations of several modern Japanese short stories and critical articles on the literature of the Meiji period (1868–1912).

Shamsur Rahman Faruqi has had a career both in government and Urdu literature. Currently posted in New Delhi, he is also the editor of an important literary magazine, *Shabkhūn*, and the author of numerous books of poetry and criticism. His most recent works include *Tafhīm-e Ghālib* (*Explicating Ghālib*) (1989) and *Shi'r-e shor angez* (*Passionate poetry*), a four-volume selection and commentary based on the work of Mīr (Vol. 1, 1990; Vol 2., 1991; Vols. 3 and 4, forthcoming). He has been named an adjunct professor at the University of Pennsylvania.

Robert P. Goldman is professor of Sanskrit and chairman of the Center for South Asia Studies at the University of California at Berkeley. He is the author of a book on the Bhṛgus of the *Mahābhārata, Gods, Priests, and Warriors* (1977), co-author of an introductory Sanskrit primer, *Devavāṇipraveśikā: An Introduction to the Sanskrit Language* (1987), and has authored many scholarly articles on Sanskrit epic studies. He is the general editor and one of the principal translators of the ongoing collaborative translation of the *Vālmīki Rāmāyaṇa* (1985).

Thomas Blenman Hare is associate professor of Japanese and of comparative literature at Stanford University. His publications include *Zeami's Style* (1986), concerning the musical and rhetorical structure of representative plays by Zeami; "Reading Kamo no Chōmei" (*Harvard Journal of Asiatic Studies* 49, no. 1 [June 1989]: 173-228), a critical essay on the writing of a thirteenth century Japanese eremite; and "Reading, Writing, and Cooking" (*Journal of Asian Studies* 49, no. 2 [May 1990]: 253-272), an examination of the epistemological ramifications of a scriptural commentary by the ninth century priest Kūkai. His current research interests include the *Tale of Genji* and the construction of subjectivities in various linguistic and cultural contexts.

John Stratton Hawley is professor and chair in the Department of Religion at Barnard College and director of the Southern Asian Institute at Columbia University. He has written on poetry and performance relating to Krishna (*At Play with Krishna* [1981]; *Krishna, the Butter Thief* [1983]) and on medieval Hindi literature and hagiography (*Sur Das* [1984]; *Songs of the Saints of India*, with Mark Juergensmeyer [1988]). His most recent edited volumes include a book on *sati* and one that investigates the ideology of gender among fundamentalist groups.

C. T. Hsia has taught at Columbia University for twenty-nine years, and is now professor emeritus of Chinese literature. An influential critic among both Chinese and Western readers, he is best known for *A History of Modern Chinese Fiction* (1961; 1971) and *The Classic Chinese Novel* (1968; 1980); is also a co-editor of *Modern Chinese Stories and Novellas, 1919-1949* (1981), a widely adopted textbook.

Theodore Huters is professor of Chinese in the Department of East Asian Languages and Literatures at the University of California at Irvine. He has written extensively on modern Chinese literature and literary history. His latest book is *Reading the Modern Chinese Short Story* (1990).

Wilt L. Idema is professor of Chinese literature in the Department of Chinese Studies at Leiden University. His publications in English include *Chinese Vernacular Fiction, The Formative Period* (1974); *Chinese Theater 1100-1450: A Source Book* (with Stephen H. West, 1981); *The Dramatic Oeuvre of Chu Yu-tan 1379-1439*

(1985); *Wang Shifu, The Moon and the Zither, the Story of the Western Wing* (with Stephen H. West, 1991). His Dutch language publications include a complete translation of Dong Jieyuan's *Xixiangji zhugongdiao* as *Het verhaal van de westerkamers in alle toonaarden* (1984) and a voluminous anthology of classical Chinese poetry entitled *Spiegel van de klassieke Chinese poëzie* (1991).

Ken K. Ito, an associate professor of Japanese language and literature at the University of Michigan, is the author of *Visions of Desire: Tanizaki's Fictional Worlds* (1991).

Donald Keene is University Professor and Shincho Professor of Japanese Literature at Columbia University. Among his many publications are *World Within Walls* (1976), *Dawn to the West* (1984), and the forthcoming *Seeds in the Heart*.

Robin Jared Lewis is associate dean of the International Affairs program at the School of International and Public Affairs, Columbia University. He was the executive editor of *The Encyclopedia of Asian History* (1988) and is the author of *E. M. Forster's Passages to India* (1979), as well as numerous articles on Indian history, literature, and culture.

Shuen-fu Lin is professor of Chinese language and literature at the University of Michigan. He is the author of *The Transformation of the Chinese Lyrical Tradition: Chiang K'uei and Southern Sung Tz'u Poetry* (1978), the co-author (with Larry Schulz) of *The Tower of Myriad Mirrors: A Supplement to "Journey to the West"* (1978; 1988), and co-editor (with Stephen Owen of Harvard University) of *The Vitality of the Lyric Voice: Shih Poetry from the Late Han to the T'ang* (1986).

Barbara Stoler Miller (1940–1993) was Samuel R. Milbank Professor and chairman of the Department of Asian and Middle Eastern Cultures at Barnard College, Columbia University. She also codirected the Barnard Centennial Scholars program. A former Guggenheim Fellow, her work received support from the Ford Foundation, the Smithsonian Institution, the National Endowment for the Humanities, and the American Council of Learned Societies. She edited and translated works of Sanskrit poetry and drama, including *Love Song of the Dark Lord* (1977), *The Hermit and the Love-Thief: Sanskrit Poems of Bhartrihari and Bilhana* (1979), *Theater of Memory: The Plays of Kālidāsa* (1984), and *The Bhagavad-Gītā* (1986); most recently she edited *The Powers of Art: Patronage in Indian Culture* (1992). Professor Miller was scholarly advisor for Peter Brook's theatrical and film version of *The Mahābhārata*.

Lucien Miller is professor of comparative literature at the University of Massachusetts, Amherst. His most recent publication is *Thrice-Told Tales: Yunnan Minority Myths, Legends, and Folktales* (forthcoming, 1993), of which he is editor and joint translator. His interests include Orientalism and Occidentalism, East-West comparative literature, Chinese fiction, Asian religion, and minority folk literatures.

Bharati Mukherjee has taught creative writing at Columbia, New York University, and Queens College and currently holds a distinguished professorship at the University of California, Berkeley. She is the author of three collections of short stories, two works of nonfiction, and two novels.

Rajagopal Parthasarathy is an associate professor of English and of Asian studies at Skidmore College, Saratoga Springs, New York. He is a poet and translator whose works include the long poem *Rough Passage* (4th printing, Oxford University Press, 1989), and the anthology *Ten Twentieth-Century Indian Poets* (11th printing, Oxford University Press, 1990). He has translated into modern English verse the sixth-century Tamil national epic, the *Cilappatikāram* (*The Epic of the Anklet*, 1993). He is preparing an English translation of the Tamil poet C. Subramania Bharati (1882-1921). His current research is focused on comparative poetics, and the epic tradition. A paper, "Tradition and the Indian Writer," appeared in the *British Journal of Aesthetics* (32.2 [April 1992]).

Andrew H. Plaks is professor of East Asian studies at Princeton University. His major publications include *Archetype and Allegory in the Dream of the Red Chamber* (1976), *Chinese Narrative: Critical and Theoretical Essays* (1977), and *The Four Masterworks of the Ming Novel* (1987).

Frances W. Pritchett is an associate professor of Urdu and Hindi language and literature in the Department of Middle East Languages and Cultures at Columbia University. She has done a fair amount of translation, and is especially interested in classical prose and poetry. Her most recent book is *The Romance Tradition in Urdu: Adventures from the Dastan of Amir Hamzah* (1991); she is now completing a book about the poetics of the ghazal, *Nets of Awareness: Urdu Poetry and Its Critics*.

William Radice is lecturer in Bengali at the School of Oriental and African Studies, University of London.

David Rubin, who has taught both Western and Indian literature at Sarah Lawrence College and Columbia University, is the author of three novels, a critical study of recent Anglo-Indian fiction, and several volumes of translations from Hindi and Nepali. His latest publications include translations of Shrilal Shukla's novel *Pahla Paṛāv* and a collection of Chayavad poetry.

Barbara Ruch is professor of Japanese literature and culture at Columbia University and director of the Institute for Medieval Japanese Studies. Until 1990 she served as founding director of the Donald Keene Center of Japanese Culture. A specialist on the popular literature and religio-secular mass media of medieval Japan, her most recent publications include "The Other Side of Culture in Medieval Japan," in *The Cambridge History of Japan* (Volume III, *Medieval Japan*) edited by Kozo Yamamura (1990), and her book in Japanese, *Mō Hitotsu no Chūsei zō* (*Medieval Japan: An Alternative Perspective*) (1991), which is a study of various neglected aspects of medieval Japanese literature, painting, and cultural history. Professor Ruch is currently directing an international research and publication project on "Women and Buddhism in Pre-Modern Japan: Research Strategies for a Newly-Developing Field."

Edward G. Seidensticker, professor emeritus of Japanese literature at Columbia University, has translated many works of Japanese literature, including novels by Kawabata Yasunari, Tanizaki Jun'ichirō, Mishima Yukio, and Murasaki Shikibu's *The Tale of Genji* (1974). He received the National Book Award for his translation of Kawabata's *The Sound of the Mountain*. His books on Japanese literature and culture include *Kafu the Scribbler* (1965), *Low City, High City: Tokyo from Edo to the Earthquake* (1983), and *Tokyo Rising: The City Since the Great Earthquake* (1990).

Haruo Shirane is an associate professor of Japanese literature in the Department of East Asian Languages and Cultures at Columbia University. He is the author of *The Bridge of Dreams: A Poetics of the Tale of Genji* (1987) and numerous articles on traditional Japanese poetry and prose.

Richard Torrance, assistant professor in the department of East Asian languages and literatures at The Ohio State University, has recently completed a study of the modern novelist Tokuda Shūsei.

John Whittier Treat is associate professor of Japanese at the University of Washington. He is the author of *Pools of Water, Pillar of Fire: The Literature of Ibuse Masuji* (1988); *The Ruin of Words: Japanese Writers and the Atomic Bomb* (forthcoming); and is currently at work on a collection of essays entitled *Governing Metaphors: Literature and the Invention of Modern Japan.*

David Der-wei Wang is associate professor of Chinese literature at Columbia University. He is the author of *Cong Liu E dao Wang Zhenhe* (*From Liu E to Wang Zhenhe*, 1986), *Zhongsheng xuanhua* (*Heteroglossia in Modern Chinese Fiction*, 1988), and *Fictional Realism in Twentieth Century China: Mao Dun, Lao She, Shen Congwen* (1992).

Burton Watson was formerly professor of Chinese literature at Columbia University. He has published over thirty volumes of translations from and studies of Chinese and Japanese poetry, philosophy, and history, including *The Complete Works of Chuang Tzu* (1968); *From the Country of Eight Islands* (1981), an anthology of Japanese poetry done in collaboration with Hiroaki Sato which won the American P.E.N. translation prize in 1982; and *The Columbia Book of Chinese Poetry* (1984).

Stephen H. West taught at the University of Arizona, Tucson, from 1972 to 1985, and is presently professor of East Asian languages at the University of California, Berkeley. His publications include "The Interpretation of a Dream: The Sources, Influence, and Evaluation of the Dongjing Meng Hua Lu," *T'oung Pao* 71 (1985); "Chilly Seas and East Flowing Rivers: Yuan Hao-wen's Poems of Lament," *Journal of the American Oriental Society* 106.1 (1986); "Zang Maoxun's Injustice to Dou E," *Journal of the American Oriental Society* 111.4 (1991); (with Wilt Idema) *Chinese Theatre 1100-1450: A Source Book* (Muenchener Ostasiatische Studien, 1982); and (with Wilt Idema) *The Moon and the Zither: Wang Shifu's Story of the Western Wing* (1991).

Anthony C. Yu is the Carl Darling Buck Distinguished Service Professor of Humanities at the University of Chicago, where he holds faculty appointments in the Divinity School, Department of East Asian Languages and Civilizations, Department of English, and the Committee on Social Thought. From 1983 to 1989, he also served as chair of the Committee on Comparative Studies in Literature. He is translator and editor of *The Journey to the West* in four volumes (1977-83). More recently, he has co-edited *Morphologies of Faith: Essays on Religion and Culture in Honor of*

Nathan A. Scott, Jr. (1990). Author of numerous essays on literature and comparative religions, he is working on a book-length
study of *Hongloumeng* (*Story of the Stone* or *Dream of the Red
Chamber*).

Pauline Yu is professor and founding chair of the Department of
East Asian Languages and Literatures at the University of Califor-
nia, Irvine. She has published numerous articles on Chinese and
comparative poetry and poetics and is the author of *The Poetry of
Wang Wei: New Translations and Commentary* (1980) and *The
Reading of Imagery in the Chinese Poetic Tradition* (1987).